The Emergence of Privateering

Legal History Library

VOLUME 62

Studies in the History of International Law

VOLUME 24

The titles published in this series are listed at *brill.com/shil*

The Emergence of Privateering

By

J.D. Ford

BRILL
NIJHOFF

LEIDEN | BOSTON

Cover illustration: A nineteenth-century depiction of the arrival at Dartmouth of the *Madre de Dios*, reckoned to be the most valuable prize taken by privately owned vessels during Elizabeth's war with Spain. It was after prizes were brought home that the legal issues dealt with in this book tended to arise.

The Library of Congress Cataloging-in-Publication Data is available online at https://catalog.loc.gov
LC record available at https://lccn.loc.gov/2023000069

Typeface for the Latin, Greek, and Cyrillic scripts: "Brill". See and download: brill.com/brill-typeface.

ISSN 1874-1793
ISBN 978-90-04-54140-5 (hardback)
ISBN 978-90-04-54141-2 (e-book)

Contents

Preface VII

Introduction 1

1 **Seizures of Ships and Goods at Sea before Privateering** 8
1 Seizures of Ships and Goods at Sea as Plunder 9
2 Acquisition of Prizes in Sixteenth-Century Scotland 24
3 Seizures of Ships and Goods at Sea as Reprisal 39
4 Authorisation of Reprisals in Sixteenth-Century Scotland 54
5 Seizures of Ships and Goods at Sea as Piracy 70
6 Apprehension of Pirates in Sixteenth-Century Scotland 86

2 **From Licit Plunder towards Licensed Privateering** 102
1 Regulation of Maritime Warfare in England 103
2 Innovation during the Reign of Elizabeth 121
3 Justification in Terms of the Practice of Nations 138
4 Justification in Terms of the Law of God 156
5 Justification in Terms of the Law of Policy 173
6 Condemnation of Pirates as Common Enemies 191

3 **Privateering in Theory and Practice *avant la lettre*** 210
1 Licensed Raiding in Jacobean Scotland 211
2 Licensed Raiding in Jacobean England 227
3 Towards a New Theory of Prize Acquisition 243
4 Towards a New Theory of International Law 258
5 Prize Litigation in Caroline England 273
6 Prize Litigation in Caroline Scotland 289

Conclusion 307

Bibliography 317
Index 408

Preface

The title of this book is intended to send three signals to readers. The first is that the book is not about the activity referred to in some later seventeenth-century sources as 'privateering', but is about the activity for which that name eventually had to be invented. In other words, its concern is not with the established activity of privateering, but is with how that activity came to be established. Had the aim been to trace the origins of privateering, some effort at least would have been devoted to clarifying the connections between the established activity and earlier activities that are described. Yet the need for a book about the emergence of privateering arises partly from a tendency in the secondary literature on the subject to look back into the past for traces of an institution found in later primary sources and to find them where they did not actually exist, with the result that what did exist is misunderstood, along with the process by which the new institution came into existence. The approach adopted here is to leave sources in which reference is made to 'privateering' aside, to endeavour to read earlier sources in their own terms and in their original contexts, without being distracted by their misunderstanding in the secondary literature, and to examine the various forms of maritime raiding described in earlier sources in the order of their development. It will be for readers to decide how successful the strategy has been, but they need to be warned in advance that they will not find a history of early privateering here. If the book is considered to be successful, it may also be considered necessary for the history of early privateering to be rewritten. That is not, however, the aim of this book, in which the examination ends at the point at which the activity later known as privateering is believed to have come into existence. If the belief is correct then the addition of chapters on early privateering would have lengthened the book without adding much of substance to its basic argument.

The second signal the title of the book is intended to send to readers is that privateering is reckoned to have emerged gradually from a series of attempts to resolve tensions between novel practices and conventional theories, and to have owed less to conscious construction than to a confusion of categories. Had privateering been created by deliberate design, or by a decisive act of legislative intervention, the transition from older forms of maritime raiding to a new institution would have been more readily identifiable, and the misunderstandings in the secondary literature would probably have been avoided. But that does not appear to have been what happened. Privateering emerged from a complicated process of development – a series of twists and turns that contemporary commentators struggled to explain – with the inevitable consequence that a book about the process is bound to be complicated as well. Readers also need to be warned that instead of describing the emergence of privateering as a linear progression from one form of maritime raiding to another, presented in a neat chronological progression and in relation to a coherent geographical area, the book approaches the subject from a variety of angles, with frequent shifts between different times and places. In an attempt to minimise the difficulty that was likely to ensue from this, the temptation to investigate tangential topics fully has been resisted, although this may mean that readers with a particular interest in those topics feel frustrated. If the book is considered to be successful, it may encourage others to rethink not only the history of early privateering but also some other aspects of maritime conflict. Even with its limited focus, the book is already longer than it was expected to be when its writing was first conceived.

The third signal the title of the book is intended to send to readers is inherent in the word 'privateering', which is used not only because the book is written in English, but also because the subject is viewed from a British perspective. Work on the subject began as part of work on another book. A treatise on maritime law written by a judge of the central admiralty court of Scotland in the later sixteenth century contains two chapters dealing with maritime raiding, neither of which describes the form of raiding that had been encountered previously during work on a treatise on Scots law written in the later seventeenth century. Preparation of an edition of the sixteenth-century treatise for publication involved investigation of the secondary literature on maritime raiding, from which it became apparent that the relationship between the forms of raiding the treatise described and the form called privateering had never been satisfactorily explained. Indeed, a book about Scottish participation in maritime conflict was published in 2010 in which readers were presented with a rather misleading account of the relationship between various legal categories. As there was not going to be an opportunity in editing the sixteenth-century treatise to clarify the relationship, an article on the subject was written in 2011, which turned out to be both too long for publication in a journal and too short for the ground to be covered adequately. The context that needed to be explored before the texts of the Scottish treatises could begin to be read accurately was proving to extend far beyond sixteenth-century Scotland, in both time and space. A longer view needed to be taken, and developments in Scotland had to be connected with developments in England, which in turn had to be connected with developments elsewhere in western Europe. The outcome is a book in which more is said about developments in England than in Scotland, but in which the subject continues to be viewed from a particular perspective. As is acknowledged at the end, the subject might well have looked rather different had it been approached from a different direction, and if readers more familiar with the histories of other countries find anything of merit in the book, they may feel inclined to revisit the subject in the light of their own interests and expertise.

At a conference held towards the end of 2013, the author ran into the editor of a journal to which the long article written in 2011 had been submitted for publication. He was told that positive reports had at last been received from both of the anonymous readers to whom it had been sent. By then, however, a paper on the subject had been presented at a seminar in London, and members of the audience had helpfully suggested that what was required was a book-length study. The editor of the journal agreed that this was probably the best way ahead, with the unfortunate consequence that the readers' reports were never seen by the author, who would no doubt have benefited from them as much as he eventually benefited from the reports of readers of the book completed at the end of 2021. Further assistance had in the meantime been received when papers were presented in Aberdeen, Exeter and Oxford, and the author is of course extremely grateful to those who invited him to speak at these venues, and who raised questions or made suggestions for improvement, even if he has not always responded to their advice in exactly the way expected. A generous invitation from Jørn Sunde to speak at Bergen not only elicited further questions and suggestions but also allowed several weeks to be devoted to work on the book there. Nevertheless, completion of the project was being delayed by other commitments, not least to the editing of the sixteenth-century treatise, which is concerned with the law of maritime commerce more than the law of maritime conflict. One interruption was caused by the appearance in 2014 of a journal article that went a long way towards clarifying the relationship between privateering and earlier forms of maritime raiding. Had that article been available four years earlier, the project that comes to fruition with the publication of this book might never have been embarked upon, and for a while it seemed doubtful whether there was any point in continuing with it. At that stage, the introduction and first two chapters of the book had already been written in pretty much the form in which they appear now, but not the third chapter and the conclusion. It was finally decided that more was worth saying about the legal significance of the new institution, which had still not been described as precisely as seemed necessary. A grant from the Leverhulme Trust had been made to fund further research for the third chapter, which was then undertaken, and sabbatical leave was afterwards granted by the University of Aberdeen to allow a final version of the text to be pulled into shape. Before the period of leave started, Covid 19 arrived in Britain, leading to the closure of libraries and archives and causing further delay. As the pandemic slowly eased, librarians and archivists proved to be even more helpful than they had been in the past, making it possible for sources to be checked despite continuing restrictions, and at this point Greg Gordon, the head of the law school at Aberdeen, was also exceptionally helpful in making more time available. The author has obviously incurred an additional debt to Koninklijke Brill NV for agreeing to publish the book, and he is especially grateful for the instructive guidance he has received from Wendel Scholma and Alessandra Giliberto and for the efforts made by the production team to reconcile the bibliography with their house style without rendering the footnotes unintelligible to readers.

Introduction

The words 'privateer' and 'privateering' came into common use in Britain in the 1660s, around the time of the Second Anglo-Dutch War, when ships in private ownership were licensed to attack the enemies of the crown and to claim title to any ships or goods they captured.[1] New terminology was being coined to describe a new practice, which would remain a feature of maritime warfare until it was declared illegal by the signatories of the Treaty of Paris at the end of the Crimean War.[2] By the end of the nineteenth century privateering in this proper sense had been abandoned by other countries too, although in recent years there has been some debate in the United States over whether a variant of the practice should be revived.[3] Partly because it is difficult to explain exactly how the licensing of private ships in the 1660s differed from earlier attempts to organise maritime warfare, the terminology coined then has often been applied to previous practice.[4] The words 'privateer' and 'privateering' have been widely used in relation to Elizabethan seafaring by historians intent on emphasising that not all depredations at sea by private parties amounted to acts of piracy.[5] As the same was true before the era of oceanic navigation, the words have understandably been used in relation to medieval practice as well.[6] Indeed, they have even been found serviceable by ancient historians.[7] Whether this expansion of the semantic range of the words matters depends on how different the new practice they were coined to describe actually was from the earlier practices to which they are now applied. There were important changes in the early-modern period in naval administration, strategy and tactics, as well as in ship design, equipment and armament, all of which (it

1 Simpson and Weiner 1993, vol. 12, pp. 519–20; Craigie, Aitken, Stevenson, Watson and Dareau 1931–2002, vol. 6, p. 238.

2 *Consolidated Treaty Series*, vol. 115, pp. 1–3.

3 Lobel 1986; Marshall 1997; De Witte 2007; Wuerth 2009; Cooperstein 2009; Staub 2009; Hutchins 2011.

4 Kemp 1976, p. 670; Hattendorf 2007, vol. 3, pp. 381–2; Gillespie 2011, vol. 1, pp. 36–7.

5 Williamson 1969, pp. 34–6, 41 and 62–3; Andrews 1984, pp. 61–2 and 118–19; Sugden 1996, pp. 44–5, 98 and 123; McDermott 2001, pp. 48–92, 268–70 and 442, and 2005, pp. 13–30, 33–5 and 57–61; Hanson 2003, pp. 52–3, 59, 86–7, 90–6 and 101; Elliott 2006, pp. 7–8, 24 and 110.

6 Pryor 1988, pp. 153–6, 171–2 and 183–6; Mollat 1993, pp. 171–2; Hutchinson 1994, pp. 73, 81 and 154; Meier 2006, pp. 146–59; Friel 2015, pp. 16, 19–20, 58–60, 100, 105 and 129; Sumption 2015, pp. 89–95.

7 Ormerod 1924, pp. 59–79, 110–14, 116–19 and 133; Jackson 1973, pp. 241–53; Casson 1991, pp. 177–8.

 | DOI:10.1163/9789004541412_002

has been forcefully pointed out) render use of the language of privateering to describe activities before the seventeenth century more than a little misleading.[8] Apart from anything else, it was not until it became normal for states to maintain fleets of ships in public ownership that it made much sense for other ships assigned an aggressive role to be distinguished as privateers.[9] Ultimately, however, terms like 'piracy' and 'privateering' were used to distinguish legal categories, and it is as legal terms that they need to be defined. It needs to be explained how the law marked one category off from another, and what the legal consequences of each categorisation were. It is this task – essentially an exercise in legal rather than maritime history – that the present book is intended to perform.[10]

If part of the difficulty in explaining how the practice called privateering differed from earlier practices is the similarity between them, and if it may be hoped that examining the regulation of the practices will bring the differences into sharper focus, a further difficulty is that privateering emerged at the same time as a new approach to the regulation of relations between nations. To understand what was different about privateering it is also necessary to understand how the type of law defining privateering as an activity with legal significance differed from the type of law governing the practices it supplanted. How modern international law differs from the approach to regulation that preceded it is itself a difficult question, for here too profound change was combined with considerable continuity.[11] Although it is not the central aim of this book to explain the origins and nature of the international law in use today, the question will inevitably arise in the course of three chapters designed to do three different things.[12] In the first chapter an overview is provided of the ways in which seizures of ships and goods at sea by private parties were categorised in the legal regime prevailing before the movement towards modern international law began. Evidence is presented here of the survival of these categories into the sixteenth century, but for the sake of clarity nothing is said at this stage about the beginnings of the movement towards modern international law in

8 Rodger 2003, pp. 240–1.

9 It complicates matters further that the word 'privateers' is sometimes used to designate ships and sometimes to designate the people who sailed them.

10 One consequence is that attention is paid here to the technicalities of documents produced on land more than to the drama of events unfolding at sea. This is a history of maritime raiding with the exciting bits left out.

11 Sereni 1943, pp. 56–67; Wijffels 1995, pp. 42–3; Grewe 2000, pp. 7–29; Steiger 2001, pp. 181–3 and 186–7; Neff 2005, pp. 85–7.

12 Again, it may seem that the most interesting aspects of the development of international law are passed over.

the same century. It is in the second chapter that this transition is first touched on, as background to an examination of significant changes made in the regulation of maritime warfare. The thesis of the second chapter is that the practice eventually designated 'privateering' started to develop in the latter half of the sixteenth century. In the third chapter the regulation of maritime warfare in the early seventeenth century is examined, and more is said about the type of law used in its regulation, the thesis being that privateering had emerged in all but name before the collapse of royal authority in Britain during the 1630s. By the time they reach the conclusion to the book readers will be able to decide for themselves whether the language of privateering should continue to be used in the anachronistic way in which it has been in the past.

As will become apparent, the problem will remain that less anachronistic language is hard to find. In a book about maritime raiding before the words 'privateer' and 'privateering' were invented, it is obviously necessary to use different vocabulary, yet the primary sources examined do not yield suitable alternatives.[13] While the expression 'maritime raiding' is itself absent from these sources, it is a convenient label for the general practice of seizing ships and goods at sea, whether it was considered to be legitimate or not. The word 'piracy' is of course used today to signify illegal seizures, but – as will be explained in the first chapter – it was not invariably used in this way. A subsidiary thesis advanced in this book is that a distinction always was drawn between legal and illegal seizures, which was one of the few aspects of legal categorisation to survive the emergence of privateering, though it was affected by an increasing emphasis on the responsibility of states to regulate conflicts at sea.[14] In the primary sources care was often taken to associate the word 'piracy' with other nouns or adjectives with less ambiguous meanings, and taking a lead from this the phrase 'criminal piracy' is used here to designate the form of raiding that was always regarded as illegitimate. The problem remains, however, of finding a suitable term to designate the legitimate form of raiding that was eventually replaced by privateering. For want of less anachronistic language, the phrase 'licit plunder' has been adopted. Although the English word 'plunder' was itself

13 The terminology used in other languages is if anything even more confusing, for rather than new terms being coined to describe the new practice, old terms tended elsewhere to be given new meanings. For example, as has often been pointed out, the French expression *guerre de course* appropriated the language of 'corsairing', which had originally had different significance (*e.g.* Rey 1992, vol. 1, pp. 504 and 516). More will be said about this in due course.

14 As will also be explained later, this runs contrary to a prominent theme in current historiography.

of later coinage, it can be applied without any great risk of confusion to the earlier practice of seizing enemy property in wartime, either on land or at sea, and it has the advantage of emphasising that an activity now considered illegal was once considered legal, at least in certain circumstances.[15] Since the words used in the primary sources to signify plunder were as ambiguous as the word piracy, the noun is again associated with an adjective.[16] The phrase 'licit plunder' is admittedly less than felicitous, and readers may be able to devise a more elegant expression, but it is used here *faute de mieux* in opposition to 'criminal piracy' and a couple of other phrases that will be encountered later in the first chapter.

Although writing this book has been conceived of as an exercise in legal rather than maritime history, it is of course appreciated that it may be of interest to historians generally, and as little prior knowledge as possible has therefore been assumed on the part of readers, irritating as this may sometimes be for specialists.[17] More specifically, work on the book began as an exercise in Scottish legal history, and explaining the development of maritime law in early-modern Scotland remains for the author its ultimate goal.[18] There are two reasons, however, why most of what is written is not focused narrowly on a small jurisdiction at the periphery of Europe. In the first place, because the conflicts with which the book is mostly concerned were wars between nations, there is a sense in which the law taken to regulate their conduct was always international.[19] Much of the book is therefore concerned with the theory and practice of maritime law in Europe generally, and readers with limited interest in Scotland may find that it enables them to understand developments elsewhere, with the specifically Scottish material providing an example of how the national and international dimensions of maritime law may be related to each other. Indeed, it is believed that viewing the subject from the perspective of a jurisdiction that had to come to terms with developments elsewhere helps to clarify the nature of those developments. In the second place, for reasons

15 More will be said about the choice of this word in due course.

16 The primary sources are much concerned, for instance, with distinguishing a just prize or *praeda iusta* from the type of *praeda* inflicted by brigands or *praedones*.

17 For an instructive review of recent work on maritime history, which tends to confirm that this exercise in legal history should be of wider interest, see Starkey 2011.

18 See the preface above for a brief outline of how the project took shape.

19 The words 'national' and 'international' are being used here rather loosely and should be taken at this stage to signify nothing more than a broad sense of the existence of territories that were governed internally by their own laws and involved externally with other similar territories. As is explained below, the word 'state' is sometimes used here in a similarly imprecise fashion.

to be explained in due course, the emergence of privateering in Scotland can only be understood properly in a British context. Much of the book is therefore concerned with developments in England, and to elucidate those developments something also has to be said about events in Spain, France and the Netherlands. To follow the argument of the book fully, readers are advised to omit nothing, yet the reality is that the sections in the first and third chapters dealing specifically with Scotland probably could be skipped over without the rest of the book becoming incomprehensible.[20] The Scottish sections, on the other hand, will be incomprehensible unless everything else is read. It should be obvious from the headings used (set out together in the table of contents) which sections concentrate on the Scottish experience of maritime conflict.

The three chapters of the book essentially form a series of essays, each with its own agenda and method, but they are all designed to address a single question, arising from a standard situation. It is envisaged that one ship is approached at sea by another. Through the use or the threat of violence, those aboard the second ship take control of the first. They retain the ship and the goods it carries, or make off with some of the goods. The situation envisaged arises at sea, not in a port, and involves the seizure of property, although people found in the first ship may also be detained.[21] The broad question addressed here is the obvious one that might have been put to a lawyer at the time: was the seizure of the ship and goods legitimate or illegitimate? More particular questions might also have been asked of legal experts: could the takers of the ship and goods be punished? could compensation be claimed from them for the losses and injuries they had inflicted? could the owners of the ship and goods recover their property? Questions like these might have been answered at two levels. On the one hand, a lawyer might have told people about the legal consequences of seizures at sea. He might, in other words, have told them about what ought to follow as a matter of law.[22] On the other hand, there might have been a divergence between what people were entitled to expect under the law and what they could actually expect to follow. A lawyer might have provided more pragmatic advice, and where there was a wide divergence between legality and reality people might actually have seen little point in consulting a lawyer. It must be borne in mind that to envisage people consulting lawyers whenever a ship and goods were seized at sea is an artificial device adopted for purposes of

20 It may be, though, that skipping the first section of the third chapter would make the rest hard to follow.

21 Compare, for example, Reyerson 2003 and Beck 2015.

22 Lawyers, in the periods studied, invariably were men.

analysis. People constantly engage today in activities governed by law without feeling any need to take advice on the law, though that is what they have to do if they want to understand what is going on more fully. It will also be seen that in responding to the questions they were actually asked, lawyers in the periods under examination often looked for answers in the customary practices of maritime communities.[23] In effect, they invited lay people to answer their own questions, and on these occasions there were answers available only because lay people were in the habit of regulating their own affairs. How they did so will be noted from time to time in the chapters that follow, and it will be seen that changes in the understanding of customary law were crucial to changes in the nature of the law regulating relations between nations. Nevertheless, both the customary practices of coastal communities and the questions they helped to answer will be approached here from the perspective of the legal experts who might have been consulted. It will be seen that while their thinking may not have been entirely consistent with the thinking of lay people, it was their thinking on which rulers generally relied in dealing with each other.[24]

Finally, in the interests of clarity, it may help to provide here some basic information about the structure of legal reasoning, although at this point readers with a legal training may need to look away in embarrassment. When asked whether the takers of a ship and goods could be punished, a lawyer would probably have considered whether they could be prosecuted by the public authorities of a state before a criminal court. One theme that needs to be explored here, however, is the extent to which it was considered legitimate to punish people outside criminal courts and without public authorisation. When asked whether compensation could be claimed from the takers of a ship and goods, a lawyer would certainly have considered whether an action could be raised against them before a civil court. Claims for compensation were made by way of 'personal actions', meaning court proceedings raised against particular persons (*personae*) who had incurred 'obligations' to those making the claims.[25] Actions of this type were distinguished from the 'real actions' that a lawyer would have thought about when asked whether the owners of a ship and goods seized at sea could recover their property. Real actions were available to owners

23 Customs tended to change in character when absorbed into the thinking of lawyers (Ibbetson 2007, p. 155; Brasington 2009, p. 89; Kadens 2016, p. 11).

24 The intention is to examine the relationship between the customary practices of maritime communities and the thinking of lawyers more fully in another book.

25 The basic theory outlined here derives from ancient Roman law, which, it will be seen, formed the foundation of much of the law examined in this book. For a lucid introduction to the subject see Nicholas 1962.

(and some other people) against anyone who interfered with the things (*res*) they owned, regardless of whether any personal relationship existed between them. As those who were 'owed' things could only claim them from the persons obliged to them, whereas those who 'owned' things could recover them from whoever happened to have them – the takers of the ship and goods, for instance, or people to whom they transferred them, or others to whom those people transferred them, and so on – 'real rights' such as ownership were generally believed to be more valuable than 'personal rights' such as claims to compensation, which would have been worthless had the person obliged disappeared or been unable to pay.[26] Consequently, as will be seen, a crucial consideration following the seizure of a ship and goods at sea was the ownership of the things taken. Although ownership tends to be acquired 'derivatively', through the transfer of title from one person to another, it can also be acquired 'originally', without one person passing it to another.[27] Most people who cook fish, for example, will have acquired it derivatively from a fishmonger, who may have acquired it derivatively from a supplier, who may even in turn have acquired it from someone else, yet ultimately the fish will have been acquired originally by the fishermen who caught it in the sea, where it was not already owned by someone else.[28] The situations in which original acquisition can occur are in practice quite limited, but it happens that in the periods dealt with here the seizure of a ship and goods at sea was in certain circumstances regarded as just such a situation. For the reasons outlined, whether ownership of a ship and goods seized at sea had been acquired was often what mattered most to people when the seizure was found to be legitimate. While the legitimacy of the seizure generally depended on the relations between the nations to which the people involved belonged, it was the relations between the people themselves that generally caused questions to be asked about the legitimacy of the seizure.[29]

26 A personal right, it is sometimes said, is only as good as the person. Of course, a real right will only be worth having while the thing exists and can be found, but ships and cargoes tended to be substantial assets.

27 The words 'title', 'ownership' and 'property' are used interchangeably here to mean the ultimate right people may have in things. People may be entitled to things (ownership) without in fact having them (possession), just as they may possess things without owning them.

28 Fish caught in fresh water are no longer acquired in precisely the same way.

29 While Koskenniemi 2011a has won adherents to the thesis that sixteenth-century theologians were responsible for the concern of modern international law with 'private rights' like property and contractual claims, the law regulating relations between nations had always revolved around these ideas to a significant extent.

CHAPTER 1

Seizures of Ships and Goods at Sea before Privateering

On 3 August 1558 the judges of the central admiralty court of Scotland, sitting in Leith, were presented with a petition by the captains and masters of two local vessels.[1] That the vessels had captains as well as masters was an indication that they had been prepared for combat, although they were not vessels owned and equipped for warfare by the state.[2] The petitioners alleged that 'thai and thair cumpany, being preparit and riggit furth in weirfair upoun inymeis of this realme, in the moneth of July lastbipast apprehendit and tuke ane Inglis prys, callit the *Grace of God* of Scarisburgh, quhilk aucht and suld be decernit to pertene to thame be ressoun of weir standand betwix this realme and the realme of Ingland'.[3] The judges confirmed that the English ship and its cargo had become the property of the petitioners after those sailing the ship, when examined by the court, 'declarit that thai, of the law of armes and be ressoun of weir standand betwix this realme and the realme of Ingland, culd nocht deny bot that thair schip and gudis ar just and lauchfull prys to the takaris thairof'. The English mariners thus conceded the legality of the claim made to their ship and goods, yet they would obviously not have been expected to know about the law of Scotland, any more than the Scottish judges would have been expected to decide the case in accordance with the law of England. The English mariners were able to express a view on the legality of the claim raised in the Scottish court because the 'law of armes' referred to was understood to have an international character.[4] As will be explained later in this book, it was not international law of the type known today, which only began to emerge towards the end of the sixteenth century. Rather, instead of all nations recognising the existence of a distinct body of norms regulating relations between them, each nation was expected to apply to disputes arising from warfare a branch of its own law, often referred to as the law of arms, which received a

1 *Acta curiae admirallatus Scotiae*, pp. 69–70.

2 Welwod, *Abridgement of all Sea-Lawes*, p. 20.

3 Here and in other quotations from primary sources liberties have occasionally been taken with both punctuation and capitalisation. Elsewhere, the use of certain letters has also been standardised.

4 Squibb 1959, pp. 162–90; Keen 1965, pp. 7–22; Meron 1993, pp. 7–16.

 | DOI:10.1163/9789004541412_003

degree of international recognition because it was developed in the light of the practices of other nations and was founded on the laws taught in universities throughout Europe. The aim of this chapter is to provide an outline of the law regulating the seizure of ships and goods at sea in medieval Europe and to consider the extent to which that law continued to be applied in practice in Scotland during the sixteenth century. The chapter alternates between sections dealing with the law taught in universities and developed in practice throughout Europe and sections dealing with the application of this law in Scotland.

1 Seizures of Ships and Goods at Sea as Plunder

Much of the ground covered by modern international law – including the formal initiation and termination of wars, and the making and keeping of treaties – was covered in ancient Rome by the *ius fetiale*, a special branch of the law concerned with the handling of relations with other nations by a dedicated class of priests (the eponymous *fetiales*).[5] War itself, however, together with some of its consequences, was thought to have arisen from a different branch of the law, known as the *ius gentium*, which encompassed all the rules and institutions believed by the Romans to be common to civilised nations (*gentes*) and not peculiar to themselves, a substantial part of the law applied to the ordinary affairs of citizens.[6] Several legal texts, preserved in the books compiled in the sixth century at the behest of the emperor Justinian and now known collectively as the *Corpus iuris civilis*, declared that 'things taken from enemies immediately become the property of the takers by *ius gentium*', in the same way that fish caught in the sea or pebbles found on a beach were understood to be acquired simply by taking them (*occupatio*).[7] Similarly, several texts declared that prisoners taken during a war would become the slaves of the takers by *ius gentium*, while an elaborate body of law dealt with the recovery of freedom by Romans who were captured and later released (*ius postliminii*), the assumption being that they too had in the meantime been the slaves of their captors.[8] On the other hand, another text indicated that land taken from an enemy during a war would become public as opposed to private property

5 Saulnier 1980; Wiedemann 1986; Watson 1993; Ferrary 1995; Santangelo 2008; Rich 2011.

6 *Digest*, 1.1.5, and *Institutes*, 1.2.2 and 2.1.17.

7 *Digest*, 41.1.5.7, 41.2.1.1 and 41.2.3.21. See too *Institutes of Gaius*, 2.69 and 4.16; Cicero, *De officiis*, 1.7.21; Quintilian, *Institutio oratoria*, 5.10.67.

8 *Digest*, 1.5.5.1, 49.15.5.2, 49.15.24 and 50.16.239.1, and *Institutes*, 1.2.2 and 2.1.17.

(*publicatur*), and it appeared to contrast private acquisition not only with the public acquisition of land but also with the acquisition of plunder (*praeda*) more generally.[9] Other texts suggested that everything captured during a war would count as plunder, described the theft of plundered things as a criminal offence, stated that the possessions of prisoners pertained to the public treasury (*fiscus*), and referred to the distribution of spoils (*spolia*) among soldiers by their commanding officers.[10] Read in isolation, these fragmentary survivals of a once extensive body of jurisprudence were difficult to understand.

Historical and literary sources shed further light on the subject. Notwithstanding certain complications, they reveal fairly clearly that Roman soldiers were required to swear an oath that they would not steal plundered things but would deliver anything of value they took from the enemy to their commanders, that their commanders were then expected to sell the plunder obtained and transfer the proceeds of the sale to the public treasury, and that the commanders were nevertheless permitted to distribute appropriate amounts of spoil as rewards among their troops.[11] Livy in particular described many occasions on which plunder was distributed by victorious generals, distinguishing the movable things that might become *praeda* from land, explaining that plunder was acquired by the Roman people by 'right of war' (*belli iure*), and praising the enemies of Rome who appreciated that 'there are certain rights of war (*belli iura*) that it is seemly to endure as well as to exercise'.[12] Modern scholars usually conclude that the legal texts relating to the acquisition of enemy things (*res hostium*) by private citizens, as if they were ownerless things (*res nullius*) open to occupation, must relate not to the acquisition of land or plunder by a campaigning army, but to the acquisition of things held by people living in Roman territory when peaceful relations with their nations broke down and recognition of their legal rights was withdrawn.[13] Of crucial importance to

9 *Digest*, 49.15.20.1.

10 *Digest*, 48.13.15, 49.14.31 and 49.15.28, and *Code*, 8.53.36.

11 Plautus, *Captives*, 1.2.110 and 2.3.453, and *Epidicus*, 1.1.43 and 64, 1.2.107, and 5.1.608 and 621; Cicero, *Letters to Atticus*, 113(5.20).5, *Letters to Friends*, 117(2.17).4, and *De inventione*, 1.45.84; Varro, *On Agriculture*, 2.10.4; *Attic Nights of Aulus Gellius*, 6.4.1–6, 13.25.24–32 and 16.4.2; Polybius, *Histories*, 6.33.1 and 10.16.2–9; Suetonius, *Lives of the Caesars*, 1.38.1; Appian, *Civil War*, 2.15.102; *Roman Antiquities of Dionysius of Halicarnassus*, 7.63.2–3; Tacitus, *Annals*, 13.39 (although Tacitus, *Histories*, 3.19 and 33–4, gives a different impression, bad practice was probably being described).

12 *Ab urbe condita*, 4.29.4, 4.53.10, 5.20.5–6, 5.25.5, 6.4.2, 6.13.6, 7.24.9–10, 7.27.8, 7.37.17, 9.1.5, 9.31.5, 9.37.10, 10.31.4, 10.45.14, 23.37.13, 24.16.5, 26.47.1–10, 27.1.2, 27.1.2, 27.19.2, 30.14.9, 31.27.4, 31.30.2–3, 37.5.3, 38.23.10, 40.16.9, 41.11.8, 45.34.4–5 and 45.40.1–5.

13 De Zulueta 1953, pp. 75–6; Berger 1953, pp. 606–7 and 678; Buckland 1963, p. 208. On the handling of plunder taken by advancing armies see too Shatzman 1972.

this interpretation is one of the legal texts, which states that enemy things 'among us' (*apud nos*) would be acquired by the takers (*occupantium*) instead of becoming public property (*publicae*).[14] If the *apud nos* requirement is read into all the other texts referring to the private acquisition of *res hostium* by *occupatio*, then those texts can easily be reconciled with the sources referring to the public acquisition of *praeda* and the distribution of *spolia* by military commanders. It took several centuries, however, for this modern interpretation to be established.

The medieval scholars who started to develop the study of Roman law as a university discipline around the beginning of the twelfth century tended to concentrate on the legal texts and to neglect the historical and literary sources.[15] To the extent that they looked beyond the *Corpus iuris civilis* it was to other legal sources, particularly those on church law incorporated into what became known as the *Corpus iuris canonici*.[16] These sources included an extract from the *Etymologiae* of Isidore of Seville in which *ius gentium* was defined as a body of law governing things like occupation, wars, captivity, slavery and *postliminium*.[17] In another extract from the same source, *ius militare* was said to provide for 'the distribution of plunder, and its just division according to the merits and efforts of the people involved, and the prince's share'.[18] This statement seemed slightly at odds with the question raised elsewhere 'whether heretics may be despoiled', which seemed to imply that fellow believers ought not to be treated in the same way.[19] Furthermore, the reference to 'the prince's share' was not easily reconciled with a passage extracted from a discussion by Ambrose of the fourteenth chapter of the book of Genesis, which described Abraham's return from a victorious war with plunder and prisoners.[20] According to the biblical text, Abraham gave 'a tithe of all the booty' to Melchizedeck, king of Salem, yet when the king of Sodom said to Abraham, 'give me the people, and you can take the property', Abraham replied that he would accept nothing that belonged to the king, while adding that his allies should receive their

14 *Digest*, 41.1.51.1.

15 Van Caenegem 1992, pp. 45–55; Robinson, Fergus and Gordon 2000, pp. 42–71; Lesaffer 2009, pp. 252–61.

16 Van Caenegem 1992, pp. 58–67; Robinson, Fergus and Gordon 2000, pp. 72–90; Lesaffer 2009, pp. 261–7.

17 *Decretum*, D. 1 c. 9; Isidore, *Etymologiae*, 5.6. The legitimacy of slavery also seemed to be conceded implicitly in *Decretum*, C. 17 q. 4 c. 37.

18 *Decretum*, D. 1 c. 10; *Etymologiae*, 5.7.

19 *Decretum*, C. 23 q. 7 pr.

20 Genesis 14.17–24. Though at this stage in the narrative Abraham was still known as Abram, his later name is used here for the sake of simplicity.

shares. Ambrose wondered why Abraham had given this reply 'when plunder was certainly in the power of the victor', to which the best answer might have been that the things captured by Abraham had actually included property taken from Sodom after a recent battle.[21] Yet the answer Ambrose provided was that 'military discipline reserves everything to the king', which was consistent neither with his own statement that plunder was in the victor's power, nor with the statement reproduced earlier that the prince was due a share of any plunder taken, nor with Abraham's ability to give a tithe of all the booty to Melchizedeck. The canon law texts thus introduced several contradictions of their own, as well as increasing the pressure on the civilian doctors to explain how the Roman law texts on the occupation of enemy things by private citizens could be reconciled with the other texts suggesting that plunder passed into public ownership.

One point was settled without much difficulty. The consensus quickly emerged that the texts relating to private acquisition were not concerned with things like land, towns or castles since 'immovable things become the property of the state declaring the war'.[22] In contrast, it was generally affirmed with some assurance that 'movable things taken from enemies become the property of the takers *iure gentium*', or that 'movable things taken in war pass into the ownership of those occupying them'.[23] In order to reconcile this common opinion with the texts relating to the distribution of spoils by commanding officers, Bartolus de Sassoferrato, the most influential of the civilian commentators, explained at one point that, strictly speaking, 'a movable thing that is taken does not become ours but is placed in common ownership and is assigned to the general'.[24] Elsewhere he repeated his observation that those who took

---

21 *Decretum*, C. 23 q. 5 c. 25; Ambrose, *De Abraham*, 3.17–18.

22 *Digestum novum*, col. 1678 (gl. 'Si quid bello' ad D.49.15.28); Bartolus de Sassoferrato, *Opera omnia*, vol. 2(1), f. 76v (ad D.41.1.5.7,), and vol. 2(2), ff. 236v-7r (ad D.49.15.26 and 49.15.28); Baldus de Ubaldis, *Commentaria super Codicem*, vol. 4, f. 158v (ad C.8.53.36); Bartolomeus de Saliceto, *Super Codicis commentaria*, vol. 4, f. 150r (ad C.8.50.12); Ioannes de Legnano, *Tractatus de bello*, p. 125; *Tractatus universi iuris*, vol. 12, f. 169v (Ioannes Lupus). For a more nuanced statement, which takes account of the tenure sometimes granted to soldiers in land occupied by the state, see Ioannes Calderinus, *Consilia*, f. 13v (n. 95, inc. 'Quis possit de iure guerram movere'). The word 'state' is of course being used rather loosely here and elsewhere – the sources refer to the *respublica, populus, civitas* or *princeps* – and it is not intended to suggest that states in the modern sense existed. Nevertheless, on the sense in which states were starting to emerge as entities in international law see Sumption 2020.

23 *Tractatus universi iuris*, f. 167r (Martinus Garatus Laudensis); *Repetitiones, disputationes necnon tractatus diversorum doctorum*, f. 100v (Angelus de Ubaldis); Bartolomeus de Bosco, *Consilia*, p. 32 (n. 24, inc. 'In quaestione Philippi de Vivaldis fuit oppositum'). Equally firm statements can be found in most of the passages cited in the preceding note.

24 *Opera omnia*, vol. 2(1), ff. 76v-7r.

things from the enemy were 'required to assign them to the general, who will later distribute them among the soldiers according to their merits', but he did not repeat his suggestion that the things had first passed into common ownership, nor was the suggestion taken up by anyone else.[25] Sometimes explaining that the pooling and redistributing of spoils was necessary to avoid soldiers being distracted from the primary task of defeating the enemy, other commentators agreed without exception that, 'to begin with, goods become the property of the takers, though afterwards they should be assigned to the general so that he may distribute them among the fighters according to their merits'.[26] This particular formulation of the opinion actually derived from a book written by Nicholas de Tudeschis, alias Panormitanus, who like other canonist doctors agreed with the civilians that military discipline reserved everything to the king only in the sense that everything was to be handed over to the royal or other commander for equitable redistribution among the troops.[27] The canonists had no doubt that it was not only a heretic who could be lawfully despoiled of a thing but any enemy, and that 'the despoiler becomes the owner of the thing'.[28]

The *res hostium* open in Roman law to private acquisition through *occupatio* were thus understood – or rather misunderstood – by the medieval doctors, both civilian and canonist, to include things plundered by troops during a war. According to them, soldiers had a right to despoil the combatants and civilians of other nations as long as there was a genuine state of war between those nations and their own. Texts in the *Corpus iuris civilis* classified enemies (*hostes*) as 'those against whom the Roman people have publicly declared war or who have themselves declared war against the Roman people'.[29] The civilian doctors consequently emphasised that the right to despoil the enemy arose only in a war that was lawful (*bellum licitum*) in the sense of being formally declared by someone who either legally or factually acknowledged no superior to whom the dispute could have been referred for resolution.[30] Under canonist

25 *Opera omnia*, vol. 2(2), ff. 236v-7r.

26 Baldus, *Commentaria super Codicem*, vol. 4, f. 158v; De Saliceto, *Super Codicis commentaria*, vol. 4, f. 150r; De Legnano, *Tractatus de bello*, p. 125; Calderinus, *Consilia*, f. 13v; *Tractatus universi iuris*, vol. 12, ff. 167r (Garatus), 169v (Lupus) and 192r (Franciscus Arias).

27 Panormitanus, *Lectura super quinque libros Decretalium*, vol. 2(2), f. 136r (ad X 2.24.29); *Decretum aureum Gratiani*, ff. 3r (gl. 'Ac principis portio' ad D. 1 c. 10) and 377 (gl. 'Omnia' ad C. 23 q. 5 c. 2); Henricus de Segusio, alias Hostiensis, *Summa aurea*, col. 286 (ad X 1.34. rub.).

28 See too *Decretum aureum Gratiani*, f. 381v (gl. 'Nunc autem' ad C. 23 q. 7 pr).

29 *Digest*, 49.15.24 and 50.16.118.

30 *Digestum vetus*, col. 57 (gl. 'Bella' ad D.1.1.5); *Digestum novum*, col. 402 (gl. 'Bello' ad D.41.2.1); *Volumen legum parvum*, pt 3, cols 17 (gl. 'Bella' ad J.1.2.2) and 128 (gl. 'Ex hostibus' ad J.2.1.17);

influence, some civilian doctors also talked about whether a war was just (*bellum iustum*) in the sense of being started for a just cause (*iusta causa*), such as defence against aggression or redress for a wrong, though the tendency among the civilians was to assume that any *bellum publicum* or *bellum licitum* would also be a *bellum iustum*.[31] This was an assumption of some importance, for a strict insistence on the justice of waging war might have led to the conclusion that only those on one side of any conflict would have been able to acquire property from the other.[32] Satisfied that those on either side of a properly initiated war could acquire property from their enemies, the civilian doctors did not make rigorous use of the concept of a just war.

As the discussion of who might possess the authority to declare a licit war suggests, the concern among the civilians was with the legitimacy of plunder not in the ancient but the contemporary world, to which they made frequent reference, for instance in noting that troops often were ordered to hand plunder over to their commanders for redistribution. Moreover, the later civilians especially were prepared to recognise that some parts of Roman law could not be applied directly to their own conditions. A pertinent example is the rule that prisoners taken in a war would become the slaves of those who captured them. Both the civilians and the canonists maintained that in theory 'a man who is taken in a war becomes a thing rather than a person', and that this theory was rightly put into practice when 'a war is declared against the Saracens'.[33] Yet they also tended to point out in a fairly standardised way that, as far as wars between Christians were concerned, 'the laws of captivity and *postliminium*

Bartolus, *Opera omnia*, vol. 2(1), f. 78r (ad D.41.2.1.1), vol. 2(2), f. 236 (ad D.49.15.24), and vol. 3 (1), f. 95v (ad D.28.1.13); Baldus, *Commentaria super Codicem*, vol. 4, f. 9r (ad C.7.14.4); *Repetitiones, disputationes necnon tractatus diversorum doctorum*, f. 100v (Angelus); De Legnano, *Tractatus de bello*, pp. 123–4; *Tractatus universi iuris*, vol. 12, ff. 159r (Paris de Puteo) and 169v (Lupus).

31 Baldus, *Commentaria super Codicem*, vol. 4, f. 158v, and *Consilia sive responsa*, vol. 2, f. 99r (n. 258, inc. 'Licet latrunculis non sit fides servanda'); De Saliceto, *Super Codicis commentaria*, vol. 4, f. 150; Bartolomeus Socinus, *Ad Digestum novum et aliquot Codicis tutulos*, ff. 2v-3r (ad D.41.2.1); *Decretum aureum Gratiani*, ff. 3r (gl. 'Servitutes' ad D. 1 c. 9) and 381v (gl. 'Nunc autem' ad C. 23 q. 7 pr); Panormitanus, *Lectura super quinque libros Decretalium*, vol. 2(2), f. 136r; Hostiensis, *Lectura in quinque Decretalium Gregorianarum libros*, vol. 1, f. 133r (ad X 2.24.29); Innocentius IV, *In quinque libros Decretalium commentaria*, f. 119r (ad X 2.24.29). On the canonist theory see Russell 1975, pp. 55–212.

32 *Cf.* Reichberg, Syse and Begby 2006, pp. 227–8, and Fedele 2021, pp. 444–72.

33 *Volumen legum parvum*, pt 3, col. 128 (gl. 'Recipiunt' ad J.2.1.17); Bartolus, *Opera omnia*, vol. 2(2), f. 236v (ad D.49.15.24); Baldus, *Consilia sive responsa*, 2.358.2; *Repetitiones, disputationes necnon tractatus diversorum doctorum*, f. 100v (Angelus); De Saliceto, *Super Codicis commentaria*, vol. 4, f. 150v; De Legnano, *Tractatus de bello*, pp. 124–5; *Tractatus universi iuris*, vol. 12, ff. 159v (De Puteo), 167v (Garatus), 169v (Lupus) and 192r (Arias).

are observed today in relation to things more than persons'. The explanation usually given was that the *ius gentium* described in the Roman texts had been introduced by ancient custom (*antiquis moribus*), that a different custom had developed in the early church and been observed in later conflicts (*mores moderni temporis et consuetudines antiquitus observatas inter Christianos*), and that it was this custom that deserved adherence (*cui consuetudini est standum*). The later custom was to detain prisoners taken in a war against Christians until a suitable ransom was paid for their release, which was itself consistent with several Roman texts referring to the payment of ransoms for the release of prisoners.[34] Without questioning the soundness of the Roman theory that prisoners of war could be enslaved, the doctors were thus able to conclude that in practice they should not be unless they were infidels. It mattered, of course, that the infidels encountered around the Mediterranean themselves preserved the practice of enslaving the Christians they captured.

Responsive to contemporary practice, the learned theory of the schools also left ample scope for local variation. Former students of the civil and canon laws often became specialists in the *ius armorum* applied in military courts.[35] Their basic assumptions in dealing with disputes were those they had imbibed as students, as is evident from a treatise written by a graduate in canon law, Honoré Bouvet, which was widely read, translated and imitated throughout Europe during the fifteenth century. One assumption – in the words of a translator into Scots, Sir Gilbert Hay, himself a 'bachilere in decreis' – was that 'gudis wonnyn apon inymyes, but ony questioun, ar thairis that wynnis thame, that is to say, meubles'.[36] The expectation was still that plunder would be handed over to royal commanders for redistribution, and it was added that things might actually belong to the king if the soldiers who took them had been in his service, but the assumption remained that things belonging to enemies were open to private acquisition through occupation.[37] Similarly, the assumption remained that while it would be wrong 'to sell a Cristyn creature that was boucht out of thraldome be the precious blude of Jhesu Crist', it was permissible to hold prisoners taken in wars waged against Christian nations to

34 *Code*, 8.50.2, 8.50.12 and 8.53.36.

35 Kilgour 1935; Contamine 1972, pp. 187–204; Wright 1976; Taylor 1977; Whetham 2009, pp. 48–70 and 166–96.

36 Bouvet, *Arbre des batailles*, sig. I4, or *Tree of Battles*, pp. 149–50; *Prose Works of Sir Gilbert Hay*, vol. 2, pp. 143–5. In Hay's Scots the word 'but' meant 'without'.

37 Bouvet, *Arbre des batailles*, sigg. G4v-5r, or *Tree of Battles*, pp. 134–5; *Prose Works of Sir Gilbert Hay*, vol. 2, pp. 113–14; Christine de Pisan, *Book of Fayttes of Armes*, vol. 1, pp. 218–20. On the distribution of spoils among troops in public employment see Powers 1988, pp. 162–87.

ransom.[38] However, these assumptions provided no more than a framework of legitimacy within which the detailed regulation of warfare required to be filled out from other sources. More detail was often provided by 'articles of war' issued at the commencement of hostilities, as when Scottish soldiers were instructed in 1448 that where one person 'takis his fallowis hors, gif he wynnis ony gudis on him, outhir presoner or uther gudis, he that aw the horse sal have the half of it', and that where one person 'strikis doun ane man of hors bak', enabling someone else to take him prisoner, 'he that strikis him doun sall have his half ransome'.[39] Otherwise advice was taken from experienced soldiers or administrators who could remember how issues had been resolved in the past, or who knew how they tended to be dealt with in other countries. In this way customary rules developed to distinguish small items that soldiers were entitled to pillage and keep for themselves from larger items that had to be pooled for redistribution as plunder, to determine the proportions in which plunder was to be shared out between those involved in a military enterprise, and to specify the means used to effect an equitable redistribution.[40] Customary rules likewise regulated the treatment of prisoners of war, indicating the levels at which ransoms ought normally to be set, and providing for the reimbursement of those who contributed towards payments made for the release of captives.[41]

To some extent the rules differed depending on whether a war was conducted on land or at sea, though either way they were developed within the same framework of legitimacy provided by the learned laws.[42] Opportunities for plunder on land tended to be open only to those who travelled into enemy territory with a campaigning army, subject to any disciplinary code enacted under the authority of the sovereign directing the war, whereas opportunities to seize ships and goods at sea were often open to mariners in the course of their ordinary business, without the necessity of service in a navy. Ships were

38 Bouvet, *Arbre des batailles*, sig. I5, or *Tree of Battles*, pp. 151–3; *Prose Works of Sir Gilbert Hay*, vol. 2, pp. 147–50; De Pisan, *Book of Fayttes of Armes*, vol. 1, pp. 222–4.

39 *Acts of the Parliaments of Scotland*, vol 1, app., pp. 350–1. Scottish as well as English practice can be found discussed in Hay 1988, pp. 265–306; Reid 1936–8, p. 216; Meron 1993, pp. 142–53. See too the ordinances reproduced and discussed in Curry 2011, along with Keen 1995 and Curry 2008.

40 Keen 1965, pp. 137–55; Bean 1989, pp. 238–44; Stacey 1994, pp. 34–5; Contamine 2000, pp. 173–9.

41 Keen 1965, pp. 156–85; Contamine 2000, pp. 164–72; King 2002, pp. 271–84. The thorough and valuable study of 'ransom culture' in Ambühl 2013 is strangely neglectful of the learned background, which among other things provided the explanation the author struggles to find of why it was thought lawful to demand a ransom (*cf.* Yamauchi 1994).

42 Maritime examples are rightly included in some of the discussions cited above.

generally armed, for reasons that will be returned to later, and they could easily be strengthened and put to sea in search of plunder as soon as a war broke out, when according to the doctrine of the schools, any enemy ships or goods captured would become the property of the captors.[43] More detailed regulations were required, however, and it was recognised throughout Europe that sovereigns could assume responsibility for the regulation of maritime warfare, and the distribution of property captured at sea, even when their own naval forces were not involved. Jurisdiction was commonly conferred on admiralty courts, staffed again with judges trained in the learned laws, who took it for granted that plunder could be lawfully acquired in wartime, and developed a fuller understanding of when exactly ships and goods should be counted as *res hostium*, when exactly they should be taken to have been occupied, and how exactly they should be divided up between their captors.[44] A share of the spoils was usually claimed by the sovereign or his admiral, typically set at a tenth, perhaps after the example of the tithe given to Melchizedeck by Abraham.[45] Gradually the language of maritime plunder became more distinctive. In the fifteenth century the word 'prise' was still used generally in Scots as well as English to signify anything taken from an enemy in a properly initiated war (from the French *prise de bonne guerre*).[46] By the sixteenth century, however, towards the end of which the spelling 'prize' first appeared in England, the word was beginning to be used more specifically in relation to the seizure of ships and goods at sea.[47]

That the fundamental assumptions of the learned laws had already been widely accepted is evident from a diplomatic exchange between the king of England and the grand master of the Teutonic Order at the beginning of the

43 Hutchinson 1994, p. 153; Sayers 2002, pp. 150–1; Rodger 2003, p. 236; Rose 2007, p. 123.

44 Sanborn 1930, pp. 60–1; Bastid 1962, pp. 183–5; Rodger 1997, p. 149; Ward 2009, pp. 33–4.

45 Obviously more would be claimed by the ruler if his own ships or employees were involved.

46 In identical entries in Robert Estienne, *Dictionaire françoislatin*, p. 391, Jean Thierry, *Dictionaire françoislatin*, p. 499, and Jean Nicot, *La grand dictionaire françoislatin*, p. 722, the phrase *emmener la prinse, pillage ou butin* is equated with the Latin *praedam agere*.

47 Simpson and Weiner 1993, vol. 12, p. 527; Craigie, Aitken, Stevenson, Watson and Dareau 1931–2002, vol. 6, pp. 231–2; Godefroy 1881–1902, vol. 6, p. 412. The English term 'prize' was thus equivalent to the Latin *praeda*, and an alternative to the terms spoils (from the Latin *spolia*) and booty (from the French *butin*). The English term 'plunder' did not come into use until the 1640s (Simpson and Weiner 1993, vol. 11, pp. 1084–5) but now seems a more natural equivalent to *praeda* than prize outwith the maritime context. Note that although the form 'prize' is said in Craigie, Aitken, Stevenson, Watson and Dareau 1931–2002 to appear in the practicks of Sir James Balfour of Pittendreich, this means the version printed in the eighteenth century, not the version written in the sixteenth century.

fifteenth century.[48] Two Prussian ships had encountered another ship at sea and taken it to Danzig, suspecting from the condition of its equipment and crew that it was in the hands of sea robbers or pirates (*raptores marini seu piratae*). On reaching port, the ship had been arrested and those on board incarcerated while the city authorities investigated the matter. Most of the sailors turned out to be from Normandy, and while they acknowledged that the ship had indeed been seized at sea and provided with a skeleton crew, they insisted that the seizure had been legitimate. When two other sailors from England were examined, they substantiated the account given by the Normans. The ship had been returning to its home port of Lynn from Newcastle with a cargo of coal when another ship, on which the Normans were sailing, approached in a hostile manner. The master of the English ship and most of his crew fled ashore, leaving the two sailors to face their assailants. A few Normans were put on board and were making off with the ship, its cargo and the two English sailors when they were met by the Prussian vessels. The English sailors had no doubt about what was happening. As everyone knew that the Normans were enemies of the English (*regis et regni Anglie notorie inimici*), it was in keeping with their law and practice that the ship would belong to the takers (*iure suo navis ista esset capientium*) and that they would themselves be held to ransom (*tenerentur eis ad exactionem more suo*). Although the authorities in Danzig were anxious to maintain their close trading relations with Lynn, they felt they had no option but to release the Normans and allow them to sell the ship and cargo and detain their English prisoners.[49] In a further twist, however, it turned out that there had been a misunderstanding, for hostilities were being encouraged in the North Sea by the king of England and the duke of Orleans, as lieutenant and captain-general of Normandy, without any formal declaration of war being issued between England and France.[50] The grand master of the Teutonic Order was relieved to be able to report that it was the city authorities in Danzig, not his own council at Marienburg, who had sent the Normans on their way. What seems striking is the assumption common to all those involved that if a war had been in existence, the seizure of a ship and the goods it carried, and also of any sailors on board the ship, would have been legitimate.

The part played by the two English sailors in this episode is especially significant, for two reasons. The first is that their readiness to acknowledge the

48 *Hanserecesse*, vol. 5, pp. 341–3. On the background to this exchange, which will be returned to later in this chapter, see Lloyd 1991, pp. 110–14.

49 On relations between Danzig and Lynn see Richards 2005, pp. 18; Jenks 2005, pp. 100–1; Parker 2008, pp. 213–14.

50 Pistono 1975; Ford 1979; Given-Wilson 2008.

legitimacy of the seizure bears testimony to the strength of the assumption shared by sailors throughout Europe, for it would obviously have been in their own interest to contest the point. The second is that their acknowledgement of the legitimacy of the seizure shows how widely the assumption was made even beyond continental Europe, notwithstanding the different impression given in the literature on prize acquisition in England.[51] It has often been suggested that ships and goods captured in wartime became the property of the English king, and that the captors of ships and goods only acquired title to them through grants made by the king.[52] It has often been suggested further that in order to receive grants from the English king mariners had to obtain licences or commmissions from him before sailing, and had to obtain court orders conferring title on them after returning to England.[53] Nothing in the evidence taken from the two sailors of Lynn supports any of this. They did not mention any requirement for a grant to be made by the king, for a licence to be held or for a court order to be obtained. Admittedly, it is not entirely clear what the sailors meant when they talked about 'their law' (*iure suo*) and 'their usage' (*more suo*), and the authorities in Danzig are less likely to have believed that the law of England should be applied to the case than their own law or even the law of Normandy. Yet the vagueness of the expressions recorded, and the failure of the English sailors to argue that a licence must be produced before a court order was made, are indicative of their acceptance that under their law, as much as the law of Danzig or Normandy, ships and goods taken from enemies in wartime became the property of the takers. In fact, no evidence has ever been adduced to demonstrate that English law deviated in any way from the theory of the law schools, and much of the evidence only makes sense on the assumption that it did not. As will be explained further in the first section of the next chapter, English kings or their officials regulated the distribution of prizes and claimed shares themselves, but only in ships and goods that mariners had acquired for themselves (*sibi adcquicierant*).[54]

The English mariners questioned in Danzig obviously did not have an opportunity to consult experts in their own law, and had they been at home

51 For a fuller discussion of this point see the first section of the next chapter, and also Ford 2018a.

52 Nicolas 1847, vol. 1, p. 140; Marsden 1909, p. 675; Holdsworth 1922–66, vol. 1, p. 140; Fermoy 1926, pp. 556–7; Schwarzenberger 1948, p. 81; Kemp 1976, p. 670; Shaw 2021, pp. 165–6.

53 Marsden 1909, p. 682; Roscoe 1924, pp. 8 and 11; Kingsford 1925, pp. 78–9; Appleby 1992, p. 90; Sayers 2002, p. 157; Starkey 2011, p. 130; Pitcaithly 2012, p. 125; Rose 2013, pp. 140–1.

54 *Documents relating to Law and Custom of the Sea*, pp. 1–2, 5–6 and 35–8; *Calendar of the Patent Rolls*, 1292–1301, p. 130; *Foedera, conventiones, litterae et cuiuscunque generis acta publica*, vol. 4, pp. 226–7.

they might still have felt little need for such advice.[55] That it was lawful to seize ships and goods from enemies in wartime, and that anything taken in these conditions could be kept, was something they would have learned when mastering their trade. That the same basic assumptions were made everywhere was something they would have been able to confirm when dealing with mariners and merchants from other nations. When they talked about 'their law' and 'their usage', they may actually have been thinking of themselves less as Englishmen than as mariners, and have been drawing attention to the common assumptions of all members of a wider seafaring community. To know that the Normans had acquired title to their ship and goods, the English mariners did not need to know that their assumptions corresponded to legal principles taught in the universities, or that technically the ship and goods were acquired by the *occupatio* of something akin to *res nullius*, or that the takers acquired real as opposed to personal rights.[56] It does not follow, however, that the legal theory lacked practical relevance. If the English mariners had understood the precise significance of the term 'enemies', for instance, they might have hesitated before conceding that the Normans had acted lawfully, and might not have lost their ship and goods, or been held to ransom.[57] Moreover, however indifferent most mariners may have been to the legal niceties of the seizures in which they were involved, when seizures were brought to the attention of government agencies, care generally was taken to understand the law correctly. The authorities in Prussia did eventually work out how the law should have been applied to the seizure made off the coast of England. Had enquiries been made there, they would have been dealt with in a specialised admiralty court, by lawyers educated at a university.[58] These lawyers would have been taught that disputes should be settled in accordance with the laws particular to the places in which they were raised (the *ius proprium*), but that the particular law

55 This point could probably be made more forcefully, for there is no direct evidence that mariners did consult lawyers. As was explained in the Introduction, however, for present purposes it is instructive to consider the advice lawyers might have given if they had been consulted.

56 Nowadays, after all, fishermen make assumptions about the legality of their trade and the ownership of catches, and need to know a fair amount about the regulations governing their activities – regulations that differ from the articles of war mentioned above in detail alone – but do not need to know about the principles underpinning the law of sea fishing – rooted again, as it happens, in the Roman lawyers' idea of the *occupatio* of *res nullius*.

57 The misunderstanding of the situation, in other words, may have been legal as well as factual.

58 Laing 1946, p. 169; Hanna 2015, p. 30; Musa 2017, p. 128.

of each place was to be examined in the light of the law common to all nations (the *ius commune*), from which it was often possible to work out solutions to problems the local sources did not cover.[59] The civil law was taken to be the common law. From a descriptive point of view, it was a discipline common to universities across Europe, and many of its principles – including those governing prize taking – were observed in practice everywhere.[60] From a prescriptive point of view, the civil law was taught in universities across Europe because it was believed to have universal validity, as the law of the empire or as a reliable guide to justice, and in international relations especially its principles were adhered to not only because they seemed sound to everyone, but also because rulers recognised a need for their dealings with each other to be governed by shared standards.

It complicates matters that the precocious centralisation of justice in England led to the development of a *ius proprium* of such sophistication that relatively little recourse was taken to the *ius commune*.[61] Indeed, the lawyers who appeared before the central courts there viewed the statutes and customs of the realm as their own 'common law'. It was in this law that prospective practitioners before these courts were educated, not at universities but at institutions known as inns of court. The common lawyers formed a separate profession from the civil lawyers in England. There was in consequence an opportunity for a distinctive law of prize acquisition to take shape, which to historians used to examining the indigenous growth of the common law may seem likely to have happened.[62] However, the opportunity does not appear to have been taken. At an early stage in the development of the common law, when royal judges were instructed to travel around the country enquiring into interference with the crown's rights, the acquisition of enemy property did receive some attention.[63] Among other things, the judges were sometimes told to find out what had become of items taken from the king's enemies in England.[64] On one occasion judges sent to the Cinque Ports were told to

59 Canning 1987, pp. 148–54; Stein 1988, pp. 83–90; Hallebeek 2018, pp. 302–7.

60 The only other law taught in the universities was the canon law of the church, though feudal law was also treated as a branch of the civil law.

61 Robinson, Fergus and Gordon 2000, pp. 125–53; Lesaffer 2009, pp. 279–83; Ascheri 2013, pp. 234–6; Wauters and De Benito 2017, pp. 144–61.

62 The widespread misunderstanding of prize law in England may have resulted to some extent from an expectation of this type. For some reason, even historians who have recognised the crucial role played by the civil lawyers in the admiralty court have paid scant attention to the civil law itself.

63 Holdsworth 1922–66, vol. 1, pp. 264–9; Milsom 1981, pp. 27–31; Hudson 2012, pp. 544–8.

64 *Eyre of Kent*, vol. 1, p. 32; *Eyre of Northamptonshire*, vol. 2, p. 778; *Rotuli litterarum clausarum*, vol. 2, p. 214; *Annales monastici*, vol. 1, p. 332; *Munimenta Gildhallae Londoniensis*,

investigate 'ships captured in war and released by William of Wrotham'.[65] It seems that William of Wrotham had been put in charge of a royal fleet, that the king's sailors had seized enemy vessels, and that some of them had been distributed without proper authority.[66] This was as close as any of the instructions – 'the articles of eyre' – came to dealing with seizures of ships and goods at sea by private parties, and the takers do not appear to have been private parties. Although the instructions are believed to have covered all the rights of the crown, none of them indicates that ships and goods taken at sea were always understood to become the property of the crown, as would later be claimed by common lawyers, after the emergence of privateering in the strict sense.[67] Until the seventeenth century, accounts of the prerogative rights of the crown did not deal with prize acquisition.[68] The legal position in medieval England appears to have been the opposite of the position in ancient Rome, since the crown confiscated anything taken from enemies at home but did not lay claim to anything taken elsewhere, unless it was taken by the king's own servants. Ironically, this was partly due to recognition that the seizure of enemy property outside England ought to be governed by the misreading of the Roman law texts in the universities.

By the sixteenth century awareness was growing that Roman practice had not in fact been consistent with the medieval reading of the Roman law texts, and some commentators on the law of arms were arguing that modern practice would be improved by being brought into line with what had really gone on in antiquity, when it was the successful nation as a whole that had been enriched with the spoils of victory.[69] Nevertheless, the theory that individual soldiers and sailors enjoyed legal rights of pillage, plunder and prize survived until the end of the century. It is true that a new approach to the

---

vol. 1, pp. 80 and 118, and vol. 2, p. 351; *Historia et cartularium monasterii Sancti Petri Gloucestriae*, vol. 2, p. 278; *Statutes of the Realm*, vol. 1, pp. 233–5; Cam 1921, pp. 19–23 and 92–5; Meekings 1961, p. 32.

65 *Bracton on the Laws and Customs of England*, vol. 2, p. 333.

66 Brooks 1925.

67 Compare, for instance, Colombos 1967, p. 814, with Baker 2003, pp. 211–12.

68 Anthony Fitzherbert, *Graunde abridgement*, pt 2, ff. 105v-6; Robert Brooke, *Graunde abridgement*, ff. 145–9r, *Statutes of the Realm*, vol. 1, pp. 226–7; *John Spelman's Reading on Quo Warranto*, pp. 26–42; *Prerogativa regis: Tertia lectura Roberti Constable de Lincolnis Inne*; Sir William Staunford, *Exposicion of the King's Prerogative*; McGlynn 1998, pp. 269–312, and 2003, pp. 261–306.

69 Raymond de Beccarie de Pavie, sieur de Fourquevaux, *Instructions sur le faict de la guerre*, f. 61, or *Instructions for the Warres*, pp. 165–6; Guillaume Joly, *Traicté de la justice militaire de France*, ff. 49–52; Balthazar de Ayala, *De iure et officiis bellicis et disciplina militari*, vol. 1, ff. 32v-54, and vol. 2, pp. 34–54.

study of Roman law had emerged in some universities, and that devotees of this approach – known as legal humanism, or as the *mos Gallicus* in contrast to the *mos Italicus* – were interested in the historical context in which the law had operated, and were keen to learn from sources other than the legal texts.[70] It is also true that Andreas Alciatus, the scholar often credited with establishing the new approach in the French universities, maintained not only that nobody taken prisoner in a war between Christian nations would become a slave, but also that no object 'taken in a war of this type becomes the taker's property', insisting that 'it is ridiculous to believe it is allowed for soldiers to despoil the subjects of each other's nations'.[71] This view was based, however, on the argument that all Christians were effectively citizens of the same state, not on a more accurate reading of the texts about private acquisition, and in general the humanist jurists continued to read even the texts about prisoners in a conventional way.[72] Furthermore, there were other scholars teaching in the universities, and practitioners who had been taught by them, who still adhered in this area to the doctrine of the medieval commentators.[73] It was still maintained by both learned lawyers and military experts that movable things taken on land or at sea became the property of the takers, subject to such duties as were imposed by the local version of the law of arms to deliver all or part of the spoils to their rulers or to those placed in authority by their rulers.[74] Despite criticism, the traditional law of arms remained in vigour throughout the sixteenth century,

70 Van Caenegem 1992, pp. 55–8; Robinson, Fergus and Gordon 2000, pp. 172–80; Lesaffer 2009, pp. 350–8.

71 *Opera omnia*, vol. 1, col. 274, and vol. 3, col. 331.

72 Iacobus Cuiacius, *Opera omnia*, vol. 2, col. 120; Franciscus Connanus, *Commentarii iuris civilis*, ff. 72r-3r and 140v; Hugo Donellus, *Commentarii de iure civili*, vol. 1, pp. 27 and 275–8. The texts about the acquisition of *res hostium* and the distribution of *spolia* do not appear to have attracted a great deal of attention at this early stage in the historical study of Roman law, though an exception that proves the rule is Pierre du Faur, *Semestrium liber secundus*, pp. 25–46, where the inconsistency between later civil law doctrine and ancient Roman law was noted, yet an attempt was made to preserve the efficacy of the civil law doctrine.

73 Claudius Cotereus, *De iure et privilegiis militum*, pp. 59 and 123; Giulio Ferretti, *Consilia et tractatus*, ff. 33, 39r and 42r; Nicolas Bohier, *Decisiones Burdegalenses*, p. 305; Petrus Gregorius Tholosanus, *Syntagma iuris universi*, pp. 250, 389–90 and 833; Caesar Costa, *Variae ambiguitates iuris*, ff. 17r and 19.

74 Pierino Belli, *De re militari et bello*, vol. 1, ff. 40v-1r, 45–7r and 52v-3r, and vol. 2, pp. 85–6, 95–9 and 115–16; Matthew Sutcliffe, *Practice, Proceedings, and Lawes of Armes*, pp. 13–15, 331, 333 and 336–8; Giulio Ferretti, *De iure et re navali*, ff. 134v-5r and 140r; *Guidon, stile et usance des marchands qui mettent à la mer*, pp. 49–50; Lancelot du Voisin, sieur de la Popelinière, *Amiral de France*, ff. 57v-8r; Henricus Bocerus, *De iure pugnae, hoc est belli et duelli*, pp. 64–73.

though subject to challenge – as will be seen in due course – from the newly emerging law of nations.[75]

2 Acquisition of Prizes in Sixteenth-Century Scotland

As the example given at the start of this chapter shows, Scotland was certainly one country in which prize acquisition continued to operate in accordance with the 'law of armes' during the sixteenth century. Although it was not then the practice for the monarch to issue written regulations to mariners at the commencement of hostilities, evidence of the unwritten rules that were taken to govern prize acquisition can be found in records of court proceedings and in books written by lawyers. The court proceedings were of various types. In the first place, for reasons that will be returned to in the third chapter, cases are recorded in which the takers of a ship or cargo sought a declaration from a court – usually the central court of admiralty, sitting in Leith or Edinburgh – that the ship or cargo constituted a just prize and therefore belonged to the takers.[76] In the second place, cases are recorded in which the lawful seizure of a ship or cargo was pled as a defence to an action raised – usually before the session, the supreme civil court of Scotland – for the restitution of property 'spoiled' from its owners.[77] In the third place, cases are recorded in which the lawful seizure of a ship or cargo was again pled as a defence, but to a complaint about piracy – made, in the few known cases, before the privy council, which functioned as a court of law as well as an administrative body.[78] The records in which examples of these types of case can be found are less informative than might have been hoped. The only surviving records of the central court of admiralty consist of summaries entered by a clerk of the court into an act book covering a period of just four and a half years, from the autumn of 1557 until the spring of 1562, and even for the period covered the summaries provide no

75 Redlich 1956, pp. 1–53; Cruickshank 1969, pp. 119–26; Contamine 2000, pp. 179–84; Trim 2002, pp. 87–9.

76 *Acta curiae admirallatus Scotiae*, pp. 10–11, 30–1, 69–70 and 72; *Registrum secreti sigili regum Scotorum*, vol. 8, p. 79; DCA, BCMB, vol. 5, 5 July 1558.

77 The many actions raised for the 'spoliation' or 'spuilzie' of a ship or cargo in which it was not pled as a defence that the seizure was lawful have been left out of this survey, but for others in which the defence may perhaps have been pled see, in addition to those mentioned below, *Extracts from the Records of the Burgh of Edinburgh*, vol. 1, pp. 122–3; *Acts of the Lords of Council in Public Affairs*, p. 250; *Practiques of Sir Richard Maitland of Lethington*, pp. 35 and 39–40.

78 Other cases relating to piracy are returned to in the final section of this chapter.

more than glimpses of the legal reasoning that motivated the decisions of the court.[79] The records of the session and privy council are more extensive – and the registers of acts and decreets of the session may contain further examples of prize litigation still to be discovered – but in their surviving form they too provide limited insight into the thinking behind decisions.[80] It seems unlikely that it was only in the few cases found in the register of the privy council that the lawful seizure of a ship or cargo was pled as a defence to a charge of piracy, and more likely that further instances would have been found in the records of the justiciary court – the highest criminal court in Scotland – if more had survived from the sixteenth century.[81] That prize litigation of which no record has survived did occur seems likely given the frequent references in other sources to seizures of ships or cargoes that are not mentioned in the court records.[82]

In addition to cases of the types mentioned, in which a court had to decide whether a seizure was lawful or not, there are also records of cases in which it was accepted by everyone concerned that a seizure was lawful and the court was asked instead to make a decision about its consequences. Although cases of the first three types were usually raised before the central courts sitting in or adjacent to Edinburgh, cases of the fourth type were also raised in the courts of

---

79 Published in 1937 by the Stair Society, the act book actually contains two gaps in its coverage, from November 1558 to February 1559 and from September 1559 to August 1560. For reviews of some of the cases recorded see Mowat 1994, pp. 118–20, and Murdoch 2010, pp. 70–6.

80 Although a protest was often entered on behalf of the admiral when the lords of session agreed to decide whether a ship or cargo had been lawfully seized (*Acts of the Lords of Council in Public Affairs*, pp. 57–8, 63–4, 539, 550 and 562; *Practicks of Sir James Balfour of Pittendreich*, vol. 2, p. 634; Sinclair's Practicks, n. 367; *Decisions of the Court of Session*, vol. 9, p. 7322; *cf.* NLS, Adv. MS 25.2.5(1), f. 32r, and Adv. MS 25.2.7, f. 19r), and although this has been taken to provide evidence of a contest over jurisdiction (Riddell 1852, vol. 1, pp. 327–31; McMillan 1936, p. 328; Dickinson 1958, pp. 398–9), the purpose of the protest was generally to protect the admiral's right to a share of any prize, not to protect his jurisdiction over all cases involving prize issues. What may not have been accidental, though, is the tendency for cases of the first type to be found in the records of the admiralty court while those of the second are more often found in the records of the session.

81 The piracy cases in the justiciary court records will be discussed in the last section of this chapter.

82 *Letters and Papers, Foreign and Domestic, of the Reign of Henry VIII*, vol. 2(1), p. 163, vol. 6, pp. 111, 129 and 201, vol. 12, p. 678, and vol. 18, pp. 12, 35, 41, 49, 61–2, 71, 74, 78, 80, 86, 93 and 180; *Acts of the Privy Council of England*, vol. 1, pp. 133 and 483–4, and vol. 6, p. 240; *Compota thesaurariorum regum Scotorum*, vol. 4, pp. 457 and 506, vol. 8, p. 275, vol. 9, pp. 58, 179, 236, 241, 253, 263, 275–7, 287, 293, 296, 303, 308–9, 311, 332, 387–8, 391, 393, 407, 409, 413, 416, 429 and 465, and vol. 10, pp. 224 and 298; *Records of the Convention of the Royal Burghs of Scotland*, vol. 1, pp. 543–4; DCA, PBD, vol. 1, f. 114r; ECA, SL1/1/3, f. 69r; Merriman 2000, pp. 181–2 and 355–6.

various coastal burghs.[83] An example may be taken from the exceptionally rich records of the courts in Aberdeen.[84] In 1548, or so a petitioner maintained, he had been 'cumand furtht of Danskyne in ane Franche schip callit the *Franceis*, amangis the company of certane merchandis and nychtbouris of the forsaid burght', when their ship came across several others belonging to 'our enemeis of Flanderis'.[85] Despite being engaged in a commercial venture, the crew and merchants took the opportunity to capture the Flemish vessels, which they brought back to Aberdeen 'as prises'. A meeting of the 'haill cumpany' was afterwards held in the home of one of the merchants, 'to mak distributioun of the geir and gudis that wes in the said pryses amangis the said company, ilkane conforme to thair estait and service done thairfor'. Because the petitioner had participated in the seizures, it was agreed that he should receive a share, and another burgess, who had been appointed 'ane of the quarter maisteris of the said schip', was instructed to pay him a share of the money he raised from the sale of part of the goods.[86] Four years later, as the petitioner complained, he was still waiting for his money, and fearing that he would never receive it he raised an action for 'compt, reknyng and payment' before the bailies of the burgh. This was a type of action commonly raised between burgesses for the recovery of sums due from one to another, and the basis of the claim was typically – as here – an agreement to which they had both been party. That the Flemish vessels and their cargoes had been acquired by their captors was taken for granted. Indeed, the merchants and mariners had felt no need to involve a court in the distribution of their gains.[87]

For obvious reasons, most of the cases connected (more or less directly) with prize acquisition arose from wars with other countries in which the Scots

---

83 *Extracts from the Records of the Burgh of Edinburgh*, vol. 1, pp. 212–14; *Extracts from the Council Register of the Burgh of Aberdeen*, vol. 1, pp. 205–6 and 304–6; ACA, CA1/1/20, pp. 368, 371, 374, 378–9, 407, 410 and 456–7; NLS, Adv. MS 25.2.5(1), f. 38r; Adv. MS 25.2.7, f. 25v. See too Frankot 2010, p. 144, and also Clark 1921, pp. 27–8, and Rae 1966, p. 48.

84 White 1985, pp. 1–3; Falconer 2013, pp. 18–20; Frankot 2017, pp. 411–12.

85 ACA, CA1/1/21, p. 184. See too CA1/1/20, pp. 130, 152, 161, 163–5, 168, 176 and 370.

86 Another case in which goods were distributed among 'the four quartar maisteris and cumpany' can be found at ACA, CA1/1/19, p. 394, and see too DCA, BCMB, vol. 3, 14 March 1552.

87 Only the petition initiating the court action was entered in the council register, where any hearings would have been noted. Presumably, lodging the petition proved to be sufficient to force the defender into making the payment required. How the bailies viewed the claim is not therefore known, but it will be seen later that a formal act of court was not considered essential to prize acquisition at this time. For a case in which a burgh court decided to wait for confirmation from a central court that a prize was just see ECA, SL1/1/2, f. 108.

were themselves involved, although Scottish courts were sometimes asked to settle disputes between foreign belligerents.[88] For much of the first sixty years of the century the Scots were at war in alliance with France, at first in the War of the League of Cambrai, then in the Habsburg-Valois War that ended in 1559, and while that was continuing in the more local conflict with England known as the Rough Wooings. After a period of internal strife brought about by the Reformation, the Scots were at peace for the remainder of the century, while gradual progress was made towards the diplomatic realignment that culminated in the union of the crowns in 1603. The lack of involvement in external wars in the last four decades of the century is one reason why most of the known prize cases were heard during its earlier years, but another is that records happen to have survived from some years rather than others. Conclusions cannot safely be deduced from the extent of known prize litigation about the extent of Scottish involvement in maritime conflict, and caution is also required in drawing conclusions about the extent to which the known cases provide an accurate impression of how the law was generally understood. The fact is, however, that a strikingly consistent impression is given by the records of well over a hundred cases raised over a period of more than fifty years. A fairly confident view may therefore be taken of how prizes were acquired in Scotland before the close of the 1560s. The records of a few cases heard in the later decades of the century are also consistent with the impression given.

In the cases in which a court was asked to decide whether a ship or cargo had been seized lawfully, the crucial question was almost always whether it had belonged to an enemy. The records of the admiralty court suggest that the question whether a ship or cargo 'be just and lauchfull pryse or nocht' was effectively equated with the question whether 'the samyn pertenis to inymeis or freindis'.[89] The answer to the question was frequently less obvious than might now be expected. It could be unclear, as a matter of fact, which country a vessel, cargo or crew came from, or whether there was a state of war between that country and the country of the takers, particularly if the parties to the action were not from Scotland.[90] Evidence could be taken from

---

88 For example, SAUL, B10/8/5, pp. 278–9, relates to the seizure of goods from a Flemish fisherman by a French mariner in 1570.

89 *Acta curiae admirallatus Scotiae*, pp. 48–9, 51–3 and 56. See too ACA, CA1/1/22, p. 596, and CA1/1/23, p. 12; NLS, Adv. MS 25.2.5(1), f. 39v, and Adv. MS 25.2.7, f. 27v.

90 *Acts of the Lords of Council in Public Affairs*, pp. 224–6 and 468; *Acta curiae admirallatus Scotiae*, pp. 1, 17–18 and 73–8; *Practicks of Sir James Balfour*, vol. 2, pp. 634 and 636; *Calendar of State Papers Relating to Scotland*, vol. 1, pp. 202–3; *Registrum secreti sigilli regum Scotorum*, vol. 2, pp. xiv-xx and 762–3, and vol. 3, pp. 50–2; *Letters and Papers, Foreign and Domestic, of the Reign of Henry VIII*, vol. 20(2), p. 69; *Extracts from the Council*

the parties themselves, who might be challenged to maintain the veracity of their allegations under oath, or inferences could be drawn from charter parties or other documents found on captured vessels, or from the destruction of documents or the precipitate flight of the crews of vessels, or a foreign court could be asked to obtain testimony abroad or to provide information it had at its disposal.[91] Even when the facts of a case were not in dispute it could remain doubtful, as a matter of law, whether a ship or cargo was to be treated as enemy property. Several cases related to seizures made after hostilities had commenced but before a formal declaration of war was issued, or after peace had been concluded but before notification was given to vessels at sea.[92] Other cases involved the question whether ships belonging to owners from friendly nations should be found to 'pertene to inymeis' if they 'ferit inymeis gudis', or to belong to 'mekle mair nor ane inemy' if they were carrying materials suitable 'for strengthening, sustening and uphalding of ony castle, towre or fortalice' in enemy hands.[93] The converse question whether friendly goods carried on an enemy ship should be treated as enemy goods was also raised, as was the question whether enemy ships or goods could be seized in neutral waters, or could be seized when a letter of safe conduct had been obtained from the takers' own ruler.[94] If letters of safe conduct could have the effect of removing ships or goods from the category of things owned by enemies, the question

Register of Aberdeen, vol. 1, pp. 304–6; ACA, CA1/1/22, pp. 590–2 and 596; Hannay 1916, pp. 63–6. *Cf.* DCA, BCMB, vol. 8, 26 May 1564; NLS, Adv. MS 25.2.5(I), f. 33v, and Adv. MS 25.2.7, f. 20.

91 *Acts of the Lords of Council in Public Affairs*, pp. 19, 530, 540, 552, 571, 592, 594, 607 and 610; *Acta curiae admirallatus Scotiae*, pp. 15–16, 19–23, 30–1, 36, 57–8 and 103; *Practiques of Sir Richard Maitland*, p. 27; NRS, SP13/72/2–4; DCA, BCMB, vol. 3, 27 June 1552; DHC, DB1/10/12/1; Finlay 2002, pp. 45–6.

92 *Acts of the Lords of Council in Public Affairs*, pp. 83, 468, 479, 493, 499, 534, 562, 578, 608, 620 and 626; *Acta curiae admirallatus Scotiae*, pp. 179–80; *Compota thesaurariorum regum Scotorum*, vol. 9, pp. 411–12, 420 and 423; *Calendar of State Papers Relating to Scotland*, vol. 1, p. 457; *Register of the Privy Council of Scotland*, vol. 1, p. 102; *Scottish Correspondence of Mary of Lorraine*, pp. 140–1; *Acts of the Privy Council of England*, vol. 3, p. 105.

93 *Acts of the Lords of Council in Public Affairs*, pp. 222, 579 and 607; *Practicks of Sir James Balfour*, vol. 2, p. 637; *Practiques of Sir Richard Maitland*, p. 95; *Acta curiae admirallatus Scotiae*, 15–16.

94 *Acts of the Lords of Council in Public Affairs*, pp. 468, 479, 493, 499, 527, 563 and 578; *Acts of the Parliaments of Scotland*, vol. 2, pp. 430–1; Records of the Parliaments of Scotland, 1543/12/26; *Practicks of Sir James Balfour*, vol. 2, p. 638; *Calendar of State Papers Relating to Scotland*, vol. 1, pp. 539, 625–6, 643–5 and 682; *Acts of the Privy Council of England*, vol. 3, p. 189; *Letters and Papers, Foreign and Domestic, of the Reign of Henry VIII*, vol. 18(2), p. 258; NRS, CS7/1/2, f. 364v; ACA, CA1/1/9, p. 598, CA1/1/18, p. 241, and CA1/1/20, pp. 8 and 17; NLS, Adv. MS 25.2.5(I), f. 39r, and Adv. MS 25.2.7, f. 27r.

was also raised whether issuing licences or commissions to mariners to sail on behalf of countries to which they did not belong could have the effect of turning the enemies of those countries into their enemies for the purposes of prize acquisition.[95] The way in which these legal questions were answered will be considered shortly, but the point that needs to be grasped at once is that they were all refinements of the more basic question whether ships or goods belonged to friends or enemies. It was on this fundamental question that the outcome of all prize cases ultimately depended.[96]

When not dealing directly with the legitimacy of seizures, courts were often concerned with the distribution of property that was assumed to have been acquired. Some cases related to rights of 'pillage' rather than 'pris'.[97] Particular members of a crew might assert rights to particular items, typically those related to their own roles, so that a master, for instance, might claim an anchor, which was understood to symbolise his authority at sea.[98] Pillage was otherwise shared out among the crew, and only the crew, which is why the distinction between pillage and prize mattered, for it was not only crew members who had a claim to a share of a prize. The owners and suppliers of the ships used in making seizures could also claim part of any ships or goods taken, the basic rule being that the master and crew were entitled to one half of every prize and the owners and suppliers to the other, which left ample scope for further controversy over the distribution of each half, to avoid which agreements were sometimes made in advance of voyages.[99] Furthermore, the rights of masters, crews, owners and suppliers were to shares in what was left of prizes after a tenth of their value had been deducted and assigned to the admiral, whose officers sometimes raised actions against mariners for 'wrangus brekking, selling and disponying upoun ane pryss' without his 'deutie' or 'admirallite' being paid.[100] On other occasions the admiral's officers acknowledged receipt of his

95 *Acta curiae admirallatus Scotiae*, pp. 139–40; *Register of the Privy Council of Scotland*, vol. 1, pp. 236–7, 241–3 and 276–7, and vol. 2, pp. 377–8; *Calendar of State Papers Relating to Scotland*, vol. 4, p. 682, and vol. 5, pp. 5–10, 14–15, 24–6, 404–5 and 428–9; *Letters and Papers, Foreign and Domestic, of the Reign of Henry VIII*, vol. 12(2), p. 359.

96 The apparent lack of engagement with the other fundamental question that might have been asked – whether ships or goods had been effectively occupied by the assailers – will be returned to later.

97 *Acts of the Lords of Council in Public Affairs*, p. 535; *Acta curiae admirallatus Scotiae*, pp. 2, 18–19 and 21–2.

98 *Acta curiae admirallatus Scotiae*, pp. 4–5, 22 and 107.

99 *Acta curiae admirallatus Scotiae*, pp. 14–15, 23–6, 28–9, 105–10, 125, 161–4, 167, 173–4 and 176–8; ACA, CA1/1/20, pp. 120, 130 and 370, and CA1/1/23, pp. 132–3, 136, 138–41, 146 and 148.

100 *Acta curiae admirallatus Scotiae*, pp. 6–8, 10, 12, 16–17, 26–7, 32–3, 37, 46–9, 56–60, 78, 80, 86, 97–8 and 101–4; ACA, CA1/1/22, pp. 662–3.

share after ships and goods were sold, formally discharging the mariners from liability.[101] That the question was raised in one instance whether the admiral was entitled to a tenth of a prize taken by a ship belonging to the queen is a reminder that what was usually at issue in prize litigation was the acquisition of enemy property by private parties, subject to a form of taxation.[102]

The distribution and taxation of prizes extended to ransoms received for the release of sailors or passengers captured on enemy ships.[103] In Dundee mariners promised each other to hold prisoners securely in their homes until ransoms were paid, 'deduceand thairof the admiralite of the samen'.[104] Prisoners held by mariners sometimes complained that they were not in fact enemy nationals, or that they were not being held in humane conditions, or that their ransoms had not been set at reasonable levels.[105] Many actions were raised to secure agreed contributions towards the ransoming of Scots imprisoned abroad, or to obtain reimbursement of ransoms paid for their release.[106] An admiralty court sitting in Dundee found that the master and crew of a Scottish ship from which a mariner had been taken prisoner by an English assailant were obliged to contribute towards the cost of his release.[107] When a French master reached Aberdeen after three members of his crew were captured by an English ship, he persuaded two burgesses of the town to pay their ransoms, providing a guarantee that he would repay them when he could.[108] When another French master brought several Flemish mariners he had captured to Aberdeen, three burgesses were persuaded to pay their ransoms too, the Franco-Scottish alliance notwithstanding, a guarantee again being provided that the burgesses would be reimbursed.[109] Indeed, when an English captor released Scottish prisoners after receiving a guarantee that their ransoms would be paid, he was able to pursue the guarantor in a Scottish court for the

101 ACA, CA1/1/17, pp. 550 and 617, CA1/1/19, pp. 354–6, and CA1/1/21, pp. 433–4; DCA, BCMB, vol. 3, 20–1 November 1550, and 5 August 1551.

102 *Acts of the Lords of Council in Public Affairs*, pp. 550–2. See too *Extracts from the Records of the Burgh of Edinburgh*, vol. 1, p. 65.

103 *Acta curiae admirallatus Scotiae*, pp. 106–7, 110–13 and 115–16; ACA, CA1/1/20, p. 120.

104 DCA, PBD, vol. 7, f. 11.

105 *Acts of the Lords of Council in Public Affairs*, pp. 275–6 and 292; Finlay 2002, pp. 42–4 and 48–9.

106 *Acta curiae admirallatus Scotiae*, pp. 51–2, 56, 88–104, 106, 114–15, 117–23 and 125–32; *Scottish Correspondence of Mary of Lorraine*, pp. 77–8 and 285–6; *Gild Court Book of Dunfermline*, p. 98; ACA, CA1/1/12/1, p. 164.

107 DCA, BCMB, vol. 3, 11 November 1546 (*sic*) and 8 June 1551.

108 ACA, CA1/1/19, p. 152.

109 ACA, CA1/1/21, p. 445, and see too CA1/1/22, pp. 64–5 and 132.

amount of the ransoms and for the expense he had incurred in looking after the prisoners.[110] An ambassador sent to England to negotiate the release of Scottish prisoners there was able to claim compensation from the prisoners for the expense he incurred in making his journey.[111]

As will by now be apparent, the cases heard in the Scottish courts often involved litigants from other countries.[112] Sir Richard Maitland of Lethington, one of the lords of session, reported a decision confirming that his court could hear actions between foreigners, remarking that they 'aught to be judged eftir the common law and not the practiqe of the realme'.[113] What was intended by this remark is not entirely clear. In one of the prize actions recorded in the registers of acts and decreets of the session, when the judges were informed that the parties involved were both 'strangearis, and may nocht byde apon lang pley', they agreed to proceed 'with expedition'.[114] They also required the defender to provide not only a guarantee that he would appear at future hearings, which was the normal practice in the session, but also a guarantee that he would be able to satisfy any award of damages made against him, which was not the normal practice there but was 'conforme to the commoun law'.[115] Moreover, the judges were asked to accept written evidence from the parties at whatever stage in the process they were able to produce it, 'nochtwithstanding ony practick observit in the contrair amangis the liegis of this realme'. This request was not immediately granted, and in general the procedure followed in cases raised between foreigners was the same as the procedure followed in other cases, yet the language used here would seem to suggest that when Maitland talked about the lords of session judging cases after the common law and not the practick of the realm, what he meant was that they had to be prepared to depart from their normal procedure in order to satisfy the special needs of foreign litigants.[116]

---

110 *Acta curiae admirallatus Scotiae*, pp. 58–9.

111 ACA, CA1/1/21, p. 387. See too CA1/1/22, pp. 630–1.

112 *Acts of the Lords of Council in Public Affairs*, pp. 176, 202–3, 212, 215, 220–1, 232–3, 242, 244, 253–4, 271, 305, 310 and 327; Hannay 1916, pp. 56–63; Finlay 2002, p. 49.

113 *Practiques of Sir Richard Maitland*, p. 25; NLS, Adv. MS 31.2.2(1), f. 3r; *Practicks of Sir James Balfour of Pittendreich*, vol. 1, p. 269.

114 *Acts of the Lords of Council in Public Affairs*, pp. 461–2 and 465–8.

115 A requirement of caution *de iudicio sisti et iudicatum solvi* was standard in the admiralty courts, and often imposed in the burgh courts when one of the parties was a stranger and doubts were raised about his solvency.

116 On this point see too ACA, CA1/1/24, pp. 429–31 and 434–6, and NLS, Adv. MS 25.2.5(1), f. 34v, and Adv. MS 25.2.7, ff. 21v-2r, along with Finlay 2002, pp. 45–6, and more generally Baker 1979 and Cordes 2003.

It is rather less likely that Maitland was thinking of departures from the substantive law applied in the Scottish courts. When another lord of session, Sir James Balfour of Pittendreich, reported a decision of the session confirming that the admiralty courts could deal with prize cases raised between foreigners, he added that the judges must deliver decisions 'conform to the lawis of this realme usit in sic caisis'.[117] In reporting a prize case heard in the session, Balfour wrote again about the determination of a substantive question 'be the lawis of this realme'. Similarly, in a case recorded in the act book of the admiralty court, it was found that the distribution of shares in a ship and cargo taken by strangers would need to be in accordance with 'the use and practik of this realme'.[118] The same records refer to the payment of admiralty duty 'conforme to the us and consuetude of this realme', and to the disposal of vessels and cargoes 'conforme to the auld usse and consuetude usit and observit in tymis bygane in siklyk casis'.[119] If doubts arose about the validity of any 'use and consuetude' alleged, the judges would take advice on the matter from experienced mariners. Thus the question whether enemy status should be inferred from the precipitate flight of sailors was referred to 'certane honest seyfarand men of the toun of Leith and utheris', while a similar inquest was invited to clarify the extent of rights of pillage under 'the usse and consuetude of seyfair, usit and observit in all tymis bygane past memor of man'.[120] In the latter case the court not only made a decision in accordance with the opinion given but also ordained 'the said usse and consuetude to be observit and kepit in all tymis to cum in siclyk caissis'.

That prize litigation was governed by the law of Scotland, subject to an expectation of flexibility in procedural matters, thus seems clear, yet there was a sense in which it might have been appropriate to talk about 'common law' even in relation to matters of substance. It is significant that when reference was made in prize litigation to 'the use and practik of this realme', an alternative expression sometimes employed was 'the us and consuetude of seyfair'.[121] If Balfour was correct that prize litigation was governed by the law of Scotland, it was governed by a special branch of that law which derived from the practices of coastal communities familiar with the usages and expectations of other

117 *Practicks of Sir James Balfour*, vol. 2, pp. 636–7.

118 *Acta curiae admirallatus Scotiae*, pp. 105–6.

119 *Acta curiae admirallatus Scotiae*, pp. 3 and 26.

120 *Acta curiae admirallatus Scotiae*, pp. 4–5, 36 and 80.

121 *Acta curiae admirallatus Scotiae*, pp. 22, 28–9 and 125; ACA, CA1/1/20, p. 120. Similar language was widely used in commercial litigation relating to navigation, as is explained in Ford 2018b, pp. xcii and xcviii.

nations.[122] The applicable law was the custom of the realm, yet in these cases it was a custom with which foreign mariners would have felt reasonably comfortable. The best way to understand this is by thinking about what the law of Scotland did and did not provide. It provided detailed rules about when ships and goods could be taken to pertain to enemies, about how ships and goods acquired through their capture from enemies should be distributed between their captors, and about how prisoners taken at sea should be detained in Scotland or repatriated from abroad. What it did not seem to provide was any rule about the legitimacy and efficacy of capturing ships, goods and prisoners from enemies. The rules articulated in the records and reports of cases heard in the courts were concerned with the practicalities of prize acquisition, but they were also dependent on assumptions that it was lawful to capture ships, goods and prisoners from enemies, that the effect of capturing ships and goods from enemies was to confer ownership on the captors, and that the capture of prisoners of war enabled ransoms for their release to be licitly demanded. Without these assumptions the rules articulated in the Scottish cases would have made little sense, yet at no stage were the assumptions themselves articulated, let alone shown to be established by local statutes or customs. One way of putting this was that the fundamental assumptions underpinning Scottish prize law formed part of the *ius commune*, as opposed to the *ius proprium*.[123] As was explained in the last section, it was the law examined in the universities that provided the basic principles of prize law, though only the basic principles, with more detailed regulation left to local lawmakers. While not entirely misleading, however, this use of the language of the law schools can be confusing. It has to be appreciated that just as the local rules were dependent on the principles provided by the common law, so the common law was dependent for its practical efficacy on its acceptance by legislators, judges and lawyers who were prepared to work on the basis of its principles.[124] Thus the law of

122 *Acta curiae admirallatus Scotiae*, pp. 15–16; *Acts of the Lords of Council in Public Affairs*, p. 535; Finlay 2002, pp. 48–9.

123 *Institutes*, 1.2.1.

124 This conception of the relationship between *ius commune* and *ius proprium* is not so far distant from what the Romans had in mind. They used the expression *ius commune* with reference to *ius naturale et gentium*, and when talking about *ius gentium* at a more practical level they both contrasted it with their *ius civile*, which was peculiarly applicable to Roman citizens, and recognised that the law of any nation consisted in part of *ius proprium* and in part of *ius commune*, meaning *ius gentium*. Thus *ius gentium* or *ius commune* was viewed both as something distinct from Roman law and as a central component of it. These distinctions will be examined more fully in the next chapter.

Scotland, by taking the theory of the law schools for granted, turned it into something more practical, and appropriated it as part of the law of Scotland.[125]

On this understanding, it is not hard to make sense of what was happening in the case mentioned at the start of this chapter.[126] The 'law of armes' that was taken to govern the case was the Scottish law of arms. The English mariners involved might not have been familiar with the particular rules governing prize acquisition in Scotland, but like the mariners involved in the Danzig case discussed in the last section they would have expected any court to apply rules of the same nature in giving effect to more basic principles with which they were familiar. As they clearly were enemies, they felt unable to deny that the seizure of their ship had been lawful. Consistently with this, an admiralty court in England declared a few years later that prize acquisition was governed 'as much by the common civil and maritime law as by our ancient, lovable and lawfully prescribed custom, hitherto used and inviolably and firmly observed since time immemorial, and upheld in contentious proceedings'.[127] The law applied in the English admiralty court was English law, worked out in detail through customary practice and forensic disputation, yet developed within the same learned framework as the law applied in the Scottish courts. When a novel question arose about the seizure of another English ship in Scotland, it was considered essential for it to be referred to the 'lerned of the session', while the English ambassador took advice from the 'doctours of the arches', meaning the civil lawyers who practised in the admiralty court in England.[128] Some years earlier an English mariner involved in litigation in Spain had similarly recognised that his case would be governed there by 'the law syvyl and of this land'.[129] Scottish mariners clearly had the same expectations of the foreign courts before which they sometimes found themselves appearing.[130]

125 The relationship, it might be said, was symbiotic, with each type of law being dependent on the other for its recognition as law that would be binding in an international setting.

126 *Acta curiae admirallatus Scotiae*, pp. 69–70.

127 *Select Pleas in the Court of Admiralty*, vol. 2, p. 95.

128 *Calendar of State Papers Relating to Scotland*, vol. 1, pp. 625–6; *Documents Relating to the Law and Custom of the Sea*, vol. 1, pp. 179–80. See too *Acts of the Privy Council of England*, vol. 7, p. 276.

129 *Letters and Papers, Foreign and Domestic, of the Reign of Henry VIII*, vol. 5, p. 415.

130 *Letters and Papers, Foreign and Domestic, of the Reign of Henry VIII*, vol. 18(1), pp. 37–8, and vol. 18(2), pp. 215–16; *Acts of the Privy Council of England*, vol. 3, p. 53; *Epistolae Iacobi Quarti, Iacobi Quinti et Mariae regum Scotorum*, vol. 1, pp. 78–80; *Letters of James the Fourth*, pp. 99–101; *Letters and Papers Illustrative of the Reigns of Richard III and Henry VII*, vol. 2, pp. 258–61; *Letters of James V*, p. 7; NLS, Adv. MS 35.5.9B, f. 213v. Other instances of the involvement of Scots in disputes overseas are given below.

Although only a handful of cases have been found in the court records from the last four decades of the sixteenth century, several treatises on maritime law were produced in Scotland during those years, all of which give at least some indication of how prize law continued to be perceived. The reports of decisions by Sir James Balfour to which reference has already been made were actually incorporated into a wider examination of the subject, which was attached as an appendix to the work known to lawyers as his 'practicks'.[131] In this treatise Balfour dealt at some length with the law governing prize acquisition.[132] Occasionally he quoted passages from, or at least mentioned, an earlier treatise on the subject by David Kintor, who appears to have been one of the judges of the central admiralty court during the period covered by the surviving act book.[133] Sadly, Kintor's treatise, which evidently did deal with prize law, has not survived. It was also known to William Welwod, who wrote another treatise on the subject while teaching at the University of St Andrews in the 1580s.[134] His *Sea-Law of Scotland*, the first legal treatise ever printed in the country, did not deal with prize law, but it was abbreviated from a longer work that touched briefly on the theme.[135] A fourth treatise was being written at about the same time by Alexander King, a court practitioner in Edinburgh, when he was removed from office as a judge of the central admiralty court.[136] He abandoned the task at this point, before writing a chapter on the law of piracy with which the treatise was supposed to conclude, but after completing a chapter on the law of prize.[137] Like many other lawyers practising before the courts in Edinburgh, King had studied the civil and canon laws at continental universities. Both Balfour and Welwod had also studied overseas, yet none of these writers spent much time in his treatise expounding the basic principles of prize acquisition he would have learned as a student.

The treatise attached to Balfour's practicks was given the title 'Sea Lawis Collectit furth of the Actis of Parliament, the Practiques, the Lawis of *Oleron*, and the Lawis of *Wisbie*, and the Constitutiounis of *Francois*, King of *France*, *annis* 1543, 1557'. The 'Practiques', by which Balfour meant the decisions of the lords of session, have been noted already to the extent that they dealt with

131 The production of this appendix is considered in Ford 2018b, pp. LXXV–VII, but needs further attention.

132 *Practicks of Sir James Balfour*, vol. 2, pp. 635–41.

133 *Practicks of Sir James Balfour*, vol. 2, pp. 614–15, 618–21, 623, 627–8, 636, 638 and 640–1.

134 Baxter 1959, pp. 246–51; Walker 1985, pp. 84–6; Matthew and Harrison 2004, vol. 58, pp. 96–8.

135 'Welwod's Treatise on Maritime Law', pp. 271–2; Stein 1988, p. 316.

136 Ford 2018b, pp. LXII–III.

137 *Alexander King's Treatise on Maritime Law*, pp. 80–95.

prize law. In fact, there were no acts of parliament dealing with the seizure of ships and goods in wartime, nor was this aspect of maritime law covered in the codes compiled at Oleron and Wisby. The source from which Balfour drew most of his material on prize law was actually French legislation, from which he quoted extensively in translation. In France, unlike Scotland, there was a tradition of legislating on maritime law, and a major restatement had been issued by Francis I in February 1544.[138] Balfour also reproduced a couple of provisions from a more obscure edict issued in 1555 or 1557, on both occasions coupling his citation of the edict with a reference to Kintor's treatise, which suggests that Kintor had already made use of French legislation.[139] Welwod's passing remarks on prize law were based entirely on a source he referred to as 'l'Admirall de France', possibly a treatise of that name in which Lancelot du Voisin, sieur de la Popelinière, reviewed an edict issued by Henry III in March 1584, which superseded Francis I's restatement.[140] Although King never cited the 1584 edict expressly in his treatise, some of the rules he stated were undoubtedly drawn from that source.[141] Indeed, it was the source from which most of his information about the regulation of prize taking was drawn, though he did also comment on the customary practices of the admiralty courts.

An obvious question to ask is why all these authors thought it appropriate to turn to French legislation when writing about the sea law of Scotland. It may be that the 'auld alliance' with France, which culminated in a brief dynastic union in the late 1550s, caused lawyers in Scotland to pay increasingly close attention to French law. The truth is, however, that the Scots had insisted on retaining their own law within the union, and there is no evidence that the edicts on maritime law in particular had come to be regarded as a part of Scots law.[142] The edicts, for example, required mariners to take any prizes they seized to their home ports, so that the admiral's officers could oversee the

138 On the legislative tradition in France see Taillemite 1993 and Allaire 2015, and on the provisions on prize law in particular see De Chastenet d'Esterre 1906, pp. 81–4, and Dumas 1908, pp. 70–116.

139 *Practicks of Sir James Balfour*, vol. 2, pp. 636 and 638. No trace of this edict has been found in the standard collections of French legislation covering this period, or in Durat-Lasalle's *Droit et législation des armées de terre et de mer*, but see Terrien, *Commentaires du droict civil de Normandie*, pp. 568–9; *Habakkuk Bisset's Rolment of Courtis*, vol. 2, pp. 235–40; *Collectanea Maritima*, p. 116; *Collection de lois maritimes antérieures au XVIIIe siècle*, vol. 4, pp. 312–13.

140 On the 1584 edict see too James 2004, pp. 32–8. On la Popelinière see Sypher 1963; Kelley 1971; Martinière 1997; Lourde 2007; Levesque 2009.

141 *Alexander King's Treatise on Maritime Law*, pp. 82–7 and 90–3.

142 On the expectations of the union so far as the laws of the two kingdoms were concerned see Ford 2015, pp. 184–8.

distribution of shares and make sure he received his 'dixiesme', adding that if it became necessary for prizes to be diverted elsewhere, this would not affect the admiral's entitlement.[143] Although this provision was reproduced by Balfour and paraphrased by King, it does not seem to have had any practical effect.[144] Prizes were taken to the most convenient ports, and no Scottish judges have been found redirecting them to others, though there was one case in which the master of a French ship was required – by David Kintor as it happens – to provide a guarantee that he would give part of his prize 'to the admirale of France for his dewite'.[145] It may be that the French legislation was also remembered when it was argued in another case that the destruction of shipping documents served as proof of enemy status, 'of the us and consuetude of seyfair, usit and observit in all realmes and cuntries'.[146] The evidentiary rule was robustly stated in a provision of the 1544 edict reproduced by Balfour, but the places mentioned here were 'Denmark, Danskin and utheris', and in the same case the court failed to adhere to another French rule, which was again reproduced from the 1544 edict by Balfour.[147] The court found that a friendly ship transporting enemy goods must be restored to its original owners, contrary to the French notion of *infection hostile*, which was never even mentioned in the record.[148] Another provision reproduced by Balfour was meant to encourage the victualling of ships by requiring prizes to be divided into four parts, of which one was due to 'le bourgeois', a part and a half to 'les victailleurs' and the remaining part and a half to 'l'equipage'.[149] It has been noted, though, that the central admiralty court in Scotland continued in the 1550s to allocate half of every prize to the master and crew, and King indicated in his treatise that this remained the rule when he was sitting in the court.[150]

143 *Edicts et ordonnances des roys de France*, vol. 2, pp. 858–9; *Recueil général des anciennes lois françaises*, vol. 12, pp. 860 and 862–3, and vol. 14, pp. 568 and 571–2; *Collection de lois maritimes*, vol. 4, pp. 307 and 309–10.

144 *Practicks of Sir James Balfour*, vol. 2, p. 641; *Alexander King's Treatise on Maritime Law*, pp. 86–7.

145 *Acta curiae admirallatus Scotiae*, p. 73.

146 *Acta curiae admirallatus Scotiae*, pp. 15–16.

147 *Practicks of Sir James Balfour*, vol. 2, pp. 637–8; *Edicts et ordonnances des roys de France*, vol. 2, pp. 859–60; *Recueil général des anciennes lois françaises*, vol. 12, pp. 864–5. See too Deák and Jessup 1932–3, pp. 496–7.

148 *Alexander King's Treatise on Maritime Law*, pp. 84–5, states that a friendly ship transporting enemy goods should be returned to its owner unless found to have 'conspired with our enemies to our ruin'.

149 *Practicks of Sir James Balfour*, vol. 2, p. 639; *Edicts et ordonnances des roys de France*, vol. 2, p. 857; *Recueil général des anciennes lois françaises*, vol. 12, pp. 858–9. Of course, the proportions were of what remained after the admiral received his tenth.

150 *Alexander King's Treatise on Maritme Law*, pp. 90–1.

The inclusion of provisions from the French edicts in Scottish books clearly cannot be taken to mean that they formed part of the law of Scotland.[151] So why was so much attention paid to them? An answer is suggested by the argument quoted a moment ago that a Scottish court should follow 'the us and consuetude of seyfair, usit and observit in all realmes and cuntries'. The rules laid down by a legislator in France could not have been directly applicable elsewhere, any more than the rules in force in Denmark, Danzig or other places could have been, nor would the adoption of an identical rule in several places have rendered it binding in others.[152] However, when members of coastal communities were asked to identify a rule, they need not have confined their attention to peculiarly Scottish customs, especially if there was no settled rule in Scotland. Attention could have been paid to foreign rules, at least if they served the function that rules were being sought to serve in Scotland. It is a notable feature of the written rules established in France – like the unwritten rules followed in Scotland – that they dealt with the practicalities of prize acquisition and never spelled out the fundamental principles on which they must have been based. They explained, for example, how shares in any prizes acquired ought to be distributed, but not how prizes were acquired in the first place, which was assumed to be established already. Having been developed on the basis of the same learned theory as the rules developed in other places, the French rules offered solutions to issues that were likely to arise wherever the learned theory was accepted. While mariners in Scotland are unlikely to have been directly acquainted with the French legislation, they may well have been involved in, or have heard about, cases decided elsewhere in which the rules enacted in France had received effect, either as legislation or as custom informed by the legislation.

For jurists writing books, rather than mariners serving on inquests, and especially for jurists like Balfour and Welwod who had little or no experience of practice in the admiralty courts, the fact that the French rules had been set down in writing would have made them particularly attractive. The French rules, moreover, had already proved to be influential in other places. They had been used as a model for legislation introduced in the Netherlands, and that legislation had since been used as a model for legislation introduced in Denmark.[153] For writers willing to go beyond describing the current state of

151 Other examples of inconsistencies between articles reproduced from the French edicts and evidence of Scottish practice can be found in *Alexander King's Treatise on Maritme Law*, pp. 82–7.

152 *Cf.* Friedland 2000; Cordes 2003 and 2017; Frankot 2012 and 2013.

153 That the Habsburg rulers of the Netherlands followed the example of earlier French kings, notably Charles V, who had issued a code of maritime law as early as 1373, was suggested

the law and to give some direction to its future development, the rules available in the French edicts provided an obvious source of guidance. Both King and Welwod worked on their treatises at a time when reform of the Scottish admiralty courts was under consideration, and Balfour may have worked on his treatise when a new admiral was coming into office and was in need of advice.[154] In 1587 that admiral was issued with new instructions in which he and his officers were specifically required to follow the example 'of the kingdoms of France, Spain, England, Denmark or other foreign nations'.[155] If this helps to explain why writers looked beyond Scotland for assistance, their understanding was that the nations listed had developed their laws within a common framework. King, for example, located his account of rules drawn from Scottish custom and French legislation between a bold statement that things seized in wartime became the property of the takers *iure gentium*, and a proposal that questions about the effective capture of ships should be resolved by comparison with Roman law texts on the *occupatio* of *res nullius*.[156] Questions of this type, which would loom large in the prize litigation of the following century, are surprisingly absent from the records of cases in the sixteenth century, but King remarked that it was 'customary for them to be disputed here', by which he must have meant at this stage in learned discussions of the subject. That his own discussion was firmly grounded on learned theory was confirmed by the next chapter of his treatise, in which he wrote about the seizure of ships and goods under letters of reprisal or marque in peacetime. For the use of these letters in Scotland to be properly understood, the theory of the continental law schools first needs to be revisited.

3 Seizures of Ships and Goods at Sea as Reprisal

The common practice of taking reprisals for losses inflicted by foreigners, for instance when pirates from one place despoiled a merchant vessel from another, caused serious difficulties for the university doctors. The practice

by Roelofsen 1984, and has been confirmed by Sicking 2004, pp. 83–4, in the course of a thorough review of the legislation at pp. 62–131. For the Danish legislation, introduced by Frederick II in 1561, see Pardesus' *Collection de lois maritimes*, vol. 3, pp. 241–68. The more obvious influence on the Danish code was the laws of Wisby, but as noted above, those laws focused more on commercial matters.

154 Ford 2018b, pp. LXXVI–VII and LXXXIII.

155 *Registrum magni sigilli regum Scotorum*, vol. 5, pp. 449–50.

156 *Alexander King's Treatise on Maritime Law*, pp. 82–3 and 94–5, citing *Institutes*, 2.1.12.

was to take reprisals not against the foreigners who had inflicted the losses – the pirates, in the same example – but against any of their compatriots who could be found – such as mariners and merchants sailing in other vessels. The problem was that the practice seemed a great deal less consistent with the written laws studied in the schools than with Germanic customary law, which recognised forms of collective responsibility.[157] It is true that before the descent of the Germanic tribes into Italy, similar practices had been known in the ancient world, and had been considered legitimate in parts of Greece.[158] Several constitutions of the later Roman emperors, however, had remarked on the 'iniquity' of holding innocent people liable for the failings of others, and one had declared it 'harsh, and contrary not only to the laws but also to natural equity, for some people to be distressed for the debts of others'.[159] The emperor Justinian himself had reiterated this view in legislating against the seizure of things belonging to innocent parties as security – the word he used was *pigneratio*, related to *pignus* or 'pledge' – for the payment of sums due from others.[160] Six hundred years later the emperor Frederick I, in an effort to encourage the recently revived study of the civil law, condemned as a *perversa consuetudo* the practice of taking reprisals against scholars from abroad simply because they happened to come from the same places as people who had failed to pay debts due to, or had committed wrongs against, citizens of university towns.[161] A vital contribution towards the rise and expansion of the European universities, this constitution was incorporated into the *Corpus iuris civilis*, on the emperor's instructions, and so itself became a subject of scholarly attention.[162] Another century later it was decided by the second general council of the church to meet at Lyons that 'although *pignerationes*, which colloquial language designates reprisals, in which one person is harassed in place of another,

157 De Mas Latrie 1866, pp. 534–5; De la Brière 1928, pp. 253–4; Jessup and Deák 1935–6, vol. 1, p. 12; Spiegel 1938, pp. 64–6; Sereni 1943, p. 44; Pollock and Maitland 2010, vol. 1, pp. 718–19.

158 Dareste 1889; Lécrivain 1897; Bravo 1980 and 1981.

159 *Code*, 3.28.33.1, 4.12–13, 11.57.1 and 12.60.4. As these constitutions were all enacted by Christian emperors, they were presumably influenced, whether directly or indirectly, by the sentiments expressed in biblical texts like Exodus 23.7, Deuteronomy 24.16 and Ezekiel 18.20.

160 *Novels*, 52.1, and see too 134.4. For the meaning of the word *pigneratio* compare *Digest*, 20.1.9.1, and see Berger 1953, p. 630; Glare 1982, p. 1378; Lewis and Short 1987, p. 1375. The spelling of the words *pigneratio* and *represalia* was variable and is standardised in the quotations that follow.

161 Koeppler 1939; Ullmann 1954; Kibre 1961, pp. 10–16.

162 *Codex Iustiniani*, cols 669–71 (C.4.13, Authentica Habita). The text of the constitution is reproduced in Koeppler 1939, pp. 606–7, as well as in Monumenta Germaniae historica, *Constitutiones et acta publica imperatorum et regum*, vol. 1, p. 249.

have been prohibited by a civil constitution as being harsh and contrary to the laws and natural equity', nevertheless it would be expedient to reinforce their prohibition 'in relation to ecclesiastical persons'.[163] A decree was therefore issued, threatening with excommunication those who took reprisals 'on the pretext of any usage, which we regard rather as an abuse', and this decree was incorporated into the *Corpus iuris canonici*, again becoming the subject of learned commentary.[164] Yet despite all this legislation, the taking of reprisals continued. The statutes of many Italian cities, in seeking to regulate or restrain the practice, afforded it a degree of recognition and legitimacy.[165] The doctors had either to accept that theory and practice were badly out of line with each other or find some means of reconciling one with the other.

By the beginning of the fourteenth century the earliest generation of canonists to comment on the Lyons decree were already finding ways of justifying the use of *pignerationes* or *represaliae* (also known, they observed, as *marchae*).[166] The civilian doctors adopted their suggestions, and the rehabilitation of the practice was consolidated towards the middle of the same century when Bartolus composed a treatise devoted to the subject.[167] Several other doctors followed his example during the next century and a half, or built discussions of the subject into their treatises on the law of war, while others outlined the new doctrine in their commentaries on Frederick's constitution and in the lectures they delivered to their students.[168] The impression is given that the treatise

163 *Sacrorum conciliorum nova et amplissimo collectio*, vol. 24, col. 101; *Disciplinary Decrees of the General Councils*, p. 358.

164 *Liber sextus*, 5.8.

165 *Volumen statutorum, legum ac iurium Venetorum*, ff. 117v-18r; *Statuta et ordinamenta comunis Cremonae*, pp. 76–7; *Statuti della Valsesia*, p. 114; *Statuta Faventiae*, pp. 338–40; *Statuta civitatis Ferentini*, pp. 109–10; *Albori del Comune di San Gimignano*, pp. 282–3; *Statuta antiqua communis Collis Vallis Else*, vol. 1, pp. 194–5; *Constitutiones sive statuta magnificae civitatis Anconae*, pp. 68–9; *Statuti della reppublica fiorentina*, vol. 2, pp. 124–6; *Respublica Mutinensis*, vol. 1, pp. 180–1 and 293, and vol. 2, pp. 12–13 and 64. See too Martines 1968, pp. 359–69, and Penna 2017.

166 *Liber sextus decretalium*, col. 687 (gl. 'Etsi' ad VI 5.8); Ioannes Andreae, *In titulum de regulis iuris commentarii*, ff. 118v-19 (ad VI 5.12.22); Guido de Baysio, *Rosarium super Decreto*, sig. 2D1v (ad C. 23 q. 2 c. 2).

167 Iacobus de Belviso, *Aurea lectura summam Autenticorum Consuetudinesque feudorum elucidans*, ff. 36v-7 (ad N.52.1); Iacobus Butrigarius, *Super Codice lectura*, f. 121r (ad C.4.13, Authentica Habita); Cinus de Pistorio, *Lectura super Codice*, f. 148v (ad C.4.13, Authentica Habita); Bartolus, *Opera omnia*, vol 5, ff. 96v-101r.

168 Ioannes de Legnano, *Tractatus de bello, de represaliis et de duello*, pp. 155–74; *Corpus selectorum tractatuum de pignoribus et hypothecis*, pp. 520–32 (Ioannes Iacobus de Canibus) and 533–8 (Martinus Garatus Laudensis); *Tractatus universi iuris*, vol. 12, f. 170v (Ioannes Lupus); Bartolomeus de Saliceto, *Super Codicis commentaria*, vol. 2, f. 116 (ad C.4.13, Authentica Habita); Baldus, *Commentaria super Codicem*, vol. 2, f. 24r (ad C.4.13,

writers relished the task of devising ways of justifying the seemingly unjustifiable, revelling in their own virtuosity in the art of accommodating local custom within learned theory, even when the custom was manifestly opposed to the texts of the law.[169] Lawyers trained in the schools of civil and canon law carried the new doctrine with them into practice, often in military tribunals, basing discussions of the subject in manuals they wrote about the law of arms on what they had been taught as students.[170] In the sixteenth century the theory developed and expounded by the late medieval commentators was still being discussed and summarised by authors who remained convinced of its practical relevance.[171] Humanist theories that the Roman concept of *pigneratio* was related to the Greek practice of *androlepsia* or the fetial institution of *clarigatio*, coupled with criticism of the commentators' preference for the 'barbarous' term *represalia*, added another dimension to the standard discussion, but its core continued to be provided by the elaborate justification of Italian practice fashioned by the commentators during the fourteenth and fifteenth centuries.[172] Since it was in France that prospective lawyers from Scotland tended to be trained in the learned laws during the sixteenth century, it is particularly important for present purposes to note that French authors continued to

Authentica Habita); Angelus de Ubaldis, *Opera omnia*, vol. 2, ff. 77v-8r (ad C.4.13, Authentica Habita).

169 Sereni 1943, pp. 43–9 and 99–102, in trying to rehabilitate the international reputation of Italy in the early 1940s, is rather misleading, but see Keen 1965, pp. 218–38; Cheyette 1970, pp. 54–64; O'Brien 2001, pp. 193–258, and 2002; Haggenmacher 2010; Van den Brande 2020; Fedele 2021, pp. 564–89.

170 Honoré Bouvet, *Arbre des batailles*, sigg. M3v-O5r, and *Tree of Battles*, pp. 173–88; *Prose Works of Sir Gilbert Hay*, vol. 2, pp. 192–228; Christine de Pisan, *Book of Fayttes of Armes*, vol. 2, pp. 252–7; Nicholas Upton, *De studio militari libri quatuor*, pp. 92–6; *Consilia domini Guidonis Papae*, f. 99; *Decisiones Guidonis Papae*, pp. 67–71.

171 Claudius Cotereus, *De iure et privilegiis militum*, pp. 185–8; Giulio Ferretti, *De iure et re navali*, ff. 55v-8; Matteo d'Afflitto, *In utriusque Siciliae Neapolisque sanctiones ac constitutiones novissima praelectio*, pt 1, ff. 50v-1r, 54 and 129r; Joos de Damhouder, *Praxis rerum criminalium*, pp. 288–94; Andreas von Gail, *Practicarum observationum libri duo*, pt 2, pp. 178–80; Matthaeus Wesenbecius, *Tractatus et responsa*, cols 1137–42; Dionysius Gothofredus, *Praxis civilis, ex antiquis et recentioribus authoribus collecta*, vol. 2, cols 753–86; Balthazar de Ayala, *De iure et officiis bellicis*, vol. 1, ff. 29–32, and vol. 2, pp. 31–3.

172 Ermolao Barbaro, *In C. Plinii Naturalis historiae libros castigationes*, pp. 482 and 515; Marcello Donati, *In Latinorum plerorumque historiae Romanae scriptorum locos obscuriores scholiae sive dilucidationes eruditissimae*, pp. 17–19; Guillaume Budé, *Altera aeditio annotationum in Pandectas*, pp. 158–9; Andreas Alciatus, *Opera omnia*, vol. 1, col. 260, and vol. 3, col. 831; Udalricus Zasius, *Opera omnia*, vol. 1, col. 277; André Tiraqueau, *Opera omnia*, vol. 5, p. 186; *Decisiones Guidonis Papae*, pp. 68–9 (annotations by Matthaeus and Ferrerius).

discuss the medieval theory in relation to local practice throughout the century.[173] In the elaborate form in which the theory would have been encountered by students attending the continental law schools from the fourteenth century onwards, several lines of argument were pursued.

The argument initially developed by the canonists, which was soon taken up by the civilians and was to remain fundamental to the whole theory, rested on comparison of the Lyons decree with another text in the *Corpus iuris canonici*. The text derived from some observations made by Augustine on the eighth chapter of the book of Joshua, in which the Israelites, some of whom had been injured by people from Ai, were ordered to destroy and plunder that city.[174] Augustine had remarked that if a war was fought to avenge injuries inflicted by people from a city or nation that then neglected to provide reparation for the injuries, 'this type of war is without doubt just'. In commenting on Augustine's remarks, as reproduced in Gratian's *Decretum*, the canonists explained that 'when a city, superior or people neglects to exercise justice on any person subject to it, in that case it appears to consent to the wrong we have suffered', and that 'the text therefore allows war to be undertaken against such a city, superior or people'.[175] Notwithstanding the Lyons decree, reproduced in the *Liber sextus*, it seemed to the canonists that this text from the *Decretum* could be taken 'to excuse the custom of Italy under which reprisals are granted against cities'. The civilians quickly adopted the thinking that a war could be waged justly 'when a city is unwilling to apply the law to its citizen', that reprisals formed 'a species of licit war', and that they were 'granted so that justice would not fail, and occasioned by a neglect of justice arising from the deficiency or negligence of rulers'.[176] By the middle of the fourteenth century, Bartolus felt able to comment that 'almost all the doctors commonly incline towards that

173 René Choppin, *De domanio Franciae libri tres*, pp. 567–71; Jean Papon, *Recueil d'arrests notables des cours souveraines de France*, vol. 1, pp. 246–50 (on the earlier cases included in Papon's collection see again *Decisiones Guidonis Papae*, pp. 67–71, together with *Questiones Johannis Galli*, pp. 233–4, 428–30 and 459–60); *Guidon, stile et usance des marchands qui mettent à la mer*, pp. 46–9; Jean de Cambolas, *Decisions notables sur diverses questions du droit*, pp. 260–1. Iacobus Cuiacius, *Opera omnia*, vol. 3, cols 1523–4, also commented on practice in France.

174 *Decretum*, C. 23 q. 2 c. 2; Augustine, *Quaestiones in Heptateuchum*, 6.10; Joshua 8.2.

175 Andreae, *In titulum de regulis iuris*, ff. 118v-19; De Baysio, *Rosarium super Decreto*, sig. 2D1v.

176 De Belviso, *Aurea lectura*, f. 36v; Butrigarius, *Super Codice lectura*, f. 121r; Cinus, *Lectura super Codice*, f. 148v; De Legnano, *Tractatus de bello, de represaliis et de duello*, pp. 156 and 167; Alexander Tartagnus, *Opera omnia*, vol. 2(1), f. 2v (ad D.24.3 rub.); *Tractatus universi iuris*, vol. 12, f. 170v (Lupus); *Corpus selectorum tractatuum*, pp. 522 and 524 (De Canibus) and 534 (Garatus).

opinion'.[177] The notion of *neglecta, denegata vel retardata iustitia* would remain central to the defence of reprisals for as long as the practice continued, though this line of argument came to be supplemented with others.[178] Some commentators drew attention to civil and canon law texts indicating that 'what anyone does for the protection of his own body, he does justly', and argued that this must be taken to extend not only to the protection of an individual's property as well as his person, but also to the protection of the body politic (*corpus mysticum*).[179] A war waged to secure justice could thus be regarded in addition as a war waged in self-defence. Another line of argument fitted better with the perception of *represaliae* as a kind of *pignerationes*. Several Roman law texts indicated – or were believed to indicate – that at least in certain circumstances it was lawful for a creditor to use force against his debtor in order to recover what was owed to him, whether by seizing the debtor personally to bring him before a court or by taking the amount due directly from his belongings.[180] The civilian doctors argued that 'a city or superior neglecting or refusing to do justice is the debtor of the party demanding justice', and concluded that anyone 'subject to that superior or people can therefore be seized', or that 'the persons or things of that people can be seized'.[181] Texts could even be found showing that 'in many cases the civil law does allow that the people of a town may be liable to make good a loss inflicted by anyone from the same town'.[182]

If these texts were hard to reconcile with the imperial constitutions that condemned the burdening of the innocent with the liabilities of the guilty, the crucial point was that those who suffered from reprisals were being held liable not so much for the failings of other individuals as for the failings of the cities or nations to which they belonged. If a city or nation failed to provide a stranger with the means to obtain redress from one of its members, the stranger could be authorised by his own city or nation to obtain redress from

---

177 Bartolus, *Opera omnia*, vol. 5, f. 97r.

178 Cotereus, *De iure et privilegiis militum*, p. 187; D'Afflitto, *In utriusque Siciliae Neapolisque sanctiones ac constitutiones*, pt 1, f. 50v; Ferretti, *De iure et re navali*, f. 56; Gail, *Practicae observationes*, pt 2, pp. 178–9; De Ayala, *De iure et officiis bellicis*, vol. 1, f. 32v, and vol. 2, p. 33.

179 Bartolus, *Opera omnia*, vol. 5, f. 97r; De Legnano, *Tractatus de bello, de represaliis et de duello*, p. 156; *Corpus selectorum tractatuum*, p. 534 (Garatus). The texts cited were *Digest*, 1.1.3, *Code*, 8.4.1, and *Liber extra*, 2.13.12. See too Giltaij 2014.

180 *Digest*, 6.1.68, 29.2.20.2 (as glossed) and 42.8.10.16, and *Code*, 1.9.14 (read *a contrario sensu*) and 3.12.9 (as glossed).

181 Bartolus, *Opera omnia*, vol. 5, f. 97r; *Corpus selectorum tractatuum*, p. 524 (De Canibus); De Legnano, *Tractatus de bello, de represaliis et de duello*, p. 157.

182 *Corpus selectorum tractatuum*, p. 524 (De Canibus), citing *Digest*, 47.9.7, and *Code*, 8.14.4, 11.59.1 and 12.62.4.

any member of the other, leaving that city or nation to redistribute the loss internally in an equitable manner. Looking at this from another angle, it was explained that while it might have been objected that the enrichment of one person at another's expense was declared by a famous text to be contrary to natural equity, 'a person making use of reprisals is not enriched at another's expense but pursues what is due to him, and afterwards the person forced to pay by way of the reprisals has a remedy against the person in whose place he was forced to pay'.[183] Provided the person forced to pay had access to the ordinary judicial process available in his own city or country, there ought in the end to be no injustice, for it would be the guilty party who was unjustly enriched at the expense of the person who fulfilled his obligation to make reparation, and the guilty party would be forced by a judge in his own city or country to make recompense for the payment made on his behalf. The practice of reprisals, it was believed, could thus be reconciled with the principles behind various imperial constitutions.

But what about the express condemnation of the practice in the *novela constitutio* issued by Justinian, in the *authentica* issued by Frederick I, and in the *canon* issued by the Second Council of Lyons? The answer, as far as Justinian's robust condemnation of *pignerationes* was concerned, was that he had intervened in significantly different circumstances, in which there could have been no *denegatio iustitiae*.[184] In Justinian's own time, it was explained, the emperor had been able to ensure that justice was never denied since all judges were ultimately answerable to him, whereas in the fourteenth century 'kings and princes and even cities, especially in Italy, do not, at least *de facto*, recognise a superior in temporal affairs, because of which recourse cannot be taken to a superior in cases of injustice'.[185] It was only with the decline of imperial authority in the west that, 'when ordinary legal remedies failed, there was a need for recourse to the extraordinary remedy of reprisals'.[186] As for the condemnations of the practice by Frederick I and the Second Council of Lyons, they could be interpreted as referring not so much to the general practice as to its particular exercise in relation to scholars and clerics.[187] 'Reprisals themselves were not

183 *Corpus selectorum tractatuum*, p. 521 (De Canibus), making allusion to *Digest*, 12.6.14 and 50.17.206.

184 Angelus, *Opera omnia*, vol. 2, ff. 77v-8r.

185 Bartolus, *Opera omnia*, vol. 5, f. 96v; De Legnano, *Tractatus de bello, de represaliis et de duello*, p. 155. Of course, whether the emperor really did exercise effective control over the entire judicial system in the early sixth century is more than a little doubtful.

186 *Corpus selectorum tractatuum*, p. 533 (Garatus).

187 Baldus, *Commentaria super Codicem*, vol. 2, f. 24r; Angelus, *Opera omnia*, vol. 2, ff. 77v-8r; De Saliceto, *Super Codicis commentaria*, vol. 2, f. 116.

generally prohibited by any of those laws', it was remarked, 'but only in certain special cases'.[188] It was argued that 'the custom in this matter is not evil or perverse generally', and that scholars and clerics were merely excluded from its normal scope, together with ambassadors, women and various other classes of person gradually added to a list of exemptions.[189] Admittedly, while it could be argued in this way that the practice of reprisals had not actually been prohibited by the civil and canon laws, what could not be argued was that those laws had made express provision for it. Yet because the pivotal canon law text was based on an instruction issued to the Israelites, it could be claimed that the practice derived from *ius divinum*, and because reprisals were understood from that text to be a species of licit war, it could further be claimed that the practice derived from *ius gentium*.[190] Moreover, while it had to be conceded that reprisals had been introduced *de aequitate iuris gentium* rather than *de iure civili positivo*, the texts allowing for the seizure of recalcitrant debtors and their goods appeared to indicate that reprisals were in some sense 'permitted by the civil law'.[191] 'Although this capability may have proceeded from *ius gentium*', one author went so far as to conclude, 'it has nevertheless received approval from the civil law, from the spirit though not the express letter of the same'.[192]

Having devised a justification for the practice of reprisals, the doctors proceeded to discuss certain implications of their theory, laying down various precepts to guide the authorisation and execution of seizures. One clear implication was that seizures had to be warranted by sovereign authority, whether by the ruler of an independent city or nation directly, or by a person or body on whom this aspect of his sovereignty had been devolved.[193] Reprisals had to be authorised by 'someone who does not acknowledge a superior, the reason being, as has been said, that reprisals are a particular species of just war (lest justice should fail), yet no one can declare war apart from someone who does not acknowledge a superior, or has a commission from him'.[194] Another implication of the theory was that since reprisals were a kind of war, things could not only be taken legitimately from citizens of the place affected but

188 *Corpus selectorum tractatuum*, p. 521 (De Canibus).

189 Bartolus, *Opera omnia*, vol. 5, ff. 99v-100r; *Corpus selectorum tractatuum*, pp. 524 and 530–2 (De Canibus) and 536–7 (Garatus).

190 Bartolus, *Opera omnia*, vol. 5, f. 96v; De Legnano, *Tractatus de bello, de represaliis et de duello*, p. 156; *Corpus selectorum tractatuum*, p. 522 (De Canibus).

191 *Corpus selectorum tractatuum*, p. 524 (De Canibus).

192 De Legnano, *Tractatus de bello, de represaliis et de duello*, p. 157.

193 Bartolus, *Opera omnia*, vol. 5, ff. 97r and 98r; De Legnano, *Tractatus de bello, de represaliis et de duello*, pp. 156–7 and 169.

194 *Corpus selectorum tractatuum*, p. 534 (Garatus).

would become the property of the takers.[195] However, the acquisition of things taken by way of reprisals in peacetime was not understood to operate in the same way as the acquisition of plunder taken during a publicly declared war. Whereas ordinary citizens were entitled to take things from each other as soon as a war was declared by one of their rulers against the other, they could not execute reprisals against each other on their own initiative (*per se*) or their own authority (*auctoritate sua*).[196] Although there were texts indicating that a creditor could sometimes take matters into his own hands by seizing the person or property of his debtor, others indicated that this was permissible only where it was impossible for him to obtain prior approval from a judge.[197] The doctors constantly insisted that for property to be acquired by way of reprisal the whole process had to be conducted under the supervision and direction of public officials (*per ministros*).[198]

The procedural model the doctors favoured was not in fact founded on the Roman law texts relating to recalcitrant debtors but on many others relating to contumacious defenders.[199] On the basis of a passing mention in one text of the need for a *secundum decretum* to be obtained before title to a defender's assets could be acquired, the early glossators and commentators had already devised a procedure to be followed when a defender summoned to appear before a court declined to do so.[200] Provided sufficient warning had been given, the next step was for the frustrated pursuer to obtain a court order (*iussus iudicis*) authorising him to take possession of property belonging to the absent defender.[201] Although a judge was supposed to issue the order, which was identified as the *primum decretum* behind the decree mentioned in the sources, the

195 Andreae, *In titulum de regulis iuris*, ff. 118v-19; De Baysio, *Rosarium super Decreto*, sig. 2D1v; *Corpus selectorum tractatuum*, pp. 522 and 524 (De Canibus).

196 De Belviso, *Aurea lectura*, f. 37v; Bartolus, *Opera omnia*, vol. 5, f. 100v.

197 *Digest*, 42.1.6.2, 42.8.10.16 and 43.24.7.4, and *Code*, 10.32.54.

198 Key texts here included *Digest*, 1.18.6, 42.1.6.2, 42.1.58 and 50.17.176.pr.

199 Bartolus, *Opera omnia*, vol. 5, ff. 100v-1r; De Legnano, *Tractatus de bello, de represaliis et de duello*, pp. 170–1; *Corpus selectorum tractatuum*, p. 537 (Garatus).

200 Odofredus, *Lectura super Digesto*, vol. 1, ff. 54v-5 (ad D.2.9.2); *Digestum novum*, cols 57–9 (gl. 'Prius' ad D.39.2.15.15); Gulielmus Durantis, *Speculum iudiciale*, vol. 2, ff. 44–56; Dinus de Mugello, *Apostille super Infortiato et Digesto novo*, sigg. R1–2 (ad D.39.2.15); Cinus, *In Codicem et aliquot titulos Digesti veteris doctissima commentaria*, vol. 2(2), ff. 44v-8r (ad D.39.2.15.16); Bartolus, *Opera omnia*, vol. 3(1), ff. 33–5 (ad D.39.2.15.16); *Tractatus universi iuris*, vol. 8, ff. 214–16r (De Belviso). For a brief summary see Engelmann 1928, pp. 489–92.

201 Odofredus, *Lectura super Digesto*, vol. 1, f. 55r; *Digestum novum*, cols 57–8; Cinus, *In Codicem et aliquot titulos Digesti veteris doctissima commentaria*, vol. 2(2), f. 45r; Bartolus, *Opera omnia*, vol. 3(1), f. 33v.

first order did not have to be issued in the course of a formal court hearing.[202] It did not enable the pursuer to become owner of the property seized, giving him nothing more than physical control (*detentatio*) over it, but it did provide a kind of security (*pignus*) for the defender's appearance, as he would need to come before the court if he wished to recover his belongings.[203] If he still declined to appear, a second court order could be obtained after a reasonable amount of time had passed, the period either being fixed by the law of the place where the court was sitting (*recurrendum est ad legem municipalem et ad consuetudinem loci*) or being left to the discretion of the judge (*committatur arbitrio iudicis*).[204] The second order would authorise the sale of the property seized, and payment of the sum due to the pursuer from the proceeds of the sale, or – typically if a suitable buyer could not be found – the appropriation of at least part of the property by the pursuer.[205] Depending on the circumstances, the buyer or pursuer would either be made owner directly (*dominium statim transferatur*) or the second order would provide a legal basis on which he could complete title after a further period of time had elapsed (*iusta causa usucapiendi vel prescribendi*). By treating the original offender in a reprisal case as a contumacious defender, and by allowing the property of his compatriots to be seized as security, the doctors were able not only to identify a convenient procedure, which gave the original offender another opportunity to respond, but also to explain how ownership of the things seized could be acquired. Clearly, in the absence of a declared war, it could not have been claimed that the things were effectively ownerless and thus open to acquisition simply by their seizure (*occupatio*). Instead, it needed to be explained how the present owner could be divested of title and how it could be conferred on someone else. Under the procedure identified this was done by means of a special type

202 Durantis, *Speculum iudiciale*, vol. 2, f. 44v; Dinus, *Apostille super Infortiato et Digesto novo*, sigg. R1v-2r; Cinus, *In Codicem et aliquot titulos Digesti veteris doctissima commentaria*, vol. 2(2), f. 45v.

203 Odofredus, *Lectura super Digesto*, vol. 1, f. 55r; *Digestum novum*, col. 59; Durantis, *Speculum iudiciale*, vol. 2, f. 49; Dinus, *Apostille super Infortiato et Digesto novo*, sig. R2v; Cinus, *In Codicem et aliquot titulos Digesti veteris doctissima commentaria*, vol. 2(2), f. 45r, and also vol. 2(1), f. 453 (ad C.7.43.8); Bartolus, *Opera omnia*, vol. 3(1), f. 35r.

204 Odofredus, *Lectura super Digesto*, vol. 1, f. 55v; *Digestum novum*, col. 58; Bartolus, *Opera omnia*, vol. 3(1), f. 34v.

205 Odofredus, *Lectura super Digesto*, vol. 1, f. 55v; *Digestum vetus*, col. 216 (gl. 'In bonis' ad D.2.9.2); *Digestum novum*, col. 58, and also col. 60 (gl. 'Dominus' ad D.39.2.15.16); Bartolus, *Opera omnia*, vol. 3(1), f. 35r; Iacobus de Arena, *Commentaria in universum ius civile*, f. 144r (ad D.39.2.5).

of judicial decision (*adiudicatio*), which had been recognised in Roman law as another way of acquiring property.[206]

The form of the judicial decision would vary from country to country or from court to court, but there was less scope for local divergence than might have been expected. Given that the practice of reprisals had not been provided for explicitly in the texts of the civil and canon laws, and that *ius gentium* had been defined there as 'what natural reason has established among all peoples', the view might easily have been taken that the practice was governed by the law of nature rather than the learned laws, and that it was up to each people to decide how the requirements of the law of nature ought to be implemented in this area.[207] As has been seen, the doctors did indeed associate the *ius gentium* under which they believed the practice of reprisals could be legitimised with *aequitas naturalis* and *ius divinum*, and sometimes they drew attention to the fact that Augustine's crucial discussion of the book of Joshua had been cited with approval not only in the *Corpus iuris canonici* but also in an account of just war theory in Thomas Aquinas' *Summa theologiae*.[208] According to Aquinas, there were three requirements for a war to be just: first, that it be waged on the authority of a ruler; secondly, that it be waged for a just cause; and thirdly, that it be waged for a sound motive.[209] As has again been seen already, the doctors of law agreed that for reprisals, a kind of limited war, to be just, the authority of a ruler was required, and also that there needed to be a just cause for their being taken, which Augustine had identified as a denial of justice. They did so, however, because these requirements were implicit in the legal sources they studied. They pointed out that Aquinas' third requirement was inconsistent with the rule stated in their sources that 'no one is punished for thinking', added that issues of motivation were a matter for the theologians who advised on the handling of cases *in foro conscientiae*, and left the works of

---

206 Jakob Spiegel, *Lexicon iuris civilis*, sigg. C1v and C2r; *Vocabularius utriusque iuris*, pp. 10–11 and 46–7; Pardoux Duprat, *Lexicon iuris civilis et canonici*, ff. 8r and 9r; Simon Schard, *Lexicon iuridicum iuris Romani simul et pontificii*, col. 115; Ioannes Calvinus, *Lexicon iuridicum*, p. 39; Jerome Verrooten, *Novum lexicon utriusque iuris*, col. 21; Cuiacius, *Opera omnia*, vol. 1, col. 1135.

207 *Digest*, 1.1.9.

208 Bartolus, *Opera omnia*, vol. 5, ff. 96v-7r, and *Corpus selectorum tractatuum*, p. 524 (De Canibus); and see too D'Afflitto, *In utriusque Siciliae Neapolisque sanctiones ac constitutiones*, pt 1, f. 50v; Damhouder, *Praxis rerum criminalium*, p. 291; Gothofredus, *Praxis civilis*, vol. 2, col. 745.

209 *Summa theologiae*, 2a2ae 40.1. Aquinas' thinking will be returned to in the next chapter when – as promised previously – the relationship between categories like *ius naturale* and *ius gentium* – crucial to the emergence of the new international law – will be examined more thoroughly.

the theologians aside while they focused on discharging their own professional responsibility of advising on the handling of cases *in foro civili*.[210] In a court of law, they conceded, no one could demand authorisation for the taking of reprisals by virtue of a right of action, or as a mandatory requirement of judicial office, since the authorisation of reprisals was seen as an equitable remedy, granted at the discretion of the judge.[211] Nevertheless, they understood the exercise of judicial discretion to be regulated by the spirit, if not by the letter, of the learned laws. Furthermore, they doubted how far even legislators could go in seeking to introduce regulations of their own devising. 'Statutes may be able to legitimise cases other than those allowed by the common law', Bartolus remarked, 'but if statutes were passed in one city in relation to reprisals granted against another free territory, then it needs to be noted that the grounds for the granting of reprisals depend on injustice done or on justice denied by the territory against which the reprisals are granted, and in relation to this statutes cannot be passed'.[212] The point was that while the practice of reprisals could be regulated locally, the theory of the schools would have to be adhered to if the legitimacy of the practice was to be recognised in other places.

In the light of this robustly stated opinion, it is no great surprise to find that studies of the practice of reprisals in medieval Europe, some of which have been detailed and rigorous, have described a fairly homogeneous system, firmly grounded on the theory worked out by the doctors.[213] Parties unable to secure justice abroad made complaints to their own rulers, or to appropriate officials appointed by their rulers. When satisfied that the parties had reasonable claims to make, and that they had been prevented from pursuing their claims through foreign courts, the rulers sent documents called 'letters of requisition' to the rulers of the foreign places, urging them to administer the justice denied. The diplomatic process was often repeated, and was sometimes reinforced in person by envoys and ambassadors, but if no satisfactory response was received, the parties themselves were eventually granted 'letters of reprisal' or 'letters of marque', which typically recounted all the efforts made to secure redress for the losses alleged, stressed that justice had been persistently denied, and declared – with protestations of reluctance on the part of the granter – that authorisation had been given for seizures of goods to be

210 *Digest*, 48.19.16.

211 *Corpus selectorum tractatuum*, p. 534 (Garatus).

212 *Opera omnia*, vol. 5, f. 97r.

213 De Mas Latrie 1866, pp. 537–67; Eiglier 1888; Sanborn 1930, pp. 224–34; Clark 1933; Gouron 1938, pp. 12–18; Timbal 1958; Chavarot 1991; Dick 2010, pp. 84–147; Fletcher 2010, pp. 111–15; Wink and Sicking 2017.

made from the compatriots of those who had inflicted the losses originally suffered and not yet redressed.[214] Care was taken to establish the extent of the losses suffered, to evaluate any goods seized, and to ensure that the holders of the letters of reprisal or marque received no more than was due to them. Goods seized, which often included ships and cargoes, had to be taken back to the countries in which the letters of reprisal or marque had been issued, and had to be accounted for before courts there. A court order was required before any goods could be sold or retained, and only as much of the proceeds of the sale or the goods themselves would be granted to the petitioners as was required to satisfy the claims recognised as genuine in the letters of reprisal or marque. If the goods produced before the courts were found insufficient to satisfy the claims, further seizures could be made, but once the claims were satisfied, the letters of reprisal or marque were cancelled.

Naturally, reprisals were not invariably taken in accordance with the theory taught in all the law schools and the practice approved in particular places, but this does not prevent the writings of the doctors and the records of diplomacy and litigation from giving a general impression of clarity and consistency. It was widely recognised that another way in which the seizure of ships and goods at sea could be legitimate was if reprisals were being taken for unredressed losses. This type of legitimate seizure was different from the plundering of enemies in several ways. First, whereas plunder was licit in wartime, reprisals were taken in peacetime. While reprisals might in principle have been taken in wartime as well, in response to denials of justice before hostilities began, there would have been no need to satisfy the more exacting requirements of the reprisal process then. Secondly, whereas the essential condition of licit plunder was the existence of a declared war, the essential condition of lawful reprisals was a denial of justice by a foreign country.[215] The civil law doctors considered plunder to be licit on either side of a declared war, yet reprisals could only be executed

214 Although several attempts have been made to distinguish between letters of reprisal and letters of marque, the words reprisal and marque seem to have been used synonymously at this stage, both being equated with the Latin term *pigneratio* and understood to denote some form of distraint (De Mas Latrie 1866, p. 537; Du Cange 1884–7, vol. 5, pp. 266–7, vol. 6, pp. 318–19, and vol. 7, p. 134; Clark 1933, pp. 700–1; Timbal 1958, pp. 113–14; Chavarot 1991, p. 52; Verzijl, Heere and Offerhaus 1998, p. 153; Niermeyer, Van de Kieft and Burgers 2002, vol. 2, pp. 853, 1038–9 and 1187). In the sixteenth century the French expression *donner marque, ou lettre de marque*, was still said to be equivalent to the Latin *dare iniectionem manuum in alium pro alio, i.e., ius pignerandi* (Thierry, *Dictionaire françois-latin*, p. 382; Nicot, *Dictionaire françois-latin*, p. 559).

215 For the civilians especially, it may be recalled, a *bellum licitum* was equivalent to a *bellum iustum*.

lawfully by a party who had been denied justice for losses sustained.[216] Thirdly, whereas the only involvement of rulers in legitimising plunder was their declaring of war against one another, more specific authorisation was required from rulers before it could be lawful to take reprisals. While rulers did often seek to regulate the conduct of warfare, they did not make possession of a licence to raid enemy shipping a condition of prize acquisition in the way that it always was in the case of reprisals. Fourthly, whereas title to plundered goods was acquired by occupation, subject to an obligation to pay shares to others, the ownership of goods seized by way of reprisal was acquired by a formal process of adjudication. Although, as will be seen further in the next chapter, mariners were often encouraged to seek judicial approval of the seizures they made in wartime, it was only in relation to reprisals that a judicial act was required for title to be acquired.

In addition to these technical – but crucially important – differences between plunder and reprisal, two differences in the way their justification was developed are worth emphasising by way of conclusion, before attention returns to Scotland. The first is that accommodating theory to practice had been more challenging where reprisals were concerned. Once the doctors had overcome the difficulty of reconciling the texts on plunder with each other, they found that their theory fitted the contemporary practice of warfare fairly well – which may of course go some way towards explaining why they read the texts in the way they did. It was necessary for them to explain that the sovereign rulers capable of declaring public wars on each other included those who did not in fact recognise any superior to whom they could make complaints, even if they were subject as a matter of law to imperial authority, and also to explain that prisoners taken in wars between Christian rulers were not to be treated as slaves, unlike those taken in wars against infidels.[217] But these were not alterations of the theory discovered in the texts so much as adjustments to its application. In contrast, it required considerable ingenuity to fashion a justification of reprisals that was consistent with the texts, some of which had to be read against the grain. In writing about the city states of northern Italy, the doctors were able to point out again that many rulers who should have been able to rely on the emperor to provide justice were unable or unwilling to do so, yet the fact also was that in many parts of Europe groups of people who

216 The denial of justice was also regarded as a just cause for waging a public war, but the point is that the civilians were not generally concerned with the existence of a just cause for war.

217 For an example of doubts left by the first point see Wubs-Mrozewicz and Wijffels 2016, pp. 27–9.

did recognise superiors waged private wars against each other, and believed they were entitled to do so.[218] They took it upon themselves to seek redress for injuries they sustained by way of reprisal, revenge or retaliation against other groups, often becoming involved in prolonged bloodfeuds.[219] Historians have connected maritime raiding in particular with the private warfare that was endemic in the border regions separating countries, identifying the seas as liquid marches (linked with the terms *marcha* and marque).[220] As the wars in which reprisals were taken by people who did recognise superiors were much harder to justify in legal terms than the limited wars authorised by superiors who claimed to be independent, it is scarcely surprising that whereas the theory of plunder had emerged and been widely accepted before the thirteenth century, it was not until the end of the same century that the doctors began to develop their theory of reprisal, which was not widely accepted until the fourteenth and fifteenth centuries.

The second difference between the justifications of plunder and reprisal that ought to be emphasised follows from the first and is its mirror image. Because the doctors struggled to accommodate their theory to the practice of reprisals, there was more need for the practice of reprisals to be accommodated to their theory than had been the case with the practice of plunder. The justification of plunder devised in the law schools had reinforced and refined rather than reformed the waging of wars. Theory and practice had come together seamlessly in the law of arms. Theory had provided principles to give coherence to the rules observed in practice, and observance of the rules had confirmed the validity of the principles, without necessarily reflecting much awareness of them. As has been seen, mariners were able to seize ships and goods at sea and to appreciate that they could be acquired from enemies without being familiar with the thinking of lawyers, or even knowing that their activity was justifiable in the minds of their rulers in terms of the laws taught in the universities. When government agencies and legal experts did become involved, this tended to result in no more than clarification of the assumptions made by mariners, as when the significance of the word 'enemy' was pinned down precisely. With regard to reprisals, however, popular practice was not able to proceed

218 Sometimes lawyers referred to these wars as *guerrae* rather than *bella*, and to their participants as *inimici* rather than *hostes*, but the usage was inconsistent (Kaminsky 2002, p. 55; Bartlett 2010, pp. 210–11; Hyams 2010, p. 166). The focus here is of course on groups recognising different superiors.

219 Wallace-Hadrill 1959; Kaueper 1988; Hyams 2003; Firnhaber-Baker 2010; Zmora 2011.

220 See especially Heebøll-Holm 2013, but also Rodger 2014, pp. 6–8, and Cordes and Höhn 2018, pp. 524–6.

in parallel with professional opinion. There had again been rules governing the practice of reprisals. Feuding was regulated by customary norms, which were sometimes ratified by the rulers whose superiority the participants in the activity recognised.[221] Border regions generally had their own regulations too, which again received ratification from rulers.[222] When maritime raiding amounted to the taking of reprisals by one coastal community against another, it was presumably governed by similar norms.[223] Yet none of these bodies of rules was consistent with the theory of reprisals worked out in the law schools, nor could the practice regulated by the rules be brought into line with the theory by means of simple adjustments and refinements. Sovereign rulers who adopted the theory were not ratifying further the existing norms but were asserting their sovereignty in taking responsibility for, and assuming control over, the practice of reprisals.[224] Under the new regime reprisals were 'limited' as opposed to 'private' wars. They could only be engaged in lawfully under the direction of government agencies, and the involvement of these agencies, along with the legal experts on whom they relied, was unavoidable. For the theory of the schools to make sense of the practice of reprisals, the practice had to be reformed and refashioned in accordance with the theory.

4 Authorisation of Reprisals in Sixteenth-Century Scotland

It is well known that reprisals were still being taken during the early sixteenth century in response to the seizure of a vessel belonging to John Barton of Leith in the reign of James III.[225] At the end of the fifteenth century, as redress had not yet been recovered, James IV had issued Barton's sons with further letters of reprisal and marque (*literae represaliae et marquae*), in which he had described the original seizure of the vessel by pirates from Portugal, had restated his

221 Miller 1990, pp. 236–9; Kaminsky 2002, pp. 59–65; Bartlett 2010, pp. 197–204; Althoff 2013, pp. 313–23; Sunderland 2017, pp. 178–85. See too Stoljar 1977.

222 Davies 1970; Neilson 1971; Neville 1988; Summerson 1991; Leeson 2009.

223 There is a tendency to assume that because the seas were similar to marches, they were governed by 'marcher law', but this is to confuse similarity with identity. Although border law might apply when people living on borders engaged in maritime raiding (*e.g.* Rae 1966, p. 48), that was another matter. *Cf.* Armstrong 2020, pp. 64–5.

224 This seems to be the point made in Heebøll-Holm 2017, although the part played in the development by learned theory is overlooked.

225 Statham 1910, pp. 19–28; Reid 1962, pp. 33–5, 41–2, 83–91 and 270–2; Mowat 1994, pp. 59, 74, 104 and 111; Macdougall 1997, pp. 238–40; Davidson 2003, pp. 30–1; Murdoch 2010, pp. 80–5.

predecessor's insistence (*requisitio*) that Barton receive the justice he had hitherto been refused (*denegata iustitia*), and had authorised Barton's sons to seize things belonging to any Portuguese mariners or merchants they encountered, up to the specified evaluation of the loss originally sustained.[226] In 1506 letters of reprisal (*represaliarum literae*) were issued again, and in the following year James IV wrote personally to the king of Portugal, warning that while the use of the letters granted to the Bartons had been frequently suspended for the sake of friendship between their nations, it was his responsibility as a king to support his subjects in the lawful claims they made in other places.[227] When the Bartons seized Portuguese vessels during the next two years, and one of the brothers was arrested in Zeeland on a charge of piracy, James promptly wrote in his support to the relevant authorities, explaining that he had reluctantly granted letters of reprisal to the brothers because they had been denied justice (*represaliarum literas ex negata iis iustitia invitus indulserit*), emphasising that they had been required to have all their seizures judicially approved, so that they would receive no more than was necessary to cover the loss originally sustained (*ad regium reportarent iudicium, ne damni dati aestimationem excederent*), and insisting that since the seizures actually made were within the terms of the letters granted, they were legally justified and did not merit punishment (*legibus fundata nullam meretur poenam*).[228]

The king of Portugal afterwards wrote to the king of Scotland to point out that reprisals were only legitimate if justice had been denied, claiming that he had received no notice of any deficiency, in accordance with the legal procedure and ancient custom observed in cases of this type (*iuris ordinem et antiquum in huiusmodi casibus morem*).[229] His objection was easily dealt with by a reminder of the already protracted history of the case, but more problematic was the Bartons' tendency to remove goods from Portuguese vessels

226 *Extracts from the Records of the Burgh of Edinburgh*, vol. 1, pp. 119–22.

227 *Acta curiae admirallatus Scotiae*, p. 202; *Documents Relating to the Law and Custom of the Sea*, vol. 1, pp. 170–2; *Epistolae Iacobi Quarti, Iacobi Quinti et Mariae regum Scotorum*, vol. 1, pp. 91–3; *Letters of James the Fourth*, pp. 81–2.

228 John Leslie, *De origine, moribus et rebus gestis Scotorum*, pp. 350–1, or *Historie of Scotland*, vol. 2, p. 130; David Chalmers, *Histoire abbregée de tous les roys de France, Angleterre et Escosse*, f. 199r; *Chronicle of the Kings of Scotland*, p. 80; *Epistolae Iacobi Quarti, Iacobi Quinti et Mariae regum Scotorum*, vol. 1, pp. 88–90 and 111–12; *Letters and Papers Illustrative of the Reigns of Richard III and Henry VII*, vol. 2, pp. 274–6; *Letters of James the Fourth*, pp. 129–31 and 134–5; NLS, Adv. MS 35.5.9B, ff. 145v and 149v; BL, Royal MS 13B II, f. 48v.

229 *Epistolae Iacobi Quarti, Iacobi Quinti et Mariae regum Scotorum*, vol. 1, pp. 103–4; *Letters of James the Fourth*, p. 156.

even when they belonged to merchants from England, France or Flanders.[230] In a famous incident preserved in folk memory, one of the Bartons was killed and two of their ships captured by an English force sent out to deal with them in 1511, after which they seem largely to have desisted from taking reprisals for the next thirty years.[231] When in 1540 a grandson of John Barton, along with the heirs of some merchants whose goods had been seized with his vessel, petitioned for renewal of the licence to take reprisals (*literae repetundarum, hoc est marcquae*), it was objected that the earlier authority would not have been permitted to lapse without reason.[232] James V, however, replied that the authority had only been permitted to lapse because the regents who had governed Scotland following his father's death in 1513 had been reluctant to have action taken against a friendly nation during his minority, and he warned that he was duty bound to grant his subjects the remedy available under *ius gentium*.[233] After a delay to give the Portuguese king time to arrange for redress to be made, new letters of reprisal (*represaliarum literae*) were finally issued in 1543, although by then James V had himself died, leaving his infant daughter Mary on the throne.[234] Contrary to the late king's reasoning, these letters were reissued in almost identical terms by various regents in 1547, 1550, 1552 and 1556.[235] First recounting the seizure of John Barton's vessel, the denial of justice he had suffered in Portugal and the exchanges between previous monarchs, the letters proceeded to confirm that the queen had reluctantly agreed

230 *Epistolae Iacobi Quarti, Iacobi Quinti et Mariae regum Scotorum*, vol. 1, pp. 120–1; *Letters of James the Fourth*, pp. 173–4 and 208–9; NLS, Adv. MS 35.5.9B, f. 163; *Acts of the Lords of Council in Public Affairs*, pp. LXI and LXIV–V; Riddell 1852, vol. 1, pp. 328–9.

231 Leslie, *De origine, moribus et rebus gestis Scotorum*, p. 355, or *Historie of Scotland*, vol. 2, p. 135; *Hall's Chronicle*, p. 525; *Letters and Papers Relating to the War with France*, pp. ix–x; *Letters and Papers, Foreign and Domestic, of the Reign of Henry VIII*, vol. 1(1), p. 452. For what appears to have been a further seizure made before 1517 see *Acts of the Lords of Council in Public Affairs*, pp. 76 and 82. For the commemoration of the 1511 incident in a popular ballad see *True Relation of the Life and Death of Sir Andrew Barton*; *Reliques of Ancient English Poetry*, pp. 134–7; *Naval Songs and Ballads*, pp. 6–15 and 340–1.

232 Leslie, *De origine, moribus et rebus gestis Scotorum*, pp. 351–2, or *Historie of Scotland*, vol. 2, pp. 131–2; *Letters and Papers, Foreign and Domestic, of the Reign of Henry VIII*, vol. 15, p. 459.

233 *Epistolae Iacobi Quarti, Iacobi Quinti et Mariae regum Scotorum*, vol. 2, pp. 76–8, 102–3, 130–2 and 147–51; *Letters of James V*, pp. 401, 403–4, 419–20, 430–1, 435, 437 and 443. On the extent to which regents were prepared to behave like kings see generally Blakeway 2015.

234 *Epistolae Iacobi Quarti, Iacobi Quinti et Mariae regum Scotorum*, vol. 2, pp. 166–8; *Warrender Papers*, vol. 1, pp. 8–9; NRS, GD1/371/3, f. 303v, and GD149/264, ff. 182v-3r.

235 *Registrum secreti sigilli regum Scotorum*, vol. 3, pp. 83–4 and 330–1, and vol. 4, pp. 111–12, 262 and 592–3; *Scottish Correpondence of Mary of Lorraine*, p. 354; *Calendar of State Papers Relating to Scotland*, vol. 1, p. 7.

to authorise the seizure of Portuguese property up to a specified evaluation of the loss sustained, and urged other rulers to recognise that when goods were seized under the letters, the intention was to execute a legal remedy (*iuris remedio*), not to engage in piracy (*pyraticam exercere*).

By the beginning of the 1560s reprisals had also been taken by Scots other than the Bartons, and against foreigners other than the Portuguese.[236] In the summer of 1530 four vessels carrying merchandise from Scotland to the Baltic had been attacked by pirates from either Friesland or Holland.[237] After prolonged diplomatic efforts failed to secure compensation, letters were issued by James V in 1539, giving the parties despoiled the right to execute reprisals (*represaliarum ius*) or wage war (*bellum agere*) against the compatriots of the pirates.[238] The letters emphasised in the usual manner that justice had been denied (*denegata iustitia*), and they exhorted any ruler whose territory the Scots visited with a prize (*praeda*) not to treat them as if they were themselves pirates. Nevertheless, complaints were received from the emperor in the following year about the seizure of ships and goods from his subjects in Flanders, Holland and Zeeland by Robert Fogo and other pirates (*piratis*), supposedly under the cover of the letters of reprisal or marque (*literae represaliarum seu de marca*) issued in 1539.[239] Faced with threats of counter-measures (*contrarii remedii*) by the emperor, James wrote at once to claim that the seizures had not been made with his authority, pointing out that Fogo, worried about the legal penalties he would face at home (*sibi a nostris legibus timens*), had taken the captured ships and goods to England, and that he had in fact been arrested as soon as he returned to Scotland, where James promised he would face justice.[240] That Fogo had not been acting within the terms of the letters granted was certainly true as far as the seizure of ships and goods from Flanders and Zeeland was concerned, and shortly afterwards, during a court action that resulted in the restoration of a vessel to its Dutch owner, evidence was produced that he had given a promise not to 'us his lattir of marque bot aganis the Fresis allanerlie'.[241] In his exchange with the emperor, James took the

236 Some of these cases are set in the context of 'reprisal wars' in Murdoch 2010, pp. 86–91.

237 *Letters of James V*, pp. 179–80.

238 *Letters of James V*, pp. 369–70; NRS, GD149/264, ff. 128–91; BL, Royal MS 18B VI, f. 199.

239 *Letters of James V*, pp. 401–2 and 404; NRS, GD149/264, ff. 55v-6.

240 *Epistolae Iacobi Quarti, Iacobi Quinti et Mariae regum Scotorum*, vol. 2, pp. 84–5 and 91–6; *Letters of James V*, pp. 407 and 413–14.

241 *Acts of the Lords of Council in Public Affairs*, pp. 496–7; see too Finlay 2002, p. 46. The suggestion in Murdoch 2010, pp. 90–1, that James' claim was an 'absolute lie', and that Fogo permitted himself to be used as a 'scapegoat', goes too far, though James clearly was troubled by the emperor's threats.

opportunity to remind him that the Scots themselves had frequently been the victims of attacks by pirates not only from Flanders, Holland and Zeeland but also from Spain, for he had already complained in 1531 about the despoiling of a ship belonging to Robert Barton by Spanish pirates, and on several occasions he had sent heralds to Spain to press for compensation.[242]

In 1539, the year in which letters were granted to Fogo and his associates, letters of reprisal or marque (*literas represaliarum sive mercae*) were also granted to Robert Barton's heirs, narrating the original seizure and subsequent denial of justice in the familiar style, and specifying the amount of compensation to be recovered through the seizure of property from any subjects of the king of Spain.[243] The use of these letters appears to have been suspended, for in the following year James wrote to the emperor to complain again about the seizure – illicit plunder (*iniqua praeda*), since it had not been justified by the law of war (*ius belli*) and was completely contrary to law and equity (*iuri et aequo maxime contraria*) – and to urge him to ensure that justice was done in Spain before James was compelled to resort to harsher measures (*ad duriora descendere*).[244] Whether the letters ever were executed is unclear, but their granting to the Bartons may help to explain the confusion that arose in a case heard by the lords of session in 1552.[245] The Spanish pursuer claimed that goods bought and sold by the defenders had been 'spuilziet fra him be ane callit Davidsone, pirat on the sea', to which it was replied that Davidson was a 'man of weire' employed by the Bartons, 'quha had ane letter of mark upon the Portingallis'. The defence failed since the pursuer was from Spain, but a vague awareness that the Bartons had been authorised to execute reprisals on both Iberian nations may have encouraged its unsuccessful presentation.[246] The letters granted to the Bartons against the Portuguese were relied on again in a case raised before the admiralty court eight years later.[247] Two Portuguese vessels had been captured by a Scottish vessel belonging in part to Robert Logan, to whom the Bartons' letters had been assigned. After the judges were presented with an 'autentik copy of the letter of mark' by the captain of the Scottish vessel, and after the crews of the captured vessels confessed under oath that they

242 *Letters of James V*, p. 194; *Acts of the Lords of Council in Public Affairs*, p. 500.

243 *Registrum secreti sigilli regum Scotorum*, vol. 2, pp. 478–9.

244 *Epistolae Iacobi Quarti, Iacobi Quinti et Mariae regum Scotorum*, vol. 2, pp. 33–5; *Letters of James V*, p. 387.

245 *Practiques of Sir Richard Maitland*, pp. 42–3.

246 By this time, of course, Spain and Portugal had the same king. On the procedural niceties see Finlay 2002, p. 44.

247 *Acta curiae admirallatus Scotiae*, pp. 182–8, 194–203, 206–8, 210 and 214–17.

'pertened to Portingallis', they were declared to be 'just and lauchfull pryissis to the said capitane and his cumpany'. Further controversy ensued over the just distribution of the prizes among interested parties, in the course of which the queen's advocate appeared in the interests of the 'commoun weill and liegis of this realme', wondering whether the sum of damages specified in the letters had not yet been fully recovered, and warning of 'trublis to cum upoun the liegis in cais the boundis thairof be excedit', which might cause the Portuguese to resort to 'just weiris, or at the leist siclik letters repressallis'.

The Logan case is particularly important for present purposes because it is the only one of which a record has survived of a court being asked to find that a ship or goods seized under letters of reprisal belonged to the takers.[248] How representative it was is hard to tell. The record is cast in a similar style to the records of cases in which ships and goods captured from enemies during wartime were found to be legitimate prizes, with the pursuer alleging that in virtue of the letters of reprisal he was 'riggit furth in weirfair' against the Portuguese, and that in view of the origins of the captured ships and goods they 'aucht and suld be decernit to the said capitane and his cumpany, takaris thairof, as just and lauchfull pryssis'. The admiralty clerk who drafted the record had a particular reason to summarise the case in terms that would emphasise the similarity between wartime seizures and peacetime reprisals, for the pursuer had claimed that the admiral was not entitled to a tenth part of the property taken, arguing that there was a difference between things acquired under letters of reprisal, which conferred a 'personale rycht' on their holder, and things acquired during a 'weir publicklie proclamit betwix realme and realme'. That the pursuer's claim was specious is evident from a contract entered into six years earlier between Logan and several captains from Leith, in which it was agreed that any property they were able to seize under the cover of his letters would be divided in certain proportions, 'all admyrall rytis and uncostis and expensis beand deducyt and rebaitit on the haill'.[249] The agreement was that the captains would try to seize Portuguese vessels and take them to ports in Scotland or France, where they would send for Logan or his agents to defend them with the 'letter of marke' and have the ships 'adjugyt gude pryses'.

The word 'adjugyt' could of course have been used simply to signify a court order, but it is rarely found in records relating to a wartime seizures, and it

248 Of the few court cases relating to reprisals of which records have survived, the others were actions brought by the alleged victims of spoliation or piracy.

249 NRS, GD172/199; and see too GD103/2/4/22, a receipt from the admiral for payment of a tenth on other goods taken by the captains.

is found again in another record concerned with reprisals.[250] In 1561 Breton merchants complained to the privy council about the seizure of their ship and goods by the sons of Walter Cant, and about the subsequent treatment of the goods by Thomas Kennedy of Bargany, an admiral depute on the west coast.[251] It was alleged, though never actually proved, that Kennedy had 'fand be sentence definitive the gudis libellit to be lauchfull pryise', on the grounds that they 'pertenit to Spanyeartis' and that the 'lettres of marque' granted to the Bartons '*contra* Spanyeartis' had been assigned to Cant.[252] The way the decrete was described at two different places in the pleadings was that Kennedy had 'adjugeit the said schip and gudis to be lauchfull pryise', and an independent reference to the case likewise stated that Kennedy was called before the council for 'adjudging' the goods to the takers.[253] Given how clearly other aspects of reprisal practice in Scotland reflected the theory of the law schools, there is reason to suppose that the term 'adjudge' was being used here in its more technical sense to signify the formal allocation of title to a new owner.[254] This supposition is reinforced by another difference between the Logan case and the cases concerned with prizes taken in wartime. In the former, the only condition attached to the court's decree was that the amount to be recovered under the letters of marque must be reduced by the amount obtained through sale of the goods taken, whereas in the latter the condition was sometimes attached that the takers must 'fynd sufficient caucioun that the samyn salbe furthcumand to ony pairty that justlie may pretend ony interes thairto in tyme cuming'.[255] Where a court merely 'discerned' the rights parties had already acquired by occupying enemy property, it was possible for mistakes to be made and for property to be reclaimed in the future. Not long before the Logan case was heard, for example, a captain in Dundee sold a ship that had been 'deliverit in

250 *Cf.* ACA, CA1/1/24, pp. 435–6, and DHC, DB1/10/12/1, where the word appears to have been used in the looser sense.

251 *Register of the Privy Council of Scotland*, vol. 1, pp. 162, 165–7, 171–82, 187–91, 195–9, 207–14, 224–7, 229–32, 234 and 238–9.

252 For a specific reference made in the pleadings to the Davidson case see the sixth section below.

253 *Calendar of State Papers Relating to Scotland*, vol. 1, p. 556.

254 The verb 'to adjudge' had been used in its looser sense in Scotland since the fourteenth century, but the noun 'adjudication' only came into use in the 1600s, to denote the allocation of a debtor's property (Craigie, Aitken, Stevenson, Watson and Dareau 1931–2002, vol. 1, pp. 22–3). Here the verb appears to have been used in a closely related sense. *Cf. Acts of the Lords of Council in Public Affairs*, pp. 254–5.

255 *Acta curiae admirallatus Scotiae*, pp. 1 and 16; *Letters of James V*, p. 139; *Aarsberetninger fra det Kongelige Geheimearchiv*, vol. 3, p. 132.

ane admerall court his just and lauchfull pryise'.[256] It later transpired that the ship had been sailing under a letter of safe conduct and ought not to have been taken. When the buyer heard that its previous possessors intended to 'persew the said schip in quhais handis thai apprehend hir', he sought an indemnity against eviction from the seller, who replied that he had sold the ship 'with all aventours, as schow wes then lyand at the schoir'. Both parties recognised that the previous possessors remained the owners and would be able to recover their property. In contrast, where parties had acquired title to a ship or goods through a formal act of 'adjudication', they were able to rely on the court's authority as the foundation of their title. It was perhaps for this reason that the Breton merchants who complained that their goods had been wrongly taken did not raise an action against the takers themselves, but instead sought compensation from the judge who was alleged to have given the takers title to the goods. That the takers had acquired title to the ship was recognised in a dispute over its ownership two years later, even though it was by then known that it should not have been adjudged to them.[257] It was not assumed, as in the Dundee case, that the illegality of the seizure prevented title from being acquired, and the obvious explanation is that title to the ship and goods was not understood to have been acquired by the seizure (*occupatio*), but by the court order (*adiudicatio*).

There is more copious evidence that reprisals were conceived of in accordance with the theory of the law schools in the correspondence of the Scottish monarchs. Letters were often sent to or received from other rulers requesting expeditious and efficacious justice in actions involving strangers.[258] Some

---

256 DCA, BCMB, vol. 5, 5 July 1558.

257 *Calendar of State Papers Relating to Scotland*, vol. 2, p. 203; *Acts of the Privy Council of England*, vol. 7, pp. 246–7.

258 *Epistolae Iacobi Quarti, Iacobi Quinti et Mariae regum Scotorum*, vol. 1, pp. 152–6, 165–7, 231–3, 299–301, 311–13, 320–1 and 348–9, and vol. 2, pp. 1–3, 49–55, 59, 79–80, 87–91, 124–6, 132–3, 162–3, 177–8, 228–9, 238–9 and 253–5; *Letters of James the Fourth*, pp. 1, 165, 228, 258–63, 270–2 and 298–9; *Letters of James V*, pp. 7, 34, 52–3, 67, 73, 106–7, 139, 141, 155, 168–9, 177–8, 185, 187, 228, 289, 327, 330–1, 339–40, 347–8, 355–6, 369, 371–3, 389–91, 394–6, 399, 407–8, 412–13, 416, 420, 428–9 and 431; *Foreign Correspondence with Marie de Lorraine*, vol. 2, pp. 60–1; *Lettres, instructions et mémoires de Marie Stuart*, vol. 1, pp. 116–17; *Forty-Seventh Annual Report of the Deputy Keeper of the Public Records*, p. 13; *Miscellany of the Maitland Club*, vol. 1, pp. 233–4; *Registrum secreti sigilli regum Scotorum*, vol. 1, p. 72; *Diplomatarium Norvegicum*, vol. 8, pp. 566 and 574–5; *Aarsberetninger fra det Kongelige Geheimearchiv*, vol. 4, p. 107; *Letters and Papers Illustrative of the Reigns of Richard III and Henry VII*, vol. 2, pp. 202–3; *Acts of the Privy Council of England*, vol. 10, pp. 34, 105 and 189; *Calendar of State Papers Relating to Scotland*, vol. 1, p. 561; BL, Royal MS 13B II, ff. 50 and 67r, and Cotton MS Caligula B VI, f. 72; NLS, Adv. MS 35.5.9B, ff. 182v-3v, 191v, 201–2r and 213v; NRS, GD149/264,

letters made it plain that justice was being requested because under *ius gentium* this was a precondition of any legitimate recourse to letters of reprisal, the use of which was at least hinted at.[259] The threat of reprisals was sometimes made explicitly, but more often it was said that the writer was reluctant to be compelled by a further denial of justice to adopt harsher measures (*duriora media*), less than friendly remedies (*remedia parum amica*) or the extreme remedies available under the law (*extrema iuris remedia*).[260] In response to threats from other rulers, Scottish monarchs typically insisted that justice had not been denied, and promised to ensure that anyone who made a complaint in Scotland would receive fair treatment in the courts.[261] When letters of reprisal had already been issued in other places, it was usually objected that they ought not to have been since the only legitimate ground for reprisals was a denial of justice (*denegata iustitia, quae causa unica est represaliarum literas decernere*) and since justice had been administered in an appropriate way.[262] Peace treaties had a similar tendency to make provision for the orderly settlement of disputes between subjects of the signatories without denying that recourse to *literae represaliarum* might ultimately be necessary *in casu denegatae aut non ministratae iustitiae*.[263]

In the complaint made by the Breton merchants in 1561 it was pointed out that in a treaty the Scottish governor had entered into with the emperor in

ff. 48, 93r, 94, 102–3r, 108–9r, 115v-16r, 127v-8r, 220, 222r, 226v-8r, 229 and 238, SP13/54 and 77, and RH9/5/17 and 22.

259 *Epistolae Iacobi Quarti, Iacobi Quinti et Mariae regum Scotorum*, vol. 1, pp. 78–80 and 235–7; *Letters and Papers Illustrative of the Reigns of Richard III and Henry VII*, vol. 2, pp. 258–61; *Letters of James the Fourth*, pp. 99–101.

260 *Epistolae Iacobi Quarti, Iacobi Quinti et Mariae regum Scotorum*, vol. 1, pp. 309–11, and vol. 2, pp. 4–8 and 126–8; *Aarsberetninger fra det Kongelige Geheimearchiv*, vol. 3, p. 207, and vol. 4, pp. 59–60; *Letters of James V*, pp. 67, 238–9, 334, 373–4 and 429–30.

261 *Epistolae Iacobi Quarti, Iacobi Quinti et Mariae regum Scotorum*, vol. 1, pp. 19–21, 106–7 and 322–3, and vol. 2, pp. 60–2, 100–1 and 240–3; *Letters and Papers Illustrative of the Reigns of Richard III and Henry VII*, vol. 2, pp. 185–7; *Letters of James the Fourth*, pp. 9–10, 19–20, 171–2 and 220; *Letters of James V*, pp. 73–4, 178–9, 396, 402–3 and 418; *Registrum secreti sigilli regum Scotorum*, vol. 5(1), pp. 412–13; *Forty-Seventh Annual Report of the Deputy Keeper of the Public Records*, p. 12; BL, Royal MS 13B II, f. 60; NRS, GD149/264, ff. 174v-5, 224 and 228.

262 *Registrum secreti sigilli regum Scotorum*, vol. 1, pp. 72–3; *Epistolae Iacobi Quarti, Iacobi Quinti et Mariae regum Scotorum*, vol. 2, pp. 137–44; *Letters of James V*, pp. 245, 370–1, 438–9 and 441–3; NRS, GD149/264, ff. 10v-11r, 94, 218–20, 331 and 409–10.

263 *Foedera, conventiones, litterae et cuiuscunque generis acta publica inter reges Angliae et alios*, vol. 12, pp. 793–800, vol. 13, pp. 631–2 and 670–2, vol. 14, pp. 86–7, 151–3, 529–37 and 786–92, and vol. 15, pp. 265–71, 513–16 and 593–7; *Corps universel diplomatique du droit des gens*, vol. 4(1), pp. 23–7, vol. 4(2), pp. 114–18 and 257–61, vol. 4(3), pp. 103–6, and vol. 5(1), pp. 29–31 and 65–7; *Letters of James V*, pp. 267–9.

1550 there was a clause providing for the suspension of all *literae represaliarum* previously issued on either side.[264] In the same year the recently returned queen of Scots received a request from her neighbour in England for assistance in responding favourably to complaints she had received about attacks on Spanish and Portuguese shipping 'by color of a letter marke'.[265] Information was supplied about the possible involvement of English sailors in seizures made by Scottish captains, and Mary declared that on reaching Scotland she had at once forbidden her subjects 'to pas to the seyis under pretence of letters of marque'.[266] Those claiming to hold the letters originally granted to the Bartons were indeed ordered to produce their copies before the privy council, together with an inventory of all the goods seized under them.[267] When they were unable to prove that their losses remained unredressed, the letters were formally cancelled. No new letters of reprisal or marque appear to have been issued in Scotland during the next thirty years.[268] Moreover, while requests for justice to be done continued to be included in the letters exchanged between rulers during this period, no clear threat that reprisals might need to be authorised has been found.[269] The nearest a Scottish ruler came to making such a threat was when merchants whose goods had been taken by English pirates asked James VI in 1580 and 1585 to authorise them 'to seek their amends at the seas'.[270] Whether they hoped to receive letters of reprisal or marque is not entirely clear, and in any event James did not accede to their request, or even warn the English queen that he was giving it consideration. By the 1580s it

264 *Corps universel diplomatique du droit des gens*, vol. 4(3), p. 124.

265 *Calendar of State Papers Relating to Scotland*, vol. 1, pp. 546–7; *Calendar of State Papers, Foreign Series, of the Reign of Elizabeth*, vol. 3, p. 584, and vol. 4, pp. 20, 54, 78, 145, 251 and 276–7; *Select Pleas in the Court of Admiralty*, vol. 2, pp. 29–31; *Tudor Royal Proclamations*, vol. 2, pp. 171–2.

266 *Lettres, instructions et mémoires de Marie Stuart*, vol. 1, pp. 105–8; *Calendar of State Papers Relating to Scotland*, vol. 1, pp. 521, 526–7, 534–6, 543 and 550.

267 *Register of the Privy Council of Scotland*, vol. 1, pp. 161–2; *Calendar of State Papers Relating to Scotland*, vol. 1, p. 553. *Cf. Extracts from the Records of the Burgh of Edinburgh*, vol. 3, pp. 111–12.

268 None has been found in the later volumes of *Registrum secreti sigilli regum Scotorum* or NRS, PS1/52–60, nor have references to letters been found in other sources.

269 *Lettres, instructions et mémoires de Marie Stuart*, vol. 1, pp. 216–18 and 253–5; *Calendar of State Papers Relating to Scotland*, vol. 2, pp. 64, 88–9, 124, 276–7 and 652, vol. 3, p. 575, vol. 5, pp. 228–9, 311, 327 and 342, vol. 6, pp. 356 and 440, vol. 7, p. 339, vol. 8, pp. 62–3, and vol. 10, pp. 70, 318, 392–3, 563 and 605–6; *Forty-Seventh Annual Report of the Deputy Keeper*, pp. 12, 24 and 26–7; NRS, GD149/265, pt 1, ff. 7v-8v, GD149/266, ff. 85 and 159v-61r, and RH9/6/4.

270 *Calendar of State Papers Relating to Scotland*, vol. 5, p. 462. This will be returned to below.

might well have been concluded by anyone investigating Scottish practice that reprisals were a thing of the past.

This may indeed have been the conclusion drawn by Sir James Balfour when he wrote the treatise on maritime law attached to his practicks. A section of the treatise headed 'Anent Lettre of Mark' consists of just two paragraphs.[271] In the first Balfour reported a case in which the lords of session found that if loss was suffered by a Scot overseas, he ought first to seek redress there, after which, if 'justice was denyit to him', he might request a 'lettre of mark' from the king, licensing him to take 'gudis and geir' from countrymen of the person who had inflicted the loss, 'ay and quhill' it was recovered. No date is provided, but the case seems to have been decided in the first half of the sixteenth century, and as reported the decision encapsulates neatly the legal theory then being put into practice in Scotland.[272] Balfour's other paragraph simply stated: 'Lettre of marque aganis the *Portugallis* dischargit. *Mar. R. fol.* 179. *act.* 23. 4 *Junii*, 1563'. The reference was to an act of parliament confirming the recalling of the Bartons' letters, but it appears to have been taken to have wider implications.[273] In 1570 a convention of the royal burghs of Scotland, on hearing that there were (as their clerk expressed it) 'certane piratt schippis in redynes in the havin of Leyth, and utheris partis of this realme, to pass furth in piracie', directed the representatives from Edinburgh to ensure that an immediate stop was put to these 'wickitt interprises', by raising a summons under the 1563 act and causing it to 'be execute upoun all schippis within the boundis of thair jurisdictionis, and speciall upoun sic as ar to pas upoun the Portingals, quhilkis ar dischargitt be the said act'.[274] Presumably the mariners in Leith meant to rely on some old letters of reprisal or marque. Alarmed by the disruption this might cause to their trade, the representatives of the burghs condemned their proposed activities as piracy, believing not only that the letters issued to the Bartons against the Portuguese had been cancelled, but also that no letters could give the mariners licence to attack foreign shipping. Balfour may have

271 *Practicks of Sir James Balfour*, vol. 2, p. 626.

272 In the printed edition the report ends: '3 *August*, – George Wallace *contra* Portugallis, 1 *t. c.* 644'. The date is also left blank in sixteenth century manuscripts of the practicks (NLS, Adv. MS 24.2.4, f. 213v, and Adv. MS 24.2.4b, f. 263r, and EUL, La. III 408, f. 104v). A George Wallace was involved in litigation overseas in 1518 and 1533, and at the latter stage in relation to *represaliarum ius* (*Epistolae Iacobi Quarti, Iacobi Quinti et Mariae regum Scotorum*, vol. 1, pp. 309–11; NRS, GD149/264, f. 11; *Letters of James V*, pp. 67 and 245), but no trace of the case was found in NRS, CS6/3. *Cf.* Gordon 2007, pp. 283–96.

273 *Acts of the Parliaments of Scotland*, vol. 2, p. 544; Records of the Parliaments of Scotland, A1563/6/25.

274 *Records of the Convention of the Royal Burghs of Scotland*, vol. 1, p. 21.

shared the view that the 1563 act had implications extending beyond the special case of the Portuguese, and may for that reason have been disinclined to devote any more space to discussion of reprisals than he did in his treatise.

A different line was taken in the treatise on maritime law written around the close of the 1580s by Alexander King.[275] After dealing with the capture of ships, goods and prisoners in wartime, King devoted a chapter of almost equal length to *pigneratio seu represalia et marqua*.[276] As his use of the word *pigneratio* signalled, he was eager to remind his readers of the learned justification of reprisals, which he rehearsed in some detail, making specific reference to Bartolus' treatise and adhering to his opinions in particular.[277] Specific reference was also made to contemporary practice in France, and to an act passed by a Scottish parliament in 1581, permitting action to be taken against any member of a 'clanne' for losses inflicted by another member, from which King felt able to conclude that the reasoning behind the legitimising of reprisals *iure gentium* was accepted in Scotland.[278] His motivation for writing as if reprisals were in active use in Scotland was hinted at when he commented in passing that it was against English mariners that they were usually required, 'for it is the English who most often indulge in piratical wickedness today'.[279] There is no doubt that English piracy posed a grave problem when King was writing, but he may also have had an ulterior motive for writing in the way that he did.[280] The excuse repeatedly offered by the English queen for the depredations of her subjects was the disorder caused by 'the civil wars in the dominions of her neighbours', which were believed to have drawn many Englishmen into the service of foreign princes, under whose authority they 'committed great spoils without difference or respect of any nation'.[281] That Elizabeth was actually content for her sailors to serve the Protestant princes of Condé and Navarre in France and Orange in the Netherlands is well known, and she was

---

275 William Welwod did not so much as mention reprisals in the earlier versions of his treatise.

276 *King's Treatise on Maritime Law*, pp. 96–109.

277 Another – though subordinate – reason for the brevity of Balfour's account may have been his usual inclination to focus on local sources to the neglect of the learned laws.

278 *King's Treatise on Maritime Law*, pp. 100–1; *Acts of the Parliaments of Scotland*, vol. 3, pp. 218–19; Records of the Parliaments of Scotland, 1581/10/35.

279 *King's Treatise on Maritime Law*, pp. 102–3.

280 The records are full of complaints, but see especially *Calendar of State Papers Relating to Scotland*, vol. 9, pp. 507, 509–15 and 546–7, and also the very helpful table of 'English Piratical Attacks upon the Scots, 1561–1603', in Murdoch 2010, pp. 363–70. Some of these records will be returned to in the final section of this chapter.

281 *Calendar of State Papers Relating to Scotland*, vol. 5, pp. 344–5, 476–7 and 510–11, and vol. 6, pp. 253 and 455; *Original Letters of Mr John Colville*, p. 21; NRS, SP13/113.

far from neutral in her attitude towards piracy.[282] Her ministers informed her that complaints about English piracy were being stirred up in Scotland by 'papists or peace-breakers', as well as 'others inclining to the French', and added that English shipping was itself at risk from 'Scottish and Dunkirk pirates'.[283] If the insinuation was that Scottish sailors were conspiring with the forces of the Catholic League, then raiding Protestant shipping from Dunkirk, it was also warned more openly that an agent of the Catholic League was recruiting pilots in Scotland to assist a new Spanish armada.[284] Since it was reported that the 'papist' Alexander King was one of those sympathetic to the Catholic League and Spain, it would appear that King's motivation for encouraging a revival of the practice of reprisals, with English shipping as its specific target, was more political than he was ready to admit.[285] If so, however, he was soon to be disappointed.

As King was probably aware, in 1589 another convention of the royal burghs, after passing an act 'thatt na maner of pirattis be ressett or interteneitt att ony frie sea poirtt within this realme', had drawn James VI's attention to serious losses suffered by many burgesses through 'the pilleage of their gudes and misusing of thair personis be certan piratt Dunkirkeris'.[286] The king had been asked to require the prince of Parma to have justice done. No relevant letters have been identified, but presumably James did write to Parma and failed to elicit a satisfactory response, for towards the end of 1590, for the first time in over thirty years, letters of reprisal or marque were issued, authorising seizures from anyone associated with the Catholic League.[287] Whether this was the response the burghs had desired, less than twenty years after they asserted that reprisals were no longer legitimate, is to say the least uncertain, but funds were raised to have vessels equipped in Scotland, and arrangements were made by the English ambassador to have ordnance supplied from south

282 This topic will be returned to in the next chapter.

283 *Calendar of State Papers Relating to Scotland*, vol. 5, p. 486, vol. 6, pp. 375–6 and 595, and vol. 10, pp. 35–6 and 216.

284 *Calendar of State Papers Relating to Scotland*, vol. 10, p. 212.

285 *Calendar of State Papers Relating to Scotland*, vol. 10, pp. 124, 138, 147 and 257. It is evident from BL, Lansdowne MS 57, f. 62, that the leaders of the Catholic League were actively considering ways of improving their effectiveness at sea in the late 1580s, when King paid a visit to Paris.

286 *Records of the Convention of the Royal Burghs*, vol. 1, pp. 305–7. On King's probable awareness of the 1589 act see Ford 2018b, p. lxiii (and the link there).

287 *Calendar of State Papers Relating to Scotland*, vol. 10, pp. 407 and 478. As the letters have not been found in the register of the privy seal, or anywhere else, their precise terms remain uncertain.

of the border.[288] The burghs soon regretted the initiative they had taken. In 1591 the privy council received a complaint from the 'haill burrowis of this realme' about the seizure from a Danzig vessel of goods belonging to the duke of Tuscany, an adherent of the Catholic League, by a merchant from Dundee called Thomas Ogilvy.[289] Their complaint was that the 'commissioun and letter of marque' on which Ogilvy had relied was 'verie generallie grantit and evill extendit', for there were 'divers princeis and potentatis undir that league standing in freindship and confederacie with his hienes, within quhais boundis and dominionis almaist the haill trafficquaris of this realme hes ane commoun and frequent trade'. Ogilvy was required by the privy council to provide security that anyone whose rights he had infringed would receive compensation, and he was instructed to execute reprisals in future only against the inhabitants of towns specifically named in the letters. Two weeks later the burghs sought further assurance that ships from places like Danzig would not be taken, 'seing thairby not onlie sall thair tred in thai pairtis be cutt of, bot a cruell wear salbe denunceit aganis his majestie'.[290] The burghs further objected that restricting the scope of the letters to the 'inhabitantis of certane townis particularlie nominat thairin, within the realme of France', would prove inadequate given that some of these towns 'of lait hes randerit thair obedience to the present king of France'. After Ogilvy had failed to appear in response to a summons, the council declared his 'letter of marque to be null hereafter', though this did not end the affair.

After another two months the owners of the ship in which the goods taken from the Danzig vessel had been carried back to Dundee complained that their ship was being held there with the goods it contained, some of which were perishable.[291] An order was issued for the release of the ship after the goods were unloaded, inventoried and, if perishable, sold.[292] At the end of the year Ogilvy himself complained that he had been 'put to the horn' for 'allegeit dissobedience', despite providing security as required and refraining from further

288 *Records of the Convention of the Royal Burghs*, vol. 1, pp. 317–18; *Calendar of State Papers Relating to Scotland*, vol. 10, pp. 407 and 433.

289 *Register of the Privy Council of Scotland*, vol. 4, pp. 615–16. See too Maxwell 1884, pp. 202–5.

290 *Register of the Privy Council of Scotland*, vol. 4, pp. 627–8. *Cf.* Ogilvie 2011, pp. 276–81.

291 *Register of the Privy Council of Scotland*, vol. 4, pp. 665–6. The authorities in Dundee had failed in a bid to gain support from neighbouring burghs (*Records of the Convention of the Royal Burghs*, vol. 1, pp. 360–1).

292 DCA, MBBC, vol. 2, pp. 60 and 62–3. Some wheat and flax had already been spoiled, but there were other items as well, including copper plate, armaments and 'certane buikes, all of ane historie anent the descriptioun of the countreis of Polonia, Muscovia, Prussia and utheris thairto adjacent'.

reprisals after the letters were revoked.[293] The horning was lifted and Ogilvie appeared in person before the council, maintaining that since he had seized the goods held in Dundee 'lauchfullie, be vertew of the said letter of marque', and had given security that anyone with an interest would receive his due, the goods ought now to be delivered to him.[294] He did not receive the goods, however. Competing claims to some of the property taken had by then been received both from the duke of Tuscany, with support from the king of Poland and Sweden, and from the owners of the Danzig vessel, with support from the city magistrates there, and the whole matter had been referred for decision to the lords of session.[295] It is disappointing for present purposes that the legal issues do not seem to have been discussed in that court before the case was urgently recalled to the privy council.[296] While the legitimacy of Ogilvy's seizure might have been hard to dispute, the fear was growing that a limited war unleashed by the granting of the letters of reprisal was about to escalate into a wider conflict, and it was decided by the council that the claims of the duke of Tuscany and the owners of the Danzig vessel should be satisfied.[297] No further letters of reprisal or marque are known to have been granted before the next century.

It may seem strange to readers familiar with the literature on the decline of feuding and the rise of the modern state in Scotland that the rulers of the country – monarchs as well as regents – became reluctant to grant letters of reprisal or marque in the later sixteenth century.[298] After all, it is at about the same time that royal authority is supposed at last to have displaced the power of regional magnates, and assuming control over the practice of reprisals is supposed to have been one way in which sovereign rulers asserted their authority. By insisting that reprisals could only be taken with their express authorisation, sovereign rulers moved towards the monopolisation of violence that is regarded as a characteristic feature of the modern state. Around the close of the sixteenth century in Scotland, after a period in which government

293 *Register of the Privy Council of Scotland*, vol. 4, pp. 707–8. To be put to the horn was to be formally denounced as a rebel.

294 *Register of the Privy Council of Scotland*, vol. 5, pp. 1 and 9–10.

295 *Register of the Privy Council of Scotland*, vol. 5, pp. 214–15.

296 *Register of the Privy Council of Scotland*, vol. 5, pp. 251–3. No trace of the case was found when the relevant volumes of the register of acts and decreets of the session were searched through, although this does not necessarily mean that the case was never heard there.

297 On this final phase see too MacLeod 1918. It is possible that the duke of Tuscany's involvement in this case established the contacts on which the negotiations covered in Mackie 1927 were based.

298 Wormald 1985; Brown 1986; Goodare 1999 and 2004; Armstrong 2010; Groundwater 2014.

agencies had cooperated with regional magnates in upholding the settlement of disputes through a regulated process of reprisal and retaliation, it became more normal for disputes to be submitted for determination to royal courts, at least in some areas of the country.[299] It was because there were other areas in which 'clannis' were not effectively 'subjectit to the ordiner cours of justice', but instead responded to actions taken against any of their members by indulging in 'deidlie feidis', that the act of parliament passed in 1581 affirmed the legitimacy of seeking redress from one member of a clan for a wrong committed by another.[300] In citing this act in his treatise King was pointing out that reprisals were an inevitable occurrence wherever parties to disputes did not live in subjection to the authority of the same sovereign ruler, as was typically the case when ships and goods were seized at sea by pirates.[301] While there was some hope of rendering the authority of the crown effective within Scotland, with seizures at sea the problem was bound to remain that there was not normally a shared superior to whom parties could submit their disputes. Either redress would have to be sought through diplomacy, backed up with the threat of authorised reprisals, or mariners and merchants would be left with little option but to settle their differences by their own means. However serious the risk of reprisals escalating from limited into public wars might have been, the alternative was a return to the private wars that were reckoned to be inconsistent with the sovereign authority of princes. This was the ostensible message delivered in King's treatise, whatever his underlying motive may have been.

The message will ring true for historians who believe that violence at sea was endemic until rulers took responsibility for the authorisation of reprisals.[302] If historians do not simply believe that the seas were an area of unregulated activity, they often talk as if the only regulation took the form of vague norms distinguishing acceptable acts of reprisal, revenge or retaliation, on the one hand, from the kinds of aggression that might foment further feuding, on the other. They recognise that parties disputed the legitimacy of particular seizures of ships and goods with each other, but insist that the violent seizure

299 Wormald 1980, though see too Godfrey 2014.

300 *Acts of the Parliaments of Scotland*, vol. 3, pp. 218–19; Records of the Parliaments of Scotland, 1581/10/35.

301 *King's Treatise on Maritime Law*, pp. 100–1, where reprisals at sea are explicitly connected with the relative lawlessness of border regions. Although the 1581 act was not specific in its terms, King took it to refer to kindreds on the borders and in the highlands and islands, where royal power was weaker. On the borders see Armstrong 2020, pp. 119–64.

302 As will be explained at the beginning of the next chapter, studies like Prétou 2016 and 2021 develop a thesis first advanced in Mollat 1976.

of ships and goods was regarded as an ordinary aspect of maritime trade.[303] Some go so far as to deny that piracy was treated as a crime, or developed as a legal category, before the sixteenth century.[304] It is certainly true that the words 'piracy' and 'pirates' were sometimes used positively or neutrally, as well as negatively, as were words like 'plunder' and 'pillage'.[305] It may have been noticed that when the burgh authorities complained in 1589 about 'piratt Dunkirkeris', they referred more specifically to the 'pilleage' of goods from ships, although it has been seen that the word 'pillage' was used more positively in relation to wartime seizures.[306] But does it follow from this ambiguous use of language that piracy only came to be categorised and condemned as a criminal activity after states started to distinguish between authorised reprisals and unauthorised plunder and pillage? The burgh authorities appear to have assumed in 1570 that unless the mariners fitting out vessels in Leith had been granted letters of reprisal or marque, any seizures they made would have amounted to acts of 'piracie'.[307] Were they able to talk about 'piracy' as an unlawful species of seizure only because they knew that 'reprisal' was considered lawful when properly authorised? It needs to be considered next whether 'piracy' was a term with precise legal significance before the sixteenth century. The investigation will begin again with the position in ancient Rome.

5 Seizures of Ships and Goods at Sea as Piracy

In both Greek and Latin the word pirate (πειρατα or *pirata*) appears to have been a relatively late addition to the vocabulary available to describe maritime activity.[308] A possible explanation is the difficulty there may have been in distinguishing between bandits or brigands on land, who sometimes took to

303 For a recent example see Höhn 2019.

304 Sayers 2002, p. 151; Pitcaithly 2012, p. 125; Haywood and Spivak 2012, pp. 7–9; Heebøll-Holm 2013, p. 13, Prétou 2014, pp. 44 and 46; Vognsen 2019, pp. 161–2. Friedland 2000, pp. 32–3, traces the development back into the fifteenth century, but sees it as a novelty then. Many historians seem to have been influenced by Rubin 1998, which is not actually reliable, as will become apparent in what follows.

305 Cheyette 1970, p. 47; Fuchs 2000, pp. 45–52; Heers 2001, p. 39; Tai 2003, p. 260–1; Kontorovich 2004, pp. 210–33; Harding 2007, pp. 20–4 and 31–3; Eddison 2013, p. 78.

306 *Records of the Convention of the Royal Burghs*, vol. 1, pp. 305–7. See too *Asloan Manuscript*, vol. 1, p. 177; Barnaby Rich, *Allarme to England*, sig. C3v; [Geoffrey Gates], *Defence of Militarie Profession*, sig. F2r. On the development of the pejorative usage see Wright 1983.

307 *Records of the Convention of the Royal Burghs of Scotland*, vol. 1, p. 21.

308 Garlan 1978, p. 2; Clavel-Lévêque 1978, p. 22; De Souza 1999, pp. 3–9 and 12–13.

the sea, and pirates at sea, who sometimes carried out raids on land. Another view, now widely held, is that there was at first a reluctance to condemn maritime raiding, which was regarded as one mode of life among others until the Romans took control of the seas around the beginning of the current era.[309] A third view, however, is that the language of piracy was invariably used in a negative way, and that piracy was invariably condemned.[310] The argument gains strength if a clear separation is maintained, as it probably ought to be, between technical and figurative uses of the vocabulary.[311] As far as the texts preserved in the *Corpus iuris civilis* are concerned, pirates were always envisaged as violent raiders who disrupted ordinary life, though raiders of this type were not invariably called 'pirates'.[312] While the words bandit (*latro*) and brigand (*praedo*) are more frequently found in the texts than pirate (*pirata*), they were not always used – as has been claimed – to the exclusion of maritime raiders, for sometimes the raiders identified as bandits or brigands can only have been operating at sea.[313] These words were sometimes used interchangeably, and bandits, brigands and pirates appear to have formed a single category in the minds of Roman lawyers.[314] If this indicates that the Romans did not have a clear conception of piracy as a separate category, it may be added that they do not seem to have regarded piracy as a distinct crime either. In a few texts there are references to *piratica* (used substantively) and to *latrocinium* as unlawful activities.[315] Generally, however, those who engaged in these

---

309 Ormerod 1924, p. 67; Jackson 1973, p. 241; Casson 1991, p. 117; De Souza 1999, pp. 19–21; McKechnie 1989, pp. 104–6. Sestier 1880, pp. 249–63 and 276–7, appears to have been influential here.

310 Avidov 1997; and see too Braund 1993.

311 Van Hooff 1998, pp. 112–14; Garraffoni 2004, pp. 370–1; Grünewald 2004, pp. 14 and 17. Even legal usage could at times be quite figurative, as in *Digest*, 4.4.3.6, 5.3.11.1–13.pr., 5.3.25, 5.3.36.3, 5.3.46, 10.3.7.4 and 41.2.5.

312 In addition to the sources cited below see *Digest*, 4.6.9, 4.9.3.1, 13.6.5.4, 16.3.31.1, 17.2.52.3–4, 19.2.9.4, 24.3.21, 27.1.13.7, 49.16.14.pr. and 50.17.23; *Code*, 4.24.6, 4.34.1, 4.65.1, 4.65.12, 5.31.8 and 6.38.1.pr.

313 *Digest*, 14.2.2.3 and 47.9.3.2.

314 Compare *Digest*, 4.3.1 with 35.2.30.pr., 4.9.3.1 with 50.17.23, and 49.15.24 with 49.15.19.2, and consider too 13.6.18.pr. and 14.2.2.3. Rubin 1998, wrongly believing there 'to be only one passage in the *Digest* in which the word *pirata* or its derivatives appears' (p. 16), goes on to draw the manifestly false conclusions that the Romans distinguished between bandits or brigands on land and pirates at sea, and that they never regarded pirates as criminals but always as lawful enemies.

315 *Digest*, 5.1.61.1, 44.7.20 and 48.19.27.2; *Code*, 4.34.1.

activities were reckoned to have committed other crimes, such as robbery, assault and murder.[316]

Nevertheless, it did make a difference in Roman law when offenders fell into the broader category of bandits, brigands and pirates.[317] Several legal texts make it clear that the apprehension of these offenders was regarded as an important responsibility of local authorities.[318] Provincial governors were authorised and encouraged to adopt dubious measures in their pursuit, such as making deals with informants or resorting to devious tricks and stratagems.[319] Once tracked down, bandits, brigands and pirates were to be subjected to torture by officials, who were assured that since harsh methods were being used to secure the just end of public safety, they would receive divine forgiveness.[320] After offenders had been interrogated, they were to face summary justice, without the usual procedural protections.[321] No appeal could be made to the emperor, nor was any other attempt to postpone punishment by having a case raised for review to be permitted.[322] Instead, severe punishments were to be imposed immediately, at least in the case of notorious offenders, the normal practice being to have them hanged where they were apprehended as an example to others.[323] In the belief that bandits, brigands and pirates would be unable to survive unless other people were prepared to trade with them, instruction was given for the receivers (*receptores*) of goods seized by these offenders to face the same strictures and penalties as they themselves faced.[324] Furthermore, quite apart from public officials being authorised to take recourse to exceptional methods in the pursuit of bandits, brigands and pirates, private citizens were authorised to attack them with impunity.[325] While to some extent a particular application of the broader approval of self-defence, the texts specifically allowed vengeance

316 *Digest*, 16.3.31.1 and 17.2.52.4 (*edict de VI bonorum raptorum*); *Digest*, 47.9.3.1 and 3 (edict *de incendio ruina naufragio rate nave expugnata*); *Digest*, 48.6.3.6 (*lex Iulia de VI publica*); *Digest*, 48.7.1 (rescript of Pius *nullam vim nautis fieri debere*); *Digest*, 48.8.1.pr. (*lex Cornelia de sicariis et veneficiis*). Robinson 1995, pp. 29–30 and 41, observes that much of the law introduced in the late republic to criminalise acts of violence was originally designed to confront the problem of armed bands; see too Riggsby 1999, p. 51.

317 Shaw 1984; Van Hooff 1998; Hopwood 1989; Grünewald 2004; Tarwacka 2009.

318 *Digest*, 1.18.6.8, 1.18.13.pr., 48.13.4.2, 48.19.27.2 and 49.1.16; *Code*, 9.39.2.3. See too Bauman 1996, p. 111, and MacMullen 1967, pp. 255–7.

319 *Digest*, 4.3.1.3 and 49.16.5.8.

320 *Code*, 3.12.8(9).

321 *Digest*, 48.3.6.

322 *Digest*, 48.19.6.pr. and 49.1.16.

323 *Digest*, 48.19.28.15, and also 47.9.7 and 48.19.27.2.

324 *Digest*, 47.9.3.3, 47.16.1–2, and 48.19.6.pr; *Code*, 9.39.1–2.

325 *Code*, 9.16.2–3.

(*ultio*) to be exacted.[326] Bandits, brigands and pirates effectively fell into the class of persons who would come to be known as outlaws.[327]

Despite pirates being treated as akin to bandits and brigands, and the aversion of the Roman jurists to defining the terms they used, the elements of a definition of the term 'piracy' could have been drawn out of the texts assembled in the *Corpus iuris*.[328] It scarcely required stating that bandits, brigands and pirates were prone to dishonesty, and that they were inclined to make use of weapons.[329] More particularly, they were described as people who banded together with a view to inflicting violence, with their forming of bands itself regarded as evidence of their intent.[330] As self-defence was permissible, carrying weapons could not on its own have served as evidence of a design to inflict violence on others, and as banding together could also have served the purpose of self-defence, it cannot always have been easy to distinguish between those intent on using violence and those prepared to use violence if they came under attack.[331] In principle, however, bandits, brigands and pirates were people who formed armed bands with the intention of taking by force things to which they knew they had no right. Bandits (*latrones*) were sometimes described more specifically as raiders who lurked around highways, and pirates (*piratae*) were always associated with raiding at sea, while brigands (*praedones*) were not specifically connected with the disruption of transport. If bandits and brigands sometimes operated at sea, when they might instead have been called pirates, those called pirates in the texts invariably operated at sea. Pirates were thus members of armed bands formed for the purpose of effecting violent seizures of ships and goods at sea, and in the legal sources they were certainly understood to engage in criminal activities, even though piracy itself was not a nominate crime.

The Roman jurists recognised that banditry, brigandage and piracy were similar in their effects, from the perspective of their victims, to plunder by enemies, since these were all overwhelming events that no one could have been expected to prevent.[332] A further similarity between pirates and enemies was reflected in a constitution enacted in the thirteenth century by the emperor

326 *Digest*, 1.1.3 and 9.2.4.pr; *Institutes*, 4.3.2; *Code*, 3.27.1–2.

327 Jaeger 1987, p. 33; Rauh 2003, p. 187; see too *Digest*, 5.1.61.

328 *Digest*, 50.17.202.

329 *Digest*, 48.6.3.6 and 50.17.126.pr. (this latter text perhaps provides another example of a more figurative use of the term *praedo*).

330 *Digest*, 48.19.11.2 and 48.19.28.10.

331 *Digest*, 48.6.11.

332 *Digest*, 3.1.1.6, 4.3.1.3, 13.6.18.pr., 23.3.5.4, 32.2.30.pr., 35.2.30.pr., 39.5.34.1, 39.6.3 and 44.7.1.4; *Code*, 6.46.6.pr.

Frederick II, which was inserted at his behest into Justinian's *Code*.[333] The emperor threatened those who plundered wrecked ships with the forfeiture of all their property, but added that the penalty would not be imposed if the ships belonged to people who engaged in piracy or were hostile to his authority or to the church (*piraticam exerceant pravitatem, aut sint nobis sive Christiano nomini inimica*).[334] Some commentators took care to distinguish the pirate ships referred to from the ships of infidels, pointing out that the latter would only be covered by the exception when there was a state of war between their country and either the empire or another Christian realm.[335] Others noted that in the emperor's ruling pirates were equated with (*aequiparantur*) or regarded as (*reputantur*) enemies of the faith.[336] The inference drawn by all the civilian doctors was that pirate vessels could be 'despoiled by everyone with impunity', or 'taken and spoiled *autoritate propria*', the reason being that every pirate was '*ipso iure* in a state of defiance'. Having renounced allegiance to their rulers, pirates had put themselves beyond the protection of the law and thus resembled enemies in being open to attack by anyone.

A connection between pirates and enemies of the faith had already been made in a decree issued by the Third Lateran Council, which was incorporated in two parts into the *Liber extra*.[337] The first part of the decree condemned those who supplied enemies of the faith with arms, then continued: 'There are even some who through greed serve as masters or pilots on the galleys or

333 *Codex Iustiniani*, col. 1192, Authentica Navigia; Monumenta Germaniae historica, *Constitutiones et acta publica imperatorum et regum*, vol. 2, p. 109.

334 As the texts cited at n. 312 above show, the Roman jurists had reckoned that offenders involved in plundering wrecks might themselves be *praedones* (*Digest*, 47.9.3.1 and 3). What seems to have been envisaged is that ships might be wrecked and then plundered in the course of an assault by pirates.

335 Odofredus de Denariis, *Lectura super Codice*, vol. 2(1), f. 11r (ad C.6.2, Authentica Navigia); *Codex Iustiniani*, col. 1192 (gl. 'Navigia' ad C.6.2, Authentica Navigia); Iacobus de Ravanis, *Lectura super Codice*, f. 251r (ad C.6.2, Authentica Navigia); Angelus de Ubaldis, *Consilia seu responsa*, f. 123v (n. 290, inc. 'Thema est tale: inter cetera capitula pacis inite').

336 Baldus de Ubaldis, *Commentaria super Codicem*, vol. 3, f. 12r (ad C.6.2, Authentica Navigia); Paulus de Castro, *Opera omnia*, vol. 3(2), f. 12v (ad C.6.2, Authentica Navigia); Bartolomeus de Saliceto, *Lectura super Codice*, vol. 2(1), f. 62r (ad C.6.2, Authentica Navigia); Iason de Maino, *Consilia sive responsa*, vol. 2, f. 65v (n. 170, inc. 'Quod praedicti Paulus et Carolus Ianuenses absolvi debeant').

337 *Sacrorum conciliorum nova et amplissimo collectio*, vol. 22, cols 230–1; *Disciplinary Decrees of the General Councils*, pp. 232–3 and 557–8, and *Decrees of the Ecumenical Councils*, vol. 1, p. 223. See too the decree issued by the Second Council of Lyons in *Decrees of the Ecumenical Councils*, vol. 1, pp. 311–12, and *Disciplinary Decrees of the General Councils*, pp. 362–3, which was not incorporated into the *Corpus iuris canonici*.

pirate ships of the Saracens'.[338] All these people were to face what the commentators envisaged as a triple penalty of excommunication by ecclesiastical authorities, confiscation of their property by secular authorities, and enslavement of their persons by anyone who managed to capture them.[339] In this first part of the decree, the word *piratica* was used quite neutrally to describe the ships used by the enemies of the church for maritime raiding, but the second part proceeded to threaten with excommunication anyone who presumed 'to capture Romans or other Christians transported on a voyage for business or other honest purposes, or to despoil them of their belongings'.[340] Although the word *piratica* did not appear in this part of the decree, no reference was made to enemies either, from which the canonist doctors concluded that the decree was also concerned with the seizure of ships and goods by pirates in peacetime.[341] What troubled the canonist doctors more was the mention of confiscation by secular authorities in an ecclesiastical decree. Comparison was made with a Roman law text threatening people who sold arms to foreigners with forfeiture of their property, which suggested that the ecclesiastical decree was merely reiterating the existing law.[342] It was also pointed out that as *miserabiles personae* the victims of piracy came under the protection of the church, and that the involvement of infidels in piracy gave the church a further interest in the matter.[343] Like the civilian commentators on Frederick II's constitution, the canonist commentators on the Third Lateran Council's decree recognised a similarity between enemies and pirates without simply collapsing the two categories into one. The crucial point for them was also that pirates, as well as

338 *Liber extra*, 5.6.6.

339 *Decretales Gregorii papae ix*, col. 1657 (ad X 5.6.6); Bernardus de Montemirato, alias Abbas antiquus, *Lectura aurea super quinque libris Decretalium*, f. 204r (ad X 5.6.6); Hostiensis, *Summa aurea*, col. 1523 (ad X 5.6); Ioannes Andreae, *In libros quintos Decretalium novella commentaria*, vol. 4, f. 41r (ad X 5.6.6); Antonius de Butrio, *In libros quintos Decretalium commentaria*, vol. 4, f. 38r (ad X 5.6.6); Franciscus Zabarella, *Super IV et V Decretalium subtilissima commentaria*, f. 59 (ad X 5.6.6).

340 *Liber extra*, 5.17.3. This part of the decree proceeded immediately to threaten those who plundered wrecks with excommunication as well.

341 *Decretales Gregorii papae ix*, col. 1727 (ad X 5.17.3); Abbas antiquus, *Lectura aurea super quinque libris Decretalium*, f. 207v (ad X 5.17.3); Andreae, *In libros quintos Decretalium novella commentaria*, vol. 4, f. 75v (ad X 5.17.3); De Butrio, *In libros quintos Decretalium commentaria*, vol. 4, f. 59r (ad X 5.17.3); Zabarella, *Super IV et V Decretalium subtilissima commentaria*, f. 83 (ad X 5.17.3).

342 *Code*, 4.41.2, cited in Hostiensis, *Summa aurea*, col. 1523. See too *Digest*, 39.4.11, and *Code*, 4.63.2 and 9.47.25, the last of which was cited in Zabarella's *Commentaria*, f. 59.

343 *Decretales Gregorii noni*, p. 974 (gl. 'Privatione' ad X 5.6.6); De Butrio, *In libros quintos Decretalium commentaria*, vol. 4, ff. 38v and 59r.

enemies, could be attacked with impunity, for the sake of *mutuo compensatio* or *compensatio doli cum dolo*.[344]

This point was not without difficulty. For one thing, there were texts in the *Digest, Code* and *Liber extra* that threatened people with the loss of title to their property if they took matters into their own hands and tried to recover things taken from them by their own efforts, on the basis that everyone should be protected against forceful dispossession.[345] From these texts the principle was extracted that *etiam praedo non sit spoliandus, immo et in sua possessione tuendus*, which was in keeping with a general tendency towards insisting on the use of judicial procedures rather than self-help.[346] Nevertheless, since Frederick II's constitution and the Third Lateran Council's decree appeared to be consistent with the *Code* text permitting vengeance to be taken against brigands, the conclusion was reached that attacking bandits, brigands and pirates was an activity covered by an exception to the normal rule.[347] It did not necessarily follow, however, that the victims of piracy would be able to recoup all the losses they had suffered if they pursued and attacked the pirates. Another difficulty with the interpretation of Frederick II's constitution and the Third Lateran Council's decree was the indication in the latter that the property of pirates would be forfeited to the civil authorities, for this meant that the pirates would lack the means to satisfy any demand made of them by their victims, who would only receive compensation if the civil authorities chose to help them.[348] Moreover, while the pirates might also have possessed goods they had seized from other victims, this was where a distinction drawn in several texts

344 Andreae, *In libros quintos Decretalium novella commentaria*, vol. 4, f. 75v; De Butrio, *In libros quintos Decretalium commentaria*, vol. 4, f. 59r; Zabarella, *Super IV et V Decretalium subtilissima commentaria*, f. 83r.

345 *Digest*, 43.16.1.31; *Code*, 8.4.7; *Liber extra*, 2.13.5. The word *praedo* had perhaps been used here in a figurative sense, but if so this usage was not differentiated from the more technical meaning.

346 De Maino, *Consilia sive responsa*, vol. 2, f. 66r; Benedictus Capra, *Consilia sive responsa*, ff. 44v (n. 32, inc. 'Casus est talis: quidam Cieschus decessit condito testamento') and 70 (n. 63, inc. 'Magister Ioannes de Caniculo deposuit apud Magistrum Iacobum'); Ioannes de Nevizanis, *Consilia sive responsa*, pp. 678–9 (n. 81, inc. 'Deum invocent adiutorem, qui eis sapientiam donavit: ideo cum Barb.'); Franciscus Bursatus, *Consilia sive responsa*, vol. 2, p. 61 (n. 8, inc. 'In causa illustriae dominae Constantiae Stranghae'); Augustinus Beroius, *Consilia sive responsa*, vol. 3, p. 225 (n. 63, inc. 'Viso toto processu causae una cum attestionibus testium').

347 *Decretales Gregorii nono*, p. 381 (gl. 'Praedo' ad X 2.13.5); Panormitanus, *Lectura super quinque libros Decretalium*, vol. 2(1), ff. 251–2 (ad X 2.13.5); Baldus, *Super Decretalibus*, f. 149 (ad X 2.13.5).

348 De Maino, *Consilia sive responsa*, vol. 2, f. 67r; Bartolomeus Socinus, *Responsa seu consilia*, vol. 1(2), ff. 119v-20r (n. 262, inc. 'In causa magnifici Petri de Medicis et sociorum').

between pirates and enemies became important.[349] Unlike enemies, pirates did not acquire title to any goods they seized, nor did any people they captured become their slaves.[350] Goods found on their ships had therefore to be restored to the original victims and could not be appropriated by later victims. The point of the comparison with enemies was simply that those who resorted to violence against pirates would not themselves be open to criminal prosecution, and would not jeopardise any rights they had in goods previously taken from them by the pirates.[351]

It may be concluded that while the medieval doctors did not develop an elaborate theory of piracy comparable to their theories of plunder and reprisal, they did develop a fairly precise understanding of piracy as a legal category and a criminal activity. They defined piracy as nautical robbery (*rapina nautica*) and pirates as maritime bandits and robbers (*latrones et derobatores maritimi*).[352] Bandits were viewed more broadly as people who lurked around public thoroughfares with a view to robbing and killing travellers.[353] They differed from thieves partly by using or threatening to use violence to achieve their gains, and partly by operating openly, not by stealth.[354] The notorious bandits or pirates who were subject to summary justice and execution by hanging wherever they were apprehended were those who made a habit of raiding people on roads or at sea (*in itineribus vel in mari*), and who had a reputation (*publica fama*) for

349 *Digest*, 28.1.13.pr., 49.15.24, 49.15.27, and 50.60.118. Contrary to the claim made in Rubin 1998, p. 16, these texts certainly did distinguish pirates (as well as bandits and brigands) from enemies.

350 *Infortiatum*, col. 368 (gl. 'Qui a latronibus' ad D.28.1.13); Bartolus, *Opera omnia*, vol. 2(2), f. 236 (ad D.49.15.24); Albericus de Rosate, *Opera omnia*, vol. 2(1), f. 97r (ad D.28.1.13).

351 Petrus de Ancharanus, *Consilia sive iuris responsa*, f. 146r (n. 277, inc. 'Ex praedicta facti narratione quis titulus criminis sive quod crimen oriatur'); Bartolomeus Caepolla, *Consilia criminalia*, f. 178v (n. 41, inc. 'Cum Petrus Malusatus olim sub pignoribus gravitate quasdam pecunias').

352 Odofredus, *Lectura super Digesto*, vol. 4, f. 115v (ad D.44.7.20); *Digestum novum*, col. 894 (gl. 'Piraticam' ad D.44.7.20); De Maino, *Consilia sive responsa*, vol. 2, f. 67r; Bartolomeus de Bosco, *Consilia*, p. 453 (n. 275, 'In pace inita inter serenissimum D. regem Aragonum'). Mere 'maritime theft' was not piracy, as Tai 2019 persists in suggesting.

353 Odofredus, *Lectura super Digesto*, vol. 1, f. 33r (ad D.1.18.13.pr.), and *Lectura super Codice*, vol. 2(1), f. 198r (ad C.9.16.3); Bartolus, *Opera omnia*, vol. 2(2), f. 206v (ad D.48.19.28.15); Beroius, *Consilia sive responsa*, vol. 3, p. 552 (n. 195, inc. 'Placet mihi conclusio, quod respectu pecuniae habitae').

354 Portius Azo, *Ad singulas leges xii librorum Codicis Iustinianei commentarius*, p. 695 (ad C.9.16.3); Albericus, *Opera omnia*, vol. 3(2), f. 204 (ad D.48.19.11.2 and 48.19.28.15); Raphael Fulgosius, *Consilia sive responsa*, ff. 212–13r (n. 157, inc. 'Supposito statuto, tenoris qui sequitur, potestate domino').

doing so.[355] Like enemies, they were open to attack by anyone, and their title to property found in their possession would not be respected. Unlike enemies, however, they would not have acquired title to anything they had despoiled, nor would anything they had lawfully obtained be open to acquisition by occupation.[356] Instead, their own property would have been forfeited to the civil authorites of the place in which they were apprehended.[357] Thus the seizure of ships and goods from pirates formed a third category of legitimate violence – after the plundering of enemies in wartime and the execution of reprisals in peacetime – while the seizure of ships and goods by pirates was itself regarded as a serious offence meriting a severe response. At least four types of seizure were therefore distinguished – licit plunder, licensed reprisal, lawful vengeance and criminal piracy – and to complicate matters further not every illegitimate seizure was taken to amount to piracy. Seizures might be made by people who had not armed themselves with a view to preying on shipping, and who could not therefore be described as pirates, yet who remained unable to justify their actions as licit plunder, licensed reprisal or lawful vengeance.

Ironically, the understanding of piracy first developed in the Italian law schools was particularly difficult to apply in the Mediterranean, where there was a perceived state of perpetual war. Conflict between Christian and Muslim nations was endemic, though peace was also believed to be possible.[358] There were periods of truce, and trade between Christians and Muslims was common, even at other times.[359] Indeed, there is evidence that Christian mariners sometimes served on Muslim ships, and vice versa, which helps to explain why the Third Lateran Council issued its decree.[360] But whereas elsewhere peace

355 Angelus *Conslia seu responsa*, f. 175v (n. 403, inc. 'Formata fuit inquisitio in hac forma'); Thomas Doctius, *Consilia vel responsa*, f. 205 (n. 192, inc. 'Pro parte dicti accusatoris in praesenti consultatione duo fundamenta sunt'); Franciscus Accoltus, *Consilia seu responsa*, f. 107r (n. 95, inc. 'Respondeo breviter dubiis eleganter motis contra partem domini Iuliani').

356 The impression given in Wortley 1947 that Bartolus coined the phrase *pirata non mutat dominium* is misleading, but that was the obvious conclusion he drew from *Digest*, 49.15.19 and 24 (*Opera omnia*, vol. 2(2), f. 236).

357 On the important difference between the acquisition of property through occupation from enemies and through forfeiture to civil authorities, which might redistribute the property, see Bossuat 1947. In the terminology of Roman law, the property of pirates – like plunder taken by campaigning armies, if properly understood – was quite literally 'confiscated', i.e. assigned to the imperial treasury (*fiscus*). As has been seen, enemy property seized in England was treated in a similar way.

358 Brundage 1976; Muldoon 1979; Lower 2006.

359 Byrne 1920; Krueger 1933; Abulafia 1994; Laiou 2001; Caselli 2013; Pita 2017.

360 Salvatori 2007.

tended to be interrupted by periods of war, in the Mediterranean war tended to be interrupted by periods of truce.[361] The boundaries between legal and illegal seizures seemed fluid because it was often difficult to tell whether ships and merchandise came from places covered by the terms of a truce, and because excuses for illegal seizures were easy to devise.[362] The description of seizures of ships and goods at sea in contemporary sources is certainly confusing, yet it clearly was understood that seizures could be legal or illegal, depending on the circumstances in which they were made.[363] The capture of prizes and prisoners from enemies in wartime was of course considered to be legal, and was subject to detailed regulation of the type discussed earlier in this chapter.[364] As was mentioned there, in wars between Christian and Muslim countries prisoners did become slaves, but otherwise the understanding of maritime plunder was the same as elsewhere.[365] Taking it for granted that *res hostium* were open to acquisition, legislators tried to avoid disputes over the division of spoils by laying down clear rules governing the seizure of plunder by those setting out *in cursum* or *ad piraticam exercendam*.[366] Different rules were taken to apply in peacetime, even though the same language tended to be used. The signatories of truces promised to take action against those who 'equipped their ship or galley in order to go *in cursum* against the Saracens', promised 'to take care of the restoring of everything that was despoiled in this sea by Christian *piratae*', and promised assistance if the other signatories sent out vessels to deal with '*cursales* or malefactors'.[367] The truces promised the execution of pirates or corsairs, the forfeiture of their belongings, the restitution of goods they seized from others and the punishment of people who purchased goods from them.

361 Fontenay and Tenenti 1976, vol. 1, p. 79; Dufourcq 1980, pp. 209–12; Greene 2010, p. 53; Jamieson 2012, pp. 13–14; Murphy 2013, pp. 23–4.

362 Ahrweiler 1976, vol. 1, pp. 15–16; Burns 1984, pp. 109–11; Simbula 2004, p. 17.

363 Wolf 1979, p. 113; Bresc 1980, p. 754; Katele 1989, pp. 88–90; Atauz 2008, pp. 61–2; Kaiser and Calafat 2014, pp. 71–2.

364 Heers 2001, pp. 168–9 and 218–19; Weiss 2011, pp. 18–19; Coleman 2013, pp. 174–5.

365 Verlinden 1980; Brodman 1985 and 1986; Meyerson 1996; Michienzi 2014; Picard 2016.

366 *Collection de lois maritimes*, vol. 2, pp. 208–12, 303–7 and 334–47, vol. 5, pp. 257–8, 396–432 and 465–72, and vol. 6, pp. 16–30 and 53; *Consulate of the Sea*, pp. 128–30, 191–4, 212–21 and 233–60; *Siete partidas*, vol. 2, pp. 462–9, and vol. 4, p. 1081; *Monumenta historiae patriae*, vol. 18, cols 760–1; Capmany 1961–3, vol. 2, pp. 66–7. Continuing use of the same terminology is probably the best explanation for the documents reproduced in Zeldes 2000, which should be compared with the document in *Medieval Trade in the Mediterranean World*, pp. 222–3.

367 *Traités de paix et de commerces*, vol. 2, pp. 34, 62, 83–4, 93–4, 120, 124, 139–40, 154, 198, 201, 205, 214, 219, 235, 247 and 352–3; *Diplomatarium Veneto-Levantinum*, vol. 1, pp. 36 and 315–16, and vol. 2, p. 29.

These promises would only be fulfilled, however, while the truces held and unless reprisals were authorised, for in other circumstances the maritime raiding described as 'corsairing' or 'piracy' was considered legitimate.

Equally confusing terminology can be found in records concerned with relations between Christian nations in the Mediterranean, although here again it is clear that seizures were considered legal or illegal depending on the circumstances.[368] Rulers promised each other that they would seek out and punish *piratae*, boasted about their efforts in hunting down those believed *crudeliter piraticam exercere*, and asserted a right to punish any *publicus cursarius* they captured, regardless of his origin.[369] When, for example, provision was made in Pisa for the maintenance of a force to protect shipping, detailed regulations were issued, with those put in command being authorised *piratas punire*.[370] The force was financed partly by a tax on shipping and partly by a levy on any goods recovered, unless they had been taken by the corsairs from foreigners, in which case they were to be restored entirely to their owners.[371] The restoration of ships and goods seized *more piratico* was frequently demanded and granted, unless the victim turned out to be a *publicus inimicus*.[372] The standard rule was that any person guilty of *raubaria, praeda vel latrocinium* would be hanged (*furca suspendatur* or *laqueo suspendatur*), to which it was sometimes added that the property of pirates would be confiscated by the civil authorites (*bona publicantur*).[373] Harsh penalties were also imposed on those who helped to finance or equip pirate voyages, who knowingly received goods taken by pirates,

368 Guiral 1980; Katele 1988; Balard 1990; Rigaud 1991; Tai 2004 and 2007.

369 *Corps universel diplomatique du droit des gens*, vol. 3(1), pp. 178–9, and vol. 3(2), pp. 407 and 399; *Diplomatarium Veneto-Levantinum*, vol. 1, pp. 130–2, 135–8 and 154–6, and vol. 2, pp. 5–6.

370 *Statuti inediti della città di Pisa*, vol. 3, pp. 612–26.

371 For the different division of ships when they were recovered from enemies see *Collection de lois maritimes*, vol. 6, p. 54; *Siete partidas*, vol. 4, p. 1082; *Monumenta historiae patriae*, vol. 18, col. 520; *Miscellanea di storia italiana*, vol. 11, p. 707; *Statuti inediti della città di Pisa*, vol. 2, p. 924.

372 *Collection de lois maritimes*, vol. 5, p. 20; *Statuta Veneta*, pt 1, f. 135v; *Statuti inediti della città di Pisa*, vol. 3, p. 364; *Diplomatarium Veneto-Levantinum*, vol. 1, pp. 125–7; *Urkunden zur älteren Handels- und Staatsgeschichte der Republik Venedig*, vol. 3, pp. 159–281; *Diplomatari de l'orient català*, p. 6; *Medieval Trade in the Mediterranean World*, pp. 318–21; De Mas Latrie 1852–61, vol. 3, pp. 728–32; Capmany 1961–3, vol. 2, pp. 206–10 and 327–8; Braunstein 1987.

373 *Statuta Veneta*, pt 1, ff. 130v-1r; *Criminalia iura serenissimae reipublicae Genuensis*, pp. 161 and 168; *Monumenta historiae patriae*, vol. 18, cols 519 and 943; *Statuta communis Parmae*, pp. 224–5; *Statuta Vallis Camonicae*, pp. 207–8; *Cronache e statuti della città di Viterbo*, p. 591; *Codice degli statuti della repubblica di Sassari*, pp. 257–8.

or who failed to take any action they might have against known pirates.[374] None of these penalties would apply, however, if seizures were made by pirates or corsairs from enemies in wartime, or under a licence to take reprisals in peacetime.[375] However difficult it could sometimes be to tell whether a pirate or corsair had been acting legally or illegally, there was no doubt that the same activity of attacking and capturing ships, goods and persons at sea would in some circumstances be legitimate and in others illegitimate.[376]

In much the same way as the words *piratae* and *cursarii* were used to describe any mariners involved in attacks on shipping in the Mediterranean, terms such as 'pirates' and 'sea rovers' were often used in sources relating to northern navigation to mean nothing more precise than 'maritime raiders'.[377] Care must therefore be taken to avoid the easy assumption that references to pirates in these sources are to people engaged in illegal activities, and more generally to ensure that distinctions are maintained here too between people engaged in licit plunder, licensed reprisal, lawful vengeance and criminal piracy.[378] Historians writing about navigation in northern waters have often neglected these distinctions, for the perfectly respectable reason that the people they study found them hard to maintain.[379] As was noted earlier, it could in practice be far from obvious to whom a ship or goods belonged, or whether a state of war existed, or how far reprisals had been licensed, to which it may now be added that knowing when raiders were open to vengeance as pirates was not straightforward either.[380] It did not help that those involved in

374 *Statuta Veneta*, pt 1, f. 131, and pt 2, f. 68v; *Criminalia iura serenissimae reipublicae Genuensis*, pp. 170–2; *Monumenta historiae patriae*, vol. 18, cols 507, 520–1, 731 and 944.

375 *Collection de lois maritimes*, vol. 5, pp. 98 and 349; *Miscellanea di storia italiana*, vol. 11, pp. 704–5 and 735–6; *Monumenta historiae patriae*, vol. 18, cols 109 and 539–40; *Actes du parlement de Paris*, pp. 23–4, 26–8, 42–3 and 50; Piergiovanni 1980, pp. 287 and 389.

376 It should by now be abundantly clear that a distinction cannot be drawn in keeping with the primary sources between legitimate 'corsairing' and illegitimate 'piracy'. The variants of these terms were used interchangeably, and with reference to legal or illegal seizures.

377 *Diplomatarium Veneto-Levantinum*, vol. 2, pp. 280–3; *Oeuvres complètes de Suger*, p. 42; *Oeuvres de Rigord et de Guillaume le Breton*, vol. 2, p. 260; Matthew Paris, *Chronica maiora*, vol. 3, p. 26; Capmany 1961–3, vol. 2, pp. 66–7.

378 For instance, mention is frequently made of a discussion in England of the question whether pirates would acquire title to things they seized if they failed to retain possession of them for at least twenty-four hours (Marsden 1894–7, vol. 1, p. xl; Sanborn 1930, pp. 282 and 311; Ward 2009, pp. 33–4). It is clear from the records relied on, however, that what was at issue here was the point at which 'enemies' would be taken to have completed title through the effective occupation of things they captured during a war (*Calendar of the Close Rolls*, 1349–54, pp. 424–5; *Second part de les reports de cases en ley*, pt 4, ff. 16v-17r).

379 Bjork 1943; Pistono 1975; Ditchburn 2000; Friedland 2000; Pitcaithly 2012; Meichsner 2019.

380 Rose 1982, pp. 21–2; Ditchburn 1992a, p. 41; Heller-Roazen 2009, p. 104.

plunder or reprisal could be tempted to stray beyond the limits of legitimacy, and might do so without banding together in precisely the way expected of pirates.[381] Nor did it help that the inveterate misconduct of professional pirates could become legitimate in wartime, and that rulers could find it expedient to tolerate or encourage their activities, recognising that however great a menace pirates might be in peacetime, they were a vital source of skilled manpower in wartime.[382] Yet the extent to which the seas were an area of lawlessness, in which might was right and legal categories had no real place, has tended to be exaggerated, for the difficulty of differentiating legal from illegal seizures, and the prevalence of the latter, appear to have been most marked in particular periods, typically when wars were beginning or ending.[383] It is doubtful, moreover, whether it may simply be assumed from the fact that merchant vessels were usually armed for defence that the opportunistic seizure of merchandice was regarded as an ordinary aspect of trade.[384] However difficult it may have been to distinguish legal from illegal seizures, distinctions certainly were drawn, and historians should resist the temptation to attribute their own uncertainties to their sources.[385]

In treaties and truces entered into between northern nations it was often promised that redress would be provided in future for *rapinas, praedas ac manifesta latrocinia* committed on either side, and to make it clear which type of offender was envisaged, explicit reference was sometimes made to *piratae, praedones vel malefactores supra mare*.[386] Complaints were often made and proceedings initiated in courts over seizures of ships and goods at sea *more piratico* or *more praedonio*.[387] Government action was promised against *piratae*

381 Schwartzenberger 1948, pp. 68–70; Kermode 1988, pp. 215–21; Ditchburn 1992b, pp. 27–30.

382 Unger 1980, pp. 259–60; Mercer 2005, p. 51; Urban 2006, p. 189.

383 Salzman 1931, pp. 254–8; Dollinger 1970, pp. 78–82; Postan 1973, pp. 112–14; Lloyd 1991, pp. 62–3 and 235–6; Meier 2006, pp. 146–59; Dotson 2003, p. 212.

384 Williamson 1913, pp. 29–30; Appleby 1992, p. 90; Rodger 2003, pp. 237–8; Sylvester 2005, pp. 164–5; Rose 2007, pp. 123–5; Ogilvie 2011, pp. 216–19; Eddison 2013, pp. 18 and 27.

385 Lewis 1937; De Roover 1945; Gardiner 1976; Jones 1987; Corsi 2012.

386 *Foedera, conventiones, litterae et cuiuscunque generis acta publica*, vol. 8, pp. 305–9 and 469–76, vol. 9, p. 483, and vol. 12, pp. 308, 385–6, 466 and 583–4; *Corps universel diplomatique du droit des gens*, vol. 2(1), pp. 286–8 and 302–6, vol. 2(2), pp. 90–1, and vol. 3(2), pp. 162, 246, 276, 321, 338–9, 376–8 and 401–2; *Hanserecesse*, vol. 2, p. 52; *Hanserecesse*, 3rd ser., vol. 2, p. 360; *Hansisches Urkundenbuch*, vol. 4, p. 13, and vol. 8, pp. 538–9; *Mémoires pour servir de preuves à l'histoire ecclésiastique et civile de Bretagne*, vol. 2, col. 883, and vol. 3, cols 178 and 515.

387 *Hanserecesse*, 2nd ser., vol. 2, p. 77; *Hanserecesse*, 3rd ser., vol. 2, p. 600, and vol. 4, pp. 312–13; *Hansisches Urkundenbuch*, vol. 3, pp. 228–30, vol. 4, p. 300, vol. 5, pp. 314–15, vol. 7, pp. 67–8, vol. 9, pp. 107–8, and vol. 11, pp. 55–6 and 469–70; *Bronnen tot de Geschiedenis van der Handel*, vol. 2, p. 1212, and 2nd ser., vol. 1, pp. 41–2; *Calendar of Early Chancery*

et mali homines who were known to be congregating at sea, or against *infestationes piratarum seu raptorum*.[388] The recognition that some pirates at least ought to be dealt with as criminals was certainly not a novelty in the sixteenth or even the fifteenth century.[389] As well as *piratae et praedones* long being subjected to punishment themselves, normally *ad mortem*, those who knowingly bought goods from pirates, who sold equipment and victuals to pirates or who helped them in other ways were also threatened with severe punishments.[390] While there is less evidence of the criminal prosecution of *piratae, praedones et malefactores* than might have been expected, there is no doubt that it did happen, and there are reasons why the paucity of evidence need not seem surprising.[391] In the absence of standing navies equipped to police the seas, the initiative lay with private parties, who can have had little incentive to bring offenders before criminal courts. For one thing, victims who wished to exact vengeance were permitted to do so directly. For another, their primary concern must usually have been to recover their property, and provided they could establish their ownership, and the seizures could not be justified as licit plunder or licensed reprisal, victims would have been able to recover their goods without having to prove that the takers had banded together for the purpose of raiding shipping.[392] Indeed, if the goods had disappeared there would not only have been little incentive to bring pirates before criminal courts, but would

Proceedings, pp. 59, 65 and 80–92; *Documents Relating to Law and Custom of the Sea*, vol. 1, pp. 10–18 and 132–6; Kingsford 1925, pp. 183–203.

388 *Hanserecesse*, vol. 1, pp. 6 and 109; *Hansisches Urkundenbuch*, vol. 4, p.13, and vol. 10, p. 398; *Documents Relating to Law and Custom of the Sea*, vol. 1, pp. 59–61.

389 In 1315, for instance, the count of Holland and Zeeland, while insisting on the innocence of certain Scottish mariners, reassured the king of England that he appreciated the need for 'depredatores vel malefactores' who preyed on shipping 'sine misericordia puniri' as an example to others (*Bronnen tot de Geschiedenis van der Handel*, vol. 1, pp. 153–4). He was satisfied that the Scots, though heavily armed, were intent on attacking their king's enemies alone. As the English king did not regard the Scots as legitimate enemies, he took a different view.

390 *Collection de lois maritimes*, vol. 2, pp. 481 and 484–5, and vol. 3, pp. 22 and 421; *Corps universel diplomatique du droit des gens*, vol. 2(2), p. 101; *Hanserecesse*, vol. 1, pp. 2, 307 and 326; *Hanserecesse*, 2nd ser., vol. 2, pp. 539–41; *Hanserecesse*, 3rd ser., vol. 2, p. 120; *Hansisches Urkundenbuch*, vol. 4, p. 480; *Documents Relating to Law and Custom of the Sea*, vol. 1, pp. 145–6.

391 *Foedera, conventiones, litterae et cuiuscunque generis acta publica*, vol. 11, pp. 767–71; *Hanserecesse*, 2nd ser., vol. 1, pp. 297–8; *Hansisches Urkundenbuch*, vol. 5, pp. 12–14; *Calendar of Early Chancery Proceedings*, pp. 4 and 83; *Select Cases in Chancery*, pp. 45–6; *Documents Relating to Law and Custom of the Sea*, vol. 1, pp. 6–7, 31–5, 74–5, 84–9 and 99–102.

392 See, for instance, *Statutes of the Realm*, vol. 1, p. 338.

actually have been a disincentive. Compensation for losses could not have been provided by takers who were declared to be pirates since their own property would have been forfeited to the civil authorities.[393]

A more optimistic view might have been encouraged by a provision found in some copies of the laws of Oleron, which stated that rules against the plundering of wrecks would not apply if the wrecked vessels belonged to pirates or enemies of the faith, for 'every one may take from suche manner of men as from dogs, and may strip them and despoil them of theyr goodes without any punishment'.[394] The implication might have been drawn that pirates' goods were open to appropriation, though the key phrase was 'without any punishment'. The obvious inspiration of the provision was Frederck II's constitution, and the possibility of its misinterpretation was precluded in places where the forfeiture of pirates' goods was explicitly threatened. That pirates could only own things they had acquired when not engaged in piracy was widely recognised, as a case involving mariners from Lynn – connected with the incident discussed near the end of the first section of this chapter – illustrates. The complaint was that the city authorities in Danzig were mishandling ships from Lynn because they were dissatisfied with the treatment of one of their ships in England.[395] Although it was admitted that the ship in question had been seized by mariners from Lynn, it was insisted that it had been in the possession not of Prussians but of Scots, with whom the English were at war (*tempore captionis navis et bonorum, de quibus nunc contenditur, invicem inimici erant*), and it had therefore been declared by an admiralty court that it was a just prize of war (*le dit prise estoit legitement fait*). It was replied that even if it were true that 'the said ship, with all the goods contained in it, was captured and despoiled at sea by Scots from the Prussians and subsequently captured and despoiled from the hands of the Scots by the English', it would still be the case that 'the restoration of a ship in this situation to the Prussians should be denied by no law'. Alluding to the principle of canon law that 'before any argument, possession ought to be restored to the person from whom it was violently taken', the Prussian envoys maintained, in language derived from the civil law, that even if their mariners had lost physical possession (*possessio corporalis*) of the ship, they would still

393 *Foedera, conventiones, litterae et cuiuscunque generis acta publica*, vol. 3(1), p. 71, and vol. 3(2), pp. 182 and 202; *Mémoires pour servir de preuves à l'histoire ecclésiastique et civile de Bretagne*, vol. 1, col. 1280; *Calendar of the Patent Rolls*, 1345–48, p. 260; *Statutes of the Realm*, vol. 2, pp. 178–81.

394 *Black Book of the Admiralty*, vol. 2, pp. 478–9; *Collection de lois maritime*, vol. 1, p. 351; *Ancient Sea-Lawes of Oleron*, p. 13; *Us et coustumes de la mer*, pp. 157–8.

395 *Hanserecesse*, vol. 5, pp. 341–7; *Hanseakten aus England*, pp. 231–2 and 235–6.

have retained possession in legal terms (*possessio civilis*) as they would not have abandoned their intention to possess (*animus possidere*).[396] Moreover, as the Scots were not at war with the Prussians (*Prutenorum amici et nullatenus inimici*), the English mariners appeared to have taken the ship from pirates (*piraticis*), and it was thus irrelevant where they came from.[397] The English mariners might have taken the ship from their enemies, but when engaging in piracy their enemies would not have acquired title to the ship by taking it from the Prussians. The English ambassadors would have found this line of reasoning comprehensible. In another case an English mariner complained that his ship was being held in Scotland because a ship seized from a Scot by English pirates had not been restored to him.[398] The ship had been recovered from the pirates but delivered to someone pretending to be the Scottish owner's agent, by whom the ship had then been sold and delivered to someone else. That buyer was required to restore the ship to its Scottish owner on the understanding that the Scottish owner had never lost title to his property.

As with the discussion of the other incident involving mariners from Lynn, what is striking about these cases is the extent to which parties from various places were able to exchange mutually intelligible arguments with each other, which casts doubt on the suggestion recently made that medieval piracy is best regarded as an instance of 'legal pluralism'.[399] What exactly is intended by this is unclear, since the concept has meant different things to different scholars.[400] In the first place, legal pluralism has been seen as a kind of 'normative pluralism', meaning that behaviour is taken to be governed by several species of rule, either legal in a strict sense or moral, religious or something of the sort. Attention will certainly need to be paid to other regimes if medieval piracy is to be understood fully as a social practice, but this can have little bearing on how piracy was viewed as a legal category.[401] In the second place, the concept

396 *Liber extra*, 3.13.1; *Digest*, 41.2.3.7–11, 41.2.8, 41.2.24 and 43.16.1.9.

397 Some of those on board the pirate vessel were alleged to be from Spain, Brittany and Flanders, and the focus on the Scots in the English pleadings seemed to the Prussians tendentious.

398 *Calendar of Early Chancery Proceedings*, pp. 72–5; *Calendar of the Patent Rolls*, 1452–61, pp. 170, 178, 224 and 301–3; *Calendar of Documents Relating to Scotland*, vol. 4, p. 265; Kingsford 1929, pp. 89–90 and 179–82.

399 Tai 2012 (endorsed in Heebøll-Holm 2017, p. 40). The concept has been developed in several fields, including legal history, where it may have had its origins (Tuori 2011; Benton 2011a; Humfress 2013).

400 Merry 1988; Griffiths 1986; Macdonald 1998; Tamanaha 2008; Twining 2009–10.

401 The same may be said in relation to the other practices examined in this chapter. Huizinga 1924, pp. 100–2, for instance, drew attention long ago to the influence of ideas chivalry on thinking about warfare, though like many historians since he tended to run together

of legal pluralism has also been used in what has been called the 'weak sense' that one system of norm generation and dispute settlement may accommodate within it other such systems. It has been seen that the laws of European nations typically contained within them particular regimes known as 'the law of arms', 'the law of the sea' and such like. Paradoxically, however, these regimes were particular within each nation precisely because there was a perceived need for them to be developed within a framework that was common to all nations. In the third place, the concept of legal pluralism is sometimes used in the 'strong sense' that within any social setting there may be competing and conflicting systems of norm generation and dispute settlement in operation. It is of course possible that the reason why seemingly similar seizures of ships and goods were sometimes judged legitimate and sometimes illegitimate was not that the circumstances of the seizures were different but that the perspectives of the judges differed. Perhaps this is why it has been suggested that medieval piracy should be regarded as an instance of legal pluralism.[402] However, while the handling of disputes over piracy may have differed from one place to another, and while more could no doubt be made of these variations, there would be a risk in attending to them of obscuring an overwhelming impression of consistency in the treatment of piracy throughout Europe. The understanding of piracy that emerged from the law schools did face opposition, but it came to be widely accepted as a basis both for the settlement of disputes and for negotiations between rulers.

6 Apprehension of Pirates in Sixteenth-Century Scotland

As was mentioned towards the end of the fourth section of this chapter, mariners who went to sea from Scotland in the later sixteenth century were constantly apprehensive of attacks by English pirates.[403] Not only were ships and

distinct modes of discourse. If it was not unfair to complain in n. 41 above about Ambühl 2013 neglecting the theory of the law schools, it must be just as fair to complain about this book neglecting other normative systems.

402 Use of the concept today, in the analysis of a globalised international order in which the authority of territorial rulers has been diminished, is encouraging its use in analysis of experience prior to the rise of the modern state (Burke-White 2003–4; Berman 2006–7; Zumbansen 2010). Not all judges handling maritime disputes then did so under the auspices of sovereign princes (for an attempt to make sense of the activities of the Hanseatic League in terms of another modern theory see Fink 2012).

403 See n. 280 above. It needs to be stressed again that the examples given below are merely examples.

goods being seized then with alarming frequency, but reports were circulating of brutal treatment being inflicted on mariners found on Scottish vessels.[404] In 1574, for instance, a ship coming home from Norway, having been driven south by 'constrarius wyndis', had been attacked by 'ane pirate Inglish ship, full of men of weir, cruell and merceles theves'.[405] According to the master, after removing visible goods and equipment, the pirates had beaten him and his crew to make them reveal the hiding place of 'mony in the said ship', had then 'thraetinit to have hangit us all', and had finally 'pat us to the see naikit, spuilzeit of our claithis, without vittuallis'. As far as the master could see, 'we ar wars handellit now then in tyme of weir, becaus gif weiris war denuncit betwix us and Ingland, thai wald do na evill to our personis, but tak us prissoneris and handell us gentillie and caus us pay ransom'. The periods of open war in the earlier decades of the century had to some extent seemed less alarming, although illegal piracy (*piratia et latrocinium*) had not been unknown then either, and had indeed been indulged in by criminals (*piratae et praedones*) from Scotland.[406] Throughout the sixteenth century Scottish rulers promised and made serious efforts to have pirates 'apprehended', put on trial and 'hanged as an example to others'.[407] Local merchants and mariners were forbidden

404 *Calendar of State Papers Relating to Scotland*, vol. 2, p. 124, vol. 4, pp. 670–1, vol. 6, pp. 216, 234–5 and 454, vol. 9, pp. 643–5, and vol. 10, pp. 70, 124, 237–8, 322, 352–4 and 533–4; *Correspondence of Robert Bowes*, pp. 127–8 and 156; *Warrender Papers*, vol. 1, pp. 166–7; *Hamilton Papers*, vol. 2, p. 659; *Acts of the Parliaments of Scotland*, vol. 3, p. 455; Records of the Parliaments of Scotland, 1587/7/61; *Calendar of the Manuscripts of the Most Honourable the Marquis of Salisbury*, vol. 3, p. 288; *Report on the Laing Manuscripts*, vol. 1, pp. 67–8; *Forty-Seventh Annual Report of the Deputy Keeper of the Public Records*, pp. 26–7; *Records of the Convention of the Royal Burghs of Scotland*, vol. 2, pp. 48–9.

405 *Calendar of State Papers Relating to Scotland*, vol. 4, pp. 683–4 (certain liberties are taken with the transcriptions below).

406 *Letters of James the Fourth*, pp. 258–9 and 261–3; *Letters and Papers, Foreign and Domestic, of the Reign of Henry VIII*, vol. 1(1), pp. 593, 602 and 620; *Epistolae Iacobi Quarti, Iacobi Quinti et Mariae regum Scotorum*, vol. 1, pp. 165–7; *Acts of the Parliaments of Scotland*, vol. 2, p. 286; Records of the Parliaments of Scotland, 1524/11/12; *Acts of the Lords of Council in Public Affairs*, p. 228; *Ancient Criminal Trials in Scotland*, vol. 1(1), p. 131; *Antiquarian Gleanings from Aberdeenshire Records*, p. 46; *Bronnen tot de Geschiedenis van den Handel met Engeland, Schotland en Ierland*, 2nd ser., vol. 1, pp. 557–8; *Foreign Correspondence with Marie de Lorraine*, vol. 2, pp. 46–8; *Acts of the Privy Council of England*, vol. 10, pp. 34 and 105; *Forty-Seventh Annual Report of the Deputy Keeper of the Public Records*, pp. 12–13; BL, Royal MS 13B II, f. 75, and Cotton MS Caligula B VI, f. 72; NLS, Adv. MS 35.5.9B, ff. 182v-3r; NRS, GD149/264, f. 238, SP13/77, RH1/2/871 and RH9/6/4; Tracy 1993, pp. 256–7 and 261–3.

407 *Calendar of State Papers Relating to Scotland*, vol. 1, pp. 550, 631, 640, 646 and 680, vol. 2, pp. 1 and 276–7, vol. 3, pp. 22–3, and vol. 10, pp. 358, 364–5, 416–17, 422, 424, 430, 442 and 454; *Register of the Privy Council*, vol. 1, pp. 104, 544–6, 557–8, 560–1 and 581–2, vol. 2, pp. 69–70 and 222–3, vol. 4, pp. 195–6 and 303, and vol. 5, pp. 40–1; *Compota thesaurariorum regum*

from assisting pirates, orders were issued for the arrest of suspected pirates when they arrived in Scotland, and commissions were granted for expeditions to sail in search of pirates. More will be said about these commissions later, but the focus of attention in this section is not on the apprehension of pirates in the sense of their capture, nor on the apprehension of pirates in the sense of fear of their activities. The focus is rather on the mental apprehension of pirates as a class of people. How was piracy understood as a legal category in sixteenth century Scotland?

It does not appear to have been assumed that any seizure of a ship and goods that did not count as licit plunder or licensed reprisal would amount to an act of criminal piracy. In 1548 a Scottish mariner was declared to be a rebel for failing to appear before the justiciary court in response to a charge that he had seized a Portuguese vessel after setting out in an armed ship 'lie weirfair'.[408] In the brief record that survives of the case it was specified that at the time of the seizure there had been 'no war or conflict declared between the realms of Scotland and Portugal', and that the accused had put his ship to sea 'without a licence from our sovereign lady the queen or her tutor and regent'. At no point, however, was use made of the words 'pirate' or 'piracy'. The explanation cannot be that the mariner had not put to sea with a view to raiding shipping, for it is made clear that this was precisely the purpose imputed to him, and he was being accused of committing a crime of some sort. An alternative explanation could perhaps be that he had believed his action to be covered by the licence granted to the Bartons, that his belief was thought to be erroneous, and that the seizure was consequently considered to be illegal, though not quite an act of piracy. No doubt the nature of the crime alleged would have become clearer if the mariner had appeared to stand trial. Another possible explanation might be that the surviving record of the case is misleading. Some cases raised before the justiciary court were noted in 'court books', running from 1493 until 1513, or in 'books of adjournal' and 'minute books', running from 1576 and 1577 respectively, and process papers also survive from some cases heard after

Scotorum, vol. 5, p. 440, vol. 9, p. 429, vol. 11, p. 254, and vol. 12, p. 33; *Ancient Criminal Trials in Scotland*, vol. 1(1), pp. 273 and 298; *Extracts from the Records of the Burgh of Edinburgh*, vol. 4, pp. 14 and 19–20; *Shetland Documents*, vol. 1, p. 152; *Forty-Seventh Annual Report of the Deputy Keeper of the Public Records*, p. 12; *Calendar of Letters and State Papers Relating to English Affairs Preserved Principally in the Archives of Simancas*, vol. 2, p. 15; *Acts of the Parliaments of Scotland*, vol. 3, p. 455; Records of the Parliaments of Scotland, 1587/7/61; [John Colville], *Historie and Life of King James the Sext*, pp. 19–20; Robert Lindesay, *Historie and Cronicles*, vol. 2, pp. 69–70, 198–200 and 315–16; NRS, GD149/265, pt 3, ff. 41–4.

408 NRS, GD149/270, pt 1, pp. 73–4.

1550.[409] There is thus a gap in the official records, between 1513 and 1550, and reliable records only really survive from before 1513 and after 1576. The 1548 case discussed here is known about only because someone made a digest of the records from 1536 to 1609 before many of them were lost.[410] It is possible that the writer omitted to note the use of the words 'pirate' and 'piracy' in the record of the 1548 case he was abbreviating, although he seems to have worked fairly carefully. In an index attached to his digest it is said that the accused was put to the horn 'for selling in ane armit schipe and be way of weirfair takeing and spuilzeing of ane Portugall schipe, being friend to this cuntrey'. Again, the impression is given that the seizure of the ship was considered to be illegal yet was not regarded as an act of piracy.

Other cases raised before the justiciary court certainly were concerned with piracy. In 1555 a vessel from Lynn was found to have been raiding shipping around Leith.[411] There was at the time no war between Scotland and England, and the mariners had to admit that since they lacked a licence from their queen, they had been acting 'contra iuris communis dispositione et reipublicae utilitate'.[412] They were explicitly accused of piracy and oppression (*piratia et oppressio*), were said to have despoiled ships with piratical force (*vis piratica*) and were hanged as pirates (*piratis laqueis suspendentur*), their property being forfeited to the crown. The difference between this case and the one raised in 1548 may have been that the mariners made no pretence of sailing under letters of reprisal. It does not seem simply to have been that the accused were present, for it is apparent from various records that in 1526 a mariner from Leith was 'dilatit as ane see pyrate, throw takin of certane schippis and gudis off frenndis', and he too was sentenced to death by hanging, but evidently *in absentia*, as he remained at liberty.[413] In 1551 another Scottish mariner was convicted of

409 The 'court books' are NRS, JC1/1–2, of which transcriptions can be found in NLS, Adv. MSS 6.1.4–6, and NRS, RH2/1/5–7. The 'books of adjournal' are NRS, JC2/1–3, and the 'minute books' begin with JC6/1, of which a more polished version can be found in JC2/1–3. The process papers from cases raised in the sixteenth century are in JC26/1–3. For a discussion of some of these records see Armstrong 2013, pp. 3–7.

410 NRS, GD149/270–2.

411 *Ancient Criminal Trials in Scotland*, vol. 1(1), pp. 379–81; NRS, GD149/270, pt 2, pp. 76–7.

412 The translation of the phrase 'contra iuris communis dispositione' in Pitcairn's *Ancient Criminal Trials in Scotland* as 'contrary to the common law of nations' is in danger of misleading. There is no reason to suppose that the common law referred to was anything other than the civil law, which would have provided a commonly recognised justification for the seizures if they had been by way of reprisal.

413 *Acts of the Lords of Council in Public Affairs*, p. 243; NRS, CS5/36, ff. 17r, 96–7, 103, 114r, 116r and 122r; *Acts of the Parliaments of Scotland*, vol. 2, p. 315; Records of the Parliaments of Scotland, 1526/11/58; *Extracts from the Records of the Burgh of Edinburgh*, vol. 1, pp. 228–9;

violent piracy (*violenta piratia*) on a French ship.[414] As he was believed to have been involved in various similar crimes (*de diversis aliis piraticis criminibus*), he was identified as a 'common pirate' and the executioner was instructed to leave his body suspended from the gallows until worne away.[415] When another Scot was 'dilaitit of the cryme of commoun piracie' in 1567, the more detailed accusation was made that he had been involved in the 'cruell invasioune be way of piracie' of several ships, often in collusion with 'commoun piratis and see revaris and thevis'.[416] Although an advocate appearing on his behalf – as it happens, the father of Alexander King, the author of the treatise on maritime law discussed earlier – pointed out that it was peculiar for a prosecution to be brought by the king's advocate instead of the victims or their families, and although he advanced a further argument that will need to be examined presently, the accused was convicted and 'hangit on ane gibbet', with his property forfeited to the crown.[417] In 1582 a mariner of Leith who had seized goods from French and Flemish ships suffered the same fate after being convicted 'of certane crymes of perasie'.[418]

In this last case an advocate objected that the accused should be transferred for trial to the admiralty court, 'in respect the cryme quhairof he is accusit is ane sefairrand mater'. The objection was dismissed in the light of previous practice, but it is evident that pirates were also prosecuted before the admiralty court.[419] When Alexander King's father advanced the argument that remains

Registrum secreti sigilli regum Scotorum, vol. 1, p. 586. Reid 1962, p. 211, is mistaken in suggesting that it was the council that passed sentence, though it will be seen shortly that it could conceivably have been the admiralty court. While the responsibility for carrying out the sentence passed to the burgh authorities in Edinburgh, this may have been because the provost at the time happened also to be an admiral depute. On the other hand, on another occasion the burgh incurred expense in buying 'cords to hang and bund uthir VI Inglismen peratts on the gallows of the Borrow Mure' (*Extracts from the Records of the Burgh of Edinburgh*, vol. 2, p. 298).

414 *Ancient Criminal Trials in Scotland*, vol. 1(1), p. 358; NRS, GD149/270, pt 2, pp. 13–14; Davidson 2003, p. 43.

415 The accused seems to have been the 'ane callit Davidsone, pirat on the sea', mentioned in a reprisal case cited at n. 245 above, which will also be returned to below.

416 *Shetland Documents*, vol. 1, pp. 122–3; *Forty-Seventh Annual Report of the Deputy Keeper of the Public Records*, p. 16; NRS, GD149/270, pt 6, pp. 30–6.

417 'Diarey of Robert Birrel', p. 12; *Registrum secreti sigilli regum Scotorum*, vol. 6, p. 12; Gore-Browne 1937, p. 395; Anderson 1982, pp. 54–5.

418 *Ancient Criminal Trials in Scotland*, vol. 1(2), pp. 93–4; *Registrum secreti sigilli regum Scotorum*, vol. 8, p. 141; NRS, JC2/1, ff. 182v and 245v-6r, and GD149/271, pt 2, pp. 31–2.

419 In 1588 the burgh court of Ayr declared that it lacked jurisdiction over piracy cases (AA, B6/11/2, f. 19r, and see too B6/11/3, f. 230v). This appears to have been the view taken in other burghs as well.

to be examined in the 1567 case, it was rejected partly 'in respect of the ordour and practik usit and observit in this court in sik causis of befoir', and partly in respect 'of the proceiding usit laitlie be the admirall in siclyke ane caus'.[420] When complaints were made in 1575 about the oppressive behaviour of the earl of Orkney, one concern was with his 'usurping the office of admiralty, in apprehending, imprisoning, adjudging and justifying of alleged pirates, and uptaking of their escheated goods'.[421] The gravamen of the complaint was that the earl had actually been encouraging piracy around the northern isles, but the significant point for present purposes is that it was the admiral's jurisdiction he was believed to have encroached upon by hearing piracy cases in his court.[422] As was mentioned in the second section of this chapter, complaints about piracy were also sometimes made to the privy council. In 1567 a mariner from Orkney complained that while his ship was passing Dundee on its way home from Hull, goods and equipment were taken from it 'be maner of plane piracie'.[423] It complicated matters that the taker, 'to cullour this his piracie', was maintaining that 'the said complenaris schip is ane piratt, quhilk gif it be trew, he salbe fugitive fra na law'. The council was asked to confirm that the mariner had always been engaged in lawful trade, and to order the restitution of his property. In 1581 merchants from Antwerp complained that two Scots, 'be way of pyracie, with thair equippage, had maisterfullie, wranguslie, and on force, spuilyeit and taken the saidis compliners guidis and merchandices upoun the seyis'.[424] One of the Scots was ordered to appear before the council, and when he failed to do so he was put to the horn. It was the other one who was convicted of piracy in the justiciary court in the following year.[425] In 1586 a merchant from Dublin complained that a mariner from Ayr, 'haveing ane cumpany and equippage of rubbaris and pyratis in his awne schip, being accouterit and furnist in hostile maner, of intentioun to persew and invade the subjectis of

420 GD149/270, pt 6, p. 33.

421 *Calendar of State Papers relating to Scotland*, vol. 5, pp. 205–9; *Shetland Documents*, vol. 1, pp. 162–7; *Oppressions of the Sixteenth Century in the Islands of Orkney and Zetland*, pp. 4–11. The word 'and' has been inserted here between 'adjudging' and 'justifying'.

422 *Register of the Privy Council of Scotland*, vol. 2, pp. 654–60; *Shetland Documents*, vol. 1, pp. 231–6; Anderson 1982, pp. 77–8 and 90. The efforts of the earl of Bothwell in the late 1580s to assert an exclusive right as admiral to try piracy cases (*Calendar of State Papers Relating to Scotland*, vol. 10, pp. 422, 442 and 454) were undermined by suspicions that he too was prepared to consort with pirates (*Calendar of State Papers Relating to Scotland*, vol. 6, pp. 25 and 189–90, vol. 9, pp. 516 and 710, and vol. 10, pp. 9, 105 and 147).

423 *Register of the Privy Council of Scotland*, vol. 1, pp. 517–18.

424 *Register of the Privy Council of Scotland*, vol. 3, pp. 368–9.

425 Prosecutions for piracy as such do not appear to have been heard by the council.

all nationis standing in amytie and freidschip with his hienes, maist cruellie and be way of piracie perseuit the said complenare and his schip'.[426] When the mariner ignored a summons to appear before the council, he was declared a rebel, but over a year later the Irish merchant had still received no redress.[427]

It is not clear in which court another case that resulted in the defenders being put to the horn was heard in 1535.[428] It was complained that on three separate occasions, and in three different ports on the west coast of Scotland, vessels belonging to a Glasgow man had been assailed by the same group of marauders. The record makes reference to 'stouthreif and oppression', 'hurting and wounding' and 'slaughter and murder', adds that the stouthreif consisted in the 'reiving' of ships and goods, but makes no mention of piracy.[429] Barely two months earlier an act of parliament had been passed because the 'crymes of thift and stouth reiff is sa commonly usit amangis the kingis liegis, and for stanching of the samyn'.[430] The act had required the employers of people accused of stouthreif to produce them before the justiciary or sheriff courts, warning that any who failed to do so would expose themselves to prosecution for complicity in the alleged offences. As some of the offenders named in the report of the 1535 case were described as 'servants' of others, and as the phrase 'art and part' recurs throughout, it could well be that the use of the language of stouthreif in the case was encouraged by this act. It could also have been encouraged by another act passed at the same time, in which provision was made for the handling of 'gret crymes'.[431] Criminal prosecutions were to be raised for 'depredationis, maisterfull reiffis and spulyeis', but only after the same matters were 'civilie decydit'. The neglected argument advanced by Alexander King's father in 1567 was that his client should not be prosecuted for piracy because that crime had 'the same nature quhilk depredatioun hes in effect', and because the matters complained about had not been 'civilie callit nor decydit befoir ony juge'.[432] As noted above, this argument was rejected in the light of practice in the justiciary and admiralty courts, but in 1535 that

426 *Register of the Privy Council of Scotland*, vol. 4, p. 72.

427 *Calendar of State Papers Relating to Scotland*, vol. 9, p. 515.

428 *Ancient Criminal Trials in Scotland*, vol. 1(1), pp. 170–1. Where Pitcairn found this record is not known.

429 The contrary impression given in Forte 2008 is misleading, though it is of course possible that it is the record (or Pitcairn's version of it) that is misleading.

430 *Acts of the Parliaments of Scotland*, vol. 2, pp. 350–1; Records of the Parliaments of Scotland, 1535/52 (*cf.* A1515/7/3).

431 *Acts of the Parliaments of Scotland*, vol. 2, p. 350; Records of the Parliaments of Scotland, 1535/51.

432 NRS, GD149/270, pt 6, p. 32.

practice had not yet had time to develop.[433] It could therefore have been considered safer to plead the Glaswegian's case in terms of stouthreif, which was dealt with in a separate act from depredation, reif and spuilzie.[434]

In general, piracy does appear to have been regarded as a special form of 'depredation', 'reif' or 'spuilzie', all of which were names for the violent seizure of property.[435] The master of the ship sailing home from Norway in 1574, it may be recalled, complained that he and his crew had been 'spuilzeit' by those aboard the 'pirate Inglish ship' that intercepted them.[436] Similarly, the merchants from Antwerp who complained in 1581 about 'pyracie', claimed that their goods had been 'spuilyeit' from them.[437] When one of those who had attacked them was convicted of 'perasie' in the following year, the charges brought against him mentioned not only 'piratia' but also 'depredatio'.[438] In another case, not yet mentioned, a man from Stirling who had bought goods from a notorious pirate was accused of complicity in 'his reif and spulzie of the saidis gudis, be way of peracie'.[439] The goods had been seized 'be way of commoun peracie, furth of the raid of Burdeaulx, from sindry the kingis confidderat freindis', and as soon as they had been unloaded from a captured ship at Kirkcaldy, the accused had assisted the pirate in sailing that ship 'unto the raid of Abirdene, quhair thai, for cullouring of their piracie and for feir of cuming thairof to Leyth, sank and drownit the said schip'. In 1594 the master and owners of a ship from Danzig complained to the privy council that while they were passing Shetland, servants of the then earl of Orkney had 'maist wrangouslie and cruellie reft, pilleit and be way of piracie maist masterfullie spuilyeit and tuke away not onlie the said ship, bot also hir haill laidning'.[440] The privy council firmly rejected the claim that the takers ought to be punished as pirates. Independent evidence

433 Mackenzie, *Observations on the Acts of Parliament*, p. 132, later remarked that 'though by this act *depredations, reiffs and spuilzies* are ordain'd to be first civily pursu'd, yet the justices use to sustain criminal pursuits for these causes in the first instance'.

434 For a later example of use of this language see DCA, PBD, vol. 17, ff. 115v-16r.

435 For a sixteenth-century discussion see Skene, *De verborum significatione*, sigg. P2v-3r, or for more recent discussions see Jackson 2013, pp. 23–5, and Simpson 2016, pp. 96–101. The language of piracy was not used when things were taken from ships by stealth rather than force (*Acta curiae admirallatus Scotiae*, p. 223; *Register of the Privy Council of Scotland*, vol. 5, pp. 371–2 and 396–7). Irons 1898, vol. 2, pp. 44–5, is therefore wrong in stating that any crime committed in relation to shipping was regarded as piracy.

436 *Calendar of State Papers Relating to Scotland*, vol. 4, p. 683.

437 *Register of the Privy Council of Scotland*, vol. 3, p. 368.

438 *Ancient Criminal Trials in Scotland*, vol. 1(2), p. 94; NRS, JC2/1, f. 182v.

439 *Ancient Criminal Trials in Scotland*, vol. 1(2), pp. 37–8; NRS, GD149/270, pt 6, p. 53.

440 *Register of the Privy Council of Scotland*, vol. 5, pp. 153 and 195–7; *Shetland Documents*, vol. 2, pp. 102–3; *Ancient Criminal Trials in Scotland*, vol. 1(2), p. 336.

raises doubts about the veracity of some of the factual allegations made, yet the complaint was not simply dismissed but was referred for consideration to the lords of session.[441] While the criminal charge of piracy, reif and spuilzie was dismissed, the possibility of a civil action for spuilzie remained open. Thus while piracy does indeed appear to have been viewed as a form of depredation, reif or spuilzie, the depredation, reif or spuilzie of a ship or goods did not necessarily amount to piracy.[442]

As was seen in the second section of this chapter, when civil actions for spuilzie were raised before the lords of session, a question sometimes asked was whether ships or goods had been seized from friends or enemies, yet it was not normally alleged that defenders who had seized property from friends were pirates.[443] In civil actions piracy was mentioned incidentally, if at all.[444] In a case heard in 1582, for example, it was alleged that goods had been seized from an English vessel 'be way of piracie', but the action concerned the receipt of goods by someone who was not himself described as a pirate.[445] Likewise, in 1528 a 'sey revair' was alleged to have 'reft and spulzeit' goods from vessels off Norway and to have had accomplices in doing so, but there was no suggestion that the 'resetters' pursued in the action were involved in the piracy.[446] When goods were brought to Scotland by pirates, the first thing the victims tended to do was to request an order from the privy council for their arrest.[447] In these cases the council records make it clear that the goods were taken 'be way of piracie', but there is no indicaton that the receivers were regarded as pirates. It does not follow that the receivers were regarded as entirely innocent. On one

441 *Memorials of the Family of Skene of Skene*, pp. 164–5; *Shetland Documents*, vol. 2, pp. 95–6; NRS, RH9/5/21.

442 For cases in which words like 'spuilzie' were used but not 'piracy' see *Acta curiae admirallatus Scotiae*, pp. 191–4; *Register of the Privy Council of Scotland*, vol. 2, pp. 653–4; *Calendar of State Papers Relating to Scotland*, vol. 5, pp. 668–9, 686 and 699, vol. 6, pp. 11 and 54, and vol. 9, p. 515; NLS, Adv. MS 6.1.5, f. 57r; NRS, JC1/2, f. 46r.

443 *Acts of the Lords of Council in Public Affairs*, p. 535; *Practiques of Sir Richard Maitland*, pp. 35, 95 and 109–10; *Shetland Documents*, vol. 1, p. 135; *Calendar of State Papers Relating to Scotland*, vol. 2, pp. 143 and 275; *Register of the Privy Council of Scotland*, vol. 4, pp. 558–9; NLS, Adv. MS 31.2.2(I), ff. 8v-9, 32v and 40v-1r; NRS, CS7/17, ff. 169v-72, and CS7/23, ff. 118–20r.

444 *Acts of the Lords of Council in Public Affairs*, pp. 461–2 and 466–8; *Registrum secreti sigilli regum Scotorum*, vol. 8, p. 141; *Practicks of Sir James Balfour*, vol. 2, p. 639 (no trace of the case reported here could be found in the register of acts and decreets); NRS, CS5/36, ff. 96–7, 103, 114r, 116r and 122r, CS7/88, f. 284r, CS7/93, ff. 276v-8, and CS7/126, ff. 348–9r.

445 NRS, CS7/88, f. 284r.

446 *Acts of the Lords of Council in Public Affairs*, pp. 299, 305, 310, 314, 326 and 353.

447 *Register of the Privy Council of Scotland*, vol. 1, pp. 239, 308–10, 347, 351–2, 429–30 and 581–2, vol. 3, pp. 446–7, and vol. 4, pp. 134–5.

occasion 'the personis byaris and intromettouris with the gudis takin in piracie be a Fransche schip of weir' were ordered to appear before the 'admirall and his deputtis, alsweill to mak suirtie that the same salbe furthcumand to the just awnaris, freindis and confiderattis of this realme, as to underly punisement for bying and resset of unlauchfull gudis upoun the streame'.[448] On another occasion it was warned that just as 'we can nocht bot maist extremelie hait the wickit depredatioun of pyrattis', so the council could 'nocht bot evin esteme thai personis that avariciouslie resettis thair gudis takin in piracie na les culpabill'.[449] Again, though, there was no indication that the resetters were themselves regarded as pirates.

In civil actions the usual aim was not to have guilty parties punished but to recover property, which would often have passed into the hands of third parties. These actions raised complications of a different nature. After a vessel from Bremen was despoiled of its cargo, which was sold at various places along the east coast of Scotland, an action was raised before the lords of session 'for the wrangous resetting, bying, intrometting, using and disponing upoun the haill laiding, guids and merchandice being within the schip'.[450] The defenders had made their purchases, it was maintained, 'upoun certane knawlege that thai wer pilleit guidis and that the personis foirsaidis committeris of the said pirosie wer oppin and notorious pirottis, haifing maid enterie nor brokin bouk at na lauchtfull harberie, and the vice of the said pirosie nocht being purgit bot the saids guidis remanand as notoriouslie knawin as pilleit and rief guidis, and the saidis pirots to be na merchandis nor traffequaris, sua that all excuse of ignorance wes tane away fra thame'. Similar language was used in other cases. In one it was alleged that the defenders had purchased goods in the knowledge that they had been taken by pirates, 'thay haveing nawayes brokin bowke nor enterit thair guidis at ane lauchfull harborie, the said vice on nawayes being purgeit, and the saidis spuilyearis to be na merchandis nor trafficquaris with sic guidis, sua that all excuse of ignorance wes takin away from thame'.[451] In another case it was argued that since the defender had bought goods from a 'manefestlie knawin pirot and revar on the sea, the vice not purgit, and disponit upon the samin at his pleassir, and was maid ritch with the pryce thairof', he was liable to the victim for the value of the goods.[452] Elsewhere it was again

448 *Register of the Privy Council of Scotland*, vol. 2, pp. 625–6, and see too vol. 1, pp. 496–7.

449 *Register of the Privy Council of Scotland*, vol. 1, pp. 336–7, 430–2, 438–9 and 503–4, and vol. 2, pp. 636–8, 645–7 and 670–1; *Calendar of State Papers Relating to Scotland*, vol. 2, pp. 111, 127–8, 194–5, 210, 286–7, 292 and 329, and vol. 5, p. 225; Rae 1966, p. 48.

450 NRS, CS7/133, f. 439, and CS7/136, ff. 150, 193v-4, 227, 250–1, 281 and 295v-8r.

451 *Register of the Privy Council of Scotland*, vol. 5, pp. 195–7.

452 *Practiques of Sir Richard Maitland*, pp. 42–3; NLS, Adv. MS 31.2.2(1), f. 11.

complained that people had intromitted with goods, 'the vice of piracie being nawayis tryit, bot bocht the same *mala fide*, far within the availl thairof'.[453]

What exactly was being argued in these cases is comprehensible if account is taken of the legal theory advocates learned in the law schools. In Roman law it was possible for buyers of goods from sellers who did not own them to complete title prescriptively by remaining in possession of the goods for a period of time, but only if the purchase was made in good faith, and if the goods had not in the past been stolen or seized by force.[454] The theft or forceful appropriation of goods was referred to as a defect (*vitium*), which remained in a thing as it passed from person to person unless the owner regained possession, which would have purged the thing of its defect (*vitium rei purgare*).[455] The medieval doctors drew a distinction between this type of defect, which affected the thing itself (*vitium reale*), and a defect such as dishonesty, which would affect a person dealing with the thing (*vitium personale*).[456] What appears to have been at issue in the reset cases in Scotland was whether the handling of the goods continued to be affected by a personal defect of dishonesty after they passed from the pirates to the receivers, for there does not seem to have been any suggestion that title to the goods might have been acquired by the receivers. The suggestion was instead that if the receivers had paid for items in good faith, so that the personal defect had been purged, they would neither have committed any wrong for which they ought to make reparation, nor have been unjustly enriched at the expense of anyone to whom they ought to make recompense. The obvious explanation for the lack of reference to title is that, in accordance with the learned theory, even if the transfer of the goods had been purged of dishonesty, the receivers would still not have been able to acquire title since the goods themselves would have been affected by the real defect of their violent seizure by pirates.[457]

It follows that proving wrongdoing in actions raised against resetters would have mattered if the property bought had been consumed, either literally or by disappearing into the hands of unknown persons. It may be recalled that in

---

453 *Register of the Privy Council of Scotland*, vol. 6, p. 14.

454 Roby 1902, vol. 1, pp. 467–83; Schulz 1951, pp. 355–60; Buckland 1963, pp. 241–52.

455 *Institutes*, 2.6.8; *Digest*, 44.3.5 and 47.2.57.2; *Code*, 7.26.7 and 7.32.11.

456 Portius Azo, *Lectura super Codicem*, p. 570 (ad C.7.32.11); Odofredus de Denariis, *Lectura super Codice*, vol. 2, ff. 107v-8r (ad C.7.32.11); Iacobus de Ravanis, *Lectura super Codice*, f. 342v (ad C.7.32.11); Cinus de Pistoria, *In Codicem et aliquot titulos Digesti veteris doctissima commentaria*, vol. 2, f. 443r (ad C.7.32.11); Albericus de Rosate, *Opera omnia*, vol. 3(1), f. 90r (ad D.41.3.4.10).

457 See too ACA, CA1/1/25, pp. 372–3, CA1/1/27, pp. 554 and 558, and CA1/1/33/1, pp. 237–8, 240–5, 248–52, 254–6 and 265; AA, B6/11/1/3, f. 477.

1561 Breton merchants complained to the privy council that Thomas Kennedy of Bargany, an admiral depute on the west coast, had improperly 'adjudged' a ship and goods to the sons of Walter Cant under the letters of marque granted to the Bartons.[458] The merchants appear to have recognised that they had been deprived of ownership by Kennedy's formal act of court, and what they actually pursued him for was the 'ressetting' of their property. It was initially argued in his defence that he had only received enough of the property to cover the admiral's entitlement to a tenth of the value of any prize, and that it had been found by the lords of session in a previous case that a defender could not be held liable for intromission with an entire cargo when he had only handled part of it.[459] As far as the pursuers were concerned, however, it was the defender's adjudication of the prize to the takers that 'gaif occasioun' to the distribution of the entire cargo, 'quhilk utherwyise wald nocht have bene done'.[460] It was then argued on Kennedy's behalf that he had committed no wrong, 'be ressone that the saidis Cantis, for the tyme, were jugeit and estemit honest personis, and justlie to have apprehendit the gudis inbrocht and takin be thame as pertening to Spanyeartis'.[461] In response it was insisted that the ship and goods had obviously belonged to Frenchmen, and that in any case the letters granted to the Bartons against the Spaniards had been deprived of validity by a treaty, as Kennedy ought to have known.[462] It was further argued on Kennedy's behalf that 'ony schip fund passand betwix realmes without coquet is jugeit to be pirate, and lesumlie may be tane be ony persone', to which it was replied that there was 'na sik law nor consuetude that will that gudis omittit out of the clerkis bukis or coquet *fiant primi occupantis*'.[463] Although pirates

458 *Register of the Privy Council of Scotland*, vol. 1, pp. 165–7.

459 *Register of the Privy Council of Scotland*, vol. 1, p. 174. The previous case was the one reported in the *Practiques of Sir Richard Maitland*, pp. 42–3, and NLS, Adv. MS 31.2.2(1), f. 11, although this line of argument was not mentioned there (the case could not be located in the register of acts and decreets). One of the other arguments presented on Kennedy's behalf was that a case of this type ought to have been raised before the lords of session.

460 *Register of the Privy Council of Scotland*, vol. 1, p. 182.

461 *Register of the Privy Council of Scotland*, vol. 1, p. 177.

462 *Register of the Privy Council of Scotland*, vol. 1, pp. 182 and 230; *Corps universel diplomatique du droit des gens*, vol. 4(3), p. 124.

463 *Register of the Privy Council of Scotland*, vol. 1, pp. 177 and 182. Kennedy's lawyers were presumably thinking of the rule that a ship taken in wartime would be presumed to belong to an enemy if its master disposed of its documentation. When that rule was rehearsed in *Acta curiae admirallatus Scotiae*, pp. 15–16, the phase was actually used that the master would be 'reput and haldin as ane pirat', presumably meaning a 'maritime raider' or enemy combatant as opposed to a neutral trader.

could be attacked with impunity, and to that extent resembled enemies in a declared war, their property was not open to acquisition by anyone who seized it. Accordingly, even if the Breton merchants had been in breach of customs regulations, and even if that meant they could be treated like pirates, which they denied, it would still not have followed that their property could be taken from them.

There is in fact ample evidence that things owned by pirates were forfeited to the crown, while things taken by pirates remained the property of their victims.[464] In 1566 a Scottish vessel was captured at sea and the crew transferred to the 'pyrats schip'.[465] Later, when most of the pirates had gone ashore, the Scots 'gave it hazard and ovirthrew the saids pirats left in the ship, and cuttit thair cable, put up saill and brought the said ship away'. After arriving in Leith, the ship was recognised by a Frenchman as one previously taken from him by pirates. Although the Scots had lost their own ship and bravely recovered another from the pirates, they were ordered by the lords of session to give the French owner the ship that still belonged to him. Something similar happened in 1574, when English vessels were driven by contrary winds into Montrose, bringing with them two Dutch vessels they had captured.[466] Shortly afterwards a Scottish ship, sailing from Danzig to Leith, was driven by the same winds into the same port. It had on board Dutch mariners who had been found drifting at sea in a boat, and who recognised in the harbour the vessels from which they had been ejected. The captors were eventually executed as pirates and left 'to hang in chaynes to the example of others'. The ships taken by them were restored to their Dutch owners, although it was pointed out that the property of convicted pirates was subject to confiscation, or more precisely that it became the property of the earl of Morton, 'as admirall of this realme, be vertew of his office'.[467] The commission granted to Morton by the crown in 1568 had mentioned *eschaetae* customarily attached to the office of admiral, which he understood to include the forfeiture of ships and goods owned by pirates, though to some extent at least this may have been an innovation.[468] In 1578, after hearing that a 'pyrat hes sauld his schip and past to Flanders to serve

464 *Calendar of State Papers Relating to Scotland*, vol. 7, pp. 516–17, vol. 8, pp. 50–1, and vol. 9, pp. 546–7; *Registrum secreti sigilli regum Scotorum*, vol. 8, p. 404; NRS, GD149/265, pt 1, ff. 7v-8r.

465 *Practiques of Sir Richard Maitland*, p. 177; NLS, Adv. MS 31.2.2(1), ff. 65v-6r. No trace of this case could be found in the register of acts and decreets.

466 *Calendar of State Papers Relating to Scotland*, vol. 4, p. 682, vol. 5, pp. 5–10, 14–15 and 24–6; *Register of the Privy Council of Scotland*, vol. 2, pp. 377–8, 404–5 and 428–9.

467 What exactly Morton thought he was entitled to is unclear. *Cf.* ACA, CA1/1/32, pp. 513–15.

468 *Registrum secreti sigilli regum Scotorum*, vol. 6, p. 21; NRS, GD150/464 and 2278.

in the weris', Morton told one of his officers to arrest the ship, remarking that 'in respect she is a pyrattis schip, bocht fra a pyrat, na doubt she is lauchfull prise and aucht to appertene unto us as admirall'.[469] Although it may normally have been considered necessary for pirates to be convicted before their ships or goods were forfeited, it was accepted in the final decades of the sixteenth century that the admiral should have at least part of their property.[470] The commission granted to the earl of Bothwell in 1587 confirmed his entitlement as admiral to a part of *piraticae naves et bona*, carefully distinguishing these things from *bona iustorum mercatorum a piratis intercepta*, which he was to restore to any *proprietarius* who claimed them within a year, after which he could put them to his own use (*propriis usibus applicare*).[471] A few years later, when it was proposed that victims of piracy should be encouraged to mount expeditions to pursue their assailants by promises that 'they might reteine and kepe to their owne uses so muche of the goodes to be founde in the pirates shipps as should amount to the value of their goodes taken by the pyrates', the plan failed because Bothwell refused to give up 'any part of the duetie belonging to him'.[472]

As was indicated earlier, mounting expeditions in pursuit of pirates was not a novel practice in the 1590s, although how they were organised does seem to have changed. In 1566 the queen licensed an experienced captain 'to reik furth and addres to the sey a weirschip or schippis with men of weir, marinaris and all necessaris, and to serche, seik, apprehend and tak all and sindrie pirattis, sey thevis, rubbaris, pilliaris, rebellis and malefactouris upoun the seyis'.[473] Those taken were to be brought before the justiciary court 'to be punist for thair demeirittis with all rigoure, in exempill of utheris', and at this stage it remained possible to promise the mariners 'the eschete of all guidis, geir, schippis and uthiris quhatsumevir pertening to the saids pirattis'. Rather

469 *Scottish Correspondence of Mary of Lorraine*, pp. 445–6.

470 *Registrum secreti sigilli regum Scotorum*, vol. 8, p. 79, though *cf.* p. 404. It is important to remember that there was a period of uncertainty after Morton lost office as admiral in 1581.

471 *Registrum magni sigilli regum Scotorum*, vol. 5, pp. 449–50. The last phrase seems to have signified something other than the acquisition of title.

472 *Calendar of State Papers Relating to Scotland*, vol. 10, pp. 328 and 330–1. It appears to have been imagined in 1589, when a master was commissioned by certain burgh authorities to sail in search of pirates, that he would be entitled to any property he seized from them (NRS, CS7/115, ff. 46v-7 and 374v-5).

473 *Registrum secreti sigilli regum Scotorum*, vol. 5(2), pp. 202–4; *Register of the Privy Council of Scotland*, vol. 1, pp. 481–2 and 544–5. The indefinite article before 'weirschip' has been added here.

surprisingly, the mariners were also promised that if any of the pirates were killed or injured in their capture, the mariners would 'incur na danger nor skaith thairfore in thair personis nor guidis, or be callit or accusit thairfore criminalie nor civilie'. A similar promise 'to releif and keip thame skaithles' was made in another licence granted in the following year, though it was in the same year that a mariner accused of taking a ship at sea claimed that it had belonged to a pirate, and that he was therefore 'fugitive fra na law'.[474] If pirates could in any case be attacked with impunity, the effect of the queen's promise would merely have been to offer additional reassurance. No such reassurance had been included in a licence granted in 1550, and at that time it had not even been considered necessary for mariners to obtain licences before sailing in pursuit of pirates.[475] A different view was being taken by the end of the 1570s, however, when victims of piracy petitioned the king 'to be licensed, or at the least overlooked, in seeking their redress'.[476] It then became normal for victims who wished to pursue pirates to 'obtene his graces power and authoritie to this effect'.[477] The pirates pursued in the closing decades of the century usually came from England, and there was evidently some concern that the king's delicate relations with the English queen should not be undermined, but there also seems to have been a growing sense that the apprehension of pirates was the king's responsibility.[478]

It has recently been suggested that the efforts made to apprehend pirates in the later sixteenth century should be viewed as a continuation of the earlier licensing of private ships to sail against the king's enemies.[479] The reason for James VI's failure to rebuild the impressive navy constructed by his

474 *Register of the Privy Council of Scotland*, vol. 1, pp. 517–18 and 544–6; *Shetland Documents*, vol. 1, pp. 249–50.

475 *Register of the Privy Council of Scotland*, vol. 1, p. 104; *Extracts from the Records of the Burgh of Edinburgh*, vol. 2, pp. 95 and 219.

476 *Calendar of State Papers Relating to Scotland*, vol. 5, p. 462; *Extracts from the Records of the Burgh of Edinburgh*, vol. 4, pp. 77–8.

477 *Register of the Privy Council of Scotland*, vol. 4, pp. 9–10; *Extracts from the Records of the Burgh of Edinburgh*, vol. 4, pp. 427–9, 494 and 500–1; *Calendar of State Papers Relating to Scotland*, vol. 7, p. 679. See too the *Autobiography and Diary of Mr James Melvill*, pp. 257–9, and *cf.* AA, B6/11/2, ff. 68v and 70v-1r.

478 *Calendar of State Papers Relating to Scotland*, vol. 5, p. 26; *Extracts from the Council Register of the Burgh of Aberdeen*, vol. 2, pp. 60–1; *Extracts from the Records of the Burgh of Edinburgh*, 2nd ser., vol. 1, p. 21; *Ayr Burgh Accounts*, p. 165; ACA, CA1/1/32, p. 298; ECA, SL1/1/9, p. 94. When a commission was granted to sail against a Danish pirate in 1580, it did not promise an indemnity from prosecution (*Register of the Privy Council of Scotland*, vol. 3, p. 255; *Shetland Documents*, vol. 1, pp. 246–7).

479 Grant 2014.

great-grandfather, it is maintained, was not the unwonted peace preserved with England during his reign, as was previously suggested, but rather the preference of all sixteenth-century monarchs after James IV for the services of licensed 'privateers'.[480] There are two problems with this thesis, or two reasons why the previous suggestion remains more plausible. The first problem is that the thesis rests partly on an assumption that pirates were regarded as a kind of enemy. From the evidence assembled here it seems that the Scots adhered to the traditional distinction between pirates and enemies. Pirates were not able to acquire title to the ships and goods they seized, nor were others who seized ships and goods belonging to pirates able to acquire title to them by *occupatio*. Moreover, when the expectation emerged that expeditions in pursuit of pirates would be licensed by the king, it was at the expense of the commonly held belief that pirates were like enemies in being open to attack without fear of civil or criminal liability for the use of force. Indeed, the other problem with the recent thesis is that it rests on the assumption that 'privateers' were employed in the sixteenth century by rulers who issued them with 'letters of marque' as opposed to the 'letters of reprisal' issued in peacetime.[481] None of the evidence cited in support of the thesis shows that letters of marque were ever issued to mariners in wartime, nor has any evidence been found to show that prize acquisition in wartime depended on possession of a licence of any kind.[482] The expressions 'letters of marque' and 'letters of reprisal' were invariably used in sixteenth-century Scotland to signify the licences that did form an essential precondition of the lawful execution of reprisals in peacetime. Ships and goods seized in reprisal for unredressed losses could only be acquired if a licence was obtained before the seizure and if a court decision was obtained afterwards, neither of which was a requirement of prize acquisition in wartime. In the sixteenth century, it may be concluded, the traditional distinctions between licit plunder, licensed reprisal, lawful vengeance and criminal piracy were still being observed in Scotland.[483]

480 The previous suggestion is attributed particularly to Dawson 2007, p. 345. On James IV's navy see Macdougall 1997, pp. 223–46.

481 This notion seems to have been imbibed uncritically from Murdoch 2010.

482 This point will be returned to in the third chapter.

483 The licensing of expeditions against pirates will also be considered further in the third chapter.

CHAPTER 2

From Licit Plunder towards Licensed Privateering

In 1975 Michel Mollat published a hugely influential essay entitled 'De la piraterie sauvage à la course réglementée'.[1] In the fourteenth and fifteenth centuries, it was maintained, unrestrained piracy, an endemic feature of maritime commerce, gradually came to be distinguished from legalised raiding. It became normal for peace treaties to commit their signatories to the suppression of piracy and the regulation of reprisals. Once orderly reprisals under letters of marque were well established, rulers began to authorise seizures of ships and goods in wartime by granting licences to mariners and regulating their exercise. By the beginning of the sixteenth century it was recognised, at least in theory, that seizures of ships and goods at sea were lawful if authorised by sovereign rulers but were otherwise unlawful acts of piracy. The crucial distinction, as many historians have accepted, was thus between authorised seizures, whether made in peacetime or wartime, and those made without any authorisation, which were to be punished as crimes.[2] Although some historians have emphasised the continuing divergence of practice from theory, and although it is known that rulers had been licensing seizures of ships and goods in wartime well before the fourteenth century, it is this understanding of legal theory that lies behind the willingness of many historians to apply the term 'privateering' to activities engaged in long before the term itself came into use.[3] An obvious problem, however, is that little attention has been paid by Mollat and his followers to the legal theory on which reliance had actually been placed throughout Europe before the sixteenth century. As was seen in the previous chapter, in the theory of the medieval law schools, the seizure of prizes in wartime had not been justified in the same way as the taking of reprisals in peacetime, nor had a distinction emerged only gradually between lawful prize taking and unlawful piracy. By declaring wars on each other, sovereign rulers had created conditions in which the plundering of enemy ships and goods was considered licit, regardless of any further authorisation the rulers provided. Consequently,

1 The version published in conference proceedings in the following year is referred to here.

2 Appleby 1992, p. 90; Thomson 1994, p. 22; Anderson 1998, pp. 29–30; Sayers 2002, p. 157; Urban 2006, p. 189; Starkey 2011, p. 130; Pitcaithly 2012, p. 125; Rose 2013, pp. 140–1; Kaiser and Calafat 2014, p. 72.

3 Stark 1897, pp. 51–2; Russon 2004, p. 299; Heebøll-Holm 2013, pp. 10–11; Sumption 2015, pp. 89–90.

 | DOI:10.1163/9789004541412_004

the problem is not to explain how the licentiousness of piracy gave way to the licensing of privateering, but is to explain how one form of legitimate prize taking came to be replaced by another. For reasons that will become clear in the next chapter, attention is focused for the time being on how the theory and practice of prize taking started to change in England during the sixteenth century. Attempts to regulate maritime warfare there before the reign of Elizabeth are first considered, to see whether the Mollat thesis may be applicable after all. Changes in practice in the closing decades of the sixteenth century are then examined, followed by changes in theory during the same period, and in this connection some attention is also paid to developments in Spain, France and the Netherlands. The Mollat thesis is returned to in the final section in connection with possible changes in the understanding of piracy.

1 Regulation of Maritime Warfare in England

In the previous chapter the regulation of maritime warfare in sixteenth-century Scotland was taken to illustrate the relationship between the general theory expounded in the law schools and the particular rules applied in local jurisdictions. It was seen that the university doctors tended to expound broad principles, leaving the detail of the law to be worked out elsewhere, while the tendency in the localities was to identify detailed rules, taking for granted the basic principles taught by the doctors. This division of labour would have made sense to lawyers educated in the universities, for they were taught to solve legal problems by moving from the particular to the general, though construing the particular in the light of the general.[4] In relation to prize taking this meant looking first at any agreement the parties to a dispute had entered into, then at any rules laid down for the particular war in which prizes had been taken, and then at any rules established to govern prize taking whenever it occurred, with each agreement and rule interpreted as an attempt to give effect to the general principles of prize acquisition accepted throughout Europe. An early example of an agreement designed to govern prize acquisition in England survives from 1295, when it was endorsed by the king and entered in his records.[5] In order to avoid quarrels at a later stage, the masters and mariners of ships preparing to depart from Bayonne had agreed that they would receive equal shares of any ships and goods they captured, except that if any of them were to be injured

4 Canning 1987, pp. 149–50; Bellomo 1995, pp. 190–5; Stein 1999, pp. 71–4.

5 *Calendar of the Patent Rolls*, 1292–1301, p. 130; *Documents Relating to Law and Custom of the Sea*, vol. 1, pp. 36–8.

or to lose a weapon in the course of an assault, they would be compensated before shares were distributed. In endorsing this agreement, the king evidently shared with its makers the assumption that ships and goods seized at sea would become their property. At other times kings took the initiative in laying down rules, for instance when assembling fleets from their own ships, from ships certain ports were bound to supply and from others they requisitioned.[6] In 1326, for instance, mariners were advised that they might retain the whole of any ships or goods they were able to acquire (*conquirere et occupare*) from the king's enemies, but were reminded that they must refrain from attacking his friends and allies.[7] On other occasions mariners were similarly encouraged to sail against the king's enemies with promises that they would not be required to share their prizes with him.[8] In 1353 mariners were instructed that if they found aboard enemy ships goods belonging to subjects of kings with whom the English king was at peace or had made a truce, the goods were to be brought back and kept safe until their owners could claim their restitution.[9]

It is at about this time that the king and his council are believed to have produced two sets of more general rules, which were incorporated in the 1420s into a handbook known as the 'Black Book of the Admiralty'.[10] The first set dealt with the responsibilities of admirals, the organisation of fleets, the payment of mariners and the distribution of prizes. One article was concerned with prizes taken by mariners 'under the king's pay', of which the king was to receive a quarter, the owners of the ships used in the seizures another quarter, and the crews of the ships the remaining half, divided among them in equal shares.[11] This rule was qualified in two ways. In the first place, the admiral of the fleet was to receive a share along with the crew members, and two shares if he was actually involved in a seizure. In the second place, other ships in the fleet were to be entitled to participate in the distribution if they had been involved in the

6 Brooks 1933, pp. 159–95; Murray 1935, pp. 2–4 and 205–17; Rose 2013, pp. 43–63.

7 *Foedera, conventiones, litterae et cuiuscunque generis acta publica*, vol. 4, pp. 226–7; *Documents Relating to Law and Custom of the Sea*, vol. 1, pp. 62–4. The earliest known articles of war issued to a fleet do not contain any provisions on prize acquisition (Benedict of Peterborough, *Chronicle of the Reigns of Henry II and Richard I*, vol. 2, pp. 110–11; *Chronica Magistri Rogeri de Hovedene*, vol. 3, p. 36), but it seems likely that others would have contained provisions like those in the articles issued to the French fleet before the battle of Sluys in 1340 (Adam Murimuth, *Continuatio chronicarum*, pp. 257–63).

8 *Calendar of the Close Rolls*, 1237–42, p. 467, and 1399–1402, pp. 168–9; *Rotuli Scotiae*, vol. 1, p. 154; *Fifth Report of the Royal Commission on Historical Manuscripts*, app., p. 501.

9 *Foedera, conventiones, litterae et cuiuscunque generis acta publica*, vol. 5, p. 719; *Documents Relating to Law and Custom of the Sea*, vol. 1, pp. 78–80.

10 Sanborn 1930, pp. 288–92; Cushway 2011, pp. 31–2; Rose 2013, pp. 116 and 149–50.

11 *Black Book of the Admiralty*, vol. 1, pp. 20–3.

seizure, even if only to the extent of sailing nearby. A different article was concerned with prizes taken by mariners 'out of the king's pay'.[12] When the takers were not in the king's service, he claimed no part of the prizes for himself, but the admiral he appointed was to receive a share or shares in the same way as if the mariners had been employed by the king. To some degree at least, these rules appear to have been a restatement of customary norms. As early as 1205 it had been declared that mariners in the king's pay would be entitled to retain half the gain they might make for themselves from his enemies (*medietatem lucri sui quod facient super inimicos nostros*), while in 1294 it had been declared that other mariners would be entitled to retain all the goods they were able to acquire for themselves (*omnia bona que sibi per se adquirere poterunt*).[13] In the later declaration – as in some of the declarations mentioned in the preceding paragraph – there was no indication that the mariners were to be remunerated by the king, though it could instead be that his employees were being offered an exceptionally generous inducement. There was no indication either that the admiral was to have an interest, perhaps because the mariners were not expected to join a royal fleet, but probably because admirals were not assigned shares until a slightly later stage, when they were also assigned a role in prize distribution.[14] What is abundantly clear is that provision was being made for the redistribution of ships and goods of which mariners were understood to have acquired ownership already by capturing them from the king's enemies.

The second set of rules produced around the middle of the fourteenth century dealt with the operation of fleets assembled under the command of the king's admirals.[15] One article provided that mariners who captured an enemy ship could keep for themselves any weapons or goods they found above the ship's hatches, in accordance with 'les aunciennes coustumes et usages de mer'.[16] Another article provided that the ship and all the other goods it contained were to be brought before the admiral so that the mariners might receive

12 *Black Book of the Admiralty*, vol. 1, pp. 22–3. Although the word 'privateers' is used in the translation provided here, it was clearly a much later insertion into an older text (*cf.* BL, Add. MS 29439, f. 164v, and Nicolas 1847, vol. 2, p. 488).

13 *Documents Relating to Law and Custom of the Sea*, vol. 1, pp. 1–2 and 35–6.

14 Separate provision was made in the 1294 declaration for seizures that happened to be made in company with ships under the command of by the barons of the Cinque Ports. It was only at the end of the thirteenth century that references to admirals began to appear in English sources, though references were previously made to *custodes maris* (Mears 1908, pp. 312–15; Fulton 1911, pp. 31–2; Sanborn 1930, pp. 278–80).

15 The early admirals were 'primarily fleet commanders', and the practice developed of appointing several to patrol separate stretches of the coast (Marsden 1907, p. 468).

16 *Black Book of the Admiralty*, vol. 1, pp. 30–3.

'ce que la loy de mer veult et demande'.[17] If mariners made off with a prize without the admiral's leave, they would be liable to pay him twice its value. Two other articles provided for situations in which it was uncertain whether a lawful prize had been taken.[18] One required mariners to bring any friendly vessel suspected of carrying enemy goods before the admiral, who would examine the officers and either send them on their way as 'loyaulx marchants et amys', or have them 'pris avec leurs biens et raensonnez, comme la loy de mer veult et demande'. Obviously, this could not happen unless English mariners were able to board foreign vessels without knowing that they belonged to, or were trading with, the king's enemies. The other article provided that if mariners encountered vessels that resisted inspection, it was lawful for them to treat the vessels as enemies (*bien lise a noz gentz les autres comme ennemys*), so long as they brought them before the admiral, 'sans eulx piller ou endommager', to have it confirmed that they were just prizes.[19] Most of these articles thus provided for the supervision of prize taking by an admiral, at least where the ships involved in seizures formed part of a fleet over which he had been put in command. The admiral's responsibility was to confirm that ships and goods had been seized in accordance with the law of the sea, and to ensure that those entitled to shares received what was due to them. Nothing in the language used suggests (as has sometimes been supposed) that prize acquisition was understood to depend on the making of judicial decisions or on formal acts of adjudication.[20] The admiral's role was simply to supervise the acquisition of prizes through acts of occupation carried out by mariners at sea and through the redistribution of their takings on land.

Another source incorporated into the 'Black Book of the Admiralty' also contained a few provisions relating to prize taking. The 'Inquisition of Queenborough' was established in 1375 to answer questions about the customary law recognised in maritime communities.[21] In the first answer the jurors gave it was stated that if a merchant ship took the opportunity to capture an enemy vessel during a voyage, 'the ship shall have two parts or shares thereof,

17 *Black Book of the Admiralty*, vol. 1, pp. 30–1. What the law of the sea provided had of course been spelled out in the first set of rules.

18 *Black Book of the Admiralty*, vol. 1, pp. 28–31.

19 That seizures of vessels resisting inspection was legitimate *iuxta legem maritimam* had been asserted in a letter sent to the king of Aragon in 1343 (*Foedera, conventiones, litterae et cuiuscunque generis acta publica*, vol. 5, pp. 376–7).

20 Marsden 1909, p. 682, and Roscoe 1924, p. 8, maintain that adjudication emerged as a requirement in the fifteenth century (itself a dubious claim, as will be seen), but they also refer for support to these articles.

21 Burwash 1947, pp. 46–7; Ward 2009, p. 23; Cushway 2011, pp. 211–12.

and the mariners the third part for their paines taken in that behalfe'.[22] This was consistent with the rule laid down earlier for seizures made by mariners 'out of the king's pay', which had not itself provided for the redistribution of prizes between shipowners and the crews they employed. It was less consistent with the further statement in the inquest's return that when prizes were taken in the admiral's absence, he was to receive his share before the remainder was divided into two parts, 'the one halfe to the ship and victualls, and the other halfe to the master, the marriners and the takers thereof'.[23] Perhaps the concern here was with captures made by ships forming part of a royal fleet, as opposed to merchant ships sailing in the ordinary course of trade, or perhaps the rule was being altered. This statement was not presented in the form of an answer to a question but as an order (*ordonne estoit*), which the king and his council were asked to impose on dissenting mariners. Some years later the same inquest was asked to report the names of 'all those who have taken upon the sea ships, goods or prisoners and have not paid to the admirall the shares due to him by his office'.[24] By the end of the fourteenth century the admiral appears to have been entitled to a share in every prize taken, which was probably expected to compensate him for the expense he incurred in supervising the acquisition and redistribution of prizes. Not surprisingly, evidence survives from the thirteenth and fourteenth centuries of efforts being made by kings to secure their portions of prizes taken by mariners in their employment.[25] Evidence also survives of grants made to deserving persons out of the king's share of goods and merchandise captured at sea from his enemies.[26] While this has often been taken to show that prize acquisition was understood to be dependent on grants from the crown, the reality is that kings were sometimes able to make grants because they had received shares in prizes acquired through the occupation of enemy property by their subjects.[27]

22 *Black Book of the Admiralty*, vol. 1, pp. 134–5; *Collection de lois maritimes*, vol. 4, p. 207.

23 *Black Book of the Admiralty*, vol. 1, pp. 144–7; *Collection de lois maritimes*, vol. 4, p. 209.

24 *Black Book of the Admiralty*, vol. 1, pp. 150–1.

25 *Calendar of the Close Rolls*, 1216–25, p. 88, 1237–42, pp. 504–5, and 1264–68, pp. 40–1; *Calendar of the Patent Rolls*, 1323–27, pp. 412–13, and 1385–89, p. 253; *Foedera, conventiones, litterae et cuiuscunque generis acta publica*, vol. 7, pp. 29–30; *Documents Relating to Law and Custom of the Sea*, vol. 1, pp. 5–6 and 8–10.

26 *Calendar of the Close Rolls*, 1247–51, p. 459, and 1253–54, p. 88; *Calendar of the Patent Rolls*, 1242–47, p. 73, 1337–39, pp. 88 and 228, and 1385–89, pp. 216, 302, 308, 338 and 364. See too Moore 2012.

27 Nicolas 1847, vol. 1, p. 140; Marsden 1909, p. 675; Holdsworth 1922–66, vol. 1, p. 562; Roscoe 1924, pp. 8–9; Fermoy 1926, pp. 556–7; Schwarzenberger 1948, p. 81; Kemp 1976, p. 670.

When the victims of seizures wished to raise objections they petitioned the king's council, which would either deal with the matter directly or refer it to the chancellor, who might then instruct someone else to conduct an investigation.[28] In 1293 a judge was appointed to hear a complaint from Iberian merchants about the capture and spoliation of a ship from Spain.[29] The captors claimed that plundering the ship had been perfectly legal, given that the king of England was at war with the king of Castile (*licuit eis lucrari super inimicos domini regis manifestos*). The captors were permitted to retain all the goods that had belonged to Spanish merchants but not those belonging to Portuguese merchants, since they were not the English king's enemies (*nunquam fuerunt inimici*). A few years later it was similarly decided that the captors of a ship could retain any goods found on board that had belonged to Spanish merchants but must return those belonging to Flemish merchants, as they were friends of England and had not lost title to their property.[30] Here, as in another case, testimony was received from a friendly ruler that some of those despoiled were his subjects.[31] In 1346 a ship from Spain was taken with a cargo of wine from Normandy.[32] As England was then at peace with Spain but at war with Normandy, the captors were allowed to keep the wine but had to return the ship and pay its master the fee he was due for its transportation.[33] Ten years later the council received a complaint from the king of Portugal about goods taken at sea from his subjects by a French vessel and subsequently taken from the French vessel by English mariners, who refused to return them to the Portuguese merchants.[34] The matter had already been considered by the admiral, who had decided that the goods could be retained by the English mariners since their king was at war with the French king. The council accepted the reasoning that the goods had belonged to enemies of their king at the time of the seizure (*in vera proprietate et possessione inimicorum nostrorum*), and that they had therefore been acquired by the English mariners when they took

28 Holdsworth 1922–66, vol. 1, pp. 530–5; Murray 1935, pp. 120–3; Gardiner 1976, pp. xi–xiv.

29 *Documents Relating to Law and Custom of the Sea*, vol. 1, pp. 12–18.

30 *Calendar of the Close Rolls*, 1296–1302, pp. 33–4; *Documents Relating to Law and Custom of the Sea*, vol. 1, pp. 42–4. See too *Select Cases Concerning the Law Merchant*, vol. 2, pp. XCIII–IV.

31 *Calendar of the Close Rolls*, 1337–39, pp. 229–30.

32 *Documents Relating to Law and Custom of the Sea*, vol. 1, pp. 75–7.

33 Whether consciously or not, the decision was made in accordance with a provision in the *Consolato del mare*, a code originating in Spain (*Collection de lois maritimes*, vol. 2, p. 304; *Consulate of the Sea*, p. 192).

34 *Foedera, conventiones, litterae et cuiuscunque generis acta publica*, vol. 6, pp. 14–15; *Documents Relating to Law and Custom of the Sea*, vol. 1, pp. 81–4.

possession of them in wartime (*per gentes nostras de bona guerra et licita fuerant acquisita*). That the English mariners were understood to have acquired the goods through occupation of enemy property was thus made clear. The weakness in the reasoning, which presumably prompted the Portuguese protest, was the bland assumption that ownership of the goods had previously passed to the French mariners. How exactly this was supposed to have happened was not explained.[35]

Although the admiral may have delivered his decision in this case in fulfilment of the supervisory function assigned to him in the rules laid down by the king in council at about the same time, the decision has been regarded as the earliest surviving evidence of the operation of admiralty courts, which certainly were in existence in the later fourteenth century.[36] In 1361 an admiralty court purported to apply the 'ley marine' in ordering the restitution of goods taken during a period of truce.[37] Regular records do not survive from this period, and it is impossible to know how active the admiralty courts were, but it is certain that other courts continued to hear prize cases at this stage. In 1375 the council ruled that while enemy goods found aboard a vessel taken at sea should be left with the takers who had acquired them (*illis ad quos pertinent*), the friendly ship itself and friendly goods it was carrying should be restored to the master, who was also to receive the freight payments due on the enemy goods.[38] Three years later it was decided that captors should not only pay the freight on enemy goods taken from a friendly ship but should also reimburse its master for the expense he incurred in raising a complaint before the council.[39] In 1385 the council dealt with a complaint concerning the capture of an English vessel by French mariners who were transporting Genoese goods.[40]

35 There may have been awareness that the king of Portugal, like the king of England, was at the time supporting the king of Castile in his war against the king of Aragon, and that the king of Aragon was supported by the king of France, from which it may have been surmised that the king of Portugal was at war with the king of France. Alternatively, it may have been found convenient to rely on the presumption that goods belonged to the parties in possession. For the strength of this presumption among English common lawyers in the fourteenth century see Seipp 1994, pp. 54–7. The Portuguese merchants were advised to pursue their complaint in France.

36 Marsden 1909, pp. 680–1; Holdsworth 1922–66, vol. 1, pp. 544–6; Sanborn 1930, pp. 282–4; Prichard and Yale 1993, p. xxx; Ward 2009, p. 34. See now Heebøll-Holm 2018, though *cf.* Cremean 2012.

37 'Early Admiralty Case, A.D. 1361', pp. 2–5.

38 *Documents Relating to Law and Custom of the Sea*, vol. 1, pp. 102–4. This decision was of course consistent with the one delivered in 1346, mentioned at n. 32 above.

39 *Documents Relating to Law and Custom of the Sea*, vol. 1, pp. 106–7.

40 *Calendar of the Close Rolls*, 1385–89, pp. 92–3.

As England was at war with France, the legitimacy of the seizure was not in question, but it was argued that the friendly merchant who had chartered the French ship should have forbidden the assault, instead of which he had actually provided assistance, in exchange for a share of the goods taken.[41] Justices appointed to hear the case persuaded the Genoese merchant to pay compensation to the English owners. Two years later another litigant from Genoa was able to recover a ship taken at sea when he proved that it was his property.[42] The crucial question here and elsewhere was whether the ships and goods taken had belonged to friends or enemies, as was spelled out by the council again in 1413, when vessels were taken during a period of truce with Flanders.[43] In the same year the council recognised that prize cases ought to be dealt with in admiralty courts, although a few months later, when it heard about several cases involving the admiral himself, it instructed someone else to determine to whom the ships and goods in question belonged (*occasione captionis et alio modo pertinent*).[44]

None of the judicial records that are known to have survived take the form of acts of adjudication, nor do any support the hypothesis that prize acquisition was dependent on grants from the crown, and nor do they ever indicate that the legitimacy of seizures was reckoned to depend on possession of a licence.[45] Nevertheless, evidence does exist that mariners were sometimes licensed to raid enemy shipping in wartime.[46] In 1242 the king granted a licence (*licentiam dedimus*) to mariners of Bayonne to annoy (*gravare*) the king of France and his subjects, with the proviso that they must not harm anyone at peace with the king of England or in possession of a letter of safe conduct issued by him.[47] In the same year other mariners were licensed to annoy the French, provided they shared half of any prizes taken with the king.[48] No mention was made

41 Reference was apparently made to 'the law of Oleroun', though it is far from clear what provision of that code, in any of its known forms, the plaintiffs could have had in mind.

42 *Calendar of the Patent Rolls*, 1385–89, p. 342.

43 *Calendar of the Close Rolls*, 1409–13, p. 376. See too Johnson 2015, pp. 420–1.

44 *Calendar of the Close Rolls*, 1413–19, p. 19; *Documents Relating to Law and Custom of the Sea*, vol. 1, pp. 124–6.

45 This last point is forcefully made in Dick 2010, pp. 25–7 and 85–6, in the course of an exceptionally accurate and perceptive review of the evidence.

46 These licences differed in form from the letters of reprisal or marque issued in peacetime, of which examples may be found in *Foedera, conventiones, litterae et cuiuscunque generis acta publica*, vol. 8, pp. 606–8 and 773, and vol. 9, pp. 125–6; *Documents Relating to Law and Custom of the Sea*, vol. 1, pp. 38–41 and 119–21; *Black Book of the Admiralty*, pp. 385–90.

47 *Foedera, conventiones, litterae et cuiuscunque generis acta publica*, vol. 1, p. 408.

48 *Calendar of the Patent Rolls*, 1232–47, pp. 328–9 and 362 (*cf.* Nicolas 1847, vol. 1, p. 239, and Stark 1897, p. 51).

of payment for their services, but it seems likely that these documents were a reminder of the obligations imposed on mariners 'under the king's pay'. In 1387 mariners were licensed to provide protection for merchant vessels, with the promise that they would be permitted to retain the whole of any prizes they took from the king's French and Scottish enemies.[49] More elaborate licences granted in the early 1400s provided that ships should be put to sea against the king's enemies, that crews could be pressed into service, that assistance should be given by royal officials, that friends and allies must not be harmed, and that either the admiral must receive his share or the captors be allowed to retain everything they were able to take (*lucrari, habere vel conqueri possint*).[50] At no point, however, did any of these documents state that the king was authorising mariners to acquire ships and goods seized from his enemies, or promise that he would make grants of ships and goods to those who seized them. The licences were designed to reinforce or modify the rules governing prize taking. They did not create the conditions in which prize acquisition was understood to occur. In contrast, when a licence was granted in 1386 to mariners from the Netherlands who had sustained losses at the hands of the king's enemies, they were explicitly authorised to seize enemy ships and goods and bring them back to England for sale.[51] Their own ruler was not at war, and these mariners were only able to prey on the king of England's enemies by being licensed to sail against them on his behalf.[52]

Significant changes were made to the regulation of maritime warfare by the 'Statute of Truces' passed by the king in parliament in 1414.[53] Aware that many people had been slain, robbed and spoiled at sea in breach of truces he or his father had made with other rulers, or contrary to letters of safe conduct they had granted to foreigners, Henry V declared that in future such actions would be taken to amount to high treason.[54] A conservator of truces and safe conducts was to be appointed in every port, with authority delegated from the admiral to investigate breaches and to hear complaints, accompanied by 'two men learned in the law'. Before any ship left port, its master (and also its owner

49 *Calendar of the Patent Rolls*, 1385–89, pp. 339 and 342.

50 *Documents Relating to Law and Custom of the Sea*, vol. 1, pp. 111–15; *Black Book of the Admiralty*, vol. 1, pp. 355–7; *Calendar of the Patent Rolls*, 1401–05, pp. 298 and 485.

51 *Documents Relating to Law and Custom of the Sea*, vol. 1, pp. 109–10.

52 Although historians sometimes refer to licences like those mentioned in this paragraph as 'letters of marque' or 'letters of reprisal', there is no evidence that they were ever labelled in this way at the time they were issued.

53 Kingsford 1925, p. 79; Gardiner 1976, pp. xiv–xv; Allmand 1992, pp. 329–31; Heebøll-Holm 2019, pp. 51–3.

54 *Statutes of the Realm*, vol. 2, pp. 178–81; *Black Book of the Admiralty*, vol. 1, pp. 414–19.

if present) was to appear before the conservator and swear an oath that he would not attempt anything contrary to a truce or safe conduct. The conservator was to maintain a record of all the voyages made from his port, noting the names of the ships, their masters and owners, and also the size of each crew. If mariners took anything during a voyage from the king's enemies or anyone else, they were required to bring it back to the same port and to inform the conservator before any attempt was made to sell or otherwise dispose of the takings, though it was accepted that rough seas, enemy action or something of the sort might at times force prizes to be brought to other ports, where notice would have to be given to different conservators. If a ship were to sail without an oath being made, or a prize to be disposed of without a report being made, the master or owner who should have sworn the oath was to be imprisoned until he paid a fine, and the prize was to be forfeited to the king, along with the ship used in its capture.[55] The loss of the prize was clearly envisaged as a punishment inflicted on disobedient mariners who had acquired title to it without fulfilling the obligation imposed by the statute. The obligation was simply to 'make full information' to the conservator. There was no requirement that the conservator issue a judicial ruling on the legitimacy of the seizure, still less that he adjudge the prize to the mariners. The 'Statute of Truces' thus contributed to the regulation of maritime warfare but did not change the fundamental principles of prize acquisition.

The appointment of conservators was not especially significant, for they had been in existence since the early fourteenth century and were mentioned routinely in truces by the early fifteenth century.[56] More genuinely novel was the treatment of breaches of truces and safe conducts as treason. Like licences authorising foreigners to annoy a ruler's enemies, truces and safe conducts created exceptions to the ordinary application of the law of arms.[57] Wars would continue, and enemies would remain enemies, but to annoy them in breach of a ruler's truce or safe conduct would be to dishonour him and could therefore be considered treasonable. One purpose of the 'Statute of Truces' was

55 Further provisions dealt with the relationship between the admiral and the Cinque Ports, which remained independent of his jurisdiction and exercised a parallel jurisdiction of their own.

56 *Rotuli Scotiae*, vol. 1, p. 397; *Foedera, conventiones, litterae et cuiuscunque generis acta publica*, vol. 8, pp. 213–14, 274–6, 282–3, 305–9, 620–3, 636–7, 641–9, 652, 659–60, 668–74, 680–1, 691–3, 710–11 and 765–6, and vol. 9, pp. 36–8, 56–60 and 114–15; Marsden 1894–7, vol. 1, p. LII.

57 As was pointed out in the last chapter, licences granted to foreigners could effectively turn their own ruler's friends into their enemies, whereas truces and safe conducts could effectively turn a ruler's enemies into his friends, albeit temporarily.

apparently to bring English law more fully into line with continental thinking on this subject.[58] Another was to secure order at sea, a particular concern of Henry V's, partly because his continental ambitions required the safe transportation of troops to France.[59] A related purpose was to uphold a series of truces lately entered into with Castile, Brittany and Burgundy, as well as France.[60] Although Henry had every intention of returning to war with France, it was a crucial component of his strategy to preserve peace with the French king's neighbours.[61] There may also have been an underlying concern with disorder on the Scottish borders, where breaches of truces and safe conducts were a regular occurrence.[62] As far as the provisions about prize taking were concerned, the statute appears to have been inspired especially by the truce concluded with the duke of Brittany on 3 January 1414.[63] This truce contained many standard clauses about not allowing ships belonging to the other party's enemies to shelter or dispose of prizes in ports, not obstructing the other party's subjects from bringing their ships and prizes into ports, and so on. But it also provided that no ships should be allowed to leave ports without undertaking to comply with the truce, and that any prizes taken should be brought home to the same ports, unless rough seas, enemy action or something of the sort made that impossible, on pain of forfeiture. These clauses were in turn reminiscent of legislation enacted in France in 1373, which had introduced the general requirements there that no one put to sea in an armed ship without promising good behaviour and obtaining permission from the admiral, and that prizes always be brought home for inspection.[64] A requirement that no

58 Keen 1965, p. 206; Bellamy 1970, pp. 128–9; Powell 1989, pp. 170–1.

59 Rodger 1997, pp. 143–5; Eddison 2013, pp. 143–4; Friel 2015, pp. 100–1. For more detail see Lambert 2017.

60 Harriss 1985, pp. 151–2; Powell 1989, pp. 201–4; Allmand 1992, pp. 67–9.

61 Vaughan 1966, pp. 205–6; Harriss 2005, pp. 540–1; Piette 2008, p. 53.

62 The point is well made in Neville 1991, although the significance of disorder on the borders is emphasised to the extent of making it seem that the primary purpose of the statute was to confront that problem.

63 *Foedera, conventiones, litterae et cuiuscunque generis acta publica*, vol. 9, pp. 80–5; *Corps universel diplomatique du droit des gens*, vol. 2(2), pp. 2–4; *Mémoires pour servir de preuves à l'histoire ecclésiastiques et civile de Bretagne*, vol. 2, cols 879–84; *Documents Relating to Law and Custom of the Sea*, vol. 1, pp. 127–30.

64 *Recueil général des anciennes lois françaises*, vol. 6, pp. 846–54; *Black Book of the Admiralty*, vol. 1, pp. 430–42. The 1373 edict was fundamental to the legislative tradition on maritime law touched on in the previous chapter (Stark 1897, pp. 91–2; Dumas 1908, p. 69; Verzijl, Heere and Offerhaus 1998, p. 44). On the inclusion of clauses similar to those in the 1414 truce in another made in 1411 with the duke of Brittany, who owed allegiance to the king of France, see Darsel 2012, p. 80.

one put to sea in an armed ship without first promising good behaviour was added to the truce already made with Castile on 12 February 1414.[65] When the 'Statute of Truces' was passed two months later it incorporated into English law, and thus made more broadly applicable, an approach to the regulation of maritime warfare that had not only been adopted in recent truces but had also been tried and tested elsewhere in Europe for over forty years.[66]

It is well known that English mariners believed nonetheless that they were being placed at a disadvantage in conflicts with mariners from other countries.[67] They complained that the sanctions threatened made it difficult for them to defend themselves against aggression, and warned that they were being discouraged from fitting out ships for the sea.[68] The statute was twice suspended, and its terms were adjusted during the next thirty years, but the new regime was reinforced at the beginning of the 1450s, subject to a softening of the threat of prosecution for treason.[69] As the recurrence of the complaints from mariners indicates, the regime was implemented to some extent, although the precise details of the legislation were not always followed. In 1417, for instance, it was ordered that no ships were to leave London without a licence from the admiral or his lieutenant.[70] Attention has often been drawn to a proclamation issued in 1426 in which the need to bring prizes home for inspection was emphasised.[71] The proclamation actually stated that goods were not to be removed from ships and sold until it was confirmed (*certifiez*) by the council, the chancellor, the admiral or his deputy that they had belonged to the king's enemies.[72] In 1437 mariners who had been licensed to put armed vessels to

65 *Foedera, conventiones, litterae et cuiuscunque generis acta publica*, vol. 9, p. 115.

66 English interest in developments in France is evident from BL, Add. MS 4598, ff. 201–2. The impression is given in *Documents Relating to Law and Custom of the Sea*, vol. 1, p. 116, that this document relates to an agreement between England and France, but it clearly relates to the treaty between France and Burgundy in *Foedera, conventiones, litterae et cuiuscunque generis acta publica*, vol. 8, pp. 548–9.

67 Kingsford 1925, pp. 80–1; Bellamy 1970, pp. 129–30; Allmand 1992, pp. 331–2.

68 *Rotuli parliamentorum*, vol. 4, pp. 67–8, 105, 351, 376–7, 448 and 492–3; *Parliament Rolls of Medieval England*, vol. 9, pp. 125–6 and 200–2, vol. 10, pp. 408 and 464, and vol. 11, pp. 132 and 188.

69 *Statutes of the Realm*, vol. 2, pp. 307–8, 315–17, 323–4, 358–9 and 363–4.

70 *Calendar of the Close Rolls*, 1413–19, pp. 340–1. On the admiralty in the fifteenth century see Sutton 2018.

71 Marsden 1909, p. 682; Runyan 1975, p. 105; Gardiner 1976, p. xvi.

72 *Calendar of the Close Rolls*, 1422–29, pp. 263–5; *Foedera, conventiones, litterae et cuiuscunque generis acta publica*, vol. 10, pp. 367–8. Friel 2015, p. 101, points out that there is no evidence that conservators discharged the responsibilities assigned to them, but the point is that the responsibilities were expected to be discharged by someone, and – to judge from the complaints – probably were being.

sea provided security that they would not plunder the king's friends or others to whom he had granted safe conducts.[73] In 1442 mariners undertook to bring prizes home for approval before they were divided up in accordance with an agreement they made before setting out.[74] In 1484 another royal proclamation required oaths to be sworn and security to be provided to the ordinary port authorities, warned that anyone who attacked a foreign vessel in breach of a treaty, truce or safe conduct would be punished as 'the kyngis rebell and traitour' and forfeit his belongings, and forbade the disposal of goods until the king or his admiral had certified their 'lawfull takyng'.[75] In 1498 a treaty entered into with France 'contra spolia maritima et pro depraedatoribus cohercendis' contained among its terms requirements that mariners swear oaths and provide security for their good behaviour to the admiral or port authorities, and forbade the disposal of goods taken at sea until the admiral or his deputies had declared them to be lawfully taken (*antequam admiraldus, viceadmiraldus aut eorum vicesgerentes declaraverint praedam et capturam iustas iusti et legitimi lucri esse*).[76] A judicial decision (*decretum*) was certainly envisaged here, not just administrative certification, but it was to take the form of a declaration that goods had been acquired, not an adjudicative act of court in the proper sense.

That the rules introduced in the fifteenth century were an addition to existing rules rather than a fundamental reworking of prize law was made clear at the beginning of the sixteenth century. When Henry VIII declared war on the French king in 1512, instructions were issued to his admiral in broadly similar terms to the rules laid down in the middle of the fourteenth century and recorded in the 'Black Book of the Admiralty' in the 1420s.[77] Provision was not made for the pillaging of weapons and goods found above a vessel's hatches, and the admiral was warned that he would have to account for any illicit plunder taken, but it was provided in the familiar way that mariners should 'receyve that the law woll and requireth', after bringing any prizes they captured before the admiral.[78] Mariners who made off with a prize without the admiral's leave would be forced 'to pay double the value of it, and of the goods so taken therin',

73 *Calendar of the Close Rolls*, 1435–41, pp. 122–3.

74 *Documents Relating to Law and Custom of the Sea*, vol. 1, pp. 130–1.

75 *Documents Relating to Law and Custom of the Sea*, vol. 1, pp. 136–8, and see too pp. 141–4, reproducing an undertaking by the authorities in Newcastle not to allow anyone to sail without providing security.

76 *Foedera, conventiones, litterae et cuiuscunque generis acta publica*, vol. 12, pp. 600–4; *Corps universel diplomatique du droit des gens*, vol. 3(2), pp. 401–2.

77 Mackie 1952, pp. 273–4; Wernham 1966, pp. 83–4; Richardson 2013, p. 16.

78 *Foedera, conventiones, litterae et cuiuscunque generis acta publica*, vol. 13, pp. 329–32. On pillage *cf.* BL, Harley MS 309, f. 13.

the assumption apparently being that the ship and goods would have become the property of the captors. Ships suspected of carrying enemy goods were also to be brought before the admiral, who was to send cargo owners on their way if found to be 'true marchauntys', but was to distribute goods appropriately if 'apperteyning to enemyes'. Ships resisting inspection could lawfully be seized, provided they were brought before the admiral 'without dispoylyng, rifelyng or enbeselyng of the goods, or doing harme to the parties'.[79] As the king would be paying the mariners' wages, he was to receive 'one half of all maner of gaynes and wynnyngs'.[80] When the war ended in 1518, a 'tractatus pro coercendis piratis' was entered into in terms similar to those agreed in 1498.[81] Before ships left harbour in either England or France, their owners and masters were to provide security to the admiral or his deputies that they would respect the peace restored between their rulers.[82] They were to swear to bring any prizes captured home for inspection, and were not to dispose of any goods until a ruling (*decretum*) was delivered confirming the legitimacy of the seizure. The requirement was again that the mariners should not transfer the title they had acquired to the goods to anyone else (*transferre, permutare, vendere vel alienare*) before the admiral or his deputy had declared the seizure to be lawful (*antequam admirallus, viceadmirallus aut eorum vicesgerentes declaraverint praedam et capturam iustas iusti et legitimi lucri esse*). If they did act precipitately they would be imprisoned and their goods would be confiscated, but any goods they had transferred would have ceased at that point to be theirs and would remain in the hands of those who had received them.

Five months after declaring war on France again in 1543, Henry VIII issued a famous proclamation encouraging mariners to annoy enemy shipping.[83] Advised that many of his subjects were 'very desirous to prepare and equipp sundry shipps and vessells att their owne costs and charges to the sea for the annoyaunce of his majesties enemies, the Frenchmen and the Scotts', he declared that they were 'att their liberties' to do so, retaining any enemy ships

79 The use of the word 'enbeselyng', and the description of the seized mariners as 'making rebellion, resistance or defence', suggests that the theory may have been revived that these ships and goods were forfeit to the crown.

80 *Foedera, conventiones, litterae et cuiuscunque generis acta publica*, vol. 13, pp. 326–9.

81 Gwyn 1990, pp. 94–5; Scarisbrick 1997, pp. 71–2; Fletcher 2009, pp. 59–60.

82 *Foedera, conventiones, litterae et cuiuscunque generis acta publica*, vol. 13, pp. 649–53; *Corps universel diplomatique du droit des gens*, vol. 4(1), pp. 280–2. Although this agreement was connected with the treaty of 'universal peace' brokered by Thomas Wolsey, the peace established was not so universal that legitimate prize taking became inconceivable.

83 Loades 1992, p. 125; Merriman 2000, p. 128; Potter 2011, p. 78.

and goods they captured for 'their owne proper use, profitt and commoditie'.[84] As incentives to action they were assured that they could put to sea 'without putting in of anie bonds of recognizance before the counsell, or in the court of the admiraltie, and without sueing forth of anie other licence', that they could seize prizes 'without making accompt in anie court or place of this realme', and that they could retain them 'without paying any parte or share to the lord admirall of England'. They were to receive no obstruction from 'his graces faithfull officers, ministers and subjectes', provided they did not 'presume to take anie thing from anie his majesties subjects, or from anie man having his graces safe conduct, upon the paines by his majesties lawes provided for the same'. This proclamation has been described as the first use of 'general reprisals' in England, and as serving the function of 'letters of marque'.[85] The truth is, however, that while the king professed to be giving 'full power and licence to all and singuler his subjects' to prey upon enemy shipping, he neither made use of the expression 'letters of marque' nor made any pretence to be authorising reprisals for losses sustained and justice denied. Indeed, the document could scarcely have done more to distance the seizures encouraged from the taking of reprisals, which is clearly not what the king had in mind. Instead, his aim was to relax the restrictions on wartime raiding that had been in place for over a century so that licit plunder could be indulged in more freely.[86] The misreading of the document is probably attributable to a whiggish inclination to identify the origins of a later practice, abetted by the loose labelling by modern editors of wartime licences as letters of marque, but it may also owe something to the terminology used in other documents issued in the prelude to the war. In the spring of 1543 the king had licensed various mariners to put to sea and take 'advantage of Frenchemen by way off reprisall and of Skottes as ennemies', subject to the requirement that they provide security before sailing not to annoy anyone else.[87] In fact, genuine letters of reprisal had been issued against the French shortly beforehand, possibly in response to letters of reprisal issued by

84 *Tudor Royal Proclamations*, vol. 1, pp. 345–6; *Documents Relating to Law and Custom of the Sea*, vol. 1, pp. 155–8.

85 Marsden 1909, p. 684; Thomson 1994, p. 23; Rodger 2003, p. 244; Gunn, Grummitt and Cools 2007, p. 61; Loades 2009, pp. 20–1; Childs 2009, pp. 185–6; Bicheno 2012, p. 45; Hanna 2015, p. 36; Scott 2018, p. 56.

86 At the moment when Henry was relaxing the restrictions in England, they were being reinforced by the new 'edit sur l'amirauté' issued by Francis I (*Recueil général des anciennes lois françaises*, vol. 12, pp. 854–69).

87 *Acts of the Privy Council of England*, vol. 1, pp. 107–10, 112 and 115; *Letters and Papers, Foreign and Domestic, of the Reign of Henry VIII*, vol. 18(1), pp. 221, 231 and 239.

the French against Henry's allies, but in the traditional form nonetheless.[88] As for the Scots, they were the king's enemies until the Treaty of Greenwich was concluded three weeks after war was declared on France.[89] A truce had in the meantime been agreed, but the licences issued in the spring nullified its effects as far as their recipients were concerned, and they also made it perfectly plain that annoying enemies was not believed to be identical with taking reprisals.[90] A contemporary chronicler understandably observed that at this stage 'there was neither peace, nor open warre', but he later added more accurately that 'this yere was open warre proclamed with Fraunce, and lycence geven to the kynges subjectes to seaze upon the Frenchemen and their goodes as in lyke cases before had been accustomed'.[91] The plundering of enemy property in Henry's last war was not founded on a new form of authorisation by the king.[92]

After the war ended in 1546, the requirements that mariners provide 'sufficient sureties' of their good behaviour and obtain 'special licens' before leaving port, whether 'uppon pretens to annoye his majesties enemyes' or for 'marchandize or any other purpose', were reintroduced.[93] When war with France and Scotland broke out again in 1557, Mary I issued a modified version of the proclamation her father had issued in 1543, relaxing the normal restrictions on sailing in the same ways, except for omission of the clause about security not being required.[94] Less than a year later, when it was found that mariners were

88 NAK, SP12/237, f. 144v; *Letters and Papers, Foreign and Domestic, of the Reign of Henry VIII*, vol. 17, p. 304.

89 An alternative explanation of the distinction drawn by the documents is proposed in Murdoch 2010, p. 44, but it does not make sense in legal terms and cannot be correct.

90 When the war began the navy was ordered 'not to take any ship of Scotland, Portingall, Spayn or Flanders', though undated instructions were also issued to 'take all Frenchmen and Scots as good prize', probably after the Treaty of Greenwich was abandoned and war was declared on the Scots towards the end of the year (*Letters and Papers, Foreign and Domestic, of the Reign of Henry VIII*, vol. 18(1), pp. 120–1 and 405–6).

91 *Hall's Chronicle*, pp. 857 and 860. In the latter passage Hall was referring to an announcement of the war in August 1543 (*Tudor Royal Proclamations*, vol. 1, pp. 320–1), but it was the same 'lycence' that was renewed in the December proclamation. On attitudes to war and peace at this time see Lowe 2000.

92 *Cf.* McDermott 2005, pp. 19–21. On the law of arms in the war on land see Murphy 2016.

93 *Acts of the Privy Council of England*, vol. 2, pp. 130–1. For an example of a licence issued at this time see *Documents Relating to Law and Custom of the Sea*, vol. 1, pp. 161–2. In 1552 it was ordered that a prize brought to Harwich by a Frenchman should be arrested until he obtained a court order confirming that it had been taken lawfully (*Acts of the Privy Council of England*, vol. 4, p. 110).

94 *Tudor Royal Proclamations*, vol. 2, pp. 79–82; *Documents Relating to Law and Custom of the Sea*, vol. 1, pp. 162–5; *Calendar of State Papers, Domestic Series, of the Reigns of Edward VI, Mary and Elizabeth*, vol. 1, p. 93. That the clause about security had not been omitted by the printer's oversight is clear from NAK, SP11/11, pp. 50–5.

reluctant to serve on naval vessels, it was announced that no one was to put a vessel to sea until 'a special licence be first obtained and had for that intent under the great seal of her majesty's admiralty, in due form to be made as in such cases it hath been used and accustomed, any proclamation made and set forth to the contrary in any wise notwithstanding'.[95] Before granting licences to mariners, the admiral insisted on being given security that he would in due course receive 'all such shares and rights as his lordship, by vertue of his office as thinges of auncyent custume dewe to the same, ought to have out of such pryces as they have latelye takyn of thenemies'.[96] After returning to port mariners sometimes sought confirmation from the admiralty court that they had seized ships and goods lawfully (*iustam predam iure belli ceperint*), though possibly only when their ownership of the property taken had been questioned by someone else.[97] It was during this war that English mariners, as was noted at the beginning of the previous chapter, acknowledged before the admiralty court in Scotland that their ship and goods had been lawfully acquired by their Scottish captors, 'of the law of armes and be ressoun of weir standand betwix this realme and the realme of Ingland'.[98] As was also noted in the previous chapter, the understanding in the admiralty court in England was that prize acquisition was governed by the *ius commune civile et maritimum* as well as by the *antiqua consuetudo* observed there since time immemorial.[99] Attention was also being paid to practice elsewhere, for the admiralty officials were being urged to adopt the French rule that a friendly ship carrying enemy goods, or friendly goods found on an enemy ship, should be treated as legitimate plunder.[100] 'The Frenshemen have lawes and doe putt the same in execution against the subjects of this realme', they were informed, 'whiche the counsell thinke convenient to be kepte lykewyse towardes them'.[101]

95 *Tudor Royal Proclamations*, vol. 2, pp. 89–90.

96 *Documents Relating to Law and Custom of the Sea*, vol. 1, pp. 166–7.

97 *Select Pleas in the Court of Admiralty*, vol. 2, pp. 106–8. In this record use was made of the verb *adiudicare* as well as *declarare*, but probably not in its proper sense since all that was asked for was confirmation that the ship and goods taken had belonged to *hostes et inimici*. Five years earlier it had been found that the goods of *piratae, praedones et malefactores* had become the king's by way of forfeiture, *et ut talia pronuncianda et adiudicanda sunt*, and here too the ruling seems to have been declaratory in character (*Select Pleas in the Court of Admiralty*, vol. 2, pp. 84–6).

98 *Acta curiae admirallatus Scotiae*, pp. 69–70.

99 *Select Pleas in the Court of Admiralty*, vol. 2, p. 95.

100 *Documents Relating to Law and Custom of the Sea*, vol. 1, pp. 165–6; *Select Pleas in the Court of Admiralty*, vol. 2, p. 22.

101 It was believed in England that the French had themselves adopted the doctrine of *infection hostile* on the basis of reciprocity with their adversaries (*Select Pleas in the Court of*

It should by now be clear that the Mollat thesis is no more consistent with the evidence available from England than from anywhere else.[102] The seizure of ships and goods at sea in wartime had not been regarded there as a manifestation of 'la piraterie sauvage', nor did it give way to 'la course réglementée' during the fourteenth and fifteenth centuries. Seizures in wartime had both been considered legitimate and been subjected to regulation since at least the thirteenth century, and their treatment was not assimilated with the treatment of reprisals in peacetime during the fourteenth and fifteenth centuries. In the middle of the sixteenth century prize taking was being dealt with in England in much the same way as it was in France, Scotland and elsewhere. The detail of the regulations introduced varied from place to place, but it was still accepted that prize taking was legitimate as soon as a war was declared between sovereign rulers. It is true that rulers were striving – despite occasional relaxation of their regulations – to increase their control over maritime conflict by insisting on the licensing of voyages and the approval of seizures, which gave rise to a superficial resemblance between plunder in wartime and reprisals in peacetime. What they were doing, however, was tightening up the existing regulation of maritime warfare, not altering the fundamental principles of prize acquisition. It cannot be emphasised enough that it is in the works of modern editors and historians, not in the original sources, that the licences granted in wartime have been called 'letters of marque', and that the proclamations issued in 1543 and 1557 have been taken to authorise 'general reprisals'. The licences examined here have none of the hallmarks of letters of marque or reprisal, no denial of justice is mentioned either there or in the proclamations referred to, and it does not appear to have been understood that mariners would acquire title to prizes taken in wartime only through a process of formal adjudication. On the contrary, the recurring threat of forfeiture of prizes makes better sense on the assumption that mariners acquired title to ships and goods as soon as they seized them from enemies, through the *occupatio* of *res hostium*. For the emergence of privateering to be accurately pinpointed, what needs to be understood is how the gradual accumulation of regulations within an unchanging framework of legitimacy eventually gave way to a fundamentally different conception of prize taking in wartime.

Admiralty, vol. 2, pp. 119–20), though no indication of any such thinking is discernible in the rule as stated in Francis I's edict (*Recueil général des anciennes lois françaises*, vol. 12, p. 864).

102 Mollat 1976 and 1980.

2 Innovation during the Reign of Elizabeth

Historians tend to agree that England was overtly at war with other countries in four periods during the reign of Elizabeth.[103] The conflict Mary entered into with France in 1557 did not end until the Habsburg-Valois War was concluded by the Treaty of Cateau-Cambrésis in April 1559, five months after Elizabeth came to the throne.[104] In the following year, English forces intervened in the struggle between the Protestant 'lords of the congregation' and the Catholic regent, Mary of Guise, in Scotland, where they were again involved in fighting with the French.[105] The conflict was terminated by the Treaty of Edinburgh in July 1560, under the terms of which both French and English forces were withdrawn from Scotland.[106] Two years later English forces were sent to France itself in support of the Huguenots, in the first of the French wars of religion.[107] After the Protestants and Catholics came to terms with each other in 1563, they combined forces to drive the English out of the towns they had occupied. For the next twenty years English governments managed to avoid overt warfare with any of their neighbours, although they continued to provide unofficial support both to the Huguenots in France and to the Protestant rebels against Spanish rule in the Netherlands.[108] In 1585 war finally broke out overtly with Spain, continuing until the end of Elizabeth's reign.[109] The wars commenced in 1560, 1562 and 1585 were 'overt' in the sense that English forces were committed to combat without any pretence that the English queen was remaining neutral. It complicated matters, however, and made the regulation of maritime warfare more confusing, that none of these wars was formally declared by one sovereign ruler against another. How maritime warfare was regulated in these overt but undeclared wars is the subject examined in this section. Consideration of the covert or unofficial conflicts of the rest of Elizabeth's reign is left aside until the next section.

Shortly after acceding to the throne in 1558, Elizabeth issued a proclamation requiring all ships to be licensed before sailing, a confirmation of the terms

103 Doran 2000; Hammer 2003; Trim 2005.

104 *Foedera, conventiones, litterae et cuiuscunque generis acta publica*, vol. 15, pp. 505–16; *Corps universel diplomatique du droit des gens*, vol. 5, pp. 28–46; *Tudor Royal Proclamations*, vol. 2, pp. 111–12 and 117.

105 McCaffrey 1968, pp. 45–92; Alford 1998, pp. 71–85; Ritchie 2002, pp. 231–44.

106 *Foedera, conventiones, litterae et cuiuscunque generis acta publica*, vol. 15, pp. 591–7; *Corps universel diplomatique du droit des gens*, vol. 5, pp. 65–7.

107 MacCaffrey 1968, pp. 128–36; Holt 2005, pp. 50–6; Heap 2019, pp. 36–44.

108 Wernham 1966, pp. 290–372; McDermott 2005, pp. 64–145; Ronald 2007, pp. 129–274.

109 Lynch 1981, vol. 1, pp. 330–50; Guy 1988, pp. 331–51; MacCaffrey 1993, pp. 235–93.

of the similar proclamation issued by her sister earlier in the year, which had lapsed on Mary's death.[110] Although peace negotiations were already under way, maritime raiding was continuing and complaints were being made by neutral countries.[111] Elizabeth declared that none of her subjects was to put a ship to sea, 'either on warfare, merchandise or otherwise', without first obtaining a 'special licence and grant' from the admiralty court, and that anyone who did venture abroad was to refrain from annoying her subjects, friends and confederates. After the war ended the requirement was relaxed to the extent that those sailing 'for trade of merchandise only' were permitted to do so without first obtaining a licence, but only if the ships were beneath a certain burden and if they sailed from certain ports.[112] 'For divers reasons', it was explained, 'it is not convenient to release the said restraint thoroughly'. The restriction on maritime raiding thus remained in place when military support was promised to the lords of the congregation in the Treaty of Berwick at the beginning of 1560.[113] Pains were taken in the treaty to explain that Elizabeth was intervening 'uponn respect of princelie honour and neyghbourheid, for defence of the just freedome of the crowne of Scotland from conquest, and not for any other sinister entent'. For their part, the lords of the congregation professed that their intention was to defend 'the just and auncient liberties' of the realm against subversion by the regent and her associates, and that they did not intend 'by this compacte to withdrawe any dew obedience from their soverane ladye the queyne, nor in any lefull thing to withstand the Frenche king, being her husband and head'. Not surprisingly, no proclamation was issued in relation to the plundering of enemy shipping, although there may have been an expectation that prizes would be taken. It was during this conflict that an undated letter is believed to have been sent from the English queen to her admiral, explaining how shares should be distributed in 'all such prises as are or shall happen to be taken upon thennemyes of our sayd navye, or by any ship or vessel of the same being in our wagis'.[114] If the letter was actually written in 1560, no attempt was made to explain how prize taking could be legitimate when war had not been declared on the monarchs of Scotland and France.

110 *Acts of the Privy Council of England*, vol. 7, p. 25; *Calendar of State Papers, Foreign Series, of the Reign of Elizabeth*, vol. 1, p. 38; *Tudor Royal Proclamations*, vol. 2, pp. 100–1.

111 Ramsay 1975, p. 125; Loades 1992, p. 209; McDermott 2005, p. 57.

112 *Tudor Royal Proclamations*, vol. 2, p. 112; *Acts of the Privy Council of England*, vol. 7, p. 73.

113 *Foedera, conventiones, litterae et cuiuscunque generis acta publica*, vol. 15, pp. 569–71; *Calendar of the Manuscripts of the Most Honourable the Marquis of Salisbury*, vol. 1, pp. 187–8.

114 *Documents Relating to Law and Custom of the Sea*, vol. 1, p. 169.

When military support was promised to the Huguenots in 1562 in the Treaty of Hampton Court, pains were taken to explain that the prince of Condé and his followers were not intent on rebelling against the authority of the French king but meant only to defend the inhabitants of Rouen, Dieppe and Le Havre 'from the slaughter and destruction that is cruelly designed against them by the duke of Guise, his brothers and other people of the Guisian faction'.[115] It is again unsurprising that Elizabeth did not issue a proclamation in relation to the plundering of enemy shipping, but maritime raiding certainly occurred, and often affected neutral vessels sailing between Spain and the Netherlands.[116] The Spanish ambassador in London understood that French and English pirates (*piratas*) were raiding in the English Channel under the cover of licences (*patentes*) granted to them by the Huguenot governor of Le Havre.[117] Elizabeth's response to the complaints she received was to issue a proclamation in 1563, insisting that she 'never knew of any such attempts intended by any of her subjects, neither gave authority or permission, nor knoweth of any given by any under her, to any person to allow or procure any such act'.[118] Sailors bringing captured goods into English ports were to be imprisoned, and the goods were to be detained until their ownership could be established before a judge. 'And for the time to come', the proclamation added, 'her majesty straightly chargeth all manner her subjects to forbear from the attempt of taking or disturbing of any ships or vessels, or from aiding of any other so to do, but to live in good peace with all manner of subjects appertaining to any prince or country with whom her majesty is in amity'. The Spanish ambassador pointed out that this was unlikely to prevent pirates from sailing out of Le Havre on French ships and from taking prizes back to French ports for disposal.[119] The French ambassador, representing a king with whom the

115 *Corps universel diplomatique du droit des gens*, vol. 5, pp. 94–5.

116 Andrews 1964, p. 16; McDermott 2001, p. 54, and 2005, pp. 59–60; Loades 1992, p. 215, and 2009, pp. 109–10.

117 *Calendar of Letters and State Papers Relating to English Affairs Preserved Principally in the Archives of Simancas*, vol. 1, pp. 299–300; *Relations politiques des Pays-Bas et de l'Angleterre*, vol. 3, pp. 238–9.

118 *Tudor Royal Proclamations*, vol. 2, pp. 208–9. This was no doubt disingenuous. For instance, the bond of recognisance granted before the admiralty court a month later by Martin Frobisher seems to be consistent with the proclamation (*Documents Relating to Law and Custom of the Sea*, vol. 1, p. 173), yet he was actually sailing under a licence issued by the Huguenot authorities in Le Havre (McDermott 2001, pp. 56–8). On the response to the proclamation in Le Havre see the *Calendar of State Papers, Foreign Series, of the Reign of Elizabeth*, vol. 6, p. 230.

119 *Calendar of Letters and State Papers Relating to English Affairs Preserved Principally in the Archives of Simancas*, vol. 1, pp. 300–1.

English queen remained formally in amity, happened to complain on the day after the proclamation was issued about the arrest of several French vessels in English ports at the behest of the mayor of London.[120] If the mayor had a grievance against somebody in France, the ambassador protested, the proper procedure was for him to seek justice there, and if that were denied, to obtain letters of reprisal at home. As the French adversaries moved towards reconciliation a month later, Elizabeth's own ambassador in Paris suggested that if the Huguenot leaders reneged on their agreement with her, she would be able to demand recompense for the expense she had incurred in supporting them, and if justice were denied in France would be able to issue letters of reprisal until the amount due was recovered.[121] It was difficult to see how else the seizure of ships and goods could have been justified in conventional terms when war had not been declared against the king of France.

Two days after Elizabeth's ambassador wrote his letter, the first religious war was brought to an end by the Peace of Amboise, after which the English forces prepared to defend their position in Le Havre.[122] Aware that the French king was licensing mariners to raid English shipping, Elizabeth issued instructions for reciprocal measures to be taken on her side of the Channel.[123] French mariners were seizing ships and holding prisoners to ransom, she noted, 'yet the king forbeareth to publish any warr against us'. In these perplexing circumstances she had decided that 'no remedy can be had but by like proceeding', and she therefore authorised the licensing of English mariners 'to repaire to the seas and to be as bold upon the French kinges subjectes, using the same in like manner as the French do'. Because of the uncertainty of the situation, however, she ordered that captured goods were not to be distributed, but were to be carefully inventoried and stored until it became clear what should be done with them. Those who received licences duly provided security before departing that they would prey only on ships from France or Brittany, not on Spanish or other friendly vessels, that they would bring any ships they captured back to the ports they sailed from, 'without spoyle, ryfflinge or other dysorder', that they would provide the admiralty court with an inventory of the goods taken, and that the goods would be kept safely 'untill farder dyrectyon and order shalbe

120 *Calendar of State Papers, Foreign Series, of the Reign of Elizabeth*, vol. 6, p. 119.

121 *Calendar of State Papers, Foreign Series, of the Reign of Elizabeth*, vol. 6, p. 208. The English ambassador, Sir Thomas Smith, had been the regius professor of civil law at Cambridge (Stein 1978).

122 Thompson 1909, pp. 191–2; Knecht 1996, pp. 37–8; Holt 2005, pp. 55–6.

123 *Documents Relating to Law and Custom of the Sea*, vol. 1, pp. 174 and 176–7; *Calendar of State Papers, Foreign Series, of the Reign of Elizabeth*, vol. 6, p. 369.

prescribed and gyven in that behalfe'.[124] In some respects these bonds for good behaviour reflected the familiar regulations governing maritime warfare, but it is notable that they were not framed in terms of 'prizes' being taken from 'enemies', any more than they were in terms of 'reprisals' being taken after a 'denial of justice'.[125] At this stage in the conflict the seizure of ships and goods at sea was being dealt with cautiously on the basis of reciprocity with the French, for as some of the bonds made clear, it was anticipated that captured goods might need in due course to be restored to their French owners. The approach was to change significantly in the summer of 1563, when Charles IX came of age and began his personal rule of France.

On 6 July 1563 Charles issued a proclamation in which he gave his subjects permission (*permis et permettons par cesdites présentes*) to set sail and annoy the queen of England and her subjects, declaring (*déclarant*) that any prizes they took (*les prinses qu'ils feront*) would be 'good and valid, and acquired by them, since plundered from enemies' (*bonnes et vallables, et à eux acquises, comme robbé d'ennemis*).[126] A week later Elizabeth announced that she had found it necessary, in view of 'this example', not only to warn her subjects on the coasts, but also to 'license' them to 'do their uttermost' against the French.[127] Whereas previously she had instructed that 'none of her subjects should spoil or rob any Frenchman by sea or land which should seek to offend them, but should only stay and preserve them and their goods in safety', she was now encouraging her subjects to prey on the French with the assurance that 'the prises taken (even as the French king hath ordered) shall be judged for good and vailable, as things taken from enemies'. For a third time, it has been suggested, the English were experimenting with 'general reprisals' under proclamation.[128] Unlike her sister in 1557, however, Elizabeth had not issued a modified version of the proclamation made by their father in 1543. She had followed explicitly the example

124 NAK, HCA25/1/1, ff. 377–9, 383–4 and 392–3.

125 A different style is used in NAK, HCA25/1/1, f. 201, a bond granted by a mariner 'entendinge to passe unto the seas uppon his owne adventure against the quenes majesties enemies', but it is undated and may have been misplaced in the file. The mariner promised not to harm the queen's subjects, friends and allies, 'utherwise then the lawes of this realme and of the sea and the leagues and intercourses doth require', and to bring 'any prize or purchase of thenemies' back to port for appraisal.

126 *Memoires de Condé*, vol. 4, pp. 551–2; *Collection of State Papers Relating to Affairs in the Reigns of Henry VIII, Edward VI, Mary and Elizabeth*, vol. 2, p. 754; *Actes royaux, depuis l'origine jusqu'à Henri IV*, col. 290.

127 *Tudor Royal Proclamations*, vol. 2, pp. 227–8.

128 Rodger 2003, p. 244, refers for support to the instructions issued earlier in the year, but seems more likely to have had this proclamation in mind; see too Scott 2013, p. 76.

of the French proclamation, in which, in any case, Charles made no more use of the language of reprisals than Henry had done. A contemporary observer, educated in the law schools of Orleans and Bourges, thought that Charles had issued a declaration of war to Elizabeth (*declara dans les formes la guerre à Elisabeth*), presumably because he could not imagine any other way in which plunder could lawfully have been taken from enemies.[129] Charles claimed to have given Elizabeth an ultimatum to withdraw her troops from France, but his proclamation was addressed to his own officers, and Elizabeth claimed to be responding reciprocally to his 'unjust provocation', not to be recognising that a state of war was formally in existence.[130] After another two weeks she issued a further proclamation to make it clear that while she had licensed maritime raiding by the inhabitants of English ports, there was no general right to attack French people wherever they could be found.[131]

It was perhaps because the situation remained rather perplexing that security continued to be provided to the admiralty court, before ships departed from England, in the form already in use, although the terms 'enemy' and 'prize' found their way into other documents.[132] While it soon became necessary to abandon Le Havre, maritime raiding remained rampant, prompting renewed complaints from neutral countries.[133] Efforts were made especially to protect vessels travelling between Spain and the Netherlands from what might amount, it was acknowledged, to piracy, but it was made clear that this protection would not extend to anyone who was found 'to colour the goods and merchandise of the French, being her majesty's enemies'.[134] In April 1564, after peace was made with the French, Elizabeth announced that she had reached an agreement with Charles that nobody should be 'impeached or molested for the taking, spoiling or detaining of any ships', whether during 'this last war, or

129 De Thou, *Histoire universelle*, vol. 3, pp. 416–17. On the writer's education see De Smet 2006, pp. 152–4.

130 For the assumption in England that civil law categories remained applicable see *Documents Relating to Law and Custom of the Sea*, vol. 1, p. 180, and *Calendar of the Manuscripts of the Most Honourable the Marquis of Salisbury*, vol. 1, pp. 298–9.

131 *Tudor Royal Proclamations*, vol. 2, p. 232.

132 *Documents Relating to Law and Custom of the Sea*, vol. 1, pp. 177–9; *Calendar of the Manuscripts of the Most Honourable the Marquis of Salisbury*, vol. 1, pp. 274 and 281–3; *Collection of State Papers*, vol. 1, pp. 402–3.

133 Wernham 1980, p. 30; Rodger 1997, p. 199; McDermott 2005, p. 58.

134 *Tudor Royal Proclamations*, vol. 2, pp. 235–6 and 243–6; *Calendar of the Manuscripts of the Most Honourable the Marquis of Salisbury*, vol. 1, pp. 286–7 and 299; *Calendar of State Papers, Foreign Series, of the Reign of Elizabeth*, vol. 7, p. 46; *Acts of the Privy Council of England*, vol. 7, pp. 141 and 146–7.

in the doubtful times before the same was published'.[135] In retrospect at least, it had been found convenient to regard the whole conflict as a declared war in which the subjects of the sovereign rulers involved had been able to acquire goods from each other. The Treaty of Troyes provided that in future mariners in England and France would be required before sailing to provide security that they would deal with their neighbours as friends, and that if disputes should arise, recourse would not be taken to letters of reprisal or marque unless justice had been denied and letters of requisition had been sent.[136] In the summer of 1564 the queen, 'being in good and perfect peace with all princes and countries, and meaning with the assistance of Almighty God to continue in the same', issued a new proclamation containing 'certain articles' to be observed by her subjects on the coasts.[137] Although ordinary trade and fishing were to be resumed without impediment, it was declared that no armed ships were to leave England without security being provided that harm would not be done to the queen's subjects or friends, with the exception of specific ships she ordered 'to be armed and pass to the seas for clearing of the same from pirates or rovers'. People residing on the coasts were not to give succour or shelter to pirates, or to purchase plundered wares from them, on pain of being prosecuted for piracy themselves. Nevertheless, as will be seen later, the view was not always taken during the next twenty years that seizures of ships and goods at sea by English sailors amounted to acts of piracy.

The return to open warfare in 1585 was precipitated by the arrest of northern ships and the imprisonment of their crews in Spanish and Portuguese ports in the summer of that year.[138] Still hoping to remain at peace, Elizabeth did not issue a proclamation on the plundering of enemy shipping, but on 9 July she did authorise her admiral, Lord Howard of Effingham, to grant 'letters of reprisall' to those whose ships, goods and employees had been 'stayed and deteyned', and who had 'no other meanes by anye order of justice to be yelded to them'.[139] Mariners were to be licensed to seize sufficient property from Philip

135 *Tudor Royal Proclamations*, vol. 2, pp. 249–50; *Acts of the Privy Council of England*, vol. 7, p. 141.

136 *Foedera, conventiones, litterae et cuiuscunque generis acta publica*, vol. 15, pp. 640–4; *Corps universel diplomatique du droit des gens*, vol. 5, pp. 126–8; *Calendar of State Papers, Foreign Series, of the Reign of Elizabeth*, vol. 7, p. 80.

137 *Tudor Royal Proclamations*, vol. 2, pp. 253–5.

138 Parker 1998, pp. 173–5; Hammer 2003, pp. 119–20; Hanson 2003, pp. 88–9.

139 NAK, C66/1263, m. 23; BL, Add. MS 29439, ff. 180–3; *Select Statutes and Other Constitutional Documents Illustrative of the Reigns of Elizabeth and James I*, pp. 464–4. On the difficulty of prohibiting trade with the 'enemy' in an undeclared war, a variant of the difficulty of justifying seizures of property from the 'enemy' in such a conflict, see Croft 1989.

II's subjects to cover the losses they had sustained, 'accordynge to suche articles and orders as shalbe agreed uppon and advised by the lordes and others of our privie councell'. On the same day the privy council issued a series of eight articles to regulate the licensing of reprisals.[140] The first required those who wished to receive letters to 'make proof before the lord admiral or his lieutenant, judge of the admiralty, that their goods have bene stayed in such sort, and of all such losses and damages as they pretend themselves to have sustained'. The second article declared that it would be 'lawfull' for those who received letters to seize ships and goods, 'in as ample and full manner as if it were in the time of open war between her majestie and the said king of Spain'. The third article required those who received letters to grant bonds to the admiralty that they would 'not break bulk' before bringing any ships and goods they seized back to an English port, that they would then provide the admiralty court with a 'true inventory' and 'true appraisement' of everything captured, and that they would not 'attempt anything' at sea against the queen's subjects or friends. After the inventory and evaluation were provided, the fourth article went on, it would be lawful for the captors to possess and enjoy what they had taken 'as lawful prizes, and as their own proper goods', which they might then dispose of 'in as ample manner as at any time heretofore hath been accustomed by the law of reprisal'. The fifth article confirmed that no one who captured ships and goods in accordance with the rules laid down would be 'reputed, taken or challenged for any offender against any her majesties laws', while the sixth confirmed that other people were free to receive captured goods 'in as ample and lawful manner as if the said goods had bene come by through the lawful traffic of merchants, or as just prizes in the time of open war'. Reverting to a preliminary stage of the process, the seventh article required those who wished to receive letters of reprisal to inform the admiral or his lieutenant of the names of the ship, its master and captain, the size of the ship and crew, and how the ship had been armed, equipped and supplied. Finally, the eighth article specified that after an inventory and evaluation had been provided, any prize taken was to be 'devided into three parts', of which one was to be assigned to the owners of the ships involved in the capture, another was to be assigned to the victuallers, and the third was to be shared among the crews.

A slightly different version of these articles also exists, which bears the same date but does not include the reference to the 'law of reprisal' in the fourth article, instead providing for the acquisition of property 'in as ample manner as at

140 NAK, SP12/280, ff. 40–2; *Papers Relating to the Navy during the Spanish War*, pp. 36–8; *Calendar of State Papers, Domestic Series, of the Reigns of Edward VI, Mary and Elizabeth*, vol. 2, p. 251.

any time heretofore hath bene accustomed in time of open warr'.[141] Since the most striking variation is a provision repeatedly made for the taking of 'gold, silver, pearle, bullion or any goods or marchandizes whatsoever belonging to the kinge of Spaine', it may be that these articles were specifically designed for ventures into the Atlantic to intercept treasure fleets from the Americas, which were by no means the only variety of maritime raiding unleashed against Spain.[142] The omission of the reference to the 'law of reprisal' in this version, however, and the use in both versions of the suppositional phrase 'as if it were in the time of open war', appear to reflect a degree of uncertainty about the legal situation in 1585. Howard's lieutenant and judge of the admiralty court, Julius Caesar, who had been educated in the law schools of Paris and Oxford, did not believe that a state of war actually existed then.[143] Asked by Howard in the autumn whether mariners were entitled to 'pillage' before prizes were distributed, Caesar replied that this was permitted to crews 'by custome in time of warre', but added that 'as this is noe tyme of open warre, soe the capitaine, master and maryners can clayme noe such custome at this tyme'.[144] If possible, he added, everything captured would be distributed in accordance with an agreement previously entered into 'for some certayntie' by the shipowners, victuallers and mariners, 'for *consensus dat legem contractui*'.[145] In the absence of such an agreement, the mariners would have to 'stand to the third parte of the whole pryze', as provided in the articles prescribed by the privy council. They would receive their portion, Caesar promised, 'your lordships tenth being first deducted', which had not in fact been provided for in the articles but was customary when prizes were taken. Thinking about the situation in the way he had been trained as a civil lawyer – moving from the particular to the general, and interpreting the regulations issued locally in the light of the theory taught in the schools – Caesar had concluded that it was indeed the 'law of reprisal' that needed to be adhered to in his court. Prizes would be dealt with as if taken

141 BL, Lansdowne MS 143, ff. 309–13. Two years later broadly similar articles were issued to the warden of the Cinque Ports (NAK, SP12/203, ff. 82–6; *Calendar of State Papers, Domestic Series, of the Reigns of Edward VI, Mary and Elizabeth*, vol. 2, p. 426). Although it is stated in *Documents Relating to Law and Custom of the Sea*, vol. 1, p. 216, that these articles were issued in 1577, this was obviously a mistake. The correct date is noted in Marsden 1909, p. 691, and also in BL, Add. MS 34150, f. 118, which appears to be notes written by Marsden.

142 Marsden 1909, pp. 689–90; Andrews 1964, pp. 3–5; Martin and Parker 1989, pp. 100–1; Loades 2000, pp. 122–3; Lenman 2001, pp. 84–5.

143 On Caesar's education see Hill 1988, pp. 6–8.

144 BL, Lansdowne MS 157, f. 318.

145 For the origins of the legal maxim cited see *Digest*, 2.14.7.5.

in the time of open war only in the sense that reprisals could properly be conceived of as a kind of limited war.

Letters of reprisal were granted in the later 1580s on the strength of warrants provided by the admiral, which typically stated that someone had sustained losses in Spain, of which he had already 'made proofe in the court of thadmiraltye', that he had been unable to 'obtaine anie restitution', despite intervention by the queen, and that it was therefore appropriate for him to be authorised to take reprisals against the king of Spain's subjects, until he recovered 'suche recompense and restitution as may countervayle his losses'.[146] Letters were then granted in the admiral's name by his lieutenant, in which it was stated that ships and goods had been seized in Spain and Portugal, 'contrarye to all order of lawe and justice', that the owners of the confiscated property lacked 'any other meanes by order of justice to be yealded to them', and that they had 'made prooef' before the admiralty court of the extent of their losses.[147] Further clauses made careful use of the language of the privy council's instructions in declaring that the holders of the letters had been authorised to seize ships and goods 'in as ample manner as yf it weare in tyme of warre', that they were to be permitted to dispose of prizes 'in as ample manner as att any tyme heretofore hathe bene accustomed by waye of reprisall', and that other people would be able to buy things from them 'in as ample and beneficiall manner as yf the sayd shipps, goodes and merchaundize had bene come by through the lawfull trafique and trade of merchauntes, or as juste prizes in the tyme of warre'. Before the letters were granted, bonds of recognisance had to be provided, guaranteeing that prizes would be brought back intact 'to some porte of this her majesties realme of Englande', that the admiralty court would then be supplied with 'a juste and perfected inventory' and 'a trewe appraisemente' of the property taken, that the admiral would receive 'the full tenthe parte' of the value calculated, and that while at sea the mariners would not 'attempte eanye thinge agaynst eany of her majestys loving subjectes, or the subjectes of eany other princes or states beinge in good leage and amity with her majestie'.[148]

146 *Documents Relating to Law and Custom of the Sea*, vol. 1, pp. 241–2; NAK, HCA25/1/2, ff. 7, 19, 24, 26, 36 and 46 (further examples can easily be found in the same file).

147 *Documents Relating to Law and Custom of the Sea*, vol. 1, pp. 237–41; *Select Statutes and Other Constitutional Documents Illustrative of the Reigns of Elizabeth and James I*, pp. 465–7. *Cf.* Berckman 1979, p. 113.

148 *Documents Relating to Law and Custom of the Sea*, vol. 1, pp. 243–7; *Select Pleas in the Court of Admiralty*, vol. 2, pp. 42–3; NAK, HCA25/1/2, ff. 1, 5, 9, 11, 16, 30, 34, 38, 42 and 44 (again, further examples can easily be found in the same file). For an example of a bond granted in relation to the seizure of property in an English port, still a different process, see *Documents Relating to Law and Custom of the Sea*, vol. 1, pp. 245–6.

A different type of bond noted that the recipients of letters had 'not made sufficient proofe as yet' of the losses they claimed to have sustained, and declared the legality of their reprisals to be conditional on 'dewe and sufficient proofe' being provided in due course.[149]

Examples survive among the records of the admiralty court of decrees confirming the proof of losses sustained in Spain or Portugal.[150] In these decrees Caesar (designated a *legum doctor*) declared that the claimants were the owners of ships or goods worth a certain amount, that the ships or goods had been unlawfully detained, and that justice had been denied by the king of Spain (*iustitia a rege Hispaniae denegata*). Not only was proof of the losses sustained actually provided in these cases, but genuine efforts seem to have been made to establish that justice had been denied after the claimants petitioned the authorities in Spain for redress.[151] As was pointed out long ago, however, decrees confirming the proof of losses are found less often among the records of the court than warrants and bonds for letters of reprisal, which suggests that letters were sometimes issued without proof of losses being provided.[152] The records also contain an exceptional decree issued on 8 December 1586, after a Spanish ship was taken with a cargo of fish off Newfoundland.[153] In this case Caesar noted that letters of reprisal (*literae reprisaliarum*) had been granted to the claimant after he provided proof of the loss (*damnum et detrimentum*) he had sustained in Spain and of the denial of justice (*denegatio iustitiae*) he had suffered there. Caesar further noted that subjects of the king of Spain were alleged to be the owners (*domini et proprietarii*) of the ship and cargo, and that both those individuals and interested parties more generally had been cited to appear and defend their interests before the court. As the claimant was now seeking to have the ship and goods adjudged (*adiudicari*) to him, a final warning was given to all interested parties to appear. Reference was made to an earlier order of the court for the preservation of the ship and cargo after they were brought back to England as a *primum decretum*, and the expectation clearly was that a *secundum decretum* would follow in the form of

149 *Documents Relating to Law and Custom of the Sea*, vol. 1, pp. 248–9 and 251–2; NAK, HCA25/1/2, ff. 3, 8, 13, 18, 28, 32 and 40 (as is becoming usual, further examples can easily be found in the same file).

150 *Select Pleas in the Court of Admiralty*, vol. 2, pp. 165–7; NAK, HCA24/54, ff. 26, 38, 40, 42 and 44.

151 These assertions may of course have been fictional, but they can be surprisingly detailed, and it is in any case significant that it was felt necessary for them to be made.

152 Andrews 1959, pp. 6–7. Copies of letters of reprisal themselves were not entered in the court records.

153 *Select Pleas in the Court of Admiralty*, vol. 2, pp. 161–3; NAK, HCA24/54, f. 245.

an act of adjudication. If such an act did follow, however, it did not find its way into the records of the court. Indeed, no acts of adjudication have been found from any cases in the records covering the first few years of the war. It seems clear that the court was operating on the assumption that seizures of Spanish ships and goods were being made by way of reprisal, and it followed from this that captors ought to have been able to acquire title to anything they captured only by way of acts of adjudication, yet this had not been mentioned in the articles issued by the privy council, and persuading mariners that they had more to do after bringing prizes home than provide the court with inventories and evaluations was proving difficult.[154]

The difficulty was addressed on 20 July 1589, when the privy council issued a revised set of articles, almost identical with those issued earlier except for the addition of a requirement that mariners promise before sailing not to distribute prizes 'untill they shall be adjudged in her majesties highe courte of the admiraltye to be lawfull prize'.[155] From this time onwards Caesar frequently passed acts of adjudication in his court, declaring that he had found ships and goods to belong to subjects of the king of Spain (*iure dominii pertinuisse*), to have been effectively captured (*capta et abducta*), and to have been seized by virtue of letters of reprisal (*virtute literarum reprisaliarum*), and therefore adjudging (*adiudicamus*) the prizes to their captors.[156] Surprisingly, he did not declare in these acts that losses had been sustained and justice denied in Spain or Portugal, and such statements seem to have disappeared from the standard styles of other documents around this time as well. The warrants obtained from the admiral tended merely to instruct that a 'comyssion of reprisall' be granted to someone to put a vessel to sea 'in warlike manner agaynste the kinge of Spayne and his subjectes'.[157] While no examples have been found of letters of reprisal granted by the court after 1589, they were probably similar

154 *Acts of the Privy Council of England*, vol. 17, pp. 412–13 and 416–19.

155 NAK, SP12/225, ff. 57–8; BL, Add. MS 12505, ff. 305 and 369–70, and Add. MS 14027, ff. 20–1; *Calendar of State Papers, Domestic Series, of the Reigns of Edward VI, Mary and Elizabeth*, vol. 2, p. 610; *Documents Relating to Law and Custom of the Sea*, vol. 1, p. 252.

156 *Documents Relating to Law and Custom of the Sea*, vol. 1, pp. 254–7, 291–3 and 306–13; NAK, HCA24/57, ff. 6–7, 24, 38–9, 40–3, 72–3 and 82 (further examples can easily be found in the same file, but it needs to be stressed that while continuous and copious records of the admiralty court survive from the 1520s onwards, it is not until the end of the 1580s that acts of adjudication start to appear); *English Privateering Voyages to the West Indies*, pp. 221–2 and 373–6.

157 *English Privateering Voyages to the West Indies*, pp. 176–7, 195, 216 and 229; NAK, HCA14/27, n. 13, and NAK, HCA25/3/1, ff. 13, 15, 27, 34, 43 and 62 (further examples can easily be found in the same file).

to several letters the queen herself is known to have granted to particularly prominent parties, which declared that authority had been given to them to fit out vessels 'in warlike sorte and manner', because they had offered service 'by the annoyinge and offendinge of the enemyes of our state'.[158] These letters required captors to account for prizes 'as in case of reprisalls oughte to be', but they made no mention of losses having been sustained or justice having been denied. In accordance with the revised version of the privy council's instructions, the bonds of recognisance submitted to the court promised that those who captured prizes would 'not breake bulcke, wast, spoile, sell or diminishe anie parte or parcell therof untill they shall be adjudged in her majesties highe courte of the admiralty to be lawfull prize'.[159] Just as the legitimacy of captures was taken to depend on letters of reprisal being granted, so the acquisition of prizes was taken to depend on acts of adjudication being passed, yet not even a pretence that losses had been sustained and justice denied was being maintained.[160] As the arrest of ships and goods and the imprisonment of crews in Spanish and Portuguese ports faded into the past, the taking of reprisals came to be separated from the conditions on which the legitimacy of the practice was understood to depend in the theory of the law schools.

Notwithstanding the continuing reliance on letters of reprisal and acts of adjudication, the initial reluctance to believe that England was at war with Spain was giving way to acceptance that prizes were being taken by ships sailing in warlike manner (*bellico more*), and from enemies (*hostes et inimici*) as opposed to friends (*amici*).[161] Aware that foreign sailors 'brought into the realme by reprisall', in order to provide evidence of the ownership of vessels and cargoes, were in a position to explore coastal areas, the privy council observed that they were actually 'enemyes unto her majesty', warned that 'upon theire retorne they may geve informacon of advantage to the enemye', and required them in future to be held in close confinement.[162] When captured

158 *Documents Relating to Law and Custom of the Sea*, vol. 1, pp. 270–2, 278–80 and 284–7.

159 *English Privateering Voyages to the West Indies*, pp. 178–9; NAK, HCA25/3, pt 1, ff. 1–7, 10–12, 14–17 and 19–20 (further examples can easily be found in the same file).

160 As Caesar made clear in opposing the suggestion that appeals should be allowed against acts of adjudication (BL, Lansdowne MS 152, ff. 152–3, and Lansdowne MS 157, ff. 254–5), the understanding in England was that captors would normally be given possession of their prizes by a court order and would become owners of them a year later, as a further court order would then confirm. See too Andrews 1959, pp. 8–9.

161 *Documents Relating to Law and Custom of the Sea*, vol. 1, pp. 293–8, 302–8, 311–13 and 322–30; *English Privateering Voyages to the West Indies*, pp. 345–61; BL, Lansdowne MS 157, f. 434.

162 *Documents Relating to Law and Custom of the Sea*, vol. 1, pp. 290–1.

ships from neutral countries were found to be supplying Spain or Portugal with military or naval equipment (*apparatus bellici aut navium usui apti et accommodandi* or *equippages de navires et autres choses necessaires à la guerre*), the court adjudged the equipment to their takers as good prize, which only made sense on the supposition that a state of war existed.[163] Prizes were distributed in accordance with the customary rules applicable 'in warlike affaers', so that if several ships 'gave chase togeather to the ennimy', they were all taken to be entitled to share in any prize taken.[164] In the 1590s, in contrast to the later 1580s, it was accepted that crews were entitled to pillage the vessels they captured before they brought them home for adjudication and distribution.[165] The 'custome in time of warre', as Caesar had called it, was now believed to be applicable.[166] Yet Caesar did not believe that mariners could simply put to sea and plunder enemy shipping. It was important to issue letters of reprisal, he advised the admiral, because unless mariners were authorised to sail, 'then shall her majestie loosse her customes, your lordship your tenthes, the shipps rott at home for want of ymployment, and the mariners either turne theire trade, or become plaine pirats, or els sell theire laboures to the enimeas to work theire pleasure'.[167] Those who put to sea and seized ships and goods without letters of reprisal from the queen or admiral – or equivalent authorisation from the king of Spain – would not only be in breach of the regulations issued to govern the conflict and be treated as pirates, but would actually be pirates.

163 *Documents Relating to Law and Custom of the Sea*, vol. 1, pp. 262–7, 282–4 and 317–20. At first, the rules on contraband were justified by reference to the open war (*la guerre ouverte*) that was taken to exist between Spain and the Netherlands, but that did not really make sense, and the simpler line was later taken that those supplying Spain and Portugal were supplying the queen's enemies.

164 *Select Pleas in the Court of Admiralty*, vol. 2, p. 44; *English Privateering Voyages to the West Indies*, pp. 134 and 138–9; BL, Lansdowne MS 73, ff. 38–9, Lansdowne MS 115, ff. 251–2, and Lansdowne MS 143, ff. 8–46. Of course, the customary rules supplemented the last of the articles laid down by the privy council, and were applicable in the absence of a 'consortship agreement' between those involved (*Documents Relating to Law and Custom of the Sea*, vol. 1, pp. 272–3 and 308–11; *English Privateering Voyages to the West Indies*, pp. 302–4).

165 *English Privateering Voyages to the West Indies*, pp. 121, 135, 137 and 142; *Naval Tracts of Sir William Monson*, vol. 4, pp. 18–19, 201 and 230; *Boteler's Dialogues*, pp. 37–40.

166 BL, Lansdowne MS 157, f. 318.

167 BL, Lansdowne MS 157, f. 446. Caesar was recommending in particular that no more security ought to be demanded than the mariners could realistically be expected to provide. Although Howard was prepared to relax some rules (*Documents Relating to Law and Custom of the Sea*, vol. 1, pp. 281–2 and 301–2), he was generally insistent on receiving his duties (*Documents Relating to Law and Custom of the Sea*, vol. 1, pp. 257–60 and 320–1; NAK, HCA14/28, n. 44, and HCA14/32, nn. 82 and 119). BL, Harley MS 598, lists vessels taken and duties paid between 1587 and 1598.

Some of those who sailed in warlike manner against the queen's enemies in the closing years of her reign did so as pirates, but many acted on the strength of letters of reprisal obtained from the admiral and sought to have their acquisition of prizes confirmed by acts of adjudication passed in his court.[168]

Having refrained from issuing a proclamation on the plundering of shipping at the start of the war, Elizabeth issued several proclamations after 1590.[169] In 1591, and again in 1599, she responded to complaints about the plundering of neutral shipping, accepting that among those who had been authorised to recover recompense for 'the notable injuries by arrests' they had suffered, 'whereof no remedy could ever be had by order of justice', there were several who 'by colour thereof' were seizing ships and goods from friendly nations.[170] It was declared that the victims should receive restitution, while the assailants should receive punishment. More significantly for present purposes, these proclamations also strengthened the requirement that the holders of letters of reprisal must satisfy the bonds they submitted to the admiralty, the standard terms of which were set out in appendices. Those who broke bulk and disposed of goods without a court order were to be imprisoned, and both their own ships and the prizes they had taken were 'to be forfeited to her majesty, whereby justice may be done to all persons that have just cause of complaint'. Owners from friendly nations could expect to have their goods restored to them, but it is significant that forfeiture was to occur 'though the prize be lawful'. As adjudication was required for title to be conferred on the captors, and the concern was with captors who had not obtained a court order, prizes obviously could not have been forfeited to the queen from the captors, yet nor would it have made sense for these ships and goods to be restored to their Spanish or Portuguese owners. The understanding thus was that ships and goods seized from the queen's enemies, but not adjudged to their captors, were to be confiscated. A further proclamation issued in 1594 warned those who received goods from a captured ship 'before it be adjudged good prize' that they would be punished and the goods would be forfeited to the queen.[171] In 1602, as both the war and the queen's reign neared their conclusion, two more

168 Andrews 1964, pp. 22–5; Spence 1995, pp. 64–5; Loades 2000, pp. 127–8; Hammer 2003, pp. 166–9; Hanson 2003, p. 95; McDermott 2005, pp. 152–3; Franks 2006, pp. 62–3.

169 Youngs 1976, pp. 95–6.

170 *Tudor Royal Proclamations*, vol. 3, pp. 71–4 and 197–9; *Documents Relating to Law and Custom of the Sea*, vol. 1, pp. 300–1; *Foedera, conventiones, litterae et cuiuscunque generis acta publica*, vol. 16, pp. 365–6. See too *Tudor Royal Proclamations*, vol. 3, pp. 99–101, 109–10 and 137–8.

171 *Tudor Royal Proclamations*, vol. 3, pp. 137–8.

proclamations were issued. One reiterated the requirements that nobody put a 'man of warre' to sea without obtaining authorisation from and giving security to the admiral, that raiding be confined to ships belonging to or collaborating with the enemy, and that prizes be adjudged to their captors by the court of admiralty before goods were sold, 'under payne of confiscation of shippe and goodes'.[172] The other proclamation was concerned more specifically with the problem of collaboration with the enemy.[173] Observing that Philip III was continuing his father's 'hostile proceadings', and that he had little prospect of success 'without the helpe and assistance of those who be her hignes confederates, frendes or allies', it explained that the best way to bring an end to 'these bloudie and unnaturall warres' was to place an embargo on trade with Spain. Warning was accordingly given to 'neighbour nations' that no one should carry goods or wares to Spain or Portugal, 'uppon paine of confiscation of the same goodes, wares and marchandises, together with the shippes or vessels wherein the same shalbe laden'. Notice was also given to all English mariners who had been authorised to annoy the enemy that they could lawfully seize ships from friendly nations if they were trading with the enemy. Such prizes were to be kept intact until 'adjudged by the judge of the high court of the admiralty of England for the time being to bee forfeited and confiscated for the causes above recited', after which they could be disposed of as freely 'as just prizes in time of open and proclaimed war'.

Following Elizabeth's death in 1603 the admiral was advised by his lieutenant and others that while the letters of reprisal issued in the queen's name had lost validity, 'the cyvell lawe' permitted any prizes already taken to be adjudged to their captors.[174] When complaints had been received from the Hanseatic League about the seizure of 'warlike provisions' from their vessels heading towards Spain, it had been answered that this was 'a course usuall amonge all Christian princes, and allowed by the lawes, as well civill as the lawe of nations'.[175] When similar complaints had been received from the Netherlands, Caesar had insisted that they be dealt with in his court 'by ordinary course of justice, which is by the civill and maritime law, the truest and most indifferent

172 *Foedera, conventiones, litterae et cuiuscunque generis acta publica*, vol. 16, pp. 436–8; *Tudor Royal Proclamations*, vol. 3, pp. 238–41.

173 *Documents Relating to Law and Custom of the Sea*, vol. 1, pp. 313–17; *Tudor Royal Proclamations*, vol. 3, pp. 255–8.

174 *Documents Relating to Law and Custom of the Sea*, vol. 1, pp. 330–1.

175 *Acts of the Privy Council of England*, vol. 18, pp. 112–13. On the understanding of the relationship between the civil law and the law of nations in England at this time see Cheyney 1905 and 1929.

judge betwene all nations'.[176] Pleadings and notes that happen to have survived from his court confirm that legal argument generally was conducted there in terms of the civil law, with reference to the literature on the taking of plunder in wartime and reprisals in peacetime.[177] Lawyers trained in the universities continued to offer their expertise to litigants in the way they were used to doing, as if a war had been declared or reprisals had been authorised. One problem, however, was that since no war had been declared it could not be claimed correctly that the property of the king of Spain's subjects had become *res hostium* open to acquisition by *occupatio*. Instead of declaring war, the queen had directed her admiral to grant letters of reprisal, and the admiralty court had then enabled prizes to be acquired by a process of *adiudicatio*. Yet a second problem was that, after the first few years of the conflict, the taking of reprisals against the king of Spain's subjects had lost any connection with losses sustained or justice denied. Although it had come to be believed that the seizure of ships and goods at sea would amount to piracy unless authorised by letters of reprisal, and although the obtaining of letters of reprisal and acts of adjudication had become mandatory, the theory of reprisals was no longer applicable, which was no doubt one reason for the increasing recourse to the language of plunder, another being the undeniable reality that England and Spain were at war. In the confusing circumstances of another undeclared war, an approach to prize taking had emerged which appeared, on the one hand, to be a hybrid of licit plunder in wartime and licensed reprisal in peacetime, yet which could not, on the other hand, be justified in terms of the traditional theory of either. In dealing with prizes that had been distributed without a court order or seized from parties trading with the enemy, the proclamations issued after 1590 had referred to the forfeiture of ships and goods to the queen, from

176 BL, Add MS 12505, ff. 377–8. By 'maritime law' Caesar probably meant what his predecessors at Doctors' Commons had referred to as 'auncient custome and the lawe of armes' (BL, Lansdowne MS 115, f. 245). Their thinking, as was noted in the last chapter, allowed for legal pluralism in the weak sense of the term. In claiming that mariners in the 1585–1604 war had a different understanding of their rights from the legal regime laid out in the official regulations, Fury 2002, pp. 102–8, may be hinting at the existence of legal pluralism in the strong sense. The evidence adduced of mariners failing to adhere to the official regulations cannot show on its own that they had a different understanding of their rights, but in this transitional period legal pluralism in the strong sense is more likely to have been developing.

177 BL, Add. MS 14027, ff. 127–9, and Lansdowne MS 129; *Consilium facultatis iuridicae Tubingensis*. For a rigorous examination of the pleadings presented in this period see Wijffels 1994a.

whom they might be adjudged to their captors.[178] If a new theory was starting to emerge here, it was not expounded clearly, though it does seem clear that for the innovation in practice that occurred in Elizabeth's reign to be convincingly justified there also needed to be significant innovation in theory.

3 Justification in Terms of the Practice of Nations

It is a striking feature of the proclamation about trading with the enemy that while some effort was made in its preamble to justify the threat of action against neutral nations, no mention was made of the civil law or the law of nations. Conscious that 'the chiefest lawe of pollicy' to be observed by any monarch was 'the safety and preservation of the kingdome and people committed to his charge', Elizabeth had decided to forbid trading with her enemies and to authorise assaults on offenders, 'according to that supreme lawe of governement, ingrafted by nature in the hart of every souverain prince, warranted by the lawe of God, and confirmed by the continuall practise of her neighbour nations in theise latter times'.[179] The preservation of her kingdom and people in safety was the 'chiefest lawe of pollicy', or the 'supreme lawe of governement', and it was a law inscribed in her heart by nature. The priority thus given to national security had also been 'warranted by the lawe of God', and had been 'confirmed by the continuall practise of her neighbour nations in theise latter times'. As the phrase 'in theise latter times' indicates, an attempt was being made to justify a recent innovation. An appeal was being made to the shared perceptions of sovereigns and to the common practice of nations, but it was not being suggested that the consensus of sovereigns and nations reflected acceptance of the civil law taught in the universities as the foundation of lawful relations between them. If there was a *ius commune* or *ius gentium*, confirmed by the practice of nations, it was the law of policy or the law of God. The legitimacy of the maritime raiding the queen was authorising could apparently be traced back to these foundations, though how was not explained

178 As was mentioned earlier, the 'Statute of Truces' had already provided for the forfeiture of prizes disposed of before the legitimacy of their acquisition was judicially confirmed, which may well have influenced the drafting of Elizabeth's proclamations on the plundering of neutral vessels. The crucial difference, however, was that both these proclamations and the proclamation on collaborating with the enemy envisaged the forfeiture of goods that still belonged to foreigners, not goods that had already been acquired by occupation from enemies.

179 *Documents Relating to Law and Custom of the Sea*, vol. 1, pp. 313–17; *Tudor Royal Proclamations*, vol. 3, pp. 255–8.

in detail in the proclamation. Later sections in this chapter will consider what may have been meant by the law of policy and the law of God, and how far a justification for maritime raiding might have been developed on the basis of these 'laws', whatever that may have meant meant. In this section consideration is given to the recent practices of neighbouring nations that Elizabeth or her draftsmen may have had in mind, and to how the adoption of these practices might have been taken to justify what was happening in England.

In the last section it was seen that during the 1560s Elizabeth sought to justify her authorisation of maritime raiding against the French as a reciprocal response to the French king's authorisation of raiding against her own subjects. In the section before that it was seen that even before Elizabeth came to the throne, reciprocity with the French had been used to encourage adoption of their doctrine of *infection hostile* – the idea that friendly ships carrying enemy goods could be acquired as *res hostium*. It was also seen there that the 'Statute of Truces' enacted in 1414, which changed the way in which maritime warfare was regulated in England during the next two centuries, was probably inspired indirectly by legislation enacted in France in 1373. To at least some extent, the French legislation had been based on existing practice, but it came itself to form the basis of the legislative tradition mentioned in the second section of the preceding chapter.[180] Three major restatements of maritime law appeared in France during the sixteenth century. The first was enacted by Francis I in 1517, in an attempt to clarify the jurisdiction of the admirals of France and Guyenne.[181] The same king took advantage of a vacancy in the admiralty of France twenty years later to pass a revised and enlarged 'edit sur l'amirauté' in 1544, reinforcing the established restraints on maritime warfare just two months after Henry VIII had relaxed the corresponding regulations in England.[182] As was noted in the preceding chapter, Henry III enacted a further revised and enlarged 'edit sur l'amirauté' in 1584, shortly before Elizabeth's war with Spain is generally believed to have started. Part of Henry's aim was to bring Brittany, which had been united with France in 1532, within the

180 The best overview of the legislative tradition remains Taillemite 1993. On the relationship between the 1373 edict and existing practice see Dumas 1908, pp. 53 and 69.

181 This edict may have had some influence on the terms of the treaty made with England in 1518 (n. 82 above), which Marsden 1909, p. 683, took to be fundamental to the articles passed by the privy council in 1585, as well as the probable cause of the resuscitation of the admiralty court in the 1520s. The latter suggestion is manifestly more plausible than the former.

182 See n. 86 above, and for the vacancy in the admiralty of France see Allaire 2015, p. 84.

jurisdiction of the admiral of France.[183] There were in fact three admiralties operating within the territory known today as France.[184] The jurisdiction of the admiral of France had previously been limited to Picardy and Normandy, facing the North Sea and English Channel, while the admiral of Guyenne had jurisdiction to the south of Brittany, on the Atlantic coast, and the admiral of Provence had jurisdiction in the south east, on the Mediterranean coast. All three admirals had to compete with other jurisdictions in their areas, and in Brittany the insistence was that the governor and lieutenant-general should continue to discharge the responsibilities of an admiral, as the duke of Brittany had done before the union.[185] It may be recalled that it was through a truce made with the duke of Brittany in 1414 that the legislation enacted in 1373 appears to have had an influence on English practice. One more observation made in the preceding chapter was that the French legislation, in its various iterations, was widely influential as an example of how the broad principles of prize acquisition taught in the law schools could be given effect in the detailed regulations governing the practice of maritime raiding.

The edicts passed in 1373, 1517, 1544 and 1584 contained essentially the same provisions in relation to prize taking. One article provided that anyone who wished to put a ship to sea at his own expense (*à ses propres despens*), in order to wage war against the king's enemies (*pour porter guerre à nos ennemis*), must first obtain the leave and consent (*congé et consentement*) of the admiral or his lieutenant.[186] Before giving his consent the admiral was to ensure that the ship was suitably equipped, after which he was to require the master and other officers to swear (*jurer*) that they would conduct themselves properly at sea, without harming the king's subjects, friends, allies or sympathisers (*sans porter dommage à nos subjets, amis, alliez ou bien-veillans*).[187] Another article

183 Anne, duc de Joyeuse, had been appointed 'l'amiral de France et de Bretagne' in 1582, but his appointment was being resisted in Brittany (James 2000, pp. 103–6, and 2004, pp. 32–8).

184 Doucet 1949, vol. 1, pp. 244–9; Zeller 1987, pp. 125–7 and 194–5; Vergé-Franceschi 1991, pp. 21–38, and 1997, pp. 35–7.

185 Darsel 2012, pp. 62–4 and 201–6.

186 *Recueil général des anciennes lois françaises*, vol. 6, pp. 848–9, vol. 12, pp. 138–9 and 855–6, and vol. 14, pp. 562–3; *Edicts et ordonnances des roys de France*, vol. 2, pp. 843–4 and 850; *Collection de lois maritimes*, vol. 4, p. 302; *Black Book of the Admiralty*, vol. 1, pp. 432–4.

187 The terms of the oath were outlined in another article, concerned with those who put ships to sea under the king's pay (*Recueil général des anciennes lois françaises*, vol. 6, p. 848, vol. 12, pp. 138 and 855, and vol. 14, p. 562; *Edicts et ordonnances des roys de France*, vol. 2, pp. 843 and 850; *Collection de lois maritimes*, vol. 4, p. 302; *Black Book of the Admiralty*, vol. 1, p. 432). In the 1517, 1544 and 1584 edicts it was added that security was to be provide (*bailler caution juratoire*) to the same effect.

provided that when prizes (*prises*) were taken, whether by vessels in the king's pay or by others under the 'cover and colour' of his wars (*sous ombre et couleur de nos guerres*), the admiral was to be presented not only with an inventory of the goods taken, from which he could calculate his own entitlement, but also with any mariners found on board, so that he could find out where they came from and to whom the goods belonged, and could thus ensure that justice was done and restitution was made to anyone who should not have been harmed (*pour garder justice, et pour restituer ceux qui sans cause auront esté endommagez*).[188] As experience had shown that mariners sometimes tried to disguise the origins of ships and goods, it was further provided in all four edicts that the admiral should be presented with any charter party found on board, so that it could be discovered whether the ship and goods really did belong to the king's enemies (*s'il y a vraye apparence qu'ils fussent de nos ennemis*).[189] As experience had also shown that when a prize was taken from the king's enemies (*quand une prise estoit faite sur nos ennemis*), the takers would sometimes dispose of goods stealthily, in defraud of the owners and victuallers, and to the possible detriment of their friendly owners, it was reaffirmed in another article that cargoes must not be interfered with until a report had been made to the admiral.[190] In the 1544 and 1584 edicts it was added that no one was to buy goods from a prize until the admiral had declared it lawful (*ait déclaré les prises estre justes et de bon et licite gain*), on pain of arrest and the confiscation of their goods (*sur peine de prise de corps et confiscation de biens*).[191] As was mentioned previously, other provisions dealt with the distribution of prizes among shipowners, victuallers and crews, the admiral's right to a tenth of each prize taken, the fate of friendly goods found on enemy ships, and related matters. While the use of the phrase 'sous ombre et couleur de nos guerres' is indicative of a

188 *Recueil général des anciennes lois françaises*, vol. 6, p. 849, vol. 12, pp. 139–40 and 856, and vol. 14, pp. 563–4; *Edicts et ordonnances des roys de France*, vol. 2, pp. 844–5; *Collection de lois maritimes*, vol. 4, p. 303; *Black Book of the Admiralty*, vol. 1, p. 434.

189 *Recueil général des anciennes lois françaises*, vol. 6, p. 850, vol. 12, pp. 140–1 and 856–7, and vol. 14, pp. 564–5; *Edicts et ordonnances des roys de France*, vol. 2, pp. 850–1; *Collection de lois maritimes*, vol. 4, pp. 303–4; *Black Book of the Admiralty*, vol. 1, p. 434.

190 *Recueil général des anciennes lois françaises*, vol. 6, p. 851, vol. 12, pp. 142 and 858, and vol. 14, pp. 565–6; *Edicts et ordonnances des roys de France*, vol. 2, pp. 845 and 851; *Collection de lois maritimes*, vol. 4, pp. 304–5; *Black Book of the Admiralty*, vol. 1, p. 436–7. It was not until the edicts of 1544 and 1584 that the requirement was generalised that captors must return with their prizes to their home ports (*Recueil général des anciennes lois françaises*, vol. 12, p. 860, and vol. 14, pp. 568–9; *Edicts et ordonnances des roys de France*, vol. 2, p. 852; *Collection de lois maritimes*, vol. 4, p. 307).

191 *Recueil général des anciennes lois françaises*, vol. 12, p. 861, and vol. 14, p. 569; *Edicts et ordonnances des roys de France*, vol. 2, pp. 852–3; *Collection de lois maritimes*, vol. 4, p. 308.

certain suspicion of private enterprise at sea, the unstated assumption behind all of these provisions remained that prize taking was lawful as soon as the king of France became involved in a war with another sovereign. The admiral had been given greater control over maritime warfare, but his judicial role was simply to maintain existing property rights, either by declaring (*déclarer*) that prizes had been lawfully taken from enemies, or by ordering their return (*restituer*) to their friendly owners.

These provisions were obviously applicable to prize taking during the wars waged by the kings of France against their neighbours during the first sixty years of the sixteenth century. When Charles IX issued his declaration on the subject in 1563, it was apparently because the legitimacy of prize taking in the undeclared war he was involved in with Elizabeth was in doubt. The basis on which licences had been granted by the Huguenot governor of Le Havre a year earlier is even less clear, although a sense of what may have been going on emerges from the much fuller documentation that survives from the third war of religion. The false peace following the brief second war in 1568 was brought to an end by an attempt to arrest the Huguenot leaders that summer.[192] Louis de Bourbon, the prince of Condé, and Gaspard de Coligny, the admiral of France, sought refuge in the Protestant stronghold of La Rochelle, where they were soon joined by Jeanne d'Albret, the queen of Navarre, accompanied by her young son Henry, who had succeeded his father as both the governor and the admiral of Guyenne.[193] After Condé was killed at the battle of Jarnac in 1569, Henry, still just fifteen years old, became the nominal leader of the Huguenot movement, supported by his cousin, Condé's son and heir, who was just sixteen.[194] It seemed important to the Huguenots that they should be led by a nobleman close to the throne, for this enabled them to maintain the pretence that they were not rebelling against royal authority but supporting a leading magnate in a legitimate enterprise to liberate the king from the control of evil counsellors who had surrounded him.[195] There were in fact few noblemen of higher rank in the kingdom than Henry of Navarre, who was next in line to the throne after Charles IX and his brothers.[196] In reality, however, it was Coligny who led the Huguenot movement in France, and Jeanne d'Albret who dealt on behalf of her son and nephew with the increasingly independent authorities in La Rochelle.[197] A council of lesser noblemen and others was formed around

192 Salmon 1975, pp. 173–5; Baumgartner 1995, pp. 214–15; Carroll 2009, pp. 180–3.

193 Sutherland 1980, pp. 166–7; Knecht 2001, pp. 348–9; Pitts 2009, pp. 42–5.

194 Buisseret 1984, p. 6; Garrisson 1995, pp. 270–1; Elliott 2000, p. 80.

195 Skinner 1978, vol. 2, pp. 302–4; Kelley 1981, pp. 282–6; Love 2001, pp. 40–4.

196 Holt 2005, pp. 38–40; Jouanna 2007, pp. 47–8; Treasure 2013, pp. 130–2.

197 Major 1994, p. 118; Meyer 1996, pp. 137–8; James 2004, p. 15.

the queen, which came to play an important part in organising the Huguenot war effort.[198] Among other things, it orchestrated a campaign of maritime raiding from the port against Catholic shipping, which was to continue throughout the third war and would also be revived in later conflicts.[199]

Among other interventions relating to prize taking, the queen's council issued instructions that no vessel should depart without the express leave and permission (*sans l'expres congé et permission*) of the queen or the admiral's lieutenant, that returning captains should provide the officers of the admiralty with an account of the prizes they had taken (*les prinses qu'ils ont fectes*), and that those officers should in turn provide regular accounts to the council (*rendre compte tous les samedys*).[200] When the queen herself gave 'congé, licence et permission' for vessels to depart and wage war against the enemies of the true religion and general cause (*faire la guerre contre les ennemis de la vraye relligion et cause générالle*), she did so explicitly under the advice and authority (*soubz l'adveu et auctorité*) of her son and nephew, and supposedly in obedience to her lord the king (*en l'obeissance du roy mon seigneur*).[201] When the lieutenant placed in charge of the admiralty gave his 'congé et permission' for vessels 'to wage war, set upon and injure the enemies and adversaries of the reformed religion and general cause', he did so simply in the name of the admiral.[202] Like the queen, he required captains to promise that they would bring their prizes back to La Rochelle, unless forced by adverse weather or similar causes into other ports, that they would surrender 'ung dixiesme' of each prize to the admiralty, and that they would also surrender 'ung autre dixiesme' to be used for the benefit of the cause (*pour estre employé au proffit de la cause*). On one occasion a captain was licensed to recover compensation for losses he had sustained (*le récompenser de plusieurs grandes pertes par luy souffertes*), but even in this exceptional case no reference was made to any denial of justice, and the goods remaining after the captain was compensated were appropriated for the cause, not returned to the victims of the seizures, who were identified in

198 Roelker 1968, pp. 311–13; Parker 1980, pp. 97–8; Robbins 1997, pp. 206–8.

199 Dietz 1952–8; De Pablo 1956; Delafosse 1963; Augeron 1997 and 2009; Poton 2004 and 2009.

200 'Conseil de la reine de Navarre à La Rochelle: Ordonnances et délibérations inédites', pp. 129–31.

201 'Régistre de l'amirauté de Guyenne au siége de La Rochelle', pp. 207–9; ADCM, B174, ff. 8v–11r and 37.

202 'Régistre de l'amirauté de Guyenne au siége de La Rochelle', pp. 204 and 223; ADCM, B174, f. 41r. For the appointment of Jacques Sores as lieutenant see the 'Régistre de l'amirauté de Guyenne au siége de La Rochelle', pp. 218–19.

the usual way as 'ennemys'.[203] Nevertheless, when prizes were brought back and reported to the authorities, decrees issued by the admiralty court not only declared (*déclairé et déclarons*) that they had been properly taken (*estre de bonne prinse, comme biens de papistes et ennemys*), but also adjudged (*adjugé et adjugeons*) them to their captors.[204] No mention of any loss sustained or justice denied was made in these decrees, which proceeded to specify that a tenth part of each prize must be surrendered to the cause as well as the admiral, an important source of revenue for the Huguenots, as contemporary observers recognised.[205] It helped that those authorised to wage war against enemies of the true religion were told they could do so 'sur tous vaisseaux et sur toutes nations indiferement'.[206] Regulations issued in the 1570s suggest that a similar approach was taken in the later wars.[207]

Eager to preserve some semblance of legality in their struggle with the Catholics, the Protestants in La Rochelle thus maintained that their mariners were sailing under licences granted on behalf of the admiral of Guyenne, who was in turn acting on behalf of the king, to whom he and his followers remained loyal.[208] A similar approach may have been taken at Le Havre during the first war, when Coligny had held office both as the governor of that port and as the admiral with jurisdiction over the area in which it lay.[209] There were problems, however, with the approach taken at La Rochelle. One was that during the third war Henry of Navarre, in common with other dignitaries who adhered to 'la nouvelle pretendue religion', was temporarily stripped of his offices by the Edict of Saint-Maur.[210] If it was possible to dismiss this edict as another measure forced upon the king by evil counsellors, a more fundamental

---

203 'Régistre de l'amirauté de Guyenne au siége de La Rochelle', pp. 210–12. See too the 'Lettres de Jeanne d'Albret, reine de Navarre, Henri, prince de Navarre, et Henri de Bourbon, prince de Condé', pp. 317–19.

204 'Régistre de l'amirauté de Guyenne au siége de La Rochelle', pp. 205, 212, 217, 222, 224–5, 227, 234–6, 238–9 and 245–7; ADCM, B174, ff. 13v-14, 30v, 37v-8, 42, 43v-4r, 45, 48v-9r, 57v-8, 60–2r, 63, 66v-8r, 80v-1r and 82v-4.

205 'Régistre de l'amirauté de Guyenne au siége de La Rochelle', pp. 240–1; La Popelinière, *L'histoire de France depuis l'an 1550 jusqu'à ces temps*, vol. 1(2), ff. 75r and 81v; Barbot, 'Histoire de La Rochelle depuis l'an 1199 jusques en 1575', vol. 17, pp. 340–1. See too Greengrass 1999, pp. 239–40, and Daussy 2015, pp. 606–7.

206 'Régistre de l'amirauté de Guyenne au siége de La Rochelle', pp. 204 and 224.

207 Barbot, 'Histoire de La Rochelle depuis l'an 1199 jusques en 1575', vol. 18, pp. 240–3; 'Rapports des Rochelais avec Henri Ier de Bourbon, prince de Condé', pp. 326–30.

208 Gouron 1938, pp. 160–2; Rambeaud 1997, p. 142; James 2004, pp. 14–16.

209 Corvisier 1983, pp. 60–1; Carroll 1998, pp. 97 and 150–1; Guillo 2016, p. 1.

210 *Receueil général des anciennes lois françaises*, vol. 14, p. 228; *Edicts et ordonnaces des roys de France* (ed. Rebuffi), pp. 1457–64; *Édits des guerres de religion*, pp. 59–66.

problem was that, far from the king having declared war against another sovereign, the Huguenots claimed to be waging war against adherents to the old religion, regardless of their national allegiance. It was probably for this reason that the admiralty court sitting in La Rochelle felt the need to proceed beyond declaring in its decisions that prizes had been lawfully taken and to adjudge them formally to their captors. Unlike the admiralty court sitting in London during the later 1580s, the authorities in La Rochelle did not pretend that reprisals were being taken for losses inflicted and justice denied, yet they do appear to have appreciated that there was a problem with maintaining that enemies were being plundered in wartime.[211] It could not have been claimed in accordance with the conventional theory of prize taking that the ships and goods of enemies (*res hostium*) were to be considered ownerless (*res nullius*) and open to acquisition through simple possession (*occupatio*), because the ships and goods did not belong to enemies in a war declared between sovereign rulers (*bellum publicum*). The licences granted under the admiral's authority, conventional as they appeared to be in form, could not have served to regulate lawful prize taking in the normal way, because the prize taking they were designed to regulate was not lawful in terms of the conventional theory. Ironically, while the legality of the maritime raiding licensed in La Rochelle was doubtful, the licences granted became more important as the only possible basis for the legality of the seizures made. How exactly they could be taken to have legitimised raiding when they were not letters of reprisal or marque was not made clear, but the task for any new theory would clearly have been to explain how a combination of licensing before seizures and adjudication afterwards could give captors title to prizes. Although the earlier practice of the Protestant authorities in France did not provide a perfect parallel with the practice of the authorities in England towards the end of the century, there were significant similarities between the approaches taken in both places.

Shortly before they withdrew to La Rochelle in 1568, Condé and Coligny had entered into a secret alliance with William of Nassau, the prince of Orange and leader of the Protestant cause in the Netherlands.[212] Maritime warfare was regulated there by an edict issued in 1540 by Charles V, a restatement with some adjustments of an edict issued in 1488 by Maximilian I, which had itself been modelled closely on the French edict issued in 1373.[213] Mariners who

211 Although editors and historians have frequently referred to the licences granted in La Rochelle as 'letters of marque', they were never called that in contemporary records, nor do they bear the hallmarks of such letters.

212 *Archives ou correspondance inédite de la maison d'Orange-Nassau*, 1st ser., vol. 3, pp. 282–6.

213 As was noted in the last chapter, the edicts issued in the Netherlands are examined in detail in Sicking 2004, pp. 62–131. That the 1488 edict had been modelled on the 1373 edict

were employed in fleets under the command of the newly created admiral of the Netherlands were required to obey the orders of any officers he appointed on their ships and to provide him with assurances of their good behaviour.[214] Mariners who proposed to sail in armed ships independently of the fleet were required to obtain licences before departing and to promise good behaviour in doing so.[215] Originally it had been the admiral or his lieutenant who had granted licences, but a significant change made in 1540 was that Charles V resumed personal responsibility for the granting of all licences, safe conducts and similar documents, which then had to be registered with the admiralty.[216] In their various French and Dutch versions, the edicts referred to the need to obtain express leave or licence (*congie et licence expesse* or *verlof en expresse toelating*) from the admiral or emperor before departing from a port in an armed ship. They provide no support for the suggestion that a distinction was already being drawn in the Netherlands between 'letters of marque', issued in wartime, and 'letters of reprisal', issued in peacetime.[217] The licensing system in the Netherlands was not only modelled on the system introduced in France but appears to have operated in much the same way. Although the admiral's responsibilities were altered in 1540, the assumption clearly remained that requiring mariners to obtain licences would encourage them to exercise in a more orderly manner than they might otherwise have done the rights of pillage and plunder they enjoyed as soon as a war was declared. The process of granting a licence enabled the authorities to acquire information about the activities of private parties and to ensure that their vessels were suitably equipped for engagements with the enemy. The process of receiving assurances of good behaviour placed pressure on mariners to conduct themselves at sea in an orderly manner. The process of supervising the distribution of prizes after they were brought back to port, which was again regulated in the Netherlands in much the same way as in France, enabled the authorities to check that the assurances they received were being honoured, and to insist on the payment

is further confirmed in Lambert 2019, pp. 120–1. For the customary law applicable before 1488 see Roelofsen 1980, and for the relationship between this law and learned theory in the practice of the courts see Roelofsen 1987, and Sicking and van Rhee 2019.

214 *Groot Placaet-Boeck*, vol. 4, pp. 1212–13; *Recueil des ordonnances de Pays-Bas*, vol. 4, pp. 271–2.

215 *Groot Placaet-Boeck*, vol. 4, pp. 1209–10; *Recueil des ordonnances de Pays-Bas*, vol. 4, p. 270.

216 *Groot Placaet-Boeck*, vol. 4, pp. 1211–12; *Recueil des ordonnances de Pays-Bas*, vol. 4, pp. 270–1.

217 The distinction is drawn repeatedly in Sicking 2004, but see especially pp. 420–80.

of shares of spoils to the admiral.[218] None of the regulations introduced in the Netherlands in 1488 and 1540 suggests that the right to acquire property from the enemy was understood to derive from the granting of a licence.

In fulfilment of his alliance with the Huguenots, William of Orange was in France during the third war of religion, and he appears to have been impressed with the arrangements made in La Rochelle to regulate maritime raiding.[219] In 1569 he began to organise maritime raiding himself.[220] In keeping with the terms of his alliance, which promised mutual assistance in the attempts the Protestants of France and the Netherlands made to liberate their rulers from the control of evil counsellors, William claimed to be resisting the tyrannous regime of the duke of Alva rather than the lawful rule of Philip II.[221] What he could not claim, however, given the changes made to the regulation of maritime warfare in 1540 by Philip's father, was that he was organising maritime raiding on the king's behalf. Instead of relying on any office or title he held in the Netherlands, he claimed to be authorising aggression at sea as a free prince of the empire (count of Nassau) and as the ruler of an independent territory in France (prince of Orange).[222] It was on this basis that he appointed an admiral of his own in 1570 and issued regulations requiring mariners who wished to sail to obtain a licence (*commissie*) from him personally or from his lieutenant, to promise (*besweren*) his admiral that they would abide by any articles of war (*ordonnantie van der oorloge*) he issued, and to have their spoils divided into three parts (*buiten sullen in drie delen gedeeit werden*), one of which he would receive himself, under the supervision of his lieutenant.[223] The licences he had started to grant a year earlier typically declared that in view of the afflictions, annoyance and iniquities (*gewelden, overlast ende ongerichticheden*) visited upon the people of the Netherlands by the duke of Alva, together with the evident commitment to the common cause (*gemeyne zaecke*) of the recipient, he was conferring power and authority (*macht ende bevel*) on him to arm a ship and annoy the duke and his adherents, 'approving and ratifying by these

218 *Groot Placaet-Boeck*, vol. 4, pp. 1210–11; *Recueil des ordonnances de Pays-Bas*, vol. 4, pp. 270–1.

219 Harrison 1902, pp. 153–4; Avermaete 1946, p. 25; De Meij 1972, pp. 329–30.

220 Motley 1882, pp. 449–50; Versteeg 1901, pp. 51–4; Van Loo 1997, pp. 174–5. Some kind of organisation had already been attempted by William's younger brother, Louis of Nassau, in 1568 (Parker 1979, pp. 121–2; French 1991, pp. 171–2; Tracy 2008, pp. 78–9).

221 Van Gelderen 1992, pp. 115–22; Israel 1998, pp. 161–2; Arnade 2008, pp. 273–6; Van der Lem 2018, pp. 83–4. For the development of Protestant propaganda in the earlier 1560s see Duke 1999 and Van Stipriaan 2007.

222 Wedgwood 1944, pp. 11–12; Geyl 2001, pp. 75–6; Geevers 2010, pp. 466–71.

223 Bor, *Oorsprongk, Begin en Vervolgh der Nederlandsche Oorlogen*, vol. 1, pp. 233–5.

everything he will do therein'.[224] William's lack of control over ports in the Netherlands limited the effectiveness of his attempt to regulate the activities of the raiders known as the *Watergeuzen* or Sea Beggars, but as the rebellion gained ground in the 1570s it became possible to establish more effective admiralties in Holland, Zeeland and Friesland.[225]

Obviously, the Spanish authorities could not have been expected to recognise the legitimacy of attacks on their shipping under licences granted by William in the Netherlands, any more than they had recognised the legitimacy of attacks under licences issued by the Huguenots in France.[226] As far as the Huguenots were concerned, quite apart from the fact that the king of France had not declared war on the king of Spain, the pretence that his admirals were issuing licences on his behalf when they were actually in rebellion against him had seemed preposterous to Spanish observers.[227] As far as the Netherlands were concerned, quite apart from the fact that the count of Nassau and prince of Orange had not in fact declared war on the king of Spain, it seemed to Spanish observers that someone whose estates were mostly situated in Brabant, Holland and Zeeland could not be a sovereign ruler capable of declaring war on the sovereign ruler of those territories.[228] From the Spanish perspective, the Protestant mariners who preyed on shipping under licences issued in France and the Netherlands were simply 'rebels, robbers and pirates'.[229] Towards the end of the sixteenth century, however, attitudes towards maritime raiding in the context of the confessional conflicts in which Philip II had become involved started to change. After recapturing Dunkirk in 1583, the duke of Parma established an admiralty there and began to assemble a fleet

224 Oudendijk 1964, pp. 139–40; De Meij 1972, p. 100; BL, Cotton MS Galba C III, f. 259, Cotton MS Galba C IV, f. 82, Add. MS 11405, ff. 280–1, and Add. MS 14027, ff. 299–301.

225 De Meij 1972, pp. 113–19; Van Vliet 1998, pp. 154–5; Enthoven 2009, pp. 109–11; Bruijn 2011, pp. 3–5; Hart 2014, p. 127. And see too Walker 2004, pp. 30–7, which includes instructive illustrations.

226 Rowen 1988, p. 13; Augeron 1996, p. 229; Weis 2003, pp. 330–1.

227 *Calendar of Letters and State Papers Relating to English Affairs Preserved Principally in the Archives of Simancas*, vol. 1, pp. 299–300.

228 *Correspondance de Philippe II sur les affaires des Pays-Bas*, vol. 2, pp. 236–7; *Relations politiques des Pays-Bas et de l'Angleterre, sous le règne de Philippe II*, vol. 6, pp. 358 and 374. Implicit in these comments was acceptance that raiding would have been legitimate had another sovereign declared war on Philip.

229 *Calendar of Letters and State Papers Relating to English Affairs Preserved Principally in the Archives of Simancas*, vol. 2, pp. 246, 250, 429–30, 432 and 434; *Relations politiques des Pays-Bas et de l'Angleterre, sous le règne de Philippe II*, vol. 6, pp. 264–5, 328–9, 341, 562, 564–5 and 568–9; *Mémoires de Viglius et d'Hopperus sur le commencement des troubles des Pays-Bas*, pp. 216–17.

known as the Armada of Flanders.[230] In the same year he issued a 'réglement pour la marine', forbidding mariners from leaving Dunkirk or other recaptured ports without first obtaining 'lettres patentes en bonne forme', and establishing a court to determine disputes over prizes 'selon droit, raison et coûtume de la mer et les ordonnances faites sur ce sujet', the judges of which were to protect the admiral's 'droit du dixiéme denier des prises'.[231] In 1590 Philip himself issued a new version of the edict of 1540 to govern maritime raiding out of Dunkirk and other ports on the Flemish coast.[232] With limited numbers of naval vessels available, the Spanish authorities took frequent recourse to the licensing of private vessels, and in the closing decades of the sixteenth century Dunkirk became an important centre of maritime raiding against Protestant shipping, as it would remain in the early seventeenth century.[233] By the 1590s, licences were also being issued to Catholic mariners sailing from ports held by the forces of the Catholic League in northern France, as well as from ports in the north of Spain itself.[234]

Had the raiding licensed by the Spanish authorities been restricted to attacks on Protestant raiders sailing from ports in France and the Netherlands, it might have been possible to justify the activity in conventional terms as a form of lawful vengeance against pirates.[235] Had the victims of the Protestant raiders been granted letters of marque after failing to obtain judicial remedies against them, it might have been possible to justify the activity instead as a form of licensed reprisal.[236] Yet the reality was that Catholic mariners were being authorised to prey more generally upon enemy ships and goods, even though the ships and goods did not pertain to enemies in the conventional sense. The renewal of Charles V's edict in 1590 indicates that maritime raiding was still

230 Malo 1913, pp. 183–4; Goodman 1997, p. 4; Parker 2004, p. 2.

231 Faulconnier, *Description historique de Dunkerque*, vol. 1, pp. 87–8.

232 Bolsée 1932, pp, 9–10; Baetens 1977, pp. 48–9; Villiers 2000, pp. 46–7.

233 Oppenheim 1968, pp. 51–2; Van Vliet 1996, pp. 155–9, and 1998, pp. 159 and 168–9; Hart 2014, pp. 135–6.

234 Stradling 1992, p. 11; Goodman 1997, pp. 13–14; James 2000, p. 109, and 2004, p. 39. For evidence that the licensing of private parties may have been considered as much as a decade earlier see the *Calendar of Letters and State Papers Relating to English Affairs Preserved Principally in the Archives of Simancas*, vol. 2, p. 688.

235 The duke of Alva appears to have had this justification in mind when he licensed armed raids on Protestant shipping in 1569 (*Calendar of State Papers, Foreign Series, of the Reign of Elizabeth*, vol. 9, p. 54; *Relations politiques des Pays-Bas et de l'Angleterre, sous le règne de Philippe II*, vol. 5, p. 453; BL, Cotton MS Galba C III, ff. 331–2r).

236 It is of course possible that this sometimes happened, but the point is that the raiding of the 'Dunkirkers' and others, already touched on in the previous chapter, was not generally regarded as a form of licensed reprisal for unredressed losses they had sustained.

believed in Spain to be lawful when one sovereign declared war on another, yet the raiding licensed in Dunkirk and other ports under Spanish control was not limited to the subjects of particular sovereigns, let alone sovereigns with whom the king of Spain was formally at war. Indeed, the United Provinces did not even begin to be recognised as an independent republic until the following century.[237] When independence had been unilaterally declared in the northern Netherlands at the beginning of the 1580s, the Protestant authorities there had issued another version of Charles V's edict to govern their own activities, again indicating that maritime raiding was believed to be a licit activity in wartime.[238] It has been supposed that the licences William of Orange granted in the 1570s amounted to letters of marque, on the basis that he had himself sustained losses at the hands of the duke of Alva and that he was authorising mariners to take reprisals on his behalf.[239] In these licences, however, no mention was made of the crucial component of a denial of justice, and there is in any case a difference between engaging in warfare as a means of recovering redress for losses, and authorising the victims of losses to secure redress for themselves in peacetime.[240] William was believed to be authorising aggression against the enemies of the Protestants in the Netherlands, albeit as the sovereign ruler of land-locked territories elsewhere.[241] Despite the use of familiar documents framed in familiar language, a new approach to the regulation of maritime warfare was being developed in the Netherlands, which again looked broadly similar to the approach being developed in England.

Elizabeth and her counsellors were certainly aware of developments in the Netherlands as well as France, not least because the Protestant raiders licensed overseas often brought their prizes into English ports for disposal.[242] Lacking

237 Parker 1979, pp. 239–40; Bonney 1991, p. 181; Prak 2005, pp. 23–4.

238 Bolsée 1932, p. 7, and Lemaire 1934, p. 162.

239 Oudendijk 1964, pp. 140–4, followed in De Meij 1972, pp. 102–4.

240 There is some evidence that the licences issued in 1568 by Louis of Nassau were conceived of as some form of authorisation of reprisals (*Calendar of State Papers, Domestic Series, of the Reigns of Edward VI, Mary and Elizabeth*, vol. 2, p. 332; *Relations politiques des Pays-Bas et de l'Angleterre, sous le règne de Philippe II*, vol. 5, pp. 380–3), and there could conceivably have been other licences like this. Again, the point is that the raiding unleashed by the Protestant authorities was not generally conceived of in this way.

241 Salmon 1975, pp. 21–2; Knecht 1994, p. 19; Parrott 1997, p. 149.

242 *Calendar of State Papers, Foreign Series, of the Reign of Elizabeth*, vol. 9, pp. 40, 82–3 and 170, and vol. 10, pp. 41–3; *Relations politiques des Pays-Bas et de l'Angleterre, sous le règne de Philippe II*, vol. 6, pp. 106, 163–4, 179–80 and 321–3; *Acts of the Privy Council of England*, vol. 8, pp. 27–8, 44, 46–7, 67, 69–70 and 85–6; *Tudor Royal Proclamations*, vol. 2, pp. 264–5 and 357–8; *Calendar of State Papers, Domestic Series, of the Reigns of Edward VI, Mary and Elizabeth*, vol. 1, p. 426; NAK, SP12/81, ff. 125–6, and SP70/107, ff. 70–1; BL, Cotton MS Galba C III, f. 291.

havens at home, the Sea Beggars had been especially frequent visitors, until they were excluded in 1572 and began to capture towns in the Netherlands.[243] In 1570 William of Orange had written personally to Elizabeth to ask what justification there could be for the arrest by one of her officers of one of his followers, whose alleged offence had been to attack the prince's enemies (*mon ennemi le duc d'Albe et ses adhérens*) in virtue of a licence he had granted (*par ma commission et charge expresse*).[244] William's admiral wrote in the same year to Elizabeth's secretary of state, maintaining that since William had effectively issued a 'juste déclaration des armes à guerre ouverte', as other rulers had effectively recognised by providing support to the Protestant cause, treating the seizures made by combatants (*les prises faictes sous l'authorité de ces guerres*) as acts of robbery (*rapts*) would be like treating other exploits of arms (*les batailles et tous aultres exploits d'armes*) as acts of murder and slaughter (*meurdres et assasinats*).[245] The language used in the admiral's letter is revealing. If it could only have been demonstrated that the wars of religion really had been declared between sovereign rulers, prize taking would have been considered legitimate 'under the authority of these wars'. Early in 1572 the admiral proposed to the English privy council that a port on the south coast be designated the official base of the Sea Beggars, and that commissioners appointed jointly by Elizabeth and William form a court there to resolve controversies over the distribution of prizes.[246] Although the proposal was not accepted, no room remained for uncertainty about what the visitors from the Continent were doing. It was well known, moreover, that English mariners were also raiding Catholic shipping under the cover of licences obtained from authorities overseas.[247] Many of these mariners saw themselves as supporters of a common

243 Black 1931; Sutherland 1984; French 1991. Since the Sea Beggars tended to refer to themselves in England as 'freebooters' (*Tudor Royal Proclamations*, vol. 2, pp. 357–8; *Acts of the Privy Council of England*, vol. 8, pp. 69–70; *Relations politiques des Pays-Bas et de l'Angleterre, sous le règne de Philippe II*, vol. 6, pp. 264–5), it is tempting to call the activity they were engaged in 'freebooting'. However, the Dutch term 'vrijbuiterij' was used to mean any kind of maritime raiding (Lunsford 2005, p. 3), much as 'piracy' had once been.

244 *Relations politiques des Pays-Bas et de l'Angleterre, sous le règne de Philippe II*, vol. 6, p. 14.

245 *Calendar of State Papers, Foreign Series, of the Reign of Elizabeth*, vol. 9, p. 256; *Relations politiques des Pays-Bas et de l'Angleterre, sous le règne de Philippe II*, vol. 5, pp. 658–9.

246 *Calendar of State Papers, Foreign Series, of the Reign of Elizabeth*, vol. 10, pp. 28 and 31; *Relations politiques des Pays-Bas et de l'Angleterre, sous le règne de Philippe II*, vol. 6, pp. 295–8 and 330–2; 'Documents tirés du Musée Britannique et du State Paper Office', pp. 423–6.

247 Rowse 1937, pp. 118–21, and 1941, pp. 389–301; Ramsay 1986, pp. 143–5; Bicheno 2012, pp. 107–8.

Protestant cause against the Catholic powers of Europe.[248] Elizabeth eventually issued a proclamation forbidding her subjects from sailing under licences granted by foreign rulers unless she gave them express permission to do so, yet in seeking to control the activity in this way she acknowledged both that she was aware of it and that she considered it lawful.[249]

It was the civil lawyers in the admiralty court who were generally asked to consider whether a mariner could rely on a licence obtained from the Huguenots 'to justifie his doinges to be lawfull', whether seizures could be authorised by William of Orange as a 'prince libre de l'empire' with a 'principaulté de tiltre en France', and similar questions.[250] The court eased the diplomatic pressure on Elizabeth by finding that ships seized under licences issued in France and the Netherlands should be released when the seizures had been made in the roads leading into English ports, but the implication was that the ships could have been retained as legitimate prizes had they been taken on the open sea.[251] Similarly, in receiving evidence that goods found aboard captured ships belonged to friends of the prince of Orange and could not be viewed as contraband, the court signalled that it would otherwise have allowed the takers to retain them.[252] It is especially significant that when the court dealt with complaints from merchants whose goods had been seized at sea, it often received testimonials from abroad declaring that the merchants were themselves members of a 'reformed congregation' or the 'reformed church', for this suggests that the enemies of the princes of Navarre and Orange were understood to be defined by religious affiliation more than national allegiance.[253]

---

248 Andrews 1964, pp. 12 and 15–17; Quinn and Ryan 1983, pp. 59 and 77; Scott 2013, pp. 77–8. Others, it ought to be added, offered to serve against the Protestants on behalf of the king of Spain (*Documents Relating to Law and Custom of the Sea*, vol. 1, pp. 199–200), or to serve his rival for the throne of Portugal, Dom Antonio, who was also a Catholic (Adams 1991, p. 53; Loades 2000, p. 125; Hanson 2003, pp. 95–6).

249 *Documents Relating to Law and Custom of the Sea*, vol. 1, pp. 202–4, and see too pp. 200–1; *Tudor Royal Proclamations*, vol. 2, pp. 395–7, and see too pp. 397–8. In giving permission to mariners Elizabeth would have been abandoning the 'plausible deniability' she had been anxious to maintain (Trim 1999).

250 *Calendar of State Papers, Foreign Series, of the Reign of Elizabeth*, vol. 10, pp. 42–3; *Relations politiques des Pays-Bas et de l'Angleterre, sous le règne de Philippe II*, vol. 6, pp. 321–3; NAK, HCA14/9, n. 196.

251 *Calendar of Letters and State Papers Relating to English Affairs Preserved Principally in the Archives of Simancas*, vol. 2, pp. 429–30, 432, 434 and 438; *Relations politiques des Pays-Bas et de l'Angleterre, sous le règne de Philippe II*, vol. 6, pp. 562, 564–5 and 568–9; NAK, HCA14/8, n. 19. See too *Documents Relating to Law and Custom of the Sea*, vol. 1, pp. 179–80.

252 NAK, HCA14/10, n. 310, HCA14/15, n. 7, and HCA14/23, n. 8.

253 NAK, HCA14/9, nn. 247–8, 314–16, 320, 327 and 333–5.

As far as the takers were concerned, the usual allegation was that they had seized enemy ships and goods 'in the service of' (or less often 'under commission from') the prince of Navarre or Orange.[254] Occasionally, the takers of ships and goods were described as operating under 'letters of marke', perhaps because genuine letters of marque or reprisal were granted to mariners who were unable to secure redress for losses they had sustained, or perhaps because lawyers who realised that the wars of religion were not actually *bella publica* supposed that the only way seizures at sea could have been justified was as acts of reprisal.[255] The supposition would not have survived close scrutiny of the licences that are actually known to have been issued in France and the Netherlands, but it would have helped to connect those licences with the letters of reprisal that the admiralty court in England purported to issue after the undeclared war with Spain began in 1585.[256]

The pretence that the queen of England was a neutral observer of the struggle between the king of Spain and his subjects in the Netherlands was finally abandoned in that year, when an English force was sent across the North Sea to support the rebels.[257] As the intervention proved ineffectual, and ports in the southern Netherlands and northern France fell into the hands of the duke of Parma and his allies, more formal provision was made for the disposal in England of 'lawfull prises' taken from the 'Dunkerkers' and other 'common enemies'.[258] Following the assassination of Henry III in 1589, Elizabeth recognised the prince of Navarre as king of France and agreed with his ambassador that further provision should be made for the disposal in England of ships and

254 *Acts of the Privy Council of England*, vol. 8, pp. 27–8, 44, 46–7 and 67; *Calendar of State Papers, Foreign Series, of the Reign of Elizabeth*, vol. 9, p. 40, and vol. 10, pp. 42–3; *Calendar of State Papers, Domestic Series, of the Reigns of Edward VI, Mary and Elizabeth*, vol. 1, p. 426; *Relations politiques des Pays-Bas et de l'Angleterre, sous le règne de Philippe II*, vol. 6, pp. 14, 295–6 and 321–3; NAK, SP12/81, ff. 125–6, HCA14/8, n. 19, HCA14/9, n. 320, HCA14/10, n. 310, and HCA14/15, n. 7; BL, Cotton MS Galba C III, f. 291.

255 *Calendar of Letters and State Papers Relating to English Affairs Preserved Principally in the Archives of Simancas*, vol. 2, p. 612; NAK, HCA14/10, nn. 166–7, and HCA14/16, n. 70.

256 Genuine letters of marque or reprisal continued to be granted in England (*Documents Relating to Law and Custom of the Sea*, vol. 1, pp. 184–9 and 288; NAK, HCA14/32, n. 145, and HCA24/23, n. 127), but the name was also applied there, as was seen in the last section of this chapter, to what were truly licences to raid enemy shipping in wartime. By the end of the century such licences were also being referred to in the Netherlands as 'brieven van marcque' (Lunsford 2005, pp. 213–15).

257 Wilson 1970, p. 86; Wernham 1980, pp. 56–7; Hammer 2003, p. 203.

258 *Documents Relating to Law and Custom of the Sea*, vol. 1, pp. 242–3; *Calendar of State Papers, Foreign Series, of the Reign of Elizabeth*, vol. 20, pp. 236–7, 239 and 296–7; *Acts of the Privy Council of England*, vol. 14, pp. 10–12 and 216; NAK, HCA14/23, n. 104, and HCA14/30, nn. 120–1.

goods taken from 'his rebells, the Leagers, and others their favorers and abettors'.[259] The French ambassador and the English admiral together drew up a series of articles, based on those issued by the privy council four years earlier to regulate the seizure of Spanish ships and goods, declaring that prizes taken from the Leaguers and their associates in accordance with the rules laid down could be disposed of 'in as ample a maner as in tyme of open warre', though without making reference to 'the law of reprisal'.[260] In the final article it was added that anyone found to be supplying the Leaguers and their associates with 'victells or municons of warr' would suffer 'forfeyture of the shipps and goods'. Over the next few years French and English mariners were licensed by the admiral 'to sett uppon by force of armes and to take and apprehend any of the shipps, goods and merchandizes of the Leagers, rebells and others whatsoever that shall ayde or assist them'.[261] It was generally stated that the recipients of licences had suffered losses at the hands of the Leaguers, but no mention was made of any denial of justice. Prizes brought to England were inventoried, appraised and adjudged to their captors, subject to the payment of duties to the French king, and sometimes with the express approval of his ambassador.[262] Serious efforts were made to ensure that the system worked effectively and that the French king received his duties.[263] By the early 1590s officials in the English admiralty saw no significant difference between someone holding a 'licence agaynest the Leagers and enimyes of the Frenche kinge' and someone holding 'letters of reprisall agayneste the kinge of Spayne and his subjects'.[264]

A significant difference was recognised after 1595, however, when Henry IV and Philip II formally declared war on each other.[265] From then onwards seizures of ships and goods from the king of Spain and his subjects by the French king's subjects (or vice versa) could have been justified in conventional terms as acts of licit plunder, and Elizabeth became worried that her subjects might prefer to offer their services to the king of France and to be licensed to raid Spanish shipping on his behalf.[266] By this stage it was possible to claim that the

259 *Documents Relating to Law and Custom of the Sea*, vol. 1, pp. 252–3; NAK, HCA14/26, n. 51.

260 BL, Lansdowne MS 148, ff. 178–9.

261 *Documents Relating to Law and Custom of the Sea*, vol. 1, pp. 273–6 and 289–90; BL, Lansdowne MS 157, ff. 364–5; NAK, HCA14/30, nn. 13, 63 and 99 (and see too HCA14/27, n. 156, HCA14/28, n. 214, HCA14/32, n. 156, and HCA25/3/1, f. 312).

262 *Documents Relating to Law and Custom of the Sea*, vol. 1, pp. 267–9 and 282–4; NAK, HCA14/27, n. 68.

263 *Documents Relating to Law and Custom of the Sea*, vol. 1, pp. 260–1; NAK, HCA14/27, nn. 33–4 and 92.

264 NAK, HCA14/27, n. 219, HCA14/28, n. 125, and HCA14/30, nn. 129 and 168.

265 Buisseret 1984, p. 57; Benedict 2002, p. 172; Pitts 2009, p. 193.

266 NAK, HCA14/32, n. 83.

licensing of maritime raiding in wars that had not been formally declared was a practice continually engaged in by the queen's 'neighbour nations in theise latter times', but the legitimacy of this practice was more difficult to justify than maritime raiding in declared wars.[267] Not only was maritime raiding in declared wars a much older practice, the legitimacy of which had been recognised in diplomatic exchanges between rulers, but their efforts to regulate the practice had been based on mutual acceptance of the legal theory taught in the law schools as a guide to legitimacy in international relations.[268] It is thus understandable that when the belligerents in the undeclared wars of the later sixteenth century sought to justify the maritime raiding they were encouraging, they did so by pretending that they were involved in something resembling declared wars, or that they were authorising something resembling peacetime reprisals.[269] They continued to employ concepts and categories conventionally adopted from the civil and canon laws, yet in contexts in which it had not been conventional for them to be employed. In eschewing reference to these laws in the proclamation she issued on trading with the enemy, Elizabeth seems to have recognised that they did not provide a secure foundation for the activity she was seeking to justify. She was able to claim instead that authorising the seizure of ships and goods from enemies or those assisting them was a practice engaged in by her neighbours. Yet this was not taken in itself to justify the activity. In her proclamation on trading with the enemy Elizabeth did not actually claim that authorising the seizure of ships and goods in undeclared wars was legitimate because it was customary in relations between nations. She did not even claim that it was a long established practice, merely remarking that it had become widespread 'in theise latter times'. Her claim was that the recent practice of nations 'confirmed' the legitimacy of an activity required by the 'lawe of pollicy' and warranted by the 'lawe of God'.[270] Attention will

267 *Documents Relating to Law and Custom of the Sea*, vol. 1, pp. 313–17; *Tudor Royal Proclamations*, vol. 3, pp. 255–8; *Proclamation of the Lords, the Generall States of the United Provinces*.

268 *Cf.* Wijffels 1993, pp. 4–7. The word 'mutual' seems more apt than 'common' as rulers expected one another to follow the same standards. The theory was common but its acceptance was mutual.

269 Undeclared wars were not, of course, a novelty in the later sixteenth century, but no trace has been found of attempts to justify maritime raiding as a legitimate activity in a different type of war from a *bellum publicum*.

270 Elizabeth, it needs to be appreciated, was saying that authorising the seizure of ships and goods had become the customary practice of nations because it was considered legitimate, not that authorising the seizure of ships and goods was legitimate because it was the customary practice of nations. As will be explained later, the distinction is of some importance in the development of the new international law.

turn next to what she or her advisers may have had in mind when she referred to the law of God.

4 Justification in Terms of the Law of God

Obvious as it is bound to seem to historians, the point is worth spelling out that most people in early modern Europe understood the legitimacy of human behaviour to be ultimately dependent on its acceptability to the Judeo-Christian God in whom they believed, more or less wholeheartedly.[271] Exponents of the art of war, aware that it was viewed with suspicion by pacific observers, often reassured their readers that warfare enjoyed this level of legitimacy. 'God is well pleased wyth wyse and wittie feates of warre', wrote Roger Ascham.[272] 'The Lorde our God', Geoffrey Gates insisted, 'useth no occupation of men in his workes and proceedings upon earth like as he doth militarie prowesse'.[273] That feats of arms were often the means by which divine providence brought order to 'rude and savage nations', executed justice on 'rebellious and faithlesse people', and defended the true church against 'the rage and violence of tyrants', was apparent both from a perusal of the scriptures and from the recollection of later events, including the recent defence of La Rochelle. Tracts justifying the Huguenot resort to arms were sometimes translated for an English audience. Hubert Languet maintained like Gates that arms were legitimately used 'to deliver the church of God from tyrannie and from the yoke of servitude'.[274] Bertrand de Loque pointed out that the scriptures made reference to 'the God of Hostes', 'the Lord God of battels' and 'the battels of God'.[275] As his English translator emphasised in presenting his work to the earl of Essex, de Loque had written about 'the ancient rules of warre, grounded on Gods holy word', which he had described as rules that 'touch simplie the conscience'.[276] A similar approach was taken in England by Lodowick Lloyd, who told his readers

271 The thesis famously defended in relation to France in Febvre 1982, pp. 335–53, could easily be extended to other European countries.

272 *Toxophilus*, pp. 70–1. In this treatise on archery, Ascham based his defence on the exploits of the Maccabees, before drawing attention to several passages in the Old Testament in which use was made of bows and arrows in battles fought at God's command.

273 *Defence of Militarie Profession*, p. 15 (slight liberties are being taken with some of the quotations here).

274 *Short Apologie for Christian Souldiours*, sig. A7.

275 *Discourses of War and Single Combat*, p. 1, citing in particular Exodus 15.3 and 2 Chronicles 20.16.

276 *Discourses of War and Single Combat*, sigg. A2 and A3v.

that 'the whole Bible is a booke of the battels of the Lord, and the whole life of man a militarie marching to these battells'.[277] To govern the conduct of these unavoidable struggles, Lloyd explained, 'the Lorde set downe certaine martiall lawes to Moses', which served as a foundation for 'the lawe of armes' still observed by modern nations.[278] John Norden agreed with Lloyd that a basic requirement of these laws was for wars to be waged only for just causes. 'When the cause is just', he declared, 'no man may question whether the warre bee lawfull', adding that as far as the conflict with Spain was concerned, 'it sufficeth us to know it is to preserve our state'.[279] The queen had issued a summons to arms on this basis, 'and wee are to obey it in a treble dutie, to God, our soveraigne, and commonweale'.

Regardless of the readership authors on the art of war were able to attract, they cannot have addressed as large an audience as the church ministers who preached at services their congregations were compelled to attend. In Elizabeth's reign ministers were only allowed to preach under licence and on approved topics, most of which were doctrinal in character, but the major exception since the time of her father had been the duty of subjects to assist in the defence of the realm.[280] 'As kynges are bound to omyt nothynge that they judge woll serve for the defence of their people', Richard Morison had explained in the 1530s, 'soo is it the bounden duetie of all subjectes, of what degree so ever they be, to serve theyr contreye in such sorte as theyr prynce and heed shall appoynt them'.[281] 'Unto this', Thomas Becon had explained further, 'doth the law both of God and nature bind us, the which to resist is extreme impiety and plain wickedness'.[282] During the late 1580s and the 1590s preachers assured their listeners that they would be doing their duty in the service of God if they took up arms 'for the maintenance of the gospel of Christ, the preservation of our noble queene Elizabeth, for the defence of our countrey, our landes, our children, our wives and our lyves, and to represse the pride of straungers'.[283] Edmund Harris reasoned that 'they which set uppon any to

277 *Stratagems of Jerusalem*, p. 1.

278 *Stratagems of Jerusalem*, pp. 50–3.

279 *Mirror of Honor*, sig. A3r. See too the same author's *Christian Familiar Comfort and Incouragement unto All English Subjects*, p. 30.

280 Jorgensen 1973; Hale 1983; Lowe 1996; Baseotto 2006.

281 *Exhortation to Styr All Englyshe Men to the Defence of Theyr Contreye*, sigg. A3v-4r.

282 *Early Works*, pp. 234–5. On Becon's *Polecy of Warre* (1542) see Lowe 2000.

283 Thomas Tymme, *Preparation against the Prognosticated Dangers of this Yeare, 1588*; E.R., *Buckler against a Spanish Brag*; John Prime, *Consolations of David, Briefly Applied to Queene Elizabeth*; Roger Hacket, *Sermon Needful for Theese Times*; Thomas Nun, *Comfort against the Spaniard*.

destroy them should have a good cause', that the aim of the Spaniards was 'the setting up againe of their Romish religion', and that in consequence 'they fight for an evill, wee for a good cause'.[284] According to Charles Gibbon, 'just warre is that which is taken in hande, at the commaundement of the magistrate, for the demaunding of things againe, or to repulse injuries, or to revenge them'.[285] On the supposition that the English had neither despoiled nor injured any of Philip II's subjects, Gibbon also concluded that 'hys cause is not just'. After Philip III's accession to the Spanish throne, Stephen Gosson similarly promised his audience that 'you shall finde the warres of the enemie, in the Indies, in Portingale, in Granada, in the Low Countries, in France, and against us, to be uncharitable and unjust'.[286] He too maintained that the English were defending themselves legitimately against unprovoked aggression, while accepting that in principle offensive wars could be waged to avenge injuries as well as to redress losses. Since superior authorities could be appealed to within states, 'a private person cannot revenge himselfe, because he may not be a judge and an actor in his owne case', yet since no one prince served 'as superiour to al other princes, war steps in in the place of just vindicative judgement', and thus 'a prince may be a judge and an actor in his owne case'.[287]

A particularly interesting contributor to this discourse for present purposes was Simon Harward, the chaplain of New College, Oxford, at the beginning of the 1590s.[288] He had previously served as a chaplain aboard a ship engaged in maritime raiding, where he had been called upon to defend the legitimacy of the activity both in sermons he delivered to the ship's company and in advice he provided to sailors with troubled consciences.[289] After returning to land he had frequently faced complaints that his previous service brought 'discredite' to the faith he was employed to promote, and he had therefore decided to reiterate the substance of his sermons and advice for a wider audience. His

284 *Sermon Preached at Brocket Hall*, sigg. B3–4r. See too Anthony Marten, *Exhortation to Stirre up the Mindes of All Her Majesties Faithfull Subjects to Defend Their Country*, sig. E4r.

285 *Watch-Worde for Warre*, sigg. E3v-4. As was typical of all these sermons, precise reference was made here to biblical texts such as Genesis 14.14 and 2 Samuel 10.7 and 18.9. But Gibbon also referred more vaguely to the works of Augustine, Isidore and Hostiensis.

286 *Trumpet of Warre*, sigg. B4-C1r.

287 Matthew Sutcliffe, *Practice, Proceedings and Lawes of Armes*, pp. 1–15, contains a defence of warfare along similar lines, but although the author was a minister, his book was not based on sermons he had delivered, and it was cited in the first chapter above because the defence of plunder it contains was mostly in line with the theory taught in the law schools.

288 Matthew and Harrison 2004, vol. 25, pp. 686–7.

289 *Solace for the Souldier and Saylour*, sig. A3. On the service of chaplains see Taylor 1978, pp. 19–26, and Rodger 1997, pp. 306–7.

first concern was to demonstrate in general 'the lawfulnes of warre and force of armes agaynst the professed enemies of Gods truth'.[290] That the 'militarie profession' was indeed lawful was 'both in the Old and New Testament sundrie waies confirmed unto us'. Melchizedek, he argued, would not have been prepared to receive a tithe of the plunder taken by Abraham's soldiers unless God had 'allowed their profession to be sacred and holy'.[291] That many biblical conflicts had been described as 'the warres of the Lord himself', and that God had prescribed 'lawes and statutes' to the Israelites to regulate their exercise of arms, provided further confirmation that wars could be lawful.[292] Some critics, Harward was aware, accepted that arms could sometimes be used 'agaynst the heathen Turkes and infidels', yet insisted that they could not be used 'against the Spaniards, professing as they say the same God with us, holding the same articles of Christian fayth, members of the same church, partakers of the same baptisme, and living in the same hope of life everlasting'.[293] To this he replied that the Spaniards 'may be in the church, but they are not of the church, and they are so much worse then the heathen infidels, as a rebell and traytor within the walles is more pernicious then a forraine or outward enemie'. Like most of the other preachers whose sermons were put into printed form, Harward assured his readers that they were fighting in God's cause when they defended the true church against its foreign oppressors.

Among those who accepted this line of argument, however, a further concern had been raised. Some people accepted that 'Antichrist and his confederates are to be beaten downe and destroyed', yet insisted that 'this should be done in warre openly proclaimed, and not in such privie intrapping and laying in waite' as was practised in 'the voyages now commonly used on the seas'.[294] If war had to be waged against the Spaniards, they complained, 'rather should their whole realme be set on, then the merchants surprised, which labour trulie and painfully for the reliefe of themselves and their families'. Harward's initial response to this complaint was to tell his readers that the merchants despoiled did not own the goods taken from them. 'Whatsoever the enemies of the grace of God doe possesse', he explained, 'yet is their possession no better then the possession of brute beasts', for true ownership was only possible 'where the

290 *Solace for the Souldier and Saylour*, sigg. B1–2.

291 Genesis 14, a favourite passage, was again cited here.

292 Deuteronomy 20.2 and 10, Judges 5.23, 2 Chronicles 20.15, Nehemiah 4.14 and 20 and Psalms 144.1 were all cited at this point.

293 *Solace for the Souldier and Saylour*, sigg. B4-C1v.

294 *Solace for the Souldier and Saylour*, sigg. B1v and D1.

faith of Christ is embraced and received'.[295] As the Spaniards were not genuine believers, whatever they might claim to own 'they possesse it as theeves and robbers, and therefore the bereaving them of it is not theft'.[296] Just as the Israelites who conquered Canaan 'tooke the labours of the people into their possession', so might English mariners appropriate from Spanish merchants things they had laboured to acquire but never actually owned.[297] From this it might have been supposed that the queen's subjects could also appropriate the possessions of 'those papists that live amongst us', but Harward warned that another prerequisite of lawful appropriation was, as Augustine had taught, 'legitima superior auctoritas aut iubens aut concedens', which in this case was lacking.[298] It was in relation to the 'lawful superior authority' of the queen that Harward developed his other major defence of maritime raiding by observing that 'there are manie things, which are in no wise lawfull in private men, that are allowed and tolerated in those which are armed with the authoritie of the publike magistrate'.[299] Whereas private people were required to forgive and forget injuries, to eschew vengeance and to deal with one another in a straightforward manner, the scriptures revealed that public magistrates were required to remember and avenge injuries inflicted on their people, and were allowed to make use of 'guilefull policie' in doing so.[300] This enabled Harward to respond directly to the specific complaint that 'the hostilitie and open enmitie betwixt us and Spaine ought first to be proclaimed before any warres ought to be taken in hand'. That ships were at sea was enough to make the enmity obvious, and if the queen, 'upon causes not knowen to us, thought good as yet no other way to proclaime the warre, we are not to busie ourselves in examining the sayd causes'. When a war was known to be waged for a just cause, people could rely on 'the authoritie of a lawfull magistrate' to justify the means by which it was waged, and it therefore sufficed for the queen to have authorised maritime raiding 'against the professed enemies of the church of God'.

It will by now be apparent that Harward and his colleagues did not seek to justify the war with Spain and the raiding of enemy shipping in terms of the theory taught in the law schools. While they sometimes referred to sources

295 Reference was made here to 1 Corinthians 3 alone, but Harward seems to have had some familiarity with the unorthodox theory of dominion expounded by theologians like John Wyclif and canonists like Hostiensis (Wilks 1965; Muldoon 1980; Dawson 1983).

296 *Solace for the Souldier and Saylour*, sig. D2v, citing 1 Samuel 30.26 and Psalms 24.1.

297 The quoted passage is from Harward's tract, but was taken there from Psalms 105.44.

298 *Contra Faustum Manichaeum*, 22.70.

299 *Solace for the Souldier and Saylour*, sigg. D1v-E1v.

300 Deuteronomy 25.17, Joshua 8.4, 2 Kings 10, Matthew 5.39 and 18.35, Luke 3.14 and Romans 12.19 and 13.5.

studied by the canonists, they relied on these biblical and patristic texts as a basis for arguments that deviated from the thinking of the lawyers in two main directions. To start with, whereas most lawyers maintained that plunder was licit in any war declared by one sovereign prince against another, the ministers made use of a broader notion of public authorisation, without attaching any special significance to declarations of war. As Harward in particular appreciated, this made it easier to defend the type of maritime raiding that was being authorised in England. Harward also deviated from the standard doctrine of the law schools in claiming that only genuine believers could own property, but at this point his reasoning appears to have been more idiosyncratic. The other way in which the ministers deviated more generally from the thinking of many lawyers was in attaching great importance to the existence of a just cause for a war to be waged. To know whether they could engage with a clear conscience in the aggressive actions their queen was authorising, people needed to know whether she had a just cause for going to war. As was seen in the last chapter, however, the civilians in particular rarely paid much attention to this issue.[301] In writing about reprisals, they sometimes mentioned that Thomas Aquinas had treated the denial of justice as a just cause for war, but they distinguished his concern with legitimacy *in foro conscientiae* from their own concern with legitimacy *in foro civili*, and did not generally talk about the causes of the wars in which they understood plunder to be licit.[302] Most civilians who mentioned Aquinas appear simply to have been following the example of Bartolus, who may have found the moral theology of Aquinas particularly interesting because it made significant use of legal ideas, and often involved discussion of legal texts.[303] As it happens, since the end of the fifteenth century Aquinas had become at least as prominent a figure among Catholic theologians as Bartolus was among civil lawyers. His *Summa theologiae* had replaced Peter Lombard's *Sententiae* as the basis of study in many theology schools, first in Italy and France, then in Spain and Portugal.[304] Around the middle of the sixteenth century he was formally adopted as a doctrinal authority by the new Society of Jesus, his thinking was frequently followed in the framing of the decrees passed by the Council of Trent, and he was officially

301 As was also mentioned, the canonists did pay more attention to the issue. The relationship between the civilians, canonists and theologians will be considered more closely later in this section.

302 See again n. 209 to the previous chapter.

303 Farrell 1975; McInerny 1982; Sigmund 1993; Baur 2012; Taitslin 2013.

304 Hamilton 1963; Pagden 1981; Fernández-Santamaria 2005; Brett 2012 and 2014; Alves and Moreira 2015.

declared a 'Doctor of the Church' by Pius V, who commissioned the printing of the first complete edition of his works.[305] His *Summa theologiae* belonged to a genre designed to provide instruction to novice priests who had to learn how to impose penance on parishioners after hearing their confessions.[306] The Spanish king had his own confessor, from whom he took advice on political as well as personal matters, and he expected public opinion to be guided by the counsel his subjects received from their confessors.[307] For a justification of the maritime raiding authorised by Elizabeth to be devised that might satisfy both conscientious believers at home and the victims of raiding overseas, it would have helped a great deal for common ground to have been discovered in the thinking of Protestant ministers and Catholic confessors.[308]

In the passage from the *Summa theologiae* referred to by Bartolus, it may be recalled, Aquinas had taught that there were three prerequisites of a just war (*bellum iustum*).[309] In explaining that the first was 'the authority of the prince (*auctoritas principis*) on whose instruction (*mandato*) the war is waged', he had made the point that while private people were meant to appeal to their superiors for justice, it was sometimes appropriate for princes who had no superior to make use of force against each other.[310] It was in explaining that the second prerequisite was a just cause (*iusta causa*) for resorting to force that Aquinas had cited Augustine's discussion of the denial of justice.[311] Unlike Bartolus and his followers, it should be noted, Aquinas was concerned here with wars in general, not with the limited wars of reprisal that might have been authorised in peacetime. His third prerequisite, with which the civilians had no concern, was that wars must be fought for a proper purpose (*intentio recta*).[312] Although he mentioned here that a perverse purpose (*prava intentio*) could render the use of force sinful even when there was both the requisite authority and a just cause for declaring war (*indicentis bellum*), it is important that Aquinas did

305 Janelle 1963, p. 209; O'Malley 1993, p. 146; Mullett 1999, p. 49; Caruana 2008, pp. 245–6; Knorn 2018, pp. 111–12.

306 Michaud-Quantin 1962; Biller 1998; Goering 2004; Decock 2013; Müller 2015.

307 Kamen 1997, pp. 233–4; Parker 1998, pp. 104 and 277, and 2014, pp. 83–4 and 345–6; O'Bannion 2012, pp. 558–9.

308 The proclamation against trading with the enemy was of course aimed partly at Elizabeth's Protestant allies, but also at other Catholic nations trading with Spain.

309 *Summa theologiae*, 2a2ae 40.1.

310 Reference was made here to Psalms 81.4 and Romans 13.4, as well as to Augustine, *Contra Faustum Manichaeum*, 22.75, a slightly later passage than the one cited by Harward from the same work.

311 *Quaestiones in Pentateuchum*, 6.10.

312 At this point reference was made to a text in Gratian's *Decretum*, C. 23 q. 1 c. 6, as well as to Augustine, *De civitate Dei*, 19.12, and *Contra Faustum Manichaeum*, 22.74.

not identify the formal declaration of war as one of his prerequisites of a *bellum iustum*. He ended his discussion by warning that wars ought to be avoided if they would result in excessive killing and looting (*occisiones et depraedationes*), which implied that killing and looting would sometimes be legitimate, as he confirmed in a later passage when he addressed the question 'whether robbery could ever be committed without sin'.[313] An obvious exception to the rule that people should not take things forcibly from one another was that princes could sometimes exact subsidies from their subjects. Another exception had been hinted at when Augustine wrote that infidels did not truly own their possessions, but Aquinas believed that infidels did have ownership unless it was decreed that they should lose their possessions by the laws of the princes of the earth (*eas secundum leges terrenorum principum amittere iussi sunt*).[314] The other major exception, however, was that it was licit to take plunder from enemies in wartime (*praedam accipere ab hostibus licitum est*).[315] Although Aquinas accepted that the things people took from enemies might become theirs (*eorum efficiuntur*), he insisted that this would only happen in a *bellum iustum*, and that even then plundering might be sinful if the plunderer's purpose were perverted by greed (*per cupiditatem*).[316]

When study of the *Summa theologiae* was revived in Italy towards the end of the fifteenth century and at the beginning of the sixteenth century, Aquinas' teaching on war and plunder was worked into penitential manuals written by theologians who were also familiar with the teaching of the law schools.[317] In writing about *auctoritas principis*, these Italian theologians often mentioned the juristic distinction between public and other wars, and made reference in doing so to the works of leading canonists and civilians, yet they insisted that wars were only legitimate if waged justly, and that they were only waged justly when the exercise of authority by a sovereign ruler coincided with a *iusta causa* and *intentio recta*.[318] Although one author described the necessary

313 *Summa theologiae*, 2a2ae 66.8.

314 *Epistolae*, 2.98.12. This was not precisely the position adopted by Harward, who seems to have believed that infidels never had true title.

315 Reference was made here to Ambrose, *De Abraham*, 1.3, a passage incorporated into the texts studied by the canonists. It is significant that no reference was made to the civil law texts on the acquisition of *res hostium*.

316 On this final point reference was made to Augustine's statement that it was a sin to fight simply for the sake of plunder (*Sermones*, 82).

317 Tavuzzi 1997, pp. 50 and 72–3, and 2007, p. 109. The Thomist revival was not initiated, as is sometimes suggested, by Pierre Crockaert in Paris at the turn of the century.

318 Pietro Maldura da Bergamo, *Tabula aurea in omnia Divi Thomae Aquinatis opera*, f. 42v; Giovanni Cagnazzo da Taggia, *Summa Tabiena, quae summa summarum merito appellatur*, pp. 160–1; Silvestro Mazzolini da Prierio, *Summa summarum, quae Silvestrina*

auctoritas principis as the *auctoritas indicendi bellum*, he did not suggest that a declaration of war was required for plunder to be lawful.[319] The legitimacy of plunder (*praeda*) was taken by these authors to depend on a coalescence of the conditions of a *bellum iustum*, not on the existence of a *bellum publicum*.[320] The question they tended to address was whether people who received plunder were obliged to restore it to those from whom it had been taken, and their usual answer was that no such obligation would arise as long as the plunder had been taken in a just war. If a war had been waged to recover redress for losses or injuries inflicted by another nation, it would not matter if the individuals plundered were personally innocent of the losses or injuries, because it was the whole nation that was regarded as the enemy (*totam habet pro hoste*).[321] Nor would it always matter if more plunder were taken than was required to provide redress for the losses or injuries sustained, because it was considered legitimate both to recover compensation for the effort of conducting a war (*operis labor*) and to impose a penalty for any failure to provide redress voluntarily (*poena contumaciae*).[322] While this left room for doubt about the legitimacy of disproportionate demands, which might be contrary to the principles of commutative and retributive justice, it was generally accepted that ordinary people could rely on the assessments made by their rulers. Furthermore, ordinary people did not need to be convinced that their rulers had a just cause for waging a war, although they could not participate in a war that they firmly believed to be unjust, 'for then they would act against their conscience and so would be sinning'.[323] If they thought a war might be just, but were motivated by greed in taking plunder, then despite the plundering of the enemy being in principle legitimate (assuming that the war was indeed just), they might still be required to return what they had received as an act of penance for their sin.[324] As for infidels, when they lived in subjection to a sovereign ruler

nuncupatur, vol. 1, f. 50v; Tommaso de Vio, Cardinal Cajetan, *Summula peccatorum*, pp. 29–30; Bartolomeo Fumo, *Summa quae aurea armilla inscribitur*, p. 89. For a different tradition, based on Lombard's *Sententiae*, compare Wilhelm Matthiae, *Libellus de bello iusto et licito*, sig. A3; Adrian VI, *Quaestiones de sacramentis in quartum Sententiarum librum*, f. 48; Gabriel Biel, *Commentarii doctissimi in quatuor Sententiarum libros*, vol. 3, pp. 313–14; Josse Clichtove, *De bello et pace opusculum*, f. 32r.

319 Cajetan, *Summula peccatorum*, p. 29.

320 Cagnazzo, *Summa Tabiena*, p. 163; Mazzolini, *Summa summarum*, vol. 1, ff. 52v-3r; Fumo, *Summa quae aurea armilla inscribitur*, pp. 90–1.

321 Cajetan, *Summula peccatorum*, p. 34.

322 Cagnazzo, *Summa Tabiena*, p. 163.

323 Fumo, *Summa quae aurea armilla inscribitur*, p. 89.

324 Mazzolini, *Summa summarum*, vol. 1, f. 52v.

against whom a war was justly waged, they could be despoiled in the normal way of things that belonged to them under their own laws.[325] 'Their ownership exists under positive law', it was explained, 'and their infidelity under divine law, which does not invalidate positive law'. Infidels living in Christian countries could only be despoiled to the extent that the laws of those countries had deprived them of their rights.

The relative insignificance for theologians of the distinction drawn by lawyers between public and other wars is especially evident in the teaching of Francisco de Vitoria, who is often credited with establishing a new approach to the analysis of international relations in the universities of Spain and Portugal.[326] In an influential lecture on the law of war, which he delivered while holding the principal chair of theology at the University of Salamanca during the late 1520s and the 1530s, Vitoria tended to assimilate wartime plunder with peacetime reprisals.[327] For one thing, when defending the thesis that offensive wars could only be waged legitimately in response to unredressed losses or injuries, he followed Aquinas' example in relating Augustine's remarks about *denegatio iustitiae* to wars in general.[328] Princes were required to ensure that justice was provided within their own territories, and when it was denied elsewhere, they were further required to ensure that it was obtained somehow by their subjects. That they could authorise the use of force both to secure redress and also to impose penalties was established 'by the law of nations and the authority of the whole world', for it was recognised everywhere that wrongdoers must be restrained, 'and this can only be through the instrumentality of princes'.[329] Although expenses could also be recovered, just as they might be if a court action were raised within a prince's territory, and although the lawyers could teach correctly that movable things taken in a war 'become the occupier's by the law of nations, even if they should exceed compensation for losses', the basic rule remained that the enemy ought to be despoiled only to the extent necessary to provide satisfaction for the losses or injuries originally

325 Cajetan, *Summa Sancti Thomae Aquinatis universam sacram theologiam complectens, cum commentariis*, vol. 2(2), pp. 229–30. On this question see too Alfonso de Castro, *Opera*, cols 1296–1312, and Alonso de la Vera Cruz, *De iusto bello contra Indos*, pp. 230–67.

326 Scott 1934a; Anghie 1996; Davis 1997; Koskenniemi 2011a; Valenzuela-Verhmehren 2013.

327 This most certainly does not mean that the legal categories were unknown to Vitoria, who made use of legal sources in writing about both plunder and reprisal. The point is rather that he did not attach much importance to the difference between them.

328 *De Indis et de iure belli relectiones*, pp. 170–1 and 279.

329 *De Indis et de iure belli relectiones*, pp. 172–3 and 280–1.

inflicted.[330] Vitoria insisted further that it was not licit for people to engage in plunder without the express authorisation of their princes or commanders, 'because they are not judges but executive officers, and those acting otherwise are bound to make restitution'.[331] As offensive wars were a kind of judicial process, the people who participated in them were effectively executing court orders, the terms of which they were not permitted to exceed. Defensive wars were not quite the same, however, and Vitoria believed that it was lawful to do everything that was necessary for the defence and preservation of a state (*omnia facere, quae ad defensionem boni publici sunt necessaria*).[332] He also believed that while in principle a war could only be waged justly on one side – only one belligerent, as he put it, could wage a *bellum iustum per se* – in practice a prince who made a genuine and plausible error could be excused for his sin – in this limited sense, he acknowledged, there could be *bella iusta ex utraque parte*.[333]

The distinction between defensive and offensive wars frequently resurfaced in works written by Thomist theologians later in the sixteenth century.[334] Princes who did have superiors, and even private people, were entitled to defend themselves and their property against aggressors, and to adopt whatever measures seemed necessary in doing so.[335] It was in offensive wars that authority had to be exercised by princes who did not have superiors to whom they could appeal for justice. As was explained with particular clarity by Domingo Bañez, one of Vitoria's successors in the principal chair of theology at Salamanca, since an offensive war was 'the ultimate act of vindicative justice', since 'such an act always pertains to a true judge', and since only a prince without a superior could be a *iudex verus* in a dispute between nations, only

330 *De Indis et de iure belli relectiones*, pp. 171, 184, 280 and 293–4. Reference was made here to legal texts on the acquisition of *res hostium* by *occupatio*, but Vitoria also connected his comments with something he had said earlier about the use letters of marque or reprisal (pp. 181 and 290). On the limitation of plunder 'quo usque secundum aequitatem sit sufficienter satisfactum de damno et iniuria', he expressed agreement with Mazzolini.

331 *De Indis et de iure belli relectiones*, pp. 185 and 295.

332 *De Indis et de iure belli relectiones*, pp. 171 and 279.

333 *De Indis et de iure belli relectiones*, pp. 173–7 and 281–6. On this point see too Winkel 2007.

334 Domingo Bañez, *Scholastica commentaria in Secundam secundae angelici doctoris Divi Thomae*, cols 1935–6; Gregorio de Valentia, *Commentariorum theologicorum libri quatuor*, vol. 3, col. 935; Luis de Molina, *De iustitia et iure*, vol. 1, col. 415; Robert Bellarmine, *Disputationes de controversiis Christianae fidei adversus huius temporis haereticos*, vol. 1, col. 1742, and *On Temporal and Spiritual Authority*, pp. 68–9; Juan Azor, *Institutiones morales*, vol. 3, col. 144.

335 Bañez, *Scholastica commentaria in Secundam secundae*, cols 1900–2; Peter Binsfeld, *Enchiridion theologiae pastoralis*, p. 334; Molina, *De iustitia et iure*, vol. 1, col. 459.

a prince of this type (also called a *princeps perfectus*) could lawfully wage a *bellum aggressivum*.[336] It followed from this, on the one hand, that if people attacked and despoiled foreigners – even 'Turks or other infidels' – without authorisation from their prince, they would not only commit a mortal sin (*peccatum mortale*) but would also be obliged to make restitution for the losses inflicted (*tenebuntur restituere damna illata*).[337] If private people sought to redress injuries on their own account (*propria auctoritate*), they would be arrogating public jurisdiction (*publicum iudicium*) to themselves, for given that – as Vitoria had pointed out – 'they are not judges, but executive officers, they ought to await the ruling of a judge'.[338] On the other hand, it followed further that authorisation to attack and despoil foreigners ought not to be granted unless a prince was convinced that he had a just cause for going to war. 'Since a prince who initiates a war is a judge with respect to another prince', Bañez stressed, 'the prince is bound to examine and investigate very carefully the causes of a just war'.[339] He ought not to resort to war over a light or slight injury (*iniuria levis aut parva*), he ought first to seek redress by every other means (*omnia media*), and he ought not to extend the conflict beyond what was necessary to recover compensation for losses (*compensatio damnorum*) and the expenses of the war (*impensae belli*), or to impose an appropriate penalty for the other prince's fault (*poena secundum proportionem culpae*).[340] Even a prince with a just cause for waging a war might end up being liable to restitution if 'either the penalty were to exceed the fault, or the compensation were to exceed the amount of the losses'. Nevertheless, as was emphasised by Domingo de Soto, another of Vitoria's successors at Salamanca, the essential position remained that 'if a war is just, plunder is licit', whereas 'if a war is unjust, robbery is committed'.[341] It seemed to some of the later Thomists that if plunder were authorised by a prince for a just cause then it would always be

336 *Scholastica commentaria in Secundam secundae*, cols 1902–4. For the view that war was an *actus iustitiae vindicativae* see too Valentia, *Commentariorum theologicorum libri quatuor*, vol. 3, col. 925.

337 Bañez, *Scholastica commentaria in Secundam secundae*, cols 1908–9.

338 Pedro de Aragón, *In Secundam secundae Divi Thomae doctoris angelici commentaria*, vol. 1, p. 251; Binsfeld, *Enchiridion theologiae pastoralis*, p. 335.

339 Bañez, *Scholastica commentaria in Secundam secundae*, cols 1911–13.

340 Valentia, *Commentariorum theologicorum libri quatuor*, vol. 3, col. 937; Molina, *De iustitia et iure*, vol. 1, cols 460–1; Bellarmine, *Disputationes de controversiis Christianae fidei adversus huius temporis haereticos*, vol. 1, col. 1742, and *On Temporal and Spiritual Authority*, p. 69.

341 *De iustitia et iure*, p. 429. See too Enrique Henríquez, *Summa theologiae moralis libri quindecim*, pp. 868–9.

licit, and there would be no liability to restitution even if it were engaged in out of greed.[342] For these theologians, *intentio recta* was not strictly speaking a prerequisite of a just war, since its absence amounted to a deficiency in charity rather than justice, which would be present as long as the *auctoritas principis* was exercised for a *iusta causa*.

Given that *literae marcharum aut represaliarum* provided explicit authorisation for maritime raiding, that they were granted by one sovereign ruler after careful investigation of an alleged *denegatio iustitiae* by another, and that the recovery of redress for losses or injuries under these letters was conceived of as a judicial process, the Thomists had little difficulty in accommodating the teaching of Bartolus and his followers on the subject of reprisals in peacetime within their moral theology.[343] Ironically, while the lawyers had found it more difficult to reconcile the taking of reprisals in peacetime with the texts they studied than the taking of plunder in wartime, it was their teaching on the taking of plunder in wartime that was more difficult to reconcile with the teaching of the theologians. Like Vitoria, the later Thomists were generally prepared to accept that 'by the law of nations, whatever movable things are taken in a just war, even if they should exceed compensation for losses, become the property of the combatants taking them'.[344] Reference was made to local *leges et consuetudines* governing the distribution of spoils among combatants, and also to the fundamental rule enunciated in the law schools that *mobilia capta in bello fiunt capientium*. It is significant, however, that the later Thomists felt the need to reiterate the clause Vitoria had inserted into his statement of the rule – 'etiamsi si excedant compensationem damnorum' – for it seemed to them that there were limits to the amount of plunder that could lawfully be taken in a war. They certainly did not accept that plunder was licit whenever a war was declared between sovereign rulers.[345] As they saw it, plunder was only licit if the prerequisites of a just war were present, which in principle

342 Aragón, *In Secundam secundae Divi Thomae doctoris angelici commentaria*, vol. 1, p. 230; Molina, *De iustitia et iure*, vol. 1, col 439; Bellarmine, *Disputationes de controversiis Christianae fidei adversus huius temporis haereticos*, vol. 1, col. 1744, and *On Temporal and Spiritual Authority*, pp. 71–2.

343 Vitoria, *De Indis et de iure belli relectiones*, pp. 181 and 290; Valentia, *Commentariorum theologicorum libri quatuor*, vol. 3, col. 937; Molina, *De iustitia et iure*, vol. 1, col. 473.

344 Bañez, *Scholastica commentaria in Secundam secundae*, col. 1934; Valentia, *Commentariorum theologicorum libri quatuor*, vol. 3, cols 939–40; Molina, *De iustitia et iure*, vol. 1, cols 461–2.

345 By the later sixteenth century it was not unusual for Thomist theologians to talk about *auctoritas principis* as *auctoritas indicendi bellum*, but there was still no move towards treating a declaration of war as a prerequisite of a just war.

could only happen on one side of a conflict. Moreover, although they accepted that compensation could be recovered for the costs of waging a war as well as for the losses or injuries originally inflicted, and that penalties could also be imposed on unjust belligerents, they still believed that justice required the harm inflicted on an enemy to be proportionate to the enemy's fault. But how could a just proportion be preserved if combatants acquired title to everything they occupied? Gregorio de Valentia, a Jesuit who had studied at Salamanca in the 1560s, was tempted by the idea that combatants did not actually acquire ownership of anything taken from the enemy until spoils were distributed by those in authority over them.[346] Luis de Molina, another Jesuit who had studied at Salamanca, connected the acquisition of plunder with the acquisition of property forfeited by criminals.[347] He did not suggest that plunder might be acquired as a result of forfeiture rather than through occupation, but he clearly did not feel comfortable with the idea that *res hostium* could be regarded as equivalent to *res nullius*.[348] He observed that plunder 'has this in common with the acquisition and loss of ownership by way of punishment, that the ownership established by the law of war is always contrary to the will of the person who loses it'. Nevertheless, instead of devising an alternative theory of the acquisition of plunder, the Thomists preferred to mention the teaching of the law schools in the course of discussions centred on the law of obligations rather than the law of property. Regardless of who owned goods plundered from the enemy, they maintained, an obligation of restitution (*obligatio restitutionis*) would arise if the goods had not been taken justly.[349]

In seeking to accommodate the teaching of the lawyers within their moral theology, the Thomists were assisted by the willingness of the canonists to make use of their vocabulary, rooted as it was in biblical and patristic sources they shared with them.[350] In the sixteenth century, indeed, there were canonists who wrote about the legitimacy of war in specifically Thomist terms.[351]

346 *Commentariorum theologicorum libri quatuor*, vol. 3, col. 940.

347 *De iustitia et iure*, vol. 1, col. 410. On Molina's theory of war see generally Fernandes 2014.

348 It may not be accidental that neither Valentia nor Molina used the words *occupare* and *occupatio* in their discussions of plunder.

349 Legal support was available from *Decretum*, C. 14 q. 6 c. 1.

350 Russell 1975, pp. 55–212; Johnson 1981, pp. 150–65; Bellamy 2008, pp. 31–7; Reid 2011, pp. 76–88; Corey and Charles 2012, pp. 67–76. For a comparison of the canonist and civilian treatments of war see Greenwood 2014.

351 Martín de Azpilcueta, *Commentaria in septem distinctiones de poenitentia*, p. 437, and *Enchiridion sive manuale confessariorum et poenitentium*, p. 275; Diego de Covarruvias, *Opera omnia*, vol. 1, pp. 540–1; Alfonso Alvarez Guerrero, *Thesaurus Christianae religionis*, p. 360.

For example, Diego de Covarruvias y Leyva, an influential member of Philip II's council of state who had attended the lectures on theology delivered at Salamanca by Vitoria and Soto, wrote that the justice of a war (*belli iustitia*) was dependent on a combination of the authority of a prince who was able to declare the war (*auctoritas principis, qui bellum indicere potest*), a just cause for declaring the war (*iusta indicendi bellum causa*) and the proper purpose of those fighting and declaring the war (*recta bellantium et indicentium bellum intentio*). Yet bringing the prerequisites of a *bellum iustum* together with the essential condition of a *bellum publicum* in this way was not in itself sufficient to resolve the differences between the theological and legal traditions, as was recognised by Martín de Azpilcueta, who had lectured to Covarruvias on the canon law at Salamanca. He was asked for advice about a question of restitution raised after a battle in North Africa, in which both goods and prisoners had been taken from the Portuguese by the Moors.[352] When some of the prisoners were released and returned home with some of the goods, which they had purchased from their captors, the original owners of the goods tried to recover them from the released prisoners. Azpilcueta explained that there were two ways of looking at the question. On the one hand, from the point of view of theologians (*theologi*), 'in order for things taken in a war to become the property of the takers, it is required that the war be just', yet the war at issue 'was unjust on the side of the Moors, because it was undertaken for the defence of lands that were not theirs but belonged to the Christians, who wished to regain them'. From this perspective, the goods purchased by the prisoners still belonged to their original owners and needed to be restored to them. On the other hand, as far as lawyers (*iurisconsulti*) were concerned, 'in order for movable things taken in a war to become the property of the takers, they do not insist on the justice of the war, but only that it was public, declared by the Roman people or by any other free people not acknowledging a superior'. From this perspective, because the war had been declared, the goods had been acquired by the Moors and title had been transferred by them to the prisoners. Azpilcueta was inclined to conclude that the goods did not need to be restored to their original owners, even if they were ready to reimburse the prisoners for the price they had paid, although he admitted to finding the question difficult. His pupil suggested a more nuanced approach, depending on whether a war had been declared in good or bad faith.[353] At least when Christian princes were

352 *Consilia et responsa*, vol. 1, pp. 122–3. See too Haggenmacher 1983, pp. 290–2, and also 1992.

353 Covarruvias, *Opera omnia*, vol. 1, pp. 553–4.

involved, Covarruvias believed that 'on account of the presumed good faith of enemies, the laws of the Romans should be observed'.[354]

The canonists tended to distinguish themselves from the civilians who concentrated on the laws of the Romans by remarking that the aim of the civil law was to promote the common good (*bonum commune*), whereas the aim of the canon law was to promote the felicity of the soul (*felicitas animi*).[355] 'Knowledge of the canon law', Fortunius Garcia remarked further in a treatise devoted to the distinction, 'is not merely practical, like knowledge of the civil law, because it partly takes account of speculation from metaphysics and theology'. Although the canonists were often concerned with how cases should be dealt with in a court of law (*forum iudiciale*), and were to this extent in a similar position to the civilians, they were sometimes concerned instead with how cases should be dealt with in a disciplinary process (*forum poenitentiale*), and to this extent they were in a similar position to the theologians.[356] As a matter of fact, the law of the church had originally been studied in the theology schools, but after the canonists began to teach in their own schools the theologians asserted the priority of their teaching, pointing out that they established at a higher level the moral principles on which the canonists relied, and complaining that the canonists, partly because they paid undue attention to the teaching of the civilians, were inclined to propose solutions to problems that were unnecessarily technical and inappropriately pragmatic.[357] In the later sixteenth century the divergence between the canon lawyers and moral theologians became more pronounced, following the decision of the Council of Trent to place greater emphasis on the secrecy of confession to a priest.[358] A distinction then emerged between the *forum internum*, in which the conscience of a believer raised a complaint privately for the examination and judgment of a confessor, and the *forum externum*, in which a complaint

354 A war against the Moors might have been a different matter, but Covarruvias did not consider that case.

355 Antonius de Butrio, *In libris quintos Decretalium commentarii*, vol. 1, ff. 77v-8r (ad X 1.4.11); Panormitanus, *Lectura super quinque libros Decretalium*, vol. 1, f. 158v (ad X 1.4.11); Angelus de Clavasio, *Summa angelica de casibus conscientiae*, f. 42v; Ioannes Paulus Lancelottus, *Institutiones iuris canonici*, pp. 71–3; Fortunius Garcia, *Tractatus de ultimo fine iuris civilis et canonici*, p. 38.

356 It is for this reason that books written by canonists, like those by Guerrero (in n. 351 above) and de Clavasio (in the preceding note), sometimes had the sort of titles theologians might have used.

357 Meyjes 1991; Shogimen 1999; Shoemaker 2010. On the situation before the disciplines diverged see Larson 2013.

358 *Canons and Decrees of the Council of Trent*, p. 197.

was dealt with publicly by a judicial or disciplinary body.[359] While reminiscent of Bartolus' distinction between the *forum conscientiae* and *forum civile*, the internal forum in which the confessor gave judgment was now differentiated more clearly from the external forum, whether judicial or penitential, in which the civilians and canonists gave advice. It was thus easier to understand how lawyers could reach one judgment – for instance, that goods taken in wartime had been acquired and could be retained by the takers – while theologians formed a different opinion – for instance, that goods taken in wartime ought to be restored to their original owners.

The increasing divergence of theological from legal thinking facilitated but also obstructed the development of a new justification for the emerging approach to maritime raiding. On the one hand, the emphasis in theological thinking on the authorisation of conduct rather than the declaration of war by princes, and the tendency to regard wars as a species of judicial process in which justice was secured from recalcitrant defenders, fitted fairly neatly the use of letters of reprisal in undeclared wars. If this usage could not really be reconciled with the principles of the civil and canon laws, it could perhaps be reconciled more readily with the principles of moral theology. Both the broader notion of *auctoritas principis*, and the treatment of wars as a response to *denegatio iustitiae*, were worked out elaborately in the treatises of the Thomist theologians, but traces of similar ideas were noted earlier in this section in the sermons of English ministers. It is indeed well known that Thomism was influencing English theology at a more systematic level in the later sixteenth century.[360] Furthermore, towards the end of the same period a new genre of literature was beginning to appear in which advice was provided on the handling of cases of conscience.[361] Although differences would remain between Catholic and Protestant moral theology, enough ground was shared for there to be a realistic prospect of a consensus being established on the legitimacy of the new approach to maritime raiding.[362] On the other hand, for any such consensus to amount to a change in the understanding of the law – human as well as divine – there would also need to be a change in how

359 Mörsdorf 1968; Bossy 1975; Myers 1996; Dürr 2014; Decock 2017.

360 Forte 1982, pp. 137–8; Voak 2003, p. 157; Kirby, 2008, pp. 253–4; Joyce 2012, pp. 73–4; Sedgwick 2019, p. 119. On *ius gentium* in particular see Richard Hooker, *Of the Lawes of Ecclesiasticall Politie*, pt 1, pp. 76–7, together with Cromartie 2000, pp. 59–61.

361 Wright 1940, p. 193; Breward 1968, pp. 5–6; Long 1989, p. 57; Keenan 1995, p. 114, and 2004, p. 17; Patterson 2014, pp. 91–2.

362 Rose 1975, pp. 187–8; Andrew 2001, pp. 28–9; Ross 2015, pp. 827–8. See, for example, William Perkins, *Discourse of Conscience*, pp. 10–12, 14 and 38.

the relationship between law and theology was understood, for the increasing prospect of a consensus being formed among moral theologians happened to coincide with an increasing divergence between the functions of theologians and lawyers.[363] Even if the new approach could be justified in terms of moral theology, it would still need to be explained why the significance of the justification was not purely moral.

5 Justification in Terms of the Law of Policy

It may be recalled that in the proclamation Elizabeth issued against trading with her enemies 'the lawe of God' was said to have 'warranted', and 'the continuall practise of her neighbour nations in theise latter times' to have 'confirmed', a precept that was taken to pertain to 'the lawe of pollicy'.[364] This precept – 'that supreme law of government ingrafted by nature in the hart of every souverain prince' – was that he must strive after 'the safety and preservation of the kingdomes and people committed to his charge'. An obvious allusion was being made here to the frequently rehearsed maxim *salus populi suprema lex esto*.[365] Although widely attributed to the XII Tables, on which the development of Roman law was believed to have been based, the maxim was actually drawn from the laws Cicero had prescribed in his *De legibus* for any

363 It is a source of some confusion that in the seventeenth and eighteenth centuries many civil lawyers became interested in connecting their subject with the moral doctrines of the theologians, partly in a bid to preserve the status of their subject as the *ius commune* of Europe (Gordley 1991; Dolezalek 1992; Decock 2012). What they sought to shore up, however, was their teaching in private law, for they had by then lost influence in the areas of public law (Wijffels 1995, p. 42) and international law (Lesaffer 2011, pp. 418–20), both of which were turned into distinct disciplines. What was diverging more clearly was the purposes pursued by lawyers and theologians, which did not prevent lawyers from paying closer attention to the teaching of the theologians.

364 *Documents Relating to Law and Custom of the Sea*, vol. 1, pp. 213–17; *Tudor Royal Proclamations*, vol. 3, pp. 255–8.

365 Richard Cosin, *Answer to the Two Fyrst and Principall Treatises of a Certaine Factious Libell*, p. 260, and *Apologie for Sundrie Proceedings by Jurisdiction Ecclesiasticall*, p. 195; William Fulbecke, *Direction or Preparative to the Study of the Lawe*, p. 2; Bartholomew Phillip, *Counseller: A Treatise of Counsels and Counsellers of Princes*, p. 134; Sir Martyn Cognet, *Politique Discourses upon Trueth and Lying*, pp. 89–90; John Tassin, *Amendment of Life, Comprised in Fower Bookes*, p. 361; Thomas Morton, *Salomon, or, A Treatise Declaring the State of the Kingdome of Israel*, p. 18; Pierre de la Primaudaye, *French Academie*, p. 742; Matthew Sutcliffe, *Briefe Replie to a Certaine Odious and Slanderous Libel*, p. 100; *Relations politiques des Pays-Bas et de l'Angleterre*, vol. 6, p. 200.

well ordered commonwealth.[366] He had been thinking of the kind of mixed constitution recommended in his *De republica*, but in this passage he had dealt in particular with the priorities of magistrates who exercised royal authority (*regium imperium*) and supreme command in wartime (*militiae summum ius*).[367] In Elizabeth's proclamation the 'soverain prince' who was to follow the *suprema lex* inscribed in his heart by nature was accordingly identified as the 'soverain commaunder'. Earlier in his *De legibus* Cicero had observed that 'the most learned men' regarded law (*lex*) as 'the highest reason, implanted in nature, which commands what ought to be done and forbids the opposite'.[368] The idea that law was the *recta ratio* implicit in the natural order is present in many of Cicero's surviving works.[369] 'True law is right reason in agreement with nature', he had declared in his *De republica*, adding there and elsewhere that it was 'of universal application, unchanging and everlasting'.[370] Because the statutes enacted by human legislators often ratified customary practices, which were in turn founded on a shared understanding of what was right or wrong, right reason could often be discerned in the laws constituted by nations for the sake of utility, yet ultimately it was 'not born of opinion, but implanted in us by a kind of innate instinct'.[371] Right reason was shared by people with the gods, and since it governed the natural order it was possible to 'conceive of this whole universe as one commonwealth of which both gods and people are members'.[372] The way Cicero sometimes put this was by saying that the gods were the authors (*auctores*) or promoters (*latores*) of a law of nature (*lex* or *ius naturae*) that governed the community they formed with other rational beings.

The broader association of law with reason and nature was something Cicero had learned from the Stoic philosophers who wrote and taught in Greek during his lifetime.[373] It was largely through the study of his own Latin works, however, together with those of Seneca, that Stoic ideas entered western theology, long before interest in Aristotelian philosophy was revived in the twelfth

366 Cicero, *De legibus*, 3.3.8; Livy, *Ab urbe condita*, 3.34.6; *Digest*, 1.2.2.6.

367 See too *Philippics*, 11.28 (and also 4.4), *In Catilinam*, 4.9, *Pro Murena*, 7, and *De lege agraria*, 2.3.7.

368 *De legibus*, 1.6.18.

369 Kesler 1985, pp. 196–206; Colish 1985, vol. 1, pp. 95–104; Van Zyl 1986, pp. 38–49; Wood 1988, pp. 70–8; Forschner 2016, pp. 51–5.

370 *De republica*, 3.22.33 (a fragment known from Lactantius, *Divinae institutiones*, 6.8), *De legibus*, 1.16.44, and *Pro Milone*, 4.10.

371 *De inventione*, 2.22.65, 2.22.67 and 2.53.160–1, and *De legibus*, 1.15.42, 2.4.8 and 2.5.13.

372 *De legibus*, 1.7.23, *De finibus*, 3.19.64, *Tusculan Disputations*, 1.13.30, and *De natura deorum*, 2.31.78–9 and 2.62.154.

373 Watson 1971; Horowitz 1974; Jacobs 2012; Alonso 2013; Atkins 2015.

century.[374] The theologians found Cicero's references to a law of nature especially instructive when reading the passage in Paul's letter to the Romans in which he had observed that 'when the Gentiles, who have no law, do by nature the things of the law', they responded to 'the law written in their hearts, their consciences bearing witness, and their reasonings mutually accusing or even excusing them'.[375] The law of nature envisaged here was somehow distinct from the law of God revealed in the scriptures. Stoic thinking also appears to have informed the comments on *ius naturale* in the writings of the Roman jurists, although they did not agree with Cicero that human laws deviating from natural reason were not true laws.[376] In fact, Cicero himself was not as exacting as he might have been, for some Stoic philosophers had insisted that only a small number of sages were capable of cultivating the virtues so successfully as to become members of the cosmopolis inhabited by the gods.[377] Cicero adopted the more moderate position that all people had sufficient reason to participate actively in the natural order shared with the gods.[378] The laws prescribed in his *De legibus* were neither the laws of the actual state in which he resided, nor those of the ideal state envisaged by some philosophers, but were laws suitable for any orderly community in the real world.[379] In some of his other works he not only distinguished the civil law of Rome from the natural law of the cosmos but also talked about the law of nations (*ius gentium*).[380] What he seems to have had in mind was a regime of the type he tried to construct in his *De legibus*, where the rules he favoured were often those in use in Rome, but were sometimes drawn instead from the practices of other states, when the laws of those states seemed to him to express more effectively the rational principles common to all nations.[381] If *ius gentium* consisted of rules that could be found

374 McNeill 1941, pp. 212–14; Verbeke 1983, pp. 14–16; Lapidge 1988, pp. 88–99; Sellars 2006, pp. 138–9; Sweeney 2012, pp. 144–5.

375 Romans 2.14–15. For Paul's own debt to Stoic thinking see Engberg-Pedersen 2000 and 2004.

376 Zuckert 1989; Vander Waerdt 1994; Kroger 2004; Honoré 2010; Brouwer 2015; Erdody 2018.

377 Schofield 1999; Obbink 1999; Sellars 2007; Vogt 2008; Dyson 2008.

378 Benardete 1987, p. 302; Harries 2002, pp. 55–6; Dyck 2004, pp. 46–7; Long 2006, pp. 346–7; Asmis 2008, pp. 21–4. For a different view see Atkins 2013, pp. 173–5.

379 Rawson 1973, p. 343; MacKendrick 1989, pp. 78–9; Powell 2001, pp. 35–7; Annas 2013, pp. 218–19; Miller 2014, pp. 331–2.

380 *De republica*, 1.2.2, *De oratore*, 1.13.56, *De partitione oratoria*, 37.129–30, *Pro Roscio Amerino*, 49.143, and *De haruspicum responsis*, 14.32.

381 The idea that some laws applied everywhere and others only in particular places was not limited to the Stoics. See, for instance, Aristotle, *Ethics*, 1134b18–1135a6, and *Rhetoric*, 1373b1–18, and also Horsley 1978.

in some form in most nations, in Cicero's writings it was associated with the idea of a global commonwealth governed by the law of nature.[382]

The law of nations was mentioned again in the most influential of Cicero's works on moral and political philosophy, an advice book he wrote for Roman statesmen.[383] At one place in his *De officiis* he observed that to profit from the despoiling of others was forbidden 'not only by nature, that is by the law of nations, but also by the statutes of peoples, through which the public interest is maintained in individual states'.[384] At another place he recalled that people belonged not only to individual cities and states but also to a global community governed by the law of nature, and observed that 'the civil law is not always identical with the law of nations, yet the law of nations ought always to be identical with the civil law'.[385] The truth was, however, that most people had access to only a shadow and inklings (*umbra et imaginibus*) of the true law (*veri iuris*), which meant that the practical advice Cicero had to offer was bound to differ from the moral theory of the sages.[386] His professed aim was not to write about the strict responsibilities (*perfecta officia*) with which a treatise on moral theory (*ad finem bonorum*) would have been concerned, but about the modest responsibilities (*media officia*) appropriate to a treatise providing instruction for everyday life (*ad institutionem vitae communis*).[387] He dealt in the first part of his treatise with the kind of morally upright or honourable behaviour (*honestum*) of which all people were capable, before proceeding in two further parts to deal first with expedient behaviour (*utile*), and then with conflicts between honourable and expedient behaviour.[388] 'The people we live with', he explained in the first part, 'are not perfect and ideally wise, but those who do very well if there is some semblance of virtue in them'.[389] These people had to think about the expediency as well as the goodness of actions, although Cicero

382 Pangle 1998; Conklin 2010; Remer 2011. This was of course the source of Vitoria's thinking on the topic.

383 Douglas 1965, p. 149; Lacey 1978, p. 173–4; Dyck 1996, p. 39; Jones 1998, pp. 131–2; Long 2008, p. 56.

384 *De officiis*, 3.5.21–3.

385 *De officiis*, 3.17.69. For the idea that people belonged to various levels of community see further *De officiis*, 1.16.50–2, 1.17.53–8, 1.41.149 and 3.6.26–8, *De finibus*, 3.19.62–3, 3.20.67–21.69, 4.2.4 and 5.23.65, *De natura deorum*, 1.2.4, *Tusculan Disputations*, 5.37.107–9, and *De amicitia*, 5.19–20.

386 Morford 2002, pp. 87–94; Atkins 2005, pp. 505–14; Lintott 2008, pp. 366–73; Bragues 2010, pp. 24–32; Aßländer 2013, pp. 754–7.

387 *De officiis*, 1.3.7–8.

388 Kidd 1971, pp. 160–2; Nicgorski 1984, pp. 561–6; Colish 1985, vol. 1, pp. 145–51; Kries 2003, pp. 382–7; Griffin 2011, pp. 313–14.

389 *De officiis*, 1.15.46.

denied that there could ever be a genuine inconsistency between expediency and goodness. 'But for all cases we have one rule', he declared, 'that what seems to be expedient may not be wrongful, or that if it is wrongful it may not seem to be expedient'. It would be inexpedient as well as wrongful, for example, to break a promise made to enemies, as opposed to brigands or pirates.[390] Cicero presented his fullest discussion of the morality of warfare when writing about the virtue of justice in the first part of his treatise.[391] Although the settlement of disputes by force was more typical of beasts than of men (*viri*, whose essential quality was *virtus*), when resort to force became necessary men were still required to abide by the laws of war (*conservanda sunt iura belli*).[392] They might fight for the sake of gaining supremacy (*imperium*) or renown (*gloria*), but they would fail to do so unless they had a just cause (*iusta causa*) for taking up arms and unless they dealt with their enemies lawfully (*iure*).[393] Cicero regarded the Roman requirement that a war be formally declared after its justice was confirmed by the *fetiales* as a manifestation of equity (*aequitas*), and he made provision in his *De legibus* for similar officials (*publici interpres*) to adjudicate on the justice of wars.[394]

With its preference for the *honestum* over the *utile*, the *De officiis* became a popular source among the authors of the advice books known as *specula principum*, in which the image of an ideal ruler, who behaved virtuously and adhered to natural law, was presented for imitation to actual rulers, who were in turn exhorted to set a suitable example for their subjects to follow.[395] Paradoxically, with its aim of providing practical advice for statesmen in the real world, Cicero's treatise also became a significant – albeit uncited – source of the notoriously subversive contribution made to the same genre by Niccolò Machiavelli at the beginning of the sixteenth century.[396] 'Because I want to write what will be useful to anyone who understands', Machiavelli explained, 'it seems to me better to concentrate on what really happens rather than on theories or speculations'.[397] Setting out like his predecessors to advise the prince on how to 'maintain his state', he advanced the novel thesis that in order

390 *De officiis*, 1.13.39, 3.20.81 and 3.29.107.

391 On the priority given to justice see Atkins 1990, and on the discussion of warfare see Keller 2012.

392 *De officiis*, 1.11.34–6, and see too 2.8.26–7.

393 *De officiis*, 1.12.38, and see too *De republica*, 3.23.34 (a fragment known from Augustine, *De civitate Dei*, 22.6.2) and 3.24.35 (a fragment known from Isidore, *Etymologiae*, 18.1.2–3).

394 *De officiis*, 1.11.36, *De legibus*, 2.14.34, and *De republica*, 2.17.31.

395 Born 1928; Gilbert 1939; Grabes 1982; Nederman 1998; Buescu 1993.

396 Colish 1978; Barlow 1999; Zerba 2004; Remer 2009; Giorgini 2014.

397 *The Prince*, pp. 54–5.

to do so he 'must be prepared to act immorally when this becomes necessary'. Machiavelli reminded his readers that there were 'two ways of contending, one by using laws, the other force', and that 'the first is appropriate for men, the second for animals'.[398] He argued, however, that men must be prepared to use both the force of the lion and the deceit of the fox. The prince must learn to appear virtuous in the conventional sense, but the *virtù* he needed to cultivate extended to political virtuosity.[399] Indeed, Machiavelli was suggesting not merely that the virtuoso prince would be prepared to neglect the conventional virtues when necessary, but also that he would appear to be virtuous at other times only because doing so was necessary in order to preserve his power. In other words, instead of necessity sometimes excusing deviant behaviour, as the lawyers and theologians were prepared to accept, necessity was regarded by Machiavelli as the guiding principle of all the prince's behaviour. His *virtù*, moreover, was expected to extend further to martial virility.[400] Since the foundations of power were 'good laws or good armies', and since it was 'impossible to have good laws if good arms are lacking', it followed that the prince must 'always be concerned with military matters'.[401] When not leading his own forces in wartime, he was to concern himself with their effective preparation.[402] Just as appearing to be virtuous would help him to achieve his political objectives, so appearing to be religious would help him to achieve his military objectives by preparing dutiful subjects to die for their country.[403]

If one striking difference between Cicero and Machiavelli was the latter's willingness to subordinate the *honestum* to the *utile*, another was his lack of interest in the law of nature and limited interest in the justification of war.[404] His realism, it is now widely believed, gave rise to an alternative way of understanding international relations, differing both from the positive jurisprudence of the lawyers and from the natural jurisprudence of the theologians.[405] He did quote with approval Livy's observation that 'war is just for whom it is necessary, and arms are pious for those whose only hope lies in arms', but far from insisting that wars could only be justified by the necessity of survival, he encouraged

398 *The Prince*, pp. 61–2.
399 Wood 1967; Hannaford 1972; Price 1973; Kahn 1986; Skinner 2018.
400 Gilbert 1944; Mallett 1990; Colish 1998; Lukes 2001 and 2004; Winter 2014.
401 *The Prince*, pp. 42–3 and 51–2, *Art of War*, p. 4, and *Discourses on Livy*, pp. 16 and 283.
402 *Discourses on Livy*, pp. 34–44 and 285–6.
403 For a detailed comparison of Machiavelli's advice on this subject with the advice offered in other *specula principum* see Gilbert 1938, pp. 62–76.
404 Mansfield 1996, p. 22; Boucher 1998, p. 133; Koskenniemi 2007, p. 11; Viroli 2010, p. 199; Roth-Isigkeit 2017, p. 19.
405 Mindle 1985; Forde 1992; Viroli 2007; Follesdal 2015; Guilhot 2016.

emulation of the wars fought by the Romans for empire and glory.[406] He also referred with approval to Livy's explanation of the sack of Rome by the Gauls as a response to the failure by the Romans to punish envoys who had acted 'against the law of nations', from which he drew the conclusion that all rulers should expect a similar response if they failed to deal lawfully with their neighbours.[407] His obvious point was that conforming to *ius gentium* would be prudent, rather than that it was morally obligatory, yet recognising the prudence of conforming to *ius gentium* would itself have given it a certain force.[408] Elsewhere, however, Machiavelli had no more to say about *ius gentium* than *ius naturale*. His advocacy of the use of devious stratagems in warfare was consistent enough with the teachings of the lawyers and theologians, nor would they have denied that whatever seemed necessary in a defensive war ought to be done, but they would not have gone so far as to say that 'where one deliberates on the safety of his homeland, there ought not to enter any consideration of either just or unjust, merciful or cruel, praiseworthy or ignominious'.[409] In protecting one's country, Machiavelli declared, 'one ought to follow entirely the policy that saves its life and maintains its liberty'. Whatever Cicero might have thought, Machiavelli was convinced by his reading of Livy that the Romans had always done what seemed most likely to serve their own interests, and his general advice to contemporary rulers was to imitate the Roman way of waging wars. Among other things, he recommended that 'all plunder should belong to the public treasury', so that it would be victorious peoples who profited from wars, not avaricious individuals, and so that there would be less need for wars to be funded through taxation.[410]

Although the astuteness of many of Machiavelli's observations was appreciated, he soon came to be condemned as an adviser who approved of any activity, however immoral, which would preserve the power of the prince, as if this end could justify recourse to any means.[411] In continental Europe the expression 'reason of state' was used to denote this type of thinking, either in an entirely negative way or in a more accommodating manner that allowed some

406 Livy, *Ab urbe condita*, 9.1.10; Machiavelli, *The Prince*, p. 88, and *Discourses on Livy*, pp. 143–7 and 248.

407 Livy, *Ab urbe condita*, 5.36.6; Machiavelli, *Discourses on Livy*, pp. 195–6 and 209–10.

408 For the (perhaps strained) reading that Machiavelli was recognising a moral obligation here see Benner 2009, pp. 309–14.

409 *Discourses on Livy*, pp. 299–302.

410 *Art of War*, pp. 140–2; *Discourses on Livy*, pp. 140–2.

411 Raab 1964; Bireley 1990; Kahn 1994a; Anglo 2005; Arienzo and Petrina 2013.

of Machiavelli's insights to be reconciled with conventional thinking.[412] In England use tended instead to be made of the familiar word 'policy'.[413] In books published there a distinction was often drawn between the 'worldly policy' taught by Machiavelli, in which considerations of 'conscience' and 'theologie' were set aside, and the 'true policy' rulers ought to pursue, in which 'prudence' was handled as an aspect of 'honestie'.[414] The Elizabethan regime was denounced by both Catholic and Puritan critics as 'a Machiavellian state', since the queen was reckoned to be lacking in genuine religious conviction.[415] While historians may find the description apt, Elizabeth and her counsellors would never have described their conduct of government in these terms.[416] Indeed, Elizabeth explicitly rejected the criticism in a speech she delivered before her parliament in 1576.[417] 'If pollicie had beene preferred before truth', she asked, would she have reintroduced the Protestant faith 'at the first beginninge' of her reign, contrary to the 'worldlie wisdoome' that innovation should be avoided by new princes.[418] 'I was not so simple', she insisted in a speech delivered ten years later, 'as not to know what danger and perill so great an alteration might procure me', adding that she had instead focused on 'those things that best fitted a kinge', enumerating the virtues Cicero had urged statesmen to cultivate.[419]

412 The expression appeared in Francesco Guicciardini, *Dialogue on the Government of Florence*, pp. 158–9, and was popularised by the widespread circulation of Giovanni Botero, *Reason of State*.

413 Praz 1928; Orsini 1946; Bawcutt 1971. On Elizabethan humanism see Peltonen 1995, pp. 18–53.

414 Matthew Parker, *Defence of Priestes Mariages Stablysshed by the Imperiall Lawes of the Realme of England*, p. 339; George Puttenham, *Arte of English Poesie*, p. 49; *Direction for Travailers Taken out of Iustus Lipsius*, sig. A3v; Robert Parsons, *Newes from Spayne and Holland*, pp. 33–4; Lambert Daneau, *Fruitfull Commentarie upon the Twelve Small Prophets*, p. 1055; William Allen, *Conference about the Next Succession to the Crowne of Ingland*, p. 217; Alexandre de Pontaymeri, *Womans Woorth Defended against All the Men in the World*, p. 69.

415 John Leslie, *Treatise of Treasons against Q. Elizabeth and the Crowne of England*, sig. A5; *Certayne Questions Demanded and Asked by the Noble Realme of Englande*, sig. A3v; Adam Blackwood, *Martyre de la royne d'Escosse, douariere de France*, pp. 36–7; *Second Admonition to the Parliament*, sig. A2; *Correspondence of Matthew Parker*, pp. 391–2; *Leicester's Commonwealth*, pp. 132 and 193.

416 The thesis that Elizabeth really did have Machiavellian tendencies was developed in Phillips 1896, pp. 912–18, has been revived more recently in Allinson 2006 and Janara 2006, and has been reasserted, though scarcely substantiated, in Hilton 2015.

417 *Proceedings in the Parliaments of Elizabeth I*, vol. 1, p. 472; *Elizabeth I: Collected Works*, p. 169.

418 Machiavelli, *The Prince*, pp. 20–1, and *Discourses on Livy*, pp. 37 and 60.

419 *Elizabeth I: Autograph Compositions*, pp. 75–6; *Elizabeth I: Collected Works*, pp. 197–8 and 202–4; *Copie of a Letter to the Right Honourable the Earle of Leycester*, pp. 30–1.

Twelve days earlier, after the condemnation of Mary Stewart for treason, Elizabeth had remarked that rulers 'stand upon stages, so that their actions are viewed and beheld of all men', and had promised her parliament that she would preserve her reputation by striving 'to do that which shall be best for the safety of my people and most for the good of the realm', or (as a printed version of her speech put it) by always doing what seemed 'just and honorable'.[420] When James VI wrote to her shortly afterwards on his mother's behalf, he reminded her 'how small difference Cicero concludis to be betwixt *utile* and *honestum* in his discourse thairof, and quhich of thaim oucht to be framed to the other'.[421] Elizabeth replied that she had been 'defending the brethe that God hath given me', and in later explaining that Mary's execution was a 'miserable accident', she claimed that she was not given to dissembling.[422] In reality, it is generally believed, dissembling was exactly what she was doing.[423] On another occasion she chided James himself for being less than straightforward with her, warning that 'we old foxes can find shiftes to save our selves by others malice, and come by knowlege of greattest secreat'.[424] When her own 'surety and estate' were at risk, the bestial devices to which she was prepared to resort included the torture of suspects.[425] Her counsellors similarly maintained that they thought 'more of honour and conscience than of profit', that they valued 'honestie and truthe more than friende or kinsman', and that they were motivated by 'a conscience to do good'.[426] Yet while Lord Burghley understood that 'Christian philosophie consisteth in difference betwixt *utile* and *honestum*', he

420 *Elizabeth I: Autograph Compositions*, pp. 70–2; *Elizabeth I: Collected Works*, pp. 188 and 193–5; *Copie of a Letter to the Right Honourable the Earle of Leycester*, pp. 16–18; *Proceedings in the Parliaments of Elizabeth I*, vol. 2, pp. 248–61.

421 BL, Cotton MS Caligula C ix, ff. 190–1; an anglicised version follows, which is reproduced in *Elizabeth I: Collected Works*, pp. 291–2.

422 *Letters of Queen Elizabeth and King James VI of Scotland*, pp. 43–5; *Letters of Queen Elizabeth I*, pp. 185–8; *Elizabeth I: Autograph Compositions*, pp. 79–80; *Elizabeth I: Collected Works*, pp. 294–6.

423 Neale 1992, pp. 288–92; MacCaffrey 1993, pp. 348–54; Guy 2017, pp. 83–92.

424 *Letters of Queen Elizabeth and King James VI of Scotland*, p. 17; *Letters of Queen Elizabeth I*, p. 163; *Elizabeth I: Autograph Compositions*, pp. 57–8; *Elizabeth I: Collected Works*, p. 262.

425 *Elizabeth I: Collected Works*, p. 127.

426 *Calendar of the Manuscripts of the Most Honourable the Marquis of Salisbury*, vol. 2, p. 421; Thomas Blundeville, *Very Briefe and Profitable Treatise Declaring Howe Many Counsells and What Maner of Counselers a Prince that Will Governe Well Ought to Have*, sigg. D2v-3r and F2v-4r; 'Nicholas Faunt's Discourse Touching the Office of Principal Secretary of Estate', p. 501. For a different understanding of 'honour', connected with the code of chivalry neglected in the previous chapter, see Sir William Segar, *Honor Military and Civill*, sig. ¶2v, along with Crane 1988, Guy 1995, and Rose 2011. And see in addition McLaren 1999.

found that knowing which to choose was in practice difficult.[427] One of his acolytes believed that a counsellor should follow his 'owne conscience', should 'decline from evil and doe good' and should 'beware of too much worldlie policie and humaine witt', yet this implied that some regard did need to be paid to political reality.[428] Burghley's son and successor as the queen's principal secretary noted that 'honest servants must strain a little when they will serve princes'.[429]

By the closing decades of the sixteenth century a more acceptable doctrine of reason of state was also beginning to take shape in Spain.[430] Pedro de Ribadeneyra, for example, rejected Machiavelli's advice that everything necessary to maintain the prince's state must be done, 'whether it is honourable or dishonourable, just and unjust indifferently, provided it is expedient', and urged the prince instead to follow Cicero's advice in cultivating a prudence that was 'true, not feigned, Christian, not political, sound virtue, not deceptive cunning'.[431] In doing so the prince was to take advice from theologians expert in matters of 'conscience' and 'divine law', but also from counsellors who had studied history and knew how impossible it was for 'true expediency to be contrary to virtue'.[432] Even Sebastián Fox Morcillo, who had written a more conventional *speculum principis* earlier in the century, had recognised a difference between the *prudentia privata* common to princes and other people, which consisted in 'fleeing from vices and pursuing virtues', and the *prudentia publica* cultivated by princes alone, which consisted in 'administering the commonwealth or preserving and extending the same'.[433] Like Ribadeneyra, Fox Morcillo had emphasised the importance for the prince of *prudentia militaris* or *militaris disciplina*.[434] Towards the end of the century Juan de Mariana urged Philip III to maintain a powerful army and navy, although he also warned him about the dangers of burdening the Spanish people with too much taxation.[435] The solution he proposed was to 'produce wars out of

427 *Letters of Lord Burghley*, p. 90. See too Read 1955, p. 30.

428 Robert Beale, 'Treatise of the Office of a Councellor and Principall Secretarie to her Majestie', vol. 1, p. 442.

429 *Calendar of the Carew Manuscripts*, vol. 4, p. 418.

430 Bleznick 1958; Soons 1979; Höpfl 2002; Fernández-Santamaria 2006; Braun 2007.

431 *Princeps Christianus adversus Nicolaum Machiavellum ceterosque huius temporis politicos*, sig. †4r and pp. 276–7.

432 *Princeps Christianus adversus Nicolaum Machiavellum*, pp. 302–4. On the relative downgrading of theological advice in Spanish practice see Marcocci 2014.

433 *De regni regisque institutione libri tres*, sigg. H2–3.

434 Ribadeneyra, *Princeps Christianus adversus Nicolaum Machiavellum*, p. 358; Fox Morcillo, *De regni regisque institutione*, sigg. K2v-4.

435 *De rege et regis institutione*, pp. 303–6, or *The King and the Education of the King*, pp. 290–1.

wars', so that his people might be enriched with 'plunder at sea and on land'. Although Mariana acknowledged that wars ought always to be waged justly, he believed that 'legitimate reasons will not indeed be lacking either for seeking to recover ancient rights or for avenging new wrongs'. Moreover, as Livy and others had realised, it would be unwise 'to allow the soldiery to grow weak in ease'.[436] Mariana particularly recommended the authorisation of maritime raiding by private parties (*praedatoriam exerceant*).[437] 'Why', he asked, 'since this liberty exists for the enemy, and their raiders (*piratae*) infest both seas every year, since they harass us often in war and spoil us of our possessions, should we wish to deprive our people completely of this privilege (*facultatem*)'. Baltasar Álamos de Barrientos offered similar advice.[438] Pointing out that Spanish shipping was preyed upon by enemy raiders (*corsarios*), he advised Philip 'to permit the subjects of your majesty to arm warships at their own expense along the whole coast of Spain to engage in maritime raiding (*anden en corso*) against the English', promising that this would 'enrich your majesty's kingdom and its inhabitants, and as a necessary corollary enrich the sovereign too with resources he could draw from his people in case of need'. The risk of the raiders putting to sea in inadequately equipped vessels, or becoming a menace to all shipping, was limited given that the king could 'give them instructions and subordinate them to naval authority'.

In England as well as Spain there were writers who maintained that wars were beneficial as a means of increasing both martial valour and military resources.[439] 'Warre is the remedy for a state surfetted with peace', wrote Sir William Cornwallis, adding that 'it is a medicine for commonwealths sicke of too much ease and tranquilitie'.[440] In an essay that would be printed in the early seventeenth century Francis Bacon agreed that 'a foreign war is like the heat of exercise and serveth to keep the body in health, for in a slothful peace both courages will effeminate and manners corrupt'.[441] It was therefore important, he explained, 'for a state to have those laws or customs which may reach

436 Livy, *Ab urbe condita*, 30.44.8; Botero, *Reason of State*, pp. 76–7; Justus Lipsius, *Sixe Bookes of Politickes or Civil Doctrine*, p. 83.

437 On the encouragement of private shipbuilding, from which the prince might reinforce his naval strength, see Casado Soto 1991, pp. 99–100; and see too Goodman 1997, p. 19.

438 *L'art de gouverner: Discours adressé à Philippe III*, pp. 109–11 and 194–211.

439 Jorgensen 1952; Waggoner 1954; Gajda 2009. On the encouragement of shipbuilding see the *Proceedings of the Parliaments of Elizabeth I*, vol. 1, pp. 103–7, discussed in Jones 2015, pp. 184–5.

440 *Discourses upon Seneca the Tragedian*, sig. H1r.

441 *Works of Francis Bacon*, vol. 6, pp. 449–51; *cf. Letters and Life of Francis Bacon*, vol. 1, pp. 174–5.

forth unto them just occasions (as may be pretended) of war', and to find just causes for conflicts, 'at the least specious', with their neighbours.[442] 'Whereas those that be strongest on land are many times nevertheless in great straits', he went on, 'he that commands the sea is at great liberty, and may take as much and as little of the war as he will'. To a queen reluctant to face the hazard of warfare on land, and eager to minimise expenditure on any engagement with the enemy, the licensing of maritime raiding by her subjects had obvious attractions.[443] The financial benefits that might accrue to the crown became especially evident following the capture in 1592 of the *Madre de Dios*, the richest prize taken in the war.[444] While the vessel was still at sea much of its cargo was removed, taken ashore and sold, 'which was not lawfull to be done by the lawes of the realme and the lawes of the sea until the whole lading were brought into the port'.[445] For 'breaking bulk', it was pointed out, 'the owner and companie deserved not only punishment but even the losse of that which were taken'.[446] The confiscation of the prize has often been misunderstood. It is not correct that 'no rules were observed' in the case, nor is it correct that the queen was entitled to the prize 'since the country was at war'.[447] It is closer to the truth to say that the 'royal prerogative' was taken to prevail over the 'common law', except that the common law referred to was actually the 'civill law', and it was 'the opynyon of the doctours' themselves that the prize must be 'adjudged to the quene'.[448] Elizabeth was advised by her counsellors that while 'in honour and profytt every thing is devolved to hir highnes disposytyon', those involved in the seizure 'wold never be induced to farther adventure if they ware not princely considered of'. All the same, the obvious implication was that if every prize taken in wartime were treated as forfeit to the crown, to be distributed according to 'honour and profytt', the queen would be in a better position to protect her own interests than she was under the traditional 'lawes of the sea'. Sir Walter Ralegh, one of those involved in the seizure, advised further that maritime raiding would be more beneficial if mariners were paid wages instead of being promised shares of prizes, 'for mercenary men are not so affectionate or religious but that they can, with safe conscience, lick their

---

442 See too Matthew Sutcliffe, *Practice, Proceedings and Lawes of Armes*, sig. A2v.

443 Wernham 1961, pp. 347–68; Croft 1991, pp. 241–3; Rodger 2004, pp. 153–7; Black 2004, pp. 36–40; Younger 2012, pp. 1–3.

444 For a contemporary account of the seizure see *The Sea-Mans Triumph*. Many of the relevant documents are gathered together in Drake 1849.

445 *Tudor Royal Proclamations*, vol. 3, pp. 109–10.

446 *Documents Relating to Law and Custom of the Sea*, vol. 1, pp. 280–1.

447 Andrews 1964, p. 73; Kelsey 1998, p. 373; Guy 2017, p. 217; Gorrochategui Santos 2018, p. 255.

448 Spence 1995, p. 108; NAK, SP12/244, f. 50; BL, Lansdowne MS 70, f. 210.

own fingers'.[449] Although mariners who worked for wages might just as easily have been described as 'mercenary men', Ralegh was using the expression in the Machiavellian sense of those who 'fight with their hands, but not with their hearts'.[450]

While Elizabeth wanted her people to be reassured that their safety was her highest priority, it is notable that in her proclamation on trading with the enemy she also claimed to know in her 'princely wisdome' that the highest priority of every prince must be the 'preservation of the kingdomes' committed to 'his' charge.[451] In describing this axiom as a 'lawe of pollicy' and 'lawe of governement' she was using language often employed to signify the 'humane wisdome and pollycy set downe by Machavel', in opposition to the 'lawe of nature' and 'lawes of God'.[452] Yet what exactly the word 'law' meant here is far from obvious. Although Machiavelli was sometimes thought to have identified what we might now call scientific laws of politics, his precepts were more accurately perceived as guidelines that princes would follow flexibly in the light of historical examples and current events.[453] Among his supposed adherents were humanist jurists who sought to construct a new universal jurisprudence by moving beyond the study of Roman law to the historical and comparative analysis of the laws all nations had found it expedient to introduce.[454] These jurists certainly claimed to be concerned with norms of the type traditionally taught in the law schools, and to be engaged in an enterprise similar to Cicero's in the *De legibus*, but was Elizabeth using the word 'law' in the same way? A few years before her proclamation was issued, when an ambassador from Poland complained about ships and goods from the Baltic being seized en route to

449 *Letters of Sir Walter Ralegh*, pp. 57, 79, 80–1 and 84.

450 *Works of Sir Walter Ralegh*, vol. 8, p. 304; Machiavelli, *The Prince*, pp. 42–51, *Discourses on Livy*, pp. 91 and 175–7, and *Art of War*, pp. 14–19; Francesco Sansovino, *Quintesence of Wit*, f. 78v; Dudley Digges, *Foure Paradoxes or Politique Discourses*, pp. 55–6; Thomas Styward, *Pathwaie to Martiall Discipline*, pp. 140–1 and 144.

451 *Documents Relating to Law and Custom of the Sea*, vol. 1, pp. 313–17; *Tudor Royal Proclamations*, vol. 3, pp. 255–8. On the use of both sermons and proclamations for purposes of propaganda see Jenkins 1942. On Elizabeth's tendency to talk about princes as essentially masculine figures (*viri*) see Heisch 1975, pp. 34–5, Marcus 1986, pp. 137–43, and Rose 2000, pp. 1079–80.

452 Robert Parsons, *Newes from Spayne and Holland*, p. 22; Jean de Serres, *Historical Collection of the Most Memorable Accidents and Tragicall Massacres of France*, p. 19; Petrus Canisius, *Summe of Christian Doctrine*, pp. 584–5; *Sermons of M. John Calvin upon the Fifth Booke of Moses Called Deuteronomie*, p. 710; George Peele, *Love of King David and Fair Bethsabe*, sig. G1r; Edmund Spenser, *Faerie Queene*, 7.6.6.

453 Lyons 1989; Hampton 1990; Kahn 1994b; Davies 2001; Almási 2018.

454 Brown 1939; Franklin 1963; Kelley 1964 and 1973; Gerbier 2009; Couzinet 2013.

Spain, the queen told him that she was permitted to interrupt the supply of provisions to her enemy by *ius naturae et gentium*.[455] Her counsellors, with advice from the doctors of law, developed three lines of argument in response to the complaint.[456] In the first place, they pointed out that the laws of nature and nations allowed people to defend themselves by repelling force with force, as was clear from one of Cicero's speeches as well as many civil and canon law texts.[457] In the second place, they pointed out that the widespread practice of preventing the provisioning of enemies was supported by many other civil and canon law texts.[458] In the third place, they pointed out that Polish kings had themselves authorised the seizure of vessels trading with their enemies, citing the maxim *quod tibi fieri non vis, alteri ne feceris*, which the canonists especially regarded as a summation of natural law.[459] None of these arguments was rehearsed in Elizabeth's own reply to the Polish ambassador, who was instead told that he would have had a better grasp of *ius naturae et gentium* if he had read 'the books of princes'. As in issuing her proclamation, the queen may have appreciated that the king of Spain was not actually her enemy in the sense in which that word was used in the legal texts. She may already have come to believe that an alternative justification could be found in 'the lawe of pollicy'. But what exactly was this law?

It has been suggested recently that a new understanding of the legitimacy of warfare was developed in a treatise on the law of arms published at the end of the sixteenth century by Albericus Gentilis, a Protestant refugee from Italy.[460]

455 *Elizabeth I: Autograph Compositions*, p. 168; *Elizabeth I: Collected Works*, p. 333; *Calendar of the Manuscripts of the Most Honourable the Marquis of Salisbury*, vol. 7, pp. 315–16. For context see Wernham 1994, pp. 199–201.

456 *Acts of the Privy Council of England*, vol. 27, pp. 307–8; *Elizabeth I: Collected Works*, pp. 334–5; *Calendar of the Manuscripts of the Most Honourable the Marquis of Salisbury*, vol. 7, pp. 320–1 and 338–9; NAK, SP82/4, f. 47, and SP88/2, ff. 15r, 40–5 and 52r. See too *Letters of Lord Burghley*, pp. 272–3; *Miscellaneous State Papers from 1501 to 1726*, vol. 1, pp. 367–8 and 370–1; NAK, SP88/2, ff. 56 and 61.

457 Cicero, *Pro Milone*, 4.10; *Digest*, 1.1.3, 4.2.12.1, 9.2.4.pr., 9.2.45.4, 43.16.1.27 and 43.16.3.9; *Code*, 8.4.1; *Decretum*, D. 1 c. 7; *Liber extra*, 2.13.12, 5.12.18 and 5.39.3. Pennington 2013 suggests that it was the canonists who first treated self-defence as a natural right, but see in particular *Digest*, 43.16.1.27.

458 *Digest*, 39.4.11.pr. and 2 and 48.4.4.pr; *Code*, 4.40.4 and 4.41.1–2; *Liber extra*, 5.6.6, 5.6.11, 5.6.12 and 5.6.17; *Extravagantes communes*, 5.2.1.

459 *Scriptores historiae augustae*, 51.7–8; *Decretales Gregorii noni*, pp. 5–6 (gl. 'Iuxta ordinatissimum' ad X 1.1.1); *Digestum vetus*, col. 60 (gl. 'Laedere' ad D.1.1.10.1); *Institutiones iuris civilis Iustiniani*, p. 11 (gl. 'Alterum non laedere' ad J.1.1.3). On the Polish practice referred to see Esper 1967.

460 Coquillette 1988, pp. 63–71; Koskenniemi 2007, pp. 12–14; Covell 2009, pp. 45–50; Capps 2011, pp. 64–70; Vollerthun 2017, pp. 106–44.

The doctorate Gentilis had received at Perugia was formally recognised at Oxford, where he began to teach the civil law in 1581, before being appointed to the regius chair of the subject in 1587.[461] In a book he published in 1582 Gentilis defended the methodology of the Italian commentators in which he had been instructed, criticising not only the legal humanists who advocated the historical recovery of ancient Roman law in place of the further refinement of the medieval *ius commune*, but also the comparative historians who advocated the discovery of genuinely common institutions through the study of 'all history, not Roman alone'.[462] Although dedicated to the earl of Leicester, the chancellor of the university, the book was not well received by the classical scholars who surrounded him.[463] It was perhaps for this reason that in a later book, dedicated in 1585 to Sir Philip Sidney, a prominent member of Leicester's circle, Gentilis praised the 'precious' discourses on Livy by Machiavelli, 'this shrewdest of men'.[464] As is evident from his treatise on the law of arms, which first appeared in 1589 and was reissued in an enlarged edition in 1598, Gentilis was also reading closely the most influential work produced by the comparative historians, Jean Bodin's *Six livres de la république*.[465] By the end of the century he was certainly prepared to make use of a wide range of historical, literary and philosophical sources in writing about law, but this was becoming common among jurists who remained fundamentally committed to the approach of the Italian commentators, and it need not mean that Gentilis' outlook had been completely transformed.[466] The suggestion recently made about him, however, is that he developed a new 'humanist' understanding of the law of war, justifying the pursuit of the national interests of both parties to a conflict, in opposition to the 'scholastic' understanding of the theologians,

---

461 Van der Molen 1968; Scattola 2012; Vadi 2014; Minnucci 2016; Wagner 2017.

462 *De iuris interpretibus dialogi sex*, p. 157.

463 Worden 1996, pp. 256–7; MacLean 2009, pp. 295–6; Craigwood 2011, pp. 86–7; Pirillo 2013, pp. 129–33; Warren 2015, pp. 34–6.

464 *De legationibus libri tres*, vol. 1, pp. 171–3, and vol. 2, pp. 156–7. See too the important findings reported in Feingold 2017.

465 Wijffels 2010; Quaglioni 2013; Vergerio 2017. For the methodology underpinning Bodin's *magnum opus* see his *Methodus ad facilem historiarum cognitionem*, sigg. *2–2*2v, or *Method for the Easy Comprehension of History*, pp. 1–8. See too Franciscus Balduinus, *De institutione historiae universae et eius cum iurisprudentia coniunctione*, sig. A3r and pp. 103, 106 and 170, and more generally Kelley 1970, pp. 116–48, Huppert 1970, pp. 88–103, and Grafton 2007, pp. 62–122.

466 On Gentilis' literary interests see Binns 1972 and Warren 2010. For the view that he was a typical legal scholar of his time see Lesaffer 2010, pp. 218–20, and Wijffels 2011, pp. 42–6.

for whom only one party could wage a war justly.[467] If this were true, his treatise would have contained a detailed account of Elizabeth's 'lawe of pollicy'.

It may easily be believed that Gentilis was moving in this direction if it is supposed that he had to make a choice between the moral theology of war, outlined in the previous section of this chapter, and the Machiavellian policy of war, outlined in the present section.[468] He did mention the theologians in his treatise, for instance in remarking that the examination of motives for fighting was their province (*quod est theologorum*), and that they ought to leave the examination of the causes of wars to the lawyers (*silete theologi in munere alieno*).[469] Furthermore, in dealing with the causes of wars he distinguished between those that were necessary (*necessariae*), expedient (*utiles*) and honourable (*honestae*).[470] The first category was grounded firmly on the legal texts permitting the use of violence to ward off violence, though reference was also made to Livy's dictum that *iustum est bellum quibus necessarium*, together with Bodin's treatment of it.[471] The causes of wars were expedient when nations resorted to arms through fear of future violence or to exact vengeance for past injuries, and were honourable when the aim was to assist allies or to uphold the international order.[472] In writing about these causes Gentilis referred to Cicero, along with other ancient authors, but his tripartite categorisation of the causes of wars was not borrowed from there, nor was it in the *De officiis* alone that he would have encountered the terms *utile* and *honestum*. As well as recognising the compelling force (*necessitas*) of self-defence, the legal texts Gentilis taught at Oxford declared that to live honourably (*honeste vivere*) was a basic requirement of the law, that not everything lawful was honourable (*non omne quod licet honestum est*), and that the introduction of human laws was driven by considerations of expediency (*utilitas*) or necessity (*necessitas*).[473] Although he was only able to find specific support in the civil law for the necessity of self-defence, his argument was that the expedient and honourable causes of wars were also necessary, since ultimately wars waged for these causes served

467 Tuck 1999, pp. 16–50, taken up in Panizza 2008 and 2013, Schröder 2010 and Piirimäe 2010.

468 Straumann 2010 rightly draws attention to the prominence of Roman law in Gentilis' thinking, but neglects the civilian tradition through which it was mediated, as is noted in Lesaffer 2011, pp. 421–2, and 2016, p. 54.

469 *De iure belli libri tres*, vol. 1, pp. 56 and 92, and vol. 2, pp. 35 and 57.

470 *De iure belli*, vol. 1, pp. 92 and 127–8, and vol. 2, pp. 58 and 79.

471 *De iure belli*, vol. 1, pp. 92–6 and 127–8, and vol. 2, pp. 58–60 and 79; Bodin, *Six livres de la république*, pp. 529 and 540, and *Six Bookes of a Commonweale*, pp. 601 and 609.

472 *De iure belli*, vol. 1, pp. 96–7, 107–8, 134 and 197–8, and vol. 2, pp. 61–2, 67, 83 and 122.

473 *Digest*, 1.1.1.2, 1.1.7.1, 1.1.11, 1.10.1 and 50.17.144.pr; *Institutes*, 1.1.3 and 1.2.2.

to defend the belligerent nations.[474] Where Gentilis undoubtedly did rely on Cicero was in a chapter of his treatise about what ought to be done 'si utile cum honesto pugnet'.[475] While acknowledging here that the maxim *necessitas non habet legem* sometimes excused deviations from justice, he was so insistent on the *honestum* prevailing over the *utile* that he warned against use of the maxim *salus populi suprema lex esto*.[476] He could scarcely have done more to signal his repudiation of the Machiavellian policy of war.

It is of course significant that Gentilis devoted another chapter of his treatise to addressing the question 'whether a war can be waged justly on both sides'.[477] It was not entirely novel for a civil lawyer to write about the just causes of war, but it was certainly unusual.[478] Although he pointed out at another place in his treatise that the word 'just' was often applied to anything that was 'lawful', Gentilis was clearly troubled by the prominence of theologians in debates over the legitimacy of wars, and he therefore considered it important to discuss the causes of wars in his capacity as a jurist (*pro officio iurisconsulti nostro*).[479] He agreed with Vitoria that while in principle there could be a just cause on only one side of any conflict, in reality there could be an excusable error on the other side, adding that this was especially likely 'si utile cum honesto pugnet'. In view of his handling of this topic in the chapter he devoted to it, the addition cannot reasonably be interpreted as an assertion that wars were just when waged in the national interest. In fact, he spelled out the proposition he meant to uphold with precision. 'This opinion of our law seems most certain to me', he stated, 'that the rights of war are attributed to both sides, that things taken on both sides belong to the takers, and that people taken on both sides are regarded as slaves'. Much of his treatise consisted of a conventional account of the law of plunder.[480] In explaining that wars had first to be declared by sovereign princes he referred to the works of Cicero, but as support for the core texts of the civil and canon laws, and he explicitly rejected the suggestion that nations should launch surprise attacks on their enemies whenever

474 *De iure belli*, vol. 1, p. 92, and vol. 2, p. 58.

475 *De iure belli*, vol. 1, pp. 570–6, and vol. 2, pp. 349–52.

476 *Decretum*, C. 1 q. 1 c. 39 and C. 23 q. 2 c. 1; *Liber extra*, 1.4.4 and 5.41.4; *Digestum vetus*, col. 124 (gl. 'Expedire' ad D.1.10.1); Roumy 2006.

477 *De iure belli*, vol. 1, pp. 45–52, and vol. 2, pp. 31–3.

478 Reichberg, Syse and Begby 2006, pp. 227–9; Szabó 2011, pp. 43–4; Greenwood 2011, pp. 50 and 84–5, and 2014, pp. 42–3 and 59–62.

479 *De iure belli*, vol. 1, pp. 17–22, and vol. 2, pp. 12–14.

480 *De iure belli*, vol. 1, pp. 327–393, 435–41, 498, 503–4, 510–11 and 534–54, and vol. 2, pp. 202–40, 265–8, 305, 310, 315 and 328–39.

this seemed expedient.[481] He did argue that waging a war against the king of Spain before he became too powerful was justifiable, but he made it clear that wars waged for this kind of *causa utilis* needed to be declared.[482] He also observed that in assuming arms in support of the rebels in the Netherlands the queen of England was actually waging war for a *causa honesta*, and he argued that there was no need to issue a new declaration of war when a prince was providing assistance in a war that had already been declared.[483] The problem remained, however, that the war in the Netherlands had not actually been declared between sovereign princes. Like the civilian doctors who practised in the admiralty court, the regius professor in Oxford discussed the legitimacy of the war, and of plunder taken in the war, in conventional terms, without providing a satisfactory explanation of how the war with Spain could be seen as a *bellum publicum*. He did not develop a new theory of prize acquisition as part of a new theory of warfare.

In consequence, it cannot be correct, as has also been suggested recently, that Gentilis' development of a Machiavellian law of arms influenced William Shakespeare in writing *The Life of Henry the Fifth*, which received its first performance in the year following the reprinting of his treatise.[484] The legitimacy of warfare was openly discussed in Shakespeare's play in terms of two of the modes of discourse considered in this and the previous chapter. First, in seeking advice from his bishops on whether he could invade France 'with right and conscience', in asserting his claim against the French king 'by the law of nature and of nations', and in assuring his soldiers that they could fight for him with clear consciences, 'his cause being just', Henry was using the language of moral theology.[485] He was claiming that his war could be justified *in foro interno*. Secondly, in threatening to sack Harfleur, in punishing a soldier for

481 *De iure belli*, vol. 1, pp. 209–18, and vol. 2, pp. 131–5, referring to Cassius Dio, *Roman History*, 52.15.1–3. The idea that plunder was licit on both sides of a *bellum publicum*, it should be remembered, was not devised by jurists like Gentilis as a means of avoiding the implications of just war theory but had always been central to the reading of the Roman law texts by the civil law doctors. *Cf.* Lesaffer 2021, pp. 435–9.

482 *De iure belli*, vol. 1, pp. 435–41, and vol. 2, pp. 265–8.

483 *De iure belli*, vol. 1, pp. 218–28, and vol. 2, pp. 136–41.

484 Camerlingo 2013 and Ragni 2016, and see too Pugliatti 2010. For the proposal that Shakespeare may have been influenced instead by Gentilis' *De armis Romanis* see Warren 2017, and for various readings of that work see Tuori 2009; Panizza 2010; Lupher 2010; Kingsbury and Straumann 2011; Wijffels 2016.

485 *Henry V*, 1.2.96, 2.4.80 and 4.1.129. Mattox 2000 reads these passages against the background of an artificial construct of 'just war theory', while Shapiro 2005, pp. 93–6, makes a more effective comparison with an address printed in Lancelot Andrews, *XCVI Sermons*, pp. 183–92.

plundering a church, and in permitting other soldiers to hold prisoners to ransom, Henry was relying on the 'law of armes', in which his captains professed to have expertise.[486] Neither the sacking of besieged towns that refused to yield, nor the execution of prisoners who posed a threat to their captors, amounted to 'war crimes' under the law of arms, as has sometimes been imagined.[487] Yet the view that acts of brutality could be excused on grounds of necessity would have been difficult to distinguish from the view that necessity should be the guiding principle of all political and military action, and it would not have been difficult to pick up hints in the play both that the reasoning of the bishops was specious and that the expertise of the captains was ridiculous.[488] Behind a suitably misleading pretence of concern with the morality and legality of warfare, the play was perhaps inviting admiration for Henry as a Machiavellian prince who did what was necessary to promote the interests of his realm.[489] As has been seen, the language of policy was certainly being used in England in the later sixteenth century.[490] At this stage, however, the law of arms had not been reworked by Gentilis or anyone else on the basis of 'the lawe of pollicy'.

6 Condemnation of Pirates as Common Enemies

Two other claims have been made for Gentilis in recent years, and it is these two claims that are examined in this final section of the present chapter. The first is that he helped to promote a new understanding of the concept of *ius gentium*, drawing upon the teaching of the schools of law and theology, yet moving in a new direction.[491] The relevant sources studied in the law schools were as usual quite confusing. Although one jurist had defined *ius naturale* as 'what nature has taught to all animals', *ius gentium* as 'what human nations put

486 *Henry V*, 3.3.1–43, 3.6.41–50 and 4.4.1–67. It is of some interest that Henry is portrayed as a king who sought to regulate the taking of plunder, given that he was in fact responsible for a major development in the regulation of maritime raiding, as was noted in the first section of this chapter.

487 Meron 1993; Spencer 1996; De Somogyi 1998; Lesaffer 2007; Condren 2009. For a textual problem with the execution of the French prisoners see Sutherland and Watts 2000, pp. 108–16.

488 Sutherland and Watts 2000, pp. 117–25; Grady 2002, pp. 204–42; Mebane 2007, pp. 256–8; Pittock 2009, pp. 178–83; Quabeck 2013, pp. 152–71; Delahunty 2014, pp. 137–60.

489 Rabkin 1977; Marx 1995; Sullivan 1996; Roe 2007; Popescu 2008.

490 For the suggestion that Shakespeare was promoting the claims of the earl of Essex see Grady 2002, pp. 204–42.

491 Panizza 2009; Wagner 2011; Iurlaro 2017; Vadi 2020.

to use', and *ius civile* as 'what neither departs from the law of nature and nations nor adheres to it altogether', another had defined *ius gentium* as 'what natural reason has constituted among all people'.[492] The compilers of Justinian's *Institutes* had not only conflated these definitions, but had also added that *ius naturale* was 'constituted by a certain divine providence', and to add to the confusion these and other texts stressed that *ius gentium*, like *ius civile*, sometimes deviated from *ius naturale* through 'urgent usage and human necessities', for instance when it introduced war in place of peace, slavery in place of personal liberty, and private property in place of common ownership.[493] The canon law sources were not much clearer. *Ius naturale* was said to be grasped 'by natural instinct', and to be 'common to all nations'.[494] *Ius civile* was defined as the particular law each nation 'constituted for itself', in contrast to *ius gentium*, which comprised various institutions 'put to use by almost all nations', such as war, slavery and private property.[495] This trichotomy of laws was derived, via the *Etymologiae* of Isidore of Seville, from Roman law, but its significance in the canon law was complicated by comparison with other sources, which described natural law as what was 'contained in the law and the gospel', and as 'arising from the creation of rational beings'.[496] Some canonists drew a distinction between the natural law grasped by an instinctive *sensualitas*, shared by people with other animals, and the natural law appreciated through exercise of a *ratio animi*, shared by people with the angels.[497] Some civilians found it equally helpful to distinguish the *ius naturale primaevum* grasped by *sensualitas* from the law appreciated by the exercise of *rationabilitas*, but they tended to focus their attention on the law that had been given practical effect in the courts, whether it was particular to the Romans or shared by them with other nations.[498] Bartolus explained that the only part of natural law with practical significance derived from natural reason (*ex ratione naturali*) but was practically significant because it was given effect by human lawmakers (*ex constitutione*).[499] A further distinction emerged between *ius gentium primarium*, in

492 *Digest*, 1.1.1.2–4, 1.1.6 and 1.1.9.

493 *Institutes*, 1.1.4–1.2.2 and 1.2.11; *Digest*, 1.1.4–5 and 1.1.11. *Cf.* Brouwer 2021, p. 129.

494 *Decretum*, D. 1 cc. 6–9.

495 The words *natio* and *gens* are being read in the same way here, perhaps a little inaccurately.

496 *Etymologiae*, 8.4–6; *Decretum*, D. 1 pr., D. 5 dict. ante c. 1, D. 6 c. 3, D. 8 dict. ante c. 1, and D. 9 c. 11.

497 Rufinus de Assisi, *Summa Decretorum*, p. 6 (ad D. 1 pr.); Stephanus Tornacensis, *Summa*, p. 7 (ad D. 1 pr.); *Decretum aureum Gratiani*, ff. 2v-3r (gl. 'Ius naturale' ad D. 1 c. 6).

498 Odofredus de Denariis, *Lectura super digesto*, vol. 1, f. 6v (ad D.1.1.5); Cinus de Pistorio, *In Codicem et aliquot titulos Digesti veteris doctissima commentaria*, vol. 2, f. 3v (ad D.1.1.1) and ff. 4v-5r (ad D.1.1.5); Albericus de Rosate, *Opera omnia*, vol. 1(1), f. 13v (ad D.1.1.5).

499 *Opera omnia*, vol. 1(1), f. 8r (ad D.1.1.5), and vol. 1(2), f. 61r (ad D.12.6.64).

which the prescriptions of natural reason were adhered to, and *ius gentium secundarium*, in which they were departed from for the sake of utility.[500] All human law was supposed to give effect to the natural law established by divine providence, but it was not human law until it was constituted among the nations of the earth, and these nations did not always follow its prescriptions precisely.[501]

In his *Summa theologiae*, in a passage devoted to distinguishing various categories of law, Aquinas had provided a strikingly different interpretation of the Roman trichotomy, which he had approached with the presuppositions of an Aristotelian philosopher.[502] He had applied the label *ius naturale* to the first principles of moral reasoning, explaining that these principles were not truly grasped by people instinctively but were rather self-evident to them as rational beings. He had applied the label *ius gentium* to conclusions that necessarily followed from the first principles, of the type produced by speculative reasoning, and *ius civile* to conclusions that probably followed from the first principles, of the type produced by practical reasoning. Viewed in this way, *ius gentium* differed from *ius naturale* only in needing to be deduced from it before it could be known, yet in a later passage Aquinas had written about *ius gentium* as if it too was sometimes derived from *ius naturale* by practical reasoning.[503] The later Thomists struggled to make sense of this inconsistency but tended to accept that *ius gentium* lay somewhere between *ius naturale* and *ius civile*.[504] In a commentary he wrote on the section of the *Summa theologiae* in which Aquinas' later passage appeared, Vitoria distinguished between rules of law that were deduced from first principles, which he regarded as part of *ius naturale*, and rules of law that were introduced by human lawmakers in order to achieve ends prescribed by *ius naturale*, at least some of which

500 Paulus de Castro, *Opera omnia*, vol. 1(1), f. 3 (ad D.1.1.1) and f. 4 (ad D.1.1.4), and vol. 1(2), f. 60 (ad D.12.6.64); Iason de Maino, *In Digestum et Codicem commentaria*, vol. 2, f. 163r (ad D.12.6.64); Fernandus Vasquius, *Controversiarum illustrium libri tres*, f. 235r; Hubertus Giphanius, *De divisionibus iuris novis interpretum quorundam, maxime glossographorum, in theses aliquot coniectis*, §§. 6–7; Ioannes Schneidewinus, *In quatuor Institutionum imperialium D. Iustiniani libros commentarii*, p. 32.

501 Brett 1997, pp. 181–6; Longfield Karr 2016, pp. 120–2, and 2018, pp. 82–3; Canning 2017, pp. 107–8, and 2018, pp. 63–4. For the survival of the distinction between primary and secondary *ius gentium* in the seventeenth century see Watson 1991, pp. 218–20, and on the relevance of *ius naturale* in practice see Helmholz 2015.

502 *Summa theologiae*, 1a2ae 90–5. See too his *Commentary on Aristotle's Nicomachean Ethics*, pp. 325–6.

503 *Summa theologiae*, 2a2ae 57.3.

504 De Aguilar 1946; De Courcelles 2005; Todescan 2014; Oliveira e Silva 2016; Bunge 2017.

he regarded as *ius gentium*.[505] Although he defined *ius gentium* elsewhere as 'what either is *ius naturale* or is derived from *ius naturale*', it was his treatment of *ius gentium* as a species of the *ius positivum* introduced by human lawmakers, as opposed to the *ius naturale* instilled in people by their creator, that was adopted by most of his successors.[506] Viewed in this way, *ius gentium* differed from *ius civile* in its generality alone, yet for the theologians, given their preoccupation with moral reasoning, this difference mattered.[507] While people were always bound in conscience to comply with positive law indirectly, because they were obliged to obey their superiors, positive law could also be binding in conscience directly to the extent that it was consistent with natural law. Since the consensus of nations provided evidence of this consistency, *ius gentium* had greater moral force than *ius civile*. For example, while the positive laws of war permitting plunder to be taken from enemies could not be regarded as logical inferences drawn from the first principles of natural law, their widespread use showed that they were generally recognised as a necessary means of securing the justice required by natural law, which meant that they were probably themselves required by natural law, and thus that they were intrinsically forceful in conscience.

Despite viewing the subject from different perspectives, the lawyers and theologians had reached the broadly consistent conclusion that while the ethical precepts of *ius naturale et gentium* were valid everywhere, they only formed part of the law of nations in a properly legal sense when they were commonly adopted by most nations. As traditionally understood, the positive law of nations was common (a *ius commune* in practice) in this descriptive sense alone, although it had no doubt become common partly because there was a more prescriptive expectation that nations would adhere to shared standards in dealing with each other. As was noted in the last chapter, for several centuries the expectation had been that rulers would base their dealings with each other on the law taught in the universities (a *ius commune* in theory). In the sixteenth century, however, tentative steps were being made towards

505 *Comentarios a la Secuna secundae de Santo Tomás*, vol. 1, pp. 12–16. For alternative readings of Vitoria see Noreña 1975, pp. 138–44; Fernández-Santamaria 1977, pp. 97–100; Boucher 2009, pp. 79–80; Brett 2011, pp. 12–14; Wagner 2018, pp. 91–3.

506 Vitoria, *De Indis et de iure belli relectiones*, pp. 151 and 257; Bañez, *Decisiones de iure et iustitia*, pp. 9–14; Aragón, *In Secundam secundae Divi Thomae doctoris angelici commentaria*, vol. 2, pp. 7–11; Valentia, *Commentariorum theologicorum libri quatuor*, vol. 2, cols 890–1 and 922–4, and vol. 3, col. 1054; Soto, *De iustitia et iure*, vol. 1, pp. 196–8; Molina, *De iustitia et iure*, vol. 1, cols 14–16.

507 Hamilton 1963, pp. 98–109; Kottman 1972, pp. 42–8; Costello 1974, pp. 217–18; Alonso-Lasheras 2011, pp. 213–15; Hill 2018, pp. 144–5.

a new conception of *ius gentium* as comprising norms that were not just descriptively common among nations but were prescriptively binding upon nations. In some of his lectures Vitoria suggested that the *consensus maiores partis totius orbis* not only provided evidence of the moral force of *ius gentium* but also gave its components legal force, on the understanding that the whole world constituted some sort of commonwealth with legislative power (*habet enim totus orbis, qui aliquo modo est una republica, potestatem ferendi leges*).[508] What exactly was envisaged here was made clear neither by Vitoria himself nor by any other theologian writing in the sixteenth century, when the obvious problem would have been to explain how anyone could possibly have had the authority to legislate for an increasingly divided continent.[509] The claim made for Gentilis, who also took up the Stoic idea of a global community governed by *ius naturale et gentium*, is that he solved the problem by taking the law of nations to comprise customary as opposed to statutory norms. It has also been seen that in many nations customary norms formed a significant part of the law regulating the seizure of ships and goods at sea, but there is a difference between nations recognising that their laws could derive to some extent from the practices and presuppositions of the people they affected, and rulers recognising that they were bound in their dealings with each other by a law that derived from their own practices and presuppositions. For the latter view to emerge, it would have been necessary for rulers themselves, or perhaps the nations they ruled, to be transformed into the key participants in the generation of customary norms.

There is some evidence that the role of rulers in international relations was starting to be seen in a new way. Not only was the practice of nations believed to provide some support for the new handling of maritime raiding, but church ministers were also advising people to leave questions about the legitimacy of warfare to their ruler's determination. If this advice may have owed something to the marginalisation of the *intentio recta* requirement in theological thought, it may have owed something to the rise of Tacitism in political thought as

508 *De Indis et de iure belli relectiones*, pp. 154 and 259–60. See too his *Relectiones theologicae per varias sectiones in duos libros divisa*, p. 120, and *Political Writings*, p. 40.

509 Much has been made of Vitoria's alteration of a quotation from a Roman text in his *De Indis et de iure belli relectiones*, pp. 151 and 257. In the statement that *ius gentium* was what 'naturalis ratio inter omnes homines constituit', Vitoria replaced the word 'homines' with 'gentes', which has been taken to mark a transformative move from people to nations as the entities governed by *ius gentium*. However, since the word 'gentes' was also used in both *Institutes*, 1.2.1, and *Digest*, 1.1.9, and had frequently been used as an alternative to 'homines' by the civilian commentators, there is an obvious danger of reading too much into a simple choice of terminology.

well.[510] Machiavelli had praised the 'golden sentence' of Tacitus that ordinary people 'ought to submit to what is present, and should wish for good princes, but whatsoever they are, endure them'.[511] From their reading of Tacitus, humanist scholars concluded that ordinary people ought to cultivate the virtue of constancy and leave their rulers to cultivate prudence, by mastering the *arcana imperii* essential to securing the national interest.[512] As has again been seen already, rulers had reason to believe that it would be in the national interest to adopt the emerging practice of authorising reprisals in wartime, while moral theologians had the means to develop a defence of what they were doing. To a civil lawyer it might well have seemed that the ethical precepts of *ius naturale et gentium* were being put into practice by rulers on grounds of expediency, and that new positive law, albeit contrary to the basic principles of the civil law, was starting to emerge among nations.[513] But did Gentilis make the crucial move to supposing that a new form of legal custom was taking shape between nations? Did he believe that once a practice was established between rulers, who considered it binding, it consequently was binding? If so, he did not set his belief down in writing. Indeed, he did not actually say that *ius gentium* was customary law but that it was 'unwritten law', in the same way that custom was (*item ut consuetudo*).[514] It could be that all he was trying to convey here was a sense that *ius gentium* was not just descriptively common but also prescriptively common insofar as rulers carried around in their heads a commitment to observing common standards. He may even have taken their commitment to encompass the particular standards they usually observed. As his handling of licit plunder in wartime shows, however, he continued to find most of these standards in the traditional teaching of the law schools. If Gentilis, like Vitoria,

510 Nash 1979; Salmon 1980; Oestreich 1982; Tuck 1993; Kraye 2001; Remer 2016.

511 Tacitus, *Histories*, 4.8; Machiavelli, *Discourses on Livy*, p. 218; *Works of Sir Walter Ralegh*, vol. 8, p. 279. For Simon Harward's acquaintance with the works of Machiavelli see Bawcutt 1969, pp. 62–4, and 2004, pp. 870–1, and Anglo 2005, pp. 370–1.

512 Benjamin 1957; Burke 1969 and 1991; Womersley 1991; Morford 1993; Parmelee 1994 (and also 1996, pp. 119–42); McCrea 1997; Papy 2001; Kewes 2011; De Landtscheer 2013; Lagrée 2016.

513 Although Gentilis made use elsewhere of the distinction drawn by the civil lawyers between a primary and a secondary law of nations, he said surprisingly little in his treatise about the possibility of *ius gentium* departing from *ius naturale* for utility's sake, possibly because he wished to avoid giving any impression of favouring the subordination of the *honestum* to the *utile* (*Lectionum et epistolarum quae ad ius civile pertinent libri quatuor*, pp. 149–50; *cf. De iure belli*, vol. 1, pp. 538–40, and vol. 2, p. 331).

514 *De iure belli*, vol. 1, pp. 10–13, and vol. 2, pp. 8–9.

was hinting at a new conception of *ius gentium*, his treatise needs to be read quite imaginatively for anything more than hints to be found there.[515]

The second (or third) claim recently made for Gentilis is that he was the first jurist to deal with piracy as a distinct category of criminal conduct.[516] Previously, it is presumed, the seas had been regarded as a lawless place where might was right, and where 'pirate' was simply a term people applied pejoratively to their opponents.[517] It is claimed that this point of view – lately dubbed 'the Augustinian paradigm' – was firmly rejected by Gentilis in favour of the alternative point of view – dubbed 'the Ciceronian paradigm' – that pirates were enemies of humanity who ought to be prosecuted and punished wherever they were found.[518] The thesis that piracy was not regarded as a crime until the sixteenth century was examined and found wanting in the last chapter, and it was partly for this reason that Mollat's representation of the medieval seas as an area characterised by 'la piraterie sauvage' was challenged at the start of this chapter. The objection to his thesis is that the seizure of ships and goods at sea was not an unregulated activity before the end of the Middle Ages, and that an extension of the licensing of reprisals into wartime did not then result in unlicensed seizures being criminalised for the first time as acts of piracy. Seizures in wartime had long been regulated, unlicensed seizures in peacetime had regularly been condemned as piracy, and the licensing of reprisals was not a device resorted to in wartime until the closing decades of the sixteenth century. Nevertheless, there may be a lingering sense that the Mollat thesis captures quite neatly what was going on in Elizabethan England. If the thesis presented here is that one way of regulating seizures in wartime

515 When Gentilis observed that 'the law of nations rests upon the association of the human race' (*De iure belli*, vol. 1, p. 107, and vol. 2, p. 67) he justified the proposition by quoting Cicero's statement that 'the agreement of all nations about a matter must be regarded as a law of nature' (*Tusculan Disputations*, 1.13.30), which was of course entirely consistent with conventional thinking.

516 Rubin 1998, pp. 28–9; Heller-Roazen 2009, pp. 105–6; Kempe 2010, pp. 355–6; Gould 2013, pp. 23 and 30; De Wilde 2018, p. 166.

517 The verb 'presume' is used here advisedly, if perhaps a little unfairly. Rubin 1998, after a discussion of 'The Greek and Roman Conception of "Piracy"' (pp. 4–13), where a partial and misleading account of Roman law is presented, leaps forward to a discussion of 'The Reorganization of the Renaissance' (pp. 13–32), though it ought to have been clear from some of the citations in the sixteenth-century sources examined that the subject had received attention from legal scholars in the intervening period. Quite why a book that leaps over the Middle Ages should have been relied on as a guide to medieval legal thought is something of a mystery.

518 The two paradigms are distinguished in Heebøll-Holm 2013, pp. 2–9, and related to each other in a different way in Sicking 2018a and 2018b.

should be understood to have been giving way to another, it may seem more accurate to conceive of the licensing of reprisals on Spanish shipping as a way of turning the licentious violence endemic at sea into a legitimate activity. After all, the licensing of reprisals enabled the 'sea dogs' who had been indulging in piracy against Spanish shipping to continue making similar seizures as a form of legitimate raiding.[519] It could therefore be that a new conception of piracy as unauthorised raiding was emerging from the recognition of authorised raiding, in wartime as much as peacetime, as the only legitimate form that the seizure of ships and goods at sea could take. The question that needs to be addressed here is whether Gentilis helped to promote this novel understanding of piracy in his treatise.

The only extended discussion of the subject appears in a chapter of the treatise devoted to the civil law distinction between enemies and pirates, in which Gentilis took the standard line that wars were not waged against brigands, bandits or pirates.[520] In composing this chapter he had referred to a *consilium* (or legal opinion) written by the humanist jurist Andreas Alciatus, in response to the question posed to him whether a pirate would be automatically deprived by the canon law of any church benefice he held.[521] Although it was clear that not everyone who committed a crime would lose a benefice *ipso iure*, it was equally clear that murderers would, and it might well have been supposed that pirates were 'maritime murderers'. Alciatus sought to subvert this supposition by drawing a series of distinctions between murderers and pirates, one of which was that 'there is no one so monstrous as to tolerate murderers, and yet pirates, provided they are not enemies, are tolerated by princes, especially here in France'. In support of this point he cited a passage from Augustine's *De civitate Dei* in which the story was told of a pirate who was brought before Alexander the Great and asked to explain why he made a nuisance of himself with his ship, to which he replied by asking Alexander to explain why he made a nuisance of himself with his fleet.[522] Gentilis was dismissive of authors like Alciatus and Augustine who admired the pirate's answer, explaining that whatever moral equivalence there arguably was between a pirate intent on petty depredation and a prince intent on global domination, there was a crucial legal distinction between a sovereign ruler who could declare war on others

519 Andrews 1985, pp. 3–4; MacCaffrey 1992, pp. 562–3; Kelsey 2003, pp. 243–4.

520 *De iure belli*, vol. 1, pp. 34–42, and vol. 2, pp. 22–6.

521 *Responsa, nunquam antehac excusa*, ff. 17v-18r.

522 *De civitate Dei*, 4.4. As Gentilis seems to have appreciated, Augustine may have been drawing on Cicero, *De republica*, 3.14.24, but it is the version of the story in the *De civitate Dei* that has been taken to form the basis of 'the Augustinian paradigm'.

and a disruptive gangster who could not be party to the type of conflict that was regulated by *ius gentium*. In support of his own distinction, Gentilis cited the opinions of two Roman lawyers and the works of a medieval civilian.[523] He cited a similar range of sources in the penultimate chapter of his treatise, where he returned briefly to the subject and rehearsed the routine propositions that pirates could be attacked with impunity, and that they could not acquire title to anything they seized.[524] Here too there was nothing remotely innovative about the substantive position defended by Gentilis, who did not in fact argue that pirates should be treated as criminals, as if they had been treated as something else in the past. In responding to Alciatus he had been drawn into examination of a source that had normally been neglected by the medieval commentators on the civil law, and it will be confirmed in a moment that he was drawn further into adopting Cicero's denunciation of pirates as everyone's enemies, but this was a matter of style more than substance. Far from making novel use of Cicero's thinking in order to contest the conventional understanding of piracy as a harsh fact of life at sea, perhaps recognised by Augustine, Gentilis made use of Cicero's language in the course of reinforcing the conventional position that piracy was an illegal species of maritime raiding, in response to Alciatus' subversive use of Augustine's story.

For Gentilis' use of Cicero's language to be properly understood, an error will first need to be corrected. It has become fashionable to credit Bartolus with coining the description of pirates as *hostes humani generis*.[525] While it is well known that Cicero, Polybius and Pliny had all described pirates as the common enemies of everyone (*communes hostes omnium*), and while similar language was used in other ancient sources, Bartolus is believed to have been

523 *Digest*, 35.2.63.pr., 49.15.27 and 50.16.118; Baldus, *Commentaria super Codicem*, vol. 3, f. 20r (ad C.6.6.4), and *Consilia sive responsa*, vol. 2, f. 71r (n. 247, inc. 'Proponitur quod Ioannes fuit captivatus'), and vol. 3, ff. 23v-4r (n. 96, inc. 'Proponitur quod consuetudo civitatis et districtus Estensis').

524 Gentilis, *De iure belli*, vol. 1, pp. 496–7, and vol. 2, pp. 423–4; *Digest*, 10.2.8, 39.5.34 and 49.15.27; Baldus, *Commentaria super Codicem*, vol. 3, f. 12r (ad C.6.2, Authentica Navigia), and *In primam Digesti veteris partem commentaria*, f. 10v (ad D.1.1.4); Angelus de Ubaldis, *Consilia seu responsa*, f. 123v (n. 290, inc. 'Thema est tale: inter cetera capitula pacis inite'); Ioannes Franciscus a Ripa, *Commentaria in primam et secundam Infortiati*, f. 48r (ad D.28.6.15).

525 Tai 2003, p. 260, and 2007, p. 215; Heller-Roazen 2009, pp. 103 and 192; Kempe 2010, p. 356; Heebøll-Holm 2013, pp. 13–14; Gould 2013, p. 30; Tirshfield 2017, p. 475; Luban 2018, p. 119; De Wilde 2018, p. 165; Sicking 2018a, p. 439, and 2018b, p. 177; Rohman 2019, p. 214.

the first author to write that pirates were the enemies of the human race.[526] The problem with this belief, however, is that Bartolus wrote nothing of the sort. In the 1490s editions of his works began to be printed with margins full of annotations, which had been written some twenty years earlier by Alexander Tartagnus.[527] Alongside Bartolus' discussion of one of the texts in which enemies were contrasted with brigands, it was noted that Frederick II had assimilated pirates with 'enemies of the faith and emperor', and it was then noted distinctly that the humanist Leonardo Bruni had denounced hypocrites as 'enemies of the human race'.[528] This annotation has been wrongly ascribed to the principal author, and not even in the annotation were pirates themselves called *hostes humani generis*. All the same, in view of the assimilation of pirates with enemies of the church and empire, both in the constitution of Frederick II referred to in the annotation, and in the decree of the Third Lateran Council with which it was compared in the last chapter, it might well be expected that the medieval doctors would have drawn attention to the idea that pirates were common enemies when dealing with these texts. The fact is, though, that a search through the commentaries of all the major civilians and canonists, and a fair number of minor jurists too, has disclosed no trace of interest in the idea. If the limited use made by the medieval civilians of philosophical, historical and literary texts may be part of the explanation, it may also be that while perfectly well aware of the idea, they were equally well aware of Cicero's acknowledgement that when the word 'enemies' was used in relation to pirates, it was not used in its strictly legal sense.[529] The doctors of law may have concluded that drawing attention to the more relaxed use of the word by lay authors would only have confused their students.[530]

It follows that when Gentilis described pirates as the common enemies of everyone he was deviating from the traditional teaching of the law schools,

---

526 Cicero, *De officiis*, 3.29.107, and *Verrine Orations*, 2.4.21 (and see too 2.5.76); Polybius, *Histories*, 2.12.6; Pliny, *Natural History*, 2.45.117; *Plutarch's Lives*, Pompey 24; Florus, *Epitome*, 1.41; Charisius, *Ars grammatica*, p. 211. See too Kowalski 2014.

527 Tartagnus taught the civil law at Bologna, Ferrara and Padua between 1450 and his death in 1477 (Padovani 2016). His 'apostillae et additiones' to Bartolus' works had been printed separately in the 1470s.

528 Bartolus, *Lectura super prima et secunda parte Digesti novi*, vol. 2, f. 383r (ad D.49.15.24); *Codex Iustiniani*, col. 1192, Authentica Navigia; Monumenta Germaniae historica, *Constitutiones et acta publica imperatorum et regum*, vol. 2, p. 109; *Pogii Florentini dialogus et Leonardi Arretini oratio adversus hypocrisim*, pt 2, p. 38. *Cf.* Edelstein 2009, pp. 30–2, and Fedele 2021, p. 274.

529 *De officiis*, 3.29.107.

530 If so, it is tempting to add, the later intrusion of Ciceronian language into legal discourse proved them right.

and he did so repeatedly. He had no sooner presented the standard legal thesis that wars were not waged against brigands, bandits and pirates than he reproduced Cicero's argument that agreements made with such people did not need to be fulfilled as they were *communes hostes omnium*.[531] Quite apart from lacking the sovereign authority necessary to declare public wars – the point made in the legal sources Gentilis cited – it seemed clear that brigands, bandits and pirates could not enjoy the protection of the law of war, 'because *ius belli* comes from *ius gentium*, and such people do not derive benefit from that law to which they are enemies' – the crucial point, as Gentilis saw it, of Cicero's argument. 'Because those people are the enemies of everyone', he reiterated later in the same chapter, 'they are unable to enjoy everyone's law'.[532] This line of reasoning made a further reappearance when Gentilis returned to the subject of piracy in his penultimate chapter, where he observed that pirates could be attacked with impunity as 'enemies'.[533] As a gloss on Frederick II's statement that pirates were 'ipso iure diffidati', he explained that 'they are scorners of *ius gentium*, so that they can have no protection under that law'. It was in a third passage, however, that the Ciceronian language was put to its most forceful use. In explaining what he meant by an 'honourable cause' for waging war, Gentilis praised the Romans for taking up arms against the pirates who had infested the ancient Mediterranean.[534] 'War is waged justly against pirates', he insisted, 'for they have violated the common law of nations'. Since piracy injured the fellowship of human society (*humanae societatis communionem*), which was held together by the law of nations, 'war by everyone is merited, for when that law is injured, everyone is injured'. Intervention in the affairs of other nations was therefore justified when it was necessary for the suppression of piracy, though Gentilis appreciated that to talk about 'enemies' in this context was potentially misleading. Properly speaking, he had already made clear, the word 'enemies' signified belligerent parties of equal status, who were capable of declaring war on each other, of entering into treaties with each other and of functioning in other ways under the law of nations,

531 *De iure belli*, vol. 1, pp. 34–5, and vol. 2, p. 22. Since enemies were people with whom peace treaties could be made as well as wars waged, Cicero's argument was, to say the least, paradoxical.

532 *De iure belli*, vol. 1, p. 35, and vol. 2, p. 23. In his *Parallele or Conference of the Civill Law, the Canon Law and the Common Law of England*, f. 6r, William Fulbecke, a keen student (as will be seen) of Gentilis, restated the argument as follows: 'to dispute of lawe is to dispute of a publike bond, whereby we are bound and obliged, but we are not bound to such lawless, disorderly and incorigible persons, by any common respecte of duetie'.

533 *De iure belli*, vol. 1, p. 696, and vol. 2, p. 423; and see too vol. 1, p. 421, and vol. 2, p. 257.

534 *De iure belli*, vol. 1, pp. 201–2, and vol. 2, p. 124. *Cf.* Panizza 2009, pp. 101–2.

which was itself a kind of agreement between nations.[535] If the meaning of the word had sometimes been extended (*communicetur*) to embrace brigands, bandits and pirates, this could not have turned them into genuine enemies. 'No one changes his name', Gentilis remarked, 'and reality along with the name'. Ancient authors had called pirates 'enemies' for rhetorical effect, in much the same way as modern politicians have declared 'war' on terrorists. Yet as recent experience has shown, an essentially stylistic change may have legal significance.[536] Three passages in which Gentilis' discussion of piracy appears to have become more topical require careful consideration.

The first passage formed an addendum to his response to the *consilium* in which Alciatus had remarked that pirates were tolerated by princes, 'especially here in France'.[537] In the light of this closing clause, Alciatus' remark should probably be read in conjunction with another distinction he had drawn between murderers and pirates, the only other one in a series of five on which Gentilis commented. 'A pirate sails a sea that is subject to no one and common by the law of nations', Alciatus had written, 'but a murderer offends in lands subject to others and against the laws of those territories'.[538] In the first half of the sixteenth century – Alciatus had died in 1550 – French navigators had embarked on trading ventures across the Atlantic and into the Caribbean, contrary to the claims of Spain and Portugal to an exclusive dominion over those waters, granted by the papacy.[539] When the French navigators met with resistance, they sought redress by seizing Spanish and Portuguese property, a practice their king had refused to condemn on the ground that a papal grant to some nations could not have deprived others of access to the seas, which were classified as *res communes* in the civil law.[540] A state of declared war had often existed between France and Spain, and when it had not letters of marque had sometimes been granted, but Alciatus appears to have been thinking of French mariners whose behaviour had been tolerated when they simply took matters into their own hands.[541] The example of these French mariners had been followed by English mariners in the second half of the century, when their behaviour had been tolerated in a similar fashion by their queen.[542] In response

535 *De iure belli*, vol. 1, pp. 40–1, and vol. 2, pp. 25–6.

536 Alfert 1992; Bassiouni 2001; Greene 2008; Ezeani 2012; Henderson 2018.

537 *De iure belli*, vol. 1, pp. 38–9, and vol. 2, p. 24.

538 *Responsa, nunquam antehac excusa*, f. 17v.

539 Lane 1998, pp. 17–28; Konstam 2008, pp. 44–8; Bicheno 2012, pp. 28–39; Martínez-Fernández 2015, pp. 11–15; Augeron and Hroděj, 2016, pp. 151–5.

540 Knecht 1994, pp. 374–5; Slattery 2005, pp. 58–9; LaMonica 2016, pp. 16–17.

541 Examples of licences have been printed in Guénin 1901, pp. 149–55, 236–42 and 249–55.

542 Parry 1963, pp. 184–5; Pérotin-Dumon 1991, pp. 208–9; Scott 2013, pp. 75–8.

to complaints about the piracy of Francis Drake, the queen had apparently answered that 'the Spaniards, by their hard dealing with the English, whom they had prohibited commerce, contrary to the law of nations, had drawn these mischiefs upon themselves'.[543] 'Seeing the use of the sea and air is common to all', she had added, 'she understood not why her or any other princes subjects should be debarred from the Indies, which she could not perswade herself the Spaniard had any just title to by the bishop of Romes donation'.[544] It was sometimes claimed at the time, and has frequently been claimed since, that the queen had authorised Drake to take reprisals against Spanish shipping, but no formal documentation has ever come to light, and when his family attempted to justify his actions, they took a different tack.[545] 'As there is a generall vengeance', it was observed, 'so is there a particular indignation engraffed in the bosom of all that are wronged, which ceaseth not seeking by all means possible to redresse or remedy the wrong received'.[546] Like Alciatus' French pirates, it might have been argued, Drake and his colleagues had been vindicating the rights of free navigation accorded to them by the law of nations, which in other respects left the seas as relatively unregulated regions of the world.[547] But Gentilis was having none of this. He commented that Alciatus reminded him of the character in Plautus' *Rudens* who thought that because the fish on market stalls had been caught in the sea, they were open to consumption by anyone.[548] Gentilis made the obvious point that once caught, fish belonged to their captors, although the issue in the play had been whether anything found floating at sea could be similarly acquired.[549] What he seems to have been driving at is that the law regulating activities at sea was more elaborate than Alciatus had suggested, that mariners who took matters into their own hands, when war had not been declared and letters of marque had not been granted,

543 William Camden, *History of the Most Renowned and Victorious Princess Elizabeth*, p. 255.

544 Allusion was clearly being made here to *Digest*, 1.8.2.1, and *Institutes*, 2.1.1, where it was said that 'by the law of nature, these things are common to everyone: the air and flowing water and the sea'.

545 MacCaffrey 1981, pp. 331–3; Corbett 1988, vol. 1, pp. 146–7; Sugden 1996, pp. 98 and 123; Hanson 2003, pp. 90–2; Chadwick 2019, p. 59.

546 Philip Nichols, *Sir Francis Drake Revived*, p. 1. According to Cummins 1995, p. 34, this book was 'possibly written and certainly checked by Drake himself'.

547 This minimalist view of *ius gentium* obviously fits with Alciatus' adoption of 'the Augustinian paradigm'.

548 Plautus, *Rudens*, 4.3. Gentilis also referred here to Priscian, *Institutiones grammaticae*, vol. 1, p. 332.

549 On the acquisition of fish Gentilis cited Athenaeus, *Deinosophists*, 8.342–3, and Baldus, *In primam Digesti veteris partem commentaria*, f. 48r (ad D.1.8.3).

were breaking the law, and that as common enemies of everyone they could claim no rights under the law of nations.[550]

Within a decade of Alciatus' death relations between France and Spain had been altered. When the Habsburg-Valois War was brought to a conclusion in 1559 at Cateau-Cambrésis, the tacit consensus among the French and Spanish negotiators was that the peace would not reach further than a line of longitude west of the Azores, so that ships and goods seized there would not need to be returned to their previous owners, an understanding eventually encapsulated in the slogan 'no peace beyond the line'.[551] There does not appear to be any basis for the belief that the understanding extended to English mariners, but as allegiances and divisions became less national than confessional, their attitudes may have been affected by a pervasive atmosphere of perpetual warfare against enemies of the faith.[552] The Atlantic and Caribbean were beginning to resemble the Mediterranean, where a distinction existed in theory between lawful raiders (historians like to call them 'corsairs') and unlicensed raiders in peacetime (often contrasted as 'pirates'), but where the distinction was not easy to apply in practice.[553] Alciatus mentioned in his *consilium* that the canon law prohibition of the sale of military resources to infidels was reinforced by the annual republication of a papal bull in which *Saraceni, Turci et alii Christi nominis inimici* were linked not only with *piratae, cursarii et latrunculi maritimi*, but also with *omni haeretici*, who in formulations issued in the later sixteenth

550 Some commentators had attempted to accommodate private warfare in their categories of lawful conflict. De Legnano, for instance, had distinguished between 'universal wars', meaning the public wars declared by princes, and 'particular wars', such as the reprisals licensed by princes, and he had linked these particular wars, fought in defence of the mystical body of the state, with other particular wars, fought in defence of an individual's natural body (*Tractatus de bello, de represaliis et de duello*, pp. 130–54 and 276–306). That self-defence was considered legitimate by lawyers (and also theologians) has already been noted more than once, but offensive operations for the sake of redress or vengeance were considered to be a different matter, and Gentilis did not himself deal with private wars as a species of legitimate conflict.

551 The first clear articulation of the understanding was found by Mattingly 1963, pp. 148–9, in letters written in the early seventeenth century. The understanding, it must be stressed, was not that the zone beyond the line was beyond the law, a free-for-all where might was right, but that a state of declared war continued to exist there, so that the ordinary law of arms continued to apply. See too Stirk 2011, and *cf.* Policante 2015.

552 Williams 1961, pp. 117–18; Elliott 2000, pp. 29–30; Manke 2002, pp. 180–1; Hammer 2003, pp. 80–1; Gould 2003, pp. 479–81; Hanna 2015, pp. 36–8.

553 Fontenay 1988, pp. 363–8; Malcolm 2015, pp. 79–81 and 327–9; White 2017, pp. 183–220.

century were expressly declared to include *Lutherani* and *Calvinistae*.[554] As the century wore on, French, Spanish and English mariners took to calling each other heretics or infidels as much as pirates or corsairs, and to making use of this terminology when defending their seizures of ships and goods, which made the term 'pirates' harder to define.[555] In examining the papal bull the canonist Petrus Rebuffus had pointed out that pirates were people who not only raided shipping without the exculpation of a declared war, but who also had no interest in anything apart from plunder, in which they indulged indiscriminately, 'like a whore who admits all men promiscuously, showing no favour to those of her own country, or to those who are attractive, or to black or white men'.[556] What set pirates apart from other maritime raiders, it might have been said, was that they were nobody's friends and therefore everybody's foes.[557] The pursuit of 'private ends' has become a crucial component of the legal definition of piracy today, and it is conceivable that Gentilis was thinking along these lines when he talked about pirates as the enemies of everyone.[558] He may have had it in mind that pirates served their own interests, not a public cause, either national or confessional. He did not write this, however, perhaps because it would not have differentiated pirates clearly enough from raiders who engaged in licit plunder, licensed reprisal or lawful vengeance, all of whom served their own interests primarily and another cause only coincidentally.

The second passage in which Gentilis' discussion of piracy became more topical appeared in the penultimate chapter of his treatise, where he wrote about two diplomatic exchanges he had come across when reading the works of humanist historians.[559] The first was connected with an incident mentioned in the previous chapter, in which vessels were dispatched from England in 1511 to apprehend raiders from Scotland led by Andrew Barton.[560] According to the

554 Alciatus, *Responsa, nunquam antehac excusa*, f. 17v; *Bullarum, privilegiorum ac diplomatum Romanorum pontificum*, vol. 4(1), pp. 140–1, and vol. 4(4), pp. 27–8; *Papal Bull In Coena Domini*, pp. 6–7 and 11–13. On the effects of the bull see Daniels 2019.

555 Gómez-Centurión Jiménez 1991; Grunberg 1997; Augeron 2004; Dimmock 2007; Adams 2009.

556 *Praxis beneficiorum*, pp. 308–9.

557 Rebuffus did not actually put it in this way, and Cicero's language is also lacking from other discussions of piracy in the sixteenth century, both by university professors (like Petrus Peckius, *Commentaria in omnes pene iuris civilis titulos ad rem nauticam pertinentes*, pp. 293–4) and by court practitioners (like Joos de Damhouder, *Enchiridion parium aut similium utriusque iuris*, pp. 111–12).

558 Johnson and Valencia 2005, p. xi; Azubuike 2009, pp. 52–3; Todd 2010, p. 5; Geiß and Petrig 2011, p. 60; Pellegrino 2012, p. 436.

559 *De iure belli*, vol. 1, pp. 696–7, and vol. 2, pp. 423–4.

560 Statham 1910, pp. 19–28; Reid 1962, p. 94–7; Macdougall 1997, p. 239–42.

Scottish humanist George Buchanan, Henry VIII knew that Barton was operating within the terms of letters of reprisal granted by James IV, but was persuaded by a Portuguese envoy to take the opportunity to rid himself of a formidable foe in the war looming against Scotland and France by pretending that he was a pirate.[561] Gentilis was convinced, probably with good reason, that Barton had exceeded the terms of his licence, and that Henry had therefore been justified in dismissing the complaint he received from James. Henry might even have gone further, according to Gentilis, and have told James that he must join him in combating piracy in a 'common war of all nations'. It was this notion that linked the first diplomatic exchange with the second, which followed an episode in the Mediterranean nearly forty years later.[562] Early in 1550 corsairs led by Turgud Reis had taken a port at what is now known as Mahdia in Tunisia, and had started to use it as a base for raids on shipping around Sicily. In the summer a fleet had been dispatched from Naples to besiege and bombard the port, which eventually surrendered in the autumn. The emperor, Charles V, had at once written to the sultan, Suleyman the Magnificent, to explain that Turgud had been indulging in piracy, contrary to the terms of their truce, and to remind him that 'the liberal chastisement of pirates and those who disturb the public peace, on private authority and with no instruction from a sovereign prince, is permitted'.[563] According to the Italian humanist Natale Conti, the Turkish sultan had been no more appeased in 1550 than the Scottish king had been in 1511, and had refused to regard Turgud and his followers as 'pirates and brigands and evil persons', insisting that it was the emperor who had 'violated the law of nations'.[564] Gentilis, however, was again satisfied that the justification of the intervention was sound. 'It is lawful', he observed, 'to destroy piratical lairs and nests infested with pirates and brigands and evil persons everywhere'.[565] He referred here to Cicero's fulsome praise of Pompey for waging a successful war (*bellum*) against the Cilician pirates, a war he had already mentioned when explaining that rulers could intervene 'honourably' in each other's affairs if that was necessary for the suppression of piracy.[566]

561 *Rerum Scoticarum historia*, pp. 374–5, and *History of Scotland*, vol. 2, pp. 247–8.

562 Monchicourt 1918, pp. 35–7; Braudel 1972, vol. 2, pp. 907–11; Coulet du Gard 1980, pp. 123–6.

563 *Correspondenz des Kaisers Karl V*, vol. 3, pp. 9–11.

564 *Universae historiae sui temporis libri triginta*, pp. 73–4.

565 For some reason, Gentilis misread Conti's ancient name for the port (*Aphrodisium*) as a reference to Durazzo in Albania, but it is his reading of the diplomatic exchange that matters.

566 *Pro lege Manilia*, 11.31. Between his discussion of the 1511 and 1550 incidents, both of which were taken to illustrate the proposition that pirates could be attacked with impunity, Gentilis interjected awkwardly an account of the proposition that pirates could acquire

Gentilis was not alone in talking about 'common enemies' in relation to the suppression of piracy. When the English admiral wondered whether he could commission mariners to pursue pirates without explicit authorisation from the queen, he was informed that he must be able to do so since it was 'lawfull for every man, by the lawes of the sea, to apprehend and take pyrats, being public enemies to all estates, without authority or commission'.[567] When a commission to pursue pirates was issued in Scotland, it was on the understanding that they were 'enemeyis to the common quietnes of all nationis', and 'commoun enemeyis to all nationis'.[568] In his otherwise conventional treatise on the law of arms, published a few years after the first edition of Gentilis' treatise appeared, Matthew Sutcliffe remarked that pirates were 'enemies of peace and civil government, and by the lawes defied and proclaimed as publike enemies of states', drawing the conclusion that it was not only 'lawful to cleare the sea of pyrates, but also honorable'.[569] Use was more often made of Ciceronian language when rulers wanted to impress upon each other their mutual responsibility to punish pirates. When Elizabeth asked the queen of Scots to prevent pirates from abusing the letters of reprisal issued by her predecessors, she reminded her that 'pyratts be counted commen ennemyes to all states'.[570] Elizabeth was herself reminded by Mary's son that pirates, according to the 'law of nations, suld be accompted ennemyes of all mankynd'.[571] 'It is moste certaine', her own officials had conceded to an envoy from Scotland, 'that amongst all nations pyratis are accompted *hostes publici*, and therefore

title to nothing they seized. The emperor's action was presented as a recent instance of the sort of action Cicero had praised, in a passage cited at the end of the discussion of Henry's action.

567 *Documents Relating to Law and Custom of the Sea*, vol. 1, p. 224. For examples of commissions of this type see *Collection of State Papers Relating to Affairs in the Reigns of Henry VIII, Edward VI, Mary and Elizabeth*, vol. 1, pp. 394–5; *Calendar of the Manuscripts of the Most Honourable the Marquis of Salisbury*, vol. 1, p. 268; *Acts of the Privy Council of England*, vol. 7, pp. 129–30; NAK, HCA25/1/1, f. 146. When Elizabeth appointed commissioners on land for 'repressinge of piraterie', she claimed to be fulfilling her 'duetye towardes God and the worlde' (*Acts of the Privy Council of England*, vol. 7, p. 278).

568 *Register of the Privy Council of Scotland*, vol. 4, pp. 195–6 (with the definite article added before 'common quietnes').

569 *Practice, Proceedings, and Lawes of Armes*, pp. 3–4.

570 *Calendar of State Papers Relating to Scotland*, vol. 1, pp. 546–7; NAK, SP52/6, f. 128v.

571 *Calendar of State Papers Relating to Scotland*, vol. 10, p. 318. The phrase *hostes humani generis* was not used by Gentilis, nor is it often found being used elsewhere in relation to pirates in this period. It is therefore of some interest that an example can be found in Buchanan, *Rerum Scoticarum historia*, p. 116, and *History of Scotland*, vol. 1, p. 235, for Buchanan had been James' tutor.

should be punished accordinglie, if they can be comprehended'.[572] Of course, to acknowledge an obligation to suppress piracy was not the same thing as to discharge the obligation.[573] Elizabeth faced repeated complaints from abroad about the toleration of 'ennemys communs de toutes gens' in her realme.[574] 'Princes ought to punish pyrates as publicke enemies to the commonwealth', it was objected, 'yet it is certein and manifest that pirats doe invade the merchants passing along by the coast of England, and are often times received in the ports of England, even by some being in authoritie'.[575] While the queen saw fit to reply that she was doing her best to fulfil her undertakings in treaties to 'punish pyrates as enemies of the commenweale', one of her counsellors pointed out that the obligation to deal firmly with offenders of this type, 'whom the civilians account to be *publici hostes societatis humanae*', did not arise from the treaties in which it was acknowledged but was owed to all princes, whether friends or foes.[576] The counsellor was Francis Bacon, a common lawyer by profession, who may not have been aware that the civil lawyers had for a long time resisted the temptation to call pirates the common enemies of everyone.[577] As Gentilis was at pains to make clear, pirates were not public enemies in the sense of opponents in a declared war (*bellum publicum*), but were rather enemies of the *humanae societatis communio* or the commonwealth (*respublica*) of nations governed by *ius gentium*.[578]

The third passage in which Gentilis' discussion of piracy became more topical appeared in the chapter he devoted to the difference between enemies and pirates, where he referred to an event described in a recent history of the regal union of Spain and Portugal.[579] In 1582, after a battle fought near São Miguel in the Azores between a Spanish fleet and a force assembled in France in support of the claim to the Portuguese throne of Dom Antonio, the prior

572 *Letters and Papers Relating to Patrick, Master of Gray*, p. 27.

573 Mathew 1924, pp. 337–9; Williams 1975, pp. 148–65; Williams 1988, pp. 232–8; Lyons 2000, pp. 21–3; Earle 2003, pp. 18–21; Snyder 2006, pp. 24–6; Murdoch 2010, pp. 113–20.

574 *Relations politique des Pays-Bas et de l'Angleterre*, vol. 6, p. 76; see too p. 315, where pirates were referred to as 'ennemis de Dieu, de toute religion et de la tranquillité publique'.

575 BL, Cotton MS Galba C III, ff. 331–2r.

576 Francis Bacon, *Letter Written out of England to an English Gentleman Remaining at Padua*, p. 11.

577 For an instructive comparison between common and civil law thinking on piracy see Youngs 1976, pp. 92–5. The interest of common lawyers resulted from an act of parliament passed in 1536 (*Statutes of the Realm*, vol. 3, p. 671). As is perfectly plain from the preamble to the act, it did not make piracy a crime for the first time.

578 Gentilis, it should be noted, did not himself refer to pirates as *hostes publici*, perhaps to avoid this confusion.

579 Kamen 1997, p. 177; Elliott 2000, pp. 189–90; Parker 2014, p. 273.

of Crato, a large number of prisoners taken by Philip II's mariners had been executed as 'enemies of the peace and the commonwealth' (*inimici del riposo, e del ben commune*).[580] According to the Italian historian Girolamo Conestaggio, the Spanish mariners had questioned the legitimacy of the executions, partly because they had hoped to enrich themselves with ransoms for the prisoners, and partly because they were not convinced that their opponents were pirates. For one thing, since significant numbers of ships and mariners had been sent out from France, it seemed that they had been engaged in an act of war rather than a pirate raid. For another, the Spanish mariners understood that licences (*patenti*) had been issued to their opponents by the king of France. Gentilis did not think the scale of the encounter mattered.[581] It had not taken place to the west of the Azores, and no new declaration of war had been made by the French or Spanish king. The executed sailors had not been enemies in a public war, yet nor had they been the common enemies of everyone, for Gentilis agreed that sailors with licences (*literae*) from their own king ought not to have been dealt with as pirates. Since it could hardly have been supposed that the French sailors had been denied justice in Spain – Gentilis knew they had been sent to assist Dom Antonio – this did not make obvious sense in conventional terms. Just as Gentilis, in claiming that Elizabeth had intervened in an existing war in 1585, evaded the issue that no war had already been declared then, so in claiming that the French king had issued licences to his sailors in 1582, he evaded the issue that there was no justification then for authorising reprisals. He was struggling to come to terms with the emerging reality that what made lawful raiding different from unlawful raiding, not only in peacetime but also in wartime, was the specific authorisation of a sovereign ruler. The meaning of the term 'piracy' may also have been changing, and to this extent there may still be some mileage in the Mollat thesis. If it is incorrect to maintain that maritime raiding in wartime was first regulated, and piracy first criminalised, only when the reprisals regime was extended to cover seizures made in wartime, it may be correct to maintain that when a transition was made from one system of wartime regulation to another, a transition was also made to a new understanding of piracy. If only licensed raiding was legitimate, then perhaps the distinguishing feature of piracy was the absence of a licence. This need not have followed, however, and for the moment the question must be left open.

580 Girolamo Conestaggio, *Dell'unione del regno di Portogallo alla corona di Castiglia*, pp. 424–6, and *Historie of the Uniting of the Kingdom of Portugall to the Crowne of Castill*, p. 294–5.

581 *De iure belli*, vol. 1, pp. 41–2, and vol. 2, p. 26.

CHAPTER 3

Privateering in Theory and Practice *avant la lettre*

No historian has provided a better account of the emergence of privateering than Nicholas Rodger.[1] In an article on 'The Law and Language of Private Naval Warfare', published in 2014, while warning that privateering in the proper sense of the word did not finally come into existence until around the time of the English Civil Wars and the Anglo-Dutch Wars, he recognised the importance of developments in Elizabethan England and located those developments within the broader context of the confessional conflicts of the later sixteenth century.[2] An attempt has been made in the second chapter of the present book to clarify the legal significance of the developments that took place in Elizabeth's reign, when two or three of the categories of maritime raiding distinguished in the first chapter came to be confused with one another.[3] In practice the boundaries between licit plunder and licensed reprisal were blurred, and doubts also arose about the legitimacy of exacting private vengeance on pirates, as rulers increasingly assumed responsibility for their suppression.[4] In theory there were various ways in which a justification might have been devised for the use of letters of reprisal or marque in wartime, but the rapid reconnaissance of these approaches undertaken in the previous chapter was inconclusive, for no legal justification appears to have been worked out before the queen's demise in 1603. Lawyers failed to close the conceptual gap that had opened between their established theory and emerging practice, preferring to avoid the issue by fudging the facts of the cases they examined, while theologians and humanists failed to explain how their moral or political justifications could be considered legal. The aim of this third chapter is to see how much further the theory and practice of maritime raiding may have advanced before the breakdown of

1 Rodger 2014.

2 Although the importance of the Elizabethan period had also been recognised in Andrews 1985, that author was criticised for making premature use of the terms 'privateering' and 'privateer'.

3 The analysis has not been entirely consistent with Rodger 2014, for the notion that English monarchs resorted to 'reprisals by general proclamation' in 1543, 1557 and 1563 has been questioned, along with the claims made by several other authors that 'letters of marque' were already being used to authorise raiding during wartime in France, Scotland and the Netherlands.

4 Ironically, given the central thrust of much recent work on piracy, the one idea that remained stable was that pirates *stricto sensu* were criminals.

 | DOI:10.1163/9789004541412_005

royal authority in Britain in the 1630s. The six sections into which the chapter is divided form three pairs, of which the first two are concerned with practice during the reign of James VI and I, the next two with theory during the same period, and the last two with practice during the first five years of the reign of Charles I, when war was resumed between England (along with Scotland) and Spain (along with France). The division between practice and theory is less than absolute, however, not least because more is said in the second section about the thinking of Albericus Gentilis. The six sections, moreover, could be organised into different pairs, since the first and last are concerned with practice in Scotland, the second and fifth with practice in England. By the seventeenth century it is impossible to make sense of Scottish experience without reference to English experience, and attending to Scottish experience helps to bring English experience into sharper focus.[5]

1 Licensed Raiding in Jacobean Scotland

In returning to Scotland, of which very little was said in the second chapter, readers need to remember that the reign of James VI, which began when he was a year old in 1567, was discussed in the first chapter without mention of the movement then under way towards a new understanding of international law, which was deliberately left aside to be discussed in the second chapter. This did not mean that developments in Scotland were examined entirely in isolation, for it was noted that when lawyers wrote about the admiral's jurisdiction in the 1580s, they made extensive use of the influential legislation on maritime warfare reissued in France. It has since been suggested that the influence of the French legislation extended to England as well as Denmark and the Netherlands. By the middle of the sixteenth century it had become a standard practice in the North Sea area for rulers, while still adhering to the traditional theory of prize acquisition taught in the law schools, to require the masters of private vessels to obtain licences before they sailed and approval of any seizures of ships and goods they made after they returned. The understanding remained that title to any ships and goods captured would be acquired by their seizure (*occupatio*) from enemies (*res hostium*), but rulers had gone some way towards increasing their control over the use of violence at sea. There is in fact evidence that efforts were being made to imitate this regime in Scotland as

5 Some readers may again prefer to skip the Scottish sections, although something will be lost in doing so.

early as 1544, when the third earl of Bothwell, after returning from a period of exile in Denmark via England, asserted a right to exercise 'his heritage of admiralite as in utheris realmes'.[6] Although regulations modelled on the French legislation were not issued in Scotland, it was apparently at the insistence of admiralty officials that some masters at least sought approval of the seizures they made after they came home.[7] Evidence also survives, from 1544 onwards, of masters obtaining licences before sailing in wartime, although there was some uncertainty over the admiral's right to grant them.[8] As was emphasised in the first chapter, there is no evidence whatsoever of these licences being regarded at the time as letters of marque, nor of prize acquisition being taken to depend either on their existence or on the adjudication of title in the proper sense.[9] When Scotland's involvement in external conflicts ended, seven years before the accession of James VI – who was of course to take great pride in his status as a *rex pacificus* – the regulation of maritime warfare was moving into line with its regulation in neighbouring countries. If the argument advanced in the second chapter is correct, the emergence of privateering as a distinct form of licensed raiding had not yet got under way. The concern of this section is with tracing the extent to which there was awareness in Scotland over the next sixty-five years of the changes initiated by the confessional conflicts of the 1560s.

There is some (albeit rather slender) evidence that the move towards licensed privateering may actually have started in Scotland itself. In August 1560 an action was raised before the central court of admiralty sitting in Edinburgh by the master of a French ship, which had been seized by an English ship while heading home from Newfoundland with a cargo of fish and oil.[10] The

6 *Acts of the Parliaments of Scotland*, vol. 2, p. 449; Records of the Parliaments of Scotland, 1544/11/28.

7 Evidence provided for the late 1550s and early 1560s by the *Acta curiae admirallatus Scotiae* was reviewed in the first chapter, though evidence was also adduced there of prizes being distributed without judicial approval. It could of course be more than a coincidence that Bothwell demanded treatment like admirals in other countries in the year that Francis I issued his revised 'edit sur l'amirauté'.

8 *Register of the Privy Council of Scotland*, vol. 1, pp. 40–1; *Compota thesaurariorum regum Scotorum*, vol. 8, p. 476, and vol. 9, p. 381; *Registrum secreti sigilli regum Scotorum*, vol. 3, pp. 418 and 404–5, and vol. 5(1), pp. 47 and 412–13; *Warrender Papers*, vol. 1, p. 15; *Letters and Papers, Foreign and Domestic, of the Reign of Henry VIII*, vol. 19(1), p. 35, vol. 19(2), p. 465, and vol. 21(2), p. 39; NRS, GD1/371, f. 304r; BL, Royal MS 18B VI, ff. 162v and 176r. *Cf. Acts of the Lords of Council in Public Affairs*, pp. 31 and 219–20.

9 The record reproduced in *Registrum secreti sigilli regum Scotorum*, vol. 2, p. xviii, provides no support for the assertion in Murdoch 2010, p. 43, that 'Patrick Loch took his ship to sea armed with letters of marque'.

10 *Acta curiae admirallatus Scotiae*, pp. 138–9.

French ship had been taken to Dundee, where the master of the English ship had refused to make its owners 'restitutioun nor deliverance of the samyn'.[11] In Edinburgh the English master claimed that the seizure had been made 'be virtew of ane licence gevin to him be the lordis of secreit counsale of Scotland, in the moneth of Marche last was, be ressoun of the grit invasionis, fyre and murthour committit be the Franchemen upoun the subjectis of this realme'.[12] The English master maintained that the licence had effectively turned him into a 'subject of the realme of Scotland for the tyme', and that he had therefore been entitled 'to pas in weirfair upoun the Franchemen as inymeis of Scotland'. It was answered for the French master that there not only was 'na inymitie declarit' between the realms of Scotland and France but could not have been, 'sen the king and quenis majestie of France war the tyme allegeit, and is yit, heidis and princis to the realmis of Scotland and France'. The seizure could not have fallen within the established category of licit plunder in wartime, and nor could it have fallen within the category of licensed reprisal in peacetime, for no attempt had been made to seek redress for a wrong inflicted on the English master in France.[13] As the licence granted has not survived, it is not known whether it contained any reference to a loss sustained by, or justice denied to, the holder, but an example does survive of a licence granted by the lords of the congregation in the same year to a Scottish master, and it simply authorised him to seize *hostium naves* on the basis of French oppression of the Scots for 'embracing the sincere religion of Christ'.[14] Although on a couple of occasions English observers referred to a licence granted by the lords of the congregation as a 'letter of marke', they appear on neither occasion to have seen the document itself, and they certainly knew that the monarchs of Scotland and France could not possibly have declared war on each other.[15] Why the English master

11 No trace has been found in the records of Dundee of any attempt to have the seizure approved there, nor was any mention made before the court in Edinburgh of approval having been obtained there.

12 *Acta curiae admirallatus Scotiae*, pp. 139–42, 147–53, 165–6, 170–2 and 174–9.

13 Had a claim for redress been presented to the king and queen of France, it was being stressed, it would also have been presented to the king and queen of Scotland.

14 *Calendar of State Papers Relating to Scotland*, vol. 1, p. 323; *Calendar of State Papers, Foreign Series, of the Reign of Elizabeth*, vol. 2, p. 403; NAK, SP52/2, f. 59. There is a gap in the register of the privy council of Scotland from 1554 to 1561. The surviving licence was addressed to the rulers of other countries and urged them not to treat the holders as *praedones* or *piratae* since they were serving their *patria* in a defensive war. It was similar in style to those surviving from the 1540s, which have been misleadingly labelled 'letters of marque' by modern scholars.

15 *Calendar of State Papers, Foreign Series, of the Reign of Elizabeth*, vol. 3, pp. 283 and 553; NAK, SP52/5, f. 27, and SP70/23, f. 96. For another reference in an English source to a

was eventually ordered to restore the ship taken to Dundee was not made clear in the decreet issued by the admiralty court.[16] A particular point of contention had been the timing of the seizure, which was made after the conclusion of the Treaty of Edinburgh but before the English master heard about the termination of hostilities.[17] It may be, however, that the judge was unconvinced by the attempt to reconcile the seizures authorised by the lords of the congregation with the familiar categories of legitimate prize taking. In any case, it is beyond doubt that the Protestant leaders in Scotland had been experimenting with the licensing of maritime raiding in a confessional conflict.

It follows that when Elizabeth and her advisers later tried to justify her proclamation against trading with the enemy in terms of the recent practice of nations, they may have been mindful of developments in Scotland as well as France, the Netherlands and Spain. For their part, the Scots were by no means ignorant of developments in these other places. In 1563 the arrival in Scotland of a ship with only four men on board raised suspicions of piracy, in response to which its master declared that he and his companions were 'faythfull obedient subjectes to the quene of Ingland, and that thai had commissioun and power of the deputie and kepar of New Havin in France to apprehend and tak as lauchfull pryise all personis and thair gudis quhilkis wer inemyis or resistaris to the religioun than professit be the prince of Condy, admirall and utheris of the congregatioun of that realme'.[18] While the authorities in Scotland waited for the licence granted at Le Havre to be produced, the warden of the West Marches of England appeared, 'avowand the said schip to be lauchfullie takin in the lait trublis in France', and it was surrendered into his custody in exchange for a guarantee that any legitimate claim made to the ship by subjects of the king of France would be respected. In 1570 several ships from Leith were arrested in London in response to the sale of two ships from London in Leith.[19] The English ships had been taken at sea by Frenchmen, 'havinge with them a lettre of marke of the queene of Navarre to take all papists goods', though why this should have been understood in Leith to justify the sale of the London ships was beyond the understanding of the English authorities. In

licence issued in Scotland by the lords of the congregation see *Calendar of State Papers Relating to Scotland*, vol. 1, p. 298; NAK, SP52/2, f. 21.

16 *Acta curiae admirallatus Scotiae*, pp. 179–80.

17 The point singled out for comment in England (*Calendar of State Papers, Foreign Series, of the Reign of Elizabeth*, vol. 3, p. 219; NAK, SP52/5, f. 6), this was also touched on in the first chapter.

18 *Calendar of State Papers Relating to Scotland*, vol. 1, pp. 236–7 and 241–3.

19 NAK, HCA14/10, n. 166.

1574, after two Dutch ships were brought into Montrose, it was found that their takers held 'a licence of the prince of Orange to take off all victuallers and others furnishers of the duke of Alva'.[20] As the licence had been purchased from a Dutch holder, and most of the takers fled from Montrose when it became apparent that the ships they had captured were themselves Dutch, the others were condemned as pirates.[21] Although the leaders of this enterprise were from England, it transpired that some of those involved were from Scotland, and in the following year another English captain, who had obtained 'a lettre of mart against the Flushingers', offered employment on his vessel to Scottish mariners.[22] He too was suspected of substantiating the English queen's supposition that piracy around the British coasts was being encouraged by 'these loose times of civil wars in foreign parts'.[23]

As was seen in the first chapter, one consequence of the commencement of hostilities between England and Spain in 1585 was the unwelcome attention received by Scottish ships from 'Leaguers' or 'Dunkirkers'.[24] When it was Scottish ships and goods that were seized, the raiders were viewed as 'pyrottis or revaris', but a different attitude came to be adopted when the victims were English or Dutch.[25] In response to a petition submitted in 1588 by a Dutch master for the restoration of a ship taken off Norway and brought into Kirkwall, the Scottish admiral noted that the taker, 'being the king of Spanys subject, obtenit a letter of merque to tak and apprehend the schippis and guidis of all personis inhabitantis of the law cuntrey of Flanderis, now dissobedient to him',

20 *Calendar of State Papers Relating to Scotland*, vol. 4, p. 682, and vol. 5, pp. 5–10, 14–15 and 24–6; *Calendar of State Papers, Foreign Series, of the Reign of Elizabeth*, vol. 10, pp. 522, 525, 530 and 533.

21 Their treatment as pirates was noted in the first chapter. It could be that the escape of some of the pirates lay behind the efforts made by the burghs around that time to mount a joint expedition with the queen of England, for some effort was also made to involve the prince of Orange (*Extracts from the Records of the Burgh of Edinburgh*, vol. 4, p. 15; *Records of the Convention of the Royal Burghs of Scotland*, vol. 1, pp. 27–9 and 44). See too *Extracts from the Records of the Burgh of Edinburgh*, vol. 3, pp. 111–12, 275 and 283–4.

22 *Calendar of State Papers Relating to Scotland*, vol. 5, pp. 27 and 178; *Calendar of State Papers, Foreign Series, of the Reign of Elizabeth*, vol. 10, p. 511, and vol. 11, p. 194; NAK, SP52/26/1, ff. 32 and 73, SP52/26/2, ff. 133r and 199, and SP70/136, f. 94. See too *Acts of the Privy Council of England*, vol. 20, pp. 151–2 , and NRS, CS7/139, ff. 341-2r, and CS7/143, ff. 251v-2r and 247v-9.

23 *Calendar of State Papers Relating to Scotland*, vol. 5, pp. 476–7, and vol. 6, pp. 253 and 455; *Original Letters of Mr John Colville*, p. 21.

24 *Calendar of State Papers Relating to Scotland*, vol. 9, pp. 149–50, and vol. 10, pp. 35–6; *Records of the Convention of the Royal Burghs of Scotland*, vol. 1, pp. 306–7; *Calendar of the Manuscripts of the Most Honourable the Marquis of Salisbury*, vol. 4, p. 218.

25 *Calendar of State Papers Relating to Scotland*, vol. 10, pp. 358 and 369; *Ancient Criminal Trials in Scotland*, vol. 1(2), p. 267.

concluding that he had seized the ship as a 'lauchfull pryse'.[26] Dunkirkers raiding in northern waters often sought to dispose of their prizes in Scotland, where Crail was found to be an especially accommodating haven.[27] In response to constant complaints from English ambassadors that the Dunkirkers deserved to be hanged as pirates, not welcomed as friends, the Scottish king observed that 'in respect of the wearis betwix them', he could not forbid the king of Spain's subjects 'to dispose of their prises here' any more than he could forbid the queen of England's.[28] James had some reason to maintain a studied neutrality, for while intercourse with Spain was being discouraged on religious grounds, the preservation of peaceful relations with Philip II was enabling Scottish merchants to exploit markets previously dominated by the English and Dutch.[29] On the other hand, James was also in amity with Elizabeth and, with an eye on the English succession, was increasingly anxious to retain her favour. He therefore undertook to persuade the Dunkirkers to restore any ships and goods they had captured, or at least to sell them back, to their English victims.[30] He warned the Dunkirkers that it would not be considered legitimate for them to seize ships or goods within his ports or coastal waters, and eventually he forbade his subjects to purchase goods from them.[31] Yet he still felt unable to deny that prizes taken by the Dunkirkers outside his waters were being

26 *Calendar of State Papers Relating to Scotland*, vol. 10, p. 854; *Register of the Privy Council of Scotland*, vol. 4, p. 331.

27 *Calendar of State Papers Relating to Scotland*, vol. 13(1), pp. 463, 512–14, 540, 648–9, 805–7 and 809; *Calendar of the Manuscripts of the Most Honourable the Marquis of Salisbury*, vol. 9, p. 222; *Records of the Convention of the Royal Burghs of Scotland*, vol. 2, pp. 42–3.

28 *Calendar of State Papers Relating to Scotland*, vol. 13(1), pp. 494–5, 568–73 and 703–4; NAK, SP52/64, f. 80, SP52/65, f. 118, and SP52/68, f. 54.

29 *Acts and Proceedings of the General Assemblies of the Church of Scotland*, vol. 2, pp. 964 and 1134; *Records of the Convention of the Royal Burghs of Scotland*, vol. 1, pp. 402–3 and 485–6, and vol. 2, p. 5; *Extracts from the Records of the Burgh of Edinburgh*, 2nd ser., vol. 1, pp. 95–6; *Register of the Privy Council of Scotland*, vol. 5, p. 398, and vol. 6, p. 88; *Calendar of State Papers Relating to Scotland*, vol. 11, pp. 36–7, 196–7 and 481, and vol. 13(1), pp. 494–5; *Early Travellers in Scotland*, pp. 86–7; *Itinerary Written by Fynes Moryson*, p. 155; [John Colville], *Historie and Life of King James the Sext*, pp. 254–5; *Aberdeen Shore Work Accounts*, pp. 31 and 33; *Compt Buik of David Wedderburne*, p. 214; BL, Lansdowne MS 142, f. 182; DCA, BCMB, vol. 19, 9 and 14 April 1596, vol. 20, 8 and 27 July and 11 and 17 October 1597, 19 June, 4 August, 11 and 20 September, 4 and 23 October 1598, and 5 March, 20 April and 7 November 1599; AA, B6/11/1/3, ff. 465v-6, and B6/11/2, f. 278r; McLaughlin 2014, pp. 59–89.

30 *Calendar of State Papers Relating to Scotland*, vol. 13(1), pp. 574–6 and 580–1, and vol. 13(2), pp. 649–57, 659–61 and 664.

31 *Calendar of State Papers Relating to Scotland*, vol. 13(1), pp. 480–1 and 566; *Register of the Privy Council of Scotland*, vol. 6, pp. 14, 43 and 113; NAK, SP52/65, f. 113. *Cf. Practicks of Sir James Balfour*, vol. 2, p. 638.

taken legitimately. If James never managed to explain how it was possible for ships and goods to be acquired from enemies when no war had been declared between Elizabeth and Philip, or between Philip and the Dutch, he at least adopted a more consistent stance than the English ambassadors, who seemed to believe that seizures licensed by Catholic authorities were acts of piracy, whereas those licensed by Protestant authorities were legitimate acts of war.[32]

As was also seen in the first chapter, another complaint raised by Elizabeth's envoys was that Scottish mariners were being found among the crews of ships sailing out of Dunkirk, and evidence does indeed survive of Scots serving under masters licensed by the king of Spain.[33] It was even rumoured that the fifth earl of Bothwell was prepared to offer his services to Philip, particularly after he fell from favour with the Scottish king.[34] While still in office as admiral of Scotland, Bothwell had instead expressed an interest in sailing against the 'Leaguers', and had enquired about obtaining the English queen's 'lettres of mark or reprisall in this behalf, and with leave and libertie to bring into, dischardge and make sale in England all suche prizes as shalbe taken'.[35] Apparently differing in this respect from the Scottish king, the Scottish admiral appreciated that the licences issued in the wars between England, Spain and the Netherlands were believed to owe something to the letters of marque or reprisal normally issued in peacetime.[36] According to his deputy, Alexander King, the admiral had spent some time studying at a continental law school, where he might have learned that prize acquisition was otherwise dependent on the existence of a *bellum publicum*.[37] He might also have learned that reprisals could only be taken legitimately after justice had been denied for losses sustained by the recipient of a licence. As was explained earlier, it was in these conventional terms that his deputy wrote about the practice, though it was suggested that in recommending its revival in response to English piracy he may have been

32 The English position makes better sense if viewed in terms of the moral theology shared with Spain, in which a just war could in principle have been waged on only one side.

33 *Calendar of State Papers Relating to Scotland*, vol. 10, pp. 36, 212, 335–6, 364–5 and 398–9, and vol. 13(2), pp. 650–7; *Register of the Privy Council of Scotland*, vol. 4, p. 331; *Warrender Papers*, vol. 2, pp. 148–9; Jack 2013.

34 *Calendar of State Papers Relating to Scotland*, vol. 11, pp. 56 and 538; *Original Letters of Mr John Colville*, p. 141; David Calderwood, *History of the Kirk of Scotland*, vol. 5, p. 19; Sáenz-Cambra 2005, pp. 141–2.

35 *Calendar of State Papers Relating to Scotland*, vol. 10, pp. 263 and 398–9; NAK, SP52/45, f. 15.

36 In 1590 Bothwell himself issued a Scot with a 'commission to serve against the Leaguers', but this probably meant a licence to pursue the Leaguers or Dunkirkers as pirates preying on Scottish vessels (*Calendar of State Papers Relating to Scotland*, vol. 10, pp. 398–9; NAK, SP52/46, f. 48).

37 *Alexander King's Treatise on Maritime Law*, pp. 42–3.

seeking to promote the interests of the Catholic League. When Dutch interference with Scottish trade led to requests for letters of marque or reprisal in 1589, Elizabeth advised James that she thought it 'a verie untimelie matter to enter into that course now, leaste yt mought be thoughte he shoulde in that action favour to muche the king of Spaigne'.[38] Letters of marque or reprisal, whether issued after a denial of justice or not, were being viewed as an instrument of war, and this was appreciated to some extent in Scotland. The embargo on trade with Spain or the southern Netherlands was causing serious problems for Scottish mariners and merchants.[39] Its legitimacy was not drawn into question, partly because sympathy was being shown towards the Scots caught up in its operation, and partly because English mariners who made unlicensed seizures were being prosecuted as pirates.[40] What James found intollerable was interference with Scottish trade by mariners licensed in the United Provinces, to which he referred derisively as a 'new erected republique, whilk consistis onlie upon rebellis and rebellioun'.[41]

On 26 March 1603, two days after Elizabeth died and ten days before James departed for England, a proclamation was issued forbidding Scottish masters from setting sail 'without his majesties licence had and obtenit to that effect', and for a brief period the authorisation of commercial ventures, a novelty north of the border, was put into practice.[42] While travelling south, James apparently issued a 'publique edict' to advise his English and Irish subjects that he was 'in good amity and freindship with all the princes of Christendome', and that therefore 'none of them, or their subjects, should by any hostile action be endamaged in their persons, territories or goods by any of our subjects, either by lande or sea'.[43] No copy of the edict has ever been found, but it was

---

38 *Collection of State Papers, Relating to Affairs in the Reigns of King Henry VIII, King Edward VI, Queen Mary and Queen Elizabeth*, vol. 2, p. 636.

39 *Extracts from the Records of the Burgh of Edinburgh*, vol. 4, pp. 466–8; *Acts of the Privy Council of England*, vol. 14, p. 216, and vol. 32, p. 154; *Calendar of State Papers, Foreign Series, of the Reign of Elizabeth*, vol. 22, p. 63; *Calendar of State Papers Relating to Scotland*, vol. 11, pp. 36–7 and 196–7; *Calendar of the Manuscripts of the Most Honourable the Marquis of Salisbury*, vol. 9, p. 103, and vol. 10, p. 350; NAK, HCA14/27, nn. 68 and 151.

40 *Acts of the Privy Council of England*, vol. 15, p. 167, and vol. 27, pp. 268–9; *Letters of Sir Walter Ralegh*, p. 17; *Documents Relating to Law and Custom of the Sea*, vol. 2, pp. 187–8.

41 *Calendar of State Papers Relating to Scotland*, vol. 13(1), pp. 494–5; *Calendar of State Papers, Foreign Series, of the Reign of Elizabeth*, vol. 22, pp. 20, 68, 82 and 221–2; NAK, SP52/64, f. 80. These entries provide support for the supposition made at the end of the last chapter, and further support is provided below.

42 *Register of the Privy Council of Scotland*, vol. 6, pp. 548 and 782–6.

43 *Foedera, conventiones, litterae et cuiuscunque generis acta publica*, vol. 16, pp. 516–17; *Documents Relating to Law and Custom of the Sea*, vol. 1, pp. 342–5; *Stuart Royal Proclamations*, vol. 1, pp. 30–2.

mentioned in another proclamation, issued in the following June, in which James acknowledged that 'the late queene of England had of long tyme warres with the kynge of Spayne, and during that tyme gave licenses and commissions to divers of her (and our nowe) subjects to set out and furnish to sea at theire charges divers shippes, warlyke appointed, for the supprising and taking of the said kings subjects and goods and for the injoying of the same, being taken and brought home as lawfull prize'.[44] Acquisitions would be respected as long as they were made before 24 April 1603, by which time mariners should have 'taken knowledge of the discontynuance of the said war'.[45] In moving south, James was able to indulge his conceit that wars were waged personally between princes, as a mystery of state on which neither members of parliament nor ministers of the church were qualified to comment.[46] Contrary to previous practice in Scotland, foreign policy came to be directed by the king, who no longer troubled to send ambassadors abroad to represent Scottish interests.[47] On reaching London the king learned that many of his new subjects welcomed peace with Spain.[48] Attention tends to be drawn by English historians to a proclamation drafted in May, advising mariners that the late queen's licences had lost validity on her death and that they must return home, as if this provided the first intimation that the war would soon be over.[49] Yet there is no evidence that this proclamation was actually pronounced, and it was the proclamation approved in June that was alluded to in the 'articles of peace, entercourse and commerce' eventually agreed with the king of Spain and the governors of the southern Netherlands, which reiterated that prize acquisitions would only be

44 *Calendar of State Papers, Domestic Series, of the Reign of James I*, vol. 1, p. 16; *Calendar of State Papers and Manuscripts, Relating to English Affairs, Existing in the Archives and Collections of Venice*, vol. 10, p. 66; Steele 1967, vol. 1, p. 109.

45 As was noted in the last chapter, the view in the English admiralty was that acquisitions could only be made up to the date of the queen's death, when the letters of marque or reprisal issued under her authority lost validity (*Documents Relating to Law and Custom of the Sea*, vol. 1, pp. 330–1).

46 *Political Works of James I*, pp. 315 and 333; *Proclamation against Excesse of Lavish and Licentious Speech of Matters of State*; *Letters of King James VI and I*, p. 374; *Poems of James VI of Scotland*, vol. 2, pp. 182–93; *Stuart Royal Proclamations*, vol. 1, pp. 495–6 and 519–21; *Letters of John Chamberlain*, vol. 2, p. 331; Thomas Fuller, *Church History of Britain*, pt 2, p. 109; Steele 1967, vol. 1, pp. 153 and 155.

47 Ferguson 1977, p. 105; Levack 1987, pp. 217–18; Goodare 2004, pp. 92–3. However, Scots did serve on the king's council in England (Goodare 2004, pp. 109–10), and they also numbered among the ambassadors sent abroad to represent English interests (Murdoch 2001, pp. 26–31).

48 Smuts 2002, pp. 374–5; Thrush 2004, pp. 301–2; Croft 2006, p. 140.

49 *Calendar of State Papers, Domestic Series, of the Reign of James I*, vol. 1, p. 12; Steele 1967, vol. 1, p. 109.

respected if made before 24 April.[50] As far as James was concerned, maritime raiding had become illegal not because Elizabeth's licences had lost validity on her death, while the war with Spain continued, but because the war with Spain had ended on her death, after which continued raiding could only have been excused by the plausible ignorance of mariners who were already at sea.

It is well known that the king's endeavour to form a closer union between his British realms was largely abandoned after 1607, but one way in which he persisted was in requiring vessels sailing from ports anywhere in Britain to fly a similar flag, which came to be known after him as the 'Union Jack'.[51] While unpopular on both sides of the border, the requirement was adhered to until the end of James' reign.[52] The flag was always flown by the publicly owned ships he had inherited on becoming king of England, and also by the additional ships occasionally hired in Scotland to supplement the force conceived of as a single royal navy.[53] The privy council in Edinburgh received notice of the king's intention 'to augment his heynes navy by building of some schippis heir', although timber felled for the purpose was instead sent to England, which remained the centre of naval activity.[54] When the Scottish council advised the king that 'some pirottis and villanes, commoun enemeyis to all lauchfull subjectis and trafficquairis, wer upoun the coastis of his mejesteis kingdome', two of his ships were sent north with instructions to capture the pirates and 'carry thame to the porte nixt adjacent to that pairt of the sea whair thay salbe apprehendit, and thair to caus thame be hangit without mercy or favoure'.[55] The council provided the English captains with pilots familiar with the east coast of Scotland, and contributed towards the costs of

50 *Foedera, conventiones, litterae et cuiuscunque generis acta publica*, vol. 16, p. 587; *Corps universel diplomatique du droit des gens*, vol. 5(1), p. 626; *Articles of Peace, Entercourse and Commerce Concluded in the Names of Kings James and Philip, and Albertus and Isabella*, sigg. B1v-2r. The June proclamation receives due attention in Allen 2000, p. 111, where the peace negotiations are examined from the Spanish point of view.

51 Galloway 1986, pp. 82–4; Wormald 1996, pp. 154–5; Nicholls 1999, pp. 150–1.

52 *Calendar of State Papers, Domestic Series, of the Reign of James I*, vol. 5, p. 425; *Stuart Royal Proclamations*, vol. 1, pp. 135–6; *Foedera, conventiones, litterae et cuiuscunque generis acta publica*, vol. 16, p. 645; *Register of the Privy Council of Scotland*, vol. 7, pp. 498–9; *Historical Works of Sir James Balfour*, vol. 2, p. 13; *Calendar of the Manuscripts of the Most Honourable the Marquess of Salisbury*, vol. 19, p. 72.

53 Goodare 1999, pp. 165–6; Murdoch 2010, pp. 127–8; Helling 2016, pp. 42–3.

54 *Register of the Privy Council of Scotland*, vol. 7, pp. 775–6, and vol. 8, pp. 234 and 277–8. Rodger 1997, p. 347, rightly remarks that the royal navy remained essentially the English navy.

55 *Register of the Privy Council of Scotland*, vol. 10, pp. 235–6.

the expedition.[56] As the pirates, again denounced as 'commoun enemyis to all lauchfull trafficquaris', withdrew towards the northern isles, the council further commissioned the earl of Caithness to equip ships 'to pas, searche, seik, follow, persew and tak the saidis pirottis quhairevir thay may be apprehendit, be sea or land, within the boundis of the cuntrey of Caithnes or on the sea and coast betwix Peterheade and Orknay', and at least one ship was taken by one of his servants.[57] Assistance had been received in the capture by a Dutch captain, sent out to protect 'the Flemes fleitt at the fischeing' off Shetland, and he too was authorised 'to searche, seik, tak and apprehend the saidis pyrattis, quhairevir or in quhat pairt soevir within the seyes or harboreis of the said cuntrey thay salhappin to convene with thame'.[58] By this stage the king's own ships had returned to England.

As well as illustrating the licensing of private vessels to compensate for the lack of naval forces in Scotland, the episode just outlined also indicates that public authorisation was considered appropriate before ships set off in pursuit of pirates.[59] As was seen in the last chapter, the irony was that the increasing identification of pirates as the common enemies of everyone involved in maritime commerce was bound up with increasing uncertainty about the legitimacy of assaulting them without prior authorisation. A few years earlier, when pirates raiding on the west coast had made their way towards the northern isles, it was remarked that 'this is a mater whiche heichlie concernis his majesteis service, and wherin his majestie is very far contempnit, in so far as ony theif or pyrott, especialie his majesteis awne subjectis, dar presome in his heynes awne watteris to committ suche robrie and spoyll upoun lauchfull subjectis'.[60] If committed around the coasts of Scotland, piracy was viewed not only as a crime against humanity but also as a personal affront to the monarch, yet there were limits to how far James could assume responsibility for its prevention. First the burgh authorities in Ayr were licensed to send out ships in pursuit of the pirates and then, after the pirates started to work their way down the

56 *Naval Tracts of Sir William Monson*, vol. 3, pp. 56–8; *Historical Works of Sir James Balfour*, vol. 2, p. 52; *Register of the Privy Council of Scotland*, vol. 10, pp. 240 and 611–12; *Letters and State Papers during the Reign of King James the Sixth*, p. 219.

57 *Register of the Privy Council of Scotland*, vol. 10, pp. 240–1 and 348.

58 *Ancient Criminal Trials in Scotland*, vol. 3(1), pp. 109–11; *Register of the Privy Council of Scotland*, vol. 10, pp. 842–3.

59 Clear evidence that it was considered essential, for instance in the form of condemnation of an expedition mounted without approval, has not been found, and a case of retrospective approval will be mentioned shortly.

60 *Register of the Privy Council of Scotland*, vol. 8, pp. 627–8. The pirates in question were 'his majesteis awne subjectis', but as king of England rather than Scotland.

east coast, the authorities in Edinburgh received a similar commission.[61] Three ships were urgently dispatched from Leith, 'your majesties awne schip at that tyme not being arryved heir', which suggests that naval assistance had been promised.[62] It was argued that the other coastal burghs should help defray the costs of the two expeditions, and eventually, after many of the pirates had been captured and their ships had been sold, provision was made for some of the proceeds of the sales to be transferred to the captors.[63] One of the ships had actually been taken on the initiative of an individual residing in Lewis, who had been in no position to obtain a licence beforehand since he had himself been put to the horn for previous 'rebellioun and disobedience', but it was decided that his 'very goode service unto his majestie and to the haill cuntrey' merited a general pardon.[64] On this and later occasions pirates were yet again described as 'profest and avowit enemeyis to all laughfull subjectis' or 'professed enemyis to all lawfull trafficquairis by sea'.[65] When it was proposed in England that the Scots ought to assist in financing an operation planned against pirates from North Africa, they too were labelled 'enemies of mankinde'.[66] In contrast, when a lawyer in Edinburgh sent James a learned treatise he had written, in which he defended the legitimacy of imposing taxes on shipping 'so that each prince's seas might be swept clean of pirates', he not only refrained from describing pirates as enemies but pointed out that at one time piracy had been regarded as an acceptable mode of life.[67]

When another lawyer dealt with maritime law in a book he was working on during the early seventeenth century, he summarised the provisions on prize

61 *Ayr Burgh Accounts*, pp. 241 and 243; *Register of the Privy Council of Scotland*, vol. 8, pp. 479–81; *Extracts from the Records of the Burgh of Edinburgh*, 2nd ser., vol. 2, p. 63.

62 *Register of the Privy Council of Scotland*, vol. 9, pp. 567–8; *Letters and State Papers during the Reign of King James the Sixth*, pp. 193–6.

63 *Register of the Privy Council of Scotland*, vol. 9, pp. 1, 18–19 and 33; *Records of the Convention of the Royal Burghs of Scotland*, vol. 2, pp. 305–6; *Extracts from the Records of the Burgh of Edinburgh*, 2nd ser., vol. 2, pp. 64–5, 67 and 342–9; *Ancient Criminal Trials in Scotland*, vol. 3(1), pp. 102–8; *Historical Works of Sir James Balfour*, vol. 2, p. 35; Calderwood, *History of the Kirk of Scotland*, vol. 7, p. 118. The rights of the admiral in relation to piracy remained uncertain (*Register of the Privy Council of Scotland*, vol. 14, p. 617). NLS, Adv. MS 6.2.1, contains 'ane abbreviat of the registers of the high court of admiralty' made before a volume beginning in 1613 was lost, but only commercial cases are mentioned between then and the end of James' reign, at ff. 20–8.

64 *Register of the Privy Council of Scotland*, vol. 9, pp. 62–3 and 395–6.

65 *Register of the Privy Council of Scotland*, vol. 12, p. 88, and vol. 13, p. 177, and see too vol. 9, pp. 395–6, 400, 546–7 and 580–1.

66 *Acts of the Privy Council of England*, vol. 35, pp. 181–2.

67 Thomas Craig, *Jus feudale tribus libris comprehensum*, pp. 14–17 and 470–1; Dodd 2016, pp. 149–50.

taking found in the French legislation, 'to knaw howe they aggrie with the sea lawes of the kingdom of Scotland'.[68] The opportunity to confirm their relevance never arose before James died in 1625 since he managed to avoid engagement in a declared war with any other nation, but the resumption of open hostilities between Spain and the United Provinces in 1621 did prompt further reflection on the law of prize acquisition.[69] It has been mentioned that as king of Scotland James had been inclined to view the Dutch as rebels against the lawful suzerainty of the king of Spain, yet as king of England he was drawn into more friendly relations with a nation that remained at war after Elizabeth's death.[70] When a truce was agreed at Antwerp in 1609, the king of Spain was forced to recognise the *de facto* independence of the United Provinces, and James was one of several foreign rulers who then recognised their *de iure* independence by sending permanent ambassadors to The Hague.[71] On the expiry of the truce in 1621, shipowners in Scotland who had bought vessels of a typically Dutch design sought certificates of ownership from their government, to protect them against seizures by raiders licensed by the rulers of Spain or the southern Netherlands.[72] In 1622 the resumed conflict was brought home to the Scots by the arrival of two vessels from Dunkirk at Leith and Aberdeen, where they were immediately blockaded by Dutch vessels.[73] The captains of the vessels were informed that while they were in Scottish waters they were obliged 'to observe his majesteis peace', which they promised to do.[74] At Aberdeen the blockade was conducted in a fairly orderly fashion, partly because the Dutch captains were offered membership of the burgh, which involved them in swearing an oath to be 'leall and trew to our most gratious soverane'.[75] In

68 *Habakkuk Bisset's Rolment of Courtis*, vol. 2, pp. 216 and 220–7.

69 Geyl 2001, pp. 372–3; Price 2000, pp. 44–5; Prak 2005, p. 37.

70 There was some awareness in Scotland of the legal implications of the continuing conflict in the Netherlands. For instance, the admiralty court in London found that a ship seized from an English owner by a Dunkirker had become the property of a Scottish buyer since it had been adjudged to the captor (NAK, HCA3/27, ff. 226v-7r, 239v, 246r, 291r and 314v, and HCA24/73, f. 179; Steckley 2020, p. 265).

71 Parker 1980, pp. 134–5; Israel 1998, pp. 405–6; Newton 2005, p. 51.

72 *Register of the Privy Council of Scotland*, vol. 13, pp. 62, 65 and 586–7; *Extracts from the Records of the Burgh of Edinburgh*, 2nd ser., vol. 2, p. 231. On the revival of raiding out of Dunkirk see Stradling 1980.

73 Gardiner 1883–4, vol. 5, pp. 79–88; Irons 1898, vol. 2, pp. 46–8; Mowat 2003, pp. 165–7.

74 *Register of the Privy Council of Scotland*, vol. 12, pp. 736–7, 739, 747 and 756, and vol. 13, pp. 26 and 33–4; *State Papers and Miscellaneous Correspondence of Thomas, Earl of Melrose*, vol. 2, pp. 457–8; *Calendar of State Papers, Domestic Series, of the Reign of James I*, vol. 3, p. 567; Calderwood, *History of the Kirk of Scotland*, vol. 7, pp. 572–3.

75 *Extracts from the Council Registers of the Burgh of Aberdeen*, vol. 2, pp. 387–8; *Register of the Privy Council of Scotland*, vol. 13, pp. 791–2; ACA, CA1/1/50, pp. 702–3.

Leith the less ingenious efforts of the Edinburgh authorities failed to prevent several violent encounters during the following months.[76] Eventually, in 1623, naval vessels were sent north to escort the Dunkirk vessels out of the king's waters.[77] They were followed at a distance by the Dutch vessels, which caused additional outrage by attacking the Dunkirk vessels before they had reached the open seas.[78] It is the legal questions that arose before the ports of Leith and Aberdeen were cleared of the belligerents that are of particular interest for present purposes.

In the summer of 1622 the privy council in Scotland had informed the king of their receipt of a petition from the captain of the Dutch vessel at Leith, requesting the release of prisoners held on the Dunkirk vessel there, 'conforme to the custome of nationis, alledgeit to be universallie observit in the lyke caise'.[79] As some of the Dutch prisoners were said to be seriously ill, the councillors had felt obliged by 'Christiane cheritie and humanitie' to send a physician aboard, but they had declined to take further action until they received the king's advice, 'becaus the mater wes a novaltie, quhairof the lyke had not occurrit in this kingdome'. Nevertheless, they had in the meantime invited the captains of the two vessels to present 'suche informatioun and probatioun anent the custome of nationis as the one will use for the laughfull detentioun of the prisonnaris, and quhairby the other will laughfullie clame their libertie'. The captain of the Dunkirk vessel claimed to have received authorisation from the king of Spain to raid enemy shipping, and to have been directed in particular to take prisoners and hold them to ransom.[80] There was of course nothing in the least novel about the practice referred to, and by this time it was well known in Scotland that it had become customary for maritime raiding to be licensed in open but undeclared wars. What had not been encountered

76 *Register of the Privy Council of Scotland*, vol. 13, pp. 36, 64, 97, 100–1, 117–18, 150, 155, 169–70, 178, 181, 211–13, 218–19, 298, 322, 376–8, 747–8 and 813–15; *Extracts from the Records of the Burgh of Edinburgh*, 2nd ser., vol. 2, pp. 242–3; *State Papers and Miscellaneous Correspondence of Thomas, Earl of Melrose*, vol. 2, pp. 512–18, 522–4, 533–5, 540–1 and 548–9; NRS, PC10/13A, ff. 22 and 88–9; ECA, SL1/1/13, pp. 426–7.

77 *Calendar of State Papers, Domestic Series, of the Reign of James I*, vol. 3, pp. 580, 587, 592–3, 598–9, 605–6, 610–12, 614–18, 620–1 and 624, and vol. 4, pp. 13, 15–16, 19–20, 26, 29–31 and 39; *Acts of the Privy Council of England*, vol. 39, p. 61.

78 *Calendar of State Papers, Domestic Series, of the Reign of James I*, vol. 4, pp. 43 and 46; *Acts of the Privy Council of England*, vol. 39, pp. 76–7; Calderwood, *History of the Kirk of Scotland*, vol. 7, pp. 577–8.

79 *State Papers and Miscellaneous Correspondence of Thomas, Earl of Melrose*, vol. 2, pp. 468–9.

80 *State Papers and Miscellaneous Correspondence of Thomas, Earl of Melrose*, vol. 2, pp. 488–90 and 497–500.

in Scotland before was the suggestion that prisoners taken into a neutral port must be released there. Furthermore, the expectation that the disagreement between the two captains would be resolved in accordance with 'the custome of nationis' may also have surprised the council. In 1607, in a final address to his English subjects about his desire for a closer union between his British realms, James had observed that while he was still learning about their common law, he was better acquainted with the civil law, 'which in the point of the conjunction of nations should beare a great sway, it being the law of nations', and in addressing the same audience two years later he had commented again that the civil law was 'in a maner *lex gentium*, and maintaineth intercourse with all forreine nations'.[81] The common lawyers present would not at the time have disagreed with him.[82] As late as 1617, when an official dispatched to demand payments from Dutch mariners fishing in Scottish waters was apprehended by the captain of a protection vessel and taken back to the Netherlands, it was the civil lawyers in England who were asked to advise on the applicable 'law of nations'.[83] Yet by 1622 it was being affirmed by a Dutch captain, and apparently accepted by his Flemish adversary, that the law of nations should be equated with the custom of nations. The question raised was never answered, for it became entangled with a broader question about the legality of blockading enemy vessels in neutral ports.

Blockading had been experienced in England between the restoration of friendship with Spain by the Treaty of London in 1604 and the suspension of hostilities between Spain and the United Provinces by the Treaty of Antwerp in 1609.[84] In the former treaty provision had been made for the free admission of foreign vessels to English ports.[85] Realising that difficulties were likely to

81 *Political Works of James I*, pp. 299 and 310.

82 Pawlisch 1985, pp. 168–70; Burgess 1992, pp. 126–30; MacMillan 2006, pp. 25–8.

83 *Register of the Privy Council of Scotland*, vol. 11, pp. 605–9; *Acts of the Privy Council of England*, vol. 35, pp. 368–9 and 402–3, and vol. 36, pp. 115 and 127; *Letters from and to Sir Dudley Carleton*, pp. 156–9, 164–5, 169–73, 175–9, 186–8, 193, 198, 200, 217, 232, 240–1 and 257–8; *Dudley Carleton to John Chamberlain*, p. 245.

84 Consistently with James' belief in the termination of Elizabeth's war at her death, attempts had been made to preserve the neutrality of his waters even before the Treaty of London was signed (*Calendar of the Manuscripts of the Most Honourable the Marquess of Salisbury*, vol. 15, p. 95; Winwood, *Memorials of Affairs of State in the Reigns of Queen Elizabeth and King James I*, vol. 2, p. 7; *Calendar of State Papers, Domestic Series, of the Reign of James I*, vol. 1, p. 41).

85 *Foedera, conventiones, litterae et cuiuscunque generis acta publica*, vol. 16, p. 588; *Corps universel diplomatique du droit des gens*, vol. 5(1), pp. 626–7; *Articles of Peace, Entercourse and Commerce Concluded in the Names of Kings James and Philip, and Albertus and Isabella*, sigg. C1v-2.

arise 'during the continuance of the warre betweene the king of Spaine and the archdukes, on the one side, and the United Provinces of the Low Countreys, on the other side', James had issued instructions in 1605 to regulate the conduct of foreign visitors.[86] Violence was not to be tolerated in or around his ports, armed ships were not to be allowed 'to hover and hang about the skirts of our ports', and if a ship 'of the one side' were to arrive at a port behind a ship 'of the other side', the first to arrive was to be 'suffered to depart a tyde or two before the other which came in last'. Difficulties did indeed arise in implementing these regulations, which were referred to at the time as 'his majesties law' or 'the laws of his kingdom', although they were also believed to be consistent with 'the rules of amity' or 'the laws of neutrality'.[87] When the privy council in Scotland sought further advice in 1622 on the handling of the blockades at Leith and Aberdeen, it was the rule that the first ship to enter a port must be permitted two tides to escape that James wanted them to implement, suggesting – unsuccessfully as it turned out – that they should negotiate the release of the Dutch prisoners without ransom as an inducement to the Dutch captains to comply.[88] It may have been as a further inducement that he identified his rule as 'the custome of nationis, universallie observit throwout all the pairtis of Europe', and as 'this allowabill custome of nationis, so weill groundit upoun infallible and goode ressonis of pollicie and state'.[89] A version of his rule did come to be recognised as part of the new *ius gentium*, but to know whether it was consciously regarded as part of a different approach to the regulation of international relations it will be necessary to examine more closely the treatment of maritime raiding during James' English reign.[90] It was certainly from

86 *Proclamation for Revocation of Mariners from Forreine Services*; *Stuart Royal Proclamations*, vol. 1, pp. 108–11; *Documents Relating to Law and Custom of the Sea*, vol. 1, pp. 354–8; Steele 1910, vol. 1, p. 117; Fulton 1911, pp. 750–3.

87 *Calendar of the Manuscripts of the Most Honourable the Marquess of Salisbury*, vol. 17, pp. 44, 227–8, 243, 252–7, 294–5, 302, 312–13, 321–2, 335–6, 420 and 602, and vol. 18, pp. 111–12, 127–8, 145–6, 148–52, 160 and 165–7; *Letters of John Chamberlain*, vol. 1, pp. 202–3 and 242; Winwood, *Memorials of Affairs of State*, vol. 2, pp. 78–84, 87–9, 94–5, 99, 104, 107 and 111; *Documents Relating to Law and Custom of the Sea*, vol. 1, pp. 351–3 and 362–5; *Report on the Manuscripts of the Duke of Buccleuch and Queensberry*, vol. 1, p. 60.

88 *Register of the Privy Council of Scotland*, vol. 12, p. 773, and vol. 13, pp. 134–6 and 205–6; *Calendar of State Papers, Domestic Series, of the Reign of James I*, vol. 3, pp. 530, 534 and 561; *Documents Relating to Law and Custom of the Sea*, vol. 1, pp. 402–4; NRS, PC10/13A, f. 72. It was remarked that order might have been given for the release of the Dutch prisoners had the Dutch captain at Leith not behaved so badly.

89 *Register of the Privy Council of Scotland*, vol. 13, pp. 135–6; NRS, PC10/13A, f. 85.

90 Verzijl 1979, pp. 58–60; Neff 2000, pp. 13–14; Schnakenbourg 2013, pp. 66–7.

England that the Scots sought instruction in the regulation of maritime conflict in the early 1620s.

2 Licensed Raiding in Jacobean England

The Treaty of London stipulated that its signatories must 'take care that their subjects abstain from all force and injury and revoke all commissions and letters, whether of reprisal or marque or of any other kind or condition, containing authorisation to take prizes'.[91] A similar clause was commonly included in articles of amity, and whatever doubts had arisen during Elizabeth's reign about the nature of the licences used to authorise prize taking, steps had already been taken, more than a year before the treaty was signed in August 1604, to put a stop to maritime raiding out of England, on the basis of a belief either that the queen's licences had been valid only during her lifetime or (as James himself believed) that the violence licensed had become illegal when the queen's death terminated her war with the king of Spain.[92] The problem that was believed to have arisen during the first year of the new king's reign was that mariners who had previously plundered shipping under licences obtained from their own queen were instead seeking licences from foreign rulers, which past experience suggested would lead to an increase in piracy around the coasts of Britain.[93] In March 1605 a proclamation was issued recalling English mariners from service elsewhere.[94] 'It hath appeared unto us', James declared, 'that many mariners and seafaring men of this realme, having gotten a custome and habite in the time of warre to make profite by spoile, doe leave their ordinary and honest vocation and trading of merchantly voyages, whereby they might both reape convenient maintenance and be serviceable to their countrey, and doe betake themselves to the service of divers forreine states'. As England was enjoying a period of 'universall peace', and as foreign

91 *Foedera, conventiones, litterae et cuiuscunque generis acta publica*, vol. 16, p. 587; *Corps universel diplomatique du droit des gens*, vol. 5(1), p. 626; *Articles of Peace, Entercourse and Commerce Concluded in the Names of Kings James and Philip, and Albertus and Isabella*, sig. B3.

92 Readers who have skipped over the previous section have missed a fuller discussion of this point.

93 *Calendar of the Manuscripts of the Most Honourable the Marquess of Salisbury*, vol. 16, p. 258.

94 *Proclamation for Revocation of Mariners from Forreine Services*; *Stuart Royal Proclamations*, vol. 1, pp. 108–11; *Documents Relating to Law and Custom of the Sea*, vol. 1, pp. 354–8; Steele 1910, vol. 1, p. 117; Fulton 1911, pp. 750–3.

licences were sometimes being used 'but for collour' of piracy, the king's subjects were ordered to return home and resume employment in maritime commerce, 'upon such paines and punishments as by the lawes of our realme may be inflicted upon them'. In future mariners were not to 'take letters of marke or reprisall, nor serve under any that hath such letters of marke or reprisall, from any forreine prince or state whatsoever, nor otherwise employ themselves in any warlike services of any forraine state upon the sea, without speciall license obtained from our selfe or from our high admirall'. In July 1605 a second proclamation was issued, reinforcing the ban on foreign service with a ban on aiding and abetting those who remained in foreign service.[95]

Another clause of the Treaty of London stipulated that 'if any dispute should be raised in connection with seizures and spoils in the kingdoms and dominions of one or other of the signatories by someone not subject to them, it must be remitted to a judge in the territory of that prince against whose subject or subjects action is taken'.[96] The new king's understanding was that the judge responsible for handling prize litigation in England sat in the admiralty court, in which the civil law was followed, although he also understood that the jurisdiction of the admiralty court was subject to the control of the common law courts.[97] The main mechanism of control, which was used aggressively in the early seventeenth century to appropriate a great deal of jurisdiction over commercial litigation for the court of common pleas, was the writ of prohibition.[98] While it was accepted that the admiralty judge ought to determine whether seizures had been lawfully made at sea (*super altum mare*), the common law judges also exploited the writ to deal with issues of ownership after prizes had been taken into ports and disposed of there or further inland.[99] Foreigners whose property had been seized at sea feared that the common law would expose them to more risk than the civil law of the insolvency of defenders,

95 *Calendar of the Manuscripts of the Most Honourable the Marquess of Salisbury*, vol. 17, pp. 211, 243 and 631; *Whereas the Kings Majestie Hath Alwayes Bene Ready to Imbrace and Cherish Such a Perfect Amitie and Friendship betweene Him and the King of Spaine*; *Stuart Royal Proclamations*, vol. 1, pp. 114–17; Steele 1910, vol. 1, pp. 117–18.

96 *Foedera, conventiones, litterae et cuiuscunque generis acta publica*, vol. 16, p. 591; *Corps universel diplomatique du droit des gens*, vol. 5(1), p. 628; *Articles of Peace, Entercourse and Commerce Concluded in the Names of Kings James and Philip, and Albertus and Isabella*, sig. E3r.

97 *Political Works of James I*, pp. 310–11. *Cf.* Christianson 1991, p. 77.

98 Prichard and Yale 1993, pp. lxxxix-xci; Levack 1973, pp. 72–81; Shavana 2015, pp. 52–8.

99 *Reports of that Learned Sir Henry Hobart*, pp. 107–9, 158–9 and 295–6; *Reports of Richard Brownlow and John Goldesborough*, pt 2, p. 29; Edward Coke, *Fourth Part of the Institutes of the Laws of England*, pp. 152–4. Examples of writs of prohibition can be found in *Hale and Fleetwood on Admiralty Jurisdiction*, pp. 287–91.

and would show more favour than the civil law to innocent purchasers of stolen goods.[100] Although the jurisdiction clause in the Treaty of London meant that actions raised against Spanish or Flemish defenders by Dutch claimants should be sent abroad for determination, the English courts still had cause to deal with prize cases arising from the continuing conflict between Spain, the southern Netherlands and the United Provinces. As early as the beginning of 1605 it was being asserted by Dutch mariners that while the king of England could regulate maritime raiding within his own waters by 'public edict', maritime raiding on the high seas was governed by 'the law of nations'.[101] But what was this law? Did they mean the civil law, and the shared standards developed in accordance with its principles, or were they referring to a new type of law, emerging from the confusion of the confessional conflicts in the past four decades? If the latter, how much understanding of the new law was there in England? Some guidance may initially be drawn from a collection of legal opinions compiled by Albericus Gentilis, after he was appointed to represent the interests of Spanish litigants in England.[102] The collection was published following Gentilis' death in 1608, but manuscript evidence tends to confirm that it provides a broadly reliable account of pleadings he presented on behalf of his clients during the last three years of his life.[103]

Many of the opinions published related to the seizure of a Portuguese vessel near the start of 1605.[104] While heading home with their prize the Dutch captors had taken shelter first at Weymouth and then off the Downs, where they had been intercepted by an English naval vessel and diverted to London. Although the Spanish ambassador believed that the English authorities were bound by their king's treaty of friendship with Spain to release the prisoners held captive by the Dutch, and to restore the property seized to its original owners, Gentilis explained that the English authorities were equally bound by their king's friendship with the United Provinces to respect any rights the Dutch captors had acquired.[105] However, as far as the prisoners were concerned, he was able to point out that according to two texts in the *Digest* a Roman citizen captured in wartime would regain his earlier status (*postliminium*) as soon as he passed

100 Marsden 1910, p. 245; Steckley 2003, pp. 59–60; Baker 2003, pp. 738–9.

101 *Calendar of the Manuscripts of the Most Honourable the Marquess of Salisbury*, vol. 17, pp. 44–5.

102 *Hispanicae advocationis libri duo*, vol. 1, sigg. *2–5r, and vol. 2, pp. III–V.

103 Simmonds 1958 and 1959.

104 For an illuminating discussion of the case, drawing extensively on the manuscript evidence, see Wijffels 1992.

105 *Hispanicae advocationis libri duo*, vol. 1, pp. 21–2, and vol. 2, pp. 24–5, citing Ambrose, *De officiis*, 3.9.59.

the borders of either his own or a friendly country.[106] In response to the suggestion that *amici nostri* should be understood to signify 'our allies', as opposed to *amici communes* or neutral nations, Gentilis invoked the civilian rule of interpretation that 'where a text does not draw a distinction, there we ought not to draw a distinction either'.[107] As far as the property was concerned, he was able to point out that while civilian authors usually wrote about the occupiers of *res hostium* acquiring title immediately (*statim*, or in medieval Latin *incontinente*), one of his texts referred to captors returning within their own defences (*intra praesidia sua*).[108] In principle, he argued, the Dutch could not have secured effective control of their prize, and thus have genuinely occupied it, until they had negotiated the hazardous passage of Dunkirk, Nieuwpoort and Ostend. He was aware of one civilian author who thought it might suffice for a prize to have been detained for a period of time, 'according to the varying practice of places and peoples', and that in England the common lawyers thought title would be acquired if a prize were held onto for a full day, as indeed was maintained in some other places too, including Spain.[109] Nevertheless, it seemed to Gentilis that any local custom requiring possession for a period of time could only be considered reasonable and applicable in a civil law court as an addition to the requirement that a prize must be carried home securely.[110] His arguments appear to have been well received in the admiralty court, which ordered the return of the ship and cargo to its original owners.[111]

For their part, the Dutch had protested against the diversion of their ship to London as an unlawful infringement of the freedom of navigation allowed

106 *Hispanicae advocationis libri duo*, vol. 1, pp. 1–4, and vol. 2, pp. 3–6, citing *Digest*, 49.15.5.1 and 49.15.19.3.

107 Portius Azo, *Brocardica sive generalia iuris*, pp. 216–17.

108 *Hispanicae advocationis libri duo*, vol. 1, pp. 5–11, and vol. 2, pp. 7–13, referring in particular to Angelus de Ubaldis, *Quaestio disputata: Renovata guerra*, col. 4; Ioannes Franciscus a Ripa, *Super Digesto novo, veteri et Codice commentaria*, f. 13r; Franciscus Accoltus, *Commentaria super titulo de acquirenda possessione*, col. 4 (ad D.41.2.1); Carolus Ruinus, *Responsa sive consilia*, vol. 5, f. 40 (n. 31, inc. 'Visa et bene intellecta facti serie, utrum dicendum'); Iason de Maino, *Commentaria in primam partem Digesti novi*, sig. A1v (ad D.41.2.1).

109 *Hispanicae advocationis libri duo*, vol. 1, pp. 12 and 97, and vol. 2, pp. 14 and 100–1; Angelus, *Quaestio disputata: Renovata guerra*, col. 5.

110 *Hispanicae advocationis libri duo*, vol. 1, pp. 11–14, and vol. 2, pp. 14–16.

111 *Documents Relating to Law and Custom of the Sea*, vol. 1, pp. 366–8. It could be that Gentilis' arguments for the release of the Portuguese prisoners were known to the Dutch mariners at Leith whose petition was discussed at the end of the last section, but if so it is significant that they were repackaged as components of the custom of nations, not the civil law.

to them by the law of nations. As was mentioned in the preceding chapter, the Roman jurists who maintained that *ius gentium* had replaced the natural *communitas* of all things with private ownership, also maintained that the sea was one thing that had remained a *res communis*.[112] It was not made clear whether the sea was common in the negative sense of belonging to nobody or in the positive sense of belonging to everybody, nor was a sharp distinction observed between *res communes* and *res publicae*, meaning things that belonged not to private individuals but to the public as a whole.[113] The early civil lawyers concluded that the word *publicae* was being used properly in relation to things shared by the people of Rome, and improperly in relation to things shared by all people, as if they formed a community comparable to Rome.[114] Strictly speaking, it was the 'use' of common things that was shared, which left open the possibility of some other sort of right being enjoyed at the same time more particularly.[115] Whereas, for instance, the use of the seashore was common to everyone, those who held the adjacent land might have a particular right 'quoad iurisdictionem'.[116] This realisation was of huge importance to the later civilians when it came to justifying the dominion claimed by the Venetians over the Adriatic Sea and by the Genoese over the Ligurian Sea, both of whom imposed taxes on mariners sailing there, and confiscated the ships and goods of any who refused to pay.[117] Attention was drawn by the doctors to the texts requiring governors to rid their provinces of brigands, bandits and pirates, and to others extending authority on land to adjacent islands.[118] Most agreed that while no one could have dominion over the sea in the sense of ownership (*proprietas*), dominion in the sense of authority to uphold law and order (*iurisdictio*) was both possible and sufficiently desirable to warrant the

112 *Institutes*, 2.1.pr.-1, and *Digest*, 1.8.2, 43.8.3.1 and 47.10.3.7.

113 *Institutes*, 2.1.2–6, and *Digest*, 1.8.1–6 and 10, 8.4.13.pr., 18.1.51, 39.2.24.pr., 41.1.14, 41.1.30.4, 41.1.50, 41.1.65.1, 41.3.45.pr., 43.8.1 and 4 and 50.19.112.

114 Petrus Placentinus, *Summa Institutionum sive elementorum*, pp. 18–19 (ad J.2.1); *Digestum vetus*, col. 74 (gl. 'Aut publicae' ad D.1.8.1); *Iustiniani imperatoris Institutionum libri quatuor Francisci Accursii glossis illustrati*, p. 141 (gl. 'Publica' ad J.2.1).

115 Odofredus de Denariis, *Lectura super Digesto*, vol. 1, ff. 24v-5r (ad D.1.8.2); *Summa Azonis*, cols 1084–5 (ad J.2.1); *Iustiniani imperatoris Institutionum libri quatuor Francisci Accursii glossis illustrati*, p. 141 (gl. 'Omnium' ad J.2.1).

116 *Iustiniani imperatoris Institutionum libri quatuor Francisci Accursii glossis illustrati*, p. 142 (gl. 'Et per hoc' ad J.2.1).

117 Baldus de Ubaldis, *In primam Digesti veteris partem commentaria*, f. 45r (ad D.1.8.1); Paulus de Castro, *Super Digesto veteri commentaria*, vol. 1, ff. 128v-9r (ad D.5.1.9); Angelus, *Lectura super secunda parte Digesti novi*, ff. 94v-5r (ad D.47.10.14).

118 *Digest*, 1.18.13, 5.1.9, 39.2.4.9, 41.1.56 and 65 and 50.16.99; *Code*, 11.13.1; *Liber extra*, 1.3.28.

imposition of taxes to pay for its exercise.[119] Gentilis' response to the Dutch protest against the interception of their prize was that they had entered the jurisdiction of the king of England, where they had been forcefully depriving other visitors of their liberty and possessions, contrary to the king's peace.[120] When the Dutch drew attention to a specific statement of the extent of the king's territorial waters, and claimed to have been intercepted outside the limits specified, Gentilis insisted that no such statement could diminish the wider jurisdiction recognised by the civilians, which was typically taken to reach as far as a hundred miles from the coastline.[121] Besides, the Dutch had been well within the king's waters, even as more narrowly defined, when they took shelter at Weymouth, and there too they had been able to retain their prize only by physically restraining the prisoners they kept on board. 'Let everyone enjoy the use of the sea', Gentilis remarked, 'but without violating the jurisdiction of another nation'.[122]

The jurisdiction of the English king was violated again in the summer of 1605, when a fleet of ships transporting troops from Portugal to Flanders was attacked by a Dutch fleet and chased into Dover, where the port authorities ordered their guns to be fired at the chasers, 'as by the laws of neutrality they were bound'.[123] The king's ministers not only confirmed that it would have been 'contrary to the rules of amity' to allow the attack to be continued inside his waters, but also pointed out that 'by this act of contempt his ordinances, which are sacred and published throughout the whole world, have been violated'.[124] While there was no doubt that those harmed in the harbour could

119 Bartolus de Sassoferrato, *Opera omnia*, vol. 5, ff. 112v-17; Baldus, *Consilia sive responsa*, vol. 2, f. 54r (n. 195, inc. 'Laudare vos et commendare ea quae dixistis'), and vol. 4, f. 15r (n. 54, inc. 'Quaeritur an Florentini vel Perusini vel similes qui conduxerunt'); Angelus, *Lectura super prima parte Digesti veteris*, f. 126r (ad D.5.1.9); Felinus Sandeus, *Singularis ac perutilis lectura super titulo de rescriptis*, sigg. O5v-6r; Bartolomeus Caepolla, *Tractatus de servitutibus, tam urbanorum quam rusticorum praediorum*, pp. 662–9.

120 *Hispanicae advocationis libri duo*, vol. 1, pp. 22–4 and 32–7, and vol. 2, pp. 25–6 and 35–9.

121 Steele 1910, vol. 1, p. 117; Fulton 1911, pp. 753–4.

122 *Hispanicae advocationis libri duo*, vol. 1, p. 37, and vol. 2, p. 38.

123 *Calendar of the Manuscripts of the Most Honourable the Marquess of Salisbury*, vol. 17, pp. 252–6, 267, 294–5 and 302.

124 Winwood, *Memorials of Affairs of State*, vol. 2, pp. 78–84, 87–9, 94–5, 99, 104, 107 and 111; *Calendar of the Manuscripts of the Most Honourable the Marquess of Salisbury*, vol. 17, pp. 312–14, 321–2, 335–6 and 420. The 'ordinances' referred to, which were outlined at the end of the first section of this chapter, were contained within the proclamation recalling mariners from foreign service discussed at the start of this section. The proclamation had of course been designed for distribution in places like the Netherlands where mariners were seeking service.

have claimed redress under 'the ordinary rules of the law', what the Spanish ambassador sought was 'some extraordinary measure' that might enable the Portuguese fleet to complete its voyage.[125] Recognising that the request needed to be handled by the king's council (*concilium*), Gentilis still thought it appropriate to offer a legal opinion (*consilium*).[126] He considered it axiomatic that 'acts violating a territory and jurisdiction may not take place in harbours, for although the use of harbours is open to all, the abuse of them is not permitted to anyone'.[127] He said nothing directly about the king's ordinances, and instead explored the learned context in which he believed they ought to be interpreted. In the *Digest*, he observed, there were texts making it clear that no one was permitted to force his way into another person's home, even for the lawful purpose of summoning him to appear in court, 'since the home should be for each person his safest refuge and shelter'.[128] The doctors of civil law had deduced from this not only that it would also be unlawful to lie in wait for someone outside his home, but also that those unlawfully deprived of their liberty should be released and given a chance to slip away.[129] Gentilis found their reasoning reminscent of an episode recounted by Livy and Appian, in which a Roman fleet had been followed by a Carthaginian fleet into a neutral port, where the two commanders had refrained from acts of hostility against each other, and where the Carthaginians had been held back long enough to enable the Romans to escape.[130] Gentilis had also heard of a previous occasion when a French ship had been pursued up the Thames by a Dutch ship, which had then been held back for a tide to enable the French ship to escape.[131] He concluded that it would be legitimate for the English government to prevent the Dutch fleet from further obstructing the completion of the Portuguese fleet's voyage, although he also recognised that whether it would be politic or practicable was another matter. If the civil lawyers appreciated that 'many things are licit

125 *Naval Tracts of Sir William Monson*, vol. 3, pp. 16–19.

126 *Hispanicae advocationis libri duo*, vol. 1, pp. 61–5, and vol. 2, pp. 65–7.

127 In the Roman sources listed at n. 112 above, ports were a standard example of *res publicae*, the use of which was said to be 'omnibus commune'.

128 *Digest*, 2.4.18, 47.10.23 and 50.17.103.

129 Tobias Nonius, *Consilia seu responsa*, f. 193v (n. 108, inc. 'Viso instrumento pacis, ac diligenter pro tenui facultate mea'); Hieronymus Schurpsius, *Consiliorum seu responsorum iuris centuria secunda*, p. 304 (n. 57, inc. 'Casus talis est: princeps N. unum ex vasallis ex praecessore investitum'); Ludovicus Romanus, *Lectura aurea et mirabilis in primam Digesti veteris partem*, f. 23v (ad D.2.4.8); Sandeus, *Commentaria in Decretalium libros quinque*, col. 1015 (ad X 2.24.4).

130 Livy, *Ab urbe condita*, 28.17.10–18.12; Appian, *Roman History*, 6.6.29–30.

131 This may have been the incident mentioned in Simmonds 1958, pp. 15–16, but since the reference provided there makes no sense it is hard to be sure.

which are not honourable', the canon lawyers appreciated that 'many things are licit which are not expedient'.[132]

Another 'edict' issued by the king of England was dealt with more directly elsewhere in Gentilis' collection.[133] In the proclamation issued in July 1605 James had warned that he was not prepared to tolerate any 'fraudulent course taken, in hope colourably to avoid the true construction of his just and necessarie ordinances'.[134] Having in a previous proclamation declared 'pyrates and rovers upon the seas to be out of his protection', he had warned in particular that he would not countenance raiding by vessels manned mostly by his subjects on the pretence that they were serving under 'captaines and commaunders belonging to some forreine prince or state, which are now or may be in termes of hostility with any of his majesties friends', and that he would 'make absolute stay of any such shippes and persons which shalbe so brought into his portes or harboroughs'.[135] When a Spanish ship was seized by a vessel 'manned by Britons alone' while operating as part of a Dutch fleet, two lines of argument were pursued against adhering to the terms of the king's proclamation.[136] First, it was argued that since the conventional law of arms allowed any combatants who assisted in a seizure to claim a share of the prize, at least part of the Spanish ship and its cargo ought to be adjudged to the commanders of the Dutch fleet, which had provided protection to the British vessel.[137] Secondly, it was argued that since the British vessel had been a component of the Dutch fleet, the sailors on board had formed a minority among those involved in the venture, in accordance with civil and canon law sources on the treatment of things such as legions and congregations as single entities.[138] Gentilis advanced three arguments to the contrary. In the first place, he pointed out that other civil law sources cautioned against reading legislation in a way that

132 *Digest*, 50.17.197; *Decretum*, C. 28 q. 1 cc. 8–9.

133 *Hispanicae advocationis libri duo*, vol. 1, pp. 44–7, and vol. 2, pp. 47–9.

134 Cited in n. 95 above. The editor of the collection mistakenly identified this as an edict issued by the king of Spain, which made a nonsense of the arguments that followed.

135 The proclamation on piracy will be returned to below.

136 The consistent use of the word *Britanni* suggests that some of the mariners may have been Scots. Although Gentilis had written in support of a closer union of James' realms in his *Regales disputationes tres*, pt 2, he did not normally use the word in his pleadings.

137 Angelus, *Quaestio disputata: Renovata guerra*, cols 7–9; Bartolomeus de Saliceto, *Opera omnia*, vol. 4, cols 738–40 (ad C.8.50.12); Baltasar de Ayala, *De iure et officiis*, vol. 1, f. 37r, and vol. 2, pp. 37–8.

138 *Digest*, 5.1.76; Hostiensis, *Lectura in quinque Decretalium Gregorianarum libros*, vol. 2, f. 172v (ad X 3.41.1).

would defeat its purpose (*fraus legis*).[139] In the second place, he drew attention to the basic principle of the civil law that no one could transfer to anyone else a better title to a thing than he had himself, reasoning that the Dutch commanders could have no right to a share of the prize when it was impossible for the British sailors to have acquired title to it by themselves.[140] In the third place, he reverted to his reasoning in relation to the Portuguese vessel diverted to London, arguing that the Dutch fleet could not have acquired title to the prize until it was brought safely within their defences, as another civil law source appeared to require.

Although several other opinions included in Gentilis' collection are also of interest for present purposes, enough ground has already been covered to give a sense of his approach to the analysis of the prize cases raised in England during the first few years of James I's reign. It seems clear that he continued to handle legal problems in the way he had been taught to as a student in Italy, albeit with increased attention paid to literary, historical and philosophical sources.[141] At other places in his collection he wrote about 'the civil law, which it seems can also be called the law of nations today and has a common bearing on all Christian nations', and about the submission of everyone in Europe 'to the civil law, especially in these nautical causes, as if to some sort of law of nations'.[142] In resisting a proposal to seek assistance from the common lawyers in determining the dispute over the Portuguese vessel taken to London, he emphasised that his concern was with the relationship between the *ius Anglicum commune* and the *ius Anglicum civile*.[143] 'I do not call the one English and the other Roman', he explained, 'for in a sovereign realm there is no law other than that of the realm itself'.[144] It was because the civil law had been 'commonly received in the west' that it had come to serve as a kind of *ius gentium*, guiding the interpretation of particular rules in particular places, and suggesting solutions to problems left unresolved by those rules. In relation to the regulation of maritime raiding, it is notable that Gentilis scarcely ever mentioned the letters of marque issued to the Dutch captains, and never

139 Petrus Corneus, *Consilia sive responsa*, vol. 3, ff. 53v-4r (n. 29, inc. 'In praesenti consultatione utrum prima fronte'); Petrus de Ancharanus, *Consilia sive iuris responsa*, ff. 6v-7r (n. 11, inc. 'Factum super quo petitur consilium tale est: sub protectione'); Raphael Fulgosius, *In Iustiniani Codicem commentaria*, vol. 1, ff. 26v-7r (ad C.1.14.5).

140 *Digest*, 50.17.54.

141 For a more expert assessment see Wijffels 2011, pp. 47–8.

142 *Hispanicae advocationis libri duo*, vol. 1, pp. 81–3 and 99, and vol. 2, pp. 87–8 and 102.

143 *Calendar of State Papers, Domestic Series, of the Reign of James I*, vol. 1, p. 216; *Documents Relating to Law and Custom of the Sea*, vol. 1, pp. 360–1.

144 *Hispanicae advocationis libri duo*, vol. 1, p. 95, and vol. 2, p. 99.

mentioned the need for formal adjudication of their prizes, instead reasoning as if they were participating in a declared war.[145] At one place he did address the question, put to him privately by another lawyer, 'whether a man born in Holland, when his father had afterwards been naturalised here, should be viewed in effect as a subject here and unable to protect himself with the Dutchmen's letters of marque'.[146] Quite apart from the possibility of inheriting citizenship, he answered, it was enough for the man to be treated as the king of England's subject for him to be domiciled in England.[147] Another argument has been taken to show that Gentilis disapproved of the new style of maritime raiding.[148] In responding to the Dutch protest against the obstruction of their freedom of navigation, he commented that while the captain who seized the Portuguese vessel was 'of course their Dutch enemy', he was also 'an unworthy belligerent, for he was engaged in banditry under letters of marque more than war'.[149] Gentilis claimed to have demonstrated in his treatise on the law of arms that it was illegal to plunder 'harmless merchants', which was exactly what was happening in 'this war of predators'. In fact, what he had demonstrated in the part of the treatise cited was that the law of arms made it illegal to plunder merchants from neutral nations.[150] Far from supporting the argument he found it convenient to advance in just one of the pleadings he presented in court, his treatise actually defended the plundering of enemy merchants in wartime. Indeed, in the same passage he explicitly defend Elizabeth's extension of maritime raiding to merchants from neutral countries who were trading with her enemies.

A petition for letters of marque to be granted in England was considered in 1607, after merchants trading in Spain complained to parliament about losses wrongfully inflicted there remaining unredressed, even though 'his majesty

145 That he did not mention the need for adjudication is especially striking, given that it would have strengthened considerably his argument that the Dutch could not have completed title to the Portuguese or Spanish prizes they seized as soon as they seized them. He clearly did not believe that the seizures were made by way of reprisal.

146 *Hispanicae advocationis libri duo*, vol. 1, p. 73, and vol. 2, p. 78.

147 Although the civil lawyers did not generally regard domicile as a sufficient ground for citizenship (Bowsky 1967; Riesenberg 1969 and 1974; Kirshner 1974 and 1979; Gilli 2000), a more relaxed view tended to be taken in relation to liability to reprisals (Kirshner 1976, pp. 88–9).

148 Simmonds 1959, p. 541.

149 *Hispanicae advocationis libri duo*, vol. 1, p. 35, and vol. 2, p. 37.

150 *De iure belli*, vol. 1, pp. 427–41, and vol. 2, pp. 261–9.

hath also written two letters to the king of Spaine himself to request justice'.[151] It was the same assembly that was reminded by James, while the petition was being considered, that the civil law was 'the law of nations', and it was from the 'doctors of the law' that the House of Commons sought advice on the legitimacy of reprisals.[152] When further advice was sought from the House of Lords, however, the response was discouraging, not least because it was felt that the authorisation of reprisals, as a kind of limited war, was 'a secreate of policie', on which the king might receive guidance from his privy council but not from his parliament.[153] James was not prepared to go beyond reminding other rulers of their shared responsibility to maintain law and order on land and sea. When he had announced in 1603 that pirates were 'out of his protection', he had added, lifting a phrase from a proclamation issued by his predecessor in 1569, that they were 'lawfully to be by any person taken, punished and suppressed with extremitie'.[154] That phrase had not reappeared in any of Elizabeth's later proclamations on piracy, and nor is it found in several proclamations on the subject issued later in James' reign, where emphasis was instead placed on the duty of coastal authorities to apprehend and punish pirates and those who gave them succour.[155] The admiral was instructed on numerous occasions to dispatch naval ships or commission private vessels to pursue pirates raiding around the British Isles.[156] Vessels were sometimes fitted out by port authorities, though it was believed that to protect merchant shipping without a licence

151 *Calendar of State Papers, Domestic Series, of the Reign of James I*, vol. 1, pp. 349 and 357; *Journals of the House of Commons*, vol. 1, pp. 340–2, 344, 355 and 372–3; Lorimer 1978, pp. 144–6; Quinn 1990, pp. 378–80; Rabb 1998, pp. 132–3.

152 James' address was mentioned in the first section at n. 81.

153 *Journals of the House of Commons*, vol. 1, pp. 374, 380–1 and 383–4; *Journals of the House of Lords*, vol. 2, pp. 521–3 and 525; *Parliamentary Diary of Robert Bowyer*, pp. 292–3, 319–20 and 332–9.

154 *Proclamation to Represse All Piracies and Depredations upon the Sea*; *Stuart Royal Proclamations*, vol. 1, pp. 53–6; *Foedera, conventiones, litterae et cuiuscunque generis acta publica*, vol. 16, pp. 542–3; *Calendar of State Papers, Domestic Series, of the Reign of James I*, vol. 1, p. 41; *Tudor Royal Proclamations*, vol. 2, pp. 313–15.

155 *Proclamation for the Search and Apprehension of Certaine Pirats* (1604); *Proclamation for the Search and Apprehension of Certaine Pirats* (1606); *Proclamation against Pirats* (1609); *Stuart Royal Proclamations*, vol. 1, pp. 98–9, 145–7 and 202–6; *Calendar of State Papers, Domestic Series, of the Reign of James I*, vol. 1, pp. 166, 321 and 485.

156 *Calendar of the Manuscripts of the Most Honourable the Marquess of Salisbury*, vol. 16, pp. 202–3; *Acts of the Privy Council of England*, vol. 38, p. 482, and vol. 39, p. 348; *Calendar of State Papers, Domestic Series, of the Reign of James I*, vol. 1, pp. 457, 534, 541 and 598, and vol. 4, pp. 146, 282 and 328; NAK, HCA14/38, n. 84. The mode of prosecution of pirates introduced in England in 1536 was extended to Ireland in 1612 (*Statutes at Large Passed in the Parliaments Held in Ireland*, vol. 1, pp. 435–7).

from the admiral would be 'dishonourable to the king'.[157] In 1611 permission was granted to Dutch vessels to pursue pirates into ports in Ireland.[158] Two years earlier vessels fitted out by the Levant Company had been authorised to seize any pirate vessels they encountered as far from the king's own waters as the Mediterranean.[159] Towards the end of James' reign a major expedition was mounted against North African pirates, in conjunction with forces from other European countries.[160] When it was reported that the North Africans 'now profess themselves the common enemies of Christendom', reference was being made to the notion of a perpetual war against infidels, but because there was in reality a state of truce with 'those of Argier and Tunis', the North African raiders were denounced in English sources as 'common enimyes of mankinde', an even more notional use of the expression.[161]

Licences to apprehend pirates were also granted to merchants trading in West Africa and Newfoundland.[162] In contrast, when English mariners continued to obtain licences from foreign rulers to raid Spanish shipping in the West Indies, the English king sympathised with their condemnation as pirates, despite the view held in some quarters that they were waging a war against infidels.[163] A strikingly different view was taken of the voyages organised by the

157 *Calendar of the Manuscripts of the Most Honourable the Marquess of Salisbury*, vol. 15, p. 168; *Acts of the Privy Council of England*, vol. 39, pp. 75–6; *Calendar of State Papers, Domestic Series, of the Reign of James I*, vol. 1, pp. 586 and 593, vol. 4, pp. 49 and 61, and vol. 5, p. 674.

158 Winwood, *Memorials of Affairs of State*, vol. 3, pp. 285–6.

159 *Documents Relating to Law and Custom of the Sea*, vol. 1, pp. 377–80; *Calendar of State Papers, Domestic Series, of the Reign of James I*, vol. 1, pp. 572–3.

160 Penn 1920, pp. 81–102; Young 1985, pp. 75–9; Hebb 1994, pp. 7–135.

161 *Cabala sive scrinia sacra*, pp. 217–18, 383 and 323–5; *Acts of the Privy Council of England*, vol. 35, pp. 181–2, 226 and 263–4, vol. 36, pp. 345–6, 358–60, 371, 376, 379–90, 392–4, 397–8, 400–1, 408–11, 416–18, 421–3, 435–7, 446–7, 449–50 and 453–4, vol. 37, pp. 61–3, 70–1, 87, 92, 105, 121–2, 126, 182, 189–90, 196–7, 200, 239–42, 247–50, 272–3, 277–8, 291 and 379–80, vol. 38, pp. 22, 27, 33–4, 39, 55–6, 59–62, 87, 139–40, 160, 196, 212–13, 238, 302 and 349, and vol. 39, pp. 149–51, 198, 374 and 379; *Naval Tracts of Sir William Monson*, vol. 3, pp. 79–85 and 94–8; *Letters of King James VI and I*, pp. 356–7.

162 *Documents Relating to Law and Custom of the Sea*, vol. 1, pp. 385–6; *Acts of the Privy Council of England*, vol. 33, pp. 145–6; *Acts of the Privy Council of England, Colonial Series*, vol. 1, pp. 5–6.

163 *Records of the Virginia Company of London*, vol. 1, p. 367, and vol. 2, p. 402; *Works of Sir Walter Ralegh*, vol. 8, p. 751; *Calendar of State Papers, Domestic Series, of the Reign of James I*, vol. 2, p. 578; *Calendar of State Papers and Manuscripts, Relating to English Affairs, Existing in the Archives and Collections of Venice*, vol. 10, p. 190, and vol. 13, pp. 266 and 347; *Cabala sive scrinia sacra*, p. 195; *Rich Papers*, pp. 141–2; Barbour 1911, pp. 534–5; Craven 1930, p. 461; Andrews 1984, pp. 286–7; Lenman 2001, p. 149; O'Hara 2010, p. 42; Hanna 2015, pp. 59 and 72–8.

East India Company.[164] In 1600 Elizabeth had granted letters of reprisal in the then familiar form to captains heading for the far east, and prizes taken there had been processed in the admiralty court in the same way as other prizes taken during the war with Spain.[165] In the commissions granted by James to the company it was stressed that 'att this present tyme wee are in amyty with all Christian princes', and aggression against Spanish and Portuguese ships was therefore forbidden, yet the commanders of the fleets were authorised not only to defend themselves against any attempt to seize their ships or goods, but also to seek 'recompence or recoverie' for any 'wronge or losse' inflicted on them, subject to the condition that any prizes taken must be 'safely brought home with their bylls of lading and charter parties, to the intent that there may be restitution made by us so soone as you shall receyve satisfaction from that state or people by whome you are damnified'.[166] It was believed in the company that when seizures were effected under these commissions the mariners involved 'had liberty to make pillage of anything that was found out of the hold', though whether the admiral was entitled to claim a tenth of everything taken was doubted.[167] When consulted on the question, the civil lawyers replied that 'the tenth part of custom belongs to the lord admiral if he gave any commission', but that they were unable to see 'any reason why the admiral should pretend any right where he gives no letters of marque'.[168] Although seizures were

164 Licences granted by foreign rulers were sometimes relied on in the far east too (Mishra 2018, p. 181), but it is the licences issued in England that are of most interest here.

165 *Register of Letters &c. of the Governour and Company of Merchants of London Trading into the East Indies*, pp. 191–6; *Documents Relating to Law and Custom of the Sea*, vol. 1, pp. 386–7.

166 *Register of Letters &c. of the Governour and Company of Merchants of London Trading into the East Indies*, pp. 50–1, 113–14, 229–30, 284–5, 357–9, 361–2, 439–40, 444–5, 451–2, 454–5 and 465–6; *Documents Relating to Law and Custom of the Sea*, vol. 1, pp. 375–6; *Letters Received by the East India Company from Its Servants in the East*, vol. 4, p. 218, and vol. 6, p. 310; *Foedera, conventiones, litterae et cuiuscunque generis acta publica*, vol. 16, pp. 775–6; *Voyage of Thomas Best to the East Indies*, pp. 230–1.

167 *Letters Received by the East India Company from Its Servants in the East*, vol. 1, pp. 219, 227–9 and 234–5, vol. 4, pp. 133, 191–2 and 260–1, and vol. 6, pp. 49, 105, 122–3, 146, 158, 163–4, 173–5, 177 and 272–5; *Documents Illustrating the Impeachment of the Duke of Buckingham*, pp. 73–82.

168 *Calendar of State Papers, Colonial Series, East Indies*, vol. 3, pp. 125, 236–7, 247–9, 252–4 and 270–4; *Documents Illustrating the Impeachment of the Duke of Buckingham*, pp. 82–7 and 115–17; *Complete Collection of State Trials and Proceedings for High Treason*, vol. 2, cols 1312–13, 1329–37 and 1431–3; *Journals of the House of Commons*, vol. 1, pp. 846–7; *Journals of the House of Lords*, vol. 3, pp. 600–3, 620–1 and 660–1; John Rushworth, *Historical Collections of Private Passages of State*, vol. 1, pp. 312–22 and 384–5; *Letters of King James VI and I*, pp. 396 and 418–19.

sometimes made in the far east in conditions close to open warfare, they were regarded by the civil lawyers as a peculiar form of reprisals, authorised by prospective licences granted on the supposition that losses might be sustained and justice denied. It mattered a great deal that the reprisals were authorised against vessels flying the flag of 'any prince or state by whose subjectes you shall susteyne any wronge or losse', for as time passed the company faced greater hostility from its Dutch than its Portuguese rivals.[169]

The legitimacy of prize taking in wartime became a practical problem in England again after the Twelve Years' Truce between Spain and the United Provinces came to an end in 1621, when the privy council and admiralty court were forced to revisit the issues resulting from the violation of territorial jurisdiction, the blockading of neutral ports and the enlistment of mariners in foreign service.[170] By this stage it appears to have been assumed that title to a prize could not have been completed until it was safely taken home by its captors.[171] Further problems were caused by the revival in the same year of licensed raiding out of La Rochelle, against mariners and merchants loyal to Louis XIII, who had attempted to impose religious toleration on areas of France that had been left by his father under Protestant control.[172] In response to a suggestion from the French ambassador that prizes brought into English ports should simply be returned to their owners, it was insisted that the correct course would be for French owners to raise actions for restitution before the admiralty court.[173] The captors were themselves reluctant to become involved in litigation there, suspecting that the legitimacy of their seizures would not be recognised. It would certainly have been difficult to justify their seizures in terms of the conventional categories of the civil law, for although it could have been conveniently forgotten that war had never been declared between

169 *Calendar of State Papers, Colonial Series, East Indies*, vol. 1, pp. 231–2, and vol. 2, p. 103; *Letters Received by the East India Company from Its Servants in the East*, vol. 6, pp. 206–7; *Acts of the Privy Council of England*, vol. 37, p. 397, vol. 38, pp. 304–5, and vol. 39, pp. 295–6 and 331–3; *Calendar of State Papers, Domestic Series, of the Reign of James I*, vol. 4, p. 485.

170 *Acts of the Privy Council of England*, vol. 38, pp. 11, 372, 455 and 468–9, and vol. 39, pp. 36–7 and 41; 'Sir John Eliot and the Vice-Admiralty of Devon', pp. 17–18 and 27–8; *Supplementary Report on the Manuscripts of the Earl of Mar and Kellie*, pp. 203 and 206; NAK, HCA24/81, ff. 106, 145 and 170.

171 It is probably for this reason that no decrees adjudicating prizes to captors have not been found in the records of the admiralty court.

172 Parker 1980, pp. 9–13; Moote 1989, pp. 124–30; Holt 2005, pp. 182–87.

173 *Acts of the Privy Council of England*, vol. 38, pp. 77, 80–1, 100, 105–6, 137–9, 141, 166, 203, 209–10, 218, 283–4, 316, 340 and 359; *Calendar of State Papers, Domestic Series, of the Reign of James I*, vol. 3, pp. 276, 305, 320–1, 326, 383–6, 389, 395–7, 399–400, 407, 420, 422, 425, 429, 435, 457, 511 and 518–19.

Spain and the United Provinces, it could not have been imagined that a state of public war existed between the king of France and the magistrates of one of his towns, nor was there a sovereign prince present in La Rochelle to grant letters of marque as originally understood. It was in these conventional terms that the civil lawyers continued to analyse the problems put to them, and why James at this point described one of the rules on blockading as 'this allowabill custome of nationis, so weill groundit upoun infallible and goode ressonis of pollicie and state', remains in need of further explanation.[174] It was to the conventional categories of the civil law that attention was turned once more after English ships were seized by French as well as Dutch captains.[175] The king of France, the magistrates of La Rochelle and the states general of the United Provinces were all warned that unless 'reall and speedie satisfaction' were provided to the English mariners and merchants who had sustained losses, James would be compelled to take recourse to 'letters of marque'.[176] In reality he remained reluctant to risk an escalation of violence, and reprisals were authorised neither against the French nor the Dutch. However, a different attitude was beginning to take shape towards Spain.

Under mounting pressure to enter the Thirty Years' War in support of his son-in-law, the elector Palatine, James' preferred strategy was to negotiate a marriage between his eldest son and the daughter of Philip IV, hoping that an alliance with Spain would enable him to put pressure on the emperor to withdraw from the Palatinate and move towards peace.[177] Charles committed himself wholeheartedly to the pursuit of the 'Spanish match', but when it failed in 1624 he reacted by encouraging the formation of a war party in the English parliament, where advice on foreign policy started to be presented openly to the king.[178] Meanwhile the seizure of ships from England and Scotland by raiders licensed in Dunkirk had resulted in demands for 'restitucion or satisfaccion' being made to the infanta Isabella in Brussels, and in January 1625 James was advised that the time had come to grant 'letters of reprisall' to those affected by

174 This was mentioned, along with other similar statements, in the closing paragraphs of the first section.

175 *Acts of the Privy Council of England*, vol. 38, pp. 97, 211 and 236, and vol. 39, pp. 22, 88, 223–4, 459, 484 and 491; *Calendar of State Papers, Domestic Series, of the Reign of James I*, vol. 4, pp. 184 and 447; *Calendar of State Papers, Colonial Series, East Indies*, vol. 3, p. 41.

176 The ambassador who delivered the warning in France one of the Scots mentioned in n. 47 above.

177 Russell 1974, pp. 290–2; Adams 1983, pp. 95–7; Croft 2003, pp. 105–10.

178 Ruigh 1971; Adams 1978; Cogswell 1989.

the seizures.[179] The privy council drew up articles to regulate their use, requiring mariners and merchants to provide proof before the admiralty court 'that their shipps and goodes have bene taken and detained from them', to enter bonds guaranteeing that any ships or goods they themselves seized would be brought back to an English port without 'the bulke thereof broken, untill jugement hath first passed in the high courte of admiraltie that the saide goodes are lawfull prize', and to refrain from harming anyone apart from 'the subjectes of the king of Spaine inhabiting the Low Countries'.[180] The recipients of the letters were assured that after goods were 'adjudged unto them', they would be able sell them to other people 'in as ample maner as at any tyme heretofore hath beene accustomed by way of reprisall, and to have and enjoy the same as lawfull prises and as their owne proper goodes'. Potential purchasers were likewise assured that if they bought goods which had been 'adjudged for lawfull prise', they would be able to enjoy them 'as if the saide goodes had bene comen by through the lawfull traffique of marchantes, or as just prises in the tyme of open warre'. The articles issued by the privy council in 1625 bore a marked resemblance to those issued during Elizabeth's war with Spain, on which they were obviously modelled, yet they ended with a new provision that made them significantly different. After ships or goods were 'adjudged for lawfull prise', it stated, 'such quantitie thereof as shall countervaile the losse and dommages of the takers shalbe delivered to them, and the residue and remainder shalbe kept in safe sequestracion and deposit for the use of the proprietors'.[181] The reprisals that were taken in the last months of James' reign thus appear to have been genuine reprisals.[182] While he had taken the risk of unleashing a war of reprisals, he was still not overtly at war with any other nation when he died towards the end of March.[183] Before his son's reign is examined, an attempt will be made to obtain a better understanding of his reference to the 'custome of

179 *Acts of the Privy Council of England*, vol. 38, p. 440, and vol. 39, pp. 228, 238–9, 281–2, 302–3, 312–13, 392, 401 and 429–30; *Calendar of State Papers, Domestic Series, of the Reign of James I*, vol. 4, pp. 305, 452 and 461.

180 *Acts of the Privy Council of England*, vol. 39, pp. 449–51; *Calendar of State Papers, Domestic Series, of the Reign of James I*, vol. 4, p. 476.

181 As stated, the article was scarcely consistent with those preceding it, which indicated that title to any ships or goods seized would have been acquired as soon as they were adjudged to their captors. The Elizabethan articles had not been reworked with due diligence.

182 *Diary of Walter Yonge*, p. 79; *Calendar of State Papers, Domestic Series, of the Reign of James I*, vol. 4, pp. 470, 482–3, 490 and 495; *Documents Relating to Law and Custom of the Sea*, vol. 1, pp. 408–9.

183 The point is neatly made in Harris 2014, p. 229.

nationis' by approaching developments during the first quarter of the seventeenth century from another angle.

3 Towards a New Theory of Prize Acquisition

On 25 February 1603 the *Santa Catarina*, a Portuguese vessel carrying silk and other fabrics, spices and other condiments, and porcelain and other Chinese wares, was seized in the Straits of Singapore by ships under the command of Jakob van Heemskerk, an employee of a Dutch trading company, in consort with ships from Johore.[184] Having been licensed by Maurice of Nassau, the admiral of Holland, not only to defend his fleet but also to seek reparation for any damage done to it, Van Heemskerk brought the *Santa Catarina* back to the Netherlands in the following summer, and on 9 September 1604 an admiralty court in Amsterdam found that the vessel, with its extremely valuable cargo, was a lawful prize, ordering the proceeds of its sale to be divided between Van Heemskerk, his employers and the state.[185] Although the finding of the court was conclusive, the Dutch East India Company – into which the body employing Van Heemskerk had been absorbed while he was away – commissioned a young advocate to compose an 'apologia' for the seizure that might satisfy the scruples of existing investors and – probably more importantly – forestall the objections of external observers.[186] If the apology drafted is not to be misconstrued, it will need to be borne in mind that its author had not spent long years in the study of law at a university.[187] Success at the Dutch bar required familiarity with the civil law, which the author certainly did acquire, but not by spending his formative years absorbing the assumptions on which instruction in the learned laws was based. As a means of keeping this crucial fact constantly in sight, the advocate will be referred to here by his vernacular name (Huig de Groot), instead of the Latinised form (Hugo Grotius) favoured in most recent writing on his life and work, Latinised names having been reserved so far for university professors alone. It may be expected, for example, that Huig

184 Detailed accounts of the seizure can be found in Borschberg 2002 and Van Ittersum 2003.

185 The admiralty court's sentence is reproduced in Hugo Grotius, *De iure praedae commentarius*, pp. 349–50, and *Commentary on the Law of Prize*, pp. 510–14.

186 Fruin 1925; Van Ittersum 2006a; Porras 2006; Wilson 2008; Borschberg 2011.

187 Knight 1965, pp. 36–8; Van Someren 1965, pp. 51–3; Edwards 1981, pp. 1–2. On the doctorate in law held by the advocate see Nellen 2018, pp. 49–50 (the best biography now available by far). While the advocate may have spent a brief period studying law in France, the degree was honorary in character.

de Groot will turn out to have viewed licensed raiding in a rather different way from Albericus Gentilis (as Alberico Gentili has been called). It seems unlikely, in any case, that the Dutch East India Company approached De Groot, who had just entered his twenties, in his capacity as a lawyer. The company is less likely to have been impressed with his limited forensic experience than with his precocious accomplishments as a humanist.[188] In executing the task assigned to him, De Groot claimed to have followed the advice given to students of rhetoric by Quintilian, who had told them that while they would later be engaged mostly in judicial oratory, focusing on what was just (*iustum*), they might also be asked to engage in censorious oratory, focusing on what was honourable (*honestum*), or in political oratory, focusing on what was expedient (*utile*), and that they would therefore need to be able to alternate between these three types of speech.[189] Since his prospective audience comprised various groups of people, De Groot undertook to examine the seizure of the *Santa Catarina* from three angles, looking first at the justice of the seizure (in the first thirteen chapters of his book), then at whether it would be honourable to keep the prize (in the fourteenth chapter), and finally at whether it would be expedient to do so (in the fifteenth).

At the start of his book De Groot warned his readers forcefully that the legitimacy of the seizure of the *Santa Catarina* could not be appraised 'solely on the basis of written laws', explaining that knowledge of *ius belli ac pacis* would have to be sought 'from some source other than the *Corpus* of Roman laws'.[190] Less assistance was provided by the doctors of civil law than by moral theologians, 'who prefer to have such questions decided on the basis of the holy scriptures', although De Groot warned further that the theologians had a tendency to confuse discussion of divine law (*ius divinum*) with discussion of the particular law of the Israelites (*ius civile Hebraeorum*). His work on another book at around the same time had drawn him into close study of the treatises written by the Spanish Thomists, to which he made frequent reference in his book about prize acquisition, now known as his *De iure praedae*.[191] He made even more frequent reference to biblical texts, but in a way that left them open to reinterpretation, regardless of any consensus that might have formed among theologians.[192] As a matter of fact, he did make extensive use of the

188 Tuck 1993, pp. 155–6; Fitzmaurice 2014, pp. 87–8; Straumann 2015, p. 2.

189 *De iure praedae commentarius*, p. 5, and *Commentary on the Law of Prize*, p. 15; Quintilian, *Institutio oratoria*, 3.4.16 and 10.1.35–6.

190 *De iure praedae commentarius*, pp. 5–7, and *Commentary on the Law of Prize*, pp. 15–17.

191 On the connection with his *Commentarius in theses xi* see Todescan 2009.

192 For a rigorous demonstration of the point see Somos 2009, and see too Somos 2011.

Roman law texts, but in a similar way, regarding them less as the foundations of the civil law tradition than as evidence of how war and peace had been regulated in antiquity.[193] 'The true way', he emphasised at the start of his book, 'has been secured for us by those jurists of antiquity whose names we revere, and who repeatedly refer the art of civil government back to the very fount of nature'. He intended to read the writings of the Roman jurists in the way recommended by Cicero in his *De legibus*, where he had concentrated on natural law but had found much of it exemplified in Roman law.[194] In moving on to a 'prolegomena', in which he identified nine rules (*regulae*) and thirteen laws (*leges*) to guide his later analysis, De Groot adopted from Cicero the rule that 'the consensus of all nations should be seen as a precept of natural law'.[195] He found the works of Cicero instructive again in identifying the natural laws that people were entitled both to defend themselves, and to take and retain whatever they required to survive.[196] When he eventually moved on in the last two chapters of his book from discussion of what was just to discussion of what was honourable and expedient, De Groot still found Cicero the most helpful guide available, citing his works in support of the theses (*problematae*) that 'it is impossible for anything just not to be honourable', and that 'whatever is honourable, the same has to be expedient'.[197] While these theses might have been thought to obviate the need for any addition to the thirteen chapters on the justice of the seizure – and help to explain why only two more chapters were added – Cicero himself had recognised the necessity of viewing subjects from various perspectives when addressing an audience with varied concerns. De Groot therefore took time at the end of his book to persuade any readers who remained in need of persuasion that the appropriation of the Portuguese vessel and its cargo was both honourable and expedient.

---

193 De Groot's use of Roman law is investigated in Straumann 2006a, 2009 and 2015, although his crucial move away from the civil law tradition is neglected. In focusing on the thinking of ancient lawyers, he was engaged in a typically humanist enterprise. He did not try to immerse himself in, and carry forward, a tradition of enquiry, a more scholastic enterprise.

194 *De legibus*, 1.5.16–17.

195 *De iure praedae commentarius*, p. 12, and *Commentary on the Law of Prize*, p. 25, citing Cicero, *Tusculan Disputations*, 1.13.30.

196 *De iure praedae commentarius*, p. 10, and *Commentary on the Law of Prize*, p. 23, citing Cicero, *De officiis*, 1.4.12 and 3.5.22, *Pro Milone*, 4.10, and *De finibus*, 4.7.16 and 5.9.24.

197 *De iure praedae commentarius*, pp. 300 and 317, and *Commentary on the Law of Prize*, pp. 438 and 463, citing Cicero, *De inventione*, 2.4.12, *De officiis*, 1.19.62 and 3.7.34, and *De finibus*, 1.16.50 and 3.21.71.

After identifying in his second chapter the rules and laws on which his account of the justice of the seizure of the *Santa Catarina* would be based, De Groot proceeded in his third chapter to discuss the general legitimacy of going to war.[198] From the laws permitting people to defend their persons and property, he maintained, it followed that they must be permitted to use force in doing so, as was widely recognised among lawyers, theologians, philosophers, historians, orators and poets. From this right to use force, he argued in his fourth chapter, it followed further that plunder was licit in wartime, as again was widely recognised.[199] Since it was by means of their belongings that enemies were able to arm themselves, 'it is no less necessary to wrest these away from them than it is to wrest a sword from a madman, if we wish to protect our property or even our personal security'. However, while this showed why it was legitimate to deprive an enemy of property during a war, it did not show why it was legitimate to retain plunder after a war ended. De Groot's solution to this problem was to follow the example of the Thomist theologians in treating just wars as a species of judicial process, to which recourse might be taken if there were no superior authority to whom disputes could be submitted for resolution.[200] In a series of chapters explaining when wars were just, he began by discussing who could go to war legitimately, distinguishing between the public wars waged by states and the private wars sometimes waged by individuals, but rejecting the civil lawyers' insistence on the former being initiated by a formal declaration. Their opinions, he remarked, 'should not carry much weight in cases concerned with public law or the law of nations'.[201] When he later returned to the same distinction, he remarked again that there was 'no reason why we should always accept the opinion of those who, content with their mastery of the civil law, have neglected to learn from the true principles of the law of nations'.[202] The important point was that neither individuals nor states could resort to arms lawfully if there was any possibility of an ordinary judicial remedy being obtained. Just as when an action was raised before a court, moreover, a war could be lawfully waged only if it served to protect persons, to recover property, to secure the payment of debts or to punish people for wrongs they had committed, although war differed to the extent that individuals enlisted to fight for a state could rely on their leader's assessment of

198 *De iure praedae commentarius*, pp. 31–42, and *Commentary on the Law of Prize*, pp. 51–67.
199 *De iure praedae commentarius*, pp. 43–57, and *Commentary on the Law of Prize*, pp. 68–88.
200 *De iure praedae commentarius*, pp. 57–9, and *Commentary on the Law of Prize*, pp. 89–91.
201 *De iure praedae commentarius*, p. 65, and *Commentary on the Law of Prize*, p. 99.
202 *De iure praedae commentarius*, p. 129, and *Commentary on the Law of Prize*, p. 193.

the justice of the cause.[203] Making reference to the practice of taking reprisals, De Groot argued that it was licit to plunder innocent parties if they came from states which failed to respect the sanctity of persons or property.[204] He also argued that while ordinary people were only supposed to engage in plunder as a means of securing the ends pursued by their leaders, the validity of any acquisitions they made would not be undermined by deficiencies in their motivation.[205] It will be apparent even from this much abbreviated outline of the fifth to ninth chapters of his book that De Groot worked through the range of topics usually covered in Thomist treatments of the subject.

At the start of his tenth chapter De Groot himself concluded that 'it should be evident from the observations already made that things seized in war and things seized on the basis of a judicial award fall into the same class'.[206] In the case of a public war, the plundering of the enemy differed 'from the execution of a judicial sentence only inasmuch as it must be carried out by armed force', while in the case of a private war, there was a temporary return to 'that early law which made each individual the judge of his own affairs'. The theory taught in the law schools was inadequate in either case. Taking private wars first, De Groot observed that comparison with the taking of reprisals was misleading since it could not have been a judicial act of adjudication that made captors the owners of whatever they seized.[207] After all, the essential condition of a private war was the absence of an effective judicial authority to which individuals could turn to have a just cause for redress vindicated. Any court ruling could only have been declaratory in nature, recognising the rights individuals had already acquired, and which they could have assigned to others.[208] On the other hand, things taken in public wars could not have been acquired by their occupation alone, as if they belonged to no one, for the truth was that they did already have owners.[209] To suppose that all rights lapsed on the outbreak of a war would have been to deny the existence of the *ius belli* recognised by

203 *De iure praedae commentarius*, pp. 67–71, and *Commentary on the Law of Prize*, pp. 102–7. For De Groot's thinking on the right to punish see Straumann 2006b and Van Nifterik 2009, and on the effect of erroneous but earnest reasoning, taken to explain how there could be a just cause on both sides of a conflict, Scattola 2009.

204 *De iure praedae commentarius*, pp. 111–12, and *Commentary on the Law of Prize*, p. 167. For De Groot's thinking on reprisals see Lesaffer 2020.

205 *De iure praedae commentarius*, pp. 122–7, and *Commentary on the Law of Prize*, pp. 182–9.

206 *De iure praedae commentarius*, p. 128, and *Commentary on the Law of Prize*, pp. 191–2.

207 *De iure praedae commentarius*, pp. 132–4, and *Commentary on the Law of Prize*, pp. 197–200.

208 *De iure praedae commentarius*, pp. 138–9, and *Commentary on the Law of Prize*, pp. 205–6.

209 *De iure praedae commentarius*, p. 139, and *Commentary on the Law of Prize*, p. 207.

classical authors.[210] As the basis for acquisition was again the existence of a just cause for redress, De Groot felt certain that 'things captured in a public war become the property of the state undertaking the war, up to the point at which the said state shall have received satisfaction', although the state too could have assigned its rights to others.[211] In a lengthy passage he pointed out that when the Roman law texts on the occupation of enemy property were read in conjunction with other classical sources it became apparent that, in antiquity, plunder fell under state ownership (*publicata*) and was surrendered to the treasury (*fiscus*), subject to the right of commanders to distribute rewards among their troops.[212] In modern times each state had its own rules for the distribution of plunder, which were best interpreted as ways of assigning or distributing spoils acquired by the state.[213] At several other places in his book De Groot stated similarly that the procedure 'under which we occupy vacant objects is insufficient for the establishment of full legal rights over enemy property', that the confiscation of enemy property by a state waging a just war 'constitutes a mode of acquiring ownership, altogether in keeping with what would happen in a legal judgment', and that individuals afterwards acquired plunder 'by public grant and as a gift, a procedure which establishes a true title'.[214] As will be seen in the next section of the present chapter, De Groot's thinking on this subject underwent significant modification over the next twenty years, but he had already gone beyond the Thomists in not only expressing doubts about the legal theory of prize acquisition but also proposing an alternative theory. Although he described his theory as a *nova sententia*, he also stressed that his aim was to revive ancient thinking after several centuries of misunderstanding.[215]

In the eleventh chapter of his book De Groot moved towards applying his new theory to the facts of the case assigned to him by recounting in detail the original outbreak of the war with Spain, the involvement of Portugal on the Spanish side, the resulting disruption of trade with Portugal itself, the efforts made by the Portuguese to exclude the Dutch from direct trade with the East Indies, and various atrocities that were alleged to have been committed against

210 Plato, *Republic*, 335e1–5; Pindar, *Isthmian Odes*, 4.48; Cicero, *De officiis*, 1.11.33; Livy, *Ab urbe condita*, 5.27.6; Seneca, *Ad Lucilium epistulae morales*, 120.6.

211 *De iure praedae commentarius*, pp. 151–2, and *Commentary on the Law of Prize*, pp. 226–7.

212 *De iure praedae commentarius*, pp. 139–51, and *Commentary on the Law of Prize*, pp. 208–26.

213 *De iure praedae commentarius*, pp. 160–2, and *Commentary on the Law of Prize*, pp. 239–42.

214 *De iure praedae commentarius*, pp. 45–6, 118–19 and 157, and *Commentary on the Law of Prize*, pp. 71–3, 176–7 and 234–5.

215 *De iure praedae commentarius*, p. 139, and *Commentary on the Law of Prize*, pp. 208.

the Dutch there.[216] In his twelfth chapter he focused on the illegality of the Portuguese efforts to monopolise trade in the far east, invoking his usual array of authors – lawyers, theologians, philosophers, historians, orators and poets – in arguing that European dominion could not be established elsewhere either by discovery or by papal grant.[217] In reality, he maintained, the Portuguese had entered into commercial treaties with several sovereign states, and they were attempting to prevent the Dutch from doing precisely the same thing. It was at this point that De Groot presented a defence of the freedom of navigation that came to attract a great deal of attention.[218] In doing so he cited the Roman law texts in which the seas were identified as *res communes*, but instead of linking the texts with their interpretation by the civilian doctors, he located them in the cultural context in which they had originated, citing passages from the *literae humaniores* in which the seas had also been described as common to everyone.[219] As he read these sources, they showed that exclusive rights of ownership had gradually emerged in primitive society when people took into their personal possession the objects they required to survive, from which he inferred that ownership could only be established in things capable of personal possession.[220] For this reason, he agreed with the civil lawyers that ownership of the seas was not possible, but while he also agreed with them that jurisdiction was a different matter, he insisted that it could only be established through agreements with other states.[221] It was also implicit in his ancient sources, he believed, that people could only be excluded from the enjoyment of things if to share them would have resulted in their diminution, so that even if the Portuguese had been able to acquire dominion over an ocean, it would still have been incumbent on them to permit other people to engage in travel, trade and fishing.[222] Pretending that no court had been available to provide redress to Van Heemskerk for the aggression he had encountered in the East Indies, De Groot concluded that he had been entitled to wage a private war against the Portuguese.[223]

216 *De iure praedae commentarius*, pp. 163–204, and *Commentary on the Law of Prize*, pp. 244–99.

217 *De iure praedae commentarius*, pp. 205–25, and *Commentary on the Law of Prize*, pp. 302–14.

218 Schermaier 2009; Zwalve 2009; Perruso 2020.

219 Cicero, *De officiis*, 1.7.20 and 1.16.51–2, and *Pro Roscio Amerino*, 26.71; Ovid, *Metamorphoses*, 6.340–59; Virgil, *Aeneid*, 7.228–30; Plautus, *Rudens*, 4.3; Seneca, *De beneficiis*, 4.28.3.

220 *De iure praedae commentarius*, p. 218, and *Commentary on the Law of Prize*, pp. 320–1.

221 *De iure praedae commentarius*, pp. 224–5 and 232–42, and *Commentary on the Law of Prize*, pp. 328–31 and 340–53.

222 *De iure praedae commentarius*, pp. 242–9, and *Commentary on the Law of Prize*, pp. 331–63.

223 *De iure praedae commentarius*, pp. 249–67, and *Commentary on the Law of Prize*, pp. 363–70.

'Although in the sense already indicated', the thirteenth chapter opened, 'this conflict could have been waged as a private war, and a just one too, it is nevertheless more accurate to say that in actual fact it is a public war'.[224] It was then insisted that the United Provinces were a sovereign state, with a just cause for war against Spain and Portugal.[225] After repeating that there was no need for a public war to be formally declared, De Groot added that in any case an 'edict issued by the states general of the United Provinces, which orders that the goods of all persons subject to the king of Spain shall be seen as spoils, is equivalent to a declaration of war'. As the losses sustained by the Dutch had not yet been fully redressed, as it was licit to seek redress from the subjects of the king of Spain and Portugal, and as the seizure was only made for the sake of securing redress, it was evident that 'by every criterion, including the criterion of conscience, the war against the Portuguese is absolutely just, and therefore the seizure of the prize in question was also just'.[226] Moving on to discuss the ownership of the prize, De Groot first observed that it was 'an acquisition of the state', then added that it was 'possible for the same prize to become the property of the East India Company in consequence of a grant made by the state'.[227] The 'edict' he had already mentioned, issued in April 1599, had authorised the seizure of ships and goods belonging to subjects of Philip III, and had further prohibited trade with Spain and Portugal by neutral ships, on pain of their forfeiture – not long afterwards, De Groot pointed out, the English queen had issued a similarly worded proclamation on trading with the enemy.[228] Far from being furnished with letters of marque in the standard form, however, Van Heemskerk and his fleet had received a commission prohibiting violence against other vessels, 'unless it should happen that someone makes a hostile bid to prevent them from engaging in navigation or commerce'.[229] De Groot claimed conveniently that it was during an assault on his fleet by the Portuguese that Van Heemskerk had seized the *Santa Catarina*, and he reckoned anyway that retrospective authorisation of the seizure could be found in the decision of the admiralty court and in a further edict of the states general expressing approval of the seizure. Furthermore, he reckoned that the

224 *De iure praedae commentarius*, p. 268, and *Commentary on the Law of Prize*, p. 392.

225 *De iure praedae commentarius*, pp. 268–78, and *Commentary on the Law of Prize*, pp. 392–406.

226 *De iure praedae commentarius*, pp. 278–80, and *Commentary on the Law of Prize*, pp. 406–8.

227 *De iure praedae commentarius*, pp. 280–7, and *Commentary on the Law of Prize*, pp. 408–18.

228 *De iure praedae commentarius*, pp. 287–96, and *Commentary on the Law of Prize*, pp. 419–32. The edict was reproduced in an appendix to the book, along with the sentence of the admiralty court and another edict, about to be mentioned below.

229 *De iure praedae commentarius*, p. 290, and *Commentary on the Law of Prize*, p. 423.

sultan of Johore had also been at war with the Portuguese, and claimed that he had assigned his right to redress for the losses inflicted upon him to Van Heemskerk.[230] In his penultimate chapter De Groot argued that quite apart from his thesis that anything just would also be honourable, the seizure of the *Santa Catarina* had involved a display of fortitude that deserved both praise and remuneration.[231] In his final chapter he argued that quite apart from his thesis that anything honourable would also be expedient, it was advantageous for the state to have its enemies annoyed and its treasury enriched at no cost to the public.[232] If his readers feared that antagonising the Portuguese might have serious repercussions, they also needed to recognise that unless the mariners who sailed to the East Indies resisted the aggression they encountered there, the Dutch would soon be deprived of access to a lucrative market.

Although a finished version of the *De iure praedae* was delivered to the East India Company in 1606, for some reason it was not published, perhaps because there were doubts about how persuasive it would seem to its intended audience. After all, readers were expected to regard both the Dutch republic and the sultanate of Johore as sovereign states, and to accept not only that no judicial process had been available to Van Heemskerk in the East Indies, but also that the sultan of Johore had assigned his right in a share of the prize to him.[233] Above all, readers were expected to abandon several centuries of reliance on the civil law tradition as a guide to the regulation of relations between nations. For whatever reason, De Groot's justification of the seizure of the *Santa Catarina* and its cargo was not widely distributed, with the exception of the central passage of the twelfth chapter in which he had focused on freedom of trade and navigation. That passage was revised for separate publication to allay anxieties expressed by the Zeeland branch of the East India Company, which was worried that access to markets in the far east might be closed off by the truce that was being negotiated with Spain in 1608.[234] The anonymous *Mare liberum, sive de iure quod Batavis competit ad Indicana commercia dissertatio*, appeared too late to have any influence on the terms of the Treaty of Antwerp, but just in time to be misread as a contribution to a controversy over fishing

230 *De iure praedae commentarius*, pp. 296–9, and *Commentary on the Law of Prize*, pp. 432–6.

231 *De iure praedae commentarius*, pp. 300–16, and *Commentary on the Law of Prize*, pp. 437–61.

232 *De iure praedae commentarius*, pp. 316–41, and *Commentary on the Law of Prize*, pp. 462–97.

233 Borschberg 1999, pp. 231–5; Keene 2002, pp. 42–52; Van Ittersum 2003, pp. 514, 535–6 and 541; Gaynor 2012, p. 838. For the limited extent of De Groot's knowledge of conditions in the far east see Borschberg 2009 and 2021.

234 Shearer 1983; Roelofsen 1989a; Edmond 1995; Thornton 2004; Wilson 2006; Gordon 2008; Van Ittersum 2009; Van Nifterik and Nijman 2009; Thumfart 2009; Somos and Margócsy 2017.

rights off the coasts of Britain.[235] A tax traditionally imposed on inshore fishermen in Scotland had been extended to offshore fishermen as well, and in May 1609, two months after De Groot's tract appeared in print, a proclamation was issued requiring foreigners to pay for licences before fishing in the vicinity of Scotland, England or Ireland.[236] The king's ministers understood that the proclamation was justified by 'what the civil law prescribeth in this case', which was that nations could exercise jurisdiction over territorial waters, and by 'what hath been the use and custome of princes in like occasions', since others had followed the example of Venice and Genoa in levying taxes on vessels entering their waters.[237] In response to pressure from the Dutch ambassador it was conceded that 'the king, for his greate love to the Low Countries, would forbeare to proceede according to the proclamacion'.[238] The proclamation was not rescinded, however, and seven years later it was revived and taken to entail that unlicensed vessels caught fishing within the prescribed limits would be forfeited to the crown.[239]

By the time the 1609 proclamation was revived, a Scottish author had replied directly to De Groot's tract.[240] After moving to England following the union of the crowns, William Welwod had publishing a revised version of the treatise on maritime law he had written in the 1580s, introducing a series of three new chapters. In the first, 'Of things taken upon sea', he ran through the conventional categories of legitimate seizures at sea, distinguishing between things 'taken from pirats and sea-thiefes', things taken from 'professed enemies in lawfull warfare', and things taken under 'the title of letters of marque, called *ius represaliarum*'.[241] In the second, 'of fishers, fishing and trafiquers therewith', he talked about the law regulating fishing, in Scotland especially.[242] In the third, 'Of the communitie and proprietie of the seas', he responded to 'a verie learned

235 Fulton 1911, pp. 118–208; Grayson 1978, pp. 241–9; Armitage 2000, pp. 108–14.

236 *Proclamation Touching Fishing*; *Stuart Royal Proclamations*, vol. 1, pp. 217–19; *Calendar of State Papers, Domestic Series, of the Reign of James I*, vol. 1, p. 509; Fulton 1911, pp. 755–6. For remarks on the composition of the proclamation see Cormack 2007, pp. 262–6.

237 Winwood, *Memorials of Affairs of State*, vol. 3, pp. 49–50; *Calendar of State Papers, Domestic Series, of the Reign of James I*, vol. 1, p. 426; NAK, SP14/32, ff. 51–2.

238 *Calendar of State Papers, Domestic Series, of the Reign of James I*, vol. 1, p. 540; NAK, SP14/47, f. 259.

239 *Calendar of State Papers, Domestic Series, of the Reign of James I*, vol. 2, p. 354, vol. 3, pp. 35–6, 222, 228, 345 and 352, and vol. 4, pp. 200 and 205. This phase of the dispute was touched on in the first section, at n. 83.

240 For a discussion of the exchange between the two authors see Van Ittersum 2006b.

241 *Abridgement of All Sea-Lawes*, pp. 53–7.

242 *Abridgement of All Sea-Lawes*, pp. 57–60.

but a subtle treatise (*incerto authore*) intituled *Mare liberum*'.[243] Dismissing the 'ridiculous pretence' that the author's purpose had been to defend freedom of navigation 'upon the ocean', which Welwod did not think anyone seriously questioned, he also criticised the author's reliance on 'the opinions and sayings of some olde poets, orators, philosophers and (wrested) jurisconsults'. While noting the consistency of several biblical texts with civil law sources, he was not much interested in 'Cicero (his man)', or in any of the other 'Grecian and Roman writers' De Groot had cited.[244] Instead, in examining the 'chiefe warrants' assembled in what had become the fifth chapter of the *Mare liberum*, Welwod concentrated on showing how the texts from the *Digest* were properly interpreted in the civil law tradition from which they had been 'wrested'.[245] De Groot answered these criticisms in a *Defensio capitis quinti Maris liberi*, explaining that his dissertation had formed part of a longer treatment of prize law, observing that freedom of navigation had unfortunately been contested in certain quarters, and pointing out that freedom of fishing had only been touched on in passing in his original discussion.[246] He defended his use of the Roman law texts he had cited, drawing support again from Cicero, Virgil, Ovid and Seneca, against whose belief that the seas remained common to everyone not a single source could be adduced 'from all antiquity'. Like his *De iure praedae*, De Groot's answer to Welwod was not published during his lifetime, but Welwod did return to the subject in a separate tract *De dominio maris*, which was published around the time that the fishery policy proclaimed in 1609 was being put into effect. The tract took the more positive form of an account of Welwod's own thinking, as opposed to a critique of someone else's views, although he reiterated his opposition to those who embraced the teachings of 'ancient jurists, poets, orators and that order of more humane writers, ignorant of the true natural law'.[247] He himself preferred to adhere to the teachings of Bartolus, 'the light of the law', along with 'the rest of the jurists', who had defended the projection of territorial jurisdiction a hundred miles into the seas.[248]

243 *Abridgement of All Sea-Lawes*, pp. 61–72.

244 Genesis 1.28, 9.1, 10.5 and 11.8; Psalms 24.1–2 and 104.9; *Digest*, 27.9.8.2 and 31.77.20; Baldus, *In primam Digesti veteris partem commentaria*, f. 45r (ad D.1.8.1).

245 *Mare liberum*, pp. 48–95, and *Free Sea*, pp. 20–37.

246 'Defensio capitis quinti Maris liberi', p. 347; 'Some Less Known Works of Hugo Grotius', p. 180; *Free Sea*, p. 104.

247 *De dominio maris*, p. 1. For the particular context in which this tract was produced see Alsop 1980.

248 *De dominio maris*, p. 5.

By the time Welwod's *De dominio maris* was printed in 1616, the author of the *Mare liberum* had visited England as a member of a delegation sent to resolve tensions between the East India companies of the two countries.[249] The Dutch company had been founded after the English company, but the success of its predecessors had already led the English company to imitate their methods, and it cannot have been purely coincidental that the commissions the English company received for its voyages contained a clause closely resembling the one De Groot mentioned in his defence of Van Heemskerk.[250] As rivalry between the two companies intensified, conferences were called to debate their differences, first at London in 1613, then at The Hague in 1615, and then at London again in 1618.[251] The basic position of the Dutch company was adumbrated by De Groot in a speech delivered before the English king at the beginning of the first conference, in which it was explained that the Dutch had fought their way into the East Indies trade during their war with Spain and Portugal, that local rulers had then promised to sell spices to them alone, that the English company was trying to work its way into the same market, and that it could not be justified in doing so unless it was at least prepared to cover part of the costs incurred by the Dutch in establishing and preserving the market.[252] On the other side it was argued that the English company had found it perfectly possible to trade peacefully in the far east, without the expense of constructing forts or hiring native troops, and that they had actually found the Portuguese to be conscientious opponents (*pii inimici*) while the Dutch were oppressive friends (*duri amici*).[253] They thought it greatly to their advantage that the freedom of trade they were asserting had been robustly defended by a Dutch author in the *Mare liberum*.[254] According to De Groot, the Dutch agreed that the English had a natural right to travel to the East Indies and to trade there, and were not minded like the Portuguese to contest that point, yet they also wished to maintain that this liberty was restricted by the contracts and treaties already entered into.[255] 'If your claim is founded on the rule of

249 Den Tex 1973, vol. 2, pp. 545–8; Patterson 1997, pp. 144–5; Nellen 2015, pp. 149–54.

250 Boxer 1965, pp. 20–4; Keay 1991, pp. 12–13; Parthesius 2010, pp. 32–5; Games 2015, pp. 180–1; Mishra 2018, pp. 25–6 and 211.

251 Clark and Van Eysinga 1951, pp. 59–81 and 96–118; Grayson 1978, pp. 250–4; Borschberg 1999, pp. 241–8; Zemanek 1999, pp. 118–19; Van Ittersum 2006b, pp. 371–96; Ruoss 2017, pp. 56–66.

252 'Colonial Conferences between England and the Netherlands in 1613 and 1615', pp. 90–3.

253 'Colonial Conferences between England and the Netherlands in 1613 and 1615', p. 199.

254 'Colonial Conferences between England and the Netherlands in 1613 and 1615', pp. 98–9, 115–16, 120, 184–5 and 219.

255 'Colonial Conferences between England and the Netherlands in 1613 and 1615', pp. 101, 109, 125–6 and 181.

the law of nations that says it is licit to trade everywhere', he explained, 'our defence is founded on the rule of the same law that says agreements ought to be fulfilled'.[256] He was not simply arguing that the rulers who had made deals with the Dutch were no longer free to sell their spices to the English, but was also insisting that it would be unconscionable for the English to entice them into breaking their bargains.[257] The civil lawyers among the English delegates must have been puzzled by the notion that a contract could limit 'the liberty in the persons contracting, and in the things concerning which the contract is made', but they were prepared to discuss the issues raised in terms of the law of nature and nations, as something distinct from the civil law.[258] What they could not understand was how any nation could have its natural liberty reduced by agreements to which it was not party.[259]

It is scarcely surprising that the two companies were unable to settle their differences in either 1613 or 1615. At the beginning of the third conference in 1618, the English king told the Dutch delegates that he did not 'expect to be taught the laws of nations by them, nor their Grotius'.[260] In fact, De Groot was not included in the delegation for the third conference, at which the two companies, by avoiding discussion of legal niceties, were able to arrive at a pragmatic (though ultimately unsuccessful) accord in 1619.[261] In the summer of that year the English king was presented with a draft of another response to the *Mare liberum*, written by the common lawyer John Selden.[262] In the form in which it was eventually published, Selden's *Mare clausum* was in two parts, the first of which assembled ancient as well as more recent sources that seemed to recognise the possibility of dominion over territorial waters.[263] In contrast to Welwod, Selden thus replied to De Groot in his own terms. Indeed, he took

256 Readers of the *Mare liberum* would not have known that the latter rule was included among those borrowed from Cicero in the *De iure praedae commentarius*, p. 18, and *Commentary on the Law of Prize*, p. 34.

257 'Colonial Conferences between England and the Netherlands in 1613 and 1615', pp. 181, 188–9 and 205.

258 For the English delegates see Clark and Van Eysinga 1951, p. 148. De Groot's reading of the texts he cited from the *Digest* will remain strange to readers versed in the civil law, but it makes better sense if it is recognised that he was advancing a Ciceronian argument about the dependence of all forms of human intercourse on good faith.

259 'Colonial Conferences between England and the Netherlands in 1613 and 1615', pp. 103–4, 120, 180, 195–6 and 218–19.

260 NAK, SP84/87, ff. 172–3.

261 Edmundson 1911, pp. 58–63; Clark and Van Eysinga 1951, pp. 130–2; Mishra 2018, pp. 214–16.

262 Berkowitz 1988, pp. 51–5; Toomer 2009, vol. 1, pp. 388–90; Thornton 2006, pp. 107–8.

263 Ziskind 1973, pp. 545–59; Christianson 1996, pp. 246–81; Somos 2012, pp. 296–326; Muldoon 2016, pp. 123–7; Haivry 2017a, pp. 113–30. See too Vieira 2003.

issue expressly with the assertion in Gentilis' treatise on the law of arms that the *Corpus iuris civilis* formed the basis of the law of nations, 'as if *ius naturale et gentium* should be drawn from these books alone'.[264] It is impossible to be sure that this passage was included in the draft submitted to the king in 1619, for when Selden's book was published in 1635 he claimed to have revised it so thoroughly that it was 'entirely new'.[265] Nevertheless, there are reasons to suppose that he had already adopted De Groot's approach to writing about the law of the sea by the time the third conference between the two East India companies ended. For one thing, in an appendix attached to another treatise he managed to publish in 1618, Selden had remarked that if the expression *ius civile Anglorum* signified anything it must be the common law, since the civil law had no binding force anywhere in Europe and was no more persuasive than the *literae humaniores*.[266] Furthermore, by the later 1630s he was coming to doubt whether any part of the law of nations could simply be found in the 'received customs of divers ages and nations, both antient and modern', as he had accepted in writing the first part of his *Mare clausum*, insisting instead that connections had to be found with the Jewish legal tradition.[267] Whatever adjustments Selden may have made to the first part of his book before it was published, its general tenor seems more consistent with the convictions he expressed around 1619 than with those he expressed in 1635. In any case, the important point for present purposes is that towards the end of James' reign awareness appears to have been growing in England of a new approach to the analysis of international relations emanating from the Netherlands. This new approach was clearly understood to owe more to the Ciceronian conception of *ius naturale et gentium* than to the traditional association of the law of nations with the civil law. Whether it was understood to operate as legal rather than moral or political analysis still needs further clarification.[268]

Having argued in the first part of his *Mare clausum* that 'the sea, by the law of nature or nations, is not common to all men but capable of private dominion', Selden proceeded to argue in the second part that 'the king of Great Britain is lord of the sea flowing about, as an inseparable and perpetual appendant of

264 *Mare clausum*, p. 102, and *Of the Dominion or Ownership of the Sea*, p. 152, citing Gentilis, *De iure belli*, vol. 1, p. 26, and vol. 2, p. 17.

265 *Mare clausum*, sig A2v-3r. By 1635 Selden had had ten years in which to come to terms with another book published by De Groot, which will be returned to in the next section.

266 *Historie of Tithes*, pp. 478–81.

267 *Mare clausum*, pp. 29–32, and *Of the Dominion or Ownership of the Sea*, pp. 42–6; *De iure naturali et gentium*, pp. 75–85; Rosenblatt 2006, pp. 158–81; Haivry 2017b, pp. 338–74.

268 Whether the references to the new approach mentioned at the end of the first section of the present chapter were fully understood in Scotland also remains less clear.

the British empire'.[269] Whether the second part of his book already existed in 1619 in anything like the form printed in 1635 remains doubtful, but it may perhaps be taken to provide some indication of the direction in which the thinking of English lawyers was beginning to move around the start of the 1620s.[270] As in the previous part, Selden assembled sources that seemed to support the thesis he was defending, including a forgotten ordinance of uncertain provenance in which it had been warned that any mariners who refused to 'stryke and lower their sailes at the command of the kyng's lieutenant' would be treated as enemies (*reputez comme ennemys*).[271] Their ships and goods would be confiscated as enemy property (*forfaitz comme biens des ennemys*), even if they belonged to friends, and the mariners themselves would be punished for their disloyalty (*pour leur rebellete*). Mention was also made of the proclamation issued in March 1604 in which it had been intimated that all mariners, regardless of nationality, were expected to submit to the English king's authority while sailing in his waters.[272] To threaten mariners who resisted the king's authority with the confiscation of their ships would have been consistent with the practice of the Venetians and Genoese, which had been defended by the doctors of civil law. To treat them as enemies when they were actually friends would have been comparable both to the treatment in recent practice of those who traded with an enemy during a war, and to the treatment in the civil and canon laws of those who gave assistance to infidels in wartime. For common lawyers like Selden, however, a more obvious comparison would have been with the confiscation of enemy property in English ports, which was apparently being extended to the waters leading into those ports, and to any mariners who seemed hostile to the English king. More generally, for common lawyers the confiscation of enemy property made better sense than its private acquisition through occupation, for their law was averse to the notion that things should be considered ownerless, and accordingly treated valuable items recovered from the sea (flotsam, jetsam and lagan, wrecked ships, whales, porpoises and such like) as the property of the crown.[273] Although the

269 *Mare clausum*, sig. B2r, and *Of the Dominion or Ownership of the Sea*, sig. E2v. The use of the terms 'Great Britain' and 'British' is of course significant.

270 A similar line of argument was advanced in John Boroughs, *Soveraignty of the British Seas*, which was said to have been 'written in the yeare 1633', when a more aggressive assertion of dominion over the seas was being encouraged by Charles I.

271 *Mare clausum*, pp. 265–6, and *Of the Dominion or Ownership of the Sea*, pp. 401–2; *Black Book of the Admiralty*, vol. 1, pp. 128–31.

272 *Mare clausum*, pp. 236–46, and *Of the Dominion or Ownership of the Sea*, pp. 363–75.

273 Thomas Digges, 'Arguments Provinge that the Quenes Highnes and Her Progenitors Are Just and Lawfull Owners of the Lands and Salte Shores Wonne oute of the Seas', pp. 185–7,

concept of confiscation had been borrowed from the civil law, it was attractive to the common lawyers because it allowed for the automatic acquisition of title.[274] Moreover, its application to things recovered from the sea was taken to demonstrate that the authority of the king and the common law was not strictly limited to the land. Had the account of prize acquisition in De Groot's *De iure praedae* been published in its initial form, not only its methodology but also some of its arguments would probably have seemed more agreeable to common lawyers like Selden than to civil lawyers like Gentilis and Welwod.

4 Towards a New Theory of International Law

In defending the seizure of the *Santa Catarina*, it may be recalled, De Groot attached some significance to an edict on licensed raiding issued by the states general of the United Provinces in 1599, which he connected with the proclamation on trading with the enemy issued by the queen of England in 1602.[275] As was seen in the last chapter, Elizabeth's proclamation had emphasised the consistency of the measures it introduced with the recent practice of neighbouring nations, a practice it had declared to be justifiable in terms of the law of God as well as the law of policy. No reference was made in the proclamation to the theory of the law schools, from which justifications of the seizure of ships and goods at sea had previously been drawn. It has now been seen that De Groot went further in his *De iure praedae* by explicitly and repeatedly rejecting the authority of the civil law as a guide to the handling of relations between nations.[276] His preferred approach was to revert to the Ciceronian foundations

190–1, 193 and 202–4; John Talbot, 'Observacions Touchinge the Kings Prerogative to Wreck of the Sea', pp. 244–6; *Reading of the Famous and Learned Robert Callis*, pp. 39–42, 45 and 54–5; *Reports of Sir Edward Coke*, vol. 3, pp. 215–17.

274 Timbal 1943–4; Parrow 1991; Kesselring 2009 and 2010; Dyjakowska 2012; Cavill 2013 and 2014.

275 The Dutch edict, reproduced in an appendix to De Groot's book, had itself drawn attention to the practice of the English queen.

276 The move away from the civil law tradition receives proper emphasis in Lesaffer 2005, pp. 35–7, though the assimilation there of De Groot and Gentilis is less helpful. It is true that both authors cited a different range of sources from the medieval cvilians, but Gentilis continued to maintain that legal authority was intrinsic to the civilian tradition, whereas De Groot attributed no more weight to civil law sources than to others (Lesaffer 2021, p. 450). Furthermore, if readers of the works of Gentilis and De Groot need to ask themselves *cui bono* (Wijffels 2021, pp. 391–2 and 404), the answer surely is that Gentilis defended the conventional claims of graduates in the civil law to advise rulers on their relations with each other, whereas De Groot advanced the claims of scholars of the humanities. It is significant that when the new understanding of *ius naturale et gentium*

of Elizabeth's law of policy, and to absorb into his argument lessons learned from the law of God by the Thomist theologians. The result was an account of prize acquisition that might have been expected to appeal both to devotees of the *studia humanitatis*, like De Groot himself, and to those who saw the seizure of the *Santa Catarina* as a case of conscience, quite possibly including readers in Spain and Portugal.[277] The account had moral as well as political resonance, and it was no doubt intended to explore dimensions neglected in the judgment of the admiralty court awarding the prize to Van Heemskerk. Nevertheless, it could be that De Groot was also intent on reinforcing the ruling of the court by replacing the reasoning of the civil lawyers with a new type of legal reasoning.[278] The aim of this section is not to contribute to the extensive literature on De Groot's role in the development of thinking about natural law but is rather to focus specifically on his understanding of the relationship between natural and positive law.[279] Did he conceive of *ius gentium* as a cogent extension of *ius naturale* or as something similar to *ius civile*? What significance did he actually attach to the practice of nations, referred to in the 1599 edict and the 1602 proclamation? Historians of international law have found these questions difficult to answer, and it complicates matters that De Groot's thinking on the topic appears to have changed within the period of James I's reign.[280] To begin with, attention will return to remarks made in the original draft of the *De iure praedae*.

In his prolegomena, presented in the second chapter of his book, De Groot explained that while his first two laws – that people were entitled to defend themselves, and to take and retain what they needed to survive – arose from the natural tendency of all created beings to preserve themselves, what turned these rights into permissive 'laws' of nature was the basic rule that 'what God has shown to be his will, that is law'.[281] From the further rule that 'what the

came to be taught in universities, it was initially in faculties of arts, and that when it was later taught in faculties of law, it was as a distinct discipline from the civil and canon laws.

277 Whether deliberately or not, De Groot was the first author to fashion a coherent defence of licensed raiding out of the diverse modes of discourse hinted at in Elizabeth's proclamation.

278 That he may have been concerned with positive law is suggested by a letter he wrote in 1606, reproduced in *Commentary on the Law of Prize*, p. 552, although its precise meaning is far from certain.

279 Chroust 1943; Crowe 1977; Tuck 1979, 1987 and 1999; Haakonssen 1985; Brett 2002, 2011 and 2019; Brouwer 2008; Brooke 2008; Tierney 2011; Straumann 2015 and 2021; Penner 2020; Jones 2021.

280 Malcolm 2002, pp. 439–40; Keene 2002, pp. 30–1; Armitage 2013, pp. 68–9.

281 *De iure praedae commentarius*, pp. 7–10, and *Commentary on the Law of Prize*, pp. 19–23.

common consent of mankind has shown to be the will of all, that is law', he then deduced the more prescriptive laws that no person should injure another, or take from him anything he had possessed.[282] It was understandable, he observed, that the consensus of nations was often described as 'the secondary law of nature, or primary law of nations'. As was noted in the last chapter, the civil lawyers were among those who made use of this phraseology, but De Groot was not using it in their way, for the example he proceeded to provide was the introduction of private property, which the civil lawyers attributed to the secondary law of nations, consisting of departures from the law of nature that most nations had found it expedient to make when creating their own civil laws. It was the Thomist theologians who viewed the introduction of private property as a derivation rather than a deviation from the law of nature, and who found in the consensus of nations confirmation of the soundness of the practical reasoning involved. Although their thinking was essentially Aristotelian, it was also consistent with Cicero's rule that 'the consensus of all nations should be seen as a precept of natural law'. So far, then, *ius gentium* was envisaged by De Groot as an extension of *ius naturale*, yet he added that 'there exists a species of mixed law, compounded of the law of nations and civil law'. Referring to this mixed law as *ius gentium secundarium*, he drew attention to the use of the phrase by a humanist lawyer in Spain, and to illustrate its significance he adopted two examples from a humanist lawyer in France, who had assembled legal, literary, historical and philosophical sources as evidence of 'the inviolability of ambassadors' and (more curiously) 'various matters relating to the burial of the dead'.[283] As a third (and for his purposes rather important) example De Groot mentioned the expectation that disputes would be submitted to judicial determination wherever possible.[284] None of his examples amounted to an expedient departure from natural law, and his concern was again with establishing a 'rule' as a basis for 'laws'. In formulating the rule that 'whatever all states have indicated to be their will, that is law in regard to all of them', he echoed Vitoria's vague idea that there was a commonwealth of nations with some kind of legislative power. The idea remained vague in the first draft of De Groot's book, though it was at least spelled out there that if the secondary law of nations were to come into conflict with the law of nature or

282 *De iure praedae commentarius*, pp. 10–14, and *Commentary on the Law of Prize*, pp. 23–7.

283 Fernandus Vasquius, *Controversiarum illustrium aliarumque usu frequentibus libri tres*, f. 113v; Pierre du Faur, *Semestrium liber secundus*, pp. 1–14. De Groot later adjusted his reference in this passage to *ius gentium secundarium*, and it is possible that he added the reference to Vasquius' book at the same time.

284 *De iure praedae commentarius*, pp. 27–9, and *Commentary on the Law of Prize*, pp. 46–8.

primary law of nations – for instance, if the submission of a dispute to judicial authority would have endangered someone's property rights – the law of nature or primary law of nations would have to take priority.[285]

It might be supposed that the explanation for the close association of *ius gentium* with *ius naturale* in the initial version of De Groot's book was his concern with the justification of a seizure made at sea, for some commentators believe that he regarded the sea as remaining in 'the state of nature'.[286] Although he never used the expression *status naturae* in his book, he certainly did maintain that the oceans were beyond the reach of any claim that might be made to territorial jurisdiction, and at one point he endorsed the opinion that they 'still remained in that primeval state in which all things had been held in common'.[287] Three different lines of argument have been advanced in support of the reading that he meant by this 'the state of nature'. In the first place, De Groot is taken to have reasoned that because in the state of nature the seas had been common to everyone, and because the seas remained common to everyone, the seas must still be in the state of nature. However, historians should obviously hesitate before attributing such a blatant fallacy to such an acute thinker. In the second place, it is pointed out that in referring to literary, historical and philosophical sources on the common ownership of the seas, De Groot was deliberately bringing to mind the mythical golden age in which human laws and institutions had not yet been created, taking his readers into a different temporal as well as spatial sphere. However, while he clearly was encouraging his readers to think about the common ownership of the seas in the ancient way, and to interpret the Roman law texts on the subject in the light of the other sources referred to, it does not follow that he wanted them to believe that the golden age still existed. It is one thing to assert that the seas remained in the primitive condition in which all things were held in common, and another to assert that they remained in the primitive condition in which there was no human law. In the third place, by insisting on the existence of an area beyond the reach of territorial jurisdiction, De Groot is taken to have envisaged an area in which there could be no jurisdiction at all, so that there was no possibility of law (*ius*) being pronounced (*dictio*). However, this line of argument rests on the assumption that territorial jurisdiction was the only

285 *De iure praedae commentarius*, pp. 29–30, and *Commentary on the Law of Prize*, pp. 48–50.

286 Kingsbury and Straumann 2010, p. 30; Brett 2011, pp. 203–4; Straumann 2015, p. 149; Kadelbach 2017, pp. 137–8; Chadwick 2019, p. 96.

287 *De iure praedae commentarius*, p. 223, and *Commentary on the Law of Prize*, p. 328. De Groot did use the expression in the later book to which attention will turn shortly, before it was made famous by Thomas Hobbes.

kind of jurisdiction possible, which was neither widely assumed at the time nor assumed by De Groot himself. The assumption widely made was that the *iurisdictio maritima* conferred on admiralty courts covered events occurring *super altum mare*, wherever that was reckoned to begin, and De Groot himself assumed that the admiralty court sitting in Amsterdam had been justified in exercising jurisdiction over the case he was discussing.[288] While he insisted that 'no one can claim special jurisdiction over the ocean with respect to locality', he recognised that a more general jurisdiction could be asserted 'with respect to persons', arguing that since the parties involved in his case were Dutch and Portuguese, and since the Portuguese courts could not be trusted to deal with the matter fairly, it was appropriate for a Dutch court to deal with it.[289]

Far from believing that the oceans remained in the state of nature and were devoid of human law, De Groot thus believed that they were an area in which the jurisdictions and laws of different nations were apt to compete with one another. As was seen in the first chapter of the present book, the traditional response to this problem was for each nation to develop and interpret its own maritime law within the common theoretical framework provided by the law schools. Each court applied its own law to cases arising from the seizure of prizes in wartime, the execution of reprisals in peacetime, and the prosecution of pirates at any time, but always in accordance with broad principles respected in every other maritime jurisdiction in Europe. The doctors of law in the universities provided guidance on how to resolve tensions not only between local laws and the common law they taught, but also between different local laws.[290] It has since been seen that the civil lawyers persisted in addressing questions in the traditional way even after the seizure of prizes in wartime was confused in practice with the execution of reprisals in peacetime. In this chapter their approach has been further exemplified by a review of some of the pleadings Gentilis submitted on behalf of Spanish litigants in relation to prizes seized by the Dutch during the first few years of James I's reign. In other pleadings that were not reviewed earlier he placed further reliance on

288 See, for instance, *Documents Relating to Law and Custom of the Sea*, vol. 2, pp. 161 and 187–8, and *Select Pleas in the Court of Admiralty*, vol. 2, pp. 84–6, 99–100, 161 and 187–8.

289 *De iure praedae commentarius*, p. 260, and *Commentary on the Law of Prize*, p. 380. *Cf.* Goodwin 2006, p. 988. More precisely, De Groot argued that had there been any relevant territorial jurisdiction it would have been exercised by the sultan of Johore, who was not interested in the case, that the Portuguese authorities in the East Indies were untrustworthy, that there was no Dutch court sitting there, and that it had therefore been appropriate for Van Heemskerk to take matters into his own hands in the Straits of Singapore, and seek judicial approval of his actions after he returned to the Netherlands.

290 Beale 1914; Thorne 1962; Clarence Smith 1970; Stein 1980; Hatzimihail 2007.

'the laws and the doctors' when addressing questions arising from the condemnation of maritime raiders as pirates.[291] Although he found it convenient to rehearse in favour of his clients arguments he had criticised in his treatise on the law of arms, he continued to conceive of piracy as the criminal activity it had always been in the minds of civil lawyers.[292] It is therefore more than a little misleading to suggest that he broke new ground in writing about pirates as criminals, that in doing so he tried to reduce the lawlessness of the oceans by projecting into them jurisdictions and laws hitherto confined to land, and that De Groot tried to do something similar in writing about the authorisation of maritime raiding on land.[293] The idea that nations could exercise jurisdiction over the seas was no more novel than the idea that piracy was a crime, and to portray Gentilis and De Groot as similarly minded innovators is to lose sight of the latter's crucial break with tradition.[294] What needs to be recognised is not that De Groot sought to solve the problem of lawlessness at sea by projecting jurisdictions and laws from the land into the sea, but that his repudiation of the civil law tradition exacerbated the problem of conflicting jurisdictions and laws that had long existed in relation to events at sea. The loss of respect for the civil law as a standard of debate shared across national boundaries created an urgent need for an alternative standard, and part of De Groot's purpose in writing his book was to identify that standard.

A better explanation for the close association of *ius gentium* with *ius naturale* in the initial version of the *De iure praedae* is that De Groot's interest in disputes resistant to judicial determination led him away from discussing the application of any *ius civile* (such as Dutch law) within a framework provided by *ius gentium* (civil law, understood as common law).[295] If he did not think the seas were still in the state of nature, he clearly did think sovereign states were. It may be recalled that when he wrote about private wars he envisaged a return to 'that early law which made each individual the judge of his own affairs', and this was the condition in which he believed sovereign states always

291 *Hispanicae advocationis libri duo*, vol. 1, pp. 50–4, 66–8 and 101–12, and vol. 2, pp. 54–6, 70–2 and 104–14. For an illuminating discussion of one of the cases see Wijffels 1994b.

292 He made use in particular of the reasoning of Alciatus mentioned in the closing section of the last chapter, where it was seen that Gentilis wrote about piracy in his treatise in a novel style, but with no great innovation in substance.

293 Benton 2005, pp. 704–6, 2010a, pp. 120–37, 2010b and 2011b.

294 A less misleading account of the relationship between them can be found in Haggenmacher 1990.

295 This also explains why his focus was on the regulation of relations between states (public international law) rather than the resolution of conflicts between jurisdictions and laws (private international law).

found themselves.[296] Citing Tacitus, he observed that 'since the state has no superior, it is necessarily the judge even of its own cause'.[297] When he made the same observation in another passage, he not only cited further classical sources in support but also advised the lawyers who tended to neglect these sources that they would find similar statements in books written by their own teachers, drawing attention especially to a passage from Baldus' commentary on Justinian's *Code* in which he had talked about the need for those claiming *suprema potestas* to rely on *ratio naturalis*.[298] In fact, elsewhere in the same commentary Baldus had clarified his position by remarking that rulers who refused to recognise the authority of the emperor were still bound to follow the civil law because that was where they would find *ratio naturalis* in the form of written law.[299] The latter passage had been subjected to devastating criticism by the humanist jurist Jean Bodin, who had objected that since law was 'nothing other than the command of a sovereign, using his power', natural reason could not have been turned into law by being set down in writing by someone who was not recognised as a sovereign.[300] Whether influenced by Bodin or not, De Groot took essentially the same line in arguing that states or individuals with no superior to whom their disputes could be submitted had no option but to fall back on natural reason for guidance on how best to conduct themselves.[301] This resort to *ius naturale et gentium* might have been satisfactory if every state had been committed to the pursuit of an ethical foreign policy, yet the obvious danger was that under some such guise states would in reality pursue their own interests, as indeed had been recommended by Machiavelli

296 *De iure praedae commentarius*, p. 128, and *Commentary on the Law of Prize*, pp. 191–2.

297 *De iure praedae commentarius*, p. 25, and *Commentary on the Law of Prize*, p. 43; Tacitus, *Annals*, 13.56.

298 *De iure praedae commentarius*, p. 6, and *Commentary on the Law of Prize*, p. 6; Cicero, *Pro Milone*, 4.10; Dio Chrysostom, *Discourses*, 76.5; Sophocles, *Antigone*, 454–5; Baldus de Ubaldis, *Commentaria super Codicem*, sig. A2v (ad Constitutio De novo); Vasquius, *Controversiarum illustrium aliarumque usu frequentium libri tres*, ff. 201v-2r.

299 *Commentaria super Codicem*, f. 44r (ad C.7.45.13).

300 *Les six livres de la république*, pp. 107–8, and *Six Bookes of a Commonweale*, pp. 107–8.

301 The relationship between Bodin, De Groot and Gentilis is examined in Quaglioni 2010 and in Domingo and Minnucci 2020. At the beginning of his treatise on the law of arms Gentilis had agreed with Bodin that the study of the *Corpus iuris civilis* provided an inadequate basis for the construction of a truly common law, recognising that 'jurists are not restricted to the books of Justinian', yet he remained critical of comparative legal historians like Bodin who seemed to him to accumulate examples without explaining how 'fixed' laws could be extracted from them (*De iure belli*, vol. 1, pp. 2–3 and 15–16, and vol. 2, pp. 4–5 and 16–17).

and his followers.[302] Affirming that the *iustum* would invariably coincide with the *honestum*, and the *honestum* with the *utile*, was unlikely to persuade readers who had moved beyond Cicero's teaching and had embraced a less moral form of reason of state doctrine. It may have been as a means of strengthening this part of his argument that De Groot traced his whole theory of *ius naturale et gentium* back to an innate desire for self-preservation, with the implication that it provided a guide to the pursuit of self-interest for states and individuals to follow, as Horace appeared to have grasped when he wrote that 'expediency might perhaps be called the mother of justice and equity'.[303] If so, however, his citation from Horace provides evidence not so much of an expectation that his readers would be convinced as of a concern that they would need convincing.

It may have been the same concern that caused De Groot to move tentatively towards identifying a more positive law of nations, which he did at several different places in his book and in two different ways. When writing about the legitimacy of warfare, he remarked that the laws of nature and nations 'cannot be invalidated by civil law', quoting for authority Cicero's statement that the law of nations ought to be (*esse debet*) part of every civil law, and referring further to statements made by Plato and Aquinas, which appeared to indicate that a human law running contrary to natural law would not be a valid law.[304] Of course, even if the texts cited had been considered authoritative by De Groot's readers, it would not actually have followed from them that the law of nature and nations necessarily formed part of every civil law, yet this was what he tried to argue when writing about the legitimacy of plunder.[305] Pointing out that approval of the practice was widespread in 'the laws and customs of individual nations', and taking this consensus to prove that it formed part of the law of nations, he concluded that 'since the despoliation of enemies is accepted under the law of nations, it must necessarily be sanctioned by civil law too'. Elsewhere in his book he reiterated his opinion that human laws could not validly deviate from natural law, but he never explained clearly why the derivation of practices from natural law among most nations would mean that the practices had to form part of the civil laws of other nations too.[306] The

302 The relationship between De Groot and Lipsius is examined in Ford 1996; Eyffinger 1998; Leira 2007; Lindberg 2011; Waszinik 2012.

303 *De iure praedae commentarius*, p. 9, and *Commentary on the Law of Prize*, p. 21; Horace, *Satires*, 1.3.98.

304 *De iure praedae commentarius*, p. 34, and *Commentary on the Law of Prize*, p. 56; Cicero, *De officiis*, 3.17.69; Plato, *Minos*, 316a-c; Aquinas, *Summa theologiae*, 1a2ae 95.2.

305 *De iure praedae commentarius*, p. 52, and *Commentary on the Law of Prize*, p. 81.

306 *De iure praedae commentarius*, pp. 232 and 236, and *Commentary on the Law of Prize*, pp. 340 and 345.

inadequacy of this mode of argument made its alternative more important. At various places in his book De Groot expressed approval of the Stoic idea of a *civitas mundi* or *respublica orbis*, as popularised by Cicero and Seneca.[307] It was this idea that lay behind Vitoria's elusive suggestion that the *consensus maiores partis totius orbis* had legal as well as moral force since the global commonwealth had the power to make laws (*potestas ferendi leges*), which in turn lay behind De Groot's equally elusive view of *ius gentium secundarium* as a mixed form of law.[308] The problem remained that to identify a legislator capable of enacting internationally binding laws was all but impossible – indeed, it was even harder for a writer working in a country that had rejected papal authority – and if it was easier to imagine some form of customary law emerging from the practice of nations, how exactly this might come about still needed to be explained. Although the laws applied by nations to their relations with one another were often of a customary character, although their shared reliance on the common theory of the schools had resulted in a body of customary law taking shape that was itself common in a descriptive sense, and although the expectation that nations would adhere to shared standards meant that in some areas – for instance, the practice of diplomacy – this customary law of nations came close to being common in a prescriptive sense, the final step remained to be taken towards a theory of customary international law.[309]

The step was taken in a treatise published by a Spanish Jesuit in 1612, on the basis of lectures he had delivered at the University of Coimbra about Aquinas' discussion of law and justice.[310] After dealing at some length with *ius naturale*, Francisco Suárez proceeded to an innovative account of *ius gentium*.[311] He first outlined the conventional view of the Thomist theologians that while *ius gentium* lay somewhere between *ius naturale* and *ius civile*, it was more closely connected with the former, then argued that it was better regarded as being more akin to the latter.[312] Everyone agreed that *ius gentium* consisted like *ius civile* of law people made for themselves, but somehow it had become common to most nations, and the challenge was to explain how,

307 *De iure praedae commentarius*, pp. 13, 93 and 331–2, and *Commentary on the Law of Prize*, pp. 27, 139 and 483.

308 De Groot's debt to Vitoria on this topic is noted in Lesaffer 2002, pp. 121–7. As was noted in the last chapter, Gentilis also made something of Vitoria's suggestion, but because De Groot repudiated the civil law as a shared standard of international relations, the pressure on him to develop Vitoria's ideas further is bound to have been much greater.

309 Queller 1967; Mattingley 1988; Hertz 1990–1; Ziegler 2004; Fedele 2016 and 2017.

310 Scott 1934b; Gordley 2012; Pace 2014; Coyle 2017; Lagerlund 2018.

311 Focarelli 2006; Tierney 2007; Bauer 2015; Kincaid 2019; Gonzalez 2019.

312 *Selections from Three Works*, vol. 1(3), pp. 180–91, and vol. 2, pp. 374–411.

given that there was no universal sovereign capable of legislating for everyone. The solution, Suárez believed, was to regard *ius gentium* as a species of *lex non scripta, quae consuetudo appellatur*, a subject he returned to at considerable length in another part of his treatise.[313] He explained there that when people behaved repeatedly in a particular manner, their behaviour eventually became habitual, and that once habitual, it was not just something that was bound to happen as a matter of fact, but was something that was bound to happen as a matter of law. Suárez is often taken to have established the doctrine found in modern international law that customs become legally binding through a combination of settled usage (*repetitio facti*) and a belief in its obligatory force (*opinio iuris*).[314] In fact, he did not express himself in precisely these terms, and what he did say is quite opaque, but for present purposes what matters is that he went on to maintain that customary laws could take shape between nations as well as between individuals.[315] He distinguished *ius gentium* in the weak or improper sense of law found among nations (*ius intra gentes*, which was common only descriptively) from *ius gentium* in the strong or proper sense of law habitually observed by nations in dealing with each other (*ius inter gentes*, which was common prescriptively).[316] Just as individuals were obliged to conform to customary usages, so too were nations, and it was the existence of these usages, it seemed to Suárez, that made it meaningful to talk about a global commonwealth.[317] While his customary *ius gentium* was in principle susceptible to alteration, he found it hard to see how it could be altered in practice since every nation would have needed to agree to the adoption of a contrary usage. As the Roman jurists had pointed out, customary law rested on the *tacitus consensus* or *tacita conventio* of all the members of the community it governed.[318]

De Groot certainly became familiar with Suárez's treatise, possibly before he made a series of amendments to his *De iure praedae*, although he may

313 *Selections from Three Works*, vol. 1(3), pp. 770–865, and vol. 2, pp. 501–752.

314 Kelly 2000, pp. 451–2; Roberts 2001, pp. 757–8; Martin 2002, pp. 354–5; Guzman 2005, p. 123; Lepard 2016, p. 62.

315 For a more careful reading see Postema 2007, pp. 279–80 and 287. Suárez is also credited with establishing the modern notion of customary international law in Ochon 2007, p. 129; Baker 2015, p. 444; Kadens 2016, p. 31; Trachtman 2016, p. 172.

316 He was therefore able to argue that the plundering of enemies in wartime had 'become a part of *ius gentium*, through common custom' (*Selections from Three Works*, vol. 1(3), pp. 814–15, and vol. 2, pp. 840–1), although his discussion of the subject ran along the usual Thomist lines. On his just war theory see Reichberg 2012.

317 Höpfl 2004, pp. 304–5; Lesaffer 2011, pp. 421–2; Brett 2012, pp. 1090–1.

318 *Digest*, 1.3.32.1 and 1.3.35.

instead have been developing his own thinking along parallel lines before 1612.[319] At some time he revisited the remarks he had made about a mixed law lying somewhere between *ius naturale* and *ius civile*, adding a new paragraph on an inserted slip of paper in which he separated this law into two types, the first taking the form of agreements between states (*pacta inter respublicas*), the second of received customs (*receptae consuetudines*).[320] He was not sure that the customs states merely shared with one another really amounted to law, 'since they were not introduced collectively but separately', so that they could be abrogated freely by any state. On the other hand, he had already mentioned that states might use agreements to create *ius gentium secundarium* in the later passage in which he defended the legitimacy of retaining plunder even after a war had ended.[321] To this passage he added another new paragraph, in which he stated that the effective seizure of any prize was a requirement introduced 'by the law of nations, not in its natural but its positive aspect, and in effect by an agreement among at least the majority of nations'.[322] In a third addition he expanded on an existing warning that the attribution of title to the occupiers of plunder derived 'not from what we have called the primary law of nations, but from positive law', explaining that this practice did not derive from 'an engagement that would bind states but from a sort of coincidental consensus, from which each nation was free to withdraw where it saw the need'.[323] By making these amendments De Groot clarified his understanding of the relationship between the consensus of nations as *ius gentium primarium*, where it served to confirm the reliability of the reasoning through which nations derived laws from *ius naturale*, and as *ius gentium secundarium*, where it served to impose obligatory laws on nations. His distinction between a coincidental consensus and a mutual undertaking – not so much a matter of *consensus*, it might have been remarked, as of *conventio* or a meeting of minds – may have strengthened his concept of *ius gentium secundarium*, but it did so at the expense of his concept of *ius gentium primarium*.[324] Moreover, by using the word *consuetudo* to

319 Kosters 1925, pp. 41–3; Waszink 2009, pp. 232–4; Borges de Macedo 2017, pp. 284–8.

320 *De iure praedae commentarius*, p. 27, and *Commentary on the Law of Prize*, pp. 45–6; LUL, BPL 917, f. 12ᵃr. For an illuminating discussion of the amendments discussed here see Haggenmacher 1981.

321 *De iure praedae commentarius*, p. 119, and *Commentary on the Law of Prize*, p. 177.

322 *De iure praedae commentarius*, pp. 121–2, and *Commentary on the Law of Prize*, p. 180–1; LUL, BPL 917, f. 53ᵃ.

323 *De iure praedae commentarius*, p. 157, and *Commentary on the Law of Prize*, p. 234–5; LUL, BPL 917, f. 69v.

324 For the latter, of course, it was important that nations reasoned independently. De Groot was contemptuous of laws that became common through thoughtless imitation, so perhaps another distinction needed to be drawn.

label the less obligatory part of *ius gentium secundarium*, he made it more difficult for his prospective readers to know what he actually had in mind when he talked about laws being formed through agreements between nations.

In his response to Welwod, written after the publication of Suárez's treatise, De Groot again distinguished between a binding form of international law (*ius gentium proprie dictum*) and an accidental form of transnational law (*ius gentium abusive dictum*), although he now noted that much of the law of nations properly so called had been 'introduced by customs', and identified the widespread reception of the civil law as a prime example of law becoming common merely 'by imitation'.[325] He returned to the significance of the term *ius gentium* in a lengthy treatise he wrote about the law of war and peace, 'whether derived from nature itself or introduced by habit and tacit agreement'.[326] Immediately contrasting his approach with the methodology of the lawyers, he declared there that he was concerned once more with the discipline Cicero had tried to extract from 'the treaties, agreements and conventions of peoples, princes and foreign nations'.[327] However, his concern was no longer with the defence of a particular seizure of a ship and goods at sea but was with the whole of *ius belli ac pacis*, and he meant to concentrate on the *iustum* alone, without talking directly about the *honestum* or *utile*.[328] Indeed, he now distanced himself from Horace's statement that expediency was the mother of justice and equity by observing that nature was the great-grandmother of *ius gentium*, for it provided the obligatory force of agreements, and it was through agreements that nations had introduced laws to regulate their dealings with each other.[329] De Groot still maintained in his *De iure belli ac pacis libri tres* that the law of nations consisted partly of precepts deduced or derived from the law of nature, and that the reliability of the precepts derived from the law of nature could be confirmed by the consensus of nations, as well as the consensus of philosophers,

325 *Defensio capitis quinti Maris liberi*, pp. 347–8 and 358–9, and 'Some Less Known Works of Hugo Grotius', pp. 181–3 and 200–1. On the relationship between De Groot, Welwod and Suárez see Haggenmacher 1983, pp. 388–97.

326 *De iure belli ac pacis*, vol. 1, sig. *4r, and vol. 2, p. 9; *Rights of War and Peace*, vol. 1, p. 75. The editions cited here are based on later versions of De Groot's treatise, which were not identical with his first edition. At this point, for instance, the later versions intruded a reference to divine law.

327 Draper 1990; Ziegler 1991–2; Yasuaki 1993; Bederman 1995–6; Bauer 2004; Stumpf 2006; Lee 2011.

328 The relationship between the two works is considered in Winkel 2009.

329 *De iure belli ac pacis*, vol. 1, sig. *5v, and vol. 2, p. 15; *Rights of War and Peace*, vol. 1, pp. 93–4. *Cf.* Straumann 2015, pp. 88–90.

historians, poets and orators.[330] But he also now maintained that part of the law of nations consisted of voluntary agreements entered into by nations, which he supported with a reference to Dio Chrysostom.[331] He identified these agreements as a species of unwritten law or custom, and he later distinguished again between this *ius gentium proprie dictum* and the customs that nations happened to have in common, typically through imitation of the civil law taught in the universities.[332] Nevertheless, he was now ready to concede that the writings of the civil lawyers sometimes provided valuable 'testimony to such a custom as forms the law of nations in our time'.[333]

This reassessment of the value of the teaching of the civil law doctors had significant repercussions on the treatment of prize acquisition in the *De iure belli ac pacis*. In his new book De Groot expressed approval of the distinction drawn by the Roman jurists between enemies and pirates, and also of the recent tendencies among nations to require licences to be obtained for expeditions against pirates, and to use property confiscated from pirates to compensate their victims.[334] He was less satisfied with the Roman definition of enemies as opponents in wars declared between sovereign nations, observing that the law of nature allowed wars to be waged for the sake of self-defence or the punishment of crimes without any announcement of hostilities, although he conceded that the law of nations required formal requests to be made for the reparation of injuries before recourse was taken to armed force.[335] It was no mere coincidence, he maintained, that rulers sent letters of requisition to each other before they authorised reprisals. De Groot's recognition of the role of agreements between nations in the formation of *ius gentium* also transformed his understanding of the plundering of enemies in wartime. Although he continued to believe that in ancient Rome plunder had been acquired by the state, he now accepted that nations could have agreed to arrange matters differently,

330 *De iure belli ac pacis*, vol. 1, sig. *7v-8r and pp. 5–6, and vol. 2, p. 23–4 and 42; *Rights of War and Peace*, vol. 1, pp. 110–13 and 159.

331 *De iure belli ac pacis*, vol. 1, pp. 6–7, and vol. 2, p. 44; *Rights of War and Peace*, vol. 1, pp. 162–3; Dio Chrysostom, *Discourses*, 76.1. Iurlaro 2018 argues that De Groot found in his source an alternative approach to the understanding of customary law from the one worked out by Suárez.

332 *De iure belli ac pacis*, vol. 1, p. 196, and vol. 2, p. 295; *Rights of War and Peace*, vol. 2, pp. 634–5.

333 *De iure belli ac pacis*, vol. 1, sig. 2*1r, and vol. 2, p. 29; *Rights of War and Peace*, vol. 1, p. 130.

334 *De iure belli ac pacis*, vol. 1, pp. 292–3, 327–8 and 449–50, and vol. 2, pp. 436–7, 485 and 630–3; *Rights of War and Peace*, vol. 2, pp. 894 and 989, and vol. 3, pp. 1247–51.

335 *De iure belli ac pacis*, vol. 1, pp. 450–4, and vol. 2, pp. 633–40; *Rights of War and Peace*, vol. 3, pp. 1262–69.

and he recognised that they had in fact agreed to treat enemy property as if it were ownerless and open to acquisition by occupation.[336] Although he continued to regard the civil law doctors as unreliable readers of the Roman law texts, he now accepted that they provided reliable evidence of the agreement nations had actually reached with each other, which was a component of *ius gentium*, unlike the rules introduced to govern the distribution of spoils, which remained part of each nation's *ius civile*, regardless of how similar they might be to each other. In response to the argument derived from Roman law that no prize was effectively occupied until brought safely home by its captors, De Groot insisted that the alternative requirement of possession for twenty-four hours had been established 'by the more recent law of nations', an indication that he was more ready than Suárez to countenance changes in the customary law of nations.[337] In response to the practice of treating friendly goods found on enemy ships as enemy goods, he insisted that it rested not on a 'fixed law' but on a rebuttable 'presumption' that the goods belonged to enemies.[338] How exactly he distinguished between practices that rested on binding agreements between nations and those that were merely widespread among nations is far from clear, and it has been pointed out that he was inclined to identify the Dutch approach as the agreed approach.[339] What matters here is that he paid a considerable amount of attention to the customary practices of nations in his new book. Whereas in his *De iure praedae* the secondary law of nations played a marginal role in a discussion focused on the law of nature and the primary law of nations, in his *De iure belli ac pacis* discussion of natural law, together with the law of nations deduced or derived from it, often gave way to an elaborate treatment of the customary practices of nations.

Unlike his *De iure praedae* and *Defensio capitis quinti Maris liberi*, De Groot's *De iure belli ac pacis* was published during his lifetime, initially around the time of the death of James VI and I.[340] As far as the regulation of maritime raiding was concerned, it delivered an ambiguous message. On the one hand, by rehabilitating the civil law doctors as commentators on the agreements reached between nations, it afforded the civil lawyers practising before the English court

336 *De iure belli ac pacis*, vol. 1, pp. 476–83, and vol. 2, pp. 670–83; *Rights of War and Peace*, vol. 3, pp. 1327–49.

337 *De iure belli ac pacis*, vol. 1, p. 474, and vol. 2, p. 666; *Rights of War and Peace*, vol. 3, pp. 1320–1.

338 *De iure belli ac pacis*, vol. 1, pp. 474–5, and vol. 2, p. 668; *Rights of War and Peace*, vol. 3, pp. 1324–5.

339 Roelofsen 1983 and 1989b.

340 Reeves 1925; Nellen 2012; Osler 2016.

of admiralty an opportunity to reposition themselves as experts in a new area of law, into which much of the learning they had already acquired had been transferred.[341] In particular, it offered them a new justification for continuing to deal with prize acquisition in terms of the occupation of enemy property, and for doing so without worrying unduly about whether an open war had ever been declared, although given that this would have involved them in a familiar mode of analysis, the likelihood is that many would still have viewed the law of nations as 'that which naturall reason hath propounded and appointed in common to all men'.[342] On the other hand, by securing the foundations of a customary law of nations, and accepting that this part of *ius gentium* was open to modification, De Groot's treatise also provided an opportunity to justify the rather different form of maritime raiding that had been taking shape in the recent practice of nations.[343] This form of maritime raiding had become quite deeply embedded in Elizabethan practice after a traditional catalogue of the admiral's responsibilities – to find out what had happened to flotsam, jetsam, lagan, wrecked ships, beached whales, and so on – was extended to require investigation of unlicensed raiding, the distribution of prizes without judicial authorisation, and so on.[344] Following the queen's death, a similar set of directions required the admiral to investigate the abuse of letters of marque during her war with Spain, as well as the service of English mariners on foreign ships, and other matters.[345] Although the new king avoided entanglement in external wars throughout his reign, it was seen earlier in this chapter that the admiralty court in England had to resolve issues arising from wars between other nations, and that licensed raiding became a feature of trade in the East Indies. To some extent at least it came to be appreciated in England that the law of nations was being viewed in the Netherlands as something distinct from the civil law, consisting partly of the customary practices of nations, and connected with

341 On the reception of De Groot's ideas in England see Barducci 2017.

342 The quotation comes from the *Direction or Preparative to the Study of the Lawe*, f. 63v, written by William Fulbecke, who epitomised Gentilis' treatise in his *Pandectes of the Law of Nations*, ff. 33v-52r (Terrill 1981, pp. 174–8; Prest 1982; Coquillette 1988, pp. 71–9; Woolf 1990, pp. 178–81). Similar definitions of the law of nations can be found in BL, Add. MS 29439, ff. 177–80r (a tract attributed to Francis Clerk in Hill 1988, p. 275, but not in Derrett 1974 or Baker 1998, pp. 71–6), and in Thomas Ridley, *View of the Civile and Ecclesiastical Law*, p. 2.

343 The emerging practice was of course more consistent with the theory of prize acquisition developed in the *De iure praedae*, but how widely this was known is unclear.

344 In BL, Add. MS 12504, f. 143, Sir Julius Caesar noted that the *Articles Concerning the Admiralty of England* printed in 1591 added six articles to a catalogue written in Latin in the fourteenth century (BL, Harley MS 2222, ff. 20–9), which was afterwards translated into French, then into English (BL, Sloane MS 1605, ff. 3–15).

345 NAK, HCA14/36, n. 132.

both the law of God and the law of policy. When war with Spain returned to the political agenda at the close of James' reign, Francis Bacon decided to publish the essay in which he had recommended frequent warfare, on whatever pretext could be manufactured, as an exercise that would keep the body politic in sound health.[346] A war fought against Spain at sea, he believed, would be 'lucrative and restorative', especially if the spoils were dealt with in the Roman way, with 'riches to the treasury' and 'donatives' to the combatants.[347] If a war were to begin, one option would have been to revert to the old justification of prize acquisition, reconceptualised as an agreement between nations, while another would have been to develop further the approach adopted in recent conflicts, on which a new agreement between nations appeared to have been emerging.

5 Prize Litigation in Caroline England

When Charles I succeeded his father on the thrones of Scotland, England and Ireland on 27 March 1625 all three realms were still at peace with their neighbours, though tensions were mounting with Spain and the southern Netherlands.[348] Since the general authorisation James had provided for the granting of letters of marque to the victims of raiders from Dunkirk was reckoned to have lapsed on his death, steps were immediately taken to provide authorisation in Charles' name.[349] The instructions reissued by the privy council again made it clear that genuine reprisals were intended, and diplomatic efforts were renewed to obtain justice in the Netherlands for those who had suffered loss.[350] Letters of marque were nonetheless granted by Sir Henry Marten, the judge of the admiralty court in London, who found it reassuring that even James, 'who was not easily drawn to write or subscribe any lines tending to extremities, gave commission to the lord admiral to issue letters

346 Wormald 1993, pp. 177–85; Peltonen 1995, pp. 193–219; Zagorin 1998, pp. 153–61; Zeitlin 2018, pp. 48–77.

347 *Letters and Life of Francis Bacon*, vol. 7, pp. 499–500; *Works of Francis Bacon*, vol. 7, pp. 451–2.

348 Carleton 1983, pp. 60–75; Cogswell 1984, pp. 242–9; Cust 2005, pp. 44–50.

349 *Acts of the Privy Council of England*, vol. 40, pp. 9 and 37; *Calendar of State Papers, Domestic Series, of the Reign of Charles I*, vol. 1, pp. 7 and 16, and vol. 3, p. 282; *Foedera, conventiones, literae et cuiuscunque generis acta publica*, vol. 18, pp. 12–13.

350 *Acts of the Privy Council of England*, vol. 40, pp. 41 and 72.

of marque'.[351] While Charles was known to favour a more aggressive policy than his father, the parliament assembled at London in the summer was reluctant to grant him the taxation he requested until there was 'a warre declared against Spaine'.[352] In the meantime preparations were made for an escalation of violence. A fleet was prepared for action by the duke of Buckingham, as admiral of England, Ireland and Wales, and mariners in foreign service were summoned home to serve their own king, on the basis that 'it would be most improper and unnaturall that his owne naturall borne subjects should upon any occasion or accedent drawe their swordes the one against the other'.[353] On 7 September the Treaty of Southampton created an 'offensive and defensive' alliance with the United Provinces, and committed its signatories to a 'guerre ouverte' against their 'commun ennemy'.[354] Viewing the appearance of a combined fleet of English and Dutch ships off Cadiz in October as 'une rupture complète avec l'Angleterre', Philip IV in Spain, and the archduchess of Austria in the Netherlands, made their own preparations for war.[355] Although no formal declaration was issued, there was no doubt that a state of open hostility existed by the end of the year, when diplomatic relations were broken off between Charles, Philip and Isabella.[356] If it might have been supposed from the Treaty of Southampton that Charles had entered the existing war between Spain and the United Provinces, it might instead have been supposed, after the

351 *Calendar of State Papers, Domestic Series, of the Reign of Charles I*, vol. 1, pp. 37, 52–3 and 285–6; *Manuscripts of the Earl Cowper*, p. 207.

352 *Journals of the House of Commons*, vol. 1, pp. 810–13; *Debates in the House of Commons in 1625*, pp. 31, 77–8, 105 and 138–41.

353 *Acts of the Privy Council of England*, vol. 40, pp. 151–2, 164 and 200–1; *Foedera, conventiones, literae et cuiuscunque generis acta publica*, vol. 18, p. 20; *Stuart Royal Proclamations*, vol. 2, pp. 59–61.

354 *Cours universel diplomatique du droit des gens*, vol. 5(2), pp. 478–81; *European Treaties Bearing on the History of the United States*, vol. 1, pp. 290–9; *State Papers Collected by Edward, Earl of Clarendon*, vol. 1, pp. 53–64; *Calendar of State Papers and Manuscripts, Relating to English Affairs, Existing in the Archives and Collections of Venice*, vol. 19, p. 167.

355 *Correspondance de la cour de l'Espagne sur les affaires des Pays-Bas au XVIIe siècle*, vol. 2, pp. 228–32, 235–6 and 240.

356 *Acts of the Privy Council of England*, vol. 40, pp. 224 and 263; *Calendar of State Papers, Domestic Series, of the Reign of Charles I*, vol. 1, p. 171; *Correspondance de la cour de l'Espagne sur les affaires des Pays-Bas au XVIIe siècle*, vol. 2, p. 235; *Calendar of State Papers and Manuscripts, Relating to English Affairs, Existing in the Archives and Collections of Venice*, vol. 19, p. 254; 'Salvetti Correspondence', p. 39. A false impression that war was declared in May is sometimes received from *Calendar of State Papers, Domestic Series, of the Reign of Charles I*, vol. 23, p. 55, but *cf. Correspondance de la cour de l'Espagne sur les affaires des Pays-Bas au XVIIe siècle*, vol. 2, p. 221.

Treaty of The Hague created an alliance with Denmark as well as the United Provinces in December, that he was entering the Thirty Years' War.[357]

Further authorisation for maritime raiding against 'the king of Spaine or his subjects, inhabitinge in sundry places under the saide kinges obedience', had already been provided in September 1625.[358] In November the privy council had issued instructions for the granting of 'letters of reprisall' by the admiralty, which had been closely modelled on those issued during Elizabeth's war, and had differed from those issued earlier in the year in failing to restrict the seizure of ships and goods to the amounts required to compensate the holders of the letters for losses they had sustained.[359] Indeed, the practice soon developed of granting letters of reprisal to anyone who asked for them, without any proof of loss, provided security was given that no seizure would be made from the king's subjects, friends or allies, and that any prize taken would be brought home intact for approval.[360] After the formal adjudication of a prize to its captors in the admiralty court, it was again declared, the captors would be entitled to dispose of it 'in as ample manner as at any tyme heretofore hath beene accustomed by way of reprisall', while its purchasers would be entitled to enjoy it 'in as ample and lawfull manner as if the said goods had bin comen by through the lawfull trafficq of merchants, or as juste prizes in the tyme of open war'.[361] In April 1626 the level of financial security required before letters of reprisal were granted was reduced, and in July 1626 the terms of the bonds of security imposed were adjusted to allow for the necessity mariners sometimes felt to dispose of prizes overseas.[362] However, a proposal that courts outside London should be authorised to adjudicate on prizes was resisted by

357 *Cours universel diplomatique du droit des gens*, vol. 5(2), pp. 482–5.

358 *Foedera, conventiones, literae et cuiuscunque generis acta publica*, vol. 18, pp. 188–9, and see too p. 222.

359 *Documents Relating to Law and Custom of the Sea*, vol. 1, pp. 410–13; *Acts of the Privy Council of England*, vol. 40, pp. 229–31; *Foedera, conventiones, litterae et cuiuscunque generis acta publica*, vol. 18, pp. 12–13; *Calendar of State Papers, Domestic Series, of the Reign of Charles I*, vol. 1, p. 142.

360 *Calendar of State Papers and Manuscripts, Relating to English Affairs, Existing in the Archives and Collections of Venice*, vol. 19, pp. 167 and 296–7; *Calendar of State Papers, Domestic Series, of the Reign of Charles I*, vol. 1, p. 457; 'Salvetti Correspondence', p. 117; Appleby 1983, vol. 1, pp. 112–13.

361 These phrases were of course carried across from the instructions issued in Elizabeth's reign, in the amended form requiring the formal adjudication of prizes.

362 *Documents Relating to Law and Custom of the Sea*, vol. 1, pp. 422–3 and 425–6; *Acts of the Privy Council of England*, vol. 40, p. 448, and vol. 41, pp. 61–2.

the admiral, who feared that he might not receive the 'tenths' he was due.[363] The admiral's right to a tenth of the value of every prize taken was traditional, unlike the imposition of customs duties on prizes, which meant that as much as a third of any prize taken was lost to the crown, leading some mariners to express regret that the king had not reverted to the practice of declaring 'a free war without any conditions'.[364] As in Elizabeth's reign, a proclamation was issued requiring the close confinement of prisoners brought back to assist in the proof of ownership, to prevent them from gathering intelligence for the enemy.[365] Towards the end of the war the bonds imposed on mariners were adjusted again to forbid raiding in the Mediterranean, which had caused difficulties for merchants trading there.[366]

Just as the regulations issued by the privy council changed after the early months of Charles' reign, so too did the form of the documents used in the admiralty. Warrants initially sent by Buckingham to Marten directed him to grant letters of reprisal or marque to mariners or merchants who had provided proof of losses they had sustained, whereas those sent from the autumn of 1625 onwards merely mentioned the authorisation the admiral had received from the king to grant letters to those who had sustained losses, without any reference to proof being provided.[367] The recurring phrase, 'to such of his majesties subjects as have suffered losse or damage by the king of Spaine, tharchdutches or anie of their subjects', was not meant seriously, as is confirmed by a letter Buckingham wrote to Marten on 29 December 1625, in which he talked about the directions he had been sending him to grant letters 'to all such persons as

363 *Calendar of State Papers, Domestic Series, of the Reign of Charles I*, vol. 1, p. 188, and vol. 4, p. 76; *Calendar of State Papers Relating to Ireland of the Reign of Charles I*, vol. 1, pp. 161, 319 and 456.

364 *Acts of the Privy Council of England*, vol. 41, pp. 64–5; *Calendar of State Papers and Manuscripts, Relating to English Affairs, Existing in the Archives and Collections of Venice*, vol. 19, p. 297. Buckingham's patent as admiral had not mentioned his right to tenths explicitly, unlike his rights to flotsam, jetsam and so on, but it had emphasised the customary character of his office (NAK, C66/2181, n. 20; and see too BL, Add. MS 37819, ff. 9v-10r, 47r, 146v and 184v).

365 *Proclamation Directing How Prisoners Shall be Ordered*; *Stuart Royal Proclamations*, vol. 2, pp. 201–2.

366 *Documents Relating to Law and Custom of the Sea*, vol. 1, pp. 456–7; *Acts of the Privy Council of England*, vol. 43, pp. 131 and 222–3, and vol. 44, pp. 56–7; *Stuart Royal Proclamations*, vol. 2, pp. 209–11.

367 A few examples of warrants can be found in NAK, HCA25/4–8, and also in SP16/115 and SP16/130, which are registers of the warrants issued in the later years of Charles' wars. A better source of early examples is BL, Add. MS 37816, the letter book of Sir Edward Nicholas, the admiral's secretary.

should desire them'.[368] Before giving effect to the warrants he received, Marten required the entry of two bonds of security in the court's records, the first promising fulfilment of the regulations issued by the privy council – to attack the king's enemies alone, to bring prizes home for appraisal, and to dispose of nothing until prizes were adjudged to the captors by the admiralty court – and the second promising payment to the admiral of a tenth of every prize taken.[369] It was of course the first type of bond that was modified towards the end of the war to give additional security against raiding in the Mediterranean. Examples of the letters of reprisal eventually granted are hard to find, but the evidence available indicates that the broad pattern of the warrants and bonds was followed in them, with the infliction of losses by subjects of the king of Spain or archduchess of Austria cited at least as a pretext, and with the restrictions imposed by the privy council carefully rehearsed.[370] While the bonds stipulated that they would remain in force until the conditions they contained were fulfilled, the letters of reprisal stipulated that they would remain in force until the conditions they contained were breached. It was thus made entirely clear that the legitimacy of maritime raiding was dependent on the validity of the commissions granted by the admiral, and that the acquisition of prizes was dependent on their adjudication to the takers by the admiralty court. Captains were licensed 'to sette uppon, take and apprehende' enemy ships and goods, yet the effective seizure or occupation of enemy property was not in itself sufficient to confer title on the takers. Despite the limitations imposed on raiders, it has been calculated from the less than comprehensive records of the admiralty that well over six hundred, and maybe as many as nine hundred and fifty captains received commissions from the admiralty during the first five years

368 BL, Add. MS 37816, f. 52r.

369 The bonds can now be found in NAK, HCA25/4–8. According to the catalogue, the last of these boxes runs on to 1650, but actually it contains just a single example from that year. The reality is that HCA25/1–3 are boxes containing bonds from 1585 to 1603, and HCA25/4–8 boxes containing bonds from 1625 to 1630, after which there is another gap in the record until the 1650s. The explanation is fairly obvious.

370 As was previously noted, letters of marque or reprisal were not routinely preserved in Elizabeth's war either. The example reproduced in *Documents Relating to Law and Custom of the Sea*, vol. 1, pp. 413–16, seems to date from early in 1625, when more genuine reprisals were envisaged. *Documents Relating to Law and Custom of the Sea*, vol. 1, pp. 457–60, reproduces a licence issued by the king himself, which proved to be rather controversial, even though Elizabeth had done something similar (Marsden 1910, p. 254; Nicholas 1955, pp. 59–60; Appleby 1983, vol. 1, pp. 91 and 113–15). As will be noted later, better examples survive from Charles' war with France.

of Charles' reign.[371] It is not obvious where the idea comes from that the duke of Buckingham was more reluctant than the earl of Nottingham had been to grant letters of reprisal or marque.[372]

After returning with prizes to English ports, captains initiated proceedings before the admiralty court in London by making a series of allegations.[373] Normally they began with an assertion that they had sailed with 'lawfull and sufficient authoritie from the kinges majestie of England, and out of the highe courte of admiraltie of England, to surprize and take as lawfull prizes the shipps and goodes of the kinge of Spaine and archduttchesse of Austria or any of their subjects', though sometimes they stated first that since October 1625 'there hath beene, and still is, warre and hostillitie betweene the kings and kingdomes of England and Spaine'. They would then add that they had seized a ship and its cargo 'on the high sea and within the jurisdiction of the admiralty of England', and that the ship and cargo had belonged to 'the subjectes of the kinge of Spaine or archduttchesse of Austria'. The authorisation of maritime raiding was already on record in the court, but evidence was adduced of ownership of the ship and goods from documents like bills of lading, many examples of which survive in the records, and from the testimony of witnesses, who were typically prisoners taken with the ships.[374] The ships were sometimes discovered to have belonged to the king of Spain himself, and often it was reported that the captain of a seized ship had been armed with 'letters of marque and commission from the kinge of Spaine, or his competent officers in that behalfe, to surprize and take as prize the shippes and goods of the Englishe, Hollanders and others the enemies of the saide kinge and kingdome of Spaine'.[375] The sentences issued by the court would usually confirm that the seizures had been made 'on the high sea and within the jurisdiction of the admiralty of England, with letters of reprisal in force', would simply add that the allegations of ownership had been verified, and would consequently adjudge (*adiudicamus*) the ships and goods to the takers as lawful prizes (*praedae legitimae*).[376] It has been

371 *Calendar of State Papers, Domestic Series, of the Reign of Charles I*, vol. 3, pp. 285–309 and 439–41, and vol. 4, pp. 151–6 and 467–71; Appleby 1983, vol. 1, pp. 186–7 and 207–8, and vol. 2, pp. 1–180.

372 Rodger 2014, p. 11. It is admittedly even harder to make accurate calculations in relation to Elizabeth's war.

373 The allegations are preserved in NAK, HCA24/81–8, along with those made in other types of case.

374 Written evidence can be found in NAK, HCA15/1–3 and HCA24/81–8, the interrogatories put to witnesses in HCA23/7–10, and their depositions in HCA13/45–8.

375 See, for instance, NAK, HCA24/86, n. 65, and HCA24/88, n. 229.

376 The sentences are included among the allegations and written evidence in NAK, HCA24/81–8. Unlike most of the documentation preserved, which was written in English – or in

established that over seven hundred acts of adjudication were passed between 1625 and 1630, and it is estimated that as many as a thousand ships may actually have been taken and acquired in this way.[377] Some other records, however, relate to actions for the restitution of ships and goods wrongly taken from the king of England's subjects, friends or allies. Others still were concerned with the distribution of prizes, and here it was alleged that for many decades 'the use and custome of the sea and admiraltie of England hath beene, and att this present is, that all prizes which have beene taken by anie man of warre, sett out by vertue of lettres of marque or reprisall, have beene, and are, divided in three partes, viz. whereof a third parte is for the owners, another third parte to the victuallers, and another third parte to the captaine and companie of such shippe which taketh such prize'.[378] Obviously the allegations made and decisions delivered in the many cases recorded varied in their details, but standard forms were used and there is a striking absence of references to losses sustained or justice denied to claimants. Prizes were adjududged to captors as long as they had been taken within the terms of the letters of reprisal or marque granted to them.

Whether the location of a seizure at sea mattered only in relation to the jurisdiction of the court or also in relation to the acquisition of the prize was debated in the autumn of 1626. During the summer of that year a Danish ship transporting timber from Norway to Spain was forced into Baltimore to have a leak repaired.[379] It was seized in the harbour by the crew of a ship whose captain had received letters of reprisal from the English admiral.[380] The captain assumed that a tenth of the value of the prize would be taken by the admiral, but the vice-admiral of Ireland had been instructed by Buckingham to ensure that the perquisites of his office were fully collected, and the question was raised whether the ship and cargo did not belong entirely to the king, who had granted a half of the value of any prizes taken in his harbours to the admiral.[381]

a foreign language, usually translated into English – on paper, the sentences of the court were written in Latin on parchment.

377 *Calendar of State Papers, Domestic Series, of the Reign of Charles I*, vol. 1, p. 345; *Documents Illustrating the Impeachment of the Duke of Buckingham*, pp. 65–9; Marsden 1910, pp. 255–6; Appleby 1983, vol. 1, pp. 252–301, and vol. 2, pp. 181–299; Andrews 1991, p. 109.

378 NAK, HCA24/85, n. 201.

379 *Calendar of State Papers Relating to Ireland of the Reign of Charles I*, vol. 1, p. 151.

380 The captain happened to be one of those who wanted a local court to be set up in Ireland (*Calendar of State Papers Relating to Ireland of the Reign of Charles I*, vol. 1, pp. 1–2, 103, 177–8 and 181–3). On this issue see Appleby and O'Dowd 1985, pp. 300–1, and Kelleher 2020, pp. 51–8.

381 *Calendar of State Papers Relating to Ireland of the Reign of Charles I*, vol. 1, pp. 37–8, 147 and 150–1.

Advice was sought from someone with 'knowledge in admiralty busines, namely Mr Clarke of Dublyn, the civill lawyer', who was eventually to become the judge of the admiralty court in London but was working at the time towards a doctorate at Cambridge.[382] During the late 1620s William Clerk wrote a tract in which he drew attention to the reliance princes placed on 'civilians' in dealing with other nations, but he did not take a narrowly civilian view of the question put to him.[383] Although the admiral had been directed by the king to authorise the seizure of enemy goods 'wheresoever they should be found', Clerk believed that enemy goods found as flotsam, jetsam or lagan would have to belong to the crown, as would goods taken in the king's harbours.[384] If the civil law showed anything relevant, it was that the rights of the king and admiral could only be taken away in express terms. Clerk's opinion was sent to Marten for comment, and his response was sent back to Clerk for further elucidation.[385] One concern raised by Marten was that the letters of reprisal granted to the captain were 'not of grace but of justice, for it is intended that none have theis letters of reprisall but such as have received losse and damage and wronges'. Since the king was fulfilling his responsibility to provide justice to his subjects, he could hardly hinder them from taking prizes wherever they were found. Clerk replied that according to 'the doctrine of the lawe', kings acted graciously when they were not required to act by law, as was the case when they condescended to grant letters of reprisal.[386] Marten also expressed concern that the king's right to ships and goods seized in his harbours was to *bona inimicorum*, yet the current conflict was not a 'solemn warr, but a reprisall warr', so that the seizure at Baltimore had not been made from enemies in the proper sense of the term. Clerk replied that if the current state of hostility between Charles and Philip 'maye not goe for open warr, at the least it resembles and equalls in substance of matter a warr denounced betweene them'. When consulted at

382 NAK, SP63/243, ff. 67r and 92r. Mr William Clark is wrongly designated a 'civil surveyor' in the calendar.

383 *Epitome of Certaine Late Aspersions Cast at Civilians*, pp. 42–4. The tract was printed in 1631, but Clerk was described on the title page as a bachelor of laws, although he had become a doctor of laws in 1629.

384 *Calendar of State Papers, Domestic Series, of the Reign of Charles I of the Reign of Charles I*, vol. 1, p. 412; NAK, SP16/34, ff. 78–9.

385 *Calendar of State Papers, Domestic Series, of the Reign of Charles I*, vol. 1, pp. 432 and 443; *Calendar of State Papers Relating to Ireland of the Reign of Charles I*, vol. 1, p. 161; *Documents Relating to Law and Custom of the Sea*, vol. 1, pp. 427–9; NAK, SP16/36, ff. 161–2r.

386 Panormitanus, *Lectura super quinque libros Decretalium*, vol. 1, f. 50v (ad X 1.3.15); *Repertorium Antonii Corseti Siculi I.U.D. praeclarissimi, ad Nicolai Abbatis Panormitani, Commentaria super Decretalium et Clementinarum libros*, sig. 2E8r.

the same time about a seizure made in another Irish port, Clerk again maintained that the king of England was at war with the king of Spain, and that the prerogative rights accorded to him by the common law of England therefore had to be recognised.[387] In defending the priority of the common law he made reference to Bodin's treatise on the sovereignty of states.[388]

An aspect of the Baltimore case that was not considered problematic was the Danish ownership of the vessel carrying the timber to Spain. An article in the Treaty of Southampton had stated that 'all contraband wares, as provisions of sustenance and warfare, ships, arms, sails, gear, gold, silver, copper, iron, lead and such like are', would be regarded as 'good prize, with the ships and persons that were carrying them'.[389] Three months later it had been decided in England that 'for avoiding of the clamour from all merchants of foreign nations, it were convenient to take the same course that Queen Elizabeth did to make a public declaration for confiscation of materials for shipping that shall go for Spain'.[390] On 24 December 1625 a proclamation had been issued forbidding English mariners from trading with Spain or other places subject to Philip IV, 'uppon payne of confiscation of theire shipps wherewith they shall soe trade', although it was later clarified that only the transportation of 'victualles, munition or other furniture for warre' was forbidden.[391] On 31 December 1625 a further proclamation had been issued to warn foreign mariners that the king of England, in response to 'the king of Spaynes restlesse ambition to aspire to an universall monarchye', was waging a defensive war against him on behalf of all 'Christian domynions', and that as it was 'neither agreeable with the rules of polycie, or law of nations, to permitt the said king or his subjects to be furnished and supplyed with corne, victual, armes or provision for his shipping, navye or armes if the same can be prevented', Charles intended to confiscate any ships found to be carrying contraband goods towards his enemy's ports, 'as other kings in like

387 *Calendar of State Papers Relating to Ireland of the Reign of Charles I*, vol. 1, pp. 149–52, 166, 171, 179, 183 and 200. See too *Documents Relating to Law and Custom of the Sea*, vol. 1, pp. 423–4 and 441–4.

388 *Cf. Manuscripts of the Earl Cowper*, vol. 1, p. 239.

389 *Cours universel diplomatique du droit des gens*, vol. 5(2), p. 480; *European Treaties Bearing on the History of the United States*, vol. 1, p. 297; *State Papers Collected by Edward, Earl of Clarendon*, vol. 1, pp. 59–60.

390 *Manuscripts of the Earl Cowper*, vol. 1, pp. 233–4; *Calendar of State Papers, Domestic Series, of the Reign of Charles I*, vol. 1, p. 178; *Acts of the Privy Council of England*, vol. 40, pp. 271 and 289–90.

391 *Foedera, conventiones, literae et cuiuscunque generis acta publica*, vol. 18, p. 251; *Stuart Royal Proclamations*, vol. 2, pp. 66–7; *Acts of the Privy Council of England*, vol. 40, pp. 408, 441–2 and 551–2.

cases have alwayes used to doe'.[392] To at least one neutral observer it seemed that this new proclamation amounted to 'the first public act declaring war'.[393] In October 1626, while the Baltimore case was being debated, ships from Baltic ports were seized on their return voyage after delivering contraband goods in Spain, and a panel of seven civil lawyers at Doctors' Commons advised that 'these shippes, thus taken, are forfeited and to be adjudged good prize'.[394] Their opinion was adopted in a proclamation issued on 4 March 1627, which also specified in detail the kinds of goods that would be regarded as contraband.[395] It was emphasised again that Charles was following the example of 'Queene Elizabeth of famous memory', and that he was introducing 'no innovation, since the same course hathe beene held, and the same penalties have beene heretofore inflicted, by other states and princes upon the like occasions, and avowed and maintained by publique writings and apologies'. Captains who seized ships sailing to or from enemy ports inserted into the allegations they presented before the admiralty court a summary of the terms of the proclamation of 31 December 1625, noting that the ships and goods taken were 'duelie forfeited for the benefitt of his majestie', but concluding on the strength of their letters of reprisal that the ships and goods should be adjudged to them as lawful prizes.[396] Since the letters of reprisal they carried warned 'all Christian people' that prizes taken from the king of Spain's subjects which were not brought home intact would be treated as 'confiscated', the thinking appears more generally to have been that adjudication conferred title on captors to ships and goods forfeited to the crown at the moment of their seizure.[397]

If prizes taken in breach of the conditions summarised in the letters of reprisal were believed to belong to the crown, the same was true of prizes taken without a valid licence, as was made clear by a series of *allegationes ex parte domini regis* presented in the admiralty court towards the end of the

392 *Calendar of State Papers, Domestic Series, of the Reign of Charles I*, vol. 1, p. 193; *Foedera, conventiones, literae et cuiuscunque generis acta publica*, vol. 18, pp. 259–60; *Stuart Royal Proclamations*, vol. 2, pp. 72–5; *Calendar of State Papers Relating to Ireland of the Reign of Charles I*, vol. 1, pp. 81–2.

393 'Salvetti Correspondence', p. 42.

394 *Calendar of State Papers, Domestic Series, of the Reign of Charles I*, vol. 1, pp. 457–8; NAK, SP16/38, ff. 6v-7r and 17.

395 *Proclamation to Prevent the Furnishing of the King of Spaine and His Subjects with Provisions for Shipping or Munition for the Warres and with Victuals*; *Foedera, conventiones, literae et cuiuscunque generis acta publica*, vol. 18, pp. 856–7; *Documents Relating to Law and Custom of the Sea*, vol. 1, pp. 433–5; *Stuart Royal Proclamations*, vol. 2, pp. 136–8.

396 See, for instance, NAK, HCA24/83/3, ff. 610–12r.

397 *Documents Relating to Law and Custom of the Sea*, vol. 1, pp. 413–16.

war.[398] It was first asserted that Charles, like previous 'kings and queenes of England, tyme out of mynde and beyond all memory of man', had the prerogative power both 'to make warr and peace with all forraigne nations', and to issue regulations 'for the managinge and orderinge of the sayd warrs'. His power had been exercised in 1625 when his privy council made provision for a war to be waged under letters of reprisal, after which no loyal subject had 'presumed to sett forth any shippe to sea' against the king of Spain or his subjects without a licence, 'nor by lawe canne sett forth any shippe to such effecte', and nor had any prize been adjudged by the admiralty court to anyone who had not 'duely obteyned letters of reprisall'. Since it was conventional for the property of pirates to be confiscated by the crown, and since pirates raided shipping without licences, it is tempting to surmise that unlicensed raiders were simply being treated as pirates.[399] In March 1626, for example, raiders from La Rochelle who were driven by bad weather into Kinsale were described as 'pirates' by the vice-admiral of Ireland.[400] Although they claimed to have been licensed by the Protestant authorities in La Rochelle, and also to have had their prizes adjudged to them by an admiralty court there, the difficulty was that a peace treaty had been signed with the king of France a month earlier, so that the validity of their licences was open to question.[401] Yet even if raiders without valid licences could have been regarded as pirates, with the implication that their property belonged to the state in which they were apprehended, it would not have followed that property they had seized from other people also belonged to that state. In fact, the allegations submitted on behalf of the English king did not refer to unlicensed raiders as pirates, nor to the forfeiture of their own property, still less of property they had seized from the king's enemies. It is revealing that the assertion actually made was that no one who had captured goods without a valid licence had ever 'beene able to obteyne any sentence for the sayd goodes *in contradictorio iudicio* against his majestye or the lord admirall'. The assumption therefore was that when prizes were adjudged to licensed raiders they were claiming a share of them from the crown, and that when they were taken without a valid licence they also

398 NAK, HCA24/87, n. 261.

399 *Documents Relating to Law and Custom of the Sea*, vol. 1, pp. 444–5; *Calendar of State Papers, Domestic Series, of the Reign of Charles I*, vol. 23, p. 71; BL, Add. MS 37817, f. 67r. There is in fact a huge amount of evidence of the presumption that unlicensed raiders were *ipso facto* pirates, though it was only a presumption.

400 *Calendar of State Papers Relating to Ireland of the Reign of Charles I*, vol. 1, pp. 94–5, 105–6, 112, 122–3 and 215–16; *Calendar of State Papers, Domestic Series, of the Reign of Charles I*, vol. 1, p. 492.

401 Moote 1989, pp. 181–2; James 2004, pp. 46–7; Holt 2005, pp. 189–90.

automatically became the property of the crown. There was not even a hint of the older notion that raiders who had acquired enemy property by occupation might be punished for breach of the king's regulations by deprivation of that property.

Since property seized from the enemy was thought to have been acquired immediately by the crown, it is understandable that naval captains were not expected to bring their prizes before the admiralty court for approval. Instead of letters of reprisal, they sailed under orders from the admiralty, which typically required them to 'assault, subdue and take' any enemy ships they encountered and bring them 'into such of his majesties portes as you shall thinke best, putting the men, shipps and goods soe taken into safe custody till further order'.[402] In the early months of the war, ships and goods seized by naval vessels, both from the enemy and from friends trading with the enemy, were duely brought back to English ports and put into safe custody there.[403] As the parliament assembled in the summer of 1625 had declined to grant the taxation requested by the king, the arrival of these prizes was welcomed as an alternative source of revenue to finance the war effort.[404] The seized ships were added to the English fleet, and money found on board was at once used to purchase arms and ammunition and to pay troops.[405] However, in response to complaints from the ambassadors of neutral countries, along with some of the king's own subjects and allies whose goods had been taken with the ships, it was accepted that the validity of all seizures ought to be examined in the admiralty court, where the process was often prolonged by the need to scrutinise documents 'written in Spanish, Italian, French, Dutch and English, and some in Arabeck'.[406] Despite the delays involved, it was feared that 'if the ambassadors have not contentment, they will make stay of the goods in France, in the

402 *Calendar of State Papers, Domestic Series, of the Reign of Charles I*, vol. 1, pp. 99 and 106; BL, Add. MS 37816, ff. 45v-6r and 90v-1r; NAK, SP16/6, ff. 39r and 124r.

403 *Calendar of State Papers, Domestic Series, of the Reign of Charles I*, vol. 1, pp. 128, 131, 135 and 137; *Manuscripts of the Earl Cowper*, vol. 1, pp. 218–19 and 221–3; *Acts of the Privy Council of England*, vol. 40, p. 215; 'Salvetti Correspondence', pp. 35 and 37; BL, Add. MS 37816, ff. 51r and 95v.

404 Lockyer 1981, pp. 277 and 294–5; Young 1986, pp. 154–6; Sharpe 1992, pp. 9–11.

405 *Calendar of State Papers, Domestic Series, of the Reign of Charles I*, vol. 1, pp. 133–4, 140 and 144; *Documents Illustrating the Impeachment of the Duke of Buckingham*, pp. 20–1; *Calendar of State Papers Relating to Ireland of the Reign of Charles I*, vol. 1, pp. 45–6; 'Salvetti Correspondence', p. 39; BL, Add. MS 37816, f. 53v.

406 *Calendar of State Papers, Domestic Series, of the Reign of Charles I*, vol. 1, pp. 144–5, 159, 161, 170, 176 and 179; *Documents Illustrating the Impeachment of the Duke of Buckingham*, pp. 21–7, 30–4, 43–53 and 59–63; *Manuscripts of the Earl Cowper*, vol. 1, pp. 225 and 238; *Acts of the Privy Council of England*, vol. 40, pp. 264 and 350; 'Salvetti Correspondence', p. 40.

United Provinces, in Denmark and in the Hans Towns, in all which places are infinite more goods of the English than in these prizes and all the rest of theirs in the kingdom'.[407] A committee was appointed to investigate the procedures followed in other countries and to propose an improved process 'for the due and speedie execution of justice, the maintenance of peace and good correspondencie with our friends and allyes, and withall for the advancement of our profit'.[408] A new set of 'instructions for the ordering of the captains and companies serving as men of warr in his majesties shipps' was drafted in 1626, though whether it was ever approved is unclear.[409] Ships and goods seized by naval vessels often were adjudged to the king in much the same way as those seized privately under letters of reprisal, but simply on the strength of their previous ownership by his enemies.[410]

It was the seizure of French ships and goods that brought Charles into the perilous state of simultaneous war with Philip IV and Louis XIII. Among the ships seized by naval vessels in the early months of the war with Philip was the *St Peter* of Le Havre, which was caught carrying a cargo laden in Spain but allegedly belonging to French merchants.[411] On advice from the privy council, Marten ordered the release of the ship and goods, but they were then arrested by admiralty officers acting under instructions from Buckingham.[412] In retaliation the *parlements* of Rouen and Rennes ordered the arrest of English ships

407 *Miscellaneous State Papers from 1501 to 1726*, vol. 2, p. 11.

408 *Calendar of State Papers, Domestic Series, of the Reign of Charles I*, vol. 1, p. 175; *Documents Illustrating the Impeachment of the Duke of Buckingham*, pp. 30–1; *Acts of the Privy Council of England*, vol. 40, p. 444; *Foedera, conventiones, literae et cuiuscunque generis acta publica*, vol. 18, pp. 731–2; *Collectanea maritima*, pp. 69–74.

409 *Calendar of State Papers, Domestic Series, of the Reign of Charles I*, vol. 1, p. 518; *Documents Relating to Law and Custom of the Sea*, vol. 1, pp. 416–22.

410 See, for instance, *Documents Relating to Law and Custom of the Sea*, vol. 1, pp. 446–7. See too *Letters and Memorials of State in the Reigns of Queen Mary, Queen Elizabeth, King James, King Charles the First, Part of the Reign of King Charles the Second and Oliver's Usurpation*, vol. 2, pp. 662–3.

411 *Documents Illustrating the Impeachment of the Duke of Buckingham*, pp. 19–20, 27–30, 35–43 and 55–9; *Acts of the Privy Council of England*, vol. 40, pp. 290 and 338–40; *Manuscripts of the Earl Cowper*, vol. 1, pp. 241 and 253; *Calendar of State Papers, Domestic Series, of the Reign of Charles I*, vol. 1, pp. 189, 192–3, 235 and 250.

412 *Journals of the House of Commons*, vol. 1, pp. 821, 823–4, 826–31, 834–5, 837–8, 845–7 and 852–3; *Journals of the House of Lords*, vol. 3, pp. 619–20; *Proceedings in Parliament 1626*, vol. 2, pp. 68, 70, 86–99, 102–10, 159–72, 200–11, 256–61 and 465–7, vol. 3, pp. 99–102, and vol. 4, pp. 381–4; Rushworth, *Historical Collections*, vol. 1, p. 309; *Documents Illustrating the Impeachment of the Duke of Buckingham*, p. 69; *Court and Times of Charles the First*, vol. 1, pp. 83–5 and 89; *Complete Collection of State Trials*, vol. 2, cols. 1311–12; 'Salvetti Correspondence', pp. 48–9.

and goods in Normandy and Brittany, the mariners and merchants affected complained to the parliament assembled at Westminster in the spring of 1626, and the arrest of the *St Peter* was added to articles of impeachment being drawn up there against the admiral.[413] Different articles were assigned for presentation to different members of the House of Commons, and responsibility for the arrest of the *St Peter* was devolved on none other than John Selden, who also remonstrated against Buckingham's failure to retain control of the English Channel, remarking that even De Groot had recognised the existence of territorial waters.[414] Selden pointed out that the admiral was required to exercise his jurisdiction *iuxta leges nostras civiles et maritimas*, and that 'by the marine laws, agreeable to the civil laws', it was only lawful to revoke an order releasing a ship and goods on the discovery of new evidence, which had not been forthcoming in the *St Peter*'s case. He further pointed out that the common law required the admiral to administer justice according to the law, and that 'the law of merchants' required him to do so swiftly as well as fairly. He insisted that the arrest of the *St Peter* had been against 'the law of nations', since it had been 'against what is agreed on by leagues betwixt us and foreign nations, that the subjects of nations in amity with us shall be well used'. His point may have been not so much that French mariners and merchants had been promised fair treatment in a treaty made with their king as that the treaties kings made with each other provided evidence of a general agreement to treat visitors from friendly countries fairly. No particular treaty was cited, and a similar line of reasoning was pursued in the admiralty court when it was argued that the rule requiring prizes to be taken *intra praesidia hostium* before they were recognised was binding 'by the use and observations of auncient treaties and leagues heeretofore made by the kinges of England with other nations', and because 'itt hath beene constantly observed, accustomed and used, and in contradictorie judgement often obtained, as a thinge agreable to the law of nations'.[415] Buckingham replied that he had followed the king's instructions as well as advice he had received from Marten, which he may genuinely have misunderstood. The attempt to have the admiral impeached failed, but in the meantime Marten had attempted to resign from office as judge of

413 Tite 1974, pp. 178–211; Lockyer 1981, pp. 308–31; Young 1986, pp. 157–67.

414 *Journals of the House of Lords*, vol. 3, pp. 598–600 and 659–60; *Proceedings in Parliament 1626*, vol. 3, pp. 182–4, 193, 195 and 425–42; Rushworth, *Historical Collections*, vol. 1, pp. 314–15 and 382–4; *Complete Collection of State Trials*, vol. 2, cols 1326, 1328 and 1429–31.

415 NAK, HCA24/87, n. 57. Just as Selden disagreed in substance but agreed in style with De Groot in his *Mare clausum*, so an argument was advanced here in De Groot's style though contrary to his preferred position on the issue raised.

the admiralty, complaining that Buckingham 'would have all to be judged gud prize which the shipps did take'.[416] On the assurance that he was merely being urged to deal with prize cases more expeditiously, he had agreed to remain in office.

After other French ships and goods were seized by English captains, after other ships and goods were arrested in retaliation in French ports, and after diplomatic efforts failed to resolve tensions, Charles and Louis found themselves in a state of open war in the spring of 1627.[417] Buckingham was authorised to grant letters of reprisal or marque for the raiding of French shipping, subject to instructions from the privy council resembling those issued in the autumn of 1625, supposedly on the basis of losses inflicted and justice denied, although the admiral was told by the king not to insist on proof of losses but to grant letters 'generally and freely to all our subjects that shall desire to take the same forthe'.[418] Warrants were sent to Marten, bonds were entered and letters were granted in the familiar forms.[419] One notable difference from the war against Philip was that licences were also granted to Protestants from France to seize ships and goods belonging to French Catholics.[420] Prizes were again adjudged not only to the holders of letters of reprisal but also to the king in relation to seizures made by naval vessels sailing under the admiral's orders.[421] Proclamations were again issued against trade with the enemy by English merchants and against the supply of contraband goods to the enemy by foreign merchants.[422] Following Buckingham's assassination in August 1628, the

416 *Calendar of State Papers, Domestic Series, of the Reign of Charles I*, vol. 2, pp. 184 and 208; Sir John Eliot, *Apology for Socrates and Negotium posterorum*, vol. 2, p. 12; BL, Add. MS 37817, f. 67r.; NAK, SP16/64, ff. 4–5, and SP16/66, f. 54.

417 Treasure 1972, pp. 99–100; Carlton 1983, p. 91; Cust 2005, p. 68.

418 *Foedera, conventiones, literae et cuiuscunque generis acta publica*, vol. 18, pp. 861 and 867; *Calendar of State Papers, Domestic Series, of the Reign of Charles I*, vol. 2, pp. 154 and 159, and vol. 23, p. 206; 'Salvetti Correspondence', p. 117; NAK, HCA25/225, ff. 1–4r (from the back of a bound volume); NAK, SP16/62, f. 1.

419 There is a clear example of a licence in NAK, HCA25/225, ff. 4v-7 (from the back), as the foundation of a register of those granted on Buckingham's instructions against the French.

420 *Documents Relating to Law and Custom of the Sea*, vol. 1, p. 437. *Cf. Calendar of State Papers, Domestic Series, of the Reign of Charles I*, vol. 2, p. 189, and *Cours universel diplomatique du droit des gens*, vol. 5(2), p. 538.

421 See, for instance, NAK, HCA24/83/2, n. 395.

422 *Proclamation Prohibiting the Importation of Any Goods or Merchandize Whatsoever in Any French Shippes or Bottomes*; *Proclamation for the Explaining of a Former Proclamation Lately Published*; *Proclamation against Unjust Pretences for Colouring of French Goods Taken by Way of Reprize*; *Proclamation Prohibiting the Transportation of Any Corne, Graine, Victuals, Ordinance, Armes or Munition of Warre into the Kingdom of France*; *Foedera,*

admiralty was placed under the control of commissioners, who were authorised to continue granting letters of reprisal.[423] The instructions issued by the privy council in the previous year were issued once more, and were declared to apply *mutatis mutandis* to mariners licensed to raid Spanish shipping.[424] Letters of reprisal were granted under warrants from the admiralty commissioners in the same manner as they had been under warrants from the late admiral.[425] Charles' war against Louis was therefore conducted in much the same way as his war against Philip, with prize acquisition operating as 'hath bin accustomed by way of reprizall' or 'in the tyme of open warr', yet in circumstances that would not have justified the use of expressions like *represaliae* or *bellum publicum* in the conventional discourse of the law schools.

The war with France was terminated on 24 April 1629 by the Treaty of Susa, in which Charles and Louis agreed to renew the 'anciennes alliances' and to reopen 'commerce seur et libre' between their realms.[426] 'And since it would be difficult', the second article stated, 'to make restitution on one side or the other of the various prizes that have been taken during the war, the two crowns have agreed that they will not do anything, and will not consent to any reprisals by sea or some other measure, in relation to what has come to pass between the two kings and their subjects during the late war'. If this article betrayed a degree of uncertainty about the legitimacy of the prizes already taken, another article stated that since there were 'many vessels at sea with letters of marque and the power to attack enemies which will not be able to learn at once of this peace', any seizures made during the next two months would not jeopardise the peace, provided the ships and goods taken were returned to their owners.[427] The war with Spain was terminated on 15 November 1530 by the

---

conventiones, literae et cuiuscunque generis acta publica, vol. 19, pp. 1–2; *Stuart Royal Proclamations*, vol. 2, pp. 141–4, 153–4 and 207–9; *Calendar of State Papers, Domestic Series, of the Reign of Charles I*, vol. 2, p. 220.

423 *Acts of the Privy Council of England*, vol. 43, pp. 96–7, 166–7 and 303; *Calendar of State Papers, Domestic Series, of the Reign of Charles I*, vol. 3, pp. 310, 316 and 333, and vol. 23, pp. 292 and 294–5; *Manuscripts of the Earl Cowper*, vol. 1, p. 367; NAK, HCA25/225, ff. 1–2r.

424 *Acts of the Privy Council of England*, vol. 43, pp. 172–4; NAK, HCA25/225, ff. 2v-5.

425 Another clear example can be found in NAK, HCA25/225, ff. 6–7, as the foundation of a register of letters granted on the commissioners' instructions.

426 *Cours universel diplomatique du droit des gens*, vol. 5(2), pp. 580–2; *European Treaties Bearing on the History of the United States*, vol. 1, pp. 300–4; *Foedera, conventiones, literae et cuiuscunque generis acta publica*, vol. 19, pp. 87–8.

427 *Calendar of State Papers, Domestic Series, of the Reign of Charles I*, vol. 3, p. 544; *Whereas There Hath Fallen out an Interruption of Amitie betweene the Kings Majestie and the Most Christian King*. It is possible that the uneasy terms of the Treaty of Troyes in 1564, discussed in the second chapter above, were revisited while the Treaty of Susa was being drafted.

Treaty of Madrid, which simply stated that Charles and Philip would 'revoke all commissions and letters whether of reprisal or marque or of any type or condition containing a power to take prizes'.[428] Whether the Spanish war had been as 'lucrative and restorative' as Francis Bacon had predicted may be open to doubt, but such 'riches' as had been acquired had certainly belonged primarily to the crown, with combatants rewarded by way of 'donatives'.[429] Although civil lawyers of an older generation like Marten may still have wished to reconcile what was happening with the conventional theory of the law schools, members of a rising generation like Clerk were more sympathetic towards the tendency among common lawyers to think in terms of forfeiture, and although no trace has been found of reference to De Groot's latest book, Selden was not the only lawyer to talk about a law of nations based on agreements between nations. If one option had been to revert to the theory that enemy property was acquired in wartime by occupation, possibly on the understanding that nations had previously agreed to treat *res hostium* as *res nullius*, that was not the option favoured in the first five years of Charles' reign. More clearly than in Elizabeth's time, ships and goods seized from the enemy were understood to belong to the crown, with maritime raiders acquiring title to prizes only by way of authorisation and approval from the state.

6 Prize Litigation in Caroline Scotland

The 'Blessed Revolution' in the last years of James' reign – when the reverential treatment of foreign policy as an *arcanum imperii* gave way to its open discussion among members of parliament, when a constant commitment to the preservation of peace in Europe gave way to the authorisation of aggression against neighbouring nations, and when the negotiation of a marriage with Philip's daughter gave way to hightening tensions with Spain in particular – was an exclusively English affair. The Scottish government had no inkling of any change of direction until September 1625, when Charles invited a convention

428 *Cours universel diplomatique du droit des gens*, vol. 5(2), pp. 620–3; *Foedera, conventiones, literae et cuiuscunque generis acta publica*, vol. 19, pp. 219–27; *European Treaties Bearing on the History of the United States*, vol. 1, pp. 305–14; *Articles of Peace, Entercourse and Commerce Concluded in the Names of the Most High and Mighty Kings Charles and Philip*, sig. C2; *Acts of the Privy Council of England*, vol. 45, pp. 140–1; *Calendar of State Papers, Domestic Series, of the Reign of Charles I*, vol. 4, p. 402; *Tudor Royal Proclamations*, vol. 2, pp. 231–3; *Historical Works of Sir James Balfour*, vol. 2, pp. 184–9.

429 Kepler 1973; Lockyer 1981, pp. 303 and 367–8; Harris 2014, pp. 248–50.

of the estates to vote on taxation that might clear some of his father's debts, cover the costs of his own coronation and finance 'suche designes as we haif in hand, bothe at home and abroade, for the weele of oure kingdomes and people'.[430] Although reference was vaguely made to 'the estate of the affaires of Christendome', no further elucidation of the king's designs was provided before the levies requested were approved.[431] Two months later the convention was reassembled and told that the king was willing to relinquish most of the levies promised in exchange for a commitment to 'the furnishing of twa thousand men with shipping for the space of thrie yeiris, to the intent thay micht be ever in reddines, alsweele for persute as defence'.[432] On this occasion it was at least explained that 'in regaird of the grite preparatioun of foreyne forceis throughout diverse pairtis of Europe' it was necessary for the Scots to be prepared 'to withstand and resist ony foreyne invasioun that sould be intendit'. They were reminded of 'the broyle whiche not long since fell out betuix the Hollanderis and Dunkirkeris in the verie haven of Leyth', and urged to consider the condition of their harbour defences and shipping. This task was remitted to the privy council and the magistrates of the coastal burghs, orders were issued for the erection of warning beacons, 'the loveable custome of wapponshawing' was revived, and careful watch was kept on vessels visiting Scotland from Dunkirk.[433] The king was advised, however, that his northern kingdom could not afford to provide the force of men he wanted.[434] Indeed, he was asked to send two of his own ships north to patrol the east coast. At the same time, he was also asked to permit Scots to purchase gunpowder in England, and since it was feared that invasion might come from Ireland, a small force was raised to serve him there.[435]

During the next four years the Scottish government continued to implement defensive measures against the purported threat of foreign invasion, but there

430 *Register of the Privy Council of Scotland*, 2nd ser., vol. 1, p. 151; *Acts of the Parliaments of Scotland*, vol. 5(1), pp. 166–7; Records of the Parliaments of Scotland, A1625/10/2.

431 Rait 1924, pp. 494–5; Lee 1985, p. 13; Macinnes 1991, p. 43.

432 *Register of the Privy Council of Scotland*, 2nd ser., vol. 1, pp. 154–7; *Acts of the Parliaments of Scotland*, vol. 5(1), pp. 175–7; Records of the Parliaments of Scotland, A1625/10/7–8, 12 and 23.

433 *Register of the Privy Council of Scotland*, 2nd ser., vol. 1, pp. 148–9, 169, 185–9, 210–15 and 224; *Acts of the Parliaments of Scotland*, vol. 5(1), p. 181; Records of the Parliaments of Scotland, A1625/10/30–1 and 33.

434 *Register of the Privy Council of Scotland*, 2nd ser., vol. 1, pp. 174–80; *Acts of the Parliaments of Scotland*, vol. 5(1), pp. 185–8; Records of the Parliaments of Scotland, A1625/10/55.

435 *Register of the Privy Council of Scotland*, 2nd ser., vol. 1, pp. 191–2 and 196–8; *Calendar of State Papers, Domestic Series, of the Reign of Charles I*, vol. 1, pp. 144, 149, 161 and 163. The need for gunpowder became apparent during the early weaponshowings.

was a marked reluctance to become involved in aggressive actions that might interfere with trade on the Continent.[436] In the spring of 1626 Charles intimated his intention to establish a council of war in Scotland, to which appointments were eventually made in the summer.[437] The council reported on the condition of harbours around the coasts, though there is no evidence that its recommendations for the strengthening of fortifications were adopted.[438] Warning beacons continued to be kept in readiness, however, and there were regular 'wapponshawings', at which efforts were made to instruct people in military discipline, 'efter the ordour in the Low Countreis'.[439] Various initiatives were taken to secure arms and ammunition, either through procurement elsewhere or through local manufacture.[440] Nevertheless, the most significant contribution to the war effort to come from Scotland took the form of troops enlisted to serve in continental armies, in the pay of Charles himself or of allies he authorised to employ them.[441] There was nothing in the least novel about troops being hired in Scotland to serve in foreign forces, which had even been authorised by Charles' father.[442] If anything was different it was the difficulty recruitment agents encountered in persuading men to enlist willingly.[443] It was reported that there was a general reluctance to serve in the war, and even

436 Brown 1991, p. 137; Goodare 1999, p. 170; Lee 2003, p. 184.

437 *Register of the Privy Council of Scotland*, 2nd ser., vol. 1, pp. 180, 285, 301–2, 334 and 337–8; *Registrum magni sigilli regum Scotorum*, vol. 8, pp. 346–7; *Stirling's Register of Royal Letters*, vol. 1, p. 62. Brief minutes of the council are preserved as NRS, PA7/2.

438 *Register of the Privy Council of Scotland*, 2nd ser., vol. 1, pp. 378–9, and vol. 2, pp. 52–4, 56–8, 62–3, 67–8, 70–5, 125–8, 133, 145–6, 149, 159–61, 181, 184–8, 225, 244–5, 285 and 556–7.

439 *Register of the Privy Council of Scotland*, 2nd ser., vol. 1, pp. 418–20, 620 and 627, and vol. 2, pp. 88–92; *Aberdeen Council Letters*, vol. 1, pp. 264–5; *Extracts from the Council Register of the Burgh of Aberdeen*, 2nd ser., vol. 1, pp. 2–7 and 10–12; *Extracts from the Burgh Records of Dunfermline*, pp. 150–1 and 159; *Shetland Documents*, vol. 3, p. 468.

440 *Register of the Privy Council of Scotland*, 2nd ser., vol. 1, pp. 377 and 380–1, and vol. 2, pp. 333–4, 337, 425–6, 434, 439–40 and 537–8; *Stirling's Register of Royal Letters*, vol. 1, p. 104, 249, 459 and 491–2; *Registrum magni sigilli regum Scotorum*, vol. 8, pp. 438–9; *Aberdeen Council Letters*, vol. 1, pp. 248–9, 260, 263 and 265–73; *Extracts from the Burgh Records of Dunfermline*, p. 155.

441 *Register of the Privy Council of Scotland*, 2nd ser., vol. 1, pp. 244–5, 247–8, 313, 315–16, 354–5, 443–5, 523–4, 531–2, 539–40, 542–4, 546–7, 550–3, 556, 560–3, 565–7, 578–81, 585, 589 and 634–6, vol. 2, pp. 27–8, 31–7, 55–6, 77–9, 147–8, 295–7, 397–8, 456–7 and 472, and vol. 3, pp. 136–8 and 208; *Acts of the Privy Council of England*, vol. 42, p. 18; *Calendar of State Papers, Domestic Series, of the Reign of Charles I*, vol. 1, pp. 389, 466 and 554, and vol. 5, pp. 122, 197 and 200; *Historical Works of Sir James Balfour*, vol. 2, pp. 133 and 138–9.

442 Bartlett 1984–5; Åberg 1990; Dunthorne 1996; Murdoch 1998; Glozier 2001; Polišenský 2001; Carswell 2012.

443 Fallon 1972, pp. 70–81; Lee 1985, pp. 81–2; Miller 2013, pp. 187–9. For a different view see Murdoch 2003, p. 211, though compare Parker 1987, pp. 194–5.

after recourse was taken to the compulsory conscription of vagabonds and convicts it was still found impossible to raise all the men desired or to prevent those raised from deserting.[444] As war got under way against France, renewed efforts were made to enlist soldiers in Scotland to serve under Buckingham on his expedition for the relief of La Rochelle.[445] Although care had been taken in France to exclude Scottish ships and goods from the retaliatory measures adopted there against the English king, the ban he had himself imposed on the import of French wine had extended to Scotland, where it caused great resentment.[446] The final outbreak of war not only caused further disruption of a market vital to the Scottish economy, but also endangered the close friendship with France maintained over many centuries.[447] Scottish trade had also been hampered since the outbreak of the war with Spain by the constant threat of capture by raiders from Dunkirk, which was discouraging mariners from venturing to sea.[448] In the spring of 1627 the king had been warned that maritime trade was 'lyke to be suppressed and cutt off by the uncontrolled power of these theivish Dunkirkeris', to the great hardship of the merchant estate, 'besydis your majesteis awne hurt in your customes and impost of wynis'.[449]

444 *Correspondence of Sir Robert Kerr, First Earl of Ancram, and His Son William, Third Earl of Lothian*, vol. 1, pp. 44–5; *Memorials of the Earls of Haddington*, vol. 2, p. 92; *Book of Carlaverock*, vol. 2, pp. 97–8; *Register of the Privy Council of Scotland*, 2nd ser., vol. 1, pp. 320–1, 329–30, 347–6, 363–4, 385, 603–5, 608, 611, 613 and 627–8, vol. 2, pp. 40–1, 113–14, 303–4, 308–9 and 325–6, and vol. 3, pp. 152 and 357–8.

445 *Acts of the Privy Council of England*, vol. 42, pp. 22, 134, 159 and 235, and vol. 43, pp. 167–8, 188, 198, 206, 208–10, 228–9, 235, 237–8, 241–2, 254–6 and 258–60; *Calendar of State Papers, Domestic Series, of the Reign of Charles I*, vol. 3, p. 375; *Register of the Privy Council of Scotland*, 2nd ser., vol. 2, pp. 37–9, 50–2, 63, 76–80, 84, 90–3, 109–10, 149 and 154–4.

446 *Historical Works of Sir James Balfour*, vol. 2, pp. 153 and 158; *Stirling's Register of Royal Letters*, vol. 1, p. 239; *Register of the Privy Council of Scotland*, 2nd ser., vol, 1, pp. 478–9, 486–7, 489, 506–7, 527–8 and 613; *Calendar of State Papers and Manuscripts, Relating to English Affairs, Existing in the Archives and Collections of Venice*, vol. 20, p. 76.

447 *Stirling's Register of Royal Letters*, vol. 1, pp. 245–6 and 267; *Register of the Privy Council of Scotland*, 2nd ser., vol. 2, pp. 242–4, 253, 265–6, 284, 305–7, 567–8 and 572–3, and vol. 3, pp. 24–5 and 44; *Calendar of State Papers and Manuscripts, Relating to English Affairs, Existing in the Archives and Collections of Venice*, vol. 21, p. 107; *Calendar of Material Relating to Ireland from the High Court of Admiralty Examinations*, p. 181; NRS, AC7/1, pp. 152–4, 232–3, 237 and 239. While Talbott 2014, pp. 107–10, sees efforts to preserve trade with France as evidence that the Scots entered the war independently and on their own terms, the conventional view that they were dragged into an English conflict to their own detriment (Lythe 1960, p. 211; Smout 1963, p. 167; Donaldson 1965, p. 387; Brown 1992, p. 105; Whyte 1995, p. 272) remains a great deal more persuasive.

448 *Register of the Privy Council of Scotland*, 2nd ser., vol. 1. pp. 225–6 and 571–2; *Stirling's Register of Royal Letters*, vol. 1, pp. 31–2.

449 *Register of the Privy Council of Scotland*, 2nd ser., vol. 1, pp. 571–2.

A possible response to the threat from Dunkirk would have been to provide protection vessels. Charles had interpreted the request he received for naval vessels to be sent north as an agreement to supply the shipping he had asked for after all.[450] The burghs were prevailed upon to increase the amount of taxation they had undertaken to collect, and three ships were purchased and equipped, two in London and the third in Leith.[451] For the next six months the three ships lay idly in the harbour at Leith, under the direction of the Earl Marischal.[452] The explanation suggested a few years later was that they had been placed under the command of captains 'quho dranke and made good cheire, bot wald not offend the enimey', and two other problems are evident in contemporary records.[453] The first is that the funds raised through an additional levy on the burghs had been exhausted by the purchase of the ships and equipment, leaving nothing to pay for their victualling.[454] The second is that sailors were no more eager to serve on naval vessels than soldiers were to serve in continental armies.[455] When asked to provide men in 1626, for example, the council of Burntisland reported that 'sic saillaris quha ar at hame, meittest to serve, hed fled the town for feir of pressing of thame'.[456] In England it was assumed that since the three ships formed part of the royal navy they could be ordered to sail south if they were needed there, though the Scottish captains were instructed to fire a gun and lower their flags if they met an English vessel, 'as accustome is of schips belonging to a foraigne prince'.[457] The ships did in fact sail south to assist with the transportation of troops to the Continent, but the operation proved to be so expensive that the king then agreed to sell them

450 *Register of the Privy Council of Scotland*, 2nd ser., vol. 1. pp. 180, 285 and 301–2; *Stirling's Register of Royal Letters*, vol. 1, pp. 41–2.

451 *Records of the Convention of the Royal Burghs of Scotland*, vol. 3, pp. 213–15; *Aberdeen Council Letters*, vol. 1, pp. 244–6; *Register of the Privy Council of Scotland*, 2nd ser., vol. 1, pp. 372 and 374; *Stirling's Register of Royal Letters*, vol. 1, pp. 41, 56–7, 107, 115 and 120; *Historical Works of Sir James Balfour*, vol. 2, p. 139.

452 *Register of the Privy Council of Scotland*, 2nd ser., vol. 1, pp. 571–2; *Stirling's Register of Royal Letters*, vol. 1, pp. 60–1.

453 *Historical Works of Sir James Balfour*, vol. 2, pp. 140–1.

454 *Stirling's Register of Royal Letters*, vol. 1, pp. 92–3, 95–6, 99, 110 and 320.

455 *Register of the Privy Council of Scotland*, 2nd ser., vol. 1, pp. 219–20, 222–3, 333–6, 390–1, 408 and 593–4, and vol. 2, pp. 71–2 and 74; *Stirling's Register of Royal Letters*, vol. 1, p. 155; *Calendar of State Papers Relating to Ireland of the Reign of Charles I*, vol. 1, p. 186; BL, Add. MS 37816, ff. 139v-40r.

456 NRS, B9/12/5, ff. 58v-9r.

457 *Acts of the Privy Council of England*, vol. 41, pp. 215–16, and vol. 42, pp. 125–6; *Stirling's Register of Royal Letters*, vol. 1, p. 99. They were promised that English ships would salute them in the same way if the encounter took place in Scottish waters.

to the Earl Marischal and the acting admiral of Scotland, the earl of Linlithgow, on the understanding that they would be operated on his behalf and with financial support from the privy council in Edinburgh.[458] In the meantime the burghs had submitted their report on the state of the nation's shipping, claiming disingenuously that the vessels found in their harbours were 'onlie small barkis, unfurnished of ordonance and unable outher to persew or defend', to which they added that they lacked the resources to fund the purchase of more ships.[459] Those they did have were sometimes requisitioned for royal service, with the justification offered that they were needed for the nation's defence, yet whereas the burghs were concerned about the defence of their commerce against maritime raiding, the king was more concerned about the defence of his southern realm against invasion through Scotland or Ireland.[460]

Notwithstanding the general reluctance to participate in aggressive actions against the king of Spain and his subjects, a small number of Scots saw an opportunity to profit from the war at sea.[461] Several Scottish ships sailing between Spain and the southern Netherlands had been caught up in the reprisals executed by English captains in 1625 and the early months of 1626.[462] After the *Blessing* of Burntisland was restored to its owner at the beginning of April 1626 its master, Andrew Watson, was himself granted letters of reprisal by Buckingham, entering bonds of security before Marten in the standard styles.[463] Three other masters from Scotland were licensed in England around

458 *Register of the Privy Council of Scotland*, 2nd ser., vol. 1, pp. 556, 560, 563–4, 579–83, 585–7, 596–7, 599–600 and 602–3, and vol. 2, pp. 22–6, 208–10 and 279–80; *Stirling's Register of Royal Letters*, vol. 1, pp. 158, 179–80, 188–9, 199–200, 229 and 233–4; *Registrum magni sigilli regum Scotorum*, vol. 8, pp. 376 and 412; NRS, AC7/1, pp. 28–30. On the acting admiral's activities at sea see too the *Wentworth Papers*, pp. 263–4.

459 *Register of the Privy Council of Scotland*, 2nd ser., vol. 1, pp. 362–3, 338–9 and 386–9; *Extracts from the Records of the Burgh of Edinburgh*, 2nd ser., vol. 8, p. 7.

460 *Register of the Privy Council of Scotland*, 2nd ser., vol. 1, pp. 381–2, 389, 430–2, 434–5, 445–6, 618–19, 630 and 669, and vol. 2, p. 75; *Stirling's Register of Royal Letters*, vol. 1, pp. 67, 78–9, 94, 291, 300 and 302; *Extracts from the Records of the Burgh of Glasgow*, vol. 1, pp. 354–5; *Aberdeen Council Letters*, vol. 1, pp. 249–50, 252–3 and 669; *Records of the Convention of the Royal Burghs of Scotland*, vol. 3, pp. 233–5, 237 and 438; *Extracts from the Records of the Royal Burgh of Stirling*, vol. 1, p. 161; *Acts of the Privy Council of England*, vol. 41, p. 271; *Historical Works of Sir James Balfour*, vol. 2, pp. 146–7.

461 For a more expansive interpretation of some of the evidence see Murdoch 2010, pp. 163–80, followed in Talbott 2014, pp. 99–101.

462 *Calendar of State Papers, Domestic Series, of the Reign of Charles I*, vol. 1, p. 37; *Acts of the Privy Council of England*, vol. 40, pp. 384–5, 387–8 and 412, and vol. 41, pp. 50–1 and 198; *Manuscripts of the Earl Cowper*, vol. 1, p. 207; 'Salvetti Correspondence', p. 35.

463 *Manuscripts of the Earl Cowper*, vol. 1, p. 226; NAK, HCA25/4/1, dated 8 April 1626; BL, Add. MS 37816, ff. 42, 48r and 80r, and Add. MS 37819, f. 22v.

the same time, and by the end of the war another eight – all from ports on the east coast between Leith and Dundee – had obtained licences there as well, a total of a dozen out of the many hundreds whose licensing remains on record.[464] These Scots were permitted to purchase ordnance and powder in England, as were others who wished to arm their merchant vessels for protection, some of whom were required to prove ownership of their vessels since they were 'Flemish builte'.[465] Near the end of April 1626, almost six months after authority to grant letters of reprisal had been issued to the English admiral, the king assented to a petition from the Scottish burghs to authorise the licensing of raiding in Scotland.[466] The privy council was told to grant letters to all his subjects there 'who sall demand the samine, provyding that you first sie thair interests, and not onlie tak thair assurance for doing of suche thingis as thay ar to performe, according to the custome in the like caises, bot also for thair prosequuting of the samine'. At this stage there was no 'custome in the like caises' as far as the Scotland was concerned. It seemed to the privy council that the burghs had made an 'errour in the termes of thair petitioun, becaus letteris of marcque ar onlie grantit aganis subjectis of nighbour princes or estaittis *ob denegatam iustitiam*', and then only to the 'particular subjectis wronged by thairis'.[467] Yet the council appreciated that it would be 'convenient to grant commissionis to suche as offered to adventure to arme shippis to persue the enemie with all hostilitie, according to the law of nationis', as long as payment was secured of the king's 'due proportioun of the pryssis, and of that portioun whiche by law belongis to the admirall'. Three weeks later the king wrote to the council again to emphasise that it would be better for mariners who were willing to sail against his enemies to be 'encouraged by further priviledgeis then to be discouraged by too strict conditionis'.[468]

It may shed light on the origins of the burghs' petition that one of the first two raiders to be licensed in Scotland was Andrew Watson, as captain of the *Blessing* of Burntisland.[469] Four of the other Scots who were granted licences

464 *Calendar of State Papers, Domestic Series, of the Reign of Charles I*, vol. 3, pp. 285, 287, 295, 301 and 307; BL, Add. MS 37816, f. 50v; Appleby 1983, vol. 2, pp. 170–2.

465 *Calendar of State Papers, Domestic Series, of the Reign of Charles I*, vol. 1, p. 374, and vol. 2, p. 281; *Acts of the Privy Council of England*, vol. 41, p. 93, and vol. 42, pp. 11–12 and 33; BL, Add. MS 37816, ff. 57r, 103v, 106v and 139v-40r, and Add. MS 37817, f. 18r.

466 *Records of the Convention of the Royal Burghs of Scotland*, vol. 3, pp. 213–14; *Register of the Privy Council of Scotland*, 2nd ser., vol. 1, pp. 237, 270–1 and 276–80. The date specified in the *Historical Works of Sir James Balfour*, vol. 2, p. 133, is out by two months.

467 *Register of the Privy Council of Scotland*, 2nd ser., vol. 1, p. 180.

468 *Register of the Privy Council of Scotland*, 2nd ser., vol. 1, pp. 300–1.

469 *Register of the Privy Council of Scotland*, 2nd ser., vol. 1, pp. 283–5; *Registrum magni sigilli regum Scotorum*, vol. 8, p. 344.

in England also took out licences at home, along with ten others – all again from Leith, the Fife ports, and Dundee – raising the number of Scottish captains licensed during the war to twenty-two.[470] In contrast to the warrants sent to the judge of the admiralty court in England, the 'signatures' issued for letters to be granted under the great seal in Scotland made no pretence of authorising reprisals for losses inflicted on and justice denied to their recipients.[471] After mentioning the 'manie grite indignities and injuries' endured by Charles and his father at the hands of Philip, they simply declared that it was 'not aggreeable with his majesteis honnour, nor reullis of pollicie, that his majestie sould ony longer forbeare these remedies whilk the law of nationis in matteris of this kynd allowis and approves'. Each captain named was accordingly being licensed to arm a named ship and 'mak his addresse to the sea, and thair to searche, seik, follow and persew with all hostilitie, and to tak or sink, the shippis or goodes of the said king of Spayne and his subjectis'. If ships and goods were taken and brought back to Scotland, the captain would be entitled 'to meddle and intromet with and to use the same shippis and goodes as pryise lawfullie foirfeytted to his majestie', and this was to extend to the ships and goods of friends if they were supplying the king's enemies with 'provisionis serveing to build, furnishe or arme any shippis of warre, or ony munitioun for the warre or materiallis for the same'. The first of the licences granted, all of which were addressed in Latin to the king's friends and allies, was labelled in the register of the great seal a 'litera represaliae', but the others were all labelled 'literae martis', an echo perhaps of 'letters of marque' but a clear indication that they were seen as 'letters of war'.[472] The justification adumbrated in the signatures was restated in the letters, including the phrase *remedia quod ius gentium in hoc fieri amat*, and reference was again made – albeit a little less precisely – to ships and goods being forfeited (*confiscatas*) to the crown and enjoyed by their takers as lawful prizes (*legitimae praedae*). Bonds of caution were entered before the council to guarantee correct use of the licences, and these promised that each captain would 'account in exchequer for his prizes, and pay to his majesty, and the lord admiral and his deputes, such proportions

470 On the involvement of a merchant from Stirling in some ventures see Morris 1919, pp. 275–83.

471 *Register of the Privy Council of Scotland*, 2nd ser., vol. 1, pp. 319, 413–14, 425–6, 447, 449, 481 and 495, and vol. 2, pp. 15–16, 20 and 23; NRS, PC7/3, ff. 80–1v, 88v-9r, 107–8, 110v-11, 115v-16, 120–1 and 140v-1.

472 *Registrum magni sigilli regum Scotorum*, vol. 8, pp. 345–7, 355, 357, 387 and 392–3; NRS, C3/2, ff. 249–50r, 262, 264v-5r, 284v-5, 288v and 290v.

thereof as are legally due'.[473] The earliest bond had actually talked about 'paying to his majesty one sixth part thereof, or less if the lords of council shall find that there is not so much due in such cases by the laws of England'. The intention was to follow the example of England, yet whatever doubts the privy councillors may have had about how prize taking was being organised there, they had no doubt that what was being organised did not amount to the taking of reprisals in the conventional sense of the term.

The hereditary admiral whose dues were being protected was at the time only fourteen years old, which is why disputes relating to seizures made by the captains were at first raised before the privy council.[474] In the autumn of 1626 seven commissioners were authorised 'to try whither the schipps takin of late by some of our subjects of that our kingdome be lawfull pryses or not'.[475] The actions pending before the council were remitted to the commissioners, who co-opted Sir Jerome Lindsay, the depute who had presided over the central court in Leith on behalf of the previous admiral, but it was objected that his appointment had lapsed on that admiral's death, and that the commissioners had not been authorised to increase their number, which was proving to be too small for a full court to be easily assembled.[476] At the end of the year the council was instructed to resume jurisdiction in several cases that had been awaiting resolution for some time, taking advice from any commissioners who happened to be present, and ensuring that while the captains who had ventured to sea had 'all the encouragments of prosecuteing the commendable course that can be convenientlie assured unto them', nothing was decided 'to the prejudice of other states against the lawis of nations and usuall course of justice'.[477] In January 1627 the earl of Linlithgow, a kinsman of the admiral, was appointed to exercise his office until he came of age.[478] The interim admiral was ordered not to 'determine upon any matters concerneing prises' without

473 *Register of the Privy Council of Scotland*, 2nd ser., vol. 1. pp. 295, 319, 426–7, 434, 458, 464, 500 and 505, and vol. 2, pp. 23, 26 and 35, and see too vol. 3, p. 144, as well as bonds of caution for the return of borrowed ordnance at vol. 1, pp. 630 and 633, vol. 2, pp. 26 and 36.

474 *Register of the Privy Council of Scotland*, 2nd ser., vol. 1, pp. 269–70, 313–14, 424, 436–8, 440–1, 454–5 and 457–8; *Stirling's Register of Royal Letters*, vol. 1, p. 56.

475 *Register of the Privy Council of Scotland*, 2nd ser., vol. 1, p. 441; *Stirling's Register of Royal Letters*, vol. 1, p. 94; *Registrum magni sigilli regum Scotorum*, vol. 8, p. 356.

476 *Register of the Privy Council of Scotland*, 2nd ser., vol. 1, pp. 446, 451, 458–63, 465–76 and 481.

477 *Register of the Privy Council of Scotland*, 2nd ser., vol. 1, pp. 482–4, 489–91, 493–4, 496–9 and 505; *Stirling's Register of Royal Letters*, vol. 1, p. 112.

478 *Registrum magni sigilli regum Scotorum*, vol. 8, p. 357; *Stirling's Register of Royal Letters*, vol. 1, pp. 114–15, 121 and 253; *Register of the Privy Council of Scotland*, 2nd ser., vol. 1, pp. 519–20; *Historical Works of Sir James Balfour*, vol. 2, p. 153.

advice from eight 'assessours', most of whom had been included among the commissioners for prizes, though the intention may have been to bring the practice of the admiralty court in Scotland into line with the practice of the court in England, where the judge usually sat with a panel of assessors.[479] 'To the effect you may know how matters of the lyk kynd have bene handled heir', the king wrote to Linlithgow at the end of the month, 'we have sent you some articles which may give you some farther light in your proceedings concerneing the saids pryses', by which he presumably meant a copy of the instructions issued by the privy council in England.[480] In April Linlithgow was praised for adopting the English practice of delivering final decrees in Latin, 'to the effect the same may be showen, if neede be, to any forrain prince or state'.[481] In the king's letters the admiral was told to decide cases 'according to the lawis in that our kingdome, and of other nightbouring nations', or more significantly 'according to the lawes of that our kingdome provyded in the like cases, or according to the lawes and custom observed in this our kingdome or by forraine princes or states'. He was also told to seek advice from the privy council on any questions of particular delicacy that arose, which he did in several cases remitted to him.[482] Although there were admiralty courts sitting elsewhere in Scotland from which no records have survived, and although there is evidence of actions being raised centrally that are not covered in the records of Linlithgow's court, those records do at least show how much of the prize litigation arising during the later stages of the wars with Spain and France was dealt with in Scotland.[483]

The first action recorded was raised, fittingly enough, by Andrew Watson, in relation to the seizure of a ship from Hamburg by the *Blessing* of Burntisland.[484] An action relating to the seizure had already been raised before the privy council, and heard by the commissioners for prizes, but a new action was initiated

479 *Stirling's Register of Royal Letters*, vol. 1, pp. 119–20; *Registrum magni sigilli regum Scotorum*, vol. 8, p. 359.

480 *Stirling's Register of Royal Letters*, vol. 1, pp. 121, 130 and 179.

481 *Stirling's Register of Royal Letters*, vol. 1, pp. 162–3.

482 *Register of the Privy Council of Scotland*, 2nd ser., vol. 1, pp. 525, 532–4, 543, 557–8, 581–2 and 588–9; *Stirling's Register of Royal Letters*, vol. 1, pp. 141, 173 and 186–7; NRS, AC7/1, pp. 6–8.

483 *Register of the Privy Council of Scotland*, 2nd ser., vol. 2, pp. 67, 69–70, 189–90, 208–9, 281–2, 564–5 and 567, vol. 3, pp. 149, 271–2, 315, 429, 446–7, 474, 521–3, 589–91, 609 and 668, and vol. 4, p. 14; *Stirling's Register of Royal Letters*, vol. 1, pp. 164, 192, 198, 245, 247, 260, 280, 290–1, 371–2 and 404–5, and vol. 2, pp. 415, 419–20, 424, 429, 435, 438, 447, 469–70, 483 and 667–8; *Shetland Documents*, vol. 2, p. 388.

484 NRS, AC7/1, pp. 2–4 and 13–17. The records are calendared in Mowat and Graham 2005.

before the admiralty court by the submission of a libel in which it was alleged that Watson had been licensed to seize friendly ships carrying contraband goods to the enemy, that he had captured the Hamburg ship on its way to Lisbon with both victuals and lead suitable for making shot, and that accordingly the ship and goods 'aucht and sould be dewlie foirfaulted and confiscat and decernit and declaired to be just and lawfull pryse at the instance of the said persewar, and theirby adjudgit to appertein to him'. In substantiation of his allegations the captain produced the 'commissioune under the great seall granted to him be his majestie' – unlike in England, of course, the licences were not already a matter of record in the court – 'twa missive letters in Dutche language', identifying the ship's destination, both of which had to be 'faithfullie translated in the Scottische language', and an 'inventrie of the goodes and geir contenit in the said schip'. On the basis of these documents William Livingston, one of two admiral deputes appointed by Linlithgow, 'withe advyse and consent of his assessours', declared the ship and goods 'to be just and lawfull pryze, and the samen to appertene to the said perseware as his awin propper schip, goodes and geir', subject to the reservation of the 'partis and portiounes' due to the king and to the admiral, 'viz. to his majestie the greit custome of the haill goodes and geir being within the said schipe, and to the said lord admirall the just tent of the said schipe and goodes'. Most of the other cases covered in the court's records were also concerned with the seizure of friendly ships. The expeditious procedure followed was later outlined in a manual written by the other admiral depute, James Roberton, who explained that there were normally just three hearings, at the first of which the court ruled on the relevancy of the libel and any defences submitted, at the second of which it received documentary evidence, and at the third of which it delivered its final decision.[485] As only the act book of the court survives, there is no direct evidence of the libels and defences submitted, but the way in which they were summarised in the court's sentences suggests that Watson's allegations formed a template for those submitted by other captains. The documents presented to the court have not been preserved either, nor have the depositions taken in some cases from witnesses. Roberton noted that one reason why the process was more expeditious than usual was that the admiral took testimony from anyone captured with a ship as soon as it arrived in Scotland, so that depositions did not have to be taken at the second stage of the process.[486] The final sentences delivered

485 'Roberton's Treatise on Court Procedure', pp. 410–24. On the authorship of the manual see Ford 2012.

486 'Roberton's Treatise on Court Procedure', p. 438.

in the other cases also followed closely the pattern of the sentence delivered in the first case.[487]

In October 1627 John Daw, licensed as the captain of the *Consort* of Crail, laid claim to another ship from Hamburg, which had not been carrying contraband goods but goods belonging to the enemy, and here too the ship and goods were found 'to be lawfull pryize, and the samen to pertein to the said persewar as taiker and apprehender thairof'.[488] In April 1628 David Robertson, licensed as the captain of the *Grace of God* of Dysart, raised an action in relation to a ship from Nieuwpoort, alleging that both the ship and its cargo belonged to subjects of the king of Spain living there, or to subjects of the king of France living in Calais, 'quhilkis king of Spaine and Frenche king ar both his majesties declaired enemeis'.[489] Despite the suggestion that wars had been declared, in this case the ship and goods were again found 'to be dewlie foirfaultit and to be gude and lawfull pryize and to pertein to the said persewar as taker and apprehender thairof'. In both cases the production of the 'lettres of mart' granted to the captain was crucial to the decision. Towards the end of 1626 the sheriff of Orkney and Shetland had seized a ship from Danzig suspected of carrying contraband goods to Spain, even though he did not hold a licence to seize ships or goods.[490] He sought and obtained a formal ratification of his conduct from the privy council, exonerating him from any charge that might have been made against him, and an action was then raised by the procurator fiscal of the admirality in relation to the ship and goods, which were found 'to be dewlie foirfeytted to our soverane lord, reserveand to the said lord admirall the just and equall tent pairt of the samin'.[491] In January 1628 a ship from Lübeck, laden with Spanish wine, was wrecked near Peterhead after being seized at sea by

487 Only one decreet was actually recorded in the act book in Latin (NRS, AC7/1, pp. 204–12), but translations could have been produced routinely without being entered in that book. Alternatively, decreets may have been issued in Latin only if the parties asked for them. It cannot be that Linlithgow's innovation was immediately set aside, because it was praised by the king in April 1627, while the surviving example is from September 1628.

488 NRS, AC7/1, pp. 92–9 and 100–6. It was similarly claimed in some of the contraband cases that goods seized belonged to the king's enemies, which was sometimes said to be shown by the destruction of crucial documents.

489 NRS, AC7/1, pp. 144–9.

490 *Register of the Privy Council of Scotland*, 2nd ser., vol. 1. pp. 468–9, 481, 498–9, 505, 525 and 558; *Shetland Documents*, vol. 3, pp. 372–3 and 376.

491 NRS, AC7/1, pp. 48–54; *Shetland Documents*, vol. 3, pp. 390–1. See too NRS, AC7/1, pp. 107–8; *Shetland Documents*, vol. 3, pp. 395–6.

merchant vessels from Montrose and St Andrews.[492] The remains of the wreck were brought to Leith, and an action was raised before the admiralty court by the masters of the merchant vessels, who had in the meantime obtained a dispensation from the king for the court to proceed 'as iff the said takers hade been sufficientlie authorized by any warrant or lettres of mark from us'.[493] In finding the ship and wine 'to be dewlie forfeytted and to be gude and lawfull pryize', the court took care to record that the king had 'frielie dispensed' with the normal requirement of authorisation by 'lettre of mart'.[494] Later in the same year the admiral recorded that a Dutch ship transporting goods for Irish merchants had been captured by a master from Glasgow, taken into the Clyde and 'alledgit lawfull pryize, quhairanent he and our deputtis have taikin sume tryall, but as yit have fund no probabill caus of pryize'.[495] It could be that the master had failed to produce any proof of collaboration with the enemy, although a more fundamental problem must have been his inability to produce a licence under the great seal.[496]

By that stage there was another possibility, at least in principle. In July 1627 the king had decided that it would be appropriate to confer the 'priviledge' of granting licences on the Scottish as well as the English admiral, 'without prejudice to us for granting of commissiones to such of our subjects ther upon whome we shall think fitt to conferre that favour'.[497] In fact, the granting of licences on the strength of authorisation from the privy council came to an end at this time, yet the Scottish admiral appears to have exercised his privilege only by granting commissions to captains already licensed under the great seal if they agreed to sail in consort with the two ships he bought from the king.[498] Sentences delivered by the admiralty court in relation to seizures made by these fleets mentioned the commissions granted to the captains in conjunction with a licence granted by the king to Linlithgow himself when

492 *Register of the Privy Council of Scotland*, 2nd ser., vol. 2, pp. 189–92, 195, 198–200, 204, 215, 219–20, 236, 238–40, 270, 274–7, 291, 564–5, 567 and 574–5, and vol. 3, pp. 209 and 268.; *Stirling's Register of Royal Letters*, vol. 1, pp. 245 and 262.

493 NRS, AC7/1, pp. 149–51 and 155–60.

494 For further difficulties arising from the case see *Register of the Privy Council of Scotland*, 2nd ser., vol. 2, pp. 417–18 and 427; *Stirling's Register of Royal Letters*, vol. 1, pp. 274, 278, 352, 595 and 597.

495 NRS, AC7/1, pp. 196–8.

496 See too *Register of the Privy Council of Scotland*, 2nd ser., vol. 1, pp. 254, 443, 617–18, 627 and 681–2.

497 *Stirling's Register of Royal Letters*, vol. 1, p. 187.

498 NRS, AC7/1, pp. 164–75, 190–5 and 198–203. *Cf. Stirling's Register of Royal Letters*, vol. 1, p. 354.

he took charge of the naval vessels, promising Charles a third of every prize taken.[499] A similar licence was granted to the Earl Marischal when he bought the other vessel, though there is no evidence that it was ever used in prize taking.[500] Both Linlithgow and the Earl Marischal received their licences at the king's direction under the great seal, as did the marquis of Hamilton, though there is again no evidence that his ship was ever used in prize taking.[501] Further licences were granted on the king's personal authority in connection with colonial enterprises.[502] When his secretary, Sir William Alexander of Menstrie, afterwards the first earl of Stirling, was put in charge of the settlement of Nova Scotia, he was created admiral of the territory and its coastal waters and authorised under the great seal to seize 'ships and vessels pertaining to the king of the Spaniards and the infanta Isabella or to whomsoever the king's declared enemies'.[503] On the basis of this licence, ships and goods seized by captains he sent across the Atlantic were found by the admiralty court in Scotland 'to be dewlie forffeytted and to be gude and lawfull pryizes'.[504] A less straightforward concession was made to Sir Robert Gordon of Lochinvar, who had been put in charge of the settlement of an Atlantic island named after the king.[505] In March 1627 a captain employed by Gordon seized a Dutch vessel near Waterford and took it back to Kirkcudbright.[506] He claimed to have acted under a licence obtained from the privy council, which Gordon had indeed requested, but had not been granted.[507] Worried about the 'foule scandall' that might follow if 'his majesteis freinds sould be mischantlie used be way of pyracie be persons not authorized with a lawfull warrant and commissioun', the

499 *Registrum magni sigilli regum Scotorum*, vol. 8, p. 412; NRS, C3/2, ff. 325v-6r.

500 *Stirling's Register of Royal Letters*, vol. 1, p. 158; *Registrum magni sigilli regum Scotorum*, vol. 8, p. 376; NRS, C3/2, ff. 284v-5.

501 *Register of the Privy Council of Scotland*, 2nd ser., vol. 2, pp. 234–5; *Registrum magni sigilli regum Scotorum*, vol. 8, p. 438; NRS, C3/2, f. 388.

502 For two cases in which licences were not in the end granted see *Register of the Privy Council of Scotland*, 2nd ser., vol. 1, pp. 357–8, 482 and 605; *Stirling's Register of Royal Letters*, vol. 1, pp. 66–7 and 78; *Shetland Documents*, vol. 3, p. 408.

503 *Stirling's Register of Royal Letters*, vol. 1, pp. 56, 118–19 and 144–5; *Registrum magni sigilli regum Scotorum*, vol. 8, p. 378; NRS, C3/2, ff. 277v-8.

504 NRS, AC7/1, pp. 109–21 and 124–8. See too *Stirling's Register of Royal Letters*, vol. 2, pp. 420 and 580.

505 *Stirling's Register of Royal Letters*, vol. 1, pp. 38–9; *Registrum magni sigilli regum Scotorum*, vol. 8, pp. 344–5.

506 *Calendar of State Papers Relating to Ireland of the Reign of Charles I*, vol. 1, pp. 220–1; *Register of the Privy Council of Scotland*, 2nd ser., vol. 1, p. 678; *Kirkcudbright Town Council Records*, vol. 2, p. 325.

507 *Register of the Privy Council of Scotland*, 2nd ser., vol. 1, p. 678.

council summoned Gordon to Edinburgh, where he admitted that a mistake had been made and that he had no legitimate claim to the prize.[508] The vessel was returned to its Dutch owners and the conduct of the captain was investigated further, but Gordon received a new commission for the settlement of Charles Island in which he was licensed to raid enemy shipping, on the basis of which his son was able to claim a prize before the admiralty court in August 1628.[509]

In the pleadings presented to the court it was usually stated that the pursuers were entitled to a prize 'ather be the lawis and practique of this kingdome of Scotland, or be the lawis of Spayne or West Flanderis, or be the lawis of other natiounes, or be the civill and commoun law, or be the articlis sent downe be his majestie to be folowit and observit be the said lord admirall whair the foirsaidis uther lawis ar deficient'.[510] The reservation of rights to the king and admiral was usually said to be 'conforme to the marine law and to the inviolabill custome observit in maters of the lyke kynd', whereas the confiscation of contraband goods was said to be founded on 'the lawis of this kingdome and utheris', and the destruction of documents to be against 'the lawes of natiounes'.[511] Whether the lawyers who presented these pleadings were thinking in terms of a *ius gentium* established by agreements between nations, or in more conventional terms of the reciprocity permitted between opponents, is hard to tell from such formulaic statements. The belief that prize taking operated in much the same way on the other side of the conflict was certainly important in a case raised in 1628, in which a captain successfully laid claim to a ship from Hamburg that had been carrying timber to the enemy, even though the ship had once belonged to Scots.[512] Two years earlier the ship had been seized 'be ane man of warre of Dunkirk', ownership had thus been lost by the Scots, and it was therefore possible for the captain to acquire title by seizing the ship from the Germans to whom it had been sold. Yet attention was also drawn to 'the lawis of other natiounes'. Whatever the king may have intended when he sent the admiral a copy of the articles issued in England, they were regarded in Scotland as a source of last resort in difficult cases, rather than as a

508 *Register of the Privy Council of Scotland*, 2nd ser., vol. 1, pp. 582, 588–9, 596–7, 601, 630 and 632–3.

509 *Register of the Privy Council of Scotland*, 2nd ser., vol. 2, pp. 9–15; *Registrum magni sigilli regum Scotorum*, vol. 8, p. 387; *Stirling's Register of Royal Letters*, vol. 1, pp. 191–2 and 211–12, and vol. 2, pp. 207–8 and 271–2; *Kirkcudbright Town Council Records*, vol. 2, pp. 364–5; NRS, C3/2, ff. 283v-4, and AC7/1, pp. 184–7.

510 See, for instance, NRS, AC7/1, pp. 14–15, 36–7, 56–7, 62–3 and 85–7.

511 See, for instance, NRS, AC7/1, pp. 14, 37, 56, 77, 85, 140, 183, 230–1 and 262.

512 NRS, AC7/1, pp. 212–18.

general guide to the regulation of prize acquisition. While the articles made it clear that title would be acquired through adjudication, and while the pleadings presented to the admiralty court in Scotland often stated that captains were meant to bring their prizes home 'to be adjudgit, ordourit and sauld as gudes dewlie foirfeyted', and asked for a ship and goods to be 'adjudged pryize', it is a notable feature of the sentences delivered that they never made use of the word 'adjudge'.[513] As there was no pretence in Scotland that reprisals were being taken, the lawyers in the court were able to deduce from their knowledge of the *ius commune* that it would suffice for title to be acquired if prizes were forfeited to the crown and granted to their takers. Nevertheless, advice was sometimes sought from England. The privy council, for example, asked whether a whole ship would be forfeit if part of its cargo was contraband or belonged to the enemy, since there were 'no praecedentis of that kynd in this cuntrey', nor was it known 'quhat wes the law and custome of that cuntrey, nor how far your majestie wald haif the same to be extendit heir'.[514] To some extent consultation was inevitable, for English ships were occasionally caught up in Scottish operations, just as Scottish ships continued to be caught up in English operations.[515] In connection with one case Roberton was advised by Marten that while the Scottish court could punish an English captain for breach of 'the law of nations', it could not punish him for breach of the English articles.[516]

Looking back on the war some years later, Roberton commented that 'England, so fare as I have seen, gave only letters of reprysall and never leters of mark, albeit reprysal be given against friends only'.[517] He recalled the handling of a dispute that arose in 1628 after a vessel was seized by masters from Hamburg in retaliation for interference with that port's trade with Flanders. After attempts to secure redress through diplomacy failed, 'letters of reprisall' were granted, because 'justice has beene ather denyed or delayed'.[518] When

513 See, for instance, NRS, AC7/1, pp. 15, 37, 110, 147, 180, 222, 228 and 230.

514 *Register of the Privy Council of Scotland*, 2nd ser., vol. 1. pp. 551–2, 597–8, 616–17; *Stirling's Register of Royal Letters*, vol. 1, pp. 177–8; NRS, PC11/2A, n. 3.

515 *Calendar of State Papers, Domestic Series, of the Reign of Charles I*, vol. 1, p. 267, vol. 3, pp. 219, 241 and 522, and vol. 5, p. 255; *Acts of the Privy Council of England*, vol. 42, p. 167, vol. 43, pp. 39, 47 and 133, and vol. 44. pp. 8–9, 227–8 and 242;; *Register of the Privy Council of Scotland*, 2nd ser., vol. 1, pp. 569–72 and 574–5, vol. 2, pp. 20–1, vol. 3, pp. 21, 32, 42, 52 and 59, and vol. 4, p. 51; *Stirling's Register of Royal Letters*, vol. 1, p. 335.

516 'Roberton's Teatise on Court Procedure', pp. 433–4; NRS, AC7/1, pp. 256–9.

517 'Roberton's Treatise on Court Procedure', p. 438. In this series of annotations on James Balfour's treatise on maritime law, Roberton was also able to compare the different way in which prizes were distributed among their takers in England (pp. 437–8).

518 *Register of the Privy Council of Scotland*, 2nd ser., vol. 2, pp. 540 and 544–5, and vol. 3, pp. 484 and 525–6; *Registrum magni sigilli regum Scotorum*, vol. 8, p. 526.

the recipients captured another ship from Hamburg in 1630, the clerks of the admiralty court made use of their usual style in drafting a decreet upholding the legitimacy of the seizure, much as their predecessors had done in similar circumstances in 1560, except that they distinguished clearly between the letters of reprisal and the licences granted to the captains of warships.[519] In fact the distinction was understood perfectly well in England, as it had to be since reprisals continued to be taken after the wars with France and Spain ended.[520] Yet Roberton had a point, for the licences that were granted in Scotland during the wars, in contrast to those granted in England, were more similar to the licences issued to the captains of warships in the 1540s and 1550s than to letters of reprisal.[521] The earlier licences had also been addressed in Latin to foreign rulers, they had explained how depredations inflicted on the Scots had forced their rulers to resort to war, and they had urged the foreign rulers to recognise that the holder of each licence was 'our subject, waging just and lawful war on the enemies of our land, not a brigand or pirate'. It continued to be believed that the licences granted to captains marked them off from pirates, but instead of spelling this out, the later licences stressed that a war was being waged under *ius gentium*, and that any ships or goods taken were considered forfeit to the king, from whom grants had been made to the takers. The new understanding of prize taking in wartime greatly increased the king's control over maritime raiding. Notwithstanding the possibility of seizures receiving retrospective ratification, prize acquisition had come to be entirely dependent on the holding of a licence granted on the conditions set by the government. In August 1627 one licence was revoked after it was reported that its recipient, 'being upoun the sea when ane of the countrie shippes wes persewit be the enemie, and he being of sufficient power to have releeved her, he shamefullie and unworthilie abandonnit his countrie shippe, made her no releefe and left her to the mercilesse crueltie of the enemie'.[522] It did not help that when called upon to serve in one of the admiral's fleets, 'he shamefullie and mischantlie refuised to joyne in that service, testifeing thairby that he wes unworthie of anie publict service or imployment in the estait'. As has been seen, despite the general reluctance of Scottish mariners to become involved in the king's wars,

519 NRS, AC7/1, pp. 278–82.

520 *Manuscripts of the Earl Cowper*, vol. 1, p. 408; *Register of the Privy Council of Scotland*, 2nd ser., vol. 4, pp. 109, 187, 413, 420–1, 484–5, 490, 524, 526 and 557–60; *Stirling's Register of Royal Letters*, vol. 2, pp. 568, 580, 593, 607, 642 and 653; *Registrum magni sigilli regum Scotorum*, vol. 8, p. 652.

521 See again the sources cited in n. 8 above.

522 *Register of the Privy Council of Scotland*, 2nd ser., vol. 2, pp. 59–60.

other recipients of *literae martis* (referred to in one source as 'freebooters') were willing to provide something like public service.[523] If the king had reason to lament the relatively 'small benefit that doth arise unto us by the prises that are taken by the subjectis of that our kingdome', it was to his advantage that he was able to demand 'a greater proportione out of the said prises then was formerlie in use to be payed unto us'.[524]

---

523 *Register of the Privy Council of Scotland*, 2nd ser., vol. 2, pp. 39–48, 59, 67, 179, 202, 261, 269–70 and 304; *Stirling's Register of Royal Letters*, vol. 1, pp. 201–2.

524 *Stirling's Register of Royal Letters*, vol. 1, p. 239.

Conclusion

Readers who have not skipped over the parts of the preceding chapters that were concerned with maritime raiding in Scotland will have noticed a sharp contrast between the handling of prize taking at the end of the 1620s and at the end of the 1550s. Having avoided involvement in wars against other nations throughout the reign of James VI, the Scots were drawn into a war initiated in England at the start of Charles I's reign. It was in fact through the licensing of maritime raiding that the war was initiated, yet several months passed before anyone thought of licensing raiding in Scotland, where the authorities were then encouraged to follow the example of England. In the records of the Scottish privy council and admiralty court, stress came to be placed on two features of prize taking that were absent from the records of the late 1550s and early 1560s.[1] In the first place, it was constantly emphasised – in directions issued by the privy council, in licences granted under the great seal and in decisions delivered by the admiralty court – that prize acquisition was dependent on the possession of a valid licence.[2] Accordingly, no one without a licence was found to have secured title to a prize. Indeed, even when it seemed convenient to ratify seizures made by unlicensed raiders and to grant them immunity from prosecution, the raiders were still not found to have secured title to the ships and goods taken. In contrast, while licences had sometimes been granted to raiders around the middle of the sixteenth century, the possession of a licence had never been identified then as a condition of prize acquisition. On the contrary, while raiders were often found by a court to have secured title to the ships and goods they had seized at sea, in no case was there even passing mention of the possession of a licence.[3] In the second place, in the late 1620s it was emphasised with unfailing regularity that ships and goods seized from the enemy, as well as contraband goods carried towards the enemy, were considered forfeit to the crown. No trace of the notion that ships and goods seized at sea from enemies were acquired by forfeiture has been found in the records of

1 While it could be that the contrast would seem less sharp if records had survived from the admiralty court for the period between 1562 and 1625, when attention might have been paid to conflicts elsewhere, there is nothing in the extensive records that have survived from the privy council for the same period to suggest that this would actually have been the case.

2 In the syllogistic reasoning of the pleadings presented to the court, the possession of a valid licence invariably formed the major premiss of the argument.

3 Not in any case arising from a seizure made in a public war, that is. As was noted at the beginning of the first section of the third chapter, a licence was mentioned in relation to a prize taken in a civil war.

 | DOI:10.1163/9789004541412_006

the sixteenth century (or any earlier period for that matter). Previously, enemy property had been considered ownerless, and raiders had been thought capable of acquiring it by occupation, as soon as their rulers created the conditions in which enemies were thought to exist. By 1630, however, no prize could be acquired merely by taking it into possession. The effective seizure of ships and goods made them the property of the crown, and they became the property of the takers only through a grant from the crown.[4] Ironically, while the Scottish understanding of prize taking had been transformed by the imitation of English practice, the corresponding transformation of English practice is harder to make out. The sharp contrast in the Scottish records between the practices documented in the late 1550s and in the late 1620s resulted from the adoption of a new practice after it had gradually emerged in England, where it retained traces of the confused process through which it had slowly come into existence. In particular, the pretence was preserved in England that the licensing of raiding in wartime had something to do with the licensing of reprisals in peacetime. It was easier for the Scots to see that a new form of wartime raiding had been developed, replacing the old form and remaining categorically distinct from reprisals in peacetime.

Around a hundred years after the new form of wartime raiding had started to emerge in the 1560s it came to be labelled, in both English and Scottish records, with the new word 'privateering'.[5] Well established in practice by the 1630s, privateering was clearly understood by the 1660s to be based in theory on 'the laws and customes of nations', conceived of as a new *ius commune*, according to which it made no difference whether a war had been declared or not.[6] Explicit reference was by then being made to De Groot's *De iure belli ac pacis* as a guide to the law of nations, yet his later theory of prize acquisition was already reckoned to be out of date.[7] Although it was believed that title to

4 There was thus a return to the Roman handling of plunder. The forfeiture was the original mode of acquisition, the grant the derivative mode, unusual in its confusion of contract with conveyance (Buckland 1963, p. 205).

5 Marsden 1911; Llewelyn Davies 1934; Carty 1981; Graham 1982; Rommelse 2003; Murdoch, Little and Forte 2003; Shavana 2015.

6 *Documents Relating to Law and Custom of the Sea*, vol. 2, pp. 5–6, 8, 23–5, 31, 49, 58, 123, 132, 149, 156 and 162; *Life of Sir Leoline Jenkins*, vol. 2, pp. 728, 732–3, 751, 759, 780 and 787; Sir James Dalrymple of Stair, *Decisions of the Lords of Council and Session*, vol. 1, pp. 234–5, 551 and 618, and vol. 2, pp. 155–6 and 213–14.

7 John Godolphin, *View of the Admiral Jurisdiction*, p. 97; Charles Molloy, *De iure maritimo et navali*, pp. 3, 10, 15, 18, 39, 59–60 and 69; *Law of Contraband of War*, pp. 254 and 256; *Documents Relating to Law and Custom of the Sea*, vol. 2, p. 143; Stair, *Decisions of the Lords of Council and Session*, vol. 1, p. 503; Sir John Nisbet of Dirleton, *Decisions of the Lords of Council and Session*, p. 55; Sir George Mackenzie of Rosehaugh, *Pleadings in Some*

prizes had previously been conferred on occupiers by 'common agreement', it was also believed that 'the present practice of the most civil and puissant soveraignties of the world hath superseded this law, and the title to enemies goods is vested in the prince, and from him derived, as other *regalia* are'.[8] In England ships and goods seized at sea in wartime had been assimilated with the *bona inimicorum* forfeited to the king under the common law, along with the *bona piratica* forfeited to the admiral, and all the other things that might have been considered ownerless had they not been brought within the royal prerogative.[9] It continued to be insisted, however, that title to prizes would not be acquired as soon as they were seized under licences promising their acquisition. In English practice prizes did not become the property of the takers 'before the same have been by law adjudged lawful to the captors and the admiral had his share', so that prizes taken in wartime were no different from reprisals executed in peacetime 'as to the divesting of the proprietor of his interest, and the investing the taker under the commission he acts by'.[10] A distinction was therefore drawn for the first time between the 'general and universal reprizals' authorised in wartime and the 'special and particular reprizals' authorised in peacetime[11] In Scotland advice was still being sought from south of the border on how prize taking should be regulated, although sometimes the Scottish judges preferred to find out for themselves, 'from the admiralties of neighbouring nations, what was the custom of nations'.[12] The practice of formally adjudging prizes to their captors was adopted in Scotland during the Anglo-Dutch Wars, perhaps because consistency with English practice was encouraged, or perhaps because it helped to ensure that the admiral received his share of any prize taken.[13] The basic understanding was that while ships or

---

Remarkable Cases, p. 124; *Decisions of the Court of Session*, vol. 14, p. 11935. Although a reference is made to De Groot's treatise in NAK, SP16/43, ff. 100–1, which is tentatively listed under 1626 in the *Calendar of State Papers, Domestic Series, of the Reign of Charles I*, vol. 1, p. 518, there is no good reason to date the document so early. As it also contains the word 'privateeres', a later date seems more likely.

8 Molloy, *De iure maritimo et navali*, p. 8; *Life of Sir Leoline Jenkins*, vol. 2, p. 765.

9 Sir Matthew Hale, *Prerogatives of the King*, p. 131; *Life of Sir Leoline Jenkins*, vol. 2, p. 765.

10 Molloy, *De iure maritimo et navali*, p. 45; *Life of Sir Leoline Jenkins*, vol. 2, p. 742.

11 Godolphin, *View of the Admiral Jurisdiction*, sig. B4v. The distinction, it should be emphasised, was between two forms of licensed raiding. It makes less sense for historians to use the same language to distinguish licensed reprisals in peacetime from unlicensed raiding in wartime, which is what they are doing when they describe the relaxation of the licensing system in the mid-sixteenth century as authorisation of general reprisals. This is most certainly not what the expression was supposed to mean when it was first used.

12 Stair, *Decisions of the Lords of Council and Session*, vol. 1, pp. 531 and 626; Ford 2005.

13 Sir John Lauder of Fountainhall, *Historical Observes of Memorable Occurrents*, p. 259. It seemed to the same author that in the second Anglo-Dutch War 'we in Scotland ware

goods seized by licensed raiders on either side of the conflict were 'confiscat as publick, belonging to the king or states, yet private persons who undertake these commissions have the expenses and profit of these seazures, paying a fifteenth part thereof to the king and a tenth part to the admiral'.[14] On both sides of the border a formal act of adjudication was thus the mechanism by which title to most of each prize was transferred from the crown to the captors.

So what exactly was privateering? The simple contrast often drawn between licensed privateering and unlicensed piracy is not entirely satisfactory.[15] On the one hand, not every licensed raider was a privateer. Attempts to exert control over maritime raiding in wartime by requiring mariners to obtain licences before sailing are found at least as early as the close of the fourteenth century, long before privateering *stricto sensu* began to emerge, and even after its emergence licences continued to be granted in peacetime for the execution of reprisals, and at any time for the mounting of expeditions against pirates.[16] On the other hand, not every unlicensed raider was a pirate. There was a crucial difference, it was observed, 'between a pirate, who is a highwayman and sets up for robbing, either having no commission at all or else hath two or three, and a lawful man of war that exceeds his commission'.[17] A privateer who failed to enter the bonds of security required before sailing was in a different position from someone who despoiled shipping 'without any commission at all', as was anyone who mistakenly believed that a licence he held was valid.[18] The question that needed to be asked was not whether raiders held valid licences but whether they 'came out *animo hostile* as privateers, not *animo furandi* as pirates'. Privateers differed from pirates in their state of mind, yet the difference between privateering and the older form of legitimate raiding in wartime cannot be explained in the same way, for raiding in wartime had always been conducted *animo hostile*. What had changed was neither the mentality of the raiders, nor the insistence on licences being obtained before they set out, but the inextricable link that had been formed between the holding of licences and prize acquisition. In the older form of raiding, prizes had been acquired

---

included and drawen to be sharers of the good and ill which follows war, contrare to our interest' (p. 255).

14 Stair, *Institutions of the Law of Scotland*, pp. 213–14.

15 Thomson 1994, p. 22; Petrie 1999, pp. 2–3; Friel 2003, p. 83; Little 2005, p. 10; Ogborn 2008, p. 23; Konstam 2008, p. 8; O'Hara 2010, p. 41; Craze 2016, p. 655; Hallwood and Miceli 2018, p. 237.

16 Molloy, *De iure maritimo et navali*, p. 52.

17 *Life of Sir Leoline Jenkins*, vol. 2, pp. 713–15.

18 *Life of Sir Leoline Jenkins*, vol. 2, p. 750; *Documents Relating to Law and Custom of the Sea*, vol. 2, pp. 142–8.

by the occupation of enemy property, and while the lack of a licence might have resulted in the confiscation of a prize as a punishment, it was the acquisition of the prize that made the punishment possible. In the new form of raiding, no one could acquire a prize without a valid licence, because it was only through the grant of a prize already acquired by the crown that it could ever be acquired by the raider. The occupation of enemy property remained a necessary condition of prize acquisition, which is one reason why a considerable amount of civil law theory found its way into the new law of nations.[19] In the new form of raiding, however, the occupation of enemy property was no longer a sufficient condition of prize acquisition, which instead hinged on forfeiture to and a gift from the king.

The distinction just drawn may seem far too technical to have significance for anyone other than a pedantic lawyer. It was admittedly in letters and treatises written by lawyers that the distinction was elaborated, and mariners who set out to raid enemy shipping may not have had a clear understanding of how they might become the owners of any ships and goods they seized. Yet merely because people acquired property without understanding the technicalities of the process does not mean that the technicalities did not exist, or that they did not matter.[20] That large numbers of mariners took the trouble both to obtain licences and to request judicial approval of the seizures they made bears witness to the importance they attached to acquiring the type of rights in prizes that could be passed on securely to other people.[21] Even though the constraints on prize taking had increased, there is actually more evidence of compliance with the conditions imposed on privateers than of compliance with the conditions imposed on their predecessors. The explanation is partly that more evidence happens to have survived from the period in which privateering came into existence, but it is also that the conditions imposed no longer had the same character. It was one thing to add a layer of regulation

19 For an illustration of the continuing importance of the civil law concept of occupation see Stair, *Decisions of the Lords of Council and Session*, vol. 2, pp. 507–10; *Decisions of the Court of Session*, vol. 14, pp. 11934–6; *Life of Sir Leoline Jenkins*, vol. 2, pp. 757–9.

20 People who feel the need when they buy houses today to pay lawyers for their services as conveyancers do so precisely because they lack the expertise to deal with the technicalities of acquisition themselves.

21 It was real rights of this type that the privy council in England was at pains to promise after ships and cargoes were formally adjudged to their captors in the admiralty court. As was remarked in the introduction to this book, these real rights would have been more valuable than the personal rights mariners could have obtained by selling ships and cargoes to buyers who were prepared to receive them without prior adjudication, and some mariners at least may have cared more generally about the legality of their behaviour.

to the practice of prize taking, threatening mariners with deprivation of the property they acquired, and another thing to change the fundamental principles of prize taking, making the acquisition of property contingent on the possession of a licence.[22] It was because prize acquisition itself had come to depend on compliance with the terms of licences that it had become possible for governments to demand larger portions of prizes, to restrict sailing to specified waters, to require assistance in naval operations, and in other ways to expect behaviour comparable to public service from privateers.[23] Making prize acquisition conditional on compliance with the terms of a licence significantly increased the control governments could exercise over maritime raiding. While the monopolisation of violence at sea was not something governments appear to have aimed at let alone achieved in the sixteenth and seventeenth centuries, the emergence of privateering moved them, however unwittingly, in that direction.[24] A product of the confessional conflicts that culminated in the Peace of Westphalia, privateering made its own contribution to the rise of the modern state.[25] In the seventeenth century, because the Scottish parliament and council had surrendered the direction of foreign policy to a monarch resident in England, privateering was already contributing to the rise of a British state of a distinctly Anglocentric variety.

Since a subsidiary thesis of this book is that piracy had always been contrasted as a criminal activity with legitimate forms of maritime raiding, more should perhaps be said by way of conclusion about the effects of the emergence of privateering on the understanding of piracy. The subsidiary thesis, which runs counter to much that has recently been written about the subject,

22 It may be accidental that examples are hard to find of prizes being confiscated from their takers before the late sixteenth century, but it does appear that the licensing of private warships became common only after possession of a licence became a fundamental condition of prize acquisition.

23 At least some economists believe that privateering was an efficient way for governments to organise maritime warfare (Anderson and Gifford 1991; Conybeare and Sandler 1993; Leeson 1995; Sechrest 2004).

24 Tilly 1985; Glete 1993 and 2002; Gallant 1998; Mabee 2009; Leira and De Carvalho 2010; Colás and Mabee 2010; Brandon 2015.

25 To look at this from a different angle, the emergence of privateering enabled states to exercise greater control over the use of violence at sea because privateering was conducted under licences attaching conditions to their exercise, because mariners were willing to do whatever was necessary to gain ownership of the ships and goods they seized, and because the new understanding of prize acquisition made compliance with licences fundamental to the acquisition of prizes. Legal technicalities thus underpinned an important change in how maritime conflict was organised in the nation states of early-modern Europe.

is that 'criminal piracy' is one category of maritime raiding that remained largely unchanged from antiquity to modernity. Whereas 'licit plunder' was supplanted in the early-modern period by 'privateering', and whereas 'licensed reprisal' later fell into disuse along with 'privateering', modern states continued to prosecute pirates as criminals.[26] The legal understanding of piracy was not transformed during the periods examined, yet it was affected by the transformation that has been identified in three ways. First, the restriction of legitimate raiding in wartime to licensed privateering expanded the area in which piracy could occur. It came to be presumed that unlicensed raiders were pirates, subject to the possibility of proof that their intentions were innocent. Secondly, the increase in state control over the use of force at sea in wartime coincided with an increasing acceptance of the responsibility of states to suppress piracy.[27] Although reliable figures cannot be calculated, especially for the earlier periods, it seems likely that the prosecution of pirates before criminal courts became more common in the early-modern period, in Britain as well as elsewhere. Thirdly, as states assumed greater responsibility for the suppression of piracy, doubts arose about the legitimacy of a fourth category of maritime raiding, referred to earlier as 'lawful vengeance'. Private parties who wished to put to sea in pursuit of pirates felt the need to obtain public authorisation before doing so, to avoid the risk of being prosecuted themselves.[28] Thus although the legal definition of piracy was not altered significantly, changes in the way in which the problem of illegal raiding was addressed provide further evidence of a gradual movement towards the monopolisation of violence at sea by modern states.

Whether the terms 'privateer' and 'privateering' should be used with greater precision in the future than they generally have been in the past is for readers to judge. Some may wish to take issue with the thesis promoted in this book, which has three obvious weaknesses (aside from those that may be less obvious to its author). The first is its limited geographical range. A desire to make sense of the legal regulation of maritime raiding in Scotland has led to an investigation of how maritime raiding was regulated in England, which in turn has involved rather limited examination of its regulation in Spain, France and the Netherlands. The whole subject might have looked quite different if

26 On the decline of 'licensed reprisal' see Wampach 2020, pp. 81–3.

27 That Cicero's condemnation of pirates as everyone's enemies was revived in connection with this transition suggests that its coincidence with the emergence of privateering was not accidental. Both developments owed a great deal to humanist learning.

28 De Groot encouraged this tendency in *De iure belli ac pacis*, vol. 1, pp. 327–8, and vol. 2, p. 485; *Rights of War and Peace*, vol. 2, p. 989.

attention had focused primarily on developments in one of these places, and more different still if it had been approached from the perspective of a place on the Mediterranean, the Baltic or some other sea.[29] The second weakness is that the enquiry has been selective and uneven in its coverage not only of space but also of time. At the risk of seeming unforgivably pretentious, it might be suggested that the enquiry has shifted between a sweeping overview of the *longue durée*, extending over several centuries, and more detailed investigation of the *moyenne durée*, lasting less than a century, with a narrower concentration on certain *événements* within the shorter period.[30] During the *moyenne durée* of the last four decades of the sixteenth century and the first three decades of the seventeenth century, it has been argued, the settled *mentalité* of the *longue durée* slowly succumbed to the demands of a succession of sudden and incompatible events that it was forced to confront in the *courte durée*. It could be, however, that instead of time actually moving at different speeds, it only appears to have done so because attention has focused on a particular development at a particular time.[31] Even if the particular development has been understood correctly, it is possible that previous developments would have looked rather different had greater attention been focused on them. The third weakness is that the thesis promoted here rests to a large degree on something that cannot be proved. It has been shown, it is believed, that in Britain, by the 1630s, privateering had emerged as a practice defined by the dependence of prize acquisition on the possession of a valid licence to raid enemy shipping, and that it was coming to be understood in theory that prizes were forfeited

29 Anxiety over Eurocentrism has been growing in recent work on the history of international law (Onuma 2000; Koskenniemi 2011b; Lorca 2012), although attempts to trace connections between Europe and developments in the far east have been less than successful (Anand 1981; Alexandrowicz 1967; Borschberg 2009 and 2021). The point has been made, moreover, that the book has failed to engage with the work of Gregor Rohmann in the way that would have been expected elsewhere.

30 Quite apart from seeming pretentious, this suggestion also fails to use the vocabulary of the *Annales* school in the way it was originally used, yet it may be a convenient way of expressing the need for legal historians, like all intellectual historians, to explain both the significance of ideas at specific times and changes in their significance from one time to another.

31 A certain amount of attention has also been paid to developments within the *longue durée*, but differentiating between periods of time has seemed less important than differentiating between modes of discourse. Confusion has been caused, it is believed, by a tendency in the secondary literature to run together the thinking of medieval theologians and lawyers (civil and canon, academic and practising) to create a monolithic construct called 'just war doctrine'. The relationships between the distinct linguistic communities that undoubtedly existed cannot be properly understood unless close attention is paid to the particular modes of discourse in which they engaged.

to the state, from which gifts were made to captors. Privateering appears to have been a new form of maritime raiding, yet its novelty is apparent from the absence of evidence of prize acquisition in wartime being taken to depend on the possession of licences before the 1560s. It is conceivable that critics will find such evidence somewhere, though it will not suffice to persist in misla-belling earlier licences as 'letters of marque', or in misappropriating the phrase 'general reprisals', or in simply reading requirements back into periods for which there is no evidence of their existence.

Bibliography

Sources cited in the footnotes to the preceding pages are listed here in three stages. Manuscript sources are listed first, under the names of the archives in which they are preserved, with a code for each archive, as used in the citations in the footnotes. Primary printed sources are then listed in alphabetical order, some by author and others by title, again as cited in the footnotes. Finally, secondary sources are listed by author's surname, followed by initials and date. Author's names appear in the third list in alphabetical order, but where several sources were written by the same person they are presented chronologically, given that the references in the footnotes are by name and date. It needs to be remembered, in relation to the primary sources especially, that authors are listed according to particular variants of their names. If they are not found under the names expected, another variant should be tried, or perhaps the title of the source.

Primary Sources (Manuscript)

Aberdeen City Archives (ACA)

CA1/1 – council register of Aberdeen.

Archives Départementales de la Charente-Maritime (ADCM)

B174 – register of the admiralty court at La Rochelle (www.bac-lac.gc.ca).

Ayrshire Archives (AA)

B6/11 – burgh court book of Ayr.

British Library (BL)

Add. MS 4598 – collections of Thomas Rymer.
Add. MS 11405 – letters and papers of Sir Julius Caesar.
Add. MS 12504 – letters and papers of Sir Julius Caesar.
Add. MS 12505 – letters and papers of Sir Julius Caesar.
Add. MS 14027 – letters and papers of Sir Julius Caesar.
Add. MS 29439 – treatises and documents relating to the admiralty court.
Add. MS 34150 – transcriptions of documents relating to the Cinque Ports.
Add. MS 37816 – letters and papers of Sir Edward Nicholas.
Add. MS 37817 – letters and papers of Sir Edward Nicholas.
Add. MS 37818 – letters and papers of Sir Edward Nicholas.
Add. MS 37819 – letters and papers of Sir Edward Nicholas.

Cotton MS Caligula B VI – royal correspondence.
Cotton MS Caligula C IX – letters and papers relating to England and Scotland.
Cotton MS Galba C III – letters and papers relating to England and the Netherlands.
Cotton MS Galba C IV – letters and papers relating to England and the Netherlands.
Harley MS 309 – letters and papers relating to military affairs.
Harley MS 598 – account of the duties received on prizes.
Harley MS 2222 – papers relating to the admiralty.
Lansdowne MS 57 – Burghley papers.
Lansdowne MS 70 – Burghley papers.
Lansdowne MS 73 – Burghley papers.
Lansdowne MS 115 – Burghley papers.
Lansdowne MS 129 – letters and papers of Sir Julius Caesar.
Lansdowne MS 143 – letters and papers of Sir Julius Caesar.
Lansdowne MS 148 – letters and papers of Sir Julius Caesar.
Lansdowne MS 152 – letters and papers of Sir Julius Caesar.
Lansdowne MS 157 – letters and papers of Sir Julius Caesar.
Royal MS 13B II – royal correspondence.
Royal MS 18B VI – royal correspondence.
Sloane MS 1605 – *De officio admiralitatis Angliae*.

Dumbarton Heritage Centre (DHC)

DB1/10 – Dumbarton town clerk's records, general series.

Dundee City Archives (DCA)

BCMB – burgh court minute book of Dundee.
MBBC – minute book of the burgh council of Dundee.
PBD – protocol books of Dundee.

Edinburgh City Archives (ECA)

SL1/1 – council register of Edinburgh.

Edinburgh University Library (EUL)

La. III 408 – Balfour's practicks.

Leiden University Library (LUL)

BPL 917 – Grotius' *De iure praedae* (www.digitalcollections.universiteitleiden.nl).

National Archives at Kew (NAK)

C66 – patent rolls.
HCA3 – act books and minutes or drafts of acts issued by the admiralty court.

HCA13 – examinations and answers of witnesses in the admiralty court.
HCA14 – exemplars of documents used in the admiralty court.
HCA15 – instance and prize papers of the admiralty court.
HCA23 – interrogatories put to witnesses in the admiralty court.
HCA24 – process papers and decrees of the admiralty court.
HCA25 – warrants and bonds for letters of marque issued by the admiralty court.
SP11 – state papers, domestic, Mary I.
SP12 – state papers, domestic, Elizabeth.
SP14 – state papers, domestic, James I.
SP16 – state papers, domestic, Charles I.
SP52 – state papers, Scotland.
SP63 – state papers, Ireland.
SP70 – state papers, foreign, Elizabeth.
SP82 – state papers, foreign, Elizabeth.
SP84 – state papers, Holland.
SP88 – state papers, foreign, Elizabeth.

National Library of Scotland (NLS)

Adv. MS 6.1.4 – transcriptions of justiciary court records.
Adv. MS 6.1.5 – transcriptions of justiciary court records.
Adv. MS 6.1.6 – transcriptions of justiciary court records.
Adv. MS 6.2.1 – extracts from the admiralty court records.
Adv. MS 24.2.4 – Balfour's practicks.
Adv. MS 24.2.4b – Balfour's practicks.
Adv. MS 25.2.5(1) – abridgement of books of sederunt.
Adv. MS 25.2.7 – abridgement of books of sederunt.
Adv. MS 31.2.2(1) – Maitland's practicks.
Adv. MS 35.5.9B – royal correspondence.

National Records of Scotland (NRS)

AC7/1 – act book of the admiralty court.
B9/12/5 – minutes of the Burntisland burgh council.
C3 – register of the great seal.
CS5 – register of acts and decreets of the lords of council and session.
CS6 – register of acts and decreets of the lords of council and session.
CS7 – register of acts and decreets of the lords of council and session.
GD1/371 – Warrender papers.
GD103/2 – Society of Antiquaries of Scotland papers.
GD149/264 – royal correspondence.
GD149/265 – royal correspondence.

GD149/266 – royal correspondence.
GD149/270 – Cuninghame of Caprington papers.
GD149/271 – Cuninghame of Caprington papers.
GD149/272 – Cuninghame of Caprington papers.
GD150/464 – Morton papers.
GD150/2275 – Morton papers.
GD172/199 – Henderson of Fordell papers.
JC1 – court books of the justiciary court.
JC2 – books of adjournal of the justiciary court.
JC6 – minute books of the justiciary court.
JC26 – process papers of the justiciary court.
PA7/2 – minutes of the council of war.
PC7 – register of commissions of the privy council.
PC10/13A – papers supplementary to the register of the privy council.
PC11/2A – papers supplementary to the register of the privy council.
PS1 – register of the privy seal.
RH1 – miscellaneous transcriptions and documents.
RH2 – miscellaneous transcriptions and documents.
RH9 – foreign papers.
SP13 – miscellaneous state papers.

Saint Andrews University Library (SAUL)

B10/8 – burgh court book of Crail.

Primary Sources

Aarsberetninger fra det Kongelige Geheimearchiv, 7 vols, ed. C.F. Wegener and A.D. Jørgensen (Copenhagen, 1852–83).

Abbas antiquus, Bernardus de Montemirato, alias, *Lectura aurea super quinque libris Decretalium* (Strasbourg, 1511).

Aberdeen Council Letters, 6 vols, ed. L.B. Taylor (London, 1942–61).

Aberdeen Shore Work Accounts, 1596–1670, ed. L.B. Taylor (Aberdeen, 1972).

Accoltus, Franciscus, *Commentaria super titulo de acquirenda possessione* (Pavia, 1502).

Accoltus, Franciscus, *Consilia seu response* (Venice, 1572).

Acta curiae admirallatus Scotiae, 6th Sept. 1557 – 11th March 1561–2, ed. T.C. Wade (Edinburgh, 1937).

Actes du parlement de Paris, 1328–42, ed. H. Furgeot (Paris, 1920).

Actes royaux, depuis l'origine jusqu'à Henri IV, ed. A. Isnard (Paris, 1910).

The Acts and Proceedings of the General Assemblies of the Church of Scotland, 1560–1618, 3 vols, ed. D. Shaw (Edinburgh, 2004).

Acts of the Lords of Council in Public Affairs, 1501–54, ed. R.K. Hannay (Edinburgh, 1932).

The Acts of the Parliaments of Scotland, 12 vols, ed. T. Thomson and C. Innes (Edinburgh, 1814–75).

Acts of the Privy Council of England, 46 vols, ed. J.R. Dasent, E.G. Atkinson, J.V. Lyle, R.F. Monger and P.E. Penfold (London, 1890–1964).

Acts of the Privy Council of England, Colonial Series, 6 vols, ed. A.W. FitzRoy, J. Munro and W.L. Grant (London, 1908–12).

Adrian VI, *Quaestiones de sacramentis in quartum Sententiarum librum* (Rome, 1522).

Álamos de Barrientos, Baltasar, *L'art de gouverner: Discours adressé à Philippe III*, ed. J.M. Guardia (Paris, 1867).

Albericus de Rosate, *Opera omnia*, 4 vols (Lyons, 1517–18).

Gli albori del Comune di San Gimignano e lo statuto del 1314, ed. M. Brogi (Siena, 1995).

Alciatus, Andreas, *Opera omnia*, 4 vols (Basel, 1549).

Alciatus, Andreas, *Responsa, nunquam antehac excusa* (Lyons, 1561).

Alexander King's Treatise on Maritime Law, ed. J.D. Ford (Edinburgh, 2018).

Allen, William, *A Conference about the Next Succession to the Crowne of Ingland* (n.p., 1595).

Ambrose, *De Abraham*, in *Patrologia Latina* (below), vol. 14.

Ambrose, *De officiis*, in *Patrologia Latina* (below) vol. 16.

Ancient Criminal Trials in Scotland, 3 vols, ed. R. Pitcairn (Edinburgh, 1833).

The Ancient Sea-Laws of Oleron, Wisby and the Hanse-Towns Still in Force, ed. Guy Miege (London, 1686).

Andreae, Ioannes, *In libros quintos Decretalium novella commentaria*, 4 vols (Venice, 1581).

Andreae, Ioannes, *In titulum de regulis iuris commentarii* (Lyons, 1551).

Angelus de Ubaldis, *Consilia seu responsa* (Lyons, 1532).

Angelus de Ubaldis, *Lectura super prima parte Digesti veteris* (Lyons, 1534).

Angelus de Ubaldis, *Lectura super secunda parte Digesti novi* (Lyons, 1534).

Angelus de Ubaldis, *Opera omnia*, 3 vols (Lyons, 1545).

Angelus de Ubaldis, *Quaestio disputata: Renovata Guerra* (Perugia, 1477).

Annales monastici, 5 vols, ed. H.R. Luard (London, 1864–9).

Antiquarian Gleanings from Aberdeenshire Records, ed. G. Turreff (Aberdeen, 1871).

Appian, *The Civil War*, 2 vols, tr. H. White (Cambridge, MA, 1913).

Appian, *Roman History*, 3 vols, tr. B.C. McGing (Cambridge, MA, 2019).

Aquinas, Thomas, *Commentary on Aristotle's Nicomachean Ethics*, tr. C.I. Litzinger (Notre Dame, IN, 1993).

Aquinas, Thomas, *Summa theologiae*, 60 vols, ed. T. Gilby (London, 1964–76).

Aragón, Pedro de, *In Secundam secundae Divi Thomae doctoris angelici commentaria*, 2 vols (Lyons, 1596–7).

Archives ou correspondance inédite de la maison d'Orange-Nassau, 8 vols, ed. G. van Prinsterer (Leiden, 1835–96).

Articles Concerning the Admiralty of England, and the Jurisdiction Thereof, 21 Julii Anno Domini 1591, Regnique Serenissimae Dominae Elizabethae Reginae Tricesimo Tertio (London, 1591).

Articles of Peace, Entercourse and Commerce Concluded in the Names of the Most High and Mighty Kings and Princes James, by the Grace of God King of Great Britaine, France and Ireland, Defender of the Faith &c., and Philip the Third King of Spaine &c., and Albertus and Isabella Clara Eugenia, Archdukes of Austrice, Dukes of Burgundie &c. (London, 1605).

Articles of Peace, Entercourse and Commerce Concluded in the Names of the Most High and Mighty Kings Charles, by the Grace of God King of Great Britaine, France and Ireland, Defender of the Faith &c., and Philip the Fourth King of Spaine &c. (London, 1630).

Ascham, Roger, *Toxophilus*, ed. E. Arber (London, 1869).

The Asloan Manuscript, 2 vols, ed. W.A. Craigie (Edinburgh, 1923–5).

Athenaeus, *The Deinosophists*, 7 vols, tr. C.B. Gulick (Cambridge, MA, 1927–41).

The Attic Nights of Aulus Gellius, 3 vols, tr. J.C. Rolfe (Cambridge, MA, 1927–52).

Augustine, *Contra Faustum Manichaeum*, in *Patrologia Latina* (below), vol. 42.

Augustine, *De civitate Dei*, in *Patrologia Latina* (below), vol. 41.

Augustine, *Epistolae*, in *Patrologia Latina* (below), vol. 33.

Augustine, *Quaestiones in Heptateuchum*, in *Patrologia Latina* (below), vol. 34.

Augustine, *Quaestiones in Pentateuchum*, in *Patrologia Latina* (below), vol. 34.

Augustine, *Sermones*, in *Patrologia Latina* (below), vol. 39.

The Autobiography and Diary of Mr James Melvill, ed. R. Pitcairn (Edinburgh, 1842).

Ayr Burgh Accounts, 1534–1624, ed. G.S. Pryde (Edinburgh, 1937).

Azo, Portius, *Ad singulas leges xii librorum Codicis Iustinianei commentaries* (Paris, 1577).

Azo, Portius, *Brocardica sive generalia iuris* (Basel, 1567).

Azo, Portius, *Lectura super Codicem* (Turin, 1577).

Azor, Juan, *Institutiones morales*, 3 vols (Rome, 1600–11).

Azpilcueta, Martín de, *Commentaria in septem distinctiones de poenitentia* (Rome, 1586).

Azpilcueta, Martín de, *Consilia et responsa*, 2 vols (Lyons, 1594).

Azpilcueta, Martín de, *Enchiridion sive manuale confessariorum et poenitentium* (Venice, 1584).

Bacon, Francis, *A Letter Written out of England to an English Gentleman Remaining at Padua* (London, 1599).

Balduinus, Franciscus, *De institutione historiae universae et eius cum iurisprudentia coniunctione* (Paris, 1561).

Baldus de Ubaldis, *Commentaria super Codicem*, 4 vols (Venice, 1500).

Baldus de Ubaldis, *Consilia sive responsa* (Venice, 1580).

Baldus de Ubaldis, *In primam Digesti veteris partem commentaria* (Venice, 1577).

Baldus de Ubaldis, *Super Decretalibus* (Lyons, 1564).

Bañez, Domingo, *Decisiones de iure et iustitia* (Venice, 1595).

Bañez, Domingo, *Scholastica commentaria in Secundam secundae angelici doctoris Divi Thomae* (Venice, 1587).

Barbaro, Ermolao, *In C. Plinii Naturalis historiae libros castigationes* (Basel, 1534).

Barbot, Amos, 'Histoire de La Rochelle depuis l'an 1199 jusques en 1575', ed. D. D'Aussy (1886) 14 *Archives historiques de la Saintonge et de l'Aunis* 1, (1889) 17 *Archives historiques de la Saintonge et de l'Aunis* 1, and (1890) 18 *Archives historiques de la Saintonge et de l'Aunis* 1.

Bartolus de Sassoferrato, *Lectura super prima et secunda parte Digesti novi*, 2 vols (Venice, 1491).

Bartolus de Sassoferrato, *Opera omnia*, 5 vols (Lyons, 1523).

Beale, Robert, 'A Treatise of the Office of a Councellor and Principall Secretarie to her Majestie', in C. Read, *Mr Secretary Walsingham and the Policy of Elizabeth*, 3 vols (Oxford, 1925), vol. 1, p. 423.

Bellarmine, Robert, *Disputationes de controversiis Christianae fidei adversus huius temporis haereticos*, 3 vols (Ingolstadt, 1586–93).

Bellarmine, Robert, *On Temporal and Spiritual Authority*, tr. S. Tutino (Indianapolis, 2012).

Belli, Pierino, *De re militari et bello tractatus*, 2 vols, ed. A. Cavaglieri and tr. H.C. Nutting (Oxford, 1936).

Benedict of Peterborough, *The Chronicle of the Reigns of Henry II and Richard I*, 2 vols, ed. W. Stubbs (London, 1867).

Beroius, Augustinus, *Consilia sive responsa*, 3 vols (Venice, 1577).

Biel, Gabriel, *Commentarii doctissimi in quatuor Sententiarum libros*, 3 vols (Brescia, 1574).

Binsfeld, Peter, *Enchiridion theologiae pastoralis* (Trier, 1609).

The Black Book of the Admiralty, 4 vols, ed. T. Twiss (London, 1871–6).

Blackwood, Adam, *Martyre de la royne d'Escosse, douariere de France* (Edinburgh, 1587).

Blundeville, Thomas, *A Very Briefe and Profitable Treatise Declaring Howe Many Counsells and What Maner of Counselers a Prince that Will Governe Well Ought to Have* (London, 1570).

Bocerus, Henricus, *De iure pugnae, hoc est belli et duelli, tractatus methodicus* (Tubingen, 1591).

Bodin, Jean, *Method for the Easy Comprehension of History*, tr. B. Reynolds (New York, 1966).

Bodin, Jean, *Methodus ad facilem historiarum cognitionem* (Paris, 1566).

Bodin, Jean, *The Six Bookes of a Commonweale*, tr. Richard Knolles (London, 1606).

Bodin, Jean, *Les six livres de la république* (Lyons, 1579).

Bohier, Nicolas, *Decisiones Burdegalenses* (Lyons, 1576).

The Book of Carlaverock: Memoirs of the Maxwells, Earls of Nithsdale, Lords Maxwell and Herries, 2 vols, ed. W. Fraser (Edinburgh, 1873).

Bor, Pieter Christiaanszoon, *Oorsprongk, Begin en Vervolgh der Nederlandsche Oorlogen*, 4 vols (Amsterdam, 1679–84).

Boroughs, Sir John, *The Soveraignty of the British Seas, Proved by Records, History and the Municipall Lawes of this Kingdome, Written in the Yeare 1633* (London, 1651).

Bursatus, Franciscus, *Consilia sive responsa*, 2 vols (Frankfurt, 1579).

Boteler's Dialogues, ed. W.G. Perrin (London, 1929).

Botero, Giovanni, *The Reason of State*, tr. P.J. and D.P. Waley (New Haven, 1956).

Bouvet, Honoré, *L'Arbre des batailles* (Paris, 1505).

Bouvet, Honoré, *The Tree of Battles*, tr. G.W. Coopland (Liverpool, 1949).

Bracton on the Laws and Customs of England, 4 vols, ed. G.E. Woodbine and tr. S.E. Thorne (Cambridge, MA, 1968–77).

Bronnen tot de Geschiedenis van der Handel met Engeland, Schotland en Ierland, 2 vols, ed. H.J. Smit (The Hague, 1928).

Bronnen tot de Geschiedenis van der Handel met Engeland, Schotland en Ierland, 2nd ser., 2 vols, ed. H.J. Smit (The Hague, 1942–50).

Brooke, Robert, *La graunde abridgement* (London, 1573).

Buchanan, George, *Rerum Scoticarum historia* (Edinburgh, 1582).

Buchanan, George, *The History of Scotland*, 2 vols, tr. J. Aikman (Glasgow, 1827).

Budé, Guillaume, *Altera aeditio annotationum in Pandectas* (Lyons, 1526).

Bullarum, privilegiorum ac diplomatum Romanorum pontificum, 14 vols, ed. C. Cocquelines (Rome, 1739–44).

Butrigarius, Iacobus, *Super Codice lectura* (Paris, 1516).

By the King, a Proclamation against Excesse of Lavish and Licentious Speech of Matters of State (London, 1620).

Cabala sive scrinia sacra: Mysteries of State and Government in Letters of Illustrious Persons and Great Ministers of State (London, 1663).

Caepolla, Bartolomeus, *Consilia criminalia* (Venice, 1575).

Caepolla, Bartolomeus, *Tractatus de servitutibus, tam urbanorum quam rusticorum praediorum* (Cologne, 1579).

Cagnazzo da Taggia, Giovanni, *Summa Tabiena, quae summa summarum merito appellatur*, 2 vols (Venice, 1580).

Cajetan, Tommaso de Vio, Cardinal, *Summula peccatorum* (Paris, 1526).

Cajetan, Tommaso de Vio, Cardinal, *Summa Sancti Thomae Aquinatis universam sacram theologiam complectens, cum commentariis Thomae de Vio, Caietani Cardinalis*, 3 vols (Lyons, 1581).

Calderinus, Ioannes, *Consilia* (Venice, 1497).

Calderwood, David, *The History of the Kirk of Scotland*, 8 vols, ed. D. Laing (Edinburgh, 1842–9).

A Calendar of Early Chancery Proceedings Relating to West Country Shipping, 1388–1493, ed. D.M. Gardiner (Torquay, 1976).

Calendar of Letters and State Papers Relating to English Affairs Preserved Principally in the Archives of Simancas, 4 vols, ed. M.A.S. Hume (London, 1892–6).

A Calendar of Material Relating to Ireland from the High Court of Admiralty Examinations, 1536–1641, ed. J.C. Appleby (Dublin, 1992).

Calendar of State Papers and Manuscripts, Relating to English Affairs, Existing in the Archives and Collections of Venice, and in Other Libraries in Northern Italy, 38 vols, ed. R. Brown, G. Bentinck, H.F. Brown and A.B. Hinds (London, 1864–1947).

Calendar of State Papers, Colonial Series, East Indies, China, Japan and Persia, 1513–1634, 5 vols, ed. W.N. Sainsbury (London, 1862–92).

Calendar of State Papers, Domestic Series, of the Reign of Charles I, 23 vols, ed. S.C. Lomas, W.D. Hamilton and J. Bruce (London, 1858–97).

Calendar of State Papers, Domestic Series, of the Reign of James I, 5 vols, ed. M.A.E. Green (London, 1857–72).

Calendar of State Papers, Domestic Series, of the Reigns of Edward VI, Mary and Elizabeth, 7 vols, ed. R. Lemon (London, 1856–71).

Calendar of State Papers, Foreign Series, of the Reign of Elizabeth, 23 vols, ed. J. Stevenson, A.J. Crosby, A.J. Butler, S.C. Lomas, A.B. Hinds and R.B. Wernham (London, 1863–1950).

Calendar of State Papers Relating to Ireland of the Reign of Charles I, 4 vols, ed. R.P. Mahaffy (London, 1900–3).

Calendar of State Papers Relating to Scotland and Mary, Queen of Scots, 1547–1603, 13 vols, ed. J. Bain, W.K. Boyd, H.W. Meikle, A.I. Cameron, M.S. Giuseppi and J.D. Mackie (Edinburgh, 1898–1969).

Calendar of the Carew Manuscripts Preserved in the Archiepiscopal Library of Lambeth, 6 vols, ed. J.S. Brewer and W. Bullen (London, 1867–73).

Calendar of the Close Rolls Preserved in the Public Record Office, 61 vols, (London, 1892–1963).

Calendar of the Manuscripts of the Most Honourable the Marquis of Salisbury, 24 vols, ed. R.A. Roberts, E. Salisbury, M.S. Giuseppi and G.D. Owen (London, 1883–1976).

Calendar of the Patent Rolls Preserved in the Public Record Office, 73 vols, (London, 1891–1986).

Calvinus, Ioannes, *Lexicon iuridicum* (Hanover, 1619).

Camden, William, *The History of the Most Renowned and Victorious Princess Elizabeth* (London, 1675).

Canisius, Petrus, *A Summe of Christian Doctrine* (n.p., 1592).

Canons and Decrees of the Council of Trent, tr. H.J. Schroeder (Rockford, IL, 1978).

Capra, Benedictus, *Consilia sive responsa* (Venice, 1566).

Cassius Dio, *Roman History*, 9 vols, tr. E. Cary (Cambridge, MA, 1914–27).

Certayne Questions Demanded and Asked by the Noble Realme of Englande (London, 1555).

Chalmers, David, *Histoire abbregée de tous les roys de France, Angleterre et Escosse* (Paris, 1579).

Charisius, *Artis grammaticae libri V*, ed. K. Heinrich (Leipzig, 1857).

Choppin, René, *De domanio Franciae libri tres* (Paris, 1574).

Chronica Magistri Rogeri de Hovedene, 4 vols, ed. W. Stubbs (London, 1868–71).

A Chronicle of the Kings of Scotland, from Fergus the First to James the Sixth (Edinburgh, 1830).

Cicero, *De amicitia*, tr. W.A. Falconer (Cambridge, MA, 1923).

Cicero, *De finibus*, tr. H. Rackham (Cambridge, MA, 1931).

Cicero, *De haruspicum responsis*, tr. N.H. Watts (Cambridge, MA, 1923).

Cicero, *De inventione*, tr. H.M. Hubbell (Cambridge, MA, 1949).

Cicero, *De lege agraria*, tr. J.H. Freese (Cambridge, MA, 1930).

Cicero, *De legibus*, tr. C.W. Keyes (Cambridge, MA, 1928).

Cicero, *De natura deorum*, tr. H. Rackham (Cambridge, MA, 1933).

Cicero, *De officiis*, tr. W. Miller (Cambridge, MA, 1913).

Cicero, *De oratore*, 2 vols, tr. E.W. Sutton and H. Rackham (Cambridge, MA, 1942).

Cicero, *De partitione oratoria*, tr. H. Rackham (Cambridge, MA, 1942).

Cicero, *De republica*, tr. C.W. Keyes (Cambridge, MA, 1928).

Cicero, *In Catilinam*, tr. C. MacDonald (Cambride, MA, 1977).

Cicero, *Letters to Atticus*, 4 vols, tr. D.R. Shackleton Bailey (Cambridge, MA, 1999).

Cicero, *Letters to Friends*, 3 vols, tr. D.R. Shackleton Bailey (Cambridge, MA, 2001).

Cicero, *Philippics*, 2 vols, tr. D.R. Shackleton Bailey, J.T. Ramsay and G. Manuwald (Cambridge, MA, 2009).

Cicero, *Pro lege Manilia*, tr. H.G. Hodge (Cambridge, MA, 1927).

Cicero, *Pro Milone*, tr. N.H. Watts (Cambridge, MA, 1931).

Cicero, *Pro Murena*, tr. C. MacDonald (Cambridge, MA, 1977).

Cicero, *Pro Roscio Amerino*, tr. J.H. Freese (Cambridge, MA, 1930).

Cicero, *Tusculan Disputations*, tr. J.E. King (Cambridge, MA, 1945).

Cicero, *Verrine Orations*, 2 vols, tr. L.H.G. Greenwood (Cambridge, MA, 1928–35).

Cinus de Pistorio, *Lectura super Codice* (Venice, 1493).

Cinus de Pistorio, *In Codicem et aliquot titulos Digesti veteris doctissima commentaria*, 2 vols (Frankfurt, 1578).

Clerk, William, *An Epitome of Certaine Late Aspersions Cast at Civilians, the Civil and Ecclesiastical Lawes, the Courts Christian, and at the Bishops and Their Chancellors* (Dublin, 1631).

Clichtove, Josse, *De bello et pace opusculum* (Paris, 1523).

Code, in the *Corpus iuris civilis* (below), vol. 2.

Codex Iustiniani (Paris, 1559).

Codice degli statuti della repubblica di Sassari, ed. P. Tola (Cagliari, 1830).

Cognet, Sir Martyn, *Politique Discourses upon Trueth and Lying* (London, 1586).

Coke, Sir Edward, *The Fourth Part of the Institutes of the Laws of England* (London, 1644).

Collectanea Maritima: Being a Collection of Public Instruments &c., Tending to Illustrate the History and Practice of Prize Law, ed. C. Robinson (London, 1801).

The Collected Dialogues of Plato, ed. E. Hamilton and H. Cairns (Princeton, 1961).

Collection de lois maritimes antérieures au XVIII*e siècle*, 6 vols, ed. J.M. Pardessus (Paris, 1828–45).

A Collection of State Papers Relating to Affairs in the Reigns of Henry VIII*, Edward* VI*, Mary and Elizabeth*, 2 vols, ed. S. Haynes and W. Murdin (London, 1740–59).

'The Colonial Conferences between England and the Netherlands in 1613 and 1615', ed. G.N. Clark and W.J.M. van Eysinga (1940) 15 *Bibliotheca Visseriana* pt 32.

Colville, John, *Historie and Life of King James the Sext*, ed. T. Thomson (Edinburgh, 1825).

A Complete Collection of State Trials and Proceedings for High Treason and Other Crimes and Misdemeanors, 21 vols, ed. T.B. Howell (London, 1816).

The Complete Works of Aristotle, 2 vols, ed. J. Barnes (Princeton, 1984).

Compota thesaurariorum regum Scotorum: Accounts of the Lord High Treasurer of Scotland, 13 vols, ed. T. Dickson, J. Balfour Paul, C.T. McInnes and A.L. Murray (Edinburgh, 1877–1978).

The Compt Buik of David Wedderburne, Merchant of Dundee, 1587–1630, ed. A.H. Millar (Edinburgh, 1898).

Conestaggio, Girolamo, *Dell'unione del regno di Portogallo all corona di Castiglia* (Milan, 1616).

Conestaggio, Girolamo, *The Historie of the Uniting of the Kingdom of Portugall to the Crowne of Castill*, tr. Edward Blount (London, 1600).

Connanus, Franciscus, *Commentariorum iuris civilis libri x* (Paris, 1558).

'Le conseil de la reine de Navarre à La Rochelle: Ordonnances et délibérations inédites, 1569–70', ed. J. de Gaulle (1854–5) 3 *Bulletin de la Société de l'histoire de protestantisme français* 123.

Consilia domini Guidonis Papae (Lyons, 1519).

Consilium facultatis iuridicae Tubingensis: A Legal Opinion on a Case of Maritime Warfare, 1593, ed. A.A. Wijffels (Leiden, 1993).

The Consolidated Treaty Series, 231 vols, ed. C. Parry (New York, 1969–81).

Constitutiones sive statuta magnificae civitatis Anconae (Ancona, 1566).

Consulate of the Sea and Related Documents, tr. S.S. Jados (University, AL, 1975).

Conti, Natale, *Universae historiae sui temporis libri triginta* (Venice, 1581).

The Copie of a Letter to the Right Honourable the Earle of Leycester (London, 1586).

Corneus, Petrus, *Consilia sive responsa*, 3 vols (Venice, 1582).

Cornwallis, Sir William, *Discourses upon Seneca the Tragedian* (London, 1601).

Corps universel diplomatique du droit des gens, 8 vols, ed. J. Dumont (Amsterdam, 1726–31).

Corpus iuris canonici, 2 vols, ed. A. Friedberg (Leipzig, 1879–81).

Corpus iuris civilis, 3 vols, ed. T. Mommsen, P. Krüger, R. Schoell and G. Kroll (Berlin, 1872–7).

Corpus selectorum tractatuum de pignoribus et hypothecis (Frankfurt, 1586).

Correspondance de la cour de l'Espagne sur les affaires des Pays-Bas au XVIIe siècle, 6 vols, ed. J. Cuvelier and J. Lefevre (Brussels, 1923–37).

Correspondance de Philippe II sur les affaires des Pays-Bas, 6 vols (Brussels, 1848–79).

Correspondence of Matthew Parker, D.D., Archbishop of Canterbury, ed. J. Bruce and T.T. Perowne (Cambridge, 1853).

The Correspondence of Robert Bowes, ed. J. Stevenson (London, 1842).

Correspondence of Sir Robert Kerr, First Earl of Ancram, and His Son William, Third Earl of Lothian, 2 vols, ed. D. Laing (Edinburgh, 1875).

Correspondenz des Kaisers Karl V, 3 vols, ed. C. Lanz (Leipzig, 1844–6).

Cosin, Richard, *An Answer to the Two Fyrst and Principall Treatises of a Certaine Factious Libell* (London, 1584).

Cosin, Richard, *An Apologie for Sundrie Proceedings by Jurisdiction Ecclesiasticall* (London, 1593).

Costa, Caesar, *Variarum ambiguitatum iuris libri tres* (Naples, 1573).

Cotereus, Claudius, *De iure et privilegiis militum libri tres* (Lyons, 1539).

The Court and Times of Charles the First, Containing a Series of Historical and Confidential Letters Transcribed from the Originals by Thomas Birch, 2 vols, ed. R.F. Williams (London, 1849).

Covarruvias y Leyva, Diego de, *Opera omnia*, 2 vols (Frankfurt, 1592).

Craig of Riccarton, Thomas, *Jus feudale tribus libris comprehensum, Book I*, tr. L. Dodd (Edinburgh, 2017).

Criminalium iurium serenissimae reipublicae Genuensis libri duo (Genoa, 1669).

Cronache e statuti della città di Viterbo, ed. I. Ciampi (Florence, 1872).

Cuiacius, Iacobus, *Opera omnia*, 4 vols (Lyons, 1614).

Cumanus, Raphael, and Fulgosius, Raphael, *Consilia sive responsa* (Venice, 1575).

D'Afflitto, Matteo, *In utriusque Siciliae Neapolisque sanctiones ac constitutiones novissima praelectio* (Venice, 1580).

Dalrymple of Stair, Sir James, *The Decisions of the Lords of Council and Session*, 2 vols (Edinburgh, 1683–7).

Dalrymple of Stair, Sir James, *The Institutions of the Law of Scotland* (Edinburgh, 1681).

Daneau, Lambert, *A Fruitfull Commentarie upon the Twelve Small Prophets* (Cambridge, 1594).

De Ancharanus, Petrus, *Consilia sive iuris responsa* (Venice, 1568).

De Arena, Iacobus, *Commentarii in universum ius civile* (Leiden, 1541).
De Ayala, Balthazar, *De iure et officiis bellicis et disciplina militari libri iii*, 2 vols, ed. J. Westlake (Washington, 1912).
Debates in the House of Commons in 1625, ed. S.R. Gardiner (London, 1873).
De Baysio, Guido, *Rosarium super Decreto* (Venice, 1495).
De Beccarie de Pavie, sieur de Fourquevaux, Raymond, *Instructions for the Warres*, (London, 1589).
De Beccarie de Pavie, sieur de Fourquevaux, Raymond, *Instructions sur le faict de la guerre*, ed. G. Dickinson (London, 1954).
De Belviso, Iacobus, *Aurea lectura summam Autenticorum Consuetudinesque feudorum elucidans* (Lyons, 1511).
De Bosco, Bartolomeus, *Consilia* (Savona, 1620).
De Butrio, Antonius, *In libros quintos Decretalium commentarii*, 4 vols (Venice, 1578).
De Cambolas, Jean, *Decisions notables sur diverses questions du droit* (Toulouse, 1659).
De Castro, Alfonso, *Opera* (Paris, 1571).
De Castro, Paulus, *Opera omnia*, 4 vols (Lyons, 1548).
De Castro, Paulus, *Super Digesto veteri commentaria*, 2 vols (Lyons, 1535).
Decisiones Guidonis Papae (Lyons, 1607).
The Decisions of the Court of Session from Its First Institution to the Present Time, 22 vols, ed. W.M. Morison (Edinburgh, 1801–4).
De Clavasio, Angelus, *Summa angelica de casibus conscientiae* (n.p., 1515).
Decrees of the Ecumenical Councils, 2 vols, ed. N.P. Tanner (London, 1990).
Decretales Gregorii noni pontificis (Lyons, 1553).
Decretales Gregorii papae ix suae integritati una cum glossis restitutae (Rome, 1582).
Decretum aureum Gratiani (Paris, 1518).
Decretum, in the *Corpus iuris canonici* (above), vol. 1.
De Damhouder, Joos, *Enchiridion parium aut similium utriusque iuris* (Antwerp, 1568).
De Damhouder, Joos, *Praxis rerum criminalium* (Antwerp, 1562).
De la Primaudaye, Pierre, *The French Academie* (London, 1586).
De la Vera Cruz, Alonso, *De iusto bello contra Indos*, ed. C. and L. Baciero, F. Maseda and L. Pereña (Madrid, 1997).
De Legnano, Ioannes, *Tractatus de bello, de represaliis et de duello*, ed. T.E. Holland (Oxford, 1917).
De Loque, Bertrand, *Discourses of Warre and Single Combat* (London, 1591).
De Maino, Iason, *Commentaria in primam partem Digesti novi* (Pavia, 1500).
De Maino, Iason, *Consilia sive responsa*, 3 vols (Venice, 1581).
De Maino, Iason, *In Digestum et Codicem commentaria*, 9 vols (Venice, 1589).
De Mugello, Dinus, *Apostille super Infortiato et Digesto novo* (Lyons, 1513).
De Nevizanis, Ioannes *Consilia sive responsa* (Lyons, 1559).

De Pisan, Christine, *Book of Fayttes of Armes and of Chyvalrye*, 2 vols, ed. A.T.P. Byles (London, 1923–37).

De Pontaymeri, Alexandre, *A Womans Woorth Defended against All the Men in the World* (London, 1599).

De Ravanis, Iacobus, *Lectura super Codice* (Paris, 1519).

De Saliceto, Bartolomeus, *Lectura super Codice*, 2 vols (Lyons, 1515).

De Saliceto, Bartolomeus, *Opera omnia*, 4 vols (Frankfurt, 1615).

De Saliceto, Bartolomeus, *Super Codicis commentaria*, 4 vols (Lyons, 1549).

De Serres, Jean, *An Historical Collection of the Most Memorable Accidents and Tragicall Massacres of France* (London, 1598).

De Thou, Jacques-Auguste, *Histoire universelle*, 11 vols (Haye, 1740).

Diary of Walter Yonge, Esq., Justice of the Peace and M.P. for Honiton, ed. G. Roberts (London, 1848).

'The Diarey of Robert Birrel', in *Fragments of Scottish History*, ed. J.G. Dalyell (Edinburgh, 1798), pt 2.

Digest, in the *Corpus iuris civilis* (above), vol. 1.

Digestum novum (Paris, 1559).

Digestum vetus (Paris, 1559).

Digges, Dudley, *Foure Paradoxes or Politique Discourses* (London, 1604).

Digges, Thomas, 'Arguments Provinge that the Quenes Highnes and Her Progenitors Kings of England Are by the Lawes of the Corone Just and Lawfull Owners of the Lands and Salte Shores Wonne by Any Person or by Any Other Meane of and oute of the Seas', in S.A. Moore, *A History of the Foreshore and the Law Relating Thereto* (London, 1888), p. 185.

Dio Chrysostom, *Discourses*, 3 vols, tr. J.W. Cohoon and H.L. Crosby (Cambridge, MA, 1932–40).

Diplomatari de l'orient català, 1301–1409, ed. A.R. y Lluch (Barcelona, 2001).

Diplomatarium Norvegicum, 22 vols, ed. C.A. Lange, C.R. Unger, H.J. Huitfeldt-Kaas and G. Storm (Oslo, 1847–1992).

Diplomatarium Veneto-Levantinum sive acta et diplomata res Venetas, Graecas atque Las siete partidas, 5 vols, tr. S.P. Scott (Philadelphia, 2001).

A Direction for Travailers Taken out of Iustus Lipsius (London, 1592).

Disciplinary Decrees of the General Councils: Text, Translation and Commentary, ed. H.J. Schroeder (London, 1937).

Doctius, Thomas, *Consilia vel responsa acutissima et quotidiana* (Venice, 1584).

Documents Illustrating the Impeachment of the Duke of Buckingham in 1626, ed. S.R. Gardiner (London, 1889).

Documents Relating to Law and Custom of the Sea, 2 vols, ed. R.G. Marsden (London, 1915–16).

'Documents tirés du Musée Britannique et du State Paper Office', ed. E. van Bruyssel (1864) 6 *Bulletin de la Commission royale d'histoire* 423.

Donati, Marcello, *In Latinorum plerorumque historiae Romanae scriptorum locos obscuriores scholiae sive dilucidationes eruditissimae* (Frankfurt, 1605).

Donellus, Hugo, *Commentariorum de iure civili libri xviii*, 3 vols (Frankfurt and Hanover, 1595–1610).

Droit et législation des armées de terre et de mer, 10 vols, ed. L. Durat-Lasalle (Paris, 1842–53).

Dudley Carleton to John Chamberlain, 1603–24: Jacobean Letters, ed. M. Lee (New Brunswick, 1972).

Du Faur, Pierre, *Semestrium liber secundus* (Lyons, 1592).

Duprat, Pardoux, *Lexicon iuris civilis et canonici* (Lyons, 1567).

Durantis, Gulielmus, *Speculum iudiciale*, 3 vols (Nuremberg, 1486).

Du Voisin, sieur de la Popelinière, Lancelot, *L'Amiral de France, et par occasion de celuy des autres nations, tant vieiles que nouvelles* (Paris, 1584).

Du Voisin, sieur de la Popelinière, Lancelot, *L'histoire de France depuis l'an 1550 jusqu'à ces temps*, 2 vols (La Rochelle, 1581).

The Earl of Stirling's Register of Royal Letters Relative to the Affairs of Scotland and Nova Scotia from 1615 to 1635, 2 vols, ed. C. Rogers (Edinburgh, 1885).

'An Early Admiralty Case, A.D. 1361', ed. C. Johnson, in *Camden Miscellany XV* (London, 1929), pt 4.

Early Travellers in Scotland, ed. P. Hume Brown (Edinburgh, 1978).

The Early Works of Thomas Becon, ed. J. Ayre (Cambridge, 1843).

Les edicts et ordonnances des roys de France, 2 vols, ed. Antoine Fontanon (Paris, 1585).

Les edicts et ordonnances des roys de France, ed. Pierre Rebuffi (Paris, 1575).

Édits des guerres de religion, ed. A. Stegman (Paris, 1979).

Eliot, Sir John, *An Apology for Socrates and Negotium posterorum*, 2 vols, ed. A.B. Grosart (London, 1881).

Elizabeth I: Autograph Compositions and Foreign Language Originals, ed. J. Mueller and L.S. Marcus (Chicago, 2003).

Elizabeth I: Collected Works, ed. L.S. Marcus, J. Mueller and M.B. Rose (Chicago, 2000).

English Privateering Voyages to the West Indies, 1588–95, ed. K.R. Andrews (Cambridge, 1959).

Epistolae Iacobi Quarti, Iacobi Quinti et Mariae regum Scotorum, 2 vols, ed. T. Ruddiman (Edinburgh, 1722–4).

E.R., *A Briefe Discourse Intituled, A Buckler against a Spanish Brag* (London, 1588).

Estienne, Robert, *Dictionaire françoislatin* (Paris, 1539).

European Treaties Bearing on the History of the United States and Its Dependencies, 4 vols, ed. F.G. Davenport and C.O. Paullin (Washington, 1917–37).

Extracts from the Burgh Records of Dunfermline in the Sixteenth and Seventeenth Centuries, ed. A. Shearer (Dunfermline, 1951).

Extracts from the Council Register of the Burgh of Aberdeen, 2 vols, ed. J. Stuart (Aberdeen, 1844–8).

Extracts from the Council Register of the Burgh of Aberdeen, 2nd ser., 2 vols, ed. J. Stuart (Aberdeen, 1871–2).

Extracts from the Records of the Burgh of Edinburgh, 5 vols, ed. J.D. Marwick (Edinburgh, 1869–92).

Extracts from the Records of the Burgh of Edinburgh, 2nd ser., 9 vols, ed. M. Wood and H. Armet (Edinburgh, 1927–67).

Extracts from the Records of the Burgh of Glasgow, 11 vols, ed. J.D. Marwick and R. Renwick (Glasgow, 1876–1916).

Extracts from the Records of the Royal Burgh of Stirling, 2 vols, ed. R. Renwick (Glasgow, 1887–9).

Extravagantes communes, in the *Corpus iuris canonici* (above), vol. 2.

The Eyre of Kent, 6 & 7 Edward II, A.D. 1313–14, 3 vols, ed. F.W. Maitland, L.W.V. Harcourt and W.C. Bolland (London, 1910–13).

The Eyre of Northamptonshire, 3–4 Edward III, A.D. 1329–30, 2 vols, ed. D.W. Sutherland (London, 1983).

Faulconnier, Pierre, *Description historique de Dunkerque*, 2 vols (Bruges, 1730).

Ferretti, Giulio, *Consilia et tractatus* (Venice, 1562).

Ferretti, Giulio, *De iure et re navali* (Venice, 1579).

Fifth Report of the Royal Commission on Historical Manuscripts (London, 1876).

Fitzherbert, Anthony, *La graunde abridgement* (London, 1577).

Florus, Lucius Annaeus, *Epitome of Roman History*, tr. J.C. Rolfe (Cambridge, MA, 1929).

Foedera, conventiones, litterae et cuiuscunque generis acta publica inter reges Angliae et alios quosvis imperatores, reges, pontifices, principes vel communitates, 20 vols, ed. T. Rymer and R. Sanderson (London, 1704–35).

Foreign Correspondence with Marie de Lorraine, Queen of Scotland, 2 vols, ed. M. Wood (Edinburgh, 1923–5).

The Forty-Seventh Annual Report of the Deputy Keeper of the Public Records (London, 1886).

Fox Morcillo, Sebastián, *De regni regisque institutione libri tres* (Antwerp, 1556).

Fulbecke, William, *A Direction or Preparative to the Study of the Lawe* (London, 1600).

Fulbecke, William, *An Historicall Collection of the Continuall Factions, Tumults and Massacres of the Romans and Italians* (London, 1601).

Fulbecke, William, *The Pandectes of the Law of Nations* (London, 1602).

Fulbecke, William, *A Parallele or Conference of the Civill Law, the Canon Law and the Common Law of England* (London, 1601).

Fulgosius, Raphael, *In Iustiniani Codicem commentaria*, 2 vols (Lyons, 1547).

Fuller, Thomas, *The Church History of Britain from the Birth of Jesus Christ until the Year 1647* (London, 1655).
Fumo, Bartolomeo, *Summa quae aurea armilla inscribitur* (Lyons, 1554).
Garcia, Fortunius, *Tractatus de ultimo fine iuris civilis et canonici* (Cologne, 1585).
Gates, Geoffrey, *The Defence of Militarie Profession* (London, 1579).
Gentilis, Albericus, *De iure belli libri tres*, 2 vols, tr. J.C. Rolfe (Oxford, 1933).
Gentilis, Albericus, *De iuris interpretibus dialogi sex*, ed. G. Astuti (Turin, 1937).
Gentilis, Albericus, *De legationibus libri tres*, 2 vols, tr. G.J. Laing (New York, 1924).
Gentilis, Albericus, *Hispanicae advocationis libri duo*, tr. F.F. Abbott (New York, 1921).
Gentilis, Albericus, *Lectionum et epistolarum quae ad ius civile pertinent libri quatuor* (London, 1583).
Gentilis, Albericus, *Regales disputationes tres* (Hanover, 1605).
Gentilis, Albericus, *The Wars of the Romans: A Critical Edition and Translation of De armis Romanis*, tr. D. Lupher (Oxford, 2011).
Gibbon, Charles, *A Watch-Worde for Warre, Not so New as Necessary* (Cambridge, 1596).
The Gild Court Book of Dunfermline, 1433–1597, ed. E.P.D. Torrie (Edinburgh, 1986).
Giphanius, Hubertus, *De divisionibus iuris novis interpretum quorundam, maxime glossographorum, in theses aliquot coniectis* (Altdorf, 1586).
Godolphin, John, *A View of the Admiral Jurisdiction* (London, 1661).
Gosson, Stephen, *The Trumpet of Warre* (London, 1598).
Gothofredus, Dionysius, *Praxis civilis, ex antiquis et recentioribus authoribus collecta*, 2 vols (Frankfurt, 1591).
Groot Placaet-Boeck, Vervattende de Placaten, Ordonnantien ende Edicten vande Hoogh-Mog, Heeren Staten Generael der Vereenighde Nederlanden ende vande Heeren Staten van Hollandt ende West-Vrieslandt, 10 vols, ed. C. Cau, S. van Leeuwen and J. Scheltus (The Hague, 1658–1705).
Grotius, Hugo, *Commentarius in theses xi: An Early Treatise on Sovereignty, the Just War and the Legitimacy of the Dutch Revolt*, tr. P. Borschberg (Berne, 1994).
Grotius, Hugo, *Commentary on the Law of Prize and Booty*, tr. G.L. Williams (Indianapolis, 2006).
Grotius, Hugo, 'Defensio capitis quinti Maris liberi', in S. Muller, *Mare clausum: Bijdrage tot de Geschiedenis der Rivaliteit van Engeland en Nederland in de Zeventiende Eeuw* (Amsterdam, 1872), p. 331.
Grotius, Hugo, *De iure belli ac pacis libri tres* (Paris, 1625).
Grotius, Hugo, *De iure belli ac pacis libri tres*, 2 vols, tr. F.W. Kelsey (Washington, 1913–25).
Grotius, Hugo, *De iure praedae commentarius*, ed. H.G. Hamaker (The Hague, 1868).
Grotius, Hugo, *The Free Sea*, tr. Richard Hakluyt (Indianapolis, 2004).
Grotius, Hugo, *Mare liberum, 1609–2009*, ed. R. Feenstra (Leiden, 2009).
Grotius, Hugo, *The Rights of War and Peace*, 3 vols, tr. John Morrice (Indianapolis, 2005).
Guerrero, Alfonso Alvarez, *Thesaurus Christianae religionis* (Cologne, 1581).

Guicciardini, Francesco, *Dialogue on the Government of Florence*, tr. A. Brown (Cambridge, 1994).

Guidon, stile et usance des marchands qui mettent à la mer (Rouen, 1619).

Habakkuk Bisset's Rolment of Courtis, 3 vols, ed. P.J. Hamilton-Grierson (Edinburgh, 1920–6).

Hacket, Roger, *A Sermon Needful for Theese Times* (Oxford, 1591).

Hale, Sir Matthew, *The Prerogatives of the King*, ed. D.E.C. Yale (London, 1976).

Hale and Fleetwood on Admiralty Jurisdiction, ed. M.J. Prichard and D.E.C. Yale (London, 1993).

Hall's Chronicle, ed. H. Ellis (London, 1809).

The Hamilton Papers, 2 vols, ed. J. Bain (Edinburgh, 1890–2).

Hanseakten aus England, 1275 bis 1412, ed. K. Kunze (Halle, 1891).

Hanserecesse: Die Recesse und andere Akten der Hansetage von 1256–1430, 8 vols, ed. W. Junghans and K. Koppmann (Leipzig, 1870–97).

Hanserecesse, 2nd ser., 7 vols, ed. G.F. von der Ropp (Leipzig, 1867–92).

Hanserecesse, 3rd ser., 9 vols, ed. D. Schäfer and F. Techen (Leipzig and Munich, 1881–1913).

Hansisches Urkundenbuch, 11 vols, ed. K. Höhlbaum, K. Kunze and W. Stein (Halle, 1876–1916).

Harris, Edmund, *A Sermon Preached at Brocket Hall* (London, 1588).

Harward, Simon, *The Solace for the Souldier and Saylour* (London, 1592).

Henríquez, Enrique, *Summa theologiae moralis libri quindecim* (Mainz, 1613).

Historia et cartularium monasterii Sancti Petri Gloucestriae, 3 vols, ed. W.H. Hart (London, 1863–7).

The Historical Works of Sir James Balfour of Denmyln and Kinnaird, 4 vols, ed. J. Haig (Edinburgh, 1824–5).

Hooker, Richard, *Of the Lawes of Ecclesiasticall Politie* (London, 1593).

Horace, *Satires*, tr. H.R. Fairclough (Cambridge, MA, 1929).

Hostiensis, Henricus de Segusio, alias, *Lectura in quinque Decretalium Gregorianarum libros*, 2 vols (Paris, 1512).

Hostiensis, Henricus de Segusio, alias, *Summa aurea* (Basel, 1573).

Infortiatum (Paris, 1559).

Innocentius IV, *In quinque libros Decretalium commentaria doctissima* (Turin, 1581).

Institutes, in the *Corpus iuris civilis* (above), vol. 1

The Institutes of Gaius, Part 1: Text with Critical Notes and Translation, ed. F. De Zulueta (Oxford, 1946).

Institutiones iuris civilis Iustiniani (Geneva, 1555).

Isidore of Seville, *Etymologiae*, in *Patrologia Latina* (below), vol. 82.

An Itinerary Written by Fynes Moryson, Gent. (London, 1617).

Iustiniani imperatoris Institutionum libri quatuor Francisci Accursii glossis illustrate (Lyons, 1577).

'James Roberton's Treatise on Court Procedure', in *Alexander King's Treatise on Maritime Law*, ed. J.D. Ford (Edinburgh, 2018), p. 407.

John Spelman's Reading on Quo Warranto, ed. J. H. Baker (London 1997).

Joly, Guillaume, *Traicté de la justice militaire de France* (Paris, 1598).

Journals of the House of Commons, 1547–1714, 17 vols (London, 1742).

Journals of the House of Lords, 1509–1714, 19 vols (London, 1767).

Kirkcudbright Town Council Records, 1576–1658, 3 vols, ed. M.B. Johnston, C.M. Armet and D. Stuart (Edinburgh, 1939).

Lactantius, *Divinae institutiones*, in *Patrologia Latina* (below), vol. 6.

Lancelottus, Ioannes Paulus, *Institutiones iuris canonici, quibus ius pontificium singulari methodo libris quatuor comprehenditur* (Lyons, 1584).

Languet, Hubert, *A Short Apologie for Christian Souldiours* (London, 1588).

Lauder of Fountainhall, Sir John, *Historical Observes of Memorable Occurrents in Church and State* (Edinburgh, 1840).

Law of Contraband of War, ed. F.T. Pratt (London, 1856).

Leicester's Commonwealth: The Copy of a Letter Written by a Master of Art of Cambridge (1584) and Related Documents, ed. D.C. Peck (Athens, OH, 1985).

Leslie, John, *De origine, moribus et rebus gestis Scotorum libri decem* (Rome, 1578).

Leslie, John, *The Historie of Scotland*, 2 vols, tr. James Dalrymple, ed. E.G. Cody and W. Murison (Edinburgh, 1888–95).

Leslie, John, *A Treatise of Treasons against Q. Elizabeth and the Crowne of England* (n.p., 1572).

The Letters and Life of Francis Bacon, 7 vols, ed. J. Spedding (London, 1862–74).

Letters and Memorials of State in the Reigns of Queen Mary, Queen Elizabeth, King James, King Charles the First, Part of the Reign of King Charles the Second and Oliver's Usurpation, 2 vols, ed. A. Collins (London, 1746).

Letters and Papers, Foreign and Domestic, of the Reign of Henry VIII, 1509–47, 21 vols, ed. J.S. Brewer, J. Gairdner and R.H. Brodie (London, 1862–1910).

Letters and Papers Illustrative of the Reigns of Richard III and Henry VII, 2 vols, ed. J. Gairdner (London, 1861–3).

Letters and Papers Relating to Patrick, Master of Gray, ed. T. Thomson (Edinburgh, 1835).

Letters and Papers Relating to the War with France, 1512–13, ed. A. Spont (London, 1897).

Letters and State Papers during the Reign of King James the Sixth, ed. J. Maidment (Edinburgh, 1838).

Letters from and to Sir Dudley Carleton, Knight, during his Embassy in Holland (London, 1775).

The Letters of James the Fourth, 1505–13, ed. R.L. Mackie (Edinburgh, 1953).

The Letters of James V, ed. R.K. Hannay and D. Hay (Edinburgh, 1954).

The Letters of John Chamberlain, 2 vols, ed. N.E. McClure (Philadelphia, 1939).

Letters of King James VI and I, ed. G.P.V. Akrigg (Berkeley, 1984).

The Letters of Lord Burghley, William Cecil, to His Son, Sir Robert Cecil, 1593–98, ed. W. Acres (Cambridge, 2017).

Letters of Queen Elizabeth and King James VI of Scotland, ed. J. Bruce (London, 1849).

The Letters of Queen Elizabeth I, ed. G.B. Harrison (London, 1968).

Letters Received by the East India Company from Its Servants in the East, 6 vols, ed. F.C. Danvers and W. Foster (London, 1896–1902).

The Letters of Sir Walter Ralegh, ed. A. Latham and J. Youings (Exeter, 1999).

'Lettres de Jeanne d'Albret, reine de Navarre, Henri, prince de Navarre, et Henri de Bourbon, prince de Condé, déclarant de bonne prise les armes capturées pendant les troubles de 1568 par Jean de Saint-Hermine, commandant à la Rochelle en l'absence du feu prince de Condé, et promettant de garantir et défendre ce commandant et les maire, échevins et pairs de la Rochelle contre toutes les recherches et répétitions qui pourraient être faites à ce sujet', (1873) 2 *Archives historiques du Poitou* 317.

Lettres, instructions et mémoires de Marie Stuart, reine d'Écosse, 7 vols, ed. A. Labanoff (London, 1844).

Liber extra, in the *Corpus iuris canonici* (above), vol. 2.

Liber sextus decretalium (Turin, 1620).

Liber sextus, in the *Corpus iuris canonici* (above), vol. 2.

The Life of Sir Leoline Jenkins, 2 vols, ed. W. Wynne (London, 1724).

Lindesay of Pitscottie, Robert, *The Historie and Cronicles of Scotland*, 3 vols, ed. A.J.G. Mackay (Edinburgh, 1899–1911).

Lipsius, Justus, *Sixe Bookes of Politickes or Civil Doctrine* (London, 1994).

Livy, *Ab urbe condita*, 14 vols, tr. B.O. Foster, F.G. Moore, E.T. Sage and A.C. Schlesinger (Cambridge, MA, 1919–59).

Lloyd, Lodowick, *The Stratagems of Jerusalem* (London, 1602).

Machiavelli, Niccolò, *The Art of War*, tr. E. Farneworth (New York, 1965).

Machiavelli, Niccolò, *Discourses on Livy*, tr. H.C. Mansfield and N. Tarcov (Chicago, 1996).

Machiavelli, Niccolò, *The Prince*, tr. R. Price (Cambridge, 1988).

Mackenzie of Rosehaugh, Sir George, *Observations on the Acts of Parliament* (Edinburgh, 1686).

Mackenzie of Rosehaugh, Sir George, *Pleadings in Some Remarkable Cases* (Edinburgh, 1672).

Maldura da Bergamo, Pietro, *Tabula aurea in omnia Divi Thomae Aquinatis opera* (Antwerp, 1612).

The Manuscripts of the Earl Cowper Preserved at Melbourne Hall, 3 vols, ed. W.D. Fane (London, 1888–9).

Mariana, Juan de, *De rege et regis institutione* (Toledo, 1599).

Mariana, Juan de, *The King and the Education of the King*, tr. G.A. Moore (Chevy Chase, MD, 1948).

Marten, Anthony, *An Exhortation to Stirre up the Mindes of All Her Majesties Faithfull Subjects to Defend Their Countrey at this Dangerous Time from the Invasion of Enemies* (London, 1588).

Matthiae, Wilhelm, *Libellus de bello iusto et licito* (Antwerp, 1514).

Mazzolini da Prierio, Silvestro, *Summa summarum, quae Silvestrina nuncupatur*, 2 vols (Lyons, 1539).

Medieval Trade in the Mediterranean World, ed. R.S. Lopez and I.W. Raymond (Oxford, 1955).

Mémoires de Condé, servant d'eclaircissement et de preuves à l'histoire de M. de Thou, 6 vols (London, 1743).

Mémoires de Viglius et d'Hopperus sur le commencement des troubles des Pays-Bas, ed. A. Wauters (Brussels, 1858).

Mémoires pour servir de preuves à l'histoire ecclésiastique et civile de Bretagne, 3 vols, ed. P.H. Morice (Paris, 1742–6).

Memorials of the Earls of Haddington, 2 vols, ed. W. Fraser (Edinburgh, 1889).

Memorials of the Family of Skene of Skene, ed. W.F. Skene (Aberdeen, 1887).

Miscellanea di storia italiana, 50 vols (Turin, 1862–1922).

Miscellaneous State Papers from 1501 to 1726, 2 vols, ed. Philip Yorke, earl of Hardwicke (London, 1778).

Miscellany of the Maitland Club, 4 vols, ed. A. Macdonald and J. Dennistoun (Edinburgh, 1840–7).

Molina, Luis de, *De iustitia et iure*, 5 vols (Mainz, 1602–9).

Molloy, Charles, *De iure maritimo et navali, or, A Treatise of Affairs Maritime and of Commerce* (London, 1682).

Monumenta Germaniae historica, *Constitutiones et acta publica imperatorum et regum*, 11 vols, ed. L. Weiland, W. Stürner, I. Schwalm, R. Bork, W. Eggeret, K. Zeumer, R. Salomon, M. Kühn and W.D. Fritz (Hanover, 1893–2003).

Monumenta historiae patriae, 22 vols (Turin, 1836–98).

Morison, Richard, *An Exhortation to Styr All Englyshe Men to the Defence of Theyr Contreye* (n.p., 1539).

Morton, Thomas, *Salomon, or, A Treatise Declaring the State of the Kingdome of Israel* (London, 1596).

Munimenta Gildhallae Londoniensis, 4 vols, ed. H.T. Riley (London, 1859–62).

Murimuth, Adam, *Continuatio chronicarum*, ed. E.M. Thompson (London, 1889).

Naval Songs and Ballads, ed. C.H. Firth (London, 1908).

The Naval Tracts of Sir William Monson in Six Books, 5 vols, ed. M. Oppenheim (London, 1902–14).

The New English Bible (Cambridge, 1970).

Nichols, Philip, *Sir Francis Drake Revived* (London, 1653).

'Nicholas Faunt's Discourse Touching the Office of Principal Secretary of Estate, &c., 1592', ed. C. Hughes (1905) 20 *English Historical Review* 499.

Nicot, Jean, *La grand dictionaire françoislatin* (Paris, 1605).

Nisbet of Dirleton, Sir John, *The Decisions of the Lords of Council and Session* (Edinburgh, 1698).

Nonius, Tobias, *Consilia seu responsa* (Venice, 1573).

Norden, John, *A Christian Familiar Comfort and Incouragement unto All English Subjects* (London, 1596).

Norden, John, *The Mirror of Honor* (London, 1597).

Novels, in the *Corpus iuris civilis* (above), vol. 3.

Nun, Thomas, *A Comfort against the Spaniard* (London, 1596).

Odofredus de Denariis *Lectura super Codice*, 2 vols (Lyons, 1552).

Odofredus de Denariis *Lectura super Digesto*, 4 vols (Lyons, 1550–2).

Oeuvres complètes de Suger, ed. A Lecoy de la Marche (Paris, 1847).

Oeuvres de Rigord et de Guillaume le Breton, 3 vols, ed. H.-F. Delaborde (Paris, 1882–5).

Oppressions of the Sixteenth Century in the Islands of Orkney and Zetland, ed. D. Balfour (Edinburgh, 1859).

Original Letters of Mr John Colville, 1582–1603, ed. D. Laing (Edinburgh, 1858).

Ovid, *Metamorphoses*, 2 vols, tr. F.J. Miller (Cambridge, MA, 1916).

Panormitanus, Nicholas de Tudeschis, alias, *Lectura super quinque libros Decretalium*, 5 vols (Lyons, 1517).

The Papal Bull In Coena Domini (London, 1848).

Papers Relating to the Navy during the Spanish War, 1585–87, ed. J.S. Corbett (London, 1898).

Papon, Jean, *Recueil d'arrests notables des cours souveraines de France*, 2 vols (Paris, 1584).

Paris, Matthew, *Chronica maiora*, 7 vols, ed. H.R. Luard (London, 1872–83).

Parker, Matthew, *A Defence of Priestes Mariages Stablysshed by the Imperiall Lawes of the Realme of England* (n.p., 1567).

The Parliamentary Diary of Robert Bowyer, 1606–7, ed. D.H. Willson (New York, 1971).

Parliament Rolls of Medieval England, 16 vols, ed. C. Given-Wilson, P. Brand, S. Phillips, M. Ormrod, G. Martin, A. Curry and R. Horrox (Woodbridge, 2005).

Parsons, Robert, *Newes from Spayne and Holland, Conteyning an Information of Inglish Affayres in Spayne, with a Conferrence Made theruppon in Amsterdame in Holland* (n.p., 1593).

Patrologia Latina, 221 vols, ed. J.-P. Migne (Paris, 1844–64).

Peckius, Petrus, *Commentaria in omnes pene iuris civilis titulos ad rem nauticam pertinentes* (Louvain, 1556).

Peele, George, *The Love of King David and Fair Bethsabe* (London, 1599).

Perkins, William, *A Discourse of Conscience* (Cambridge, 1596).

Phillip, Bartholomew, *The Counseller: A Treatise of Counsels and Counsellers of Princes* (London, 1589).

Pindar, *Isthmian Odes*, tr. W.H. Race (Cambridge, MA, 1997).

Placentinus, Petrus, *Summa Institutionum sive elementorum* (Mainz, 1535).

Plautus, *The Captives*, tr. P. Nixon (Cambridge, MA, 1916).

Plautus, *Epidicus*, tr. P. Nixon (Cambridge, MA, 1917).

Plautus, *Rudens*, tr. W.D.C de Milo (Cambridge, MA, 2012).

Pliny, *Natural History*, 10 vols, tr. H. Rackham and W.H.S. Jones (Cambridge, MA, 1938–63).

Plutarch's Lives, 11 vols, tr. B. Perrin (Cambridge, MA., 1914–26).

The Poems of James VI of Scotland, 2 vols, ed. J. Craigie (Edinburgh, 1955–8).

Pogii Florentini dialogus et Leonardi Arretini oratio adversus hypocrisim (Lyons, 1579).

The Political Works of James I, ed. C.H. McIlwain (Cambridge, MA, 1918).

Polybius, *The Histories*, 6 vols, tr. W.R. Paton (Cambridge, MA, 1922–7).

The Practicks of Sir James Balfour of Pittendreich, 2 vols, ed. P.G.B. McNeill (Edinburgh, 1962–3).

The Practiques of Sir Richard Maitland of Lethington, ed. R.S. Sutherland (Edinburgh, 2007).

Prerogativa regis: Tertia lectura Roberti Constable de Lincolnis Inne, Anno 11 H. 7, ed. S.E. Thorne (New Haven, 1949).

Prime, John, *The Consolations of David, Briefly Applied to Queene Elizabeth* (Oxford, 1588).

Priscian, *Institutiones grammaticae*, 2 vols, ed. A. Krehl (Leipzig, 1819–20).

Proceedings in Parliament 1626, 4 vols, ed. W.B. Bidwell and M. Jansson (New Haven, 1992–6).

Proceedings in the Parliaments of Elizabeth I, 3 vols, ed. T.E. Hartley (Leicester, 1981–95).

A Proclamation against Excesse of Lavish and Licentious Speech of Matters of State (London, 1620).

A Proclamation against Pirats (London, 1609).

A Proclamation against Unjust Pretences for Colouring of French Goods Taken by Way of Reprize (London, 1627).

A Proclamation Directing How Prisoners Shall be Ordered Which Are Taken at Sea by Men of Warre (London, 1628).

A Proclamation for Revocation of Mariners from Forreine Services (London, 1605).

A Proclamation for the Explaining of a Former Proclamation Lately Published (London, 1627).

A Proclamation for the Search and Apprehension of Certaine Pirats (London, 1604).

A Proclamation for the Search and Apprehension of Certaine Pirats (London, 1606).

A Proclamation of the Lords, the Generall States of the United Provinces, whereby the Spaniards and All Their Goods are Declared To Be Lawfull Prize (London, 1599).

A Proclamation Prohibiting the Importation of Any Goods or Merchandize Whatsoever in Any French Shippes or Bottomes (London, 1627).

A Proclamation Prohibiting the Transportation of Any Corne, Graine, Victuals, Ordinance, Armes or Munition of Warre into the Kingdom of France (London, 1628).

A Proclamation to Prevent the Furnishing of the King of Spaine and His Subjects with Provisions for Shipping or Munition for the Warres and with Victuals (London, 1627).

A Proclamation to Represse All Piracies and Depredations upon the Sea (London, 1603).

A Proclamation Touching Fishing (London, 1609).

The Prose Works of Sir Gilbert Hay, 3 vols, ed. J.A. Glenn (Edinburgh, 1993–2005).

Puttenham, George, *The Arte of English Poesie* (London, 1589).

Questiones Johannis Galli, ed. M. Boulet (Paris, 1945).

Quintilian, *Institutio oratoria*, 4 vols, tr. H.E. Butler (Cambridge, MA, 1920–2).

'Rapports des Rochelais avec Henri Ier de Bourbon, prince de Condé, 1576–77', (1873) 2 *Archives historiques du Poitou* 326.

The Reading of the Famous and Learned Robert Callis, Esq., upon the Statute of 23 H. 8 Cap. 5 of Sewers (London, 1686).

Rebuffus, Petrus, *Praxis beneficiorum* (Lyons, 1599).

Records of the Convention of the Royal Burghs of Scotland, 8 vols, ed. J.D. Marwick and T. Hunter (Edinburgh, 1870–1918).

The Records of the Parliaments of Scotland, ed. K.M. Brown (www.rps.ac.uk).

The Records of the Virginia Company of London, 4 vols, ed. S.M. Kingsbury (Washington, 1906–35).

Recueil des ordonnances de Pays-Bas, 1506–1700, 7 vols, ed. J. Lameere, C. Laurent and H. Simont (Brussels, 1893–1957).

Recueil général des anciennes lois françaises, 29 vols, ed. F.-A. Isambert, M. Jourdan and M. Decrusy (Paris, 1822–33).

The Register of Letters &c. of the Governour and Company of Merchants of London Trading into the East Indies, 1600–19, ed. G. Birdwood and W. Foster (London, 1893).

The Register of the Privy Council of Scotland, 14 vols, ed. J.H. Burton and D. Masson (Edinburgh, 1877–98).

The Register of the Privy Council of Scotland, 2nd ser., 8 vols, ed. D. Masson and P. Hume Brown (Edinburgh, 1899–1908).

'Régistre de l'amirauté de Guyenne au siége de La Rochelle, 1569–70', ed. A. Bardonnet (1878) 7 *Archives historique de Poitou* 191.

Registrum magni sigilli regum Scotorum: The Register of the Great Seal of Scotland, 11 vols, ed. J. Balfour Paul, J.M. Thomson, J.H. Stevenson and W. K. Dickson (Edinburgh, 1984).

Registrum secreti sigilli regum Scotorum: The Register of the Privy Seal of Scotland, 7 vols, ed. M. Livingston, G. Donaldson, J. Beveridge and D.H. Fleming (Edinburgh, 1908–66).

Relations politiques des Pays-Bas et de l'Angleterre sous le règne de Philippe II, 11 vols, ed. J.M.B.C. Kervyn de Lettenhove and L. Gilliodts van Severen (Brussels, 1882–1900).

Reliques of Ancient English Poetry, ed. T. Percy (London, 1845).

Repertorium Antonii Corseti Siculi I. U. D. praeclarissimi, ad Nicolai Abbatis Panormitani, Commentaria super Decretalium et Clementinarum libros (Venice, 1588).

Repetitiones, disputationes necnon tractatus diversorum doctorum (Venice, 1472).

Report on the Laing Manuscripts Preserved in the University of Edinburgh, 2 vols, ed. H. Paton (London, 1914).

Report on the Manuscripts of the Duke of Buccleuch and Queensberry, 3 vols, ed. R.E.G. Kirk (London, 1899–1926).

The Reports of Richard Brownlow and John Goldesborough (London, 1675).

The Reports of Sir Edward Coke, 6 vols, ed. R.P. Tyrwhitt, J.F. Fraser and J.H. Thomas (London, 1826).

The Reports of that Learned Sir Henry Hobart (London, 1641).

Respublica Mutinensis, 2 vols, ed. E.P. Vicini (Milan, 1929–30).

Ribadeneyra, Pedro de, *Princeps Christianus adversus Nicolaum Machiavellum ceterosque huius temporis politicos*, tr. Jean Oran (Antwerp, 1603).

Rich, Barnaby, *Allarme to England, Foreshewing What Perilles Are Procured, Where the People Live Without Regarde to Martiall Lawe* (London, 1578).

The Rich Papers: Letters from Bermuda, 1615–1646, ed. V.A. Ives (Toronto, 1984).

Ridley, Sir Thomas, *A View of the Civile and Ecclesiastical Law* (London, 1607).

Ripa, Ioannes Franciscus a, *Commentaria in primam et secundam Infortiati* (Lyons, 1537).

Ripa, Ioannes Franciscus a, *Super Digesto novo, veteri et Codice commentaria* (Lyons, 1538).

The Roman Antiquities of Dionysius of Halicarnassus, 7 vols, tr. E. Cary (Cambridge, MA, 1937–50).

Romanus, Ludovicus, *Lectura aurea et mirabilis in primam Digesti veteris partem* (Lyons, 1547).

Rotuli litterarum clausarum in Turri Londinensi asservati, 2 vols, ed. T.D. Hardy (London, 1833–44).

Rotuli parliamentorum, 6 vols (London, 1783).

Rotuli Scotiae in Turri Londinensi et in Domo Capitulari Westmonsteriensi asservati, 2 vols, ed. D. Macpherson, J. Caley and W. Illingworth (London, 1814–19).

Rufinus de Assisi, *Summa Decretorum*, ed. H. Singer (Aalen, 1902).

Ruinus, Carolus, *Responsa sive consilia*, 6 vols (Venice, 1579).

Rushworth, John, *Historical Collections of Private Passages of State, Weighty Matters in Law, Remarkable Proceedings in Five Parliaments*, 8 vols, ed. G. Thomason (London, 1659–1701).

Sacrorum conciliorum nova et amplissimo collectio, 56 vols, ed. G.D. Mansi, P. Labbe, G. Cossart and N. Coleti (Florence, Venice and Paris, 1759–1927).

'Salvetti Correspondence', ed. H.B. Tomkins, in *Eleventh Report of the Historical Manuscripts Commission* (London, 1887), app., pt 1.

Sandeus, Felinus, *Commentaria in Decretalium libros quinque*, 3 vols (Venice, 1570).

Sandeus, Felinus, *Singularis ac perutilis lectura super titulo de rescriptis* (Milan, 1499).

Sansovino, Francesco, *The Quintesence of Wit, Being a Corrant Comfort of Conceites, Maximies and Poleticke Devises*, tr. Robert Hitchcock (London, 1590).

Schard, Simon, *Lexicon iuridicum iuris Romani simul et pontificii* (Basel, 1582).

Schneidewinus, Ioannes, *In quatuor Institutionum imperialium D. Iustiniani libros commentarii* (Strasbourg, 1592).

Schurpsius, Hieronymus, *Consiliorum seu responsorum iuris centuria secunda* (Frankfurt, 1551).

The Scottish Correspondence of Mary of Lorraine, ed. A.I. Cameron (Edinburgh, 1927).

Scriptores historiae augustae, 3 vols, tr. D. Magie (Cambridge, MA, 1921–3).

The Sea-Mans Triumph (London, 1592).

A Second Admonition to the Parliament (n.p., 1572).

Le second part de les reports des cases en ley, que fuerent argue en le temps de le tres haut et puissant prince, Roy Edward le Tierce (London, 1619).

Segar, Sir William, *Honor Military and Civill, Contained in Foure Bookes* (London, 1602).

Selden, John, *De iure naturali et gentium, iuxta disciplinum Ebraeorum, libri septem* (London, 1640).

Selden, John, *The Historie of Tithes* (London, 1618).

Selden, John, *Mare clausum seu de domnio maris libri duo* (London, 1635).

Selden, John, *Of the Dominion or Ownership of the Sea*, tr. Marchamont Needham (London, 1652).

Select Cases Concerning the Law Merchant, 3 vols, ed. H. Hall (London, 1908–32).

Select Cases in Chancery, 1364–1471, ed. W.P. Baildon (London, 1896).

Select Pleas in the Court of Admiralty, 2 vols, ed. R.G. Marsden (London, 1894–7).

Select Statutes and Other Constitutional Documents Illustrative of the Reigns of Elizabeth and James I, ed. G.W. Prothero (Oxford, 1913).

Seneca, *Ad Lucilium epistulae morales*, 3 vols, tr. R.M. Gummere (Cambridge, MA, 1917–25).

Seneca, *De beneficiis*, tr. J.W. Basore (Cambridge, Mass., 1935).

The Sermons of M. John Calvin upon the Fifth Booke of Moses Called Deuteronomie (London, 1583).

Shakespeare, William, *Henry V*, ed. J. Fisher (Harlow, 1994).

Shetland Documents, 3 vols, ed. J.H. Ballantyne and B. Smith (Lerwick, 1994–2016).

Sinclair's Practicks, ed. A.L. Murray and G. Dolezalek (www.home.uni-leipzig.de/jura rom/ scotland/dat/sinclair).

'Sir John Eliot and the Vice-Admiralty of Devon', ed. H. Hulme, in *Camden Miscellany XVII*, Shakespeare, William (London, 1940), pt 3.

Skene of Curriehill, Sir John, *De verborum significatione* (Edinburgh, 1597).

Socinus, Bartolomeus, *Ad Digestam novum et aliquot Codicis titulus* (Lyons, 1564).

'Some Less Known Works of Hugo Grotius', ed. H.F. Wright (1928) 7 *Bibliotheca Visseriana* pt 18.

Sophocles, *Antigone*, tr. H. Lloyd-Jones (Cambridge, MA, 1994).

Soto, Domingo de, *De iustitia et iure libri decem* (Salamanca, 1556).

Spenser, Edmund, *The Faerie Queene*, ed. A.C. Hamilton, H. Yamashita and T. Suzuki (Harlow, 2007).

Spiegel, Jakob, *Lexicon iuris civilis* (Basel, 1549).

State Papers and Miscellaneous Correspondence of Thomas, Earl of Melrose, 2 vols, ed. J. Maidment (Edinburgh, 1837).

State Papers Collected by Edward, Earl of Clarendon, Commencing from the Year 1621, 3 vols, ed. R. Scrope and T. Monkhouse (Oxford, 1767).

Statuta antiqua communis Collis Vallis Else, 1307–1407, 2 vols, ed. R. Ninci (Rome, 1999).

Statuta civitatis Ferentini, ed. M. Vendittelli (Rome, 1988).

Statuta communis Parmae (Parma, 1840).

Statuta et ordinamenta comunis Cremonae, ed. G. Solazzi (Milan, 1952).

Statuta Faventiae, ed. G. Rossini (Bologna, 1930).

Statuta Vallis Camonicae (Brescia, 1624).

Statuta Veneta (Venice, 1606).

The Statutes at Large Passed in the Parliaments Held in Ireland, 21 vols (Dublin, 1786).

The Statutes of the Realm, 11 vols (London, 1810–28).

Statuti della reppublica fiorentina, 2 vols, ed. R. Caggese, G. Pinto, F. Salvestrini and A. Zorzi (Florence, 1999).

Statuti della Valsesia, ed. C.G. Mor (Milan, 1932).

Statuti inediti della cittá di Pisa dal XII *al* XIV *secolo*, 3 vols, ed. F. Bonaini (Florence, 1854–7).

Staunford, Sir William, *An Exposicion of the King's Prerogative, Collected out of the Great Abridgement of Justice Fitzherbert* (London, 1567).

Stuart Royal Proclamations, 2 vols, ed. J.F. Larkin and P.L. Hughes (Oxford, 1973–83).

Styward, Thomas, *The Pathwaie to Martiall Discipline* (London, 1582).

Suárez, Francisco, *Selections from Three Works*, 2 vols, tr. G.L. Williams, A. Brown and J. Waldron (Oxford, 1944).

Suetonius, *The Lives of the Caesars*, 2 vols, tr. J.C. Rolfe (Cambridge, MA, 1914–51).

Summa Azonis, locuples iuris civilis thesaurus (Basel, 1563).

Supplementary Report on the Manuscripts of the Earl of Mar and Kellie, ed. H. Paton (London, 1930).

Sutcliffe, Matthew, *A Briefe Replie to a Certaine Odious and Slanderous Libel* (London, 1600).

Sutcliffe, Matthew, *The Practice, Proceedings, and Lawes of Armes* (London, 1593).

Tacitus, *The Annals*, 3 vols, tr. J. Jackson (Cambridge, MA, 1931–7).

Tacitus, *The Histories*, 2 vols, tr. C.H. Moore (Cambridge, MA, 1925–31).

Talbot, John, 'Observacions Touchinge the Kings Prerogative to Wreck of the Sea', in S.A. Moore, *A History of the Foreshore and the Law Relating Thereto* (London, 1888), p. 244.

Tartagnus, Alexander, *Opera omnia*, 3 vols (Lyons, 1520).

Tassin, John, *The Amendment of Life, Comprised in Fower Bookes* (London, 1595).

Terrien, Guillaume, *Commentaires du droict civil tant public que privé, observé au pays et duché de Normandie* (Rouen, 1654).

Thierry, Jean, *Dictionaire françoislatin* (Paris, 1564).

Tholosanus, Petrus Gregorius, *Syntagma iuris universi* (Frankfurt, 1611).

Tiraqueau, André, *Opera omnia*, 7 vols (Frankfurt, 1616).

Tornacensis, Stephanus, *Summa*, ed. J.F. von Schulte (Aalen, 1891).

Tractatus universi iuris, 18 vols (Lyons, 1549).

Traités de paix et de commerce et documents divers concernant les relations des Chrétiens avec les Arabs de l'Afrique septentroniale au Moyen Age, 2 vols, ed. L. de Mas Latrie (Paris, 1866).

A True Relation of the Life and Death of Sir Andrew Barton, a Pirate and Rover on the Sea (London, 1630).

Tudor Royal Proclamations, 3 vols, ed. P.L. Hughes and J.F. Larkin (New Haven, 1964–9).

Tymme, Thomas, *A Preparation against the Prognosticated Dangers of this Yeare, 1588* (London, 1588).

Upton, Nicholas, *De studio militari libri quatuor* (London, 1654).

Urkunden zur älteren Handels- und Staatsgeschichte der Republik Venedig, 3 vols, ed. G.L.F. Tafel and G.M. Thomas (Vienna, 1856–57).

Us et coustumes de la mer, ed. Estienne Cleirac (Bordeaux, 1661).

Valentia, Gregorio de, *Commentariorum theologicorum libri quatuor*, 4 vols (Ingolstadt, 1603).

Varro, *On Agriculture*, tr. W.D. Hooper (Cambridge, MA, 1967).

Vasquius, Fernandus, *Controversiarum illustrium aliarumque usu frequentibus libri tres* (Venice, 1564).

Verrooten, Jerome, *Novum lexicon utriusque iuris* (Paris, 1574).

Virgil, *Aeneid*, 2 vols, tr. H.R. Fairclough (Cambridge, MA, 1918).

Vitoria, Francisco de, *Comentarios a la Secunda secundae de Santo Tomás*, 6 vols, ed. V. Beltrán de Heredia (Salamanca, 1932–52).

Vitoria, Francisco de, *De Indis et de iure belli relectiones*, tr. J.P. Bate (Washington, 1917).

Vitoria, Francisco de, *Political Writings*, ed. A. Pagden and J. Lawrance (Cambridge, 1991).

Vitoria, Francisco de, *Relectiones theologicae per varias sectiones in duos libros divisa* (Lyons, 1586).

Vocabularius utriusque iuris (Lyons, 1559).

Volumen legum parvum (Paris, 1559).
Volumen statutorum, legum ac iurium Venetorum (Venice, 1564).
Von Gail, Andreas, *Practicarum observationum libri duo* (Amsterdam, 1663).
The Voyage of Thomas Best to the East Indies, 1612–14, ed. W. Foster (London, 1932).
The Warrender Papers, 2 vols, ed. A.I. Dunlop (Edinburgh, 1931–2).
Welwod, William, *An Abridgement of all Sea-Lawes* (London, 1613).
Welwod, William, *De dominio maris, iuribusque ad dominium praecipue spectantibus assertio brevis et methodica* (London, 1616).
Welwod, William, *The Sea-Law of Scotland* (Edinburgh, 1590).
'Welwod's Treatise on Maritime Law', in *Alexander King's Treatise on Maritime Law*, ed. J.D. Ford (Edinburgh, 2018), p. 351.
Wentworth Papers, 1597–1628, ed. J.P. Cooper (London, 1973).
Wesenbecius, Matthaeus, *Tractatus et responsa, quae vulgo consilia iuris appellantur* (Basel, 1575).
Whereas the Kings Majestie Hath Alwayes Bene Ready to Imbrace and Cherish such a Perfect Amitie and Friendship betweene Him and the King of Spaine (London, 1605).
Whereas There Hath Fallen out an Interruption of Amitie betweene the Kings Majestie and the Most Christian King (London, 1629).
Winwood, Sir Ralph, *Memorials of Affairs of State in the Reigns of Queen Elizabeth and King James I*, 3 vols, ed. E. Sawyer (London, 1725).
The Works of Francis Bacon, 7 vols, ed. J. Spedding, R.L. Ellis and D.D. Heath (London, 1857–61).
The Works of Sir Walter Ralegh, 8 vols (Oxford, 1829).
XCVI Sermons by the Right Honourable and Reverend Father in God, Lancelot Andrewes, (London, 1632).
Zabarella, Franciscus, *Super IV et V Decretalium subtilissima commentaria* (Venice, 1602).
Zasius, Udalricus, *Opera omnia*, 7 vols (Lyons, 1550–1).

Secondary Sources

Åberg, A. (1990), 'Scottish Soldiers in the Swedish Armies in the Sixteenth and Seventeenth Centuries', in G.G. Simpson, *Scotland and Scandinavia, 800–1800*, Edinburgh, p. 90.
Abulafia, D. (1994), 'The Role of Trade in Muslim-Christian Contact during the Middle Ages', in D.A. Agius and R. Hitchcock (eds), *The Arab Influence in Medieval Europe*, Reading,
Adams, A.L. (2009), 'So Many Thieves and Lutherans at Sea: Spain's Reaction to the Emergence of French Huguenots in the New World', MA dissertation, Missouri State University, Springfield, p. 1.

Adams, S. (1978), 'Foreign Policy and the Parliaments of 1621 and 1624', in K.M. Sharpe (ed.), *Faction and Parliament: Essays on Early Stuart History*, Oxford, p. 139.

Adams, S. (1983), 'Spain or the Netherlands? The Dilemmas of Early Stuart Foreign Policy', in H. Tomlinson (ed.), *Before the English Civil War: Essays on Early Stuart Politics and Government*, London, p. 79.

Adams, S. (1991), 'The Outbreak of the Elizabethan Naval War against the Spanish Empire: The Embargo of May 1585 and Sir Francis Drake's West Indies Voyage', in M.J. Rodriguez-Salgado and S. Adams (eds), *England, Spain and the Gran Armada, 1585–1604*, Edinburgh, p. 45.

Ahrweiler, H. (1976), 'Course et piraterie dans la Méditerranée orientale aux IVème-XVème siècles (Empire Byzantin)', in M. Mollat (ed.), *Course et piraterie: Études présentées pendant le XIVe Congrès Internationale des Sciences Historiques (San Francisco, août 1975)*, 3 vols, Paris, vol. 1, p. 7.

Alexandrowicz, C.H. (1967), *An Introduction to the History of the Law of Nations in the East Indies*, Oxford.

Alfert, R. (1992), '*Hostes humani generis*: An Expanded Notion of US Counterterrorist Legislation', 6 *Emory International Law Review* 171.

Alford, S. (1998), *The Early Elizabethan Polity: William Cecil and the British Succession Crisis, 1558–69*, Cambridge.

Allaire, B. (2015), 'Between Oléron and Colbert: The Evolution of French Maritime Law until the Seventeenth Century', in M. Fusaro, B. Allaire, R. Blakemore and T. Vanneste (eds), *Law, Labour and Empire: Comparative Perspectives on Seafarers, c.1500–1800*, Basingstoke, p. 79.

Allen, P.C. (2000), *Philip III and the Pax Hispanica, 1598–1621: The Failure of Grand Strategy*, New Haven.

Allinson, R. (2006), '*The Prince* and Queen Elizabeth I: A New Perspective on the Development of English Machiavellism', 34 *Melbourne Historical Journal* 19.

Allmand, C.T. (1992), *Henry V*, London.

Almási, G. (2018), 'Machiavelli's Scientific Method: A Common Understanding of his Novelty in the Sixteenth Century', 44 *History of European Ideas* 1.

Alonso, F.L. (2013), 'Cosmopolitanism and Natural Law in Cicero', in F. Contreras (ed.), *The Threads of Natural Law: Unravelling a Philosophical Tradition*, Dordrecht, p. 27.

Alonso-Lasheras, D. (2011), *Luis de Molina's De iustitia et iure: Justice as Virtue in an Economic Context*, Leiden.

Alsop, J.D. (1980), 'William Welwood, Anne of Denmark and the Sovereignty of the Sea', 49 *Scottish Historical Review* 171.

Althoff, G. (2013), 'The Rules of Conflict among the Warrior Aristocracy of the High Middle Ages', in K. Esmark, L. Hermanson, H.J. Orning and H. Vogt (eds), *Disputing Strategies in Medieval Scandinavia*, Leiden, p. 313.

Alves, A.A. and Moreira, J.M. (2015), *The Salamanca School*, New York.

Ambühl, R. (2013), *Prisoners of War in the Hundred Years War: Ransom Culture in the Late Middle Ages*, Cambridge.

Anand, R.P. (1981), 'Maritime Practice in South-East Asia until 1600 AD and the Modern Law of the Sea', 30 *International and Comparative Law Quarterly* 440.

Anderson, G.M. and Gifford, A. (1991), 'Privateering and the Private Production of Naval Power', 11 *Cato Journal* 99.

Anderson, M.S. (1998), *The Origins of the Modern European State System, 1494–1618*, London.

Anderson, P.D. (1982), *Robert Stewart, Earl of Orkney, Lord of Shetland, 1533–93*, Edinburgh.

Andrew, E.G. (2001), *Conscience and Its Critics: Protestant Conscience, Enlightenment Reason and Modern Subjectivity*, Toronto.

Andrews, K.R. (1959), 'Introduction', in *English Privateering Voyages to the West Indies, 1588–95*, Cambridge, p. 1.

Andrews, K.R. (1964), *Elizabethan Privateering: English Privateering during the Spanish War, 1585–1603*, Cambridge.

Andrews, K.R. (1984), *Trade, Plunder and Settlement: Maritime Enterprise and the Genesis of the British Empire, 1480–1630*, Cambridge.

Andrews, K.R. (1985), 'Elizabethan Privateering', in J. Youings (ed.), *Raleigh in Exeter 1985: Privateering and Colonisation in the Reign of Elizabeth I*, Exeter, p. 1.

Andrews, K.R. (1991), *Ships, Money and Politics: Seafaring and Naval Enterprise in the Reign of Charles I*, Cambridge.

Anghie, A. (1996), 'Francisco de Vitoria and the Colonial Origins of International Law', 5 *Social and Legal Studies* 321.

Anglo, S. (2005), *Machiavelli – The First Century: Studies in Enthusiasm, Hostility and Irrelevance*, Oxford.

Annas, J. (2013), 'Plato's *Laws* and Cicero's *De legibus*', in M. Schofield (ed.), *Aristotle, Plato and Pythagoreanism in the First Century BC*, Cambridge, p. 206.

Appleby, J.C. (1983), 'English Privateering during the Spanish and French Wars, 1625–30', 2 vols, PhD dissertation, University of Hull.

Appleby, J.C. (1992), 'Devon Privateering from Early Times to 1688', in M. Duffy (ed.), *The New Maritime History of Devon, vol. 1: From Early Times to the Late Eighteenth Century*, London, p. 90.

Appleby, J.C. and O'Dowd, M. (1985), 'The Irish Admiralty: Its Organisation and Development, c. 1570–1640', 24 *Irish Historical Studies* 299.

Arienzo, A. and Petrina, A., eds, (2013), *Machiavellian Encounters in Tudor and Stuart England: Literary and Political Influences from the Reformation to the Restoration*, Farnham.

Armitage, D. (2000), *The Ideological Origins of the British Empire*, Cambridge.

Armitage, D. (2013), *Foundations of Modern International Thought*, Cambridge.

Armstrong, J.W. (2010), 'The "Fyre of Ire Kyndild" in the Fifteenth-Century Scottish Marches', in S.A. Throop and P.R. Hyams (eds), *Vengeance in the Middle Ages: Emotion, Religion and Feud*, Farnham, p. 51.

Armstrong, J.W. (2013), 'The Justice Ayre in the Border Sheriffdoms, 1493–8', 92 *Scottish Historical Review* 1.

Armstrong, J.W. (2020), *England's Northern Frontier: Conflict and Local Society in the Fifteenth-Century Scottish Marches*, Cambridge.

Arnade, P. (2008), *Beggars, Iconoclasts and Civic Patriots: The Political Culture of the Dutch Revolt*, Ithaca.

Ascheri, M. (2013), *The Laws of Late Medieval Italy, 1000–1500: Foundations for a European Legal System*, Leiden.

Asmis, E. (2008), 'Cicero on Natural Law and the Laws of the State', 27 *Classical Antiquity* 1.

Aßländer, M.S. (2013), 'Honorableness or Beneficialness? Cicero on Natural Law, Virtues, Glory and (Corporate) Reputation', 116 *Journal of Business Ethics* 751.

Atauz, A.D. (2008), *Eight Thousand Years of Maltese Maritime History: Trade, Piracy and Naval Warfare in the Central Mediterranean*, Gainesville.

Atkins, E.M. (1990), '*Domina et regina virtutum*: Justice and *Societas* in *De officiis*', 35 *Phronesis* 258.

Atkins, E.M. (2005), 'Cicero', in C. Rowe and M. Schofield (eds), *The Cambridge History of Greek and Roman Political Thought*, Cambridge, p. 477.

Atkins, J.W. (2013), *Cicero on Politics and the Limits of Reason: The Republic and Laws*, Cambridge.

Atkins, J.W. (2015), 'Zeno's *Republic*, Plato's *Laws* and the Early Development of Stoic Natural Law Theory', 32 *Polis* 166.

Augeron, M. (1996), 'Course et Protestantisme à La Rochelle, vus par les Espagnols, d'après les archives du *Consejo de Estado*, 1568–1628', in D. Guillemet and J. Peret (eds), *Les sociétés littorales du centre-ouest atlantique: De la préhistoire à nos jours*, Poitiers, p. 215.

Augeron, M. (1997), 'Coligny et les Espagnols à travers la course, c. 1560–72: Une politique maritime au service de la cause protestante', in M. Acerra and G. Martinière (eds), *Coligny, les protestants et la mer*, Paris, p. 155.

Augeron, M. (2004), 'Violences théâtralisées, violences sacralisées: Les marins Huguenots face aux 'papistes' dans la seconde moitié du XVIe siècle', in idem, *La violence et la mer dans l'espace atlantique, XIIe–XIXe siècle*, Rennes, p. 285.

Augeron, M. (2009), 'Pour "la défense et l'advencement de la yraye religion": Jacques de Sores, un corsaire au service de la cause protestante', in M. Augeron, D. Poton and B. van Ruymbeke (eds), *Les Huguenots et l'Atlantique, vol. 1: Pour Dieu, la cause ou les affaires*, Paris, p. 189.

Augeron, M. and Hroděj, P. (2016), 'Entre course, contrebande et piraterie, la conquête des mers lointaines au XVIe siècle', in G. Buti and P. Hroděj (eds), *Histoire des pirates et des corsairs de l'antiquité à nos jours*, Paris, p. 151.

Avermaete, R. (1946), *Les Gueux de mer et la naissance d'une nation*, Brussels.

Avidov, A. (1997), 'Were the Cilicians a Nation of Pirates?', 12 *Mediterranean Historical Review* 5.

Azubuike, L. (2009), 'International Law Regime against Piracy', 15 *Annual Survey of International and Comparative Law* 43.

Baetens, R. (1977), 'The Organisation and Effects of Flemish Privateering in the Seventeenth Century', 8 *Acta historiae Neerlandicae* 48.

Baker, J.H. (1979), 'The Law Merchant and the Common Law before 1700', 38 *Cambridge Law Journal* 295.

Baker, J.H. (1998), *Monuments of Endlesse Labours: English Canonists and Their Work, 1300–1900*, London.

Baker, J.H. (2003), *The Oxford History of the Laws of England: Volume VI, 1483–1558*, Oxford.

Baker, R.B. (2015), 'Customary International Law: A Reconceptualisation', 41 *Brooklyn Journal of International Law* 439.

Balard, M. (1990), 'Course et piraterie à Genes à la fin du Moyen Âge', in G.L. Nadal (ed.), *El comerç alternatiu: Corsarisme i contraban, ss. XV–XVIII*, Palma, p. 29.

Barbour, V. (1911), 'Privateers and Pirates of the West Indies', 16 *American Historical Review* 523.

Barducci, M. (2017), *Hugo Grotius and the Century of Revolution, 1613–1718: Transnational Reception in English Political Thought*, Oxford.

Barlow, J.J. (1999), 'The Fox and the Lion: Machiavelli Replies to Cicero', 20 *History of Political Thought* 627.

Bartlett, I.R. (1984–5), 'Scottish Mercenaries in Europe, 1570–1640: A Study in Attitude and Policies', 13 *Scottish Tradition* 18.

Bartlett, R. (2010), '"Mortal Enmities": The Legal Aspects of Hostility in the Middle Ages', in B.S. Tuten and T.L. Billado (eds), *Feud, Violence and Practice: Essays in Medieval Studies in Honor of Stephen D. White*, Farnham, p. 197.

Baseotto, P. (2006), 'Fighting the "Warres of the Lord": Incitement to War in Elizabethan Devotional Literature', in G. Teulié (ed.), *Religious Writings and War*, Montpellier, p. 37.

Bassiouni, M.C. (2001), 'Universal Jurisdiction for International Crimes: Historical Perspectives and Contemporary Practice', 42 *Virginia Journal of International Law* 81.

Bastid, S. (1962), 'Le droit de la guerre dans des documents judiciaries français du XIVe siècle', 8 *Annuaire français de droit international* 181.

Bauer, D. (2004), 'The Importance of Medieval Canon Law and the Scholastic Tradition for the Emergence of the Early Modern International Legal Order', in R. Lesaffer (ed.), *Peace Treaties and International Law in European History*, Cambridge, p. 198.

Bauer, D. (2015), 'Custom in Francisco Suárez's *De lege non scripta*: Between Factuality and the Legal Realm', 4 *Anuario de derecho canónico* 351.

Bauman, R.A. (1996), *Crime and Punishment in Ancient Rome*, London.

Baumgartner, F.J. (1995), *France in the Sixteenth Century*, Basingstoke.

Baur, M. (2012), 'Law and Natural Law', in B. Davies and E. Stump (eds), *The Oxford Handbook of Aquinas*, Oxford, p. 238.

Bawcutt, N.W. (1969), 'Some Elizabethan Allusions to Machiavelli', 20 *English Miscellany* 53.

Bawcutt, N.W. (1971), '"Policy", Machiavellism and the Earlier Tudor Drama', 1 *English Literary Renaissance* 195.

Bawcutt, N.W. (2004), 'The "Myth of Gentillet" Reconsidered: An Aspect of Elizabethan Machiavellianism', 99 *Modern Language Review* 863.

Baxter, J.H. (1959), 'William Welwood of St Mary's College', in *Ecclesia: Een Bundel Opstellen aangeboden aan Prof. dr J.N. Bakhuizen van den Brink*, The Hague, p. 241.

Beale, J.H. (1914), *Bartolus on the Conflict of Laws*, Cambridge, MA.

Bean, J.M.W. (1989), *From Lord to Patron: Lordship in Late Medieval England*, Manchester.

Beck, C. (2015), 'Common Good and Private Justice: Letters of Marque and the *Utilitas publica* in Fourteenth-Century Marseilles', 41 *Journal of Medieval History* 88.

Bederman, D. (1995–6), 'Reception of the Classical Tradition in International Law: Grotius' *De iure belli ac pacis*', 16–17 *Grotiana* 3.

Bellamy, A.J. (2008), *Just Wars: From Cicero to Iraq*, Cambridge.

Bellamy, J.G. (1970), *The Law of Treason in England in the Later Middle Ages*, Cambridge.

Bellomo, M. (1995), *The Common Legal Past of Europe, 1000–1800*, tr. L.G. Cochrane, Washington.

Benardete, S. (1987), 'Cicero's *De legibus* I: Its Plan and Intention', 108 *American Journal of Philology* 295.

Benedict, P. (2002), 'The Wars of Religion, 1562–98', in M.P. Holt (ed.), *Renaissance and Reformation France, 1500–1648*, Oxford, p. 147.

Benjamin, E.B. (1957), 'Sir John Hayward and Tacitus', 8 *Review of English Studies* 275.

Benner, E. (2009), *Machiavelli's Ethics*, Princeton.

Bennett, M. (2010), 'Legality and Legitimacy in War and Its Conduct, 1350–1650', in F. Tallett and D.J.B. Trim (eds), *European Warfare, 1350–1750*, Cambridge, p. 264.

Benton, L. (2005), 'Legal Spaces of Empire: Piracy and the Origins of Ocean Regionalism', 47 *Comparative Studies in Society and History* 700.

Benton, L. (2010a), *A Search for Sovereignty: Law and Geography in European Empires, 1400–1900*, Cambridge.

Benton, L. (2010b), 'Legalities of the Sea in Gentili's *Hispanica advocatio*', in B. Kingsbury and B. Straumann (eds), *The Roman Foundations of the Law of Nations: Alberico Gentili and Justice of Empire*, Oxford, p. 269.

Benton, L. (2011a), 'Historical Perspectives on Legal Pluralism', 3 *Hague Journal on the Rule of Law* 57.

Benton, L. (2011b), 'Towards a New Legal History of Piracy: Maritime Legalities and the Myth of Universal Jurisdiction', (2011) 23 *International Journal of Maritime History* 225.

Berckman, E. (1979), *Victims of Piracy: The Admiralty Court, 1575–1678*, London.

Berger, A. (1953), *Encyclopaedic Dictionary of Roman Law*, Philadelphia.

Berkowitz, D.S. (1988), *John Selden's Formative Years: Politics and Society in Early Seventeenth Century England*, Washington.

Berman, P.S. (2006–7), 'Global Legal Pluralism', 80 *California Law Review* 1155.

Bicheno, H. (2012), *Elizabeth's Sea Dogs: How the English Became the Scourge of the Seas*, London.

Biller, P. (1998), 'Confession in the Middle Ages: Introduction', in P. Biller and A.J. Minnis (eds), *Handling Sin: Confession in the Middle Ages*, Woodbridge, p. 3.

Binns, J.W. (1972), 'Alberico Gentili in Defence of Poetry and Acting', 19 *Studies in the Renaissance* 224.

Bireley, R. (1990), *The Counter-Reformation Prince: Anti-Machiavellianism or Catholic Statecraft in Early Modern Europe*, Chapel Hill, NC.

Bjork, D.K. (1943), 'Piracy in the Baltic, 1375–98', 18 *Speculum* 39.

Black, J. (2004), *The British Seaborne Empire*, New Haven.

Black, J.B. (1931), 'Queen Elizabeth, the Sea Beggars and the Capture of Brille, 1572', 46 *English Historical Review* 30.

Blakeway, A. (2015), *Regency in Sixteenth-Century Scotland*, Woodbridge.

Bleznick, D.W. (1958), 'Spanish Reaction to Machiavelli in the Sixteenth and Seventeenth Centuries', 19 *Journal of the History of Ideas* 542.

Bolsée, J. (1932), *Inventaire des archives des conseils et sièges d'amirauté*, Tongres.

Bonney, R. (1991), *The European Dynastic States, 1494–1660*, Oxford.

Borges de Macedo, P.E.V. (2017), *Catholic and Reformed Traditions in International Law: A Comparison between the Suarezian and Grotian Concept of Ius gentium*, Cham.

Born, L.K. (1928), 'The Perfect Prince: A Study in Thirteenth and Fourteenth Century Ideals', 3 *Speculum* 470.

Borschberg, P. (1999), 'Grotius, East India Trade and the King of Johor', 30 *Journal of Southeast Asian Studies* 225.

Borschberg, P. (2002), 'The Seizure of the *Sta Catarina* Revisited: The Portuguese Empire in Asia, VOC Politics and the Origins of the Dutch-Johor Alliance', 33 *Journal of Southeast Asian Studies* 31.

Borschberg, P. (2009), 'Grotius, Maritime Intra-Asian Trade and the Portuguese *Estado da Índia*: Problems, Perspectives and Insights from *De iure praedae*', in H.W. Blom (ed.), *Property, Piracy and Punishment: Hugo Grotius on War and Booty in De iure praedae – Concepts and Contexts*, Leiden, p. 31.

Borschberg, P. (2011), *Hugo Grotius, the Portuguese and Free Trade in the East Indies*, Singapore.

Borschberg, P. (2021), 'Grotius and the East Indies', in R. Lesaffer and J. Nijman (eds), *The Cambridge Companion to Hugo Grotius*, Cambridge, p. 65.

Bossuat, A. (1947), 'La règlement des confiscations sous le règne de Charles VII', 91 *Comptes-rendus des séances de l'Académie des Inscriptions et Belles-Lettres* 6.

Bossy, J. (1975), 'The Social History of Confession in the Age of the Reformation', 25 *Transactions of the Royal Historical Society* 21.

Boucher, D. (1998), *Political Theories of International Relations*, Oxford.

Boucher, D. (2009), *The Limits of Ethics in International Relations: Natural Law, Natural Rights and Human Rights in Transition*, Oxford.

Bowsky, W.M. (1967), 'A New *Consilium* of Cino of Pistoia (1324): Citizenship, Residence and Taxation', 42 *Speculum* 431.

Boxer, C.R. (1965), *The Dutch Seaborne Empire, 1600–1800*, London.

Bragues, G. (2010), 'Profiting with Honor: Cicero's Vision of Leadership', 97 *Journal of Business Ethics* 21.

Brandon, P. (2015), *War, Capital and the Dutch State, 1588–1795*, Leiden.

Brasington, B.C. (2009), '*Antiquis fas erat*: Reflections on Custom in Glosses to Ivo of Chartres' *Panormia*', in P. Andersen and M. Münster-Swendson (eds), *Custom: The Development and Use of a Legal Concept in the Middle Ages*, Copenhagen, p. 81.

Braudel, F. (1972), *The Mediterranean and the Mediterranean World in the Age of Philp II*, 2 vols, tr. S. Reynolds, London.

Braun, H.E. (2007), *Juan de Mariana and Early Modern Spanish Political Thought*, Aldershot.

Braund, D. (1993), 'Piracy under the Principate and the Ideology of Imperial Eradication', in J. Rich and G. Shipley (eds), *War and Society in the Roman World*, London, p. 195.

Braunstein, P. (1987), 'La capture d'un coque vénetienne sur la route de Flandre au début du XVe siècle', in H. Dubois, J.-C. Hocquet and A. Vauchez (eds), *Horizons marins, itinéraires spirituels, Ve–XVIIIe siècles*, 2 vols, Paris, vol. 2, p. 123.

Bravo, B. (1980), 'Sulân: Représailles et justice privée contre des étrangers dans les citées grecques (étude du vocabulaire et des institutions)', 10 *Annali della Scuola Normale Superiore di Pisa* 705.

Bravo, B. (1981), 'Androlèpsia: La 'prise d'hommes' comme vengeance d'un meurtre commis dans une cité étrangère', in J. Modrzejewski and D. Liebs (eds), *Symposion 1977: Vorträge zur Griechischen und Hellenistischen Rechtsgeschichte*, Cologne, p. 131.

Bresc, H. (1980), 'Course et piraterie en Sicile, 1250–1450', 10 *Anuario de estudios medievales* 751.

Brett, A.S. (1997), *Liberty, Right and Nature: Individual Rights in Later Scholastic Thought*, Cambridge.

Brett, A.S. (2002), 'Natural Right and Civil Community: The Civil Philosophy of Hugo Grotius', 45 *Historical Journal* 31.

Brett, A.S. (2011), *Changes of State: Nature and the Limits of the City in Early-Modern Natural Law*, Princeton.

Brett, A.S. (2012), 'Francisco de Vitoria (1483–1546) and Francisco Suárez (1548–1617)', in B. Fassbender and A. Peters (eds), *The Oxford Handbook of the History of International Law*, Oxford, p. 1086.

Brett, A.S. (2014), 'Luis de Molina on Law and Power', in M. Kaufmann and A. Aichele (eds), *A Companion to Luis de Molina*, Leiden, p. 155.

Brett, A.S. (2019), 'The Subject of Sovereignty: Law, Politics and Moral Reasoning in Hugo Grotius', 17 *Modern Intellectual History* 619.

Breward, I. (1968), 'William Perkins and the Origins of Reformed Casuistry', 40 *Evangelical Quarterly* 3.

Brodman, J.W. (1985), 'Municipal Ransoming Law on the Medieval Spanish Frontier', 60 *Speculum* 318.

Brodman, J.W. (1986), *Ransoming Captives in Crusader Spain: The Order of Merced on the Christian-Islamic Frontier*, Philadelphia.

Brooke, C. (2008), 'Grotius, Stoicism and *Oikeiosis*', 29 *Grotiana* 25.

Brooks, F.W. (1925), 'William de Wrotham and the Office of Keeper of the King's Ports and Galleys', 40 *English Historical Review* 570.

Brooks, F.W. (1933), *The English Naval Forces, 1199–1272*, London.

Brouwer, R. (2008), 'On the Ancient Background of Grotius' Notion of Natural Law', 29 *Grotiana* 1.

Brouwer, R. (2015), 'Ulpian's Appeal to Nature: Roman Law as Universal Law', 83 *Tijdschrift voor Rechtsgeschiedenis* 60.

Brouwer, R. (2021), *Law and Philosophy in the Late Roman Republic*, Cambridge.

Brown, J.L. (1939), *The Methodus ad facilem historiarum cognitionem of Jean Bodin: A Critical Study*, Washington.

Brown, K.M. (1986), *Bloodfeud in Scotland, 1573–1625: Violence, Justice and Politics in an Early-Modern Society*, Edinburgh.

Brown, K.M. (1991), 'From Scottish Lords to British Officers: State Building, Elite Integration and the Army in the Seventeenth Century', in N. Macdougall (ed.), *Scotland and War, AD 79–1918*, Edinburgh, p. 133.

Brown, K.M. (1992), *Kingdom or Province? Scotland and the Regal Union, 1603–1715*, Basingstoke.

Bruijn, J.R. (2011), *The Dutch Navy of the Seventeenth and Eighteenth Centuries*, St John's, NL.

Brundage, J.A. (1976), 'Holy War and the Medieval Lawyers', in T.P. Murphy (ed.), *The Holy War*, Columbus, OH, p. 99.

Buckland, W.W. (1963), *A Text-Book of Roman Law from Augustus to Justinian*, Cambridge.

Buescu, A.I. (1993), 'The Utopia of a Perfect Prince: Recurrences in Modern Europe's "Mirrors for the Prince"', 16 *History of European Ideas* 599.

Buisseret, D. (1984), *Henry IV, King of France*, London.

Bunge, K. (2017), 'Francisco de Vitoria: A Redesign of Global Order on the Threshold of the Middle Ages to Modern Times', in S. Kadelbach, T. Kleinlein and D. Roth-Isigkeit (eds), *System, Order and International Law: Legal Thought from Machievelli to Hegel*, Oxford, p. 38.

Burgess, G. (1992), *The Politics of the Ancient Constitution: An Introduction to English Political Thought, 1603–42*, Basingstoke.

Burke, P. (1969), 'Tacitism', in T.A. Dorey (ed.), *Tacitus*, London, p. 149.

Burke, P. (1991), 'Tacitism, Scepticism and Reason of State', in J.H. Burns (ed.), *The Cambridge History of Political Thought, 1450–1700*, Cambridge, p. 479.

Burke-White, W.W. (2003–4), 'International Legal Pluralism', 25 *Michigan Journal of International Law* 963.

Burns, R.I. (1984), *Muslims, Christians and Jews in the Crusader Kingdom of Valencia: Societies in Symbiosis*, Cambridge.

Burwash, D. (1947), *English Merchant Shipping, 1460–1540*, Toronto.

Byrne, E.H. (1920), 'Genoese Trade with Syria in the Twelfth Century', 25 *American Historical Review* 191.

Cam, H.M. (1921), *Studies in the Hundred Rolls: Some Aspects of Thirteenth-Century Administration*, Oxford.

Camerlingo, R. (2013), '*Henry V* and the Just War: Shakespeare, Gentili and Machiavelli', in A. Arienzo and A. Petrina (eds), *Machiavellian Encounters in Tudor and Stuart England: Literary and Political Influences from the Reformation to the Restoration*, Farnham, p. 103.

Canning, J. (1987), *The Political Thought of Baldus de Ubaldis*, Cambridge.

Canning, J. (2017), 'The Medieval Roman and Canon Law Origins of International Law', in W. Bain (ed.), *Medieval Foundations of International Relations*, Abingdon, p. 102.

Canning, J. (2018), 'The Universal Rule of Law in the Thought of the Late Medieval Jurists of Roman and Canon Law', in A. Carty and J. Nijman (eds), *Morality and Responsibility of Rulers: European and Chinese Origins of a Rule of Law as Justice for World Order*, Oxford, p. 55.

Capmany y de Monpalar, A. de (1961–3), *Memorias históricas sobre la marina, commercio y artes de la antigua ciudad de Barcelona*, 3 vols, ed. E. Giralt y Raventós and C. Batlle y Gallart, Barcelona.

Capps, P. (2011), 'Natural Law and the Law of Nations', in A. Orakhelashvili (ed.), *Research Handbook on the Theory and History of International Law*, Cheltenham, p. 61.

Carleton, C. (1983), *Charles I: The Personal Monarch*, London.

Carroll, S. (1998), *Noble Power during the French Wars of Religion: The Guise Affinity and the Catholic Cause in Normandy*, Cambridge.

Carroll, S. (2009), *Martyrs and Murderers: The Guise Family and the Making of Europe*, Oxford.

Carswell, A. (2012), '"Mercenaries": The Scottish Soldier in Foreign Service, 1568–1860', in E.M. Spiers, J.A. Craig and M.J. Strickland (eds), *A Military History of Scotland*, Edinburgh, p. 248.

Carty, A.J. (1981), 'The Law of Nature and Nations as a Source', in D.M. Walker (ed.), *Stair Tercentenary Studies*, Edinburgh, p. 127.

Caruana, L. (2008), 'The Jesuits and the Quiet Side of the Scientific Revolution', in T. Worcester (ed.), *The Cambridge Companion to the Jesuits*, Cambridge, p. 243.

Casado Soto, J.L. (1991), 'Atlantic Shipping in Sixteenth Century Spain and the 1588 Armada', in M.J. Rodriguez-Salgado and S. Adams (eds), *England, Spain and the Gran Armada, 1585–1604*, Edinburgh, p. 95.

Caselli, C. (2013), 'Genoa, Genoese Merchants and the Ottoman Empire in the First Half of the Fifteenth Century: Rumours and Reality', 25 *Al-Masāq* 252.

Casson, L. (1991), *The Ancient Mariners: Seafarers and Sea Fighters of the Mediterranean in Ancient Times*, Princeton.

Cavill, P.R. (2013), 'Heresy and Forfeiture in Marian England', 56 *Historical Journal* 879.

Cavill, P.R. (2014), 'Heresy, Law and the State: Forfeiture in Late Medieval and Early Modern England', 129 *English Historical Review* 270.

Chadwick, M. (2019), *Piracy and the Origins of Universal Jurisdiction: On Stranger Tides?*, Leiden.

Chavarot, M.-C. (1991), 'La pratique des lettres de marque d'après les arrêts du parlement, XIIIe-début XVIe siècle', 51 *Bibliothèque de l'École des Chartes* 51.

Cheyette, F.L. (1970), 'The Sovereign and the Pirates, 1332', 45 *Speculum* 40.

Cheyney, E.P. (1929), 'England and Denmark in the Later Days of Queen Elizabeth', 1 *Journal of Modern History* 9.

Cheyney, E.P. (1905), 'International Law under Queen Elizabeth', 20 *English Historical Review* 659.

Childs, D. (2009), *Tudor Sea Power: The Foundation of Greatness*, Barnsley.

Christianson, P. (1991), 'Royal and Parliamentary Voices in the Ancient Constitution, c. 1604–21', in L. Levy Peck (ed.), *The Mental World of the Jacobean Court*, Cambridge, p. 71.

Christianson, P. (1996), *Discourse on History, Law and Governance in the Public Career of John Selden, 1610–35*, Toronto.

Chroust, A.H. (1943), 'Hugo Grotius and the Scholastic Natural Law Tradition', 17 *New Scholasticism* 101.

Clarence Smith, J.A. (1970), 'Bartolo on the Conflict of Laws', 14 *American Journal of Legal History* 157.

Clark, G. (1933), 'The English Practice with Regard to Reprisals by Private Persons', 27 *American Journal of International Law* 694.

Clark, G.N. and van Eysinga, W.J.M. (1951), 'The Colonial Conferences between England and the Netherlands in 1613 and 1615', 17 *Bibliothecha Visseriana* pt 34.

Clark, V.E. (1921), *The Port of Aberdeen: A History of Its Trade and Shipping from the 12th Century to the Present Day*, Aberdeen.

Clavel-Lévêque, M. (1978), 'Brigandage et piraterie: Représentations idéologiques et pratiques impérialistes au dernier siècle de la république', 4 *Dialogues d'histoire ancienne* 17.

Cogswell, T. (1984), 'Foreign Policy and Parliament: The Case of La Rochelle, 1625–6', 99 *English Historical Review* 214.

Cogswell, T. (1989), *The Blessed Revolution: English Politics and the Coming of War, 1621–4*, Cambridge.

Colás, A. and Mabee, B. (2010), 'The Flow and Ebb of Private Seaborne Violence in Global Politics: Lessons from the Atlantic World, 1689–1815', in A. Colás and B. Mabee (eds), *Mercenaries, Pirates, Bandits and Empires: Private Violence in Historical Context*, London, p. 83.

Coleman, D. (2013), 'Of Corsairs, Converts and Renegades: Forms and Functions of Coastal Raiding on Both Sides of the Far Western Mediterranean, 1490–1540', 19 *Medieval Encounters* 167.

Colish, M.L. (1978), 'Cicero's *De officiis* and Machiavelli's *Prince*', 9 *Sixteenth Century Journal* 80.

Colish, M.L. (1985), *The Stoic Tradition from Antiquity to the Early Middle Ages*, 2 vols, Leiden.

Colish, M.L. (1998), 'Machiavelli's Art of War: A Reconsideration', 51 *Renaissance Quarterly* 1151.

Colombos, C.J. (1967), *The International Law of the Sea*, London.

Condren, C. (2009), 'Understanding Shakespeare's Perfect Prince: Henry V, the Ethics of Office and the French Prisoners', 9 *Shakespeare International Yearbook* 195.

Conklin, W.E. (2010), 'The Myth of Primordialism in Cicero's Theory of *Ius gentium*', 23 *Leiden Journal of International Law* 479.

Contamine, P. (1972), *Guerre, état et société à la fin du Moyen Âge: Études sur les armées des rois de France, 1337–1494*, Paris.

Contamine, P. (2000), 'The Growth of State Control: Practices of War, 1300–1800 – Ransom and Booty', in P. Contamine (ed.), *War and Competition between States*, Oxford, p. 163.

Conybeare, J.A.C. and Sandler, T. (1993), 'State-Sponsored Violence as a Tragedy of the Commons: England's Privateering Wars with France and Spain, 1625–30', 77 *Public Choice* 879.

Cooperstein, T.M. (2009), 'Letters of Marque and Reprisal: The Constitutional Law and Practice of Privateering', 40 *Journal of Maritime Law and Commerce* 221.

Coquillette, D.R. (1988), *The Civilian Writers of Doctors' Commons, London: Three Centuries of Juristic Innovation in Comparative, Commercial and International Law*, Berlin.

Corbett, J.S. (1988), *Drake and the Tudor Navy*, 2 vols, Aldershot.

Cordes, A. (2003), 'The Search for a Medieval *Lex mercatoria*', 5 Oxford University Comparative Law Forum (www.ouclf.iuscomp.org/articles/cordes).

Cordes, A. (2017), '*Lex maritima*? Local, Regional and Universal Maritime Law in the Middle Ages', in W. Blockmans, M. Kron and J. Wubs-Mrozewicz (eds), *Routledge Handbook of Maritime Trade around Europe, 1300–1600: Commercial Networks and Urban Autonomy*, Abingdon, p. 69.

Cordes, A. and Höhn, P. (2018), 'Extra-Legal and Legal Conflict Management among Long-Distance Traders, 1250–1650', in H. Pihlajamäki, M.D. Dubber and M. Godfrey (eds), *The Oxford Handbook of European Legal History*, Oxford, p. 509.

Corey, D.D. and Charles, J.D. (2012), *Just War Tradition: An Introduction*, Wilmington, DE.

Cormack, B. (2007), *A Power to Do Justice: Jurisdiction, English Literature and the Rise of Common Law, 1509–1625*, Chicago.

Corsi, M.R.D. (2012), 'Piracy or Policy? Lübeck's 1249 Attack on Copenhagen', 8 *Viking and Medieval Scandinavia* 53.

Corvisier, A. (1983), 'Une ville nouvelle au destin ambitieux', in A. Corvisier (ed.), *Histoire du Havre et de l'estuaire de la Seine*, Toulouse, p. 45.

Costello, F.B. (1974), *The Political Philosophy of Luis de Molina, S.J., 1535–1600*, Rome.

Coulet du Gard, R. (1980), *La course et la piraterie en Méditerranée*, Paris.

Couzinet, M.D. (2013), 'On Bodin's Method', in H.A. Lloyd (ed.), *The Reception of Bodin*, Leiden, p. 39.

Covell, C. (2009), *The Law of Nations in Political Thought: A Critical Survey from Vitoria to Hegel*, Basingstoke.

Coyle, S. (2017), 'Natural Law in Aquinas and Suárez', 8 *Jurisprudence* 319.

Craigie, W., Aitken, A.J., Stevenson, J.A.C., Watson, H.D. and Dareau, M.G., eds, (1931–2002), *A Dictionary of the Older Scottish Tongue from the Twelfth Century to the End of the Seventeenth*, 12 vols, Chicago, London and Aberdeen.

Craigwood, J. (2011), 'Sidney, Gentili and the Poetics of Embassy', in R. Adams and R. Cox (eds), *Diplomacy and Early Modern Culture*, Basingstoke, p. 82.

Crane, M.T. (1988), '*Video et taceo*: Elizabeth I and the Rhetoric of Counsel', 28 *Studies in English Literature* 1.

Craven, F.W. (1930), 'The Earl of Warwick, a Speculator in Piracy', 10 *Hispanic American Historical Review* 457.

Craze, S. (2016), 'Prosecuting Privateers for Piracy: How Piracy Law Transitioned from Treason to a Crime against Property', 28 *International Journal of Maritime History* 654.

Cremean, D.J. (2012), 'Historic Origins of the Admiralty Court', *Journal of Business Law* 350.

Croft, P. (1989), 'Trading with the Enemy, 1585–1604', 32 *Historical Journal* 281.

Croft, P. (1991), 'English Commerce with Spain and the Armada War, 1558–1603', in M.J. Rodriguez-Salgado and S. Adams (eds), *England, Spain and the Gran Armada, 1585–1604*, Edinburgh, p. 236.

Croft, P. (2003), *King James*, Basingstoke.

Croft, P. (2006), '*Rex pacificus*, Robert Cecil and the 1604 Peace with Spain', in G. Burgess, R. Wymer and J. Lawrence (eds), *The Accession of James I*, Basingstoke, p. 140.

Cromartie, A. (2000), 'Theology and Politics in Richard Hooker's Thought', 21 *History of Political Thought* 41.

Crowe, M.B. (1977), *The Changing Profile of the Natural Law*, The Hague.

Cruickshank, C.G. (1969), *Army Royal: Henry VIII's Invasion of France, 1513*, Oxford.

Cummins, J. (1995), *Francis Drake: The Lives of a Hero*, London.

Curry, A. (2008), 'The Military Ordinances of Henry V: Texts and Contexts', in C. Given-Wilson, A. Kettle and L. Scales (eds), *War, Government and Aristocracy in the British Isles, c. 1150–1500: Essays in Honour of Michael Prestwich*, Woodbridge, p. 214.

Curry, A. (2011), 'Disciplinary Ordinances for English and Franco-Scottish Armies in 1385: An International Code?', 37 *Journal of Medieval Studies* 269.

Cushway, G. (2011), *Edward III and the War at Sea: The English Navy, 1327–77*, Woodbridge.

Cust, R. (2005), *Charles I: A Political Life*, Harlow.

Daniels, T. (2019), 'Popes and Pirates: Vatican Sources Regarding Violence at Sea', in T. Heebøll-Holm, P. Höhn and G. Rohmann (eds), *Merchants, Pirates and Smugglers: Criminalisation, Economics and the Transformation of the Maritime World, 1200–1600*, Frankfurt, p. 75.

Dareste, R. (1889), 'Le droit de représailles', 2 *Revue des études grecques* 305.

Darsel, J. (2012), *L'Amirauté en Bretagne des origines à la fin du XVIIIe siècle*, Rennes.

Daussy, H. (2015), 'Financing the Huguenot War Effort during the Early Wars of Religion, 1562–70', 38 *French Historical Studies* 593.

Davidson, J.D.J. (2003), *Scots and the Sea*, Edinburgh.

Davies, C. (2001), 'Baltasar Álamos de Barrientos and the Nature of Spanish Tacitism', in N. and C Griffin, E. Southworth and C. Thompson (eds), *Culture and Society in Habsburg Spain*, London, p. 57.

Davies, R.R. (1970), 'The Law of the March', 5 *Welsh History Review* 1.

Davis, G.S. (1997), 'Conscience and Conquest: Francisco de Vitoria on Justice in the New World', 13 *Modern Theology* 476.

Dawson, J.D. (1983), 'Richard FitzRalph and the Fourteenth-Century Poverty Controversies', 34 *Journal of Ecclesiastical History* 315.

Dawson, J.E.A. (2007), *Scotland Re-Formed, 1488–1587*, Edinburgh.

De Aguilar, J.M. (1946), 'The Law of Nations and the Salamanca School of Theology', 9 *Thomist* 186.

Deák, F. and Jessup, P.C. (1932–3), 'Prize Law Procedure at Sea: Its Early Development', 7 *Tulane Law Review* 488.

De Chastenet d'Esterre, J. (1906), *Histoire de l'amirauté en France*, Paris.

Decock, W. (2012), *Theologians and Contract Law: The Moral Transformation of the 'Ius commune', ca. 1500–1650*, Leiden.

Decock, W. (2013), 'Adrian of Utrecht (1459–1523) at the Crossroads of Law and Morality: Conscience, Equity and the Legal Nature of Early-Modern Practical Theology', 81 *Tijdschrift voor Rechtsgeschiedenis* 573.

Decock, W. (2017), 'Collaborative Legal Pluralism: Confessors as Law Enforcers in Mercado's Advice on Economic Governance (1571)', 25 *Rechtsgeschichte* 103.

De Courcelles, D. (2005), 'Managing the world: The Development of *Ius gentium* by the Theologians of Salamanca in the Sixteenth Century', 38 *Philosophy and Rhetoric* 1.

De la Brière, Y. (1928), 'Évolution de la doctrine et de la pratique en matière de représailles', 22 *Recueil des cours* 241.

Delafosse, M. (1963), 'Les corsaires protestants à La Rochelle, 1570–7', 121 *Bibliothèque de l'École des Chartes* 187.

Delahunty, R.J. (2014), 'The Conscience of a King: Law, Religion and War in Shakespeare's King Henry V', 53 *Journal of Catholic Legal Studies* 129.

De Landtscheer, J. (2013), 'On Good Government: Erasmus' *Institutio principis Christiani* versus Lipsius' *Politica*', in K.A.E. Enenkel (ed.), *The Reception of Erasmus in the Early Modern Period*, Leiden, p. 179.

De Mas Latrie, L. (1852–61), *Histoire de l'île de Chypre sous le règne des princes de la maison de Lusignan*, 3 vols, Paris.

De Mas Latrie, R. (1866), 'Du droit de marque ou droit de représaille au Moyen Âge', 27 *Bibliothèque de l'École des chartes* 529.

De Meij, J.C.A. (1972), *De Watergeuzen en de Nederlanden, 1568–72*, Amsterdam.

Den Tex, J. (1973), *Oldenbarnevelt*, 2 vols, tr. R.B. Powell, Cambridge.

De Pablo, J. (1956), 'L'armée de mer huguenote pendant la troisième guerre de religion', 47 *Archiv für Reformationsgeschichte* 64.

De Roover, F.E. (1945), 'A Prize of War: A Painting of Fifteenth Century Merchants', 19 *Bulletin of the Business Historical Society* 3.

Derrett, J.D.M. (1974), 'The Works of Francis Clerke, Proctor', 40 *Studia et documenta historiae et iuris* 52.

De Smet, I.A.R. (2006), *Thuanus: The Making of Jacques-Auguste de Thou, 1553–1617*, Geneva.

De Somogyi, N. (1998), *Shakespeare's Theatre of War*, Aldershot.

De Souza, P. (1999), *Piracy in the Graeco-Roman World*, Cambridge.

De Wilde, M (2018), 'Enemy of All Humanity: The Dehumanizing Effects of a Dangerous Concept', 47 *Netherlands Journal of Legal Philosophy* 158.

De Witte, R.P. (2007), 'Let Privateers Marque Terrorism: A Proposal for a Reawakening', 82 *Indiana Law Journal* 131.

De Zulueta, F. (1953), *The Institutes of Gaius, Part II: Commentary*, Oxford.

Dick, B.D. (2010), '"Framing Piracy": Restitution at Sea in the Later Middle Ages', PhD dissertation, University of Glasgow.

Dickinson, W.C. (1958), 'Courts of Special Jurisdiction', in G.C.H. Paton (ed.), *An Introduction to Scottish Legal History*, Edinburgh, p. 396.

Dietz, B. (1952–8), 'The Huguenot and English Corsairs during the Third Civil War in France, 1568 to 1570', 19 *Proceedings of the Huguenot Society of London* 278.

Dimmock, M. (2007), 'Crusading Piracy? The Curious Case of the Spanish in the Channel, 1590–95', in C. Jowett (ed.), *Pirates? The Politics of Plunder, 1550–1650*, Basingstoke, p. 74.

Ditchburn, D. (1992a), 'Piracy and War at Sea in Late-Medieval Scotland', in T.C. Smout (ed.), *Scotland and the Sea*, Edinburgh, p. 35.

Ditchburn, D. (1992b) 'The Pirate, the Policeman and the Pantomime Star: Aberdeen's Alternative Economy in the Early Fifteenth Century', 12 *Northern Scotland* 19.

Ditchburn, D. (2000), 'Bremen Piracy and Scottish Periphery: The North Sea World in the 1440s', in A.I. Macinnes, T. Riis and F.G. Pedersen (eds), *Ships, Guns and Bibles in the North Sea and the Baltic States, c.1350-c.1700*, East Linton, p. 1.

Dodd, L. (2016), 'Thomas Craig's Aetiology of Law and Society: Literary Dependence and Independence in the *Jus feudale*', 37 *Journal of Legal History* 121.

Dolezalek, G. (1992), 'The Moral Theologians' Doctrine of Restitution and Its Juridification in the Sixteenth and Seventeenth Centuries', *Acta Juridica* 104.

Dollinger, P. (1970), *The German Hansa*, tr. D.S. Ault and S.H. Steinberg, London.

Domingo, R. and Minnucci, G. (2020), 'Alberico Gentili and the Secularisation of the Law of Nations', in R. Domingo and J. Witte (eds), *Christianity and Global Law: An Introduction*, Abingdon, p. 98.

Donaldson, G. (1965), *Scotland: James V to James VII*, Edinburgh.

Doran, S. (2000), *Elizabeth I and Foreign Policy, 1558–1603*, London.

Dotson, J.E. (2003), 'Commercial Law in Fourteenth-Century Merchant Manuals', 9 *Medieval Encounters* 204.

Doucet, R. (1948), *Les institutions de la France au XVIe siècle*, 2 vols, Paris.

Douglas, A.E. (1965), 'Cicero the Philosopher', in T.A. Dorey (ed.), *Cicero*, New York, p. 135.

Drake, W.R. (1849), 'Notes upon the Capture of the "Great Carrack" in 1592', 33 *Archaeologia* 209.

Draper, G.I.A.D. (1990), 'Grotius' Place in the Development of Legal Ideas about War', in H. Bull, B. Kingsbury and A. Roberts (eds), *Hugo Grotius and International Relations*, Oxford, p. 177.

Du Cange, Charles du Fresne, sieur (1884–7), *Glossarium mediae et infimae Latinitatis*, 10 vols, Niort.

Dufourcq, C.E. (1980), 'Chrétiens et Musulmans durant les derniers siècles du Moyen Âge', 10 *Anuario de estudios medievales* 207.

Duke, A. (1999), 'Dissident Propaganda and Political Organisation at the Outbreak of the Revolt of the Netherlands', in P. Benedict, G. Marnef, H. van Nierop and M. Venard (eds), *Reformation, Revolt and Civil War in France and the Netherlands, 1555–85*, Amsterdam, p. 115.

Dumas, A. (1908), *Étude sur le jugement des prises maritimes en France jusqu'à la suppression de l'office d'amiral, 1627*, Paris.

Dunthorne, H. (1996), 'Scots in the Wars of the Low Countries, 1572–1648', in G.G. Simpson (ed.), *Scotland and the Low Countries, 1124–1994*, East Linton, p. 109.

Dürr, R. (2014), 'Confession as an Instrument of Church Discipline: A Study of Catholic and Lutheran Confessional Manuals from the 16th and 17th Centuries', in S. Müller and C. Schweiger (eds), *Between Creativity and Norm-Making: Tensions in the Early-Modern Era*, Leiden, p. 215.

Dyck, A.R. (1996), *A Commentary on Cicero's De officiis*, Ann Arbor.

Dyck, A.R. (2004), *A Commentary on Cicero, De legibus*, Ann Arbor.

Dyjakowska, M. (2012), 'Fund Collection through Litigation by the State Treasury in the Roman Empire (with Special Reference to the First Three Centuries AD)', 2 *Studia Ceranea* 27.

Dyson, H. (2008), 'What Kind of Cosmopolitans Were the Stoics? The Cosmic City in the Early Stoa', 25 *Polis* 182.

Earle, P. (2003), *The Pirate Wars*, London.

Eddison, J. (2013), *Medieval Pirates: Pirates, Raiders and Privateers, 1204–1453*, Stroud.

Edelstein, D. (2009), *The Terror of Natural Right: Republicanism, the Cult of Nature and the French Revolution*, Oxford.

Edmond, G. (1995), 'The Freedom of Histories: Reassessing Grotius on the Sea', 2 *Law/Text/Culture* 179.

Edmundson, G. (1911), *Anglo-Dutch Rivalry during the First Half of the Seventeenth Century*, Oxford.

Edwards, C.S. (1981), *Hugo Grotius, the Miracle of Holland: A Study of Political and Legal Thought*, Chicago.

Eiglier, J. (1888), *Étude historique sur le droit de marque ou de représailles a Marseilles aux XIIIe, XIVe et XVe siècles*, Marseilles.

Elliott, J.H. (2000), *Europe Divided, 1559–98*, Oxford.

Elliott, J.H. (2006), *Empires of the Atlantic World: Britain and Spain in America, 1492–1830*, New Haven.

Engberg-Pedersen, T. (2000), *Paul and the Stoics*, Edinburgh.

Engberg-Pedersen, T. (2004), 'Stoicism in the Apostle Paul: A Philosophical Reading', in S.K. Strange and J. Zupko (eds), *Stoicism: Traditions and Transformations*, Cambridge, p. 52.

Engelmann, A. (1928), *A History of Continental Civil Procedure*, London.

Enthoven, V. (2009), 'A Diabolical Dilemma: Zeeland and the Command of the Scheldt River, 1572–1609', 21 *International Journal of Maritime History* 101.

Erdody, J. (2018), 'Understanding the Concept of *Ius naturale* in Ancient Roman Law', 9 *Journal on European History of Law* 178.

Esper, T. (1967), 'A Sixteenth-Century Anti-Russian Arms Embargo', 15 *Jahrbücher für Geschichte Osteuropas* 180.

Eyffinger, A. (1998), '*Amoena gravitate morum spectabilis*: Justus Lipsius and Hugo Grotius', in M. Laureys (ed.), *The World of Justus Lipsius: A Contribution Towards His Intellectual Biography*, Brussels, p. 297.

Ezeani, E.C. (2012), 'The 21st Century Terrorist: *Hostis humani generis*', 3 *Beijing Law Review* 158.

Falconer, J.R.D. (2013), *Crime and Community in Reformation Scotland: Negotiating Power in a Burgh Society*, London.

Fallon, J.A. (1972), 'Scottish Mercenaries in the Service of Denmark and Sweden, 1626–32', PhD dissertation, University of Glasgow.

Farrell, P.M. (1957), 'Sources of St Thomas' Concept of Natural Law', 20 *Thomist* 237.

Febvre, L. (1982), *The Problem of Unbelief in the Sixteenth Century: The Religion of Rabelais*, tr. B. Gottlieb, Cambridge, MA.

Fedele, D. (2016), 'The Status of Ambassadors in Lucas de Penna's Commentary on the *Tres libri*', 84 *Tijdschrift voor Rechtsgeschiedenis* 165.

Fedele, D. (2017), *Naissance de la diplomatie moderne, XIIIe–XVIIe siècles: L'ambassadeur au croisement du droit, de l'éthique at de la politique*, Baden-Baden.

Fedele, D. (2021), *The Medieval Foundations of International Law: Baldus de Ubaldis (1327–1400), Doctrine and Practice of the Ius gentium*, Leiden.

Feingold, M. (2017), 'What's in a Date? Alberico Gentili and the Genesis of *De legationibus libri tres*', 64 *Notes and Queries* 312.

Ferguson, W. (1977), *Scotland's Relations with England: A Survey to 1707*, Edinburgh.

Fermoy, B.E.R. (1926), 'A Maritime Indenture of 1212', 41 *English Historical Review* 556.

Fernandes, J.M.A.A. (2014), 'Luis de Molina: On War', in M. Kaufmann and A. Aichele (eds), *A Companion to Luis de Molina*, Leiden, p. 228.

Fernández-Santamaría, J.A. (1977), *The State, War and Peace: Spanish Political Thought in the Renaissance, 1516–59*, Cambridge.

Fernández-Santamaría, J.A. (2005–6), *Natural Law, Constitutionalism, Reason of State and War: Counter-Reformation Spanish Political Thought*, 2 vols, New York.

Ferrary, J.-L. (1995), '*Ius fetiale* et diplomatie', in E. Frézouls and A. Jacquemin (eds), *Les relations internationales*, Strasbourg, p. 411.

Fink, A. (2012), 'The Hanseatic League and the Concept of Functional Overlapping Competing Jurisdictions', 65 *Kyklos* 194.

Finlay, J. (2002), 'Foreign Litigants before the College of Justice in the Sixteenth Century', in H.L. MacQueen (ed.), *Stair Society: Miscellany Four*, Edinburgh, p. 37.

Firnhaber-Baker, J. (2010), 'Seigneurial War and Royal Power in Later Medieval Southern France', 208 *Past and Present* 37.

Fitzmaurice, A. (2014), *Sovereignty, Property and Empire, 1500–2000*, Cambridge.

Fletcher, C. (2010), 'La communauté anglaise face à l'étranger: La loi de marque, le bien commun et la dot de Lucia Visconti († 1422)', 19 *Cahiers de recherches médiévales et humanistes* 105.

Fletcher, S. (2009), *Cardinal Wolsey: A Life in Renaissance Europe*, London.

Focarelli, C. (2006), 'Customary Foundations of *Ius gentium* in Francisco Suárez's Thought and the Concept of International Community in Contemporary International Law', 16 *Italian Yearbook of International Law* 41.

Follesdal, A. (2015), 'Machiavelli at 500: From Cynic to Vigilant Supporter of International Law', 28 *Ratio Juris* 242.

Fontenay, M. (1988), 'Corsaires de la foi ou rentiers du sol? Les chevaliers de Malte dans le 'corso' méditerranéen au XVIIe siècle', 35 *Revue d'histoire moderne et contemporaine* 361.

Fontenay, M. and Tenenti, A. (1976), 'Course et piraterie méditerranéennes de la fin du Moyen Âge au début du XIXème siècle', in M. Mollat (ed.), *Course et piraterie: Études présentées pendant le XIVe Congrès Internationale des Sciences Historiques (San Francisco, août 1975)*, 3 vols, Paris, vol. 1, p. 78.

Ford, C.A. (1996), 'Preaching Propriety to Princes: Grotius, Lipsius and Neo-Stoic International Law', 28 *Case Western Reserve Journal of International Law* 313.

Ford, C.J. (1979), 'Piracy or Policy: The Crisis in the Channel, 1400–3', 29 *Transactions of the Royal Historical Society* 63.

Ford, J.D. (2005), 'The Law of the Sea and the Two Unions', 127 *Proceedings of the British Academy* 127.

Ford, J.D. (2012), 'A Guide to the Procedure of the Admiralty Court', 18 *Scottish Archives* 95.

Ford, J.D. (2013), 'William Welwod's Treatises on Maritime Law', 34 *Journal of Legal History* 171.

Ford, J.D. (2015), 'Four Models of Union', in H.L. MacQueen (ed.), *Stair Society: Miscellany Seven*, Edinburgh, p. 179.

Ford, J.D. (2018a), 'Some Dubious Beliefs about Medieval Prize Law', in A. Musson and N. Ramsay (eds), *Courts of Chivalry and Admiralty in Late-Medieval Europe*, Woodbridge, p. 215.

Ford, J.D. (2018b), 'Introduction', in *Alexander King's Treatise on Maritime Law*, Edinburgh, p. IX.

Forde, S. (1992), 'Varieties of Realism: Thucydides and Machiavelli', 54 *Journal of Politics* 372.

Forschner, B. (2016), 'Law's Nature: Philosophy as a Legal Argument in Cicero's Writings', in P.J. du Plessis (ed.), *Cicero's Law: Rethinking Roman Law of the Late Republic*, Edinburgh, p. 50.

Forte, A.D.M. (2008), 'A Preliminary Account of an Early Sixteenth-Century Episode of Highland Piracy', 24 *Scottish Gaelic Studies* 207.

Forte, P.E. (1982), 'Richard Hooker's Theory of Law', 12 *Journal of Medieval and Renaissance Studies* 133.

Franklin, J.H. (1963), *Jean Bodin and the Sixteenth Century Revolution in the Methodology of Law and History*, New York.

Frankot, E.B.I. (2010), 'Maritime Law and Practice in Late-Medieval Aberdeen', 89 *Scottish Historical Review* 136.

Frankot, E.B.I. (2012), *'Of Laws of Ships and Shipmen': Medieval Maritime Law and Its Practice in Urban Northern Europe*, Edinburgh.

Frankot, E.B.I. (2013), '*Der ehrbaren Hanse-Städte Schiffs-Ordnung und See-Recht*: Diversity and Unity in Hanseatic Maritime Law', in J. Wubs-Mrozewicz and S. Jenks (eds), *The Hanse in Medieval and Early Modern Europe*, Leiden, p. 109.

Frankot, E.B.I. (2017), 'Aberdeen and the East Coast of Scotland', in W. Blockmans, M. Kron and J. Wubs-Mrozewicz (eds), *Routledge Handbook of Maritime Trade around Europe, 1300–1600: Commercial Networks and Urban Autonomy*, Abingdon, p. 411.

Franks, M. (2000), *The Basingstoke Admiral: A Life of Sir James Lancaster, c. 1554–1618* Salisbury.

French, M.J. (1991), 'Privateering and the Revolt of the Netherlands: The *Watergeuzen* or Sea Beggars in Portsmouth, Gosport and the Isle of Wight, 1570–1', 47 *Proceedings of the Hampshire Field Club and Archaeological Society* 171.

Friedland, K. (2000), 'Maritime Law and Piracy: Advantages and Inconveniences of Shipping in the Baltic', in A.I. Macinnes and F.G. Pedersen (eds), *Ships, Guns and Bibles in the North Sea and Baltic States, c. 1350-c. 1700*, East Linton, p. 30.

Friel, I. (2003), *Maritime History of Britain and Ireland, c. 400–2001*, London.

Friel, I. (2015), *Henry V's Navy: The Sea-Road to Agincourt and Conquest, 1413–22*, Stroud.

Fruin, R. (1925), 'An Unpublished Work of Hugo Grotius', 5 *Bibliotheca Visseriana* pt. 10.

Fuchs, B. (2000), 'Faithless Empires: Pirates, Renegados and the English Nation', 67 *English Literary History* 45.

Fulton, T.W. (1911), *The Sovereignty of the Sea*, Edinburgh.

Fury, C.A. (2002), *Tides in the Affairs of Men: The Social History of Elizabethan Seamen, 1580–1603*, Westport.

Gajda, A. (2009), 'Debating War and Peace in Late-Elizabethan England', 52 *Historical Journal* 851.

Gallant, T.W. (1998), 'Brigandage, Piracy, Capitalism and State Formation: Transnational Crime from a Historical World-Systems Perspective', in J.M. Heyman (ed.), *States and Illegal Practices*, Oxford, p. 25.

Galloway, B. (1986), *The Union of England and Scotland, 1603–8*, Edinburgh.

Games, A. (2015), 'Anglo-Dutch Maritime Interactions in the East Indies during the Early Seventeenth Century', in P.C. Mancall and C. Shammas (eds), *Governing the Sea in the Early-Modern Era: Essays in Honor of Robert C. Ritchie*, San Marino, p. 171.

Gardiner, D.M. (1976), 'Introduction', in *A Calendar of Early Chancery Proceedings Relating to West Country Shipping, 1388–1493*, Torquay, p. VII.

Gardiner, S.R. (1883–4), *History of England from the Accession of James I to the Outbreak of the Civil War, 1603–42*, 10 vols, London.

Garlan, Y. (1978), 'Signification historique de la piraterie grecque', 4 *Dialogues d'histoire ancienne* 1.

Garraffoni, R. (2004), 'Robbers and Soldiers: Criminality and Roman Army in Apuleius' *Metamorphoses*', 22 *Gerión* 367.

Garrisson, J. (1995), *A History of Sixteenth Century France, 1483–1598*, Basingstoke.

Gaynor, J.L. (2012), 'Piracy in the Offing: The Law of Lands and the Limits of Sovereignty at Sea', 85 *Anthropological Quarterly* 817.

Geevers, L. (2010), 'Family Matters: William of Orange and the Habsburgs after the Abdication of Charles V, 1555–67', 63 *Renaissance Quarterly* 459.

Geiß, R. and Petrig, A. (2011), *Piracy and Armed Robbery at Sea: The Legal Framework for Counter-Piracy Operations in Somalia and the Gulf of Aden*, Oxford.

Gerbier, L. (2009), 'Une méthod pour interpréter les histoires: Machiavel et Jean Bodin', 61 *Revue de métaphysique et de morale* 151.

Geyl, P. (2001), *History of the Dutch-Speaking Peoples, 1555–1648*, London.

Gilbert, A.H. (1938), *Machiavelli's Prince and Its Forerunners: The Prince as a Typical Book De regimine principum*, New York.

Gilbert, F. (1939), 'The Humanist Concept of the Prince and *The Prince* of Machiavelli', 11 *Journal of Modern History* 449.

Gilbert, F. (1944), 'Machiavelli: The Renaissance of the Art of War', in D.M. Earle (ed.), *Makers of Modern Strategy: Military Thought from Machiavelli to Hitler*, Princeton, p. 3.

Gillespie, A. (2011), *A History of the Laws of War*, 3 vols, Oxford.

Gilli, P. (2000), 'Comment cesser d'être étranger: Citoyens et non-citoyens dans la pensée juridique italienne de la fin du Moyen Âge', in P. Gauvard (ed.), *L'étranger au Moyen Âge: XXXe Congrès de la S.H.M.E.S. (Göttingen, juin 1999)*, Paris, p. 59.

Giltaij, J. (2014), 'Roman Law and the *Causa legitima* for Reprisal', 20 *Fundamina* 349.

Giorgini, G. (2014), 'Cicero and Machiavelli: Two Visions of Statesmanship and Two Educational Projects Compared', 16 *Etica & Politica* 506.

Given-Wilson, C. (2008), '"The Quarrels of Old Women": Henry IV, Louis of Orléans and Anglo-French Chivalric Challenges in the Early Fifteenth Century', in G. Dodd and D. Briggs (eds), *The Reign of Henry IV: Rebellion and Survival, 1403–13*, Woodbridge, p. 28.

Glare, P.G.W., ed. (1982), *Oxford Latin Dictionary*, Oxford.

Glete, J. (1993), *Navies and Nations: Warships, Navies and State Building in Europe and America, 1500–1860*, 2 vols, Stockholm.

Glete, J. (2002), *War and the State in Early Modern Europe: Spain, the Dutch Republic and Sweden as Fiscal-Military States, 1500–1600*, London.

Glozier, M. (2001), 'Scots in the French and Dutch Armies', in S. Murdoch (ed.), *Scotland and the Thirty Years War, 1618–48*, Leiden, p. 122.

Godefroy, F. (1881–1902), *Dictionnaire de l'ancienne langue française*, 10 vols, Paris.

Godfrey, A.M. (2014), 'Rethinking the Justice of the Feud in Sixteenth-Century Scotland', in S. Boardman and J. Goodare (eds), *Kings, Lords and Men in Scotland and Britain, 1300–1625*, Edinburgh, p. 136.

Goering, J. (2004), 'The Internal Forum and the Literature of Penance and Confession', 59 *Traditio* 175.

Gómez-Centurión Jiménez, C. (1991), 'The New Crusade: Ideology and Religion in the Anglo-Spanish Conflict', in M.J. Rodríguez-Salgado and S. Adams (eds), *England, Spain and the Gran Armada, 1585–1604*, Edinburgh, p. 264.

Gonzalez, M.R. (2019), 'The Common Law of Nations: The *Ius gentium* in the Political Thought of Francisco Suárez, S.J.', MA dissertation, Baylor University, Waco.

Goodare, J. (1999), *State and Society in Early Modern Scotland*, Oxford.

Goodare, J. (2004), *The Government of Scotland, 1560–1625*, Oxford.

Goodman, D. (1997), *Spanish Naval Power, 1589–1665: Reconstruction and Defeat*, Cambridge.

Goodwin, J.M. (2006), 'Universal Jurisdiction and the Pirate: Time for an Old Couple to Part', 39 *Vanderbilt Journal of Transnational Law* 973.

Gordley, J. (1991), *The Philosophical Origins of Modern Contract Law*, Oxford.

Gordley, J. (2012), 'Suárez on Natural Law', in B. Hill and H. Lagerlund (eds), *The Philosophy of Francisco Suárez*, Oxford, p. 209.

Gordon, E. (2008), 'Grotius and the Freedom of the Seas in the Seventeenth Century', 16 *Williamette Journal of International Law and Dispute Resolution* 252.

Gordon, W.M. (2007), *Roman Law, Scots Law and Legal History: Selected Essays*, Edinburgh.

Gore-Browne, R. (1937), *Lord Bothwell*, London.

Gorrochategui Santos, L. (2018), *The English Armada: The Greatest Naval Disaster in English History*, tr. P.J. Gold, London.

Gould, E.H. (2003), 'Zones of Law, Zones of Violence: The Legal Geography of the British Atlantic, circa 1772', 60 *William and Mary Quarterly* 471.

Gould, H.D. (2013), 'Cicero's Ghost: Rethinking the Social Construction of Piracy', in M.J. Struett, J.D. Carlson and M.T. Nance (eds), *Maritime Piracy and the Construction of Global Governance*, London, p. 23.

Gouron, M. (1938), *L'Amirauté de Guienne, depuis le premier amiral anglais en Guienne jusqu'à la Révolution*, Paris.

Grabes, H. (1982), *The Mutable Glass: Mirror Imagery in Titles and Texts of the Middle Ages and the English Renaissance*, Cambridge.

Grady, H. (2002), *Shakespeare, Machiavelli and Montaigne: Power and Subjectivity from Richard II to Hamlet*, Oxford.

Grafton, A. (2007), *What Was History? The Art of History in Early-Modern Europe*, Cambridge.

Graham, E.J. (1982), 'The Scottish Marine during the Dutch Wars', 61 *Scottish Historical Review* 67.

Grant, S.K. (2014), 'Scotland and the Early Modern Naval Revolution, 1488–1603', MA dissertation, University of Guelph.

Grayson, J.C. (1978), 'From Protectorate to Partnership: Anglo-Dutch Relations, 1598–1625', PhD dissertation, University of London.

Greene, J. (2008), '*Hostis humani generis*', 34 *Critical Inquiry* 683.

Greene, M. (2010), *Catholic Pirates and Greek Merchants: A Maritime History of the Mediterranean*, Princeton.

Greengrass, M. (1999), 'Financing the Cause: Protestant Mobilisation and Accountability in France, 1562–89', in P. Benedict, G. Marnef, H. van Nierop and M. Venard (eds), *Reformation, Revolt and Civil War in France and the Netherlands, 1555–85*, Amsterdam, p. 233.

Greenwood, R.M. (2011), 'Law and War in Late-Medieval Italy: The *Ius commune* on War and Its Application in Florence, c. 1150–1450', PhD dissertation, University of Toronto.

Greenwood, R.M. (2014), 'War and Sovereignty in Medieval Roman Law', 32 *Law and History Review* 31.

Grewe, W.G. (2000), *The Epochs of International Law*, tr. M. Byers, Berlin.

Griffin, M. (2011), 'The Politics of Virtue: Three Puzzles in Cicero's *De officiis*', in B. Morison and K. Ierodiakonou (eds), *Episteme, etc: Essays in Honour of Jonathan Barnes*, Oxford, p. 310.

Griffiths, J. (1986), 'What Is Legal Pluralism?', 24 *Journal of Legal Pluralism and Unofficial Law* 1.

Groundwater, A. (2014), '"We Bund and Obleiss Us Never More to Quarrell": Bonds, Private Obligations and Public Justice in the Reign of James VI', in S. Boardman and J. Goodare (eds), *Kings, Lords and Men in Scotland and Britain, 1300–1625*, Edinburgh, p. 173.

Grunberg, B. (1997), 'Corsaires français et 'Luthéranisme' au Mexique en 1560', in M. Acerra and G. Martinière (eds), *Coligny, les protestants et la mer*, Paris, p. 81.

Grünewald, T. (2004), *Bandits in the Roman Empire: Myth and Reality*, London.

Guénin, E. (1901), *Ango et ses pilotes d'après des documents inédites*, Paris.

Guilhot, N. (2016), 'The First Modern Realist: Felix Gilbert's Machiavelli and the Realist Tradition in International Thought', 13 *Modern Intellectual History* 681.

Guillo, L. (2016), 'Le Cantique sur la prinse du Havre de Grâce (1563): Une oeuvre inconnue de Claude Goudimel?' (www.hal.archives-ouvertes.fr/hal-01487085).

Guiral, J. (1980) 'Course et piraterie à Valence de 1410 à 1430', 10 *Anuario de estudios medievales* 759.

Gunn, S., Grummitt, D. and Cools, H. (2007), *War, State and Society in England and the Netherlands, 1477–1559*, Oxford.

Guy, J. (1988), *Tudor England*, Oxford.

Guy, J. (1995), 'The Rhetoric of Counsel in Early Modern England', in D. Hoak (ed.), *Tudor Political Culture*, Cambridge, p. 292.

Guy, J. (2017), *Elizabeth: The Forgotten Years*, Harmondsworth.

Guzman, A.T. (2005), 'Saving Customary International Law', 27 *Michigan Journal of International Law* 115.

Gwyn, P. (1990), *The King's Cardinal: The Rise and Fall of Thomas Wolsey*, London.

Haakonssen, K. (1985), 'Hugo Grotius and the History of Political Thought', 13 *Political Theory* 239.

Haggenmacher, P. (1981), 'Genèse et signification du concept de *ius gentium* chez Grotius', 2 *Grotiana* 44.

Haggenmacher, P. (1983), *Grotius et la doctrine de la guerre juste*, Paris.

Haggenmacher, P. (1990), 'Grotius and Gentili: A Reassessment of Thomas E. Holland's Inaugural Lecture', in H. Bull, B. Kingsbury and A. Roberts (eds), *Hugo Grotius and International Relations*, Oxford, p. 133.

Haggenmacher, P. (1992), 'Just War and Regular War in Sixteenth-Century Spanish Doctrine', 32 *International Review of the Red Cross* 434.

Haggenmacher, P. (2010), 'L'ancêtre de la protection diplomatique: Les représailles de l'ancien droit, XIIe–XVIIIe siècles', 143 *Relations internationales* 7.

Haivry, O. (2017a), 'John Selden and the Jewish Religious Fountainhead of the International Law of the Sea', in M. Koskenniemi, M. García-Salmones and P.

Amorosa (eds), *International Law and Religion: Historical and Contemporary Perspectives*, Oxford, p. 111.

Haivry, O. (2017b), *John Selden and the Western Political Tradition*, Cambridge.

Hale, J.R. (1983), 'Incitement to Violence? English Divines on the Themes of War, 1578 to 1631', in idem, *Renaissance War Studies*, London, p. 487.

Hallebeek, J. (2018), 'Structure of Medieval Roman Law: Institutions, Sources and Methods', in H. Pihlajamäki, M.D. Dubber and M. Godfrey (eds), *The Oxford Handbook of European Legal History*, Oxford, p. 286.

Hallwood, P. and Miceli, T. (2018), 'Piracy and Privateers in the Golden Age: Lessons for Today', 49 *Ocean Development and International Law* 236.

Hamilton, B. (1963), *Political Thought in Sixteenth-Century Spain: A Study of the Political Ideas of Vitoria, Soto, Suárez and Molina*, Oxford.

Hammer, P.E.J. (2003), *Elizabeth's Wars: War, Government and Society in Tudor England, 1544–1604*, Basingstoke.

Hammer, P.E.J. (2005), 'The Crucible of War: English Foreign Policy, 1589–1603', in S. Doran and G. Richardson (eds), *Tudor England and Its Neighbours*, Basingstoke, p. 235.

Hampton, T. (1990), *Writing from History: The Rhetoric of Exemplarity in Renaissance Literature*, Ithaca, NY.

Hanna, M.G. (2015), *Pirate Nests and the Rise of the British Empire, 1570–1740*, Chapel Hill, NC.

Hannaford, I. (1972), 'Machiavelli's Concept of *Virtù* in *The Prince* and *The Discourses* Reconsidered', 20 *Political Studies* 185.

Hannay, R.K. (1916), 'Shipping and the Staple, AD 1515–31', 9 *Book of the Old Edinburgh Club* 49.

Hanson, N. (2003), *The Confident Hope of a Miracle: The True Story of the Spanish Armada*, London.

Harding, C. (2007), '*Hostis humani generis*: The Pirate as Outlaw in the Early-Modern Law of the Sea', in C. Jowitt (ed.), *Pirates? The Politics of Plunder, 1550–1650*, Basingstoke, p. 20.

Harries, J. (2002), 'Cicero and the Defining of the *Ius civile*', in G. Clark and T. Rajak (eds), *Philosophy and Power in the Graeco-Roman World: Essays in Honour of Miriam Griffin*, Oxford, p. 51.

Harris, T. (2014), *Rebellion: Britain's First Stuart Kings, 1567–1642*, Oxford.

Harrison, W. (1902), *William the Silent*, London.

Harriss, G.L. (1985), 'The Management of Parliament', in G.L. Harriss (ed.), *Henry V: The Practice of Kingship*, Oxford, p. 137.

Harriss, G.L. (2005), *Shaping the Nation: England, 1360–1461*, Oxford.

Hart, M. 't (2014), *The Dutch Wars of Independence: Warfare and Commerce in the Netherlands, 1570–1680*, Abingdon.

Hattendorf, J.B., ed. (2007), *The Oxford Encyclopedia of Maritme History*, 4 vols, Oxford.

Hatzimihail, N.E. (2007), 'Bartolus and the Conflict of Laws', 60 *Revue hellenique de droit international* 12.

Hay, D. (1988), *Renaissance Essays*, London.

Haywood, R. and Spivak, R. (2012), *Maritime Piracy*, Abingdon.

Heap, W.A. (2019), *Elizabeth's French Wars, 1562–98*, London.

Hebb, D.D. (1994), *Piracy and the English Government, 1616–42*, Aldershot.

Heebøll-Holm, T.K. (2013), *Ports, Piracy and Maritime War: Piracy in the English Channel and the Atlantic, c. 1280-c. 1330*, Leiden.

Heebøll-Holm, T.K. (2017), 'Law, Order and Plunder at Sea: A Comparison of England and France in the Fourteenth Century', 32 *Continuity and Change* 37.

Heebøll-Holm, T.K. (2018), 'The Origins and Jurisdiction of the English Court of Admiralty in the Fourteenth Century', in A. Musson and N. Ramsay (eds), *Courts of Chivalry and Admiralty in Late Medieval Europe*, Woodbridge, p. 149.

Heebøll-Holm, T.K. (2019), 'Piracy, Patriotism and Profit in England around 1400', in T. Heebøll-Holm, P. Höhn and G. Rohmann (eds), *Merchants, Pirates and Smugglers: Criminalisation, Economics and thc Transformation of the Maritime World, 1200–1600*, Frankfurt, p. 33.

Heebøll-Holm, T., Höhn, P. and Rohmann, G. (2019), 'Introduction', in T. Heebøll-Holm, P. Höhn and G. Rohmann (eds), *Merchants, Pirates and Smugglers: Criminalisation, Economics and the Transformation of the Maritime World, 1200–1600*, Frankfurt, p. 9.

Heers, J. (2001), *Les Barbaresques: La course et la guerre en Méditerranée, XIVe–XVIe siècle*, Paris.

Heisch, A. (1975), 'Queen Elizabeth I: Parliamentary Rhetoric and the Exercise of Power', 1 *Signs* 31.

Heller-Roazen, D. (2009), *The Enemy of All: Piracy and the Law of Nations*, New York.

Helling, C. (2016), 'The Royal Navy and Scotland, 1603–1714: Naval and State Development in a Regal Union', PhD dissertation, University of Aberdeen.

Helmholz, R.H. (2015), *Natural Law in Court: A History of Legal Theory in Practice*, Cambridge, MA.

Henderson, C.S. (2018), 'Taking off the Gloves: Terrorists as *Hostis humani generis*', 4 *Baku State University Law Review* 2.

Hertz, A.Z. (1990–1), 'Medieval Treaty Obligation', 6 *Connecticut Journal of International Law* 425.

Hill, B. (2018), 'Domingo de Soto', in R. Domingo and J. Martínez-Torrón (eds), *Great Christian Jurists in Spanish History*, Cambridge, p. 134.

Hill, L.M. (1988), *Bench and Bureaucracy: The Public Career of Sir Julius Caesar, 1580–1636*, Stanford.

Hilton, L. (2015), *Elizabeth: Renaissance Prince*, Boston, MA.

Höhn, P. (2019), 'Pirate Places, Merchant Spaces? Distribution and Criminalisation in the Late-Medieval Baltic Sea', in T. Heebøll-Holm, P. Höhn and G. Rohmann (eds), *Merchants, Pirates and Smugglers: Criminalisation, Economics and the Transformation of the Maritime World, 1200–1600*, Frankfurt, p. 127.

Holdsworth, W.S. (1922–66), *A History of English Law*, 16 vols, London.

Holt, M.P. (2005), *The French Wars of Religion, 1562–1629*, Cambridge.

Honoré, T. (2010), 'Ulpian, Natural Law and Stoic Influence', 78 *Tijdschrift voor Rechtsgeschiedenis* 199.

Höpfl, H. (2002), 'Orthodoxy and Reason of State', 23 *History of Political Thought* 211.

Höpfl, H. (2004), *Jesuit Political Thought: The Society of Jesus and the State, c. 1540–1630*, Cambridge.

Hopwood, K. (1989), 'Bandits, Elites and Rural Order', in A. Wallace-Hadrill (ed.), *Patronage in Ancient Society*, London, p. 171.

Horowitz, M.C. (1974), 'The Stoic Synthesis of the Idea of Natural Law in Man: Four Themes', 35 *Journal of the History of Ideas* 3.

Horsley, R.A. (1978), 'The Law of Nature in Philo and Cicero', 71 *Harvard Theological Quarterly* 35.

Houlbrooke, R. (2011), *Britain and Europe, 1500–1780*, London.

Hudson, J. (2012), *The Oxford History of the Laws of England: Volume II, 871–1216*, Oxford.

Huizinga, J. (1924), *The Waning of the Middle Ages: A Study of the Forms of Life, Thought and Art in France and the Netherlands in the Fourteenth and Fifteenth Centuries*, tr. F. Hopman, London.

Humfress, C. (2013), 'Thinking through Legal Pluralism: "Forum Shopping" in the Later Roman Empire', in J. Duindam, J.D. Harris and C. Humfress (eds), *Law and Empire: Ideas, Practices, Actors*, Leiden, p. 225.

Huppert, G. (1970), *The Idea of Perfect History: Historical Erudition and Historical Philosophy in Renaissance France*, Urbana, IL.

Hutchins, T.E. (2011), 'Structuring a Sustainable Letters of Marque Regime: How Commissioning Privateers Can Defeat the Somali Pirates', 99 *California Law Review* 819.

Hutchinson, G. (1994), *Medieval Ships and Shipping*, London.

Hyams, P.R. (2003), *Rancor and Reconciliation in Medieval England*, Ithaca, NY.

Hyams, P.R. (2010), 'Was There Really Such a Thing as Feud in the High Middle Ages?', in S.A. Throop and P.R. Hyams (eds), *Vengeance in the Middle Ages: Emotion, Religion and Feud*, Farnham, p. 151.

Ibbetson, D.J. (2007), 'Custom in Medieval Law', in A. Perreau-Saussine and J.B. Murphy (eds), *The Nature of Customary Law*, Cambridge, p. 151.

Irons, J.C. (1898), *Leith and Its Antiquities from the Earliest Times to the Close of the Nineteenth Century*, 2 vols, Edinburgh.

Israel, J.I. (1998), *The Dutch Republic: Its Rise, Greatness and Fall, 1477–1806*, Oxford.

Iurlaro, F. (2017), 'The Burden of Reason: *Ratio probabilis*, *Consensio omnium* and the Impact of *Humanitas* on Alberico Gentili's Theory of Customary International Law', 38 *History of Political Thought* 409.

Iurlaro, F. (2018), 'Grotius, Dio Chrysostom and the Invention of Customary *Ius gentium*', 39 *Grotiana* 15.

Jack, R.D.S. (2013), 'Montgomerie and the Pirates', 5 *Studies in Scottish Literature* 133.

Jackson, A.H. (1973), 'Privateers in the Ancient Greek World', in M.R.D. Foot (ed), *War and Society: Historical Essays in Honour and Memory of J.R. Western*, London, p. 241.

Jacobs, J.A. (2012), 'Stoic Eudaimonism and the Natural Law Tradition', in J.A. Jacobs (ed.), *Reason, Religion and Natural Law: From Plato to Spinoza*, Oxford, p. 57.

Jaeger, G.A. (1987), *Pirates, flibustiers et corsaires: Histoire et légendes d'une société d'exception*, Avignon.

James, A. (2000), 'Between "Huguenot" and "Royal": Naval Affairs during the Wars of Religion', in K. Cameron, M. Greengrass and P. Roberts (eds), *The Adventure of Religious Pluralism in Early Modern France*, Oxford, p. 101.

James, A. (2004), *Navy and Government in Early Modern France, 1572–1661*, Woodbridge.

Jamieson, A.G. (2012), *Lords of the Sea: A History of the Barbary Corsairs*, London.

Janara, L. (2006), 'Machiavelli, Elizabeth I and the Innovative Historical Self: A Politics of Action, not Identity', 27 *History of Political Thought* 455.

Janelle, P. (1963), *The Catholic Reformation*, Milwaukee.

Jenkins, G. (1942), 'Ways and Means in Elizabethan Propaganda', 26 *History* 105.

Jenks, S. (2005), 'Trade and Relations between Lynn and the Hanse in the Middle Ages', in K. Friedland and P. Richards (eds), *Essays in Hanseatic History*, Dereham, p. 94.

Jessup, P.C. and Deák, F. (1935–6), *Neutrality: Its History, Economics and Law*, 4 vols, New York.

Johnson, D., and Valencia, M. (2005), *Piracy in Southeast Asia: Status, Issues and Responses*, Singapore.

Johnson, J.T. (1981), *Just War Tradition and the Restraint of War: A Moral and Historical Inquiry*, Princeton.

Johnson, T. (2015), 'Medieval Law and Materiality: Shipwrecks, Finders and Property on the Suffolk Coast, ca. 1380–1410', 120 *American Historical Review* 407.

Jones, H. (1998), *Master Tully: Cicero in Tudor England*, Nieuwkoop.

Jones, M. (1987), 'Roches *contra* Hawley: la cour anglaise de chevalerie et un cas de piraterie à Brest, 1386–1402', 64 *Mémoires de la Société d'Histoire et d'Archéologie de Bretagne* 53.

Jones, M. (2021), 'Natural Law as True Law', in R. Lesaffer and J. Nijman (eds), *The Cambridge Companion to Hugo Grotius*, Cambridge, p. 138.

Jones, N. (2015), *Governing by Virtue: Lord Burghley and the Management of Elizabethan England*, Oxford.

Jorgensen, P.A. (1952), 'Theoretical Views of War in Elizabethan England', 13 *Journal of the History of Ideas* 469.

Jorgensen, P.A. (1973), 'Elizabethan Religious Literature for Time of War', 37 *Huntingdon Library Quarterly* 1.

Jouanna, A. (2007), *The Saint Bartholomew's Day Massacre: The Mysteries of a Crime of State, 24 August 1572*, tr. J. Bergin, Manchester.

Joyce, A.J. (2012), *Richard Hooker and Anglican Moral Theology*, Oxford.

Kadelbach, S. (2017), 'Hugo Grotius: On the Conquest of Utopia by Systematic Reasoning', in S. Kadelbach, T. Kleinlein and D. Roth-Isigkeit (eds), *System, Order and International Law: The Early History of International Legal Thought from Machiavelli to Hegel*, Oxford, p. 134.

Kadens, E. (2016), 'Custom's Past', in C.A. Bradley (ed.), *Custom's Future: International Law in a Changing World*, Cambridge, p. 11.

Kahn, V. (1986), '*Virtù* and the Example of Agathocles in Machiavelli's *Prince*', 13 *Representations* 63.

Kahn, V. (1994a), *Machiavellian Rhetoric: From the Counter-Reformation to Milton*, Princeton.

Kahn, V. (1994b), 'Reading Machiavelli: Innocent Gentillet's Discourse on Method', 22 *Political Theory* 539.

Kaiser, W. and Calafat, G. (2014), 'Violence, Protection and Commerce: Corsairing and *Ars piratica* in the Early-Modern Mediterranean', in S.E. Amirell and L. Müller (eds), *Persistent Piracy: Maritime Violence and State-Formation in Global-Historical Perspective*, Basingstoke, p. 69.

Kamen, H. (1997), *Philip of Spain*, New Haven.

Kaminsky, H. (2002), 'The Noble Feud in the Later Middle Ages', 177 *Past and Present* 55.

Katele, I.B. (1988), 'Piracy and the Venetian State: The Dilemma of Maritime Defense in the Fourteenth Century', 63 *Speculum* 865.

Katele, I.B. (1989), 'Captains and Corsairs: Distinguishing Protection and Aggression', in K. Friedland (ed.), *Maritime Aspects of Migration*, Cologne, p. 87.

Kaueper, R.W. (1988), 'Private War', in idem, *War, Justice and Public Order: England and France in the Later Middle Ages*, Oxford, p. 225.

Keay, J. (1991), *The Honourable Company: A History of the English East India Company*, London.

Keen, M.H. (1965), *The Laws of War in the Late Middle Ages*, London.

Keen, M.H. (1995), 'Richard II's Ordinances of War of 1385', in R.E. Archer and S. Walker (eds), *Rulers and Ruled in Late-Medieval England: Essays Presented to Gerald Harriss*, London, p. 33.

Keenan, J.F. (1995), 'William Perkins (1558–1602) and the Birth of British Casuistry', in J.F. Keenan and T.A. Shannon (eds), *The Context of Casuistry*, Washington, p. 105.

Keenan, J.F. (2004), 'Was William Perkins' *Whole Treatise of Cases of Conscience* Casuistry? Hermeneutics and British Practical Divinity', in H.E. Braun and E. Vallance (eds), *Contexts of Conscience in Early Modern Europe, 1500–1700*, Basingstoke, p. 17.

Keene, E. (2002), *Beyond the Anarchical Society: Grotius, Colonialism and Order in World Politics*, Cambridge.

Kelleher, C. (2020), *The Alliance of Pirates: Ireland and Atlantic Piracy in the Early Seventeenth Century*, Cork.

Keller, A. (2012), 'Cicero: Just War in Classical Antiquity', in H.G. Justenhoven and W.A. Barbieri (eds), *From Just War to Modern Peace Ethics*, Berlin, p. 9.

Kelley, D.R. (1964), '*Historia integra*: François Baudouin and His Conception of History', 35 *Journal of the History of Ideas* 35.

Kelley, D.R. (1970), *Foundations of Modern Historical Scholarship: Language, Law and History in the French Renaissance*, New York.

Kelley, D.R. (1971), 'History as a Calling: The Case of La Popelinière', in A. Molho and J.A. Tedeschi (eds), *Renaissance Studies in Honor of Hans Baron*, Florence, p. 773.

Kelley, D.R. (1973), 'The Development and Context of Bodin's Method', in H. Denzer (ed.), *Jean Bodin: Verhandlungen der Internationalen Bodin Tagung*, Munich, p. 123.

Kelley, D.R. (1981), *The Beginning of Ideology: Consciousness and Society in the French Reformation*, Cambridge.

Kelly, J.P. (2000), 'The Twilight of Customary International Law', 40 *Virginia Journal of International Law* 449.

Kelsey, H. (1998), *Sir Francis Drake: The Queen's Pirate*, New Haven.

Kelsey, H. (2003), *Sir John Hawkins: Queen Elizabeth's Slave Trader*, New Haven.

Kemp, P., ed. (1976), *The Oxford Companion to Ships and the Sea*, Oxford.

Kempe, M. (2010), '"Even in the Remotest Corners of the World": Globalised Piracy and International Law, 1500–1900', 5 *Journal of Global History* 353.

Kepler, J.S. (1973), 'The Value of the Ships Gained and Lost by the English Shipping Industry during the Wars with Spain and France, 1624–30', 59 *Mariner's Mirror* 218.

Kermode, J. (1998), *Medieval Merchants: York, Beverley and Hull in the Later Middle Ages* Cambridge.

Kesler, C.R. (1985), 'Cicero and the Natural Law', PhD dissertation, Harvard University.

Kesselring, K.J. (2009), 'Felony Forfeiture in England, c. 1170–1870', 30 *Journal of Legal History* 201.

Kesselring, K.J. (2010), 'Felony Forfeiture and the Profits of Crime in Early Modern England', 53 *Historical Journal* 271.

Kewes, P. (2011), 'Henry Savile's Tacitus and the Politics of Roman History in Late-Elizabethan England', 74 *Huntington Library Quarterly* 515.

Kibre, P. (1961), *Scholarly Privileges in the Middle Ages: The Rights, Privileges and Immunities of Scholars and Universities at Bologna, Padua, Paris and Oxford*, London.

Kidd, I.G. (1971), 'Stoic Intermediates and the End for Man', in A.A. Long (ed.), *Problems in Stoicism*, London, p. 150.

Kilgour, R. (1935), 'Honoré Bonet: A Fourteenth-Century Critic of Chivalry', 50 *Publications of the Modern Languages Association of America* 352.

Kincaid, E.R. (2019), 'Settling Law: Francisco Suárez's Theory of Custom for Contemporary Contexts', in R.A. Maryks and J.A. Senent de Frutos (eds), *Francisco Suárez (1548–1617): Jesuits and the Complexities of Modernity*, Leiden, p. 178.

King, A. (2002), '"According to the Custom Used in French and Scottish Wars": Prisoners and Casualties on the Scottish Marches in the Fourteenth Century', 28 *Journal of Medieval History* 263.

Kingsbury, B. and Straumann, B. (2010), 'The State of Nature and Commercial Sociability in Early Modern International Legal Thought', 31 *Grotiana* 22.

Kingsbury, B. and Straumann, B. (2011), 'Introduction: Roman Wars and Roman Laws', in Alberico Gentili, *The Wars of the Romans: A Critical Edition and Translation of De armis Romanis*, Oxford, p. x.

Kingsford, C.L. (1925), *Prejudice and Promise in Fifteenth-Century England*, Oxford.

Kirby, W.J.T. (2008), 'Reason and Law', in W.J.T. Kirby (ed.), *A Companion to Richard Hooker*, Leiden, p. 251.

Kirshner, J. (1974), '*Ars imitatur naturam*: A *Consilium* of Baldus on Naturalization in Florence', 5 *Viator* 289.

Kirshner, J. (1976) 'A *Consilium* of Rosello dei Roselli on the Meaning of *Florentinus*, *De Florentia* and *De populo*', 6 *Bulletin of Medieval Canon Law* 87.

Kirshner, J. (1979), 'Between Culture and Nature: An Opinion of Baldus of Perugia on Venetian Citizenship', 9 *Journal of Medieval and Renaissance Studies* 179.

Knecht, R.J. (1994), *Renaissance Warrior and Patron: The Reign of Francis I*, Cambridge.

Knecht, R.J. (1996), *The French Wars of Religion, 1559–98*, Harlow.

Knecht, R.J. (2001), *The Rise and Fall of Renaissance France, 1483–1610*, Oxford.

Knight, W.S.M. (1965), *The Life and Works of Hugo Grotius*, London.

Knorn, B. (2018), 'Theological Renewal after the Council of Trent? The Case of Jesuit Commentaries on the *Summa theologiae*', 79 *Theological Studies* 107.

Koeppler, H. (1939), 'Frederick Barbarossa and the Schools of Bologna: Some Remarks on the *Authentica Habita*', 54 *English Historical Review* 577.

Konstam, A. (2008), *Piracy: The Complete History*, Oxford.

Kontorovich, E. (2004), 'The Piracy Analogy: Modern Universal Jurisdiction's Hollow Foundation', 45 *Harvard International Law Journal* 183.

Koskenniemi, M. (2007), '"Not Excepting the Iroquois Themselves ...": Machiavelli, Pufendorf and the Prehistory of International Law' (www.cadmus.eui.eu).

Koskenniemi, M. (2011a), 'Empire and International Law: The Real Spanish Contribution', 61 *University of Toronto Law Journal* 1.

Koskenniemi, M. (2011b), 'Histories of International Law: Dealing with Eurocentrism', 19 *Rechtsgeschichte* 152.

Kosters, J. (1925) 'Les Fondements du droit des gens', 4 *Bibliotheca Visseriana* pt 9.

Kottman, K.A. (1972), *Law and Apocalypse: The Moral Thought of Luis de Leon, 1527?-91*, Dordrecht.

Kowalski, J.-M. (2014), 'Du héros épique à l'ennemi public: Évolution des représentations antiques du pirate', in M. Battesti (ed.), *La piraterie au fil de l'histoire: Un défi pour l'état*, Paris, p. 25.

Kraye, J. (2001), 'Stoicism in the Renaissance from Petrarch to Lipsius', 22 *Grotiana* 21.

Kries, D. (2003), 'On the Intention of Cicero's *De officiis*', 65 *Review of Politics* 375.

Kroger, J.R. (2004), 'The Philosophical Foundations of Roman Law: Aristotle, the Stoics and Roman Theories of Natural Law', *Wisconsin Law Review* 905.

Krueger, H.C. (1933), 'Genoese Trade with Northwest Africa in the Twelfth Century', 8 *Speculum* 377.

Lacey, W.K. (1978), *Cicero and the End of the Roman Republic*, London.

Lagerlund, H. (2018), 'Francisco Suárez', in R. Domingo and J. Martinez-Torrón (eds), *Great Christian Jurists in Spanish History*, Cambridge, p. 210.

Lagrée, J. (2016), 'Justus Lipsius and Neostoicism', in J. Sellars (ed.), *The Routledge Handbook of the Stoic Tradition*, London, p. 160.

Laing, L.H. (1946), 'Historic Origins of Admiralty Jurisdiction in England', 45 *Michigan Law Review* 163.

Laiou, A.E. (2001), 'Byzantine Trade with Christians and Muslims and the Crusades', in A.E. Laiou and R.P. Mottahedeh (eds), *The Crusades from the Perspective of Byzantium and the Muslim World*, Washington, p. 157.

Lambert, B. (2019), 'Cargoes, Courts and Compromise: The Management of Maritime Plunder in the Burgundian Low Countries', in T. Heebøll-Holm, P. Höhn and G. Rohmann (eds), *Merchants, Pirates and Smugglers: Criminalisation, Economics and the Transformation of the Maritime World, 1200–1600*, Frankfurt, p. 107.

Lambert, C. (2017), 'Henry V and the Crossing to France: Reconstructing Naval Operations for the Agincourt Campaign, 1415', 43 *Journal of Medieval History* 24.

LaMonica, M. (2016), 'The Predecessors of Grotius: The Use of Piracy in Contests over Sovereignty, Empire and State-Building in the Early-Modern French Atlantic', MA dissertation, McGill University, Montreal.

Lane, K.E. (1998), *Pillaging the Empire: Piracy in the Americas, 1500–1750*, New York.

Lapidge, M. (1988), 'The Stoic Inheritance', in P. Dronke (ed.), *A History of Twelfth-Century Philosophy*, Cambridge, p. 81.

Larson, A.A. (2013), 'The Reception of Gratian's *Tractatus de penitentia* and the Relationship between Canon Law and Theology in the Second Half of the Twelfth Century', 37 *Journal of Religious History* 457.

Lécrivain, C.A. (1897), 'Le droit de se faire justice soi-même et les représailles dans les relations internationales de la Grèce', 9 *Mémoires de l'Académie des Sciences de Toulouse* 277.

Lee, D. (2011), 'Popular Liberty, Princely Government and the Roman Law in Hugo Grotius *De iure belli ac pacis*', 72 *Journal of the History of Ideas* 371.

Lee, M. (1985), *The Road to Revolution: Scotland under Charles I, 1625–37*, Urbana, IL.

Lee, M. (2003), *The 'Inevitable' Union and Other Essays on Early Modern Scotland*, East Linton.

Leeson, P.T. (1995), 'Was Privateering Plunder Efficient?', 26 *Journal of Economic Behaviour and Organization* 303.

Leeson, P.T. (2009), 'The Laws of Lawlessness', 38 *Journal of Legal Studies* 471.

Leira, H. (2007), 'At the Crossroads: Justus Lipsius and the Early Modern Development of International Law', 20 *Leiden Journal of International Law* 65.

Leira, H. and de Carvalho, B. (2010), 'Privateers of the North Sea: At Worlds End – French Privateers in Norwegian Waters', in A. Colás and B. Mabee (eds), *Mercenaries, Pirates, Bandits and Empires: Private Violence in Historical Context*, London, p. 55.

Lemaire, L. (1934), 'L'amirauté de Dunkerque, 1579–1791', 31 *Bulletin de l'Union Faulconnier* 155.

Lenman, B. (2001), *England's Colonial Wars, 1550–1688: Conflicts, Empire and National Identity*, Harlow.

Lepard, B.D. (2016), 'Customary International Law as a Dynamic Process', in C.A. Bradley (ed.), *Custom's Future: International Law in a Changing World*, Cambridge, p. 62.

Lesaffer, R.C.H. (2002), 'The Grotian Tradition Revisted: Change and Continuity in the History of International Law', 73 *British Yearbook of International Law* 103.

Lesaffer, R.C.H. (2005), 'Argument from Roman Law in Current International Law: Occupation and Acquisitive Prescription', 16 *European Journal of International Law* 25.

Lesaffer, R.C.H. (2007), 'Siege Warfare in the Early Modern Age: A Study on the Customary Laws of War', in A. Perreau-Saussine and J.B. Murphy (eds), *The Nature of Customary Law*, Cambridge, p. 176.

Lesaffer, R.C.H. (2009), *European Legal History: A Cultural and Political Perspective*, Cambridge.

Lesaffer, R.C.H. (2010), 'Alberico Gentili's *Ius post bellum* and Early-Modern Peace Treaties', in B. Kingsbury and B. Straumann (eds), *The Roman Foundations of the Law of Nations: Alberico Gentili and the Justice of Empire*, Oxford, p. 210.

Lesaffer, R.C.H. (2011), 'The Classical Law of Nations, 1500–1800', in A. Orakhelashvili (ed.), *Research Handbook on the Theory and History of International Law*, Cheltenham, p. 408.

Lesaffer, R.C.H. (2016), 'Roman Law and the Intellectual History of International Law', in A. Orford and F. Hoffmann (eds), *The Oxford Handbook of the Theory of International Law*, Oxford, p. 38.

Lesaffer, R.C.H. (2020), 'Grotius on Reprisal', 41 *Tijdschrift voor Rechtsgeschiedenis* 330.

Lesaffer, R.C.H. (2021), 'The Laws of War- and Peace-Making', in R. Lesaffer and J. Nijman (eds), *The Cambridge Companion to Hugo Grotius*, Cambridge, p. 433.

Levack, B.P. (1973), *The Civil Lawyers in England, 1603–41: A Political Study*, Oxford.

Levack, B.P. (1987), *The Formation of the British State: England, Scotland and the Union, 1603–1707*, Oxford.

Levesque, R. (2009), 'En quête du troisième monde, Lancelot Voysin, seigneur de la Popelinière', in M. Augeron, D. Poton and B. van Ruymbeke (eds), *Les Huguenots et l'Atlantique, vol. 1: Pour Dieu, la cause ou les affaires*, Paris, p. 171.

Lewis, C.T. and Short, C. (1987), *A Latin Dictionary*, Oxford.

Lewis, E. (1937), 'Responsibility for Piracy in the Middle Ages', 19 *Journal of Comparative Legislation and International Law* 77.

Lindberg, B. (2011), 'Stoicism in Political Humanism and Natural Law', in E. De Bom, M. Janssens, T. Van Houdt and J. Papy (eds), *(Un)Masking the Realities of Power: Justus Lipsius and the Dynamics of Political Writing in Early Modern Europe*, Leiden, p. 73.

Lintott, A. (2008), *Cicero as Evidence: A Historian's Companion*, Oxford.

Little, B. (2005), *The Sea Rover's Practice: Pirate Tactics and Techniques, 1630–1730*, Washington.

Llewelyn Davies, D.J. (1934), 'Enemy Property and Ultimate Destination during the Anglo-Dutch Wars, 1664–67 and 1672–74', 15 *British Yearbook of International Law* 21.

Lloyd, T.H. (1991), *England and the German Hanse, 1157–1611*, Cambridge.

Loades, D. (1992), *The Tudor Navy: An Administrative, Political and Military History*, Aldershot.

Loades, D. (2000), *England's Maritime Empire: Seapower, Commerce and Policy, 1490–1690*, Harlow.

Loades, D. (2009), *The Making of the Elizabethan Navy, 1540–90: From the Solent to the Armada*, Woodbridge.

Lobel, J. (1986), 'Covert War and Congressional Authority: Hidden War and Forgotten Power', 134 *University of Pennsylvania Law Review* 1035.

Lockyer, R. (1981), *Buckingham: The Life and Political Career of George Villiers, First Duke of Buckingham, 1592–1628*, London.

Long, A.A. (2006), *From Epicurus to Epictetus: Studies in Hellenistic and Roman Philosophy*, Oxford.

Long, A.A. (2008), 'The Concept of the Cosmopolitan in Greek and Roman Thought', 137 *Daedalus* 50.

Long, J. (1989), 'William Perkins: "Apostle of Practical Divinity"', 103 *Churchman* 53.

Longfield Karr, S. (2016), 'Redefining *Ius* to Restore Justice: The Centrality of *Ius gentium* in Humanist Jurisprudence', in P.J. du Plessis and J.W. Cairns (eds), *Reassessing Legal Humanism: Petere fontes?*, Edinburgh, p. 108.

Longfield Karr, S. (2018), '"The Law of Nations Is Common to All Mankind": *Ius gentium* in Humanist Jurisprudence', in A. Carty and J. Nijman (eds), *Morality and Responsibility of Rulers: European and Chinese Origins of a Rule of Law as Justice for World Order*, Oxford, p. 73.

Lorca, A.B. (2012), 'Eurocentrism in the History of International Law', in B. Fassbender and A. Peters (eds), *The Oxford Handbook of the History of International Law*, Oxford, p. 1034.

Lorimer, J. (1978), 'The English Contraband Tobacco Trade in Trinidad and Guiana, 1590–1617', in K.R. Andrews, N.P. Canny and P.E.H. Hair (eds), *The Westward Enterprise: English Activities in Ireland, the Atlantic and America, 1480–1650*, Liverpool, p. 124.

Lourde, B. (2007), 'L'Avent-discourse de *L'Amiral de France* (1584) de La Popelinière: Une défense et illustration de la langue française', 69 *Bibliothèque d'humanisme et de renaissance* 103.

Love, R.S. (2001), *Blood and Religion: The Conscience of Henri IV*, Montreal.

Lowe, B. (1996), 'Religious wars and the "Common Peace": Anglican Anti-War Sentiment in Elizabethan England', 28 *Albion* 415.

Lowe, B. (2000), 'A War to End All Wars? Protestant Subversions of Henry VIII's Final Scottish and French Campaigns (1542–45)', in D. Wolfthal (ed.), *Peace and Negotiation: Strategies for Coexistence in the Middle Ages and the Renaissance*, Turnhout, p. 179.

Lower, M. (2006), 'Tunis in 1270: A Case Study of Interfaith Relations in the Late Thirteenth Century', 28 *International History Review* 504.

Luban, D. (2018), 'The Enemy of All Humanity', 47 *Netherlands Journal of Legal Philosophy* 112.

Lukes, T.J. (2001), 'Lionizing Machiavelli', 95 *American Political Science Review* 561.

Lukes, T.J. (2004), 'Martialling Machiavelli: Reassessing the Military Reflections', 66 *Journal of Politics* 1089.

Lunsford, V.W. (2005), *Piracy and Privateering in the Golden Age Netherlands*, Basingstoke.

Lupher, D. (2010), 'The *De armis Romanis* and the *Exemplum* of Roman Imperialism', in B. Kingsbury and B. Straumann (eds), *The Roman Foundations of the Law of Nations: Alberico Gentili and the Justice of Empire*, Oxford, p. 85.

Lynch, J. (1981), *Spain under the Habsburgs*, 2 vols, Oxford.

Lyons, J.D. (1989), *Exemplum: The Rhetoric of Example in Early-Modern France and Italy*, Princeton.

Lyons, M.A. (2000), 'Maritime Relations between Ireland and France, c. 1480-c. 1630', 27 *Irish Economic and Social History* 1.

Lythe, S.G.E. (1960), *The Economy of Scotland in Its European Setting, 1550–1625*, London.

Mabee, B. (2009), 'Pirates, Privateers and the Political Economy of Private Violence', 21 *Global Change, Peace and Security* 139.

MacCaffrey, W.T. (1968), *The Shaping of the Elizabethan Regime: Elizabethan Politics, 1558–72*, Princeton.

MacCaffrey, W.T. (1981), *Queen Elizabeth and the Making of Policy, 1572–88*, Princeton.

MacCaffrey, W.T. (1992), *Elizabeth I: War and Politics, 1588–1603*, Princeton.

MacCaffrey, W.T. (1993), *Elizabeth I*, London.

Macdonald, R.A. (1998), 'Metaphors of Multiplicity: Civil Society, Regimes and Legal Pluralism', 15 *Arizona Journal of International and Comparative Law* 69.

Macdougall, N. (1997), *James IV*, Edinburgh.

Macinnes, A.I. (1991), *Charles I and the Making of the Covenanting Movement, 1625–41*, Edinburgh.

MacKendrick, P. (1989), *The Philosophical Books of Cicero*, London.

Mackie, J.D. (1927), *Negotiations between King James VI and I and Ferdinand I, Grand Duke of Tuscany*, Oxford.

Mackie, J.D. (1952), *The Early Tudors, 1485–1558*, Oxford.

MacLean, I. (2009), *Learning and the Market Place: Essays in the History of the Early-Modern Book*, Leiden.

MacLeod, J. (1918), 'The Duke of Tuscany and His Shipwrecked Cargo', 15 Scottish Historical Review 245.

MacMillan, K. (2006), *Sovereignty and Possession in the English New World: The Legal Foundations of Empire, 1576–1640*, Cambridge.

MacMullen, R. (1967), *Enemies of the Roman Order: Treason, Unrest and Alienation in the Empire*, Cambridge, MA.

Major, J.R. (1994), *From Renaissance Monarchy to Absolute Monarchy: French Kings, Nobles and Estates*, Baltimore, MD.

Malcolm, N. (2002), *Aspects of Hobbes*, Oxford, 2002.

Malcolm, N. (2015), *Agents of Empire: Knights, Corsairs, Jesuits and Spies in the Sixteenth-Century Mediterranean World*, London.

Mallett, M. (1990), 'The Theory and Practice of Warfare in Machiavelli's Republic', in G. Bock, Q. Skinner and M. Viroli (eds), *Machiavelli and Republicansim*, Cambridge, p. 173.

Malo, H. (1913), *Les corsaires dunkerquois et Jean Bart, des origines à 1662*, Paris.

Manke, E. (2002), 'Empire and State', in D. Armitage and M.J. Braddick (eds), *The British Atlantic World, 1500–1800*, Basingstoke, p. 175.

Mansfield, H.C. (1996), *Machiavelli's Virtue*, Chicago.

Marcocci, G. (2014), 'Conscience and Empire: Politics and Moral Theology in the Early Portuguese World', 18 *Journal of Early Modern History* 473.

Marcus, L.S. (1986), 'Shakespeare's Comic Heroines, Elizabeth I and the Political Uses of Androgyny', in M.B. Rose (ed.), *Women in the Middle Ages and the Renaissance: Literary and Historical Perspectives*, Syracuse, NY, p. 135.

Marsden, R.G. (1894–7), 'Introduction', in *Select Pleas in the Court of Admiralty*, 2 vols, London, vol. 1, p. XI.

Marsden, R.G. (1907), 'The Vice-Admirals of the Coast', 22 *English Historical Review* 468.

Marsden, R.G. (1909), 'Early Prize Jurisdiction and Prize Law in England', 24 *English Historical Review* 675.

Marsden, R.G. (1910), 'Early Prize Jurisdiction and Prize Law in England, Part II', 25 *English Historical Review* 243.

Marsden, R.G. (1911), 'Early Prize Jurisdiction and Prize Law in England, Part III', 26 *English Historical Review* 34.

Marshall, C.K. (1997), 'Putting Privateers in Their Place: The Applicability of the Marque and Reprisal Clause to Undeclared Wars', 64 *University of Chicago Law Review* 953.

Martin, C. and Parker, G. (1989), *The Spanish Armada*, London.

Martin, F.F. (2002), 'Delineating a Hierarchical Outline of International Law Sources and Norms', 65 *Saskatchewan Law Review* 333.

Martines, L. (1968), *Lawyers and Statecraft in Renaissance Florence*, Princeton.

Martínez-Fernández, L. (2015), 'Far beyond the Line: Corsairs, Privateers, Buccaneers and Invading Settlers in Cuba and the Caribbean, 1529–1670', 75 *Revista de Indias* 7.

Martinière, G. (1997), 'Autour de La Popelinière', in M. Acerra and G. Martinière (eds), *Coligny, les protestants et la mer*, Paris, p. 45.

Marx, S. (1995), 'Holy War in *Henry V*', 48 *Shakespeare Survey* 85.

Mathew, D. (1924), 'The Cornish and Welsh Pirates in the Reign of Elizabeth', 39 *English Historical Review* 337.

Matthew, H.C.G. and Harrison, B.H., eds, (2004), *Oxford Dictionary of National Biography*, 61 vols, Oxford.

Mattingly, G. (1963), 'No Peace beyond What Line?', 13 *Transactions of the Royal Historical Society* 145.

Mattingly, G. (1988), *Renaissance Diplomacy*, New York.

Mattox, J.M. (2000), 'Henry V: Shakespeare's Just Warrior', 12 *War, Literature and the Arts* 30.

Maxwell, A. (1884), *The History of Old Dundee*, Edinburgh.

McCrea, A. (1997), *Constant Minds: Political Virtue and the Lipsian Paradigm in England, 1584–1650*, Toronto.

McDermott, J. (2001), *Martin Frobisher: Elizabethan Privateer*, New Haven.

McDermott, J. (2005), *England and the Spanish Armada: The Necessary Quarrel*, New Haven.

McGlynn, M. (1998), 'The King and the Law: *Prerogativa regis* in Early Tudor England', PhD dissertation, University of Toronto.

McGlynn, M. (2003), *The Royal Prerogative and the Learning of the Inns of Court*, Cambridge.

McInerny, R. (1982), *Ethica Thomistica: The Moral Philosophy of Thomas Aquinas*, Washington.

McKechnie, P. (1989), *Outsiders in the Greek Cities in the Fourth Century BC*, London.

McLaren, A.N. (1999), *Political Culture in the Reign of Elizabeth I: Queen and Commonwealth, 1558–85*, Cambridge.

McLaughlin, C. (2014), 'Scottish Commercial Contacts with the Iberian World, 1581–1730', PhD dissertation, University of St Andrews.

McMillan, A.R.G. (1936), 'Admiralty and Maritime Law', in H. McKechnie (ed.), *An Introductory Survey of the Sources and Literature of Scots Law*, Edinburgh, p. 325.

McNeill, J.T. (1941), 'Natural Law in the Thought of Luther', 10 *Church History* 211.

Mears, T.L. (1908), 'The History of the Admiralty Jurisdiction', in *Select Essays in Anglo-American Legal History*, Cambridge, vol. 2, p. 312.

Mebane, J.S. (2007), '"Impious War": Religion and the Ideology of Warfare in *Henry V*', 104 *Studies in Philology* 250.

Meekings, C.A.F. (1961), *Crown Pleas of the Wiltshire Eyre, 1249*, Devizes.

Meichsner, M. (2019), 'Islands and Maritime Conflicts: Gotland around 1500', in T. Heebøll-Holm, P. Höhn and G. Rohmann (eds), *Merchants, Pirates and Smugglers: Criminalisation, Economics and the Transformation of the Maritime World, 1200–1600*, Frankfurt, p. 189.

Meier, D. (2006), *Seafarers, Merchants and Pirates in the Middle Ages*, Woodbridge.

Mercer, M. (2005), 'The Administration of the Cinque Ports in the Early Lancastrian Period', in K. Dockray and P. Fleming (eds), *People, Places and Perspectives: Essays on Late-Medieval and Early-Tudor England in Honour of Ralph A. Griffiths*, Stroud, p. 47.

Meron, T. (1993), *Henry's Wars and Shakespeare's Laws: Perspectives on the Law of War in the Later Middle Ages*, Oxford.

Merriman, M. (2000), *The Rough Wooings: Mary Queen of Scots, 1542–51*, East Linton.

Merry, S.E. (1988), 'Legal Pluralism', 22 *Law and Society Review* 869.

Meyer, J.P. (1996), *Reformation in La Rochelle: Tradition and Change in Early-Modern Europe, 1500–68*, Geneva.

Meyerson, M.D. (1996), 'Slavery and Solidarity: Mudejars and Foreign Muslim Captives in the Kingdom of Valencia', 2 *Medieval Encounters* 286.

Meyjes, G.M.M.P. (1991), 'Exponents of Sovereignty: Canonists as Seen by Theologians in the Later Middle Ages', Subsidia 9 *Studies in Church History* 299.

Michaud-Quantin, P. (1962), *Sommes de casuistique et manuels de confession au Moyen Âge*, Louvain.

Michienzi, I.H. (2014), '"Que Dieu les engloutisse!": Les reactions des milieu marchands italiens face à la guerre de course et à la piraterie en Méditerranée, fin XIVe-début XVe siècle', in M. Battesti (ed.), *La piraterie au fil de l'histoire: Un défi pour l'état*, Paris, p. 299.

Miller, F.D. (2014), 'The Rule of Reason in Cicero's Philosophy of Law', 33 *University of Queensland Law Journal* 321.

Miller, J. (2013), 'The Scottish Mercenary as a Migrant Labourer in Europe, 1550–1650', in E.J. Zürcher (ed.), *Fighting for a Living: A Comparative Study of Military Labour, 1500–2000*, Amsterdam, p. 169.

Miller, W.I. (1990), *Bloodtaking and Peacemaking: Feud, Law and Society in Saga Iceland*, Chicago.

Milsom, S.F.C. (1981), *Historical Foundations of the Common Law*, London.

Mindle, G.B. (1985), 'Machiavelli's Realism', 47 *Review of Politics* 212.

Minnucci, G. (2016), 'Alberico Gentili', in S. Dauchy, G. Martyn, A. Musson, H. Pihlajamäki and A. Wijffels (eds), *The Formation and Transmission of Western Legal Culture: 150 Books that Made the Law in the Age of Printing*, Cham, p. 149.

Mishra, R. (2018), *A Business of State: Commerce, Politics and the Birth of the East India Company*, Cambridge, MA.

Mollat, M. (1976), 'De la piraterie sauvage à la course réglementée, XIVe–XVe siècle', in M. Mollat (ed.), *Course et piraterie: Études présentées pendant le XIVe Congrès international des sciences historiques (San Francisco, août 1975)*, 3 vols, Paris, vol. 1, p. 162.

Mollat, M. (1980), 'Essai d'orientation pour l'étude de la guerre de course et la piraterie, XIIIe–XVe siècles', 10 *Anuario de estudios medievales* 743.

Mollat, M. (1993), *Europe and the Sea*, Oxford.

Monchicourt, C. (1918), 'Épisodes de la carrière tunisienne de Dragut, 1550–51', 25 *Revue tunisienne* 35.

Moore, T.K. (2012), 'The Cost-Benefit Analysis of a Fourteenth-Century Naval Campaign: Margate/Cadzand, 1387', in R. Gorski (ed.), *Roles of the Sea in Medieval England*, Woodbridge, p. 103.

Moote, A.L. (1989), *Louis XIII, the Just*, Berkeley.

Morford, M. (1993), 'Tacitean *Prudentia* and the Doctrines of Justus Lipsius', in T.J. Luce and A.J. Woodman (eds), *Tacitus and the Tacitean Tradition*, Princeton, p. 129.

Morford, M. (2002), *The Roman Philosophers, from the Time of Cato the Censor to the Death of Marcus Aurelius*, London.

Morris, D.B. (1919), *The Stirling Merchant Gild and the Life of John Cowane*, Stirling.

Mörsdorf, K. (1968), 'Forum', 2 *Sacramentum Mundi* 344.

Motley, J.L. (1882), *The Rise of the Dutch Republic: A History*, London.

Mowat, S. (1994), *The Port of Leith*, Edinburgh.

Mowat, S. and Graham, E.J. (2005), High Court of Admiralty Scotland Records, 1627–1750, CDROM.

Muldoon, J. (1979), *Popes, Lawyers and Infidels*, Liverpool.

Muldoon, J. (1980), 'John Wyclif and the Rights of the Infidels: The *Requerimiento* Reexamined', 36 *Americas* 301.

Muldoon, J. (2016), 'Is the Sea Open or Closed? The Grotius-Selden Debate Revisited', in K. Pennington and M.H. Eichbauer (eds), *Law as Profession and Practice in Medieval Europe: Essays in Honor of James A. Brundage*, Abingdon, p. 117.

Müller, W.P. (2015), 'The Internal Forum of the Later Middle Ages: A Modern Myth?', 33 *Law and History Review* 887.

Mullett, M.A. (1999), *The Catholic Reformation*, London.

Murdoch, S. (1998), 'The House of Stuart and the Scottish Professional Soldier, 1618–40: A Conflict of Nationality and Identities', in B. Taith and T. Thornton (eds), *War: Identities in Conflict, 1300–2000*, Stroud, p. 37.

Murdoch, S. (2001), 'Scottish Ambassadors and British Diplomacy, 1618–35', in S. Murdoch (ed.), *Scotland and the Thirty Years War, 1618–48*, Leiden, p. 27.

Murdoch, S. (2003), *Britain, Denmark-Norway and House of Stuart, 1603–60*, East Linton.

Murdoch, S. (2010), *The Terror of the Seas? Scottish Maritime Warfare, 1513–1713*, Leiden.

Murdoch, S., Little, A. and Forte, A. (2003), 'Scottish Privateering, Swedish Neutrality and Prize Law in the Third Anglo-Dutch War, 1672–74', 59 *Forum Navale* 37.

Murphy, M.N. (2013), 'The Barbary Pirates', 24 *Mediterranean Quarterly* 19.

Murphy, N. (2016), 'Violence, Colonisation and Henry VIII's Conquest of France, 1544–46', 233 *Past and Present* 13.

Murray, K.M.E. (1935), *The Constitutional History of the Cinque Ports*, Manchester.

Musa, S. (2017), 'Victims of Maritime Conflict, Compensation Claims and the Role of the Admiralty Courts in the Early Modern Period', 5 *Comparative Legal History* 125.

Myers, W.D. (1996), *'Poor Sinning Folk': Confession and Conscience in Counter-Reformation Germany*, Ithaca, NY.

Nash, J.C. (1979), 'Stoicism and the Stoic Theme of *Honestum* in Early French Renaissance Literature', 76 *Studies in Philology* 203.

Neale, J.E. (1992), *Queen Elizabeth I*, Chicago.

Nederman, C.J. (1998), 'The Mirror Crack'd: The *Speculum principum* as Political and Social Criticism in the Late Middle Ages', 3 *European Legacy* 18.

Neff, S.C. (2000), *The Rights and Duties of Neutrals: A General History*, Manchester.

Neff, S.C. (2005), *War and the Law of Nations: A General History*, Cambridge.

Neilson, G. (1971), 'The March Laws', in I.D. Willock (ed.), *Stair Society: Miscellany One*, Edinburgh, p. 12.

Nellen, H.J.M. (2012), 'On the Occasion of the Acquisition of the First Edition of *De iure belli ac pacis* by the Peace Palace Library', 33 *Grotiana* 1.

Nellen, H.J.M. (2018), *Hugo Grotius: A Lifelong Struggle for Peace in Church and State, 1583–1645*, Leiden.

Neville, C.J. (1988), 'Border Law in Late-Medieval England', 9 *Journal of Legal History* 335.

Neville, C.J. (1991), 'The Law of Treason in the English Border Counties in the Later Middle Ages', 9 *Law and History Review* 1.

Newton, D. (2005), *The Making of the Jacobean Regime*, Woodbridge.

Nicgorski, W. (1984), 'Cicero's Paradoxes and His Idea of Utility', 12 *Political Theory* 557.

Nicholas, B. (1962), *An Introduction to Roman Law*, Oxford.

Nicholas, D. (1955), *Secretary Nicholas, 1593–1669: His Life and Letters*, London.

Nicholls, A.D. (1999), *The Jacobean Union: A Reconstruction of British Civil Policies under the Early Stuarts*, Westport, CT.

Nicolas, N.H. (1847), *A History of the Royal Navy*, 2 vols, London.

Niermeyer, J.F., van de Kieft, C. and Burgers, J.W.J. (2002), *Mediae Latinitatis lexicon minus*, 2 vols, Leiden.

Noreña, C.G. (1975), *Studies in Spanish Renaissance Thought*, The Hague.

O'Banion, P.J. (2012), 'Only the King Can Do It: Adaptations and Flexibility in Crusade Ideology in Sixteenth-Century Spain', 81 *Church History* 552.

Obbink, D. (1999), 'The Stoic Sage in the Cosmic City', in K. Ierodiakonou (ed.), *Topics in Stoic Philosophy*, Oxford, p. 178.

O'Brien, J.G. (2001), 'The *Ius Commune* Law of War: Giovanni da Legnano's *De bello* and the Medieval Origins of International Public Law', PhD dissertation, University of Kansas.

O'Brien, J.G. (2002), 'In Defense of the Mystical Body: Giovanni da Legnano's Theory of Reprisals', 1 *Roman Law Tradition* 25.

Ochon, C. (2007), 'The Individual and Customary International Law Formation', 48 *Virginia Journal of International Law* 119.

Oestreich, G. (1982), *Neostoicism and the Early-Modern State*, tr. D. McLintock, Cambridge.

Ogborn, M. (2008), *Global Lives: Britain and the World, 1550–1800*, Cambridge.

Ogilvie, S. (2011), *Institutions and European Trade: Merchant Guilds, 1000–1800*, Cambridge.

O'Hara, G. (2010), *Britain and the Sea since 1600*, Basingstoke.

Oliveira e Silva, P. (2016), 'The Concept of *Ius gentium*: Some Aspects of Its Doctrinal Development from the School of Salamanca to the Universities of Coimbra and Evora', in K. Bunge, M.J. Fuchs, D. Simmermacher and A. Spindler (eds), *The Concept of Law (Lex) in the Moral and Political Thought of the 'School of Salamanca'*, Leiden, p. 106.

O'Malley, J.W. (1993), *The First Jesuits*, Cambridge, MA.

Onuma, Y., ed. (1993), *A Normative Approach to War: Peace, War and Justice in Hugo Grotius*, Oxford.

Onuma, Y., ed. (2000), 'When Was the Law of International Society Born? An Inquiry of the History of International Law from an Intercivilizational Perspective', 2 *Journal of the History of International Law* 1.

Oppenheim, M.M. (1968), *The Maritime History of Devon*, Torquay.

Ormerod, H.A. (1924), *Piracy in the Ancient World: An Essay in Mediterranean History*, Liverpool.

Orsini, N. (1946), '"Policy", or the Language of Elizabethan Machiavellianism', 9 *Journal of the Warburg and Courtauld Institutes* 122.

Osler, D.J. (2016), 'The Restless Mind and the Living Text: The First Edition of Grotius' *De iure belli ac pacis*', 37 *Grotiana* 1.

Oudendijk, J.K. (1964), 'De Kaperbrieven van Willem van Oranje', 19 *Bijdragen voor de Geschiedenis der Nederlanden* 133.

Pace, P. (2014), 'Suárez on the Natural Law', in V. Salas and R. Fastiggi (eds), *A Companion to Francisco Suárez*, Leiden, p. 274.

Padovani, A. (2016), '*Liber primus (-septimus) consiliorum Alexandri Imolensis*', in S. Dauchy, G. Martyn, A. Musson, H. Pihlajamäki and A. Wijffels (eds), *The Formation and Transmission of Western Legal Culture: 150 Books that Made the Law in the Age of Printing*, Cham, p. 53.

Pagden, A. (1981), 'The search for Order: The "School of Salamanca" and the *Ius naturae*', in F.W. Hodcroft (ed.), *Medieval and Renaissance Studies on Spain and Portugal in Honour of P.E. Russell*, Oxford, p. 155.

Pangle, T.L. (1998), 'Socratic Cosmopolitanism: Cicero's Critique and Transformation of the Stoic Ideal', 31 *Canadian Journal of Political Science* 235.

Panizza, D. (2008), 'Gentili and the Theological Tradition of War: The Critical Points of a Change of Paradigm', in *Alberico Gentili: La salvaguardia dei beni culturali nel diritto internazionale*, Milan, p. 145.

Panizza, D. (2009), 'The "Freedom of the Sea" and the "Modern Cosmopolis" in Alberico Gentili's *De iure belli*', 30 *Grotiana* 88.

Panizza, D. (2010), 'Alberico Gentili's *De armis Romanis*: The Roman Model of the Just Empire', in B. Kingsbury and B. Straumann (eds), *The Roman Foundations of the Law of Nations: Alberico Gentili and the Justice of Empire*, Oxford, p. 53.

Panizza, D. (2013), 'Political Theory and Jurisprudence in Gentili's *De iure belli*: The Great Debate between "Theological" and "Humanist" Perspectives from Vitoria to Grotius', in P.-M. Dupuy and V. Chetail (eds), *Les fondements du droit international: Liber amicorum Peter Haggenmacher*, Leiden, p. 211.

Papy, J. (2001), 'Lipsius' (Neo-)Stoicism: Constancy between Christian Faith and Stoic Virtue', 22 *Grotiana* 47.

Parker, D. (1980), *La Rochelle and the French Monarchy: Conflict and Order in Seventeenth-Century France*, London.

Parker, G. (1979), *The Dutch Revolt*, Harmondsworth.

Parker, G. (1980), *Europe in Crisis, 1598–1648*, Brighton.

Parker, G. (1987), *The Thirty Years War*, London.

Parker, G. (1998), *The Grand Strategy of Philip II*, New Haven.

Parker, G. (2004), *The Army of Flanders and the Spanish Road, 1567–1659*, Cambridge.

Parker, G. (2014), *Imprudent King: A New Life of Philip II*, New Haven.

Parker, K. (2008), 'Politics and Patronage in Lynn, 1399–1416', in G. Dodd and D. Briggs (eds), *The Reign of Henry IV: Rebellion and Survival, 1403–13*, Woodbridge, p. 210.

Parmelee, L.F. (1994), 'Neostoicism and Absolutism in Late-Elizabethan England', in A.E. Bakos (ed.), *Politics, Ideology and the Law in Early-Modern Europe*, Rochester, NY, p. 3.

Parmelee, L.F. (1996), *Good Newes from Fraunce: French Anti-League Propaganda in Late-Elizabethan England*, Rochester, NY.

Parrott, D. (1997), 'A "Prince Souverain" and the French Crown: Charles de Nevers, 1580–1637', in R. Oresko, G.C. Gibbs and H.M. Scott (eds), *Royal and Republican Sovereignty in Early-Modern Europe: Essays in Memory of Ragnhild Hatton*, Cambridge, p. 149.

Parrow, K.A. (1991), 'Neither Treason nor Heresy: Use of Defense Arguments to Avoid Forfeiture during the French Wars of Religion', 22 *Sixteenth Century Journal* 705.

Parry, J.H. (1963), *The Age of Reconnaissance: Discovery, Exploration and Settlement, 1450–1650*, London.

Parthesius, R. (2010), *Dutch Ships in Tropical Waters: The Development of the Dutch East India Company (VOC) Shipping Network in Asia, 1595–1660*, Amsterdam.

Patterson, W.B. (1997), *King James VI and I and the Reunion of Christendom*, Cambridge.

Patterson, W.B. (2014), *William Perkins and the Making of a Protestant England*, Oxford.

Pawlisch, H.S. (1985), *Sir John Davies and the Conquest of Ireland: A Study of Legal Imperialism*, Cambridge.

Pellegrino, F. (2012), 'Historical and Legal Aspects of Piracy and Armed Robbery against Shipping', 43 *Journal of Maritime Law and Commerce* 429.

Peltonen, M. (1995), *Classical Humanism and Republicanism in English Political Thought, 1570–1640*, Cambridge.

Penn, C.D. (1920), *The Navy under the Early Stuarts and Its Influence on English History*, London.

Penna, D. (2017), 'Piracy and Reprisal in Byzantine Waters: Resolving a Maritime Conflict between Byzantines and Genoese at the end of the Twelfth Century', 5 *Comparative Legal History* 36.

Penner, S. (2020), 'Making Use of the Testimonies: Suárez and Grotius on Natural Law', 41 *Grotiana* 108.

Pennington, K. (2013), '*Moderamen inculpatae tutelae*: The Jurisprudence of a Justifiable Defence', 24 *Rivista internazionale di diritto comune* 27.

Pérotin-Dumon, A. (1991), 'The Pirate and the Emperor: Power and the Law on the Seas, 1450–1850', in J.D. Tracy (ed.), *The Political Economy of Merchant Empires*, Cambridge, p. 196.

Perruso, R. (2002) 'The Development of the Doctrine of *Res communes* in Medieval and Early-Modern Europe', 70 *Tijdschrift voor Rechtsgeschiedenis* 69.

Petrie, D.A. (1999), *The Prize Game: Lawful Looting on the High Seas in the Days of Fighting Sail*, New York.

Phillips, W.A. (1896), 'The Influence of Machiavelli on the Reformation in England', 40 *Nineteenth Century* 907.

Picard, C. (2016), 'La piraterie musulman en Méditerranée au Moyen Âge', in G. Buti and P. Hroděj (eds), *Histoire des pirates et des corsairs de l'antiquité à nos jours*, Paris, p. 129.

Piergiovanni, V. (1980), *Gli statuti civili e criminali di Genova nel Medioevo*, Genoa.

Piette, G. (2008), *Brittany: A Concise History*, Cardiff.

Piirimäe, P. (2010), 'Alberico Gentili's Doctrine of Defensive War and Its Impact on Seventeenth Century Normative Views', in B. Kingsbury and B. Straumann (eds), *The Roman Foundations of the Law of Nations: Alberico Gentili and the Justice of Empire*, Oxford, p. 187.

Pirillo, D. (2013), 'Republicanism and Religious Dissent: Machiavelli and the Italian Protestant Reformers', in A. Arienzo and A. Petrina (eds), *Machiavellian Encounters in Tudor and Stuart England: Literary and Political Influences from the Reformation to the Restoration*, Farnham, p. 121.

Pistono, S.P. (1975), 'Henry IV and the English Privateers', 90 *English Historical Review* 322.

Pita, V.O. (2017), 'Commercial Litigation across Religious Borders: Rendering Justice for Valencian Merchants in Fifteenth-Century North Africa and Granada', 5 *Comparative Legal History* 88.

Pitcaithly, M. (2012), 'Piracy and Anglo-Hanseatic Relations, 1385–1420', in R. Gorski (ed.), *Roles of the Sea in Medieval England*, Woodbridge, p. 125.

Pittock, M. (2009), 'The Problem of *Henry V*', 93 *Neophilologus* 175.

Pitts, V.J. (2009), *Henri IV of France: His Reign and Age*, Baltimore.

Policante, A. (2015), *The Pirate Myth: Genealogies of an Imperial Concept*, London.

Polišenský, J.V. (2001), 'A Note on Scottish Soldiers in the Bohemian War, 1619–22', in S. Murdoch (ed.), *Scotland and the Thirty Years War, 1618–48*, Leiden, p. 109.

Pollock, F. and Maitland, F.W. (2010), *The History of English Law before the Time of Edward I*, 2 vols, Indianapolis.

Popescu, O.A. (2008), '*Henry V*: The Machiavellian Production of an Ideal King', 10 *University of Bucharest Review* 130.

Porras, I.M. (2006), 'Constructing International Law in the East Indian Seas: Property, Sovereignty, Commerce and War in Hugo Grotius' *De iure praedae – The Law of Prize and Booty, or "On How to Distinguish Merchants from Pirates"*', 31 *Brooklyn Journal of International Law* 742.

Postan, M.M. (1973), *Medieval Trade and Finance*, Cambridge.

Postema, G.J. (2007), 'Custom in International Law: A Normative Practice Account', in A. Perreau-Saussine and J.B. Murphy (eds), *The Nature of Customary Law*, Cambridge, p. 279.

Poton, D. (2004), 'Des corsaires bretons au service de la cause huguenote: Les Trimault de Croisic', in E. Berriot-Salvadore, P. Chareyre and C. Martin-Ulrich (eds), *Jeanne d'Albret et sa cour*, Paris, p. 59.

Poton, D. (2009), 'Des corsaires bretons au service de la cause: Les Trimault de Croisic', in M. Augeron, D. Poton and B. van Ruymbeke (eds), *Les Huguenots et l'Atlantique, vol. 1: Pour Dieu, la cause ou les affaires*, Paris, p. 213.

Potter, D. (2011), *Henry VIII and Francis I: The Final Conflict, 1540–47*, Leiden.

Powell, E. (1989), *Kingship, Law and Society: Criminal Justice in the Reign of Henry V*, Oxford.

Powell, J.G.F. (2001), 'Were Cicero's *Laws* the Laws of Cicero's *Republic*?', in J.G.F, Powell and J. North (eds), *Cicero's Republic*, London, p. 17.

Powers, J.F. (1988), *A Society Organized for War: The Iberian Militias in the Central Middle Ages, 1000–1284*, Berkeley.

Prak, M. (2005), *The Dutch Republic in the Seventeenth Century*, tr. D. Webb, Cambridge.

Praz, M. (1928), 'Machiavelli and the Elizabethans', 13 *Proceedings of the British Academy* 3.

Prest, W. (1982), 'William Fulbecke (1560–1616)', 3 *Journal of Legal History* 172.

Prétou, P. (2014), 'Du "larron écumeur de mer" aux "pirathes": Les genèses de l'accusation en piraterie à la fin du Moyen Âge français', in M. Battesti (ed.), *La piraterie au fil de l'histoire: Un défi pour l'état*, Paris, p. 37.

Prétou, P. (2016), 'L'essor de la piraterie en Europe du XIIIe au XVe siècle', in G. Buti and P. Hroděj (eds), *Histoire des pirates et des corsairs de l'antiquité à nos jours*, Paris, p. 93.

Prétou, P. (2021), *L'invention de la piraterie en France au Moyen Âge*, Paris.

Price, J.L. (2000), *Dutch Society, 1588–1713*, Cambridge.

Price, R. (1973), 'The Senses of *Virtù* in Machiavelli', 3 *European Studies Review* 315.

Prichard, M.J. and Yale, D.E.C. (1993), 'Introduction', in *Hale and Fleetwood on Admiralty Jurisdiction*, London.

Pryor, J.H. (1988), *Geography, Technology and War: Studies in the Maritime History of the Mediterranean, 649–1571*, Cambridge.

Pugliatti, P. (2010), *Shakespeare and the Just War Tradition*, Farnham.

Quabeck, F. (2013), *Just and Unjust Wars in Shakespeare*, Berlin.

Quaglioni, D. (2010), 'Pour une histoire du droit de guerre au début de l'âge modern: Bodin, Gentili, Grotius', 10 *Laboratoire italien* 27.

Quaglioni, D. (2013), 'The Italian 'Readers' of Bodin, 17th-18th Centuries: The Italian Readers out of Italy – Alberico Gentili', in H.A. Lloyd (ed.), *The Reception of Bodin*, Leiden, p. 371.

Queller, D.E. (1967), *The Office of Ambassador in the Middle Ages*, Princeton.

Quinn, D.B. (1990), *Explorers and Colonies: America, 1500–1625*, London.

Quinn, D.B. and Ryan, A.N. (1983), *England's Sea Empire, 1550–1642*, London.

Raab, F. (1964), *The English Face of Machiavelli: A Changing Interpretation, 1500–1700*, London.

Rabb, T.K. (1998), *Jacobean Gentleman: Sir Edwin Sandys, 1561–1629*, Princeton.

Rabkin, N. (1977), 'Rabbits, Ducks and *Henry V*', 28 *Shakespeare Quarterly* 279.

Rae, T.I. (1966), *The Administration of the Scottish Frontier, 1513–1603*, Edinburgh.

Ragni, C. (2016), 'Shakespeare's "Quarrel Honourable" and Gentili's "Iusta Contentio": *Henry V* and the Forging of the Nation', 16 *Studies in Ethnicity and Nationaliam* 218.

Rait, R.S. (1924), *The Parliaments of Scotland*, Glasgow.

Rambeaud, P. (1997), 'L'amiral à La Rochelle: L'union du ciel et de la mer', in M. Acerra and G. Martinière (eds), *Coligny, les protestants et la mer*, Paris, p. 131.

Ramsay, G.D. (1975), *The City of London in International Politics at the Accession of Elizabeth Tudor*, Manchester.

Ramsay, G.D. (1986), *The Queen's Merchants and the Revolt in the Netherlands*, Manchester.

Rauh, N.K. (2003), *Merchants, Sailors and Pirates in the Roman World*, Stroud.

Rawson, E. (1973), 'The Interpretation of Cicero's *De legibus*', 1 *Aufsteig und Niedergang der römischen Welt* 334.

Read, C. (1955), *Mr Secretary Cecil and Queen Elizabeth*, London.

Redlich, F. (1956), *De praeda militari: Looting and Booty, 1500–1815*, Wiesbaden.

Reeves, J.S. (1925), 'The First Edition of Grotius' *De iure belli ac pacis*, 1625', 19 *American Journal of International Law* 12.

Reichberg, G.M. (2012), 'Suárez on Just War', in D. Schwartz (ed.), *Interpreting Suárez: Critical Essays*, Cambridge, p. 185.

Reichberg, G.M., Syse, H. and Begby, E. (2006), *The Ethics of War: Classic and Contemporary Readings*, Oxford.

Reid, C.R. (2011), 'The Rights of Self-Defence and Justified Warfare in the Writings of the Twelfth- and Thirteenth-Century Canonists', in K. Pennington and M.H. Eichbauer (eds), *Law as Profession and Practice in Medieval Europe: Essays in Honor of James A. Brundage*, Farnham, p. 73.

Reid, R.C. (1936–8), 'The Merkland Cross', 21 *Transactions of the Dumfriesshire and Galloway Natural History and Antiquarian Society* 216.

Reid, W.S. (1962), *Skipper from Leith: The History of Robert Barton of Over Barton*, Philadelphia.

Remer, G. (2009), 'Rhetoric as a Balancing of Ends: Cicero and Machiavelli', 42 *Philosophy and Rhetoric* 1.

Remer, G. (2011), 'Ciceronian *Ius gentium* and World Legislation', 8 *International Organizations Law Review* 225.

Remer, G. (2016), 'Justus Lipsius, Morally Acceptable Deceit and Prudence in the Ciceronian Tradition', 37 *History of Political Thought* 238.

Rey, A., ed. (1992), *Dictionnaire historique de la langue française*, 2 vols, Paris.

Reyerson, K.L. (2003), 'Commercial Law and Merchant Disputes: Jacques Coeur and the Law of Marque', 9 *Medieval Encounters* 244.

Rich, J. (2011), 'The *Fetiales* and Roman International Relations', in J.H. Richardson and F. Santangelo (eds), *Priests and State in the Roman World*, Stuttgart, p. 187.

Richards, P. (2005), 'The Hinterland and Overseas Trade of King's Lynn, 1205–1537: An Introduction', in K. Friedland and P. Richards (eds), *Essays in Hanseatic History*, Dereham, p. 10.

Richardson, G. (2013), *The Field of Cloth of Gold*, New Haven.

Riddell, J. (1852), *Inquiry into the Law and Practice on Scottish Peerages*, 2 vols, Edinburgh.

Riesenberg, P. (1969), 'Civism and Roman Law in Fourteenth-Century Italian Society', 7 *Explorations in Economic History* 237.

Riesenberg, P. (1974), 'Citizenship at Law in Late-Medieval Italy', 5 *Viator* 333.

Rigaud, P. (1991), 'Pirates et corsaires sur le bas-Rhône, IXe–XVe siècles', in M. Vergé-Franceschi (ed.), *Guerre et commerce en Méditerranée, IX–XX siècles*, Paris, p. 37.

Riggsby, A.M. (1999), *Crime and Community in Ciceronian Rome*, Austin.

Ritchie, P.E. (2002), *Mary of Guise in Scotland, 1548–60: A Political Career*, East Linton.

Robbins, K.C. (1997), *City on the Ocean Sea: La Rochelle, 1530–1650*, Leiden.

Roberts, A.E. (2001), 'Traditional and Modern Approaches to Customary International Law: A Reconciliation', 95 *American Journal of International Law* 757.

Robinson, O.F. (1995), *The Criminal Law of Ancient Rome*, London.

Robinson, O.F., Fergus, T.D. and Gordon, W.M. (2000), *European Legal History: Sources and Institutions*, London.

Roby, H.J. (1902), *Roman Private Law in the Times of Cicero and of the Antonines*, 2 vols, Cambridge.

Rodger, N.A.M. (1997), *The Safeguard of the Sea*, London.

Rodger, N.A.M. (2003), 'The New Atlantic: Naval Warfare in the Sixteenth Century', in J.B. Hattendorf and R.W. Unger (eds), *War at Sea in the Middle Ages and the Renaissance*, Woodbridge, p. 233.

Rodger, N.A.M. (2004) 'Queen Elizabeth and the Myth of Sea Power in English History', 14 *Transactions of the Royal Historical Society* 153.

Rodger, N.A.M. (2014) 'The Law and Language of Private Naval Warfare', 100 *Mariner's Mirror* 6.

Roe, J. (2007), 'Shakespeare and Machiavelli: *The Prince* and the History Plays', in P. Vilches and G. Seaman (eds), *Seeking Real Truths: Multidisciplinary Perspectives on Machiavelli*, Leiden, p. 357.

Roelker, N.L. (1968), *Queen of Navarre: Jeanne d'Albret, 1528–72*, Cambridge, MA.

Roelofsen, C.G. (1980), 'Early Dutch Prize Law: Some Thoughts on a Case before the Court of Holland and the Grand Council of Mechelen, 1477–82', 27 *Netherlands International Law Review* 218.

Roelofsen, C.G. (1983), 'Some Remarks on the "Sources" of the Grotian System of International Law', 30 *Netherlands International Law Review* 73.

Roelofsen, C.G. (1984), 'L'amirauté à Veere, considérée dans ses attributions judiciaires, XVe–XVIe siècles', 24 *Publications du Centre Européen d'Études Bourguignonnes (XIV–XVI siècles)* 67.

Roelofsen, C.G. (1987), 'La relation entre le droit romain et le droit coutumier dans quelques procès de prise maritime devant la Cour de Hollande et le Grand Conseil de Malines', in G. Marcours (ed.), *Cornua legum*, Antwerp, p. 167.

Roelofsen, C.G. (1989a), 'The Sources of *Mare liberum*: The Contested Origins of the Doctrine of the Freedom of the Seas', in W.P. Heere (ed.), *International Law and Its Sources: Liber amicorum Maarten Bos*, The Hague, p. 93.

Roelofsen, C.G. (1989b), 'Grotius and the State Practice of His Day', 10 *Grotiana* 3.

Rohman, G. (2019), 'The Making of Connectivity: How Hamburg Tried to Gain Control over the Elbe River (13th 16th Centuries)', in T. Heebøll-Holm, P. Höhn and G. Rohmann (eds), *Merchants, Pirates and Smugglers: Criminalisation, Economics and the Transformation of the Maritime World, 1200–1600*, Frankfurt, p. 207.

Rommelse, G. (2003), 'English Privateering against the Dutch Republic during the Second Anglo-Dutch War, 1664–7', 22 *Tijdschrift voor Zeegeschichte* 17.

Ronald, S. (2007), *The Pirate Queen: Elizabeth I, Her Pirate Adventurers and the Dawn of Empire*, Stroud.

Roscoe, E.S. (1924), *A History of the English Prize Court*, London.

Rose, E. (1975), *Cases of Conscience: Alternatives Open to Recusants and Puritans under Elizabeth I and James I*, Cambridge.

Rose, J. (2011) 'Kingship and Counsel in Early-Modern England', 54 *Historical Journal* 47.

Rose, M.B. (2000) 'The Gendering of Authority in the Public Speeches of Elizabeth I', 115 *Publications of the Modern Language Association of America* 1077.

Rose, S. (1982), 'Introduction', in *The Navy of the Lancastrian Kings*, London, p. 1.

Rose, S. (2007), *The Medieval Sea*, London.

Rose, S. (2013), *England's Medieval Navy, 1066–1509: Ships, Men and Warfare*, Barnsley.

Rosenblatt, J.P. (2006), *Renaissance England's Chief Rabbi: John Selden*, Oxford.

Ross, R.J. (2015), 'Binding in Conscience: Early-Modern English Protestants and Spanish Thomists on Law and the Fate of the Soul', 33 *Law and History Review* 803.

Roth-Isigkeit, D. (2017), 'Niccolò Machiavelli's International Legal Thought: Culture, Contingency and Construction', in S. Kadelbach, T. Kleinlein and D. Roth-Isigkeit (eds), *System, Order and International Law: The Early History of International Legal Thought from Machiavelli to Hegel*, Oxford, p. 19.

Roumy, F. (2006), 'L'origine et la diffusion de l'adage canonique *Necessitas non habet legem,* VIIIe–XIIIe siècles', in W.P. Müller and M.E. Sommar (eds), *Medieval Church Law and the Origins of the Western Legal Tradition: A Tribute to Kenneth Pennington*, Washington, p. 301.

Rowen, H.H. (1988), *The Prince of Orange: The Stadholders in the Dutch Republic*, Cambridge.

Rowse, A.L. (1937), *Sir Richard Grenville of the Revenge: An Elizabethan Hero*, London.

Rowse, A.L. (1941), *Tudor Cornwall: Portrait of a Society*, London.

Rubin, A.P. (1998), *The Law of Piracy*, New York.

Ruigh, R.E. (1971), *The Parliament of 1624: Politics and Foreign Policy*, Cambridge, MA.

Runyan, T.J. (1975), 'The Rolls of Oleron and the Admiralty Court in Fourteenth-Century England', 19 *American Journal of Legal History* 95.

Ruoss, A. (2017), 'Competitive Collaboration: The Dutch and English East India Companies and the Forging of Global Corporate Political Economy, 1650–1700', PhD dissertation, Duke University.

Russell, C. (1974), *The Crisis of Parliaments: English History, 1509–1660*, Oxford.

Russell, F.H. (1975), *The Just War in the Middle Ages*, Cambridge.

Russon, M. (2004), *Les côtes guerrières: Mer, guerre et pouvoirs au Moyen Âge*, Rennes.

Sáenz-Cambra, C. (2005), *Scotland and Philip II, 1580–98*, Sevenoaks.

Salmon, J.H.M. (1975), *Society in Crisis: France in the Sixteenth Century*, London.

Salmon, J.H.M. (1980), 'Cicero and Tacitus in Sixteenth Century France', 85 *American Historical Review* 307.

Salvatori, E. (2007), 'Corsairs' Crews and Cross-Cultural Interactions: The Case of the Pisan Trapelcinus in the Twelfth Century', 3 *Medieval Encounters* 32.

Salzman, L.F. (1931), *English Trade in the Middle Ages*, Oxford.

Sanborn, F. (1930), *Origins of the Early English Maritime and Commercial Law*, New York.

Santangelo, F. (2008), 'The Fetials and Their *Ius*', 51 *Bulletin of the Institute of Classical Studies* 63.

Saulnier, C. (1980), 'Le rôle des prêtres fétiaux et l'application du *ius fetiale* à Rome', 58 *Revue historique du droit français et étranger* 171.

Sayers, W. (2002), 'Chaucer's Shipman and the Law Marine', 37 *Chaucer Review* 145.

Scarisbrick, J.J. (1997), *Henry VIII*, New Haven.

Scattola, M. (2009), 'Law, War and Method in the *Commentary on the Law of Prize* by Hugo Grotius', in H.W. Blom (ed.), *Property, Piracy and Punishment: Hugo Grotius on War and Booty in De iure praedae – Concepts and Contexts*, Leiden, p. 79.

Scattola, M. (2012), 'Alberico Gentili (1552–1608)', in B. Fassbender and A. Peters (eds), *The Oxford Handbook of the History of International Law*, Oxford, p. 1092.

Schermaier, M.J. (2009), '*Res communes omnium*: The History of an Idea from Greek Philosophy to Grotian Jurisprudence', 30 *Grotiana* 20.

Schnakenbourg, E. (2013), *Entre la guerre et la paix: Neutralité et relations internationales, XVIIe–XVIIIe siècles*, Rennes.

Schofield, M. (1999), *The Stoic Idea of the City*, Chicago.

Schröder, P. (2010), 'Taming the Fox and the Lion: Some Aspects of the Sixteenth Century's Debate on Inter-State Relations', in O. Asbach and P. Schröder (eds), *War, the State and International Law in Seventeenth-Century Europe*, Farnham, p. 83.

Schulz, F. (1951), *Classical Roman Law*, Oxford.

Schwarzenberger, G. (1948), 'International Law in Early English Practice', 25 *British Yearbook of International Law* 52.

Scott, D. (2013), *Leviathan: The Rise of Britain as a World Power*, London.

Scott, D. (2018), 'The Spanish Armada and England's Conflict with Spain, 1585–1604', in J. Davey (ed.), *Tudor and Stuart Seafarers: The Emergence of a Maritime Nation, 1485–1707*, London, p. 54.

Scott, J.B. (1934a), *The Spanish Origins of International Law: Francisco de Vitoria and His Law of Nations*, Oxford.

Scott, J.B. (1934b), *The Catholic Conception of International Law*, Washington.

Sechrest, L.J. (2004), 'Public Goods and Private Solutions in Maritime History', 7 *Quarterly Journal of Austrian Economics* 3.

Sedgwick, P.H. (2019), *The Origins of Anglican Moral Theology*, Leiden.

Seipp, D.J. (1994), 'The Concept of Property in the Early Common Law', 12 *Law and History Review* 29.

Sellars, J. (2006), *Stoicism*, Chesham.

Sellars, J. (2007), 'Stoic Cosmopolitanism and Zeno's *Republic*', 28 *History of Political Thought* 1.

Sereni, A.P. (1943), *The Italian Conception of International Law*, New York.

Sestier, J.M. (1880), *La piraterie dans l'antiquité*, Paris.

Shapiro, J. (2005), *1599: A Year in the Life of William Shakespeare*, London.

Sharpe, K. (1992), *The Personal Rule of Charles I*, New Haven.

Shatzman, I. (1972), 'The Roman General's Authority over Booty', 21 *Zeitschrift für Alte Geschichte* 177.

Shavana, M. (2015), 'Tides and Tribulations: English Prize Law and the Law of Nations in the Seventeenth Century', 17 *Journal of the History of International Law* 47.

Shaw, B.D. (1984), 'Bandits in the Roman Empire', 105 *Past and Present* 3.

Shaw, T.J. (2021), *The Legal History of Pirates and Privateers*, n.p.

Shearer, I. (1983), 'Grotius and the Law of the Sea', *Bulletin of the Australian Society of Legal Philosophy* 46.

Shoemaker, K. (2010), 'When the Devil Went to Law School: Canon Law and Theology in the Fourteenth Century', in S.E. Young (ed.), *Crossing Boundaries at Medieval Universities*, Leiden, p. 255.

Shogimen, T. (1999), 'The Relationship between Theology and Canon Law: Another Context of Political Thought in the Early Fourteenth Century', 60 *Journal of the History of Ideas* 417.

Sicking, L.H.J. (2004), *Neptune and the Netherlands: State, Economy and War at Sea in the Renaissance*, Leiden.

Sicking, L.H.J. (2018a), 'The Pirate and the Admiral: Europeanisation and Globalisation of Maritime Conflict Management', 20 *Journal of the History of International Law* 429.

Sicking, L.H.J. (2018b), '"God's Friend, the Whole World's Enemy": Reconsidering the Role of Piracy in the Development of Universal Jurisdiction', 47 *Netherlands Journal of Legal Philosophy* 176.

Sicking, L.H.J. and van Rhee, R. (2019), 'Prize Law, Procedure and Politics: The Settlement of a Prize Case before the Admiralty Court and the Great Council of the Netherlands', in H. Dondorp, M. Schermaier and B. Sirks (eds), *De rebus divinis et humanis: Essays in Honour of Jan Hallebeek*, Göttingen, p. 303.

Sigmund, P.E. (1993), 'Law and Politics', in N. Kretzmann and E. Stump (eds), *The Cambridge Companion to Aquinas*, Cambridge, p. 217.

Simbula, P.F. (2004), 'Îles, corsaires et pirates dans la Méditerranée médiévale', 47 *Médiévales* 17.

Simmonds, K.R. (1958), 'Alberico Gentili at the Admiralty Bar, 1605–8', 7 *Archiv des Völkerrechts* 3.

Simmonds, K.R. (1959), 'The Gentili Manuscripts', 76 *Zeitschrift der Savigny-Stiftung für Rechtsgeschichte (Romanistische Abteilung)* 534.

Simpson, A.R.C. (2016), 'Procedures for Dealing with Robbery in Scotland before 1400', in A.R.C. Simpson, S.C. Styles, E. West and A.L.M. Wilson (eds), *Continuity, Change and Pragmatism in the Law: Essays in Memory of Professor Angelo Forte*, Aberdeen, p. 95.

Simpson, J.A. and Weiner, E.S.C., eds (1993), *The Oxford English Dictionary*, 20 vols, Oxford.

Skinner, Q. (1978), *Foundations of Modern Political Thought*, 2 vols, Cambridge.

Skinner, Q. (2018), 'Machiavelli on Misunderstanding Princely *Virtù*', in idem, *From Humanism to Hobbes: Studies in Rhetoric and Politics*, Cambridge, p. 15.

Slattery, B. (2005), 'Paper Empires: The Legal Dimensions of French and English Ventures in North America', in J. McLaren, A.R. Buck and N.E. Wright (eds), *Despotic Dominion: Property Rights in British Settler Societies*, Vancouver, p. 50.

Smout, T.C. (1963), *Scottish Trade on the Eve of the Union, 1660–1707*, Edinburgh.

Smuts, M. (2002), 'The Making of *Rex pacificus*: James VI and I and the Problem of Peace in an Age of Religious War', in D. Fisclin and M. Fortier (eds), *Royal Subjects: Essays on the Writings of James VI and I*, Detroit, p. 378.

Snyder, A.J. (2006), 'The Politics of Piracy: Pirates, Privateers and the Government of Elizabeth I, 1558–88', MA dissertation, University of North Carolina, Wilmington.

Somos, M. (2009), 'Secularisation in *De iure praedae*: From Bible Criticism to International Law', in H.W. Blom (ed.), *Property, Piracy and Punishment: Hugo Grotius on War and Booty in De iure praedae – Concepts and Contexts*, Leiden, p. 147.

Somos, M. (2011), *Secularisation and the Leiden Circle*, Leiden.

Somos, M. (2012), 'Selden's *Mare clausum*: The Secularisation of International Law and the Rise of Soft Imperialism', 14 *Journal of the History of International Law* 287.

Somos, M. and Margócsy, D. (2017), 'Pirating *Mare liberum* (1609)', 38 *Grotiana* 176.

Soons, A. (1979), *Juan de Mariana*, Boston, MA.

Spence, R.T. (1995), *The Privateering Earl: George Clifford, 3rd Earl of Cumberland, 1558–1605*, Stroud.

Spencer, J.M. (1996), 'Princes, Pirates and Pigs: Criminalizing Wars of Conquest in *Henry V*', 47 *Shakespeare Quarterly* 160.

Spiegel, H.W. (1938), 'Origin and Development of Denial of Justice', 32 *American Journal of International Law* 63.

Squibb, G.D. (1959), *The High Court of Chivalry: A Study in the Civil Law in England*, Oxford.

Stacey, R.C. (1994), 'The Age of Chivalry', in M. Howard, G.J. Andreopoulos and M.R. Shulman (eds), *The Laws of War: Constraints on Warfare in the Western World*, New Haven.

Stark, F.R. (1897), *The Abolition of Privateering and the Declaration of Paris*, New York.

Starkey, D.J. (2011), 'Voluntaries and Sea Robbers: A Review of the Academic Literature on Privateering, Corsairing, Buccaneering and Piracy', 97 *Mariner's Mirror* 127.

Statham, E.P. (1910), *Privateers and Privateering*, Cambridge.

Staub, D.J. (2009), 'Letters of Marque: A Short-Term Solution to an Age-Old Problem', 40 *Journal of Maritime Law and Commerce* 261.

Steckley, G.F. (2003), 'Collisions, Prohibitions and the Admiralty Court in Seventeenth-Century London', 21 *Law and History Review* 41.

Steckley, G.F. (2020), 'Ownership in the Seventeenth-Century Admiralty Court', 41 *Journal of Legal History* 257.

Steele, R. (1967), *A Bibliography of Royal Proclamations of the Tudor and Stuart Sovereigns and of Others Published under Authority*, 3 vols, New York.

Steiger, H. (2001), 'From the International Law of Christianity to the International Law of the World Citizen: Reflections on the Formation of the Epochs of the History of International Law', 3 *Journal of the History of International Law* 180.

Stein, P.G. (1978), 'Sir Thomas Smith: Renaissance Civilian', *Acta Juridica* 79.

Stein, P.G. (1980), 'Bartolus, the Conflict of Laws and Roman Law', in P. Feuerstein and C. Parry (eds), *Multum non multa: Festscrift für Kurt Lipstein*, Heidelberg, p. 251.

Stein, P.G. (1988), *The Character and Influence of the Roman Civil Law: Historical Essays*, London.

Stein, P.G. (1999), *Roman Law in European History*, Cambridge.

Stirk, P. (2011), 'No Peace beyond the Line', in S. Legg (ed.), *Spatiality, Sovereignty and Carl Schmitt: Geographies of the Nomos*, Abingdon, p. 276.

Stoljar, S. (1977), 'How Can Feud-Law Be Law Properly So Called?', 13 *University of Western Australia Law Review* 262.

Stradling, R.A. (1980), 'The Spanish Dunkirkers, 1621–48: A Record of Plunder and Destruction', 95 *Tijdschrift voor Geschiedenis* 541.

Stradling, R.A. (1992), *The Armada of Flanders: Spanish Maritime Policy and European War, 1568–1668*, Cambridge.

Straumann, B. (2006a), '"Ancient Caesarian Lawyers" in a State of Nature: Roman Tradition and Natural Rights in Hugo Grotius' *De iure praedae*', 34 *Political Theory* 328.

Straumann, B. (2006b), 'The Right to Punish as a Just Cause of War in Hugo Grotius' Natural Law', 2 Studies in the History of Ethics (www.historyofethics).

Straumann, B. (2009), 'Natural Rights and Roman Law in Hugo Grotius' *Theses lvi*, *De iure praedae* and *Defensio capitis quinti Maris liberi*', in H.W. Blom (ed.), *Property, Piracy and Punishment: Hugo Grotius on War and Booty in De iure praedae – Concepts and Contexts*, Leiden, p. 341.

Straumann, B. (2010), 'The *Corpus iuris* as a Source of Law between Sovereigns in Alberico Gentili's Thought', in B. Kingsbury and B. Straumann (eds), *The Roman Foundations of the Law of Nations: Alberico Gentili and the Justice of Empire*, Oxford, p. 101.

Straumann, B. (2015), *Roman Law in the State of Nature: The Classical Foundations of Hugo Grotius' Natural Law*, Cambridge.

Straumann, B. (2021), 'Sociability', in R. Lesaffer and J. Nijman (eds), *The Cambridge Companion to Hugo Grotius*, Cambridge, p. 157.

Stumpf, C.A. (2006), *The Grotian Theology of International Law: Hugo Grotius and the Moral Foundations of International Relations*, Berlin.

Sugden, J. (1996), *Sir Francis Drake*, London.

Sullivan, V. (1996), 'Princes to Act: Henry V as the Machiavellian Prince of Appearance', in J. Alulis and V. Sullivan (eds), *Shakespeare's Political Pageant: Essays in Literature and Politics*, London, p. 125.

Summerson, H. (1991), 'The early Development of the Laws of the Anglo-Scottish Marches, 1249–1448', in W.M. Gordon and T.D. Fergus (eds), *Legal History in the Making*, London, p. 29.

Sumption, J. (2015), *The Hundred Years War, Volume IV: Cursed Kings*, Philadelphia.

Sumption, J. (2020), 'Anglo-Scottish Relations, 1290–1513, and the Beginnings of International Law', in A.M. Godfrey (ed.), *Stair Society: Miscellany Eight*, Edinburgh, p. 1.

Sunderland, L. (2017), *Rebel Barons: Resisting Royal Power in Medieval Culture*, Oxford.

Sutherland, J. and Watts, C.T. (2000), *Henry V, War Criminal? and Other Shakespeare Puzzles*, Oxford.

Sutherland, N.M. (1980), *The Huguenot Struggle for Recognition*, New Haven.

Sutherland, N.M. (1984), 'The Foreign Policy of Queen Elizabeth, the Sea Beggars and the Capture of Brill, 1572', in idem, *Princes, Politics and Religion, 1547–89*, London, p. 183.

Sutton, A.F. (2018), 'The Admiralty and Constableship of England in the Later Fifteenth Century: The Operation and Development of These Offices, 1462–85, under Richard, Duke of Gloucester and King of England', in A. Musson and N. Ramsay (eds), *Courts of Chivalry and Admiralty in Late Medieval Europe*, Woodbridge, p. 187.

Sweeney, E.C. (2012), 'Thomas Aquinas on the Natural Law Written in Our Hearts', in J.A. Jacobs (ed.), *Reason, Religion and Natural Law: From Plato to Spinoza*, Oxford, p. 133.

Sylvester, D.G. (2005), 'Communal Piracy in Medieval England's Cinque Ports', in N. Christie and M. Yazigi (eds), *Noble Ideals and Bloody Realities: Warfare in the Middle Ages*, Leiden, p. 163.

Sypher, G.W. (1963), 'La Popelinière's *Histoire de France*: A Case of Historical Objectivity and Religious Censorship', 24 *Journal of the History of Ideas* 41.

Szabó, K.T. (2011), *Anticipatory Action in Self-Defence*, The Hague.

Tai, E.S. (2003), 'Piracy and Law in Medieval Genoa: The *Consilia* of Bartolomeo Bosco', 9 *Medieval Encounters* 256.

Tai, E.S. (2004), 'Restitution and the Definition of a Pirate: The Case of Sologrus de Nigro', 19 *Mediterranean Historical Review* 34.

Tai, E.S. (2007), 'Marking Water: Piracy and Property in the Premodern West', in J.H. Bentley, R. Bridenthal and K. Wigen (eds), *Seascapes: Maritime Histories, Littoral Cultures and Transoceanic Exchanges*, Honolulu, p. 35.

Tai, E.S. (2012), 'The Legal Status of Piracy in Medieval Europe', 10 *History Compass* 838.

Tai, E.S. (2019), 'Pirates on the Coast: Littoral Expansion and Maritime Predation in Liguria and Dalmatia, 1300–1600', in T. Heebøll-Holm, P. Höhn and G. Rohmann (eds), *Merchants, Pirates and Smugglers: Criminalisation, Economics and the Transformation of the Maritime World, 1200–1600*, Frankfurt, p. 165.

Taillemite, E. (1993), 'Les ordonnance de marine au XVIe siècle', in P. Masson and M. Vergé-Franceschi (eds), *La France et la mer au siècle des grandes découvertes*, Paris, p. 55.

Taitslin, A. (2013), 'The Competing Sources of Aquinas' Natural Law: Aristotle, Roman Law and the Early Church Fathers', in F.J. Contreras (ed.), *The Threads of Natural Law: Unravelling a Philosophical Tradition*, Dordrecht, p. 47.

Talbott, S. (2014), *Conflict, Commerce and Franco-Scottish Relations, 1560–1713*, Abingdon.

Tamanaha, B.Z. (2008), 'Understanding Legal Pluralism: Past to Present, Local to Global', 30 *Sydney Law Review* 375.

Tarwacka, A. (2009), *Romans and Pirates: Legal Perspective*, Warsaw.

Tavuzzi, M. (1997), *Prierias: The Life and Works of Silvestro Mazzolini da Prierio, 1456–1527*, Durham, NC.

Tavuzzi, M. (2007), *Renaissance Inquisitors: Dominican Inquisitors and Inquisitorial Districts in Northern Italy, 1474–1527*, Leiden.

Taylor, G. (1978), *The Sea Chaplains: A History of the Chaplains of the Royal Navy*, Oxford.

Taylor, M.A. (1977), 'A Critical Edition of Geoffroy de Charny's *Livre Charny* and the *Demandes pour la joute, les tournois et la guerre*', PhD dissertation, University of North Carolina, Chapel Hill.

Terrill, R.J. (1981), 'The Application of the Comparative Method by English Civilians: The Case of William Fulbecke and Thomas Ridley', 2 *Journal of Legal History* 169.

Thompson, J.W. (1909), *The Wars of Religion in France, 1559–76: The Huguenots, Catherine de Medici and Philip II*, Chicago.

Thomson, J.E. (1994), *Mercenaries, Pirates and Sovereigns: State-Building and Extraterritorial Violence in Early-Modern Europe*, Princeton.

Thorne, S.E. (1962), 'Sovereignty and the Conflict of Laws', in *Bartolo de Sassoferrato: Studi e documenti per il VI centenario, vol. 2*, Milan, p. 675.

Thornton, H. (2004), 'Hugo Grotius and the Freedom of the Seas', 16 *International Journal of Maritime History* 17.

Thornton, H. (2006), 'John Selden's Response to Hugo Grotius: The Argument for Closed Seas', 18 *International Journal of Maritime History* 105.

Thrush, A. (2004), 'The Parliamentary Opposition to Peace with Spain in 1604: A Speech of Sir Edward Hoby', 23 *Parliamentary History* 301.

Thumfart, J. (2009), 'On Grotius' *Mare liberum* and Vitoria's *De Indis*, Following Agamben and Schmitt', 30 *Grotiana* 65.

Tierney, B. (2007), 'Vitoria and Suárez on *Ius gentium*, Natural Law and Custom', in A. Perreau-Saussine and J.B. Murphy (eds), *The Nature of Customary Law*, Cambridge, p. 101.

Tierney, B. (2011), *The Idea of Natural Rights: Studies on Natural Rights, Natural Law and Church Law, 1150–1625*, Grand Rapids, MI.

Tilly, C. (1985), 'War Making and State Making as Organised Crime', in P.B. Evans, D. Rueschemeyer and T. Skocpol (eds), *Bringing the State back in*, Cambridge, p. 169.

Timbal, P.C. (1943–4), 'La confiscation dans le droit français des XIIIe et XIVe siècles', 21 *Revue historique de droit français et étranger* 44, and 22 *Revue historique de droit français et étranger* 35.

Timbal, P.C. (1958), 'Les lettres de marque dans le droit de la France medievale', 10 *Recueils de la Societé Jean Bodin* 109.

Tirshfield, J.T. (2017), 'The Socio-Historical Case for the Existence of a Nexus Requirement in the Application of Universal Jurisdiction to Maritime Piracy', 19 *Journal of the History of International Law* 467.

Tite, C.G.C. (1974), *Impeachment and Parliamentary Judicature in Early Stuart England*, London.

Todd, P. (2010), *Maritime Fraud and Piracy*, London.

Todescan, F. (2009), '*Sequuntur dogmatica de iure praedae*: Law and Theology in Grotius' Use of Sources in *De iure praedae*', in H.W. Blom (ed.), *Property, Piracy and Punishment: Hugo Grotius on War and Booty in De iure praedae – Concepts and Contexts*, Leiden, p. 281.

Todescan, F. (2014), '*Ius gentium medium est intra ius naturale et ius civile*: La 'double face' du droit des gens dans la scolastique espagnole du 16ème siècle', in P.M. Dupuy and V. Chetali (eds), *The Roots of International Law: Liber amicorum Peter Haggenmacher*, Leiden, p. 121.

Toomer, G.J. (2009), *John Selden: A Life in Scholarship*, 2 vols, Oxford.

Trachtman, J.P. (2016), 'The Growing Obsolescence of Customary International Law', in C.A. Bradley (ed.), *Custom's Future: International Law in a Changing World*, Cambridge, p. 172.

Tracy, J.D. (1993), 'Herring Wars: The Hapsburg Netherlands and the Struggle for Control of the North Sea, ca. 1520 60', 24 *Sixteenth Century Journal* 249.

Tracy, J.D. (2008), *The Founding of the Dutch Republic: War, Finance and Politics in Holland, 1572–88*, Oxford.

Treasure, G.R.R. (1972), *Cardinal Richelieu and the Development of Absolutism*, London.

Treasure, G.R.R. (2013), *The Huguenots*, New Haven.

Trim, D.J.B. (1999), 'The "Secret War" of Elizabeth I: England and the Huguenots during the Early Wars of Religion, 1562–77', 27 *Proceedings of the Huguenot Society* 189.

Trim, D.J.B. (2002), 'Fighting "Jacob's War": The Employment of English and Welsh Mercenaries in the European Wars of Religion', PhD dissertation, University of London.

Trim, D.J.B. (2005), 'Seeking a Protestant Alliance and Liberty of Conscience on the Continent, 1558–85', in S. Doran and G. Richardson (eds), *Tudor England and Its Neighbours*, Basingstoke, p. 139.

Tuck, R. (1979), *Natural Rights Theories: Their Origin and Development*, Cambridge.

Tuck, R. (1987), 'The "Modern" Theory of Natural Law', in A. Pagden (ed.), *The Languages of Political Theory in Early-Modern Europe*, Cambridge, p. 99.

Tuck, R. (1993), *Philosophy and Government, 1572–1651*, Cambridge.

Tuck, R. (1999), *The Rights of War and Peace: Political Thought and the International Order from Grotius to Kant*, Oxford.

Tuori, K. (2009), 'Alberico Gentili and the Criticism of Expansion in the Roman Empire: The Invader's Remorse', 11 *Journal of the History of International Law* 205.

Tuori, K. (2011), 'The Disputed Roots of Legal Pluralism', 9 *Law, Culture and the Humanities* 330.

Twining, W. (2009–10), 'Normative and Legal Pluralism: A Global Perspective', 20 *Duke Journal of Comparative and International Law* 473.

Ullmann, W. (1954), 'The Medieval Interpretation of Frederick I's Authentic *Habita*', in *L'Europa e il diritto romano: Studi in memoria di Paulo Koschaker*, 2 vols, Milan, vol. 1, p. 100.

Unger, R.W. (1980), *The Ship in the Medieval Economy, 600–1600*, London.

Urban, W. (2006), *Medieval Mercenaries: The Business of War*, Barnsley.

Vadi, V. (2014), 'At the Dawn of International Law: Alberico Gentili', 40 *North Carolina Journal of International Law and Commercial Regulation* 135.

Vadi, V. (2020), *War and Peace: Alberico Gentili and the Early-Modern Law of Nations*, Leiden.

Valenzuela-Verhmehren, L. (2013), 'The Origin and Nature of the State in Francisco de Vitoria's Moral Philosophy', 62 *Ideas y valores* 81.

Van Caenegem, R.C. (1992), *An Historical Introduction to Private Law*, tr. D.E.L. Johnston, Cambridge.

Van den Brande, P.C. (2020), '*Remedium repraesaliarum*: The Medieval and Early-Modern Practice and Theory of Reprisal within the Just War Doctrine', 41 *Grotiana* 305.

Van der Lem, A. (2018), *Revolt in the Netherlands: The Eighty Years War, 1568–1648*, tr. A. Brown, London.

Van der Molen, G. (1968), *Alberico Gentili and the Development of International Law*, Leiden.

Vander Waerdt, P.A. (1994), 'Philosophical Influence on Roman Jurisprudence? The Case of Stoicism and Natural Law', 36 *Aufsteig und Niedergang der römischen Welt* 4851.

Van Gelderen, M. (1992), *The Political Thought of the Dutch Revolt, 1555–90*, Cambridge.

Van Hooff, A.J.L. (1998), 'Ancient Robbers: Reflections behind the Facts', 19 *Ancient Society* 105.

Van Ittersum, M.J. (2003), 'Hugo Grotius in Context: Van Heemskerck's Capture of the *Santa Catarina* and Its Justification in *De iure praedae*, 1604–6', 31 *Asian Journal of Social Science* 511.

Van Ittersum, M.J. (2006a), *Profit and Principle: Hugo Grotius, Natural Rights Theories and the Rise of Dutch Power in the East Indies, 1595–1615*, Leiden.

Van Ittersum, M.J. (2006b), '*Mare liberum* versus the Propriety of the Seas? The Debate between Hugo Grotius (1583–1645) and William Welwood (1552–1624) and Its Impact on Anglo-Scotto-Dutch Fishery Disputes in the Second Decade of the Seventeenth Century', 10 *Edinburgh Law Review* 239.

Van Ittersum, M.J. (2009), 'Preparing *Mare liberum* for the Press: Hugo Grotius' Rewriting of Chapter 12 of *De iure praedae* in November-December 1608', in H.W.

Blom (ed.), *Property, Piracy and Punishment: Hugo Grotius on War and Booty in De iure praedae – Concepts and Contexts*, Leiden, p. 246.

Van Loo, I. (1997), 'For Freedom and Fortune: The Rise of the Dutch Privateering in the First Half of the Dutch Revolt, 1568–1609', in M. van der Hoeven (ed.), *Exercise of Arms: Warfare in the Netherlands, 1568–1648*, Leiden, p.173.

Van Nifterik, G. (2009), 'Grotius and the Origin of the Ruler's Right to Punish', in H.W. Blom (ed.), *Property, Piracy and Punishment: Hugo Grotius on War and Booty in De iure praedae – Concepts and Contexts*, Leiden, p. 396.

Van Nifterik, G. and Nijman, J. (2009), '*Mare liberum* Revisited, 1609–2009', 30 *Grotiana* 3.

Van Someren, L. (1965), *Umpire to the Nations: Hugo Grotius*, London.

Van Stipriaan, R. (2007), 'Words at War: The Early Years of William of Orange's Propaganda', 11 *Journal of Early Modern History* 331.

Van Vliet, A.P. (1996), 'The Influence of Dunkirk Privateering on the North Sea (Herring) Fishery during the Years 1580–1650', in J. Roding and L.H. van Voss (eds), *The North Sea and Culture, 1550–1800*, Hilversum, p. 150.

Van Vliet, A.P. (1998), 'Foundation, Organisation and Effects of the Dutch Navy, 1568–1648', in M. van der Hoeven (ed.), *Exercise of Arms: Warfare in the Netherlands, 1568–1648*, Leiden, p. 153.

Van Zyl, D.H. (1986), *Cicero's Legal Philosophy*, Roodepoort.

Vaughan, R. (1966), *John the Fearless: The Growth of Burgundian Power*, London.

Verbeke, G. (1983), *The Presence of Stoicism in Medieval Thought*, Washington.

Vergé-Franceschi, M. (1991), *Marine et education sous l'Ancien Régime*, Paris.

Vergé-Franceschi, M. (1997), 'L'amirauté de France dans la deuxième moitié du XVIe siècle: Un enjeu entre catholiques et protestants', in M. Acerra and G. Martinière (eds), *Coligny, les protestants et la mer*, Paris, p. 35.

Vergerio, C. (2017), 'Alberico Gentili's *De iure belli*: An Absolutist's Attempt to Reconcile the *Ius gentium* and the Reason of State Tradition', 19 *Journal of the History of International Law* 429.

Verlinden, C. (1980), 'Aspects quantitatifs de l'esclavage méditerranéen au bas Moyen Âge', 10 *Anuario de estudios medievales* 769.

Versteeg, D. (1901), *The Sea Beggars: Liberators of Holland from the Yoke of Spain*, New York.

Verzijl, J.H.W. (1979), *International Law in Historical Perspective, Part IX–B: The Law of Neutrality*, Alphen aan den Rijn.

Verzijl, J.H.W., Heere, W.P. and Offerhaus, J.P.S. (1998), *International Law in Historical Perspective, Part IX–C: The Law of Maritime Prize*, Leiden.

Vieira, M.B. (2003), '*Mare liberum* vs *Mare clausum*: Grotius, Freitas and Selden's Debate on Dominion over the Seas', 64 *Journal of the History of Ideas* 361.

Villiers, P. (2000), *Les corsaires du littoral: Dunkerque, Calais, Boulogne, de Philippe II à Louis XIV, 1568–1713*, Villeneuve d'Ascq.

Viroli, M. (2007), 'Machiavelli's Realism', 14 *Constellations* 466.

Viroli, M. (2010), *Machiavelli's God*, Princeton.

Voak, N. (2003), *Richard Hooker and Reformed Theology: A Study of Reason, Will and Grace*, Oxford.

Vognsen, F.L. (2019), 'Conceptualising Danish "Piracy", c. 1460–1525: A Criminalised Economy or a Circular Exchange of Goods, Money and People?', in T. Heebøll-Holm, P. Höhn and G. Rohmann (eds), *Merchants, Pirates and Smugglers: Criminalisation, Economics and the Transformation of the Maritime World, 1200–1600*, Frankfurt, p. 145.

Vogt, M. (2008), *Law, Reason and the Cosmic City: Political Philosophy in the Early Stoa*, Oxford.

Vollerthun, U. (2017), *The Idea of International Society: Erasmus, Vitoria, Gentili and Grotius*, Cambridge.

Waggoner, G.R. (1954), 'An Elizabethan Attitude toward Peace and War', 33 *Philological Quarterly* 20.

Wagner, A. (2011), 'Francisco de Vitoria and Alberico Gentili on the Legal Character of the Global Commonwealth', 31 *Oxford Journal of Legal Studies* 565.

Wagner, A. (2017), 'Alberico Gentili: Sovereignty, Natural Law and the System of Roman Civil Law', in S. Kadelbach, T. Kleinlein and D. Roth-Isigkeit (eds), *System, Order and International Law: The Early History of International Legal Thought from Machiavelli to Hegel*, Oxford, p. 92.

Wagner, A. (2018), 'Francisco de Vitoria', in R. Domingo and J. Martínez-Torrón (eds), *Great Christian Jurists in Spanish History*, Cambridge, p. 84.

Walker, B. (2004), *The Seafarers: Armada*, London.

Walker, D.M. (1985), *The Scottish Jurists*, Edinburgh.

Wallace-Hadrill, J.M. (1959), 'The Bloodfeud of the Franks', 41 *Bulletin of the John Rylands Library* 459.

Wampach, C. (2020), *Armed Reprisals from Medieval Times to 1945*, Baden-Baden.

Ward, R. (2009), *The World of the Medieval Shipmaster: Law, Business and the Sea, c. 1350–1450*, Woodbridge.

Warren, C.N. (2010), 'Gentili, the Poets and the Laws of War', in B. Kingsbury and B. Straumann (eds), *The Roman Foundations of the Law of Nations: Alberico Gentili and the Justice of Empire*, Oxford, p. 146.

Warren, C.N. (2015), *Literature and the Law of Nations, 1580–1680*, Oxford.

Warren, C.N. (2017), '*Henry V*, Anachronism and the History of International Law', in L. Hutson (ed.), *The Oxford Handbook of English Law and Literature, 1500–1700*, Oxford, p. 709.

Waszink, J. (2009), 'Using the Work: Remarks on the Text of *De iure praedae*', in H.W. Blom (ed.), *Property, Piracy and Punishment: Hugo Grotius on War and Booty in De iure praedae – Concepts and Contexts*, Leiden, p. 215.

Waszink, J. (2012), 'Lipsius and Grotius: Tacitism', 12 *History of European Ideas* 1.

Watson, A. (1991), *Roman Law and Comparative Law*, Athens, GA.

Watson, A. (1993), *International Law in Archaic Rome*, Baltimore, MD.

Watson, G. (1971), 'The Natural Law and Stoicism', in A.A. Long (ed.), *Problems in Stoicism*, London, p. 216.

Wauters, B. and de Benito, M. (2017), *The History of Law in Europe: An Introduction*, Cheltenham.

Wedgwood, C.V. (1944), *William the Silent: William of Nassau, Prince of Orange, 1533–84*, London.

Weis, M. (2003), *Les Pays-Bas espagnols et les Etats du Saint Empire, 1559–79: Priorités et enjeux de la diplomatie en temps de troubles*, Brussels.

Weiss, G.L. (2011), *Captives and Corsairs: France and Slavery in the Early-Modern Mediterranean*, Stanford.

Wernham, R.B. (1961), 'Elizabethan War Aims and Strategy', in S.T. Bindoff, J. Hurstfield and C.H. Williams (eds), *Elizabethan Government and Society: Essays Presented to Sir John Neale*, London, p. 340.

Wernham, R.B. (1966), *Before the Armada: The Growth of English Foreign Policy, 1485–1588*, London.

Wernham, R.B. (1980), *The Making of Elizabethan Foreign Policy, 1558–1603*, Berkeley.

Wernham, R.B. (1984), *After the Armada: Elizabethan England and the Struggle for Western Europe, 1588–95*, Oxford.

Wernham, R.B. (1994), *The Return of the Armadas: The Last Years of the Elizabethan War against Spain, 1595–1603*, Oxford.

Whetham, D. (2009), *Just Wars and Moral Victories: Surprise, Deception and the Normative Framework of European War in the Later Middle Ages*, Leiden.

White, A. (1985), 'Religion, Politics and Society in Aberdeen, 1543–93', PhD dissertation, University of Aberdeen.

White, J.M. (2017), *Piracy and Law in the Ottoman Mediterranean*, Stanford.

Whyte, I.D. (1995), *Scotland before the Industrial Revolution: An Economic and Social History, c. 1050-c. 1750*, Harlow.

Wiedemann, T.E.J. (1986), 'The *Fetiales*: A Reconsideration', 36 *Classical Quarterly* 478.

Wijffels, A.A. (1992), *Alberico Gentili and Thomas Crompton: An Encounter between an Academic Jurist and a Legal Practitioner*, Leiden.

Wijffels, A.A. (1993), 'Introduction', in *Consilium facultatis iuridicae Tubingensis*, ed. A.A. Wijffels, Leiden, p. 1.

Wijffels, A.A. (1994a), '*Ius gentium* in the Practice of the Court of Admiralty around 1600', in A.D.E. Lewis and D.J. Ibbetson (eds), *The Roman Law Tradition*, Cambridge, p. 119.

Wijffels, A.A. (1994b), 'Sir Julius Caesar and the Merchants of Venice', in F. Battenberg and F. Ranieri (eds), *Geschichte der Zentraljustiz in Mitteleuropa: Festschrift für Bernard Diestelkamp zum 65 Geburtstag*, Weimar, p. 195.

Wijffels, A.A. (1995), 'Early-Modern Literature on International Law and the *Usus modernus*', 16 *Grotiana* 35.

Wijffels, A.A. (2010), 'From Perugia to Oxford: Past and Present of Political Paradigms', in F. Treggiari (ed.), *Alberico Gentili: La tradizione giuridica perugina e la fondazione del diritto internazionale*, Perugia, p. 60.

Wijffels, A.A. (2011), 'Early-Modern Scholarship on International Law', in A. Orakhelashvili (ed.), *Research Handbook on the Theory and History of International Law*, Cheltenham, p. 23.

Wijffels, A.A. (2016), '*Antiqui et recentiores*: Alberico Gentili – Beyond *Mos Italicus* and Legal Humanism', in P.J. du Plessis and J.W. Cairns (eds), *Reassessing Legal Humanism and Its Claims: Petere fontes?*, Edinburgh, p. 11.

Wijffels, A.A. (2021), 'Legal Scholastic and Humanist Influences on Grotius', in R. Lesaffer and J. Nijman (eds), *The Cambridge Companion to Hugo Grotius*, Cambridge, p. 387.

Wilks, M. (1965), 'Predestination, Property and Power: Wyclif's Theory of Dominion and Grace', 2 *Studies in Church History* 220.

Williams, N. (1961), *Captains Outrageous: Seven Centuries of Piracy*, London.

Williams, N. (1975), *The Sea Dogs: Privateers, Plunder and Piracy in the Elizabethan Age*, London.

Williams, N.J. (1988), *The Maritime Trade of the East Anglian Ports, 1550–90*, Oxford.

Williamson, J.A. (1913), *Maritime Enterprise, 1485–1558*, Oxford.

Williamson, J.A. (1969), *Hawkins of Plymouth*, London.

Wilson, C. (1970), *Queen Elizabeth and the Revolt in the Netherlands*, London.

Wilson, E. (2006), 'Erasing the Corporate Sovereign: Intertextuality and an Alternative Explanation for the Publication of Hugo Grotius' *Mare liberum* (1609)', 30 *Itinerario* 78.

Wilson, E. (2008), *Savage Republic: De Indis of Hugo Grotius, Republicanism and Dutch Hegemony within the Early Modern World System, c.1600–1619*, Leiden.

Wink, J., and Sicking, L.H.J. (2017), 'Reprisal and Diplomacy: Conflict Resolution within the Context of Anglo-Dutch Commercial Relations, c. 1300-c. 1415', 5 *Comparative Legal History* 53.

Winkel, L. (2007), 'Francisco de Vitoria on Just War on Both Sides and on the Legal Position of Burgundy', 75 *Tijdschrift voor Rechtsgeschiedenis* 355.

Winkel, L. (2009), 'Problems of Legal Systematization from *De iure praedae* to *De iure belli ac pacis*: *De iure praedae* Chapter II and the Prolegomena of *De iure belli ac pacis* Compared', in H.W. Blom (ed.), *Property, Piracy and Punishment: Hugo Grotius on War and Booty in De iure praedae – Concepts and Contexts*, Leiden, p. 61.

Winter, Y. (2014), 'The Prince and His Art of War: Machiavelli's Military Populism', 81 *Social Research* 165.

Wolf, J.B. (1979), *The Barbary Coast: Algiers under the Turks, 1500–1830*, New York.

Womersley, D. (1991), 'Sir Henry Savile's Translation of Tacitus and the Political Interpretation of Elizabethan Texts', 42 *Review of English Studies* 313.

Wood, N. (1967), 'Machiavelli's Concept of *Virtù* Reconsidered', 15 *Political Studies* 159.

Wood, N. (1988), *Cicero's Social and Political Thought*, Berkeley.

Woolf, D.R. (1990), *The Idea of History in Early Stuart England: Erudition, Ideology and 'The Light of Truth' from the Accession of James I to the Civil War*, Toronto.

Worden, B. (1996), *The Sound of Virtue: Philip Sidney's Arcadia and Elizabethan Politics*, New Haven.

Wormald, B.H.G. (1993), *Francis Bacon: History, Politics and Science, 1561–1626*, Cambridge.

Wormald, J. (1980), 'Bloodfeud, Kindred and Government in Early-Modern Scotland', 87 *Past and Present* 54.

Wormald, J. (1985), *Lords and Men in Scotland: Bonds of Manrent, 1442–1603*, Edinburgh.

Wormald, J. (1996), 'James VI, James I and the Identity of Britain', in B. Bradshaw and J. Morrill (eds), *The British Problem, c. 1534–1707: State Formation in the Atlantic Archipelago*, Basingstoke, p. 148.

Wortley, B.A. (1947), '*Pirata non mutat dominium*', 24 *British Yearbook of International Law* 258.

Wright, L.B. (1940), 'William Perkins: Elizabethan Apostle of Practical Divinity', 3 *Huntington Library Quarterly* 171.

Wright, N.A.R. (1976), 'The *Tree of Battles* of Honoré Bouvet and the Laws of War', in C.T. Allmand (ed.), *War, Literature, and Politics in the Late Middle Ages*, Liverpool, p. 12.

Wright, N.A.R. (1983), '"Pillagers" and "Brigands" in the Hundred Years War', 9 *Journal of Medieval History* 15.

Wubs-Mrozewicz, J. and Wijffels, A.A. (2016), 'Diplomacy and Advocacy: The Case of the *King of Denmark* v. *Dutch Skippers* before the Danzig City Council, 1564–67', 84 *Tijdschrift voor Rechtsgeschiedenis* 1.

Wuerth, I. (2009), 'The Captures Clause', 76 *University of Chicago Law Review* 1683.

Yamauchi, S. (1994), 'Looting of Men and Legal Theories in Medieval and Early-Modern Europe', 23 *Hitotsubashi Journal of Law and Politics* 13.

Yasuaki, O. (ed.) *A Normative Approach to War: Peace, War and Justice in Hugo Grotius* (Oxford, 1993).

Young, M.B. (1986), *Servility and Service: The Life and Work of Sir John Coke*, Woodbridge.

Younger, N. (2012), *War and Politics in the Elizabethan Counties*, Manchester.

Youngs, F.A. (1976), *The Proclamations of the Tudor Queens*, Cambridge.

Zagorin, P. (1998), *Francis Bacon*, Princeton.

Zeitlin, S.G. (2018), 'War and Peace in the Political Thought of Francis Bacon', PhD dissertation, University of California, Berkeley.

Zeldes, N. (2000), '*Ad piraticam exercendam*: Two "Piratical" Contracts from Early Sixteenth Century Sicily', 15 *Mediterranean Historical Review* 111.

Zeller, G. (1987), *Les institutions de la France au XVIe siècle*, Paris.

Zemanek, K. (1999), 'Was Hugo Grotius Really in Favour of the Freedom of the Seas?', 1 *Journal of the History of International Law* 48.

Zerba, M. (2004), 'The Frauds of Humanism: Cicero, Machiavelli and the Rhetoric of Imposture', 22 *Rhetorica* 215.

Ziegler, K.H. (1991–2), 'Grotius Topical, or the Import of Antiquity into the International aw of Europe', 12–13 *Grotiana* 78.

Ziegler, K.H. (2004), 'The Influence of Medieval Roman Law on Peace Treaties', in R. Lesaffer (ed.), *Peace Treaties and International Law in European History from the Late Middle Ages to World War One*, Cambridge, p. 147.

Ziskind, J. (1973), 'International Law and Ancient Sources: Grotius and Selden', 35 *Review of Politics* 537.

Zmora, H. (2011), *The Feud in Early-Modern Germany*, Cambridge.

Zuckert, M.P. (1989), '"Bringing Philosophy down from the Heavens": Natural Right in the Roman Law', 51 *Review of Politics* 70.

Zumbansen, P. (2010), 'Transnational Legal Pluralism', 1 *Transnational Legal Theory* 141.

Zwalve, W.J. (2009), 'The *Introduction to the Jurisprudence of Holland* and the Doctrine of the Free Seas', 30 *Grotiana* 49.

Index

Aberdeen 26, 30, 93, 223–4, 226
Abraham (patriarch) 11–12, 17, 159
Adjudication (*adiudicatio*) 48–9, 52, 59–61, 97, 106, 110, 112, 115, 119–20, 131–8, 144–5, 154, 184, 212, 223, 234, 236, 240, 242, 247, 275, 277–9, 282–3, 285, 287, 299, 304, 309–11
Admiralty (or admiral) 17, 29, 98–9, 104–9, 114, 140–3, 146, 154, 207, 212, 215, 217, 219, 228, 237–8, 274–7, 279–80, 286–8, 295, 297, 299–303, 305
  Admiral's share of prize 17, 29–30, 36–7, 59, 97, 104, 107, 111, 117, 119, 129–30, 134, 141, 143–4, 149, 239, 277, 279, 297, 299–300, 309–10
  See too Courts, admiralty
Adriatic Sea 231
Ai 43
Álamos de Barrientos, Baltasar (Spanish author) 183
Albania 206
Alciatus, Andreas (civil lawyer) 23, 198–9, 202–4, 263
Alexander the Great (Greek king) 198
Alva, Fernando Álvarez de Toledo y Pimentel, duke of (governor of the Netherlands) 147, 149–51, 215
Ambrose of Milan (church father) 11–12
Amsterdam 243, 262
Androlepsia 42
Antwerp 91, 93
Appian (Greek historian) 233
Aquinas, Thomas (theologian) 49, 161–3, 165, 193, 265–6
Aragon 106, 109
Archdukes, Albert VII of Austria and Isabella Clara Eugenia (governors of the Netherlands) 226, 241, 274, 276–8, 302
Algiers 238
Aristotle (Greek philosopher) 174, 193, 260
Articles of eyre 22
Art of war 156–7
Ascham, Roger (English author) 156
Atlantic Ocean 129, 140, 202, 204, 302
Augustine of Hippo (church father) 43, 49, 158, 160, 162–3, 165, 197–9
Ayr 90–1, 221
Azores 204, 208–9
Azpilcueta, Martín de (canon lawyer) 170

Bacon, Francis (English author) 183–4, 208, 273, 289
Baldus de Ubaldis (civil lawyer) 264
Balfour, Sir James, of Pittendreich (Scottish author) 17, 32, 35, 37–9, 64–5, 304
Baltic Sea 185, 282, 314
Baltimore 279–82
Bandits (*latrones*) 71–3, 77, 198, 201–2, 231
Bañez, Domingo (theologian) 166–7
Bartolus de Sassoferrato (civil lawyer) 12–13, 41, 43–4, 50, 65, 161–2, 168, 172, 192, 199–200, 253
Bartons (Scottish mariners) 54–8, 63–4, 88, 97, 205–6
Bayonne 103, 110
Becon, Thomas (English author) 157
Black Book of the Admiralty 104, 106, 115
Blessing (Scottish ship) 294–5, 298
Blockade of neutral ports 223–6, 233–4, 240–1
Bodin, Jean (French lawyer) 187–8, 264, 281
Bologna 200
Bonds of security 130–1, 133, 135, 242, 277, 287, 294, 296, 310
Bordeaux 93
Bothwell, Francis Stewart, earl of (Scottish admiral) 99, 217
Bothwell, Patrick Hepburn, earl of (Scottish admiral) 212
Bourges 126
Bouvet, Honoré (French author) 15–16
Brabant 148
Breaking bulk 29, 95, 128, 133, 135–6, 141, 184, 242, 275, 277, 282
Bremen 95
Brigands (*praedones*) 71–3, 82–3, 87, 119, 177, 198, 201–2, 206, 213, 231, 305
Brittany 60–2, 85, 97–8, 113, 124, 139–40, 286
Bruni, Leonardo (Italian author) 200

Brussels 241
Buchanan, George (Scottish author) 206–7
Buckingham, George Villiers, duke of (English admiral) 274, 276, 278–9, 285–7, 292, 294
Bull *In coena domini* 204–5
Bull *Inter caetera* 202–3, 249
Burghley, William Cecil, lord (English statesman) 181–2
Burgundy 113–14
Burntisland 293–5, 298

Cadiz 274
Caesar, Sir Julius (English judge) 129, 131–4, 136–7, 272
Caithness, George Sinclair, earl of (Scottish nobleman) 221
Cambridge 124, 280
Canaan 160
Canon law (or canon lawyers) 11–13, 21, 40–50, 74–8, 84, 155, 160–2, 169, 171–2, 178–9, 186, 189, 192, 198, 200, 204–5, 211, 234, 257, 259, 314
Cant, Walter (Scottish mariner) 60, 97
Caribbean Sea 202, 204
Carthage (or Carthaginians) 233
Castile 108–9, 113–14
Catholic League 66–7, 149, 154, 215, 217–18
Charles I (Scottish and English king) 211, 241–2, 257, 273–4, 276–85, 287–9, 291, 293, 295–6, 298, 301–2, 306–7
Charles V (French king) 38, 113
Charles V (Holy Roman Emperor) 145–7, 149–50, 206
Charles IX (French king) 125–6, 142
Charles Island 302–3
China 243
Chivalry 181
Cicero (Roman author) 173–82, 185–6, 188–9, 197, 199–201, 206–7, 245, 253, 256, 258, 260, 265–6, 269, 313
Cilician pirates 206
Cinque Ports 21, 105, 112, 129
Civil law (or civil lawyers) 11–15, 21, 34, 39–50, 73–8, 84–5, 96, 102–3, 129, 133, 136–8, 152, 155, 162, 171–2, 178–9, 184, 186–211, 225, 228–37, 239–41, 243–9, 251–3, 255–60, 262–4, 270–1, 280, 282, 286, 288–9, 311, 314
Clarigatio 42
Clerk, Francis (English author) 272
Clerk, William (English author) 280–1, 289
Clyde 301
Coimbra 266
Coligny, Gaspard de (French admiral) 142, 144–5, 214
Common law (English) 21, 31, 208, 225, 228, 230, 235, 255–8, 280–1, 286, 289, 309
Common law (*ius commune*) 21, 33, 50, 89, 119, 138, 173, 184, 187, 194, 235, 262–3, 266, 303–4
See too Canon law, Civil law
Common ownership 12–13, 192, 202–3, 230–3, 249, 252–3, 260–1
Comparative legal history 185, 187, 264
Condé, Louis de Bourbon (*père*), prince of (Huguenot leader) 123, 142, 145, 214
Condé, Louis de Bourbon (*fils*), prince of (Huguenot leader) 65, 142–3
Conestaggio, Girolamo (Italian author) 209
Confiscation 9–11, 22, 74–6, 78–80, 84, 89, 98–9, 112–13, 115–16, 119–20, 130, 135–7, 141, 154, 169, 184, 231, 248, 252, 257–8, 270, 281–3, 289, 296, 299–305, 307–11, 314
Conservator of truces 111–12
Consort (Scottish ship) 300
Conti, Natale (Italian author) 206
Contraband 28, 134, 136, 152, 173, 185–6, 214, 218, 236, 250, 257–8, 281–2, 284, 287, 296, 299–301, 303–4, 307
Convention of the royal burghs 64, 66, 70
Cornwallis, Sir William (English author) 183
Corpus iuris canonici 11, 41, 43, 49, 74, 76
Corpus iuris civilis 9, 11, 13, 40, 71, 73, 244, 256, 264
Corsairing (*guerre de course*) 3, 79–81, 102, 120, 183, 204–6
Council of Trent 161, 171
Courts
admiralty 8–9, 17, 24–5, 27, 30–2, 34–5, 37–9, 58–9, 61, 84, 90–2, 95, 97–9, 109–10, 116–17, 119, 122–4, 126, 128–32, 135–7, 144, 152–3, 190, 211–12, 214, 223, 228, 230, 239–40, 242–3, 250, 259, 262, 271–3,

Courts (*cont.*)
275, 277–8, 280, 282–4, 286–7, 296–305, 307, 311
bailie 26, 31
common pleas 228
justiciary 25, 88–9, 92, 99
military 15, 42
privy council 24–5, 60, 67–8, 90–2, 94–5, 117, 128–9, 132–4, 151, 154, 213, 220, 224, 226, 237, 240, 242, 273, 275–7, 283, 285, 287–8, 290, 294–5, 297–8, 300–2, 304, 307, 311–12
session 24–5, 31, 34, 58, 64, 68, 94–5, 97–8
sheriff 92
Covarruvias, Diego de, y Leyva (canon lawyer) 170–1
Crail 216, 300
Crockaert, Pierre (theologian) 163
Customary law 6, 15–16, 32–4, 36–40, 42–3, 46, 48, 55, 97, 105–6, 119, 129–30, 134, 137, 146, 149, 155, 168, 174, 195–6, 224–5, 227, 230, 239, 252, 256, 265, 276, 279, 293, 295, 298, 303–4
See too Practice of nations, Practick

Danzig 18–19, 26, 34, 37–8, 67–8, 84, 93, 98, 300
Daw, John (Scottish mariner) 300
De Clavasio, Angelus (canon lawyer) 171
De Groot, Huig (Dutch author) 243–56, 258–71, 286, 289, 308–9, 313
De Legnano, Ioannes (civil lawyer) 204
Denmark (or Danes) 37–9, 100, 211–12, 275, 279, 281, 285
Dio Chrysostom (Greek author) 270
Doctors' Commons 34, 137, 282
Dom Antonio, prior of Crato (claimant to Portuguese throne) 152, 208–9
Dover 232
Downs 229
Drake, Sir Francis (English mariner) 203
Dublin 91
Dundee 30, 60–1, 67–8, 91, 213–14, 295–6
Dunkirk (or Dunkirkers) 66, 70, 148–50, 153, 215–17, 223–4, 230, 241, 273, 290, 292–3, 303
Durazzo 206
Dutch East India Company 243–4, 250–1, 254–6
Dysart 300

Earl Marischal, William Keith (Scottish statesman) 293–4, 302
East Indies 248–9, 251, 254, 262, 272
Edict of Saint-Maur 144
Edits sur l'amirauté 211–12, 222–3
Charles V (1373) 38, 113, 139–41, 145
Francis I (1517) 139–41
Francis I (1544) 35–7, 117, 120, 139–41, 212
Henry III (1584) 36, 139–41
Edinburgh 24–5, 64, 90, 212–13, 220, 222, 224, 294, 303
Elector Palatine, Frederick V (German prince) 241
Elizabeth (English queen) 63, 65, 100, 103, 121–7, 133, 135–9, 142, 150–5, 157, 162, 173–4, 180–1, 184–6, 188, 190, 202–3, 207–10, 214, 216–20, 223, 225, 227, 236–7, 239, 242, 250, 258–9, 272, 275–8, 281–2, 289
England (or Englishmen) 5, 8, 17–22, 31, 39, 56–7, 63, 65, 83–7, 89, 94, 100–1, 103–39, 145, 150–4, 156–61, 172–3, 180–4, 197, 202–8, 210–23, 225–43, 252, 254–7, 272–90, 292–7, 303–5, 309, 311–13
English Channel 140, 286
English East India Company 239, 254–6
Essex, Robert Devereux, earl of (English nobleman) 156, 191
Expediency (*utile*) 176–8, 181–2, 188–90, 196, 234, 244–5, 251, 260, 265, 269

Ferrara 200
Fetiale law (*ius fetiale*) 9, 42, 177
Feuding 53–4, 68–9
Fife 296
Flanders (or Flemings) 26, 56–8, 85, 90, 98, 108, 110, 118, 149, 215, 221, 225, 229, 232, 295, 303–4
Flotsam, jetsam and lagan 257, 272, 276, 280
Flushing (or Flushingers) 215
Fogo, Robert (Scottish mariner) 57
Forfeiture, *see* Confiscation
Forum conscientiae vel civile 49–50, 161, 172
Forum externum vel internum 172, 190

Fox Morcillo, Sebastián (Spanish author) 182
France (or Frenchmen) 5, 35–9, 42, 56, 59, 65, 67, 89, 95, 97–8, 103, 109–10, 113–22, 124–7, 139–50, 152–4, 156, 158, 161, 190, 198, 202–6, 208–14, 233, 240–1, 243, 260, 277, 283–8, 292, 298, 300, 305, 313
Franceis (French ship) 26
Francis I (French king) 35–7, 117, 120, 139, 212
Frederick I (Holy Roman Emperor) 40–1, 45
Frederick II (Danish king) 39
Frederick II (Holy Roman Emperor) 73–6, 84, 200–1
Freebooting (*vrijbuiterij*) 151, 306
Freedom of navigation and trade 230–1, 236, 249, 251, 253–5
Friesland 57, 148
Frobisher, Martin (English mariner) 123
Fulbecke, William (English author) 201, 272

Garcia, Fortunius (canon lawyer) 171
Gates, Geoffrey (English author) 156
Gauls 179
General reprisals 117, 120, 125, 210, 309, 315
Genoa (or Genoese) 109–10, 231, 252, 257
Gentilis, Albericus (civil lawyer) 186–91, 195–209, 211, 229–30, 232–6, 244, 257–8, 262–4
Germany (or Germans) 303
Gibbon, Charles (English author) 158
Glasgow 92–3, 301
Global commonwealth (*respublica orbis*) 174–6, 195, 201, 208, 260, 266–7
Gordon, Sir Robert, of Lochinvar (Scottish laird) 302–3
Gosson, Stephen (English author) 158
Grace of God (English ship) 8
Grace of God (Scottish ship) 300
Granada 158
Greece 40
Grotius, Hugo, *see* De Groot, Huig.
Guerrero, Alfonso Alvarez (canon lawyer) 171
Guyenne 139–40, 144

Hamburg 298–300, 303–5
Hamilton, James Hamilton, marquis of (Scottish nobleman) 302
Hanseatic League 136, 285
Harfleur 190
Harris, Edmund (English author) 157–8
Harward, Simon (English author) 158–63, 196
Harwich 118
Hay, Sir Gilbert (Scottish author) 15–16
Henry III (French king) 36, 139, 153
Henry IV (French king) 65, 67, 142–4, 152–4
Henry V (English king) 111, 113, 190–1
Henry VIII (English king) 115–16, 118, 125–6, 139, 157, 206–7
Hobbes, Thomas (English author) 261
Holland 57–8, 83, 148, 236
Honourableness (*honestum*) 176–8, 180–2, 184, 188–90, 196, 201, 206–7, 234, 244–5, 251, 265, 269
Horace (Roman author) 265, 269
Hostiensis, Henricus de Segusio, Cardinal (canon lawyer) 158, 160
Howard of Effingham, lord, *see* Nottingham, earl of
Huguenots 121, 123–4, 142–5, 148, 152, 156
Hull 91

Indies 158, 203
See too East Indies, West Indies
Infanta Isabella, *see* Archdukes
Infection hostile 37, 119–20, 139
Infidels (Saracens or Turks) 14–15, 74–5, 79, 167, 204–5, 238, 257
Inns of court 21
Inquisition of Queenborough 106–7
International law (*ius inter gentes*) 2–4, 6, 8–9, 24, 155, 173, 211, 259, 263, 265–72, 304–5, 308–9, 311, 314
Ireland (or Irishmen) 218, 237–8, 252, 273–4, 279–81, 283, 290, 294, 301
Isidore of Seville (church father) 11, 158, 192
Israel (or Israelites/Jews) 159–60, 244, 256
Italy 41, 161–2, 186, 235
Ius militare 11
Ius proprium 21, 33

James III (Scottish king) 54
James IV (Scottish king) 54–5, 101, 206
James V (Scottish king) 56–8

James VI and I (Scottish and English king) 63, 66, 100, 181, 207, 211–12, 216–20, 222–3, 225–7, 234–5, 237–9, 242, 254–6, 259, 262, 271–3, 289, 291, 296, 307
Jarnac 142
Johore 243, 251, 262
Justinian (Roman emperor) 9, 40, 45, 74, 192, 264

Kennedy, Thomas (Scottish judge) 60, 97
King, Alexander (Scottish author) 35–7, 39, 65–6, 69, 90, 92, 217
Kinsale 283
Kintor, David (Scottish author) 35–7
Kirkcaldy 93
Kirkcudbright 302
Kirkwall 215

Languet, Hubert (French author) 156
La Popelinière, Lancelot du Voisin, sieur de (French author) 36
La Rochelle 142–5, 147, 156, 240–1, 283, 292
Law of arms (*ius armorum*) 8, 15–16, 23–4, 34, 42, 53, 58, 86, 112, 119, 137, 157, 186–7, 191, 204, 207, 234, 236, 256, 263
Law of God (*ius divinum*) 46, 49, 138–9, 155–73, 175, 182, 185, 244, 258–9, 273
Law of nations (*ius gentium*) 9, 11–12, 15, 33, 39, 46, 49, 56, 62, 65, 138, 165, 168, 172, 175–6, 179, 186, 190–7, 199, 201, 203, 206, 208, 225–6, 229, 231, 235, 237, 246, 255, 256, 258–61, 264–9, 272, 281, 286, 295–7, 303
Law of nature, *see* Natural law
Law of policy 138–9, 155, 173–91, 258–9, 273, 281, 296
Law of war (*ius belli*) 10, 177, 201, 244, 247–8, 269
Laws of Oleron 35–6, 84, 110
Laws of Wisby 35–6, 39
Legal pluralism 85–6, 137
Le Havre 123–4, 126, 142, 144, 214, 285
Leicester, Robert Dudley, earl of (English statesman) 187
Leith 8, 24, 32, 54, 59, 64, 70, 89–90, 93, 98, 214, 222–4, 226, 230, 290, 293, 295–7, 301
Letters or reprisal or marque 39, 50–1, 54–9, 62–4, 66–8, 70, 89, 97, 101–2, 111, 117, 120, 124, 127–8, 130–7, 145–6, 149–50, 153, 166, 168, 172, 202–3, 206–7, 210, 212–15, 217–19, 227–8, 235–6, 239, 241, 250, 252, 272–80, 282–5, 287–9, 294–6, 300–1, 304–6, 315
Letters of requisition 50, 61–2, 127, 270
Levant Company 238
Lewis 222
Licences to sail 19, 28–9, 99–102, 110–12, 117–18, 120–5, 140, 142–3, 145–50, 152–5, 209, 211–12, 214, 219, 221, 228, 238–40, 270, 307, 310–12, 314–15
Ligurian Sea 231
Lindsay, Sir Jerome (Scottish judge) 297
Linlithgow, Alexander Livingston, earl of (Scottish admiral) 294, 297–302
Lipsius, Justus (Dutch author) 265
Lisbon 299
Livingston, William (Scottish judge) 299
Livy (Roman historian) 10, 178–9, 183, 187–8, 233
Lloyd, Lodowick (English author) 156–7
Loch, Patrick (Scottish mariner) 212
Logan, Robert (Scottish mariner) 58–9
Lombard, Peter (theologian) 161
London 114, 145, 214, 219, 223, 229–30, 235, 254, 273–5, 278, 280, 293
Loque, Bertrand de (French author) 156
Lords of the congregation 121–2, 213–14
Louis of Nassau (Dutch leader) 147, 150
Louis XIII (French king) 240, 285, 287–8
Lübeck 300
Lynn 18–19, 84–5, 89

Maccabees (Jewish leaders) 156
Machiavelli, Niccolò (Italian author) 177–80, 182, 185, 187–91, 196, 264
Madre de Dios (Portuguese ship) iv, 184
Mahdia 206
Maitland, Sir Richard, of Lethington (Scottish author) 31–2
Marches 53–4, 69, 214
Mariana, Juan de (Spanish author) 182–3
Marienburg 18
Marten, Sir Henry (English judge) 273, 276–7, 280, 285–7, 289, 294, 304

Mary I (English queen) 118, 121–2, 125
Mary I (Scottish queen) 56, 63, 99, 181, 207
Mary of Guise (Scottish queen) 121
Maximilian I (Holy Roman Emperor) 145
Mazzolini, Silvestro, da Prierio (theologian) 166
Mediterranean Sea 15, 78–81, 140, 201, 204, 206, 238, 276–7, 314
Melchizedeck (biblical king) 11–12, 17, 159
Mirrors of princes (*specula principum*) 177–8, 182, 186
Molina, Luis de (theologian) 169
Mollat, Michel (historian) 102–3, 120, 197, 209
Montrose 98, 215, 301
Moors 170–1
Morison, Richard (English author) 157
Morton, James Douglas, earl of (Scottish admiral) 98–9
Moses (Jewish leader) 157
Muscovy 67
Mysteries of state (*arcana imperii*) 196, 219, 237, 289
See too Reason of state

Naples 206
Nassau, Maurice of (Dutch admiral) 243
Natural law (*ius naturale*) 33, 49, 157, 173–6, 178–9, 185–6, 190, 192–7, 245, 253, 255–6, 258–61, 264–5, 268–71
Navarre, prince of, *see* Henry IV (French king)
Navarre, Jeanne d'Albret, queen of (Huguenot leader) 142–3, 214
Netherlands (or Dutchmen) 5, 38, 98, 103, 111, 121, 123, 126, 134, 136, 145–53, 158, 190, 210–11, 214–19, 221, 223–6, 229–30, 232–6, 238, 240–3, 248–9, 251–2, 254–6, 262–3, 271–4, 278, 290–1, 294, 301–3, 313
See too Flanders (or Flemings) Friesland, Holland, United Provinces of the Netherlands, Zeeland
Newcastle 18, 115
Newfoundland 131, 212, 238
Nicholas, Sir Edward (English official) 276
Nieuwpoort 230, 300
Norden, John (English author) 157
Normandy 18–19, 108, 140, 286
North Africa 170, 222, 238
North Sea 140, 153, 211
Norway 87, 93–4, 215, 279
Nottingham, Charles Howard, earl of (English admiral) 127, 129, 134, 278
Nova Scotia 302

Occupation (*occupatio*) 9–11, 13, 17, 20, 29, 39, 48, 52, 60–1, 78, 81, 97, 101, 104, 106–7, 109, 120, 137–8, 145, 165–6, 168–9, 211, 230, 247–8, 257, 268, 271–2, 277, 284, 289, 307, 311
Ogilvie, Thomas (Scottish mariner) 67–8
Orange, William of Nassau, prince of (Dutch leader) 65, 145, 147–8, 150–3, 215
Orkney 91, 93, 221, 300
Orleans 126
Ostend 230
Ovid (Roman author) 253
Oxford 129, 158, 187–8, 190

Padua 200
Panormitanus, Nicholas de Tudeschis, alias (canon lawyer) 13
Paris 129, 163
Parliament 35–6, 64–5, 69, 92, 208, 236–7, 241, 274, 284, 286, 289, 312
Parma, Alexander Farnese, duke of (governor of the Netherlands) 66, 148–9, 153
Paul (apostle) 175
Perugia 187
Peterhead 221, 300
Philip II (Spanish king) 127–8, 147–9, 154, 158, 170, 209, 216–17
Philip III (Spanish king) 136, 158, 182–3, 250
Philip IV (Spanish king) 241, 274, 276–8, 280–1, 285, 287–9, 296, 302
Picardy 140
Pillage 16, 22, 29, 70, 95, 115, 129, 134, 146, 239
Piracy (or pirates) 3, 17, 24–5, 35, 39–40, 55–6, 58, 64, 66, 69–103, 119–20, 123, 126–7, 134–5, 137, 148–9, 177, 197–210, 213–18, 222, 227–8, 231, 234, 237, 252, 262–3, 270, 283, 302, 305, 310, 312–13
Pirates as common enemies (*communes hostes*) 197, 199–202, 204–5, 207–9, 220–2, 238, 313
See too Vengeance on pirates

Pisa 80
Pius v (pope) 162
Plato (Greek philosopher) 265
Plautus (Roman author) 203
Pliny (Roman author) 199
Plunder (*praeda*) 3–4, 10–11, 16–17, 22, 51, 70, 78–9, 81–2, 101, 117, 120, 122–3, 127, 135, 137, 145–6, 154, 158, 161–2, 164–8, 179, 183, 189, 191, 194, 196, 205, 210–11, 213, 227, 236, 246–7, 262, 268, 270, 308, 313
Poland 67–8, 185–6
Polybius (Greek historian) 199
Pompey (Roman statesman) 206
Portugal (or Portuguese) 54–9, 64, 88–9, 108–9, 118, 127, 130–1, 132–6, 152, 158, 161, 165, 170, 202, 206, 208–9, 229–30, 232–3, 235–6, 239–40, 243, 245, 248–51, 254, 259, 262
Postliminium 9, 14–15, 229–30
Practice of nations 138–9, 154–6, 195–6, 214, 226, 241–3, 258–9, 265–72, 289, 309
Practick 31–2, 35, 91
Prisoners 10, 14, 16, 23, 33, 52, 75, 77, 79, 87, 133, 170, 189, 191, 209, 224–5, 226, 229, 232, 276, 278
See too Postliminium, Ransom
Privateering 1–3, 5, 22, 101–3, 105, 210, 212, 308–15
Provence 140
Prussia 17–21, 67, 84–5

Quintilian (Roman author) 244

Ralegh, Sir Walter (English mariner) 184–5
Ransom 15, 18, 20, 30, 33, 209, 224, 226
Reason of state 179–80, 182, 226, 241, 265
See too Mysteries of state (*arcana imperii*)
Rebuffus, Petrus (canon lawyer) 205
Receivers (*receptores*) of pirated goods 72, 79–80, 83, 94–7, 127
Rennes 285
Reis, Turgud (Turkish mariner) 206
Reprisal (*pigneratio*) 39–70, 78, 81–2, 88–9, 101–2, 117, 120, 125, 128–33, 137, 149–50, 153, 155, 161–2, 168, 196–8, 203–5, 209–10, 213, 217, 236–7, 240–2, 247, 252, 262, 273, 275, 288, 294, 297, 304–5, 308–10, 313
See too Letters of reprisal and marque
Res hostium 10–11, 13, 17, 23, 60, 79, 120, 137, 139, 145, 163, 166, 169, 211, 213, 230, 248, 272, 277, 284, 289, 311
Res nullius 10, 20, 39, 48, 145, 169, 271, 289, 307
Ribadeneyra, Pedro de (Spanish author) 182
Roberton, James (Scottish judge) 299, 304–5
Robertson, David (Scottish mariner) 300
Robbery (*rapina*) 72, 77, 151, 160, 162, 167
Rodger, Nicholas (historian) 210
Roman law 6–7, 9–11, 70–3, 173, 175, 185, 187, 190–2, 197, 199, 231, 233, 244–5, 248, 253, 261, 267, 270–1, 273, 308
Rouen 285
Royal council (English) 108–10, 219, 233

Salamanca 165–7, 169–70
Salisbury, Robert Cecil, earl of (English statesman) 182
Santa Catarina (Portuguese ship) 243–4, 246, 250–1, 258–9
São Miguel 208
Scarborough 8
Scotland (or Scotsmen) 4–5, 8–9, 15–16, 24–39, 42, 52, 54–70, 83–101, 103, 111, 113, 116–18, 120–2, 205–7, 210–27, 234, 241, 252, 256, 273, 289–309, 312–13
Sea Beggars 148, 151
Second Council of Lyons 40–1, 45, 74
Selden, John (English author) 255–8, 286, 289
Seneca (Roman author) 174, 253, 266
Shakespeare, William (English author) 190–1
Shetland 93, 221, 300
Sicily 206
Sidney, Sir Philip (English author) 187
Sluys 104
Smith, Sir Thomas (English ambassador) 124
Society of Jesus (or Jesuits) 161, 169, 266
Soto, Domingo de (theologian) 167–8, 170
Spain (or Spaniards) 5, 39, 58, 60, 85, 97, 103, 108, 118, 121, 123–4, 126–37, 139, 148–50, 152, 154, 157–62, 165, 182–3, 186, 190, 198, 202–5, 208–9, 214–20, 223–30, 233–4, 236–42, 248, 250–1, 254, 259–60,

Spain (or Spaniards) (*cont.*)
262, 272–5, 279, 281–3, 285, 288–9, 292, 294, 296, 298, 300, 302–3, 305, 313
Spoils (*spolia*) 10–11, 17, 23
Spuilzie 24, 87, 91–5
St Andrews 301
State of nature 261–3
Statute of Truces 111–14, 138–9
Stirling 93
Stirling, William Alexander, earl of (Scottish statesman) 302
Stoicism 174–5, 195, 266
Stouthreif 92–3
St Peter (French ship) 285–6
Straits of Singapore 243, 262
Suárez, Francisco (Spanish author) 266–7, 269–71
Suleyman the Magnificent (Ottoman emperor) 206
Supreme law (*salus populi*) 138, 173–4, 185, 189
Sutcliffe, Matthew (English author) 207
Sweden 68

Tacitus (Roman author) 195–6, 264
Tartagnus, Alexander (civil lawyer) 200
Territorial waters 152, 216, 221, 223–5, 229, 232, 240, 252–3, 257, 261–2, 286
Thames 233
Theft (*furtum*) 10, 77, 96, 160
The Hague 223, 254
Theology (or theologians) 49–50, 161–73, 175, 178–9, 182, 187–8, 190–1, 193–4, 196, 204, 210, 217, 244, 246–8, 259–60, 266–7, 314
Third Lateran Council 74–6, 78, 200
Treason 111–12, 114–15, 159
Treaties 102, 113–16, 201, 208, 286
  Amboise 124
  Antwerp 223, 225, 251
  Berwick 122
  Cateau-Cambrésis 121, 204
  Edinburgh 121, 214
  Greenwich 118
  Hampton Court 123
  London 219–20, 225, 227–9
  Madrid 289
  Paris 1
  Southampton 274, 281
  Susa 288
  The Hague 275
  Troyes 127, 288
  Westphalia 312
Tunis 238
Tunisia 206
Tuscany, duke of 67–8

Union Jack 220
Union of Scottish and English crowns 27, 218–120, 225, 234
Union of Scottish and French crowns 36, 213
United Provinces of the Netherlands 150, 218, 223, 225, 229, 240–1, 250, 258, 274–5, 285
United States of America 1

Valentia, Gregorio de (theologian) 169
Van Heemskerk, Jakob (Dutch mariner) 243, 249–51, 254, 259, 262
Vasquius, Fernandus (civil lawyer) 260
Vengeance on pirates 72–3, 76, 78, 81, 84, 98, 100–1, 149, 199, 201, 205–7, 210, 221, 237, 313
Venice (or Venetians) 231, 252, 257
Virgil (Roman author) 253
Virtue (*virtus*) 177, 182, 196
Virtuosity (*virtù*) 178
Vitoria, Francisco de (theologian) 165–8, 170, 176, 189, 193–6, 260, 266

Wales 274
Wars
  Anglo-Dutch 1, 210, 309
  Crimean 1
  English Civil 210
  French religious 121, 142–5
  Habsburg-Valois 27, 121, 204
  just 13–14, 51, 156–73
  public 13–14, 51–2, 69, 145, 153, 155, 163–5, 170, 190, 208–9, 217, 241, 246–8, 250, 288, 307
  of the League of Cambrai 27
  private 54, 69, 246–7, 249–50, 263
  Rough Wooings 27
  Thirty Years' 241, 275

Waterford 302
Watson, Andrew (Scottish mariner) 294–5, 298–9
Weaponshowings 290–1
Welwod, William (Scottish author) 35–6, 38–9, 65, 252–5, 258, 269
West Africa 238
West Indies 238
Westminster 286
Weymouth 229, 232
William of Wrotham (English admiral) 22
Wolsey, Thomas (English statesman) 116
Wyclif, John (theologian) 160

Zeeland 55, 57–8, 83, 148, 251